J Torrend

## A Comparative Grammar of the South African Bantu Languages

Comprising those of Zanzibar, Mozambique, the Zambesi, Kafirland, Benguela, Angola, the Congo, the Ogowe, the Cameroons, the lake region

J Torrend

**A Comparative Grammar of the South African Bantu Languages**
*Comprising those of Zanzibar, Mozambique, the Zambesi, Kafirland, Benguela, Angola, the Congo, the Ogowe, the Cameroons, the lake region*

ISBN/EAN: 9783337085148

Printed in Europe, USA, Canada, Australia, Japan

Cover: Foto ©Paul-Georg Meister /pixelio.de

More available books at **www.hansebooks.com**

# A COMPARATIVE GRAMMAR

OF THE

# SOUTH-AFRICAN BANTU LANGUAGES

COMPRISING THOSE OF

ZANZIBAR, MOZAMBIQUE, THE ZAMBEZI, KAFIRLAND, BENGUELA, ANGOLA, THE CONGO, THE OGOWE, THE CAMEROONS, THE LAKE REGION, ETC.

BY

J. TORREND, S.J.,

OF THE ZAMBEZI MISSION,

AUTHOR OF "AN OUTLINE OF A XOSA-KAFIR GRAMMAR

LONDON
KEGAN PAUL, TRENCH, TRÜBNER & CO., L$^{TD}$.
PATERNOSTER HOUSE, CHARING CROSS ROAD.
1891.

# PREFACE.

However favourably my friends may have thought of this work when still in manuscript, I cannot flatter myself that it comes near to the perfection to which I should have wished to have been able to bring it. Any criticisms, corrections, additions, or suggestions, will be received with hearty thanks.

There is no need to call the attention of any one to the importance of the study of Bantu. Independently of its scientific interest, it is a key for opening one half of an immense continent to Christian civilization.

I will only add a word of thanks to all those to whom I am indebted for help, whether from their published works in the same line as this, or from private advice and information.

I feel particularly indebted to the following friends :

The Rev. J. T. Walford, S. J., for having very kindly looked over, and corrected, the greater part of the English of my MSS. and proofsheets.

Dr. R. N. Cust, for having no less kindly given me a number of modern publications on the Bantu languages, among others most of those of the S. P. C. K. His " *Sketch of the Modern Languages of Africa* " has also been to me an invaluable guide throughout.

The Revv. Fathers Causse, Temming, Ronchi, André, S. J., for information or MSS. regarding the Kafir, Chwana, Senna, and Kilimane languages, respectively.

The Rev. Father Lévesque, of the *Société de Notre-Dame des Missions d'Afrique*, for having kindly sent me all the publications of his Society on the Bantu languages.

The Rev. Father L. Cheikho, S. J., for copious information on South-Africa derived from the ancient Arab writers.

The Custodian of the Grey Library in Capetown, and the officials of the British Museum.

Above all, the Rev. Father Depelchin, S. J., the founder of the Zambezi Mission, at whose bidding I undertook these studies. When he came back to the Cape Colony in 1883 from his laborious missionary explorations in the far interior with broken health, but an undaunted spirit, I had the advantage of enjoying his company for nearly two months at St. Aidan's College, Grahamstown. All this time he was constantly saying to me: " For the love of God learn the native languages. I have come across millions of men who need but to hear Our Lord's words and deeds to become so many good and happy Christians ". These words have been ringing in my ears ever since that time, giving me courage and strength to persevere in my attempt to do so. But for them, this work probably never would have been undertaken; certainly it would not have been brought to an end.

I pass by some other friends, who will not allow their names to appear in these pages, but whose kind help will not be forgotten.

God grant that this little work be not useless to the evangelization and civilization of Africa!

*St. Aloysius' College, Jersey.*

*Whit-Sunday, May 17, 1891.*

# SOUTH-AFRICA

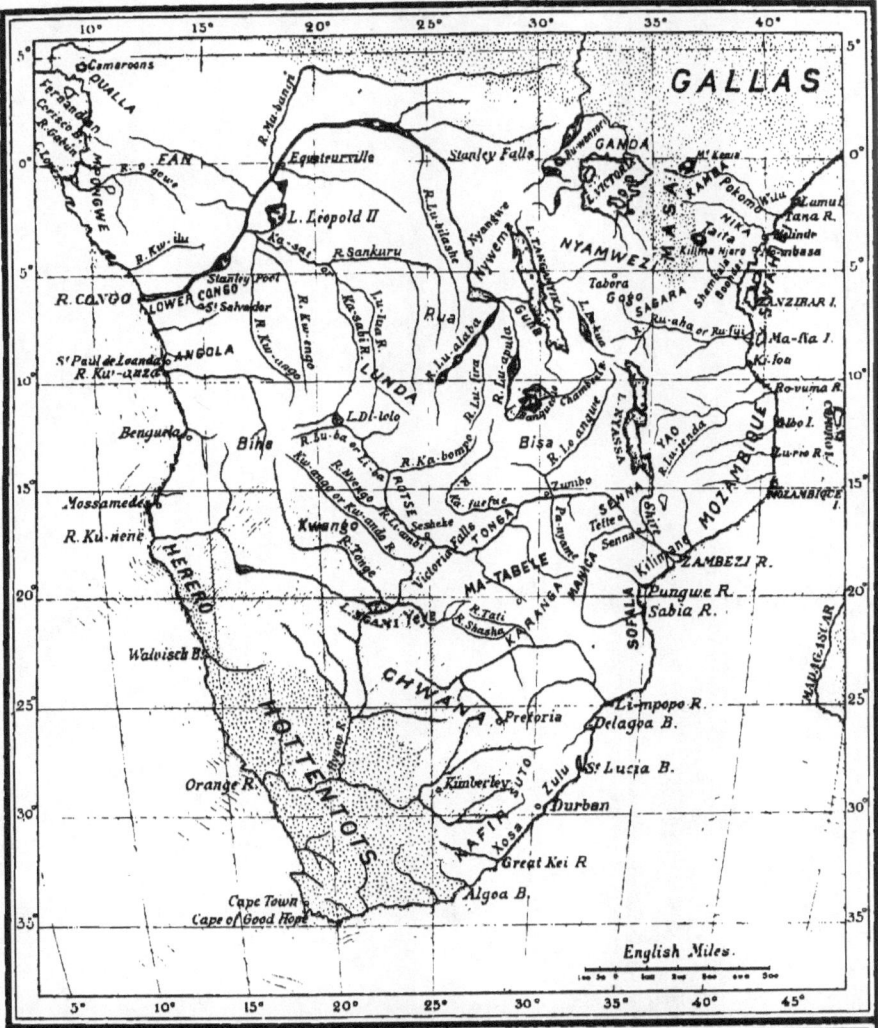

## REFERENCE MAP
TO ACCOMPANY THE
### COMPARATIVE GRAMMAR
OF THE
### SOUTH-AFRICAN BANTU LANGUAGES
BY
J. TORREND, S. J.

N. B. *The names printed in red are those of the languages more particularly dealt with in this work.*

Non-Bantu Languages;   Bantu intermixed with non-Bantu Languages.

# CONTENTS.

## INTRODUCTION.

I. Division of the South-African Languages ... ... ... ...
II. Bantu Literature. — Sources ... ... ... ... ... ...
III. The Origin of the Bantu.... ... ... ... ... ... ...

## Chapter I.

### GENERAL PRINCIPLES AND PHONETICS....

I. Alphabet. ... ... ... ... ... ... ... ... ... ... ...
II. Characteristic Features of the Bantu Family of Languages.
   First principle. ... ... ... ... ... ... ... ... ... ...
   Second principle... ... ... ... ... ... ... ... ... ...
   Third principle. ... ... ... ... ... ... ... ... ... ...
   Fourth principle.... ... ... ... ... ... ... ... ... ...
III. Comparative Phonetics of the Principal Bantu Languages...
   Tonga. ... ... ... ... ... ... ... ... ... ... ... ...
   Yao... ... ... ... ... ... ... ... ... ... ... ... ...
   Nyamwezi. ... ... ... ... ... ... ... ... ... ... ...
   Sagara, and Gogo... ... ... ... ... ... ... ... ... ...
   Shambala, and Boondei. ... ... ... ... ... ... ... ...
   Taita. ... ... ... ... ... ... ... ... ... ... ... ...
   Kamba. ... ... ... ... ... ... ... ... ... ... ... ...
   Swahili. ... ... ... ... ... ... ... ... ... ... ... ...
   Nyika, or Nika, and Pokomo. ... ... ... ... ... ... ...
   Senna (including Tette and Nyassa). ... ... ... ... ...
   Karanga (*alias* Kalaka). ... ... ... ... ... ... ... ...
   Ganda. ... ... ... ... ... ... ... ... ... ... ... ...
   Kafir (Xosa, Zulu, and Tebele)... ... ... ... ... ... ...
   Herero. ... ... ... ... ... ... ... ... ... ... ... ...
   Bihe. ... ... ... ... ... ... ... ... ... ... ... ...
   Mbunda, Lojazi, Nano, and Ndonga. ... ... ... ... ...
   Rotse. ... ... ... ... ... ... ... ... ... ... ... ...
   Runda, or Lunda, and Luba. ... ... ... ... ... ... ...
   Rua... ... ... ... ... ... ... ... ... ... ... ... ...
   Angola, Mbamba, and Fiote, or Lower Congo. ... ... ...
   Middle Congo Languages... ... ... ... ... ... ... ...
   Nywema. ... ... ... ... ... ... ... ... ... ... ... ...
   Kua, or Mozambique, and Chwana... ... ... ... ... ...
   Tshagga, and Hinzua... ... ... ... ... ... ... ... ...
   Mpongwe. ... ... ... ... ... ... ... ... ... ... ...
   Dualla. ... ... ... ... ... ... ... ... ... ... ... ...
   Fan... ... ... ... ... ... ... ... ... ... ... ... ...

|   |   | Page |
|---|---|---|
| Fernandian (Fernando Po). | ... | 49 |
| Languages of the Congo Forest. | ... | 50 |
| Semi-Bantu. | ... | 51 |
| Conclusion. | ... | 51 |
| IV. More General Phonetic Changes. | ... | 53 |
| § 1. Changes caused by the Collision of two Vowels... | ... | 53 |
| § 2. Various Phonetic Changes... | ... | 56 |
| V. On Accentuation in Bantu... | ... | 61 |

## Chapter II.

### ON SUBSTANTIVES. ... ... ... ... ... ... 63

| I. On Articles... | ... | 64 |
|---|---|---|
| II. The MU-BA Class and the Sub-classes connected with it... | ... | 67 |
| § 1. Transformations of the Classifier MU-... | ... | 68 |
| § 2. Transformations of the Classifier BA-. | ... | 70 |
| § 3. The Sub-Class — -BA... | ... | 71 |
| § 4. The Sub-Class MU-MA. | ... | 72 |
| § 5. Substantives which belong to the MU-BA Class and the Sub-Classes connected with it. | ... | 72 |
| § 6. Etymologies. — Varia... | ... | 73 |
| III. The MU-MI Class... | ... | 76 |
| § 1. Transformations of the Classifier MU-... | ... | 76 |
| § 2. Transformations of the Classifier MI-. | ... | 77 |
| § 3. Substantives which belong to the MU-MI Class... | ... | 79 |
| § 4. Etymologies. — Varia... | ... | 80 |
| IV. The IN-ZIN Class. | ... | 82 |
| § 1. Transformations of the Singular Classifier IN-. | ... | 82 |
| § 2. Transformations of the Plural Classifier (Z)IN-... | ... | 84 |
| § 3. Substantives which belong to the IN-(Z)IN Class. | ... | 85 |
| § 4. Etymologies. — Varia... | ... | 86 |
| V. The LI-MA Class. | ... | 88 |
| § 1. Transformations of the Classifier LI-. | ... | 88 |
|     I. Polysyllabic stems which begin with a consonant | ... | 88 |
|     II. Monosyllabic stems. | ... | 90 |
|     III. Stems which begin with a vowel. | ... | 91 |
| § 2. Transformations of the Classifier MA-. | ... | 91 |
| § 3. Substantives which belong to the LI-MA Class... | ... | 91 |
| § 4. Etymologies. — Varia... | ... | 93 |
| VI. The BU-MA Class and the Sub-classes connected with it. | ... | 96 |
| § 1. Forms in the Class BU-MA and the Sub-class MA. | ... | 97 |
| § 2. The Sub-classes BU without plural, and BU-(Z)IN. | ... | 94 |
| § 3. Substantives which belong to the BU-MA Class and the Sub-Classes connected with it. | ... | 99 |
| § 4. Etymologies. — Varia... | ... | 100 |
| VII. The KU-MA Class... | ... | 102 |
| § 1. Forms. | ... | 102 |
| § 2. Substantives which belong to the KU-MA Class... | ... | 103 |
| § 3. Etymologies. — Varia... | ... | 103 |

|     |     | Page |
| --- | --- | --- |
| VIII. | The LU-(ZIN) Class and the Sub-classes connected with it... ... ... | 104 |
|  | § 1. Transformations of the Classifier LU-... ... ... ... ... ... | 104 |
|  | § 2. Plural Classifiers corresponding to LU-... ... ... ... ... | 105 |
|  | § 3. Substantives belonging to cl. LU-... ... ... ... ... ... | 106 |
|  | § 4. Etymologies. — Varia... ... ... ... ... ... ... ... | 107 |
| IX. | The CI-ZI Class. ... ... ... ... ... ... ... ... ... | 109 |
|  | § 1. Transformations of the Classifier CI-. ... ... ... ... ... | 109 |
|  | § 2. Transformations of the Classifier ZI-. ... ... ... ... ... | 111 |
|  | § 3. Substantives which belong to the CI-ZI Class. ... ... ... | 112 |
|  | § 4. Etymologies. — Varia... ... ... ... ... ... ... ... | 113 |
| X. | The diminutive Class KA-TU and the Sub-classes connected with it. | 115 |
|  | § 1. Forms. ... ... ... ... ... ... ... ... ... ... | 115 |
|  | § 2. Substantives which belong to the KA-TU Class and the Sub-Classes connected with it. ... ... ... ... ... ... ... ... | 119 |
|  | § 3. Etymologies. — Varia... ... ... ... ... ... ... ... | 120 |
| XI. | Locative Classifiers, and Prepositions... ... ... ... ... ... | 122 |
|  | § 1. Transformations of the Locative Classifier PA-... ... ... | 123 |
|  | § 2. Transformations of the Locative Classifier KU-... ... ... | 127 |
|  | § 3. Transformations of the Locative Classifier MU-... ... ... | 128 |
|  | § 4. Plural Locative Classifiers... ... ... ... ... ... ... | 129 |
|  | § 5. Effects of the Locative Classifiers on the other Prefixes of the Substantives. | 129 |
|  | § 6. On the Use of the Locative Classifiers... ... ... ... ... | 130 |
|  | § 7. Prepositions which are not Classifiers... ... ... ... ... | 131 |
|  | § 8. The Particles -LI, -NA, etc., in Locative Expressions... ... | 133 |
|  | § 9. Etymologies. — Varia... ... ... ... ... ... ... ... | 134 |
| XII. | Copulative Prefixes before substantives.. ... ... ... ... ... | 136 |
| XIII. | The Particles which introduce Substantives after Passive Verbs... | 138 |
| XIV. | Suffixes of Substantives. ... ... ... ... ... ... ... ... | 138 |
| XV. | Onomatopoetic Substantives. ... ... ... ... ... ... ... | 139 |
| XVI. | Retrospect. — Varia. ... ... ... ... ... ... ... ... | 140 |

## Chapter III.

### ON ADJECTIVES... ... ... ... ... ... 142

|     |     |     |
| --- | --- | --- |
| I. | Quantitative Adjectives. ... ... ... ... ... ... ... ... | 144 |
|  | § 1. Adaptation of the Quantitative Adjectives to the different Classes of Nouns... ... ... ... ... ... ... ... ... ... | 144 |
|  | § 2. Effects of the Phonetic Laws upon the Forms of Quantitative Adjectives. | 145 |
|  | § 3. On the Use of Quantitative Adjectives as Epithets. ... ... | 146 |
|  | § 4. On the Use of Quantitative Adjectives as Predicates... ... | 148 |
| II. | Non-Quantitative Adjectives. ... ... ... ... ... ... ... | 149 |
| III. | Comparatives and Superlatives... ... ... ... ... ... ... | 150 |

## Chapter IV.

### ON PRONOUNS... ... ... ... ... ... 152

|     |     |     |
| --- | --- | --- |
| I. | Connective Pronouns. ... ... ... ... ... ... ... ... | 152 |
|  | § 1. Forms. ... ... ... ... ... ... ... ... ... ... | 153 |
|  | § 2. Connective Pronouns prefixed to verbs as Subjects. ... ... | 155 |

|  | Page |
|---|---|
| § 3. Connective Pronouns prefixed to verbs as Objects. | 157 |
| § 4. Reflexive Pronouns. | 158 |
| II. Substantive Personal Pronouns. | 159 |
| § 1. Forms. | 160 |
|     I. Enclitic Forms. | 160 |
|     II. Self-standing Forms. | 162 |
|     III. Copula-containing Forms. | 164 |
| § 2. Use of the different Forms. | 165 |
|     I. Self-standing Forms. | 165 |
|     II. Enclitic Forms. | 167 |
|     III. Copula-containing Forms. | 169 |
| § 3. Varia. | 169 |
| III. Demonstrative Pronouns. | 170 |
| § 1. Fundamental Forms. | 171 |
|     I. Formation of these pronouns. | 173 |
|     II. Use and place of these pronouns. | 174 |
| § 2. Emphatic Forms. | 177 |
| § 3. Copula-containing Forms. | 178 |
| IV. Relative Pronouns, and Relative Particles. | 181 |
| § 1. Forms of the Relative Particles. | 181 |
| § 2. Use of Relative Particles and Construction of Relative Clauses in General. | 184 |
|     I. Relative clauses in which the antecedent is represented by the subject of the verb. | 184 |
|     II. Relative clauses in which the antecedent is represented by an object of the verb. | 186 |
| V. Pronouns in Possessive Expressions. | 189 |
| § 1. General Principle. | 189 |
| § 2. Connective Pronouns Suppressed. | 190 |
| § 3. Possessive Expressions after Locatives. | 191 |
| VI. Relative and Possessive Expressions used Substantively. | 194 |
| VII. Relative and Possessive Expressions equivalent to our Adjectives. | 197 |
| VIII. Pronouns referring to Substantives understood, and Pronouns used as Conjunctions. | 198 |
|     Appendix on the Lunda Language. | 201 |
| IX. Numerals. | 203 |
| § 1. Bantu Numeration. | 203 |
| § 2. Formation and Use of the Numbers from "One" to "Six". | 206 |
| § 3. Formation and Use of the Numbers above "Six". | 207 |
| § 4. Complex Numbers. | 207 |
| § 5. Ordinal Numbers and Numerical Adverbs. | 208 |
|     The negative particle before the number "one". | 208 |
| X. Interrogative Pronouns and Various Determinatives. | 208 |
| § 1. The Pronoun "How many?". | 209 |
| § 2. The Pronoun and Adjective "What? What sort of...?". | 209 |
| § 3. The Pronoun "Who?". | 211 |
| § 4. The Discriminative Pronoun "Which?". | 211 |
| § 5. Interrogative Pronouns used Indefinitely. | 212 |
| § 6. The Pronoun and Adjective "All, whole". | 212 |
| § 7. The Pronoun *A— -like* "Alone, By himself". | 213 |
| § 8. The Pronouns *A-a-la-kue* "He also", *A-ba-la-bo* "They also," etc. | 214 |
| § 9. The Pronouns rendering "Self." | 215 |
| § 10. The Pronoun *-mbi* "Other, Different, Foreign." | 216 |
| § 11. The Pronouns "One... another", "Some... others." | 216 |
| Retrospect on the Article. | 217 |

# Chapter V.

## ON VERBS ... 219

**I. Fundamental Forms of the Simple Verb.** ... 219
   § 1. Principal Parts of the Verbs in Bantu. ... 219
   § 2. Fundamental Forms derived from *-bona* ... 221
      I. Imperative form *bona* " see ". ... 221
      II. Indicative form *ndi-bona* " I see ". ... 222
      III. Infinitive form *ku-bona* " to see ". ... 225
   § 3. Subjunctive Form *ndi-bone*... ... 225
   § 4. Perfect Form *ndi-bonide*. ... 227
   § 5. The Forms *ndi-bonanga* and *ndi-bonaga*... ... 229
   § 6. The Negative Form *(ta) ndi-boni*. ... 230

**II. Auxiliaries**... ... 231
   § 1. General Principles. ... 231
   § 2. The Negative Auxiliaries... ... 232
      I. Forms.... ... 232
         *A*. Absolute indicative clauses... ... 233
         *B*. Relative clauses... ... 233
         *C*. Subjunctive clauses. ... 234
         *D*. Imperative clauses and the infinitive. ... 234
      II. Examples. ... 235
   § 3. The Auxiliary *-A*.. ... 237
   § 4. The Auxiliary *YA* " to Go "... ... 242
   § 5. The Auxiliary *ENDA* " to Go ", and various Continuative Auxiliaries... 243
   § 6. The Auxiliaries *KALA* and *NNA* " to Sit, to Remain "... ... 247
   § 7. The Auxiliary *ZA* or *IZA* " to Come "... ... 248
   § 8. The Auxiliary *KUE*.... ... 251
   § 9. The Auxiliary *KA*. ... 251
   § 10. The Auxiliary *INSI*... ... 254
   § 11. The Auxiliaries *MA* and *BA* " to Stand, to Stop. "... ... 255
   § 12. The Auxiliaries *CI, KI, SI, SA*, etc. ... 256
   § 13. The Auxiliary *NGA*... ... 258
   § 14. The Auxiliary *TI* " to Say. "... ... 260
   § 15. The Auxiliary *BUYA* " to Come back. ". ... 261
   § 16. The Auxiliary *MANA* " to Come to an End. "... ... 262
   § 17. Various Auxiliaries. ... 263

**III. The Verbs " To Be " and " To Have. "**... ... 263
   § 1. Copula Understood. ... 264
   § 2. The verbal Forms *LI, LE, ELE, IRI*, etc., used as the Copula. ... 264
   § 3. The Verb *KU-BA* " to Become, to Come to be, " used as the Copula. ... 266
   § 4. The Verbs *-KALA* and *-NNA* or *-INA* " to Sit, " used as the Copula... 267
   § 5. The Verb *-ENDA* used as the Copula... ... 268
   § 6. Various Copulative Particles. ... 268
   § 7. The Copula in Negative clauses.. ... 269
   § 8. The Verb " To Have. ". ... 270
   § 9. The Verbs " To Be " and " To Have " in Locative Expressions... ... 271

**IV. Derivative Verbs.** ... 272
   § 1. Passive Verbs.. ... 272
   § 2. Other Derivative Verbs. ... 275

|  | Page |
|---|---|
| I. Applicative verbs. | 276 |
| II. Causative verbs... | 277 |
| III. Intensive verbs... | 279 |
| IV. Reversive and expansive verbs... | 279 |
| V. Reciprocal verbs.. | 280 |
| Conclusion.. | 280 |
| Retrospect on Adverbs, Prepositions, and Conjunctions. | 281 |
| **Appendix I. Ethnographical Notes in Tonga.** | 283 |
| I. On the Rotse. | 283 |
| II. On the Karanga.... | 286 |
| III. On the Tonga. | 289 |
| **Appendix II. Specimens of Kafir Folk-Lore.** | 296 |
| I. The Bird that made Milk... | 296 |
| II. Mlonjaloniani, his Sister, and a Mbulu... | 300 |
| III. The Gqongqos and Qajana. | 305 |
| IV. Tanga-lo-mlibo. ... | 314 |
| **Alphabetical Index.** | |

# INTRODUCTION.

## I. Division of the South-African Languages.

*1.* Whatever may be the correct division of the native races of South-Afrika, the languages of this country constitute three plainly distinct groups viz. the Hottentot-Bushman, the Masai, and the Bantu. With the first two I have not to deal in this work. If they are mentioned here, it is only to set them soon aside.

*2. The Hottentot-Bushman group.* — This comprises the languages spoken mostly by nomadic, or only half-settled people, who are found in the least accessible parts of the South-African deserts. Living in caves or in wretched huts, too lazy to cultivate the soil, eating such food as bull-frogs and lizards, wanting in what the Kafirs call marriage-laws, having no notion of political union, they are generally despised, and persecuted, or kept in subjection, by their Bantu neighbours. They are of every description with regard to colour, stature, physique, and dispositions. Some are yellow-white, others red, others reddish-black. Most of them are dwarfish in size, scarcely above four feet, but they also number fine specimens of humanity, such as the six-foot Lange Berg Bushmen near the Orange River. Some have fine proportions; others are of the very lowest type, with short foreheads, and hair on their bodies and legs. Some are of gentle disposition, ready to do any service; others wage war on all living beings, and cannot be trusted with anything (¹).

*3.* They used to be found in ancient times — as possibly they may be found yet — even in the north-eastern deserts of Africa, and from the fact of their living in caves (διὰ τὸ τρώγλας ὑποδεδυκέναι. (²)) were known to the Greeks under the name of Troglodytes. The most generic name they have among their Bantu neighbours is that of *Ba-tua*, or in Chwana pronunciation *Ba-roa*, which now means " slaves ", and is synonymous with *ba-bua*, or *in-ja*, " dogs ". Southern Kafirs distinguish, as we do, between the pure Bushmen and the more civilized Hottentots, whom they consider to be a mixed race. These they call *a Ma-lawu*, which according to regular phonetic changes seems to stand for *Arabu*, as if they once had had something to do with the Arabs. Probably the southern Bushmen are related as a race to the dwarfs who live on the north-eastern affluents of the Congo. The latter, however, seem to speak semi-Bantu languages (n. 242 of this work).

---

1. See Anderson's *Twenty-five Years in a Waggon*, London, 1887, vol. I, pp. 282, 296, etc., and vol. II, p. 74; also the *Proceedings of the R. G. S.*, 1886, p. 438.
2. *Geogr. Graeci Minores*, Didot, 1861, vol. II, p. 248.

There is ground to believe that either these, or the Bantu proper, have preserved the original language of South-Africa the best, while the southern Bushmen, whose ancestors were, perhaps, the slaves of foreign gold and diamond diggers, have forgotten it entirely.

*4.* The most prominent features which distinguish the languages of the Hottentot-Bushman group from Bantu are : — 1°) a great abundance of those peculiar consonants which are termed clicks (nn. 35-38), and have been compared by Herodotus to the screeching of bats, τετρίγασι καθάπερ αἱ νυκτερίδες (IV, 183); — 2°), a grammatical system built nearly exclusively on sex-denoting suffixes, while the Bantu mechanism consists mostly of prefixes which imply no such reference.

*5.* On the whole this group of languages differs perhaps more from the generality of the Bantu languages than from any other. The late Professor Bleek has remarked in it signs of affinity with some North-African languages ([1]). He has even come to the remarkable conclusion that " all those sex-denoting languages known to us in Africa, Asia, and Europe, are members of one large family, of which the primitive type has, in most respects, been best preserved to us in the Hottentot language ([2]) ".

*6. The Masai group.* — The Masai are warlike tribes with pastoral and nomadic habits, which occupy a large belt of ground south of the equator from Mount Kenia to south of Mount Njaro, or Kilima-Njaro. They are said to resemble in a high degree the Somali. They are divided into Masai proper and Kwafi ([3]). H. H. Johnston has observed that Latuka, 5° north of the equator, and Bari, on the White Nile, between 4° and 6° Lat., are members of the Masai family of languages ([4]).

Many points of contact might be shown to exist between Masai and Bantu, but, as it would require a somewhat lengthy explanation to bring them out, I have thought it better not to touch them in this work. It has certainly more in common with Galla than with Bantu.

*7. The Bantu group.* — The third, and more important, group of languages spoken in South-Africa, the one which I have attempted to describe in this work, may be said to comprise the idioms spoken by all the agricultural black tribes of this country. Bleek, who did more than any one else to throw light on its numerous ramifications, proposed to the scientific world to term it Bantu, because this word, which properly means " people " in most of the languages of this group (n. 322*), is principally used by the natives when speaking of themselves in contradiction to white people ([5]). This term, whatever may be thought of its correctness, has been adopted on so good an authority, and is now the current name.

*8.* There can be no doubt that these people must be identified with the

---

1. *Comparative Grammar of South-African Languages*, I, p. VIII.
2. See *Reynard the Fox in South-Africa*, pp. XIV-XIX.
3. See Introduction to the *Vocabulary of the Engutuk Eloikob*, by the Rev. L. Krapf, Tübingen, 1854.
4. *The Kilimanjaro Expedition*, London, 1886, p. 450.
5. MS. 214 of the Grey Library, Capetown, entitled " *Thirty chapters of Zulu Tradition* ", chapter v.

*Zindj* of the ancient Arab geographers. I grant that I find no distinct mention made by them of the western Bantu, but they distinctly include under the name of Zindj all the eastern tribes dwelling between the Juba River and Delagoa Bay; and this says enough, as it means all the Bantu tribes known to them.

9. It also seems certain that "the large country called *Agi-sumba*, or *Agi-symba*", by Ptolemy, the existence of which was known to this geographer as far as the 16th parallel of south latitude (¹), is no other than the Bantu field. The Masai still call the Swahili *La-shumba-n*, and the Kavirondo, a non-Bantu tribe dwelling north-west of Lake Victoria Nyanza, call them *Wa-ki-chumbi*. A few Bantu tribes also call themselves *Ma-zimba*, or in Mozambique pronunciation *Ma-rimba* (n. 173), which, perhaps, may be etymologically identified with these words. Then there are the *Ki-rimba* or *Ki-zimba* islands north of Mozambique. In some parts of the Congo basin the chief-town of a king is still called *Mu-sumba*, as formerly that of the Monomotapa was called *Zimba*, or *Zimba-we*, or *Zimba-bye*, — all words in which we probably find the element *sumba*, or *symba*, of Ptolemy's *Agi-sumba* (²).

10. It has been repeatedly said that the Bantu have no generic national name for themselves. This is not quite correct. My native informants, those of the Zambezi as well as those of Kafraria, gave me independent evidence that all the native tribes of which they had any knowledge, the Bushmen and Hottentots excepted, were included under the generic name of *Ba-nsundu*. This is the word which is variously pronounced *Ba-sutu*, *Be-suto*, *Ba-suto*, *A-sutu*. I do not know whether it may not be traced in *Ba-sundi*, which is the name of a large Bantu tribe on the Congo. Certainly it must be identified with the word *A-suut*, or *A-suur*, of the Fan tribe on the Upper Ogowe. It seems to mean "the dark-brown tribes". This at least is the meaning which southern Kafirs assign to it. I should not be astonished if it were found to be related to the word *Soudan*, "Blacks", of the Arabs.

11. Languages distinctly Bantu are heard in all the well-watered parts of South-Africa from the Keiskamma River in Cape Colony to the equator in the east, and from Walfish Bay to the Old Kalabar River on the 5th parallel of north latitude in the west. In most parts of Central Africa the Bantu field extends but little north of the equator. There are some Bantu enclaves in the Soudan, on the Niger, and further to the west. Philological science has not yet determined what is the exact relation of the languages of the other black tribes in the north-west to Bantu. For myself, I have come to the conclusion that several of them have at least as much in common with the southern Bantu languages as certain Aryan languages between themselves, English and Greek for instance. But, except for a few

---

1. *Geogr.*, I, 8 and 10; IV, 9.
2. In several eastern Bantu languages, the word *simba* means "lion", which is synonymous with "king". Perhaps it is also related to *Agi-sumba*.

short digressions on this subject (nn. 245, 598, and 830), I have limited my field of study to those languages which differ from one another no more than English does from German.

*12. Classification of the Bantu languages.* — Notwithstanding the existence of a considerable amount of literature, the study of the Bantu languages in general must still be said to be in its infancy, and I think that any attempt at their scientific classification must fail for some time. Bleek attempted one. It is not only inadequate, but entirely misleading from beginning to end to one who has comparative philology in view. He does not seem to have noticed, for instance, that Chwana has much more affinity with Kua of Mozambique than with Zulu, nor that Mpongwe differs more from most of the languages of the Congo than from those of Mozambique. When I began these comparative studies, one of the first things which struck me was the existence of a group embracing Chwana, Mozambique, and Mpongwe, and further researches have only confirmed this view. But I have found no other neatly defined group. Hence, taking all the languages that have some particular affinity with those of Mozambique to form the Kua, or Chwana-Mozambique-Mpongwe, group (169 and 246), nearly all the others may be provisionally considered as forming the main group. Those of Fernando Po, and, probably, certain little known Bantu languages of the Cameroons and the Soudan, do not come well into either the main or the Kua group. They also provisionally may be considered as forming the Fernandian group.

*13.* Dr. Robert Needham Cust, dealing with these languages in his "*Sketch of the Modern Languages of Africa*", follows a geographical method throughout. Hence his classification necessarily has its defects, but less than any other that I know of; and I think it may be adopted until more is known of some languages, principally those of the Congo basin. Only it should be so modified as to pay due regard to the existence of the Chwana-Mozambique-Mpongwe group, and to certain obvious affinities between various languages. Thus, instead of a general division of these languages into a Southern, an Eastern, and a Western branch, I should begin with their division into the main and the Kua group, with the addition of the Fernandian. Then each of the first two I should subdivide into an Eastern and a Western half-group. The meridian of the Victoria Falls would be the approximate line of demarcation between east and west, as nearly all the tribes to the west of this limit are included by the natives under the names of *Ma-mbunda* or *Ma-mbundu, Ma-kwango, E-xi-kongo,* and *Am-pongwe,* all of which mean "western people" (¹). The word *Si-ongo,* which is the native name of the Falls, seems even to mean "the separation, or beginning, of the west."

---

1. It appears that in the Portuguese colony of Angola the word *A-mbundu,* or *A-mbunda,* is thought to mean "the invaders". This certainly cannot be its original meaning : for the simpler word *mbunda* means "back", hence "west", in several of the *Mbunda,* or *Mbundu,* languages.

Each of the half-groups may further be subdivided into clusters, according to the greater or lesser affinity of the various languages.

*14.* Hence the following might serve as a provisional classification of the best known among these : —

## I. Main Group.

### Eastern Half.

**Kafir Cluster.**
- Xosa or Kafir proper, spoken in Kafraria and the Transkei.
- Zulu, in Natal and Zululand.
- Mfengu, in Swaziland.
- Tabele, or Tebele, in Matabeleland.

**Karanga Cluster.**
- Vumbe (the Se-kalaka of the Bechwana) in Southern Matabeleland
- Shona, in Eastern Matabeleland.
- Karanga proper, by Wange's people north of the Middle Zambezi.
- Yeye, on the Zouga River and round Lake Ngami.

**Tonga Cluster.**
- Tonga proper, between the Kafuefue and the Zambezi.
- Lea, east of the Victoria Falls.
- Subia, west of the Victoria Falls.
- Bue, on the Zambezi, north-east of Moemba's.
- Kova, between the Kafuefue and the Loangwe River.
- Bisa, between the Loangwe and the Chambezi River.
- Bemba, north-west of the Chambezi River.
- Nyassa Tonga, east of the Loangwe River.

**Senna Cluster.**
- Senna proper, at Senna.
- Shire, on the Shire River.
- Sofala, at Sofala.
- Tette, at Tette.
- Zumbo, or Ntsua, at Zumbo.
- Nyassa, on Lake Nyassa.
- Gindo, from the Rufiji to the Lindi River.

**Viti Cluster.**
- Ngoni, west of Lake Nyassa.
- Viti proper, on the Upper Rufiji.
- Bunga, north-east of Lake Nyassa.

**Gangi Cluster.**
- Gangi proper, or Henge,
- Ziraha,
- Kwenyi,
- Nkwifiya,
- Ndunda,    } on the Upper Rufiji and its affluents.
- Bena,
- Sango,
- Kimbu,
- Nyaturu,

**Ungu Cluster.** { Ungu, Fipa } on Lake Rukua and its affluents.

**Sagara Cluster.**
- Kaguru, or Sagara proper,
- Itumba,
- Kondoa,      } in Usagara.
- Kami,
- Khutu,
- Gogo, in Ugogo,
- Hehe, on the Upper Rufiji.

NYAMWEZI CLUSTER. { Nyanyembe, Sumbua, Sukuma, } in Unyamwezi.
Tusi, or Ila, north-east of Lake Tanganyika.
Regga, or Legga, west of Lake Mut'a nzige.
GANDA CLUSTER. { Ganda, north of Lake Victoria Nyanza.
Nyambu, south-west of Lake Victoria Nyanza.
TAITA CLUSTER. { Pare, near Kilima Njaro.
Tambi, Teri, Jiri, } on the hills between Kilima Njaro and Mombasa.
NIKA, or NYIKA, CLUSTER. { Daruma, Rabai, Giriama, Digo, } round Mombasa.
Pokomo, on the Tana, or Pokomo, River.
Kamba, from Mount Kenia to Kilima Njaro.
SWAHILI CLUSTER. { Lamu, in Lamu Island.
Gunya, in Patta Island.
Mvita, at Mombasa.
Pemba, in Pemba Island.
Unguja, at Zanzibar.
SHAMBALA CLUSTER. { Shambala proper, on the Shambala hills.
Boondei, between the coast and the Shambala hills.
Zegula, inland from Zanzibar.
Nguru, west of the Zegula.
IBO CLUSTER. { Lima, on the coast opposite Zanzibar.
Ibo, in Ibo Island (12° 20′ S. lat.).
Zaramo, in Uzaramo, south of Zanzibar.
Konde, on the Lower Rovuma.
Yao, between the Upper Rovuma and the Lujenda River.

## WESTERN HALF.

HERERO CLUSTER. { Herero, in Damaraland.
Ndonga, on the Kunene River.
Lojazi, near the sources of the Kwando, or Southern Kwango, River.
BENGUELA CLUSTER. { Bihe, on the Upper Kwanza.
Nano, in the district of Benguela.
Kwango, or Mbunda proper, west of the Rotse Valley.
ROTSE CLUSTER. { Rotse, on the Upper Zambezi.
Nyengo, on the Nyengo River, west of the Rotse.
(CI-)BOKO CLUSTER. { (Ci-)Boko, between the Upper Kwanza and the Upper Kasai.
Yakka (?), on the Northern Kwango River.
ANGOLA CLUSTER. { Angola proper, Mbamba } in the district of S$^t$ Paul de Loanda.
Mbangala, at Kasanje.
Sertão, at Ambaka.
Lower Congo, or Fiote, at, and round, S. Salvador.
Lunda, between the Upper Kasai and the Upper Lualaba.
GUHA CLUSTER. { Guha, Rungu, } east of the Upper Lualaba.
NYWEMA CLUSTER. { Bamba, east of the Lualaba, north of the Lukuga River.
Kusu, west of Nyangwe.

Rua, west of the Middle Lualaba.
Luba, on the Lower Kasai and the Lulua River.

YANSI CLUSTER. { Teke, round Stanley Pool.
{ Yansi, spoken by the native traders above Stanley Pool.

## II. Rua Group.

### EASTERN HALF.

CHWANA CLUSTER. { Tlhaping, or Chwana proper, } 
{ Rolong, } in Bechwanaland, and the Transvaal
{ Mangwato, }
{ Suto, in Basutoland, and the Orange Free State.
{ Kololo, on the Zambezi, above the Victoria Falls.

NYAMBANE CLUSTER. { Gwamba, south-west of the Lower Limpopo.
{ Nyambane, at, and round, Inyambane.
{ Chiloane, in, and round, the islands of Chiloane.

MOZAMBIQUE CLUSTER. { Kilimane, on the Kwakwa River.
{ Tugulu, in, and round, the island of Mozambique.
{ Gunda (?), on the Lukugu River (?). See n. 97.
{ Mbwabe, } inland from Ibo Island.
{ Medo, }
{ Masasi, north of the Lower Rovuma.

TSHAGGA CLUSTER. { Tshagga } near Kilima Njaro.
{ Gweno }

COMORO CLUSTER. { Hinzua, in Hinzua Island.
{ Angazidja (?), in Great Comoro Island.

### WESTERN HALF.

Buma, on the Congo, at, and round, Bolobo.

MPONGWE CLUSTER. { Mpongwe, on the Lower Ogowe and the Gabún.
{ Shekiani, or Bulu, on the River Gabún.

DUALLA CLUSTER. { Kele, or Kali, along the Bembo River.
{ Benga, on the islands of Corisco Bay.
{ Dualla, round the Cameroon Mountains.
{ Subu, or Isubu, north of the Dualla.

Fan, or Pahuin, on the Upper Ogowe.

## III. Fernandian Group.

FERNANDIAN CLUSTER. { Banapa }
{ Banni } in Fernando Po Island.
{ Ureka }

*15.* The length of this list of languages might lead the reader to think that it implies a great diversity between them, something like that existing between the Indo-European languages. This would be a false notion. In general the languages of the same cluster must be considered as mere dialectic varieties. This, for instance, is the case with Xosa, Zulu, and Tebele, in the Kafir cluster; with Tlhaping, Rolong, Suto, and Kololo, in the Chwana cluster, etc. There are even several clusters which might quite appropriately be said to form together a single language. For instance, the differences between the Senna, Gangi, Nika, Shambala, Sagara, and Ibo, clusters cannot be said by any means to be as great as those which may be remarked between several French *patois*. The greatest noticeable divergencies are found to exist between the Mpongwe cluster and the languages of the main group. These may be said to amount to something like the difference between Latin and French, or between English and German.

## II. Bantu Literature. — Sources.

*16.* Writing is unknown to the Bantu in general. According to my Tonga informants from the Middle Zambezi, God said to the Ma-nkua (the whites) that they must learn to write, and to the Tonga that they must learn to speak. The only Bantu known to write are those among the coast tribes which have fallen most under foreign influence. On the west coast Roman characters alone are known. On the east coast the Arabic alphabet has probably long been in use and is still prevailing. Daniel J. Rankin, M. R. A. S., formerly Acting British Consul at Mozambique, says that even the Makua of the coast of Mozambique, though they have so long been under Portuguese influence know how to write only in Arabic characters. " In most of the large villages ", he adds, " the children of the better class receive lessons in reading and writing, the universal and only lesson-book being the Koran. Beginners are taught to read and write the alphabet and simple sentences on religious subjects by means of a board called " ubáu ", formed of a hard kind of wood — answering in its use to the slate of European schools — from which ink-marks can be effaced when desired. This stage passed, a well-thumbed copy of the Koran does duty as a reading-book. The Arabic alphabet having been learned, and pronunciation of the words acquired, the education of the average native ceases. Correspondence is afterwards carried on in Swahili by those who have attained greater proficiency in their studies ([1]) ".

*17.* We do not know when Bantu thus began to be written on the east coast. No Bantu literature originally writen in Arabic characters has been preserved, except two small poems in Old Swahili, published in Roman characters by Dr. Steere in his collection of Swahili tales ([2]), and a longer one, left in manuscript by Dr. L. Krapf, and lately published in the *Zeitschrift für afrikanische Sprachen*, 1887.

*18.* Still less do we possess anything of the period preceding the occupation of Eastern Africa by the Arabs. Not a few remarkable monuments of an ancient civilization have indeed been discovered in the Bantu field south of

---

1. *Arab Tales translated from Swahili into the Tugulu dialect of the Makua Language*, by Daniel J. Rankin, 1886.
2. *Swahili Tales*, by Edward Steere, 2d edition, London, 1889.

the Zambezi, but either no inscriptions have been found near them, or, if any have been noticed, there is every appearance that they are not in Bantu. Thus, if we may rely on a paper of Farini, which was read in 1886 before the Royal Geographical Society, this traveller (?) had then discovered in the Kalahari desert about 23°½ S. lat. by 21°½ E. long. what may have been the work of ancient diamond-diggers, the right place, it seemed, to look for inscriptions, but he found none. " It had evidently been ", he writes, " a huge walled inclosure, elliptical in form, and about the eighth of a mile in length. The masonry was of a Cyclopean character; here and there the gigantic square blocks still stood on each other, and in one instance the middle stone being of a softer nature was weatherworn... In the middle of the ellipse was a kind of pavement of long narrow square blocks neatly fitted together, forming a cross, in the centre of which was what seemed to have been a base for either a pedestal or monument. We unearthed a broken column, a part of which was in a fair state of preservation, the four flat sides being fluted... We sought diligently for inscriptions, but we could find none (¹) ". Several descriptions have also been given by various writers of the ruins of Zimbabye, near the gold-fields of Mashonaland, but no inscription has ever been mentioned, unless we may consider as such certain carvings found there by the traveller Anderson : " There are, " he writes, " several beams inserted in the walls, projecting eight feet, composed of a hard and fine-grained stone of a dark colour. Upon one of them are carvings, diamond-shaped, one within another, separated by wavy lines... Several old diggings are in the vicinity ". The same writer, after having mentioned a large number of old ruins and forts in the vicinity of various ancient gold-diggings, speaks also of numerous rocks somewhere near the Limpopo " with carvings of animals, snakes, and figures, on them ", which may turn out to be some kind of hieroglyphics. He mentions one circular rock in particular, with " no other stones near it, fifteen feet in diameter, similar to a ball cut in the centre..., covered with carvings... representing paths with trees and fruits on each side ". " Upon one of the trees, " he adds, " is a snake crawling down with a fruit or round ball in its mouth ; near it is a figure, and a little distance off another figure with wings, almost like an iguana, flying towards a man who is running away. His left foot is similar to that of a horse, the right one has two points... the intermediate spaces have many stars. " The writer adds that, though the rock is very hard, some portions of the carvings have been rendered nearly smooth by large animals rubbing against it, from which he concludes that they must be very ancient (²). Mr. O'Neil, formerly consul at Mozambique, writes that he was told by the Capitão-mor of Gorongoza of many ancient inscriptions to be seen in the Manica gold-fields, and that, judging from the description given of them, he thought they were in cuneiform or wedge-shaped

---

1. *Proceedings of the R. G. S.*, 1886, p. 447.
2. Anderson's *Twenty-five Years in a Waggon*, Vol. I, pp. 196, 197, Vol. II, pp. 150, 201, 202, etc.

characters (¹). But of course, so long as our knowledge ends there, we must rest satisfied with a " perhaps ", as far as this has anything to do with Bantu. Perhaps on those rocks and ruins we have ancient inscriptions, and, if so, since they are in the Bantu field, perhaps they are couched in Bantu. Probably they are not. What is certain is that no native can give any account of their origin. Neither could the Arabs do so 400 years ago, when they were first met with by Vasco de Gama near the coast of Sofala.

Certain drawings were found on rocks near the Congo by Captain Tuckey in 1816, and they have been compared by Mr. de Laborde to similar drawings which are mixed up with the inscriptions of Wadi Mokatteb in Arabia (²). There is even less probability of these being Bantu inscriptions than there is in the case of those mentioned by Anderson and O'Neil.

It therefore seems that, waiting further discoveries, the history of Bantu literature must begin with the first Christian Missions to South-Africa.

*19. Bantu Literature of the seventeenth Century.* — It appears that two catechisms were written in the seventeenth century by Dominican missionaries stationed at Tette on the Zambezi, but they never have been published (³). This cannot be too much regretted. To preach God's Word to the natives of Africa, then to go off without having given it to them in writing, and yet to expect that these material people and their children will abide permanently by it, is to expect from God's grace as great a miracle as if they were to embrace the faith without anybody preaching it to them. The missionaries of Angola and the Congo did more permanent work, as is well known, and I have little doubt that the result was due in a great measure to the works they published.

*20.* The first Bantu work ever printed seems to have been a translation into the language of S¹ Salvador of Father Jorge's treatise on Christian Doctrine. It was made by the priests at the court of Congo with the aid of Fr. Matthaeus Cardozo, S. J., and published at Lisbon in 1624 (⁴).

*21.* In 1642 there was printed at Lisbon a catechism in the language of Angola, written by Father Pacconio, S. J., and abridged by Father de Coucto, S. J. This work has passed through several editions. Father Cannecattim, writing in 1805, finds it full of defects, such as laconicisms, redundancy and useless circumlocutions, neglect of the grammatical rules laid down at the end of its Roman edition, etc. But Héli Chatelain, author of two Angola Grammars, justly remarks that Cannecattim's criticisms are not only excessive, but unjust (⁵). It may be added in particular that the rules laid down at the end of the Roman edition are not Father de Coucto's, but of the Capuchin editor, and that the greatest defect of the work might have been its agreement with those rules, as they are more artificial than correct. Indeed

---

1. *Proceedings of the R. G. J.*, 1885, p. 443.
2. *Voyage de l'Arabie Pétrée*, par L. de Laborde et Linant, Paris, 1830, p. 71, and Illustrations.
3. *Études religieuses, philosophiques, historiques et littéraires*, 1878, p. 797.
4. Bentley's *Dictionary and Grammar of the Kongo Language*, p. XI.
5. *Grammatica elementar do Kimbundu*, p. XV.

as far as I am able to judge, Father de Coucto's catechism is still now one of the best Bantu works we possess. I have made use of it constantly in writing this work.

22. In 1650 the Capuchin Father Hyacinth Busciotto de Vetralla published in Rome a vocabulary in four columns, Congo, Portuguese, Latin, and Italian. I have not seen this work.

In 1659 the Propaganda at Rome published a Congo Grammar of the same author, entitled "*Regulae quaedam pro difficillimi Congensium idiomatis faciliori captu ad Grammaticae normam redactae.*" This is a good work, and one which shows much insight into the language. It has been lately translated into English by Mr. H. Grattan Guinness, of the Livingstone Congo Mission.

23. In 1697 Father Pedro Dias, S. J., published at Lisbon an Angola Grammar entitled "*Arte da lingua de Angola*". According to Héli Chatelain the author of this little work shows that he understood well the mechanism of the language with which he dealt ([1]). I have found in it several precious observations which I have noticed nowhere else.

The first series of publications in and on the languages of South-Africa seems to have come to an end with this book, unless we add to it an abridged grammar of the language of Kakongo, which forms the 19th chapter of a *History of Loango* published in 1776 ([2]). About this time a very good French-Congo Dictionary was ready for the press. Unfortunately it is still in manuscript, waiting in the British Museum for publication ([3]). Its counterpart, the Congo-French Dictionary, has been discovered at Rome by Père Duparquet, of the Congregation of the Holy Ghost ([4]).

24. *The revival of Bantu Literature.* — Bantu studies were finally resumed at the beginning of this century by the Capuchin Father Bernardo Maria de Cannecattim. He published at Lisbon in 1804 an Angola Dictionary, and in 1805 an Angola Grammar. He undoubtedly must be praised for his initiative, but his works cannot be said to be as valuable as the preceding. His Dictionary is one of those dry collections of words without a single example to establish the proper value of any one of them. His Grammar is retrograde as compared with the little work of Father Pedro Dias, which he does not seem to have known.

Since then Bantu literature has been steadily increasing in the number of its volumes until such publications have become matters of frequent occurrence.

25. The most famous is Bleek's *Comparative Grammar of South-African Languages.* This work was intended to reveal to the scientific world the extent, as well as the proper features, of the great Bantu family of languages, and at the same time to determine its relation to the Hottentot-

---

1. *Grammatica elementar do Kimbundu*, p. xvi.
2. *Histoire de Loango*, par M. l'abbé Proyart, Paris, 1776.
3. Add. Mss. 33, 779, Grenville Library.
4. *Missions Catholiques*, 1886, p. 400.

Bushman family, and, perhaps, to other families as well. It was to be published in four parts. The first appeared in 1862. It contains a classification of the South-African languages best known at the time, followed by a study of their phonetics. The first section of the second part was published in 1869. It is a very careful comparative study of the prefixes and suffixes of substantives both in Bantu and Hottentot. Unfortunately Bleek died before he could carry his work any further than this first section. His premature loss will ever be a matter of regret to the scientific world.

*26.* The other treasures of Bantu literature down to 1883 have been described at length in Dr. Cust's classical " *Sketch of the Modern Languages of Africa* ". This is not the place to do the same work over again. It is simply astonishing that Dr. Cust was so successful in picking up the vast amount of information on Bantu languages and their literature which he has embodied in his work. I cannot say I have got at all the available sources mentioned by him for the study of these languages. I think, however, I have perused nearly all those which were to my purpose. The want of the others, if want it be, is compensated, at least in part, by the information I have obtained directly from natives of various parts of Africa, by the possession of several works which have appeared since 1883, and by the perusal of certain MSS. of Livingstone and other travellers which are in the Grey Library in Capetown.

In mentioning the materials which I have thus had at my disposal, I refer the reader for further information to Dr. Cust's work.

*27. Sources for the Kafir cluster.* — See Cust, pp. 301 (Xosa) and 299 (Zulu).

1. Doehne's *Zulu-Kafir Dictionary*, Capetown, 1857.
2. Davies's *Kafir Dictionary, Xosa and Zulu*, London, 1872.
3. Callaway's *Nursery Tales of the Zulus*, Natal, 1868.
4. „ *Religious system of the Zulus*, Natal, 1868.
5. Appleyard's *The Kafir Language*, King William's Town, 1850.
6. Grout's *Grammar of the Zulu Language*, Natal, 1861, etc., etc.

Kafir is the Bantu language I know best, having learnt it through five years' intercourse with the Xosa-Kafirs, during which purposely I never spoke to them but in their language. Most of the Kafir sentences given in this work are taken from tales which I wrote under their dictation, or which they wrote for me. One of these was published in 1886 in my " *Outline of a Xosa-Kafir Grammar.* " Four others are appended to this work as specimens of the traditional literature of these people.

*28. Sources for the Karanga cluster.* — See Cust, pp. 307 (Kalaka), 310 (Yeye), and 307 (Shona).

When I had learned Tonga from the three Zambezi boys whom I shall mention hereafter, one of them gave me the Karanga translation of most of what I had written in Tonga. He was a very intelligent native, about thirty years of age, belonging to the family of Wange, whom he made out to be the direct representative of the old house of Monomotapa, and about whom more may be seen in the second section of the first appendix to this work. He therefore belonged to those Karanga who crossed to the north of the Zambezi, when driven by Mzilikazi out of what is now Matabeleland. His native name was *Siacibi*. I do not know that anything has ever been published on the dialects of the important Karanga cluster. There is a Vocabulary of Yeye in Livingstone's Vocabulary (MS.) to be mentioned hereafter.

29. *Sources for the Tonga cluster.* — See Cust, pp. 322 (Toka, *alias* Tonga), 325 (Bisa), 329 (Tonga), and 364 (Bemba).

This again is an important cluster on which nothing worth notice has yet been published. I take Tonga as the standard language throughout this work ([1]). I learned what I know of it in 1884 from three natives who had come down to the Cape Colony from the Interior in the company of Fathers Depelchin and Croonenberghs, S. J. One of the three was the Karanga named Siacibi mentioned just above. He pretended to speak pure Tonga like the other two, saying that all the subjects of Wange have learned to speak this language since they crossed the Zambezi, though they all know Karanga also. As I told him I had heard that they had adopted the Kololo language, he said that this was quite false, and that not a single subject of Wange knew Kololo, adding that this language was very difficult to learn, while Tonga was easy. Whenever he gave me any information in Tonga, I got his two companions to repeat what he had said, in order to make sure of the correctness of his idiom. The second of these "boys", as they are called in South-Africa, belonged to the *Lea* tribe *(alias Ba-lea, Ma-leya,* etc.), dwelling below the Victoria Falls. His own native language was Lea, which is a Tonga dialect, but he was quite used to speak pure Tonga, according to the standard received on the Middle Zambezi. His pronunciation was somewhat indistinct. The third of the three, whom we only knew by the name of Joe, was one of the independent Tonga who recognise Monze as their paramount rain-maker ([2]). His immediate chief was the well-known Sinamane, on the Zambezi River. His pronunciation was wonderfully clear and distinct. Unfortunately he was too young to give

---

1. I believe it will readily be seen by those who will peruse this work that the Tonga language of the Middle Zambezi represents well the proper features of the larger number of the Bantu languages. As the name of *Ba-tonga* is common to several South-African tribes, it may be as well for me to state here what I think of them. I consider the Tonga of the Middle Zambezi, who have no other name than this, to be the purest representative of the original Bantu. They alone, it seems, have never been tributary to any empire: they say that they have never had any but independent chieftains, or patriarchs, who may recognise a paramount rain-maker, but no king in the proper sense of this word. Neither slavery, nor anything like higher and lower class, is known amongst them, they all are the "children" of the chiefs. Then, well protected in their peninsula by the Kafuefue on one side and the Zambezi on the other, they may easily have guarded themselves against invaders, as they do in our own days. The other tribes known by the name of Tonga in other parts of South-Africa I should equally consider to represent the aborigines with respect to their neighbours, or to the upper classes intermixed with them. They are all peaceful agricultural tribes. Such are, for instance, the Tonga of Sofala and the Lower Limpopo, also called *Ma-Gwamba* or *Ma-kwapa* "people of the place", and *Ma-hlengwe*, or, as the Xosa-Kafirs pronounce this word, *a Ma-mfenqu;* the Tonga of Lake Nyassa, also called *Wa-kamanga;* the *Tonga* or *Tanga* of the Katanga; the *Tonga* or *Tanga* of the Gabún, also called *Naku,* etc.

2. See the third section of the first Appendix to this work.

much information, being at the time only thirteen or fourteen years of age. Some specimens of the kind of information I obtained from these natives are appended to this work (Appendix I.) Livingstone has written a great deal about the Tonga in his " *Missionary Travels* ". He writes their name *Ba-toka* according to Chwana pronunciation, instead of *Ba-tonga*.

In January 1885 I was kindly allowed to copy in the Grey Library in Capetown a MS. of Livingstone which contains a Tonga vocabulary. It is entitled " A Comparative Vocabulary of the Languages of the *Ba-khoba* or *Ba-yeye*, *Ba-shubea* (= *Ba-subia*), *Ba-lojazi*, *Ba-ponda* ( = *Mambunda*), *Ba-rotse*, *Ba-toka* (= *Ba-tonga*), *Ba-nyeñko*, *Be-chuana*, and English. " Too many words in this MS. remind one of the Chwana scholar, but with this exception it is sufficiently reliable.

I have no other source than this MS. for Subia. For Bisa and Bemba there are short collections in Last's precious *Polyglotta Africana Orientalis*, a work to be often referred to hereafter. Another collection of Bisa words is found in Stanley's Comparative Vocabulary at the end of " *Through the Dark Continent* ". With regard to the Tonga dialect of Lake Nyassa, see n. 65.

*30. Sources for the Senna cluster.* — See Cust, pp. 307 (Zizulu = Tette) and 323 (Nyai = Tette and Zumbo), 326 (Ravi = Nyassa), 330 (Nganga = Nyassa), and 331 (Sena).

In 1885 a native of Kilimane, by name Justino, whom I met in the Cape Colony, wrote out for me vocabularies, dialogues, fables, and a short history of the life and passion of Our Lord, in Senna and Portuguese. I have mostly made use of these MSS., all well written and perfectly consistent. My other sources are : —

1. MSS. kindly lent to me by Father Ronchi, S. J., containing vocabularies, fables, etc.
2. *Elementos de Grammatica Tetense*, pelo R. P. Victor José Courtois, S. J., Moçambique, 1889.
3. *A Grammar of the Chinyanja Language as spoken at Lake Nyassa*..., by Alexander Riddel, of the Livingstonia Mission, Edinburgh, 1880.
4. *Dictionary of the Kiniassa Language*, by the Rev. John Rebman, Basle, 1877.
5. Specimens of Gindo in Dr. Steere's *Short specimens of three African Languages*, 1869, and in Last's *Polygl.*, pp. 90-92.
6. Bleek's *Languages of Mozambique*, London, 1856.
7. *The Tette Language*, MS. in the Grey Library, Capetown, attributed to Livingstone.
8. *The Senna, Tette, and Maravi, Languages*, MS. attributed to Rebmann, kindly lent to me by the late Father Weld, S. J.

*31. Sources for the Viti cluster.* — See Cust, p. 301 (Ngoni).

1. A few words here and there in Montagu Kerr's *Far Interior*.
2. Last's *Polyglotta Afr. Or.*, pp. 139-141 (Bunga).
3. Stanley's *Viti* or *Tuta* Vocabulary at the end of the *Dark Continent*.

*32. Sources for the Gangi cluster.* — See Cust, pp. 343 (Henge), 362 (Bena), 363 (Sango).

1. Last's *Polygl. Afr. Or.*, pp. 93-96 (Gangi), 105-108 (Ziraha), 117-120 (Kwenyi), 109-112 (Nkwifiya), 113-116 (Ndunda), 121-123 (Bena), 124-127 and 225-226 (Sango), 231 (Kimbu), 157-159 (Nya-turu).

*33. Sources for the Ungu cluster.* —

*Introduction.* XXIX

1. Stanley's *Voc.* in the *Dark Continent*, (Fipa, Rungu (?)).
2. Last's *Polygl. Afr. Or.*, p. 128-130 (Ungu).

*34. Sources for the Sagara cluster.* — See Cust, p. 352 (Sagara), p. 362 (Hehe), p. 365 (Gogo).

1. Stanley's *Voc.* in the *Dark Continent*, (Sagara, Gogo).
2. Last's *Grammar of the Kaguru Language*, London, 1886. See note to n. 77.
3. Last's *Polygl. Afr. Or.*, pp. 57-60, 221-222, and 233 (Kaguru), 61-64 (Itumba), 65-68 (Kondoa), 69-72 (Kami), 73-74 (Khutu), 97-100 and 223-224 (Gogo), 101-104 and 227 (Hehe).

*35. Sources for the Nyamwezi cluster.* — See Cust, pp. 365 (Nyamwezi), 367 (Tusi), and 373 (Sukuma).

1. Stanley's *Sukuma Voc.* in the *Dark Continent*.
2. Dr. Steere's *Collections for a Grammar of the Nyamwezi Language*, London (no date).
3. Last's *Polygl. Afr. Or.*, pp. 146-149 (Sukuma), 150-153 (Sumbwa), and 154-156 (Tusi, or Ha).

*36. Source for Regga.* — See Cust, p. 377 (Regga).

Last's *Polygl.*, pp. 203-212.

*37. Sources for the Ganda cluster.* — See Cust, pp. 374 (Ganda), and 373 (Zongora = Nyambu). I have mostly availed myself of the excellent " *Essai de Grammaire Ruganda*, par un Père de la Société des Missions d'Afrique, Paris, 1885. " My other sources are : —

1. *Katekismu Ruganda*, Alger, 1887.
2. *St Matthew's Gospel in Ganda*, British and Foreign Bible Society, 1888.
3. *An Outline Grammar of the Luganda Language*, by Rev. C. T. Wilson, M. A., F. R. G. S., C. M. S. Missionary to Uganda, London, 1882.
4. Stanley's *Voc.* in the *Dark Continent* (Ganda, Nyambu).
5. Last's *Pol. Afr. Or.*, pp. 173-175 (Ganda), and 160-163 (Nyambu).

*38. Sources for the Taita cluster.* See Cust, pp. 350 (Teita), 357 (Taveta), and 354 (Pare).

1. *A pocket Vocabulary of the Ki-swahili, Ki-nyika, Ki-taita, and Ki-kamba Languages*, compiled by A. Downes Shaw, C. M. S. Missionary in East-Africa, London, 1885.
2. *Wörterverzeichnis aus dem Kidschagga und Pare*, in the *Zeitschrift für afrikanische Sprachen*, 1887-1888, pp. 72-76.
3. *Ki-taveita Vocabulary* in H. H. Johnston's *Kilimanjaro Expedition*, London, 1886, pp. 521-540.

*39. Sources for the Nika cluster.* — See Cust, p. 355 (Nyika or Nika).

1. Downes Shaw's *Pocket Dictionary*, just mentioned.
2. *A Nika-English Dictionary*, compiled by the late Rev. Dr. L. Krapf and the late Rev. J. Rebmann, edited by the Rev. T. H. Sparshott, S. P. C. K., 1887.

*40. Sources for Pokomo.* — See Cust, p. 359.

1. *Zur Grammatik des Ki-pokomo*, in the *Zeitschrift f. a. S.*, 1888-89, pp. 161-189.
2. *Kipokomo Wörterverzeichnis*, von Missionar Ferd. Würtz, *Ibid.* 1889-90, pp. 81-105.

*41. Sources for Kamba.* — See Cust, p. 359.

1. Last's *Polygl. Afr. Or.*, pp. 53-56 and 217-218.
2. Last's *Grammar of the Kamba Language*, London, 1885.
3. Shaw's *Pocket Vocabulary* already mentioned.
4. Krapf's *Deutch Ki-kamba Wörterbuch* in the *Zeitschrift f. a. S.*, 1887-88, pp. 81-123.

*42. Sources for the Swahili cluster.* — See Cust, p. 345.

Swahili I have studied mostly from Dr. Steere's " *Swahili Tales as told by Natives of Zanzibar*, 2$^d$ ed., London, 1889, " and the " *Arab Tales, translated from ...Swahili... into the Tugulu dialect of the Makua Language*, by

Daniel J. Rankin, M. R. A. S., ex-Acting British Consul at Mozambique, London, 1886." My other sources are the three following remarkable works:

1. Krapf's *Dictionary of the Swahili Language* (London, 1882), which, with its copious examples intended to bring out the proper meaning of the words, is a good specimen of what every Bantu Dictionary should be.

2. *A Handbook of the Swahili Language as spoken at Zanzibar*, by the late Edward Steere, LL. D., Missionary Bishop for Central Africa, 3ᵈ edition,... by A. C. Madan, M. A., London, 1885.

3. *Grammaire Kisuahili*, par le Père Delaunay, de la Société des Missionnaires de N.-D. des Missions d'Afrique, Paris, 1885.

*43. Sources for the Shambala cluster.* — See Cust, pp. 351 (Zeguha and Nguru), and 353 (Boondei and Shambala).

1. Dr. Steere's *Collections for a Handbook of the Shambala Language*, 1867.
2. Last's *Polygl. Afr. Or.*, pp. 41-44 (Shambala), 49-52 and 213-214 (Zeguha=Zegula), 45-48 and 215-216 (Nguru), and 37-40 (Boondei).
3. *Collections for a Handbook of the Boondei Language*, by Rev. H. W. Woodward, of the Universities' Mission to Central Africa, S. P. C. K., 1882.

*44. Sources for the Ibo cluster.* —

1. *Ibo Vocabulary* in Rankin's *Arab Tales*, mentioned above, pp. 43-46.
2. Last's *Polygl. Afr. Or.*, pp. 33-36 (Lima).

*45. Source for Zaramo.* — See Cust, p. 344.

1. Dr. Steere's *Short specimens of three... African Languages*, London, 1869.

*46. Sources for Konde.* — See Cust, pp. 341 (Konde), and 343 (Donde).

1. Last's *Polygl. Afr. Or.*, pp. 77-80.
2. *Konde Vocabulary* in Rankin's *Arab Tales* mentioned above, pp. 43-46.

*47. Sources for Yao.* — See Cust, p. 334.

1. *Introductory Handbook of the Yao Language*, by the Rev. Alexander Hetherwick, M. A., F. R. G. S., S. P. C. K. 1889.
2. Dr. Steere's *Collections for a Handbook of the Yao Language*, S. P. C. K., 1871.
3. Last's *Polygl. Afr. Or.*, p. 87-89.

*48. Sources for the Herero cluster.* — See Cust, pp. 309 (Herero), and 311 (Ndonga).

1. *An English-Herero Dictionary*, by the Rev. F. W. Kolbe, Capetown, 1883.
2. Dr. Bütner's *Sprachführer für Reisende in Damaraland*, and *Märchen der Ova-herero* in the *Zeitschrift f. a. S.*, 1887-88, pp. 252-294, 189-216, and 295-307.
3. Bleek's note on *Sindonga* in his *Comparative Grammar* (212-216).
4. *Lojazi Vocabulary* in Livingstone's *Comparative Voc.* MS. mentioned above.

*49. Sources for the Benguela cluster.* — See Cust, p. 390 (Nano).

1. Bleek's note on Nano in his *Comparative Gr.*, pp. 216-220.
2. *Pangela Vocabulary* in Koelle's *Polyglotta Africana*, London, 1854.
3. Stover's *Observations on the Grammatical structure of the Umbundu Language*, Boston, 1885.
4. Sander's *Vocabulary of the Umbundu Language*, Boston, 1885.

*50. Source for Kwango, or Mbunda proper.* — See Cust, p. 390 (Ponda or Mbunda).

*Mbunda Vocabulary* in Livingstone's *Comparative Voc.* MS. mentioned above.

*51. Sources for the Rotse cluster.* — See Cust, p. 389 (Luina).

1. *Barotse Language translated into the Sichuana*, MS. in the Grey Library, Capetown, attributed to Livingstone.
2. *Rotse Vocabulary* in Livingstone's *Comp. Voc.* MS. mentioned above.
3. *Nyengo Vocabulary* in the same MS.

*52. Sources for the (Ci-)boko cluster.* — See Cust, p. 397 (Kioko), and p. 399 (Yakka).

*Quioco Vocabulary* in Capello and Ivens' *From Benguella to the Territory of Yacca*, London, 1882, pp. 327-330.

*53. Sources for the Angola cluster.* — See Cust, p. 393 (Bunda = Angola).

1. *Arte da lingua de Angola*, pelo P. Pedro Dias, S. J. Lisboa, 1697, *supra*, n. *23*.
2. Father de Coucto's *Catechism*, 1661, *supra*, n. *21*.
3. Héli Chatelain's *Grammatica elementar do Kimbundu*, Genebra, 1888-89.
  Do. *Die Grundzüge des Kimbundu*, in the *Zeitschrift f. a. S.*, 1889-90.
  Do. *Sammlung von Mbamba und Mbangala Wörtern*, ibid. 1889.
4. *N-bunda Vocabulary* in Capello and Iven's *From Benguela...*, pp. 304-325.
5. *Colleçao de Observaçoes grammaticaes sobre a lingua Bunda*, por Fr. Bernardo Maria de Cannecattim, Capuchino..., Lisboa, 1805.
6. Cannecattim's *Diccionario da lingua Bunda ou Angolense*, Lisboa, 1804.
7. *Kasands Vocabulary* in Koelle's *Polygl. Afr.*, London, 1854.

*54. Sources for Lower Congo.* See Cust, p. 405.

1. MS. French-Congo Dictionary, 1772, British Museum.
2. Bentley's *Dictionary and Grammar on the Kongo Language*, Baptist Miss. Soc., 1887.
3. *Grammaire Fiote*, par le Rév. P. Alexandre Visseq, de la Congrégation du Saint-Esprit, Paris, 1889.
4. *Regulae quaedam... pro... Congensium idiomatis... captu*, a P. Hyacintho Brusciotto a Vetralla, Concionatore Capucino, Romae, 1659, *supra* n. *22*.

*55. Sources for Lunda.* — See Cust, p. 399.

1. *Ruunda Vocabulary* in Koelle's *Polyglotta Africana*.
2. *Lunda Vocabulary* in Capello and Ivens *From Benguela...*, pp. 329-331.
3. Carvalho's *Methodo pratico para fallar a lingua da Lunda*, Lisbon, 1890. See n. 78S[bis].

*56. Sources for the Guha cluster.* — See Cust, pp. 371 (Guha), and 363 (Rungu).

1. Last's *Polygl. Afr. Or.*, pp. 170-172 (Guha).
2. Stanley's *Comparative Voc.* in the *Dark Continent* (Guhha, and Rungu (?) ).

*57. Sources for the Nywema cluster.* — See Cust, p. 372 (Nywema, and Kusu).

1. Last's *Polygl. Afr. Or.*, pp. 183-187 and 232-233.

*58. Sources for Rua..* — See Cust, p. 371.

1. Cameron's *Kirua Vocabulary* in *Across Africa*, London, 1877.
2. Last's *Polygl. Afr. Or.*, pp. 167-169.

*59. Sources for Luba.* — See Cust, p. 400.

Dr. Büttner's *Zur Grammatik der Balubasprache* in the *Zeitschrift f. a. S.*, 1888-89, pp. 220-233.

*60. Source for the Yansi cluster.* — See Cust, pp. 409 (Teke) and 410 (Yanzi).

See nn. 159-162.

*61. Sources for the Chwana cluster.* — See Cust, p. 305.

In 1885 I collected some materials for the study of Chwana with the help of a native of the Ba-kwena tribe from Pretoria, and a Mo-suto subject of the late Moshesh. But in writing this work I have not made so much use of these as of the "*Notes towards a Secoana Grammar*, collected by the Rev. William Crisp, Canon and Chancellor of Bloemfontein Cathedral

(2d edition, London, 1886)," and of the Chwana Catechism of Father Temming, S. J. My other sources are: —

1. *An English and Secwana Vocabulary*, by the Rev. John Brown, London, 1876.
2. *The Chwana New Testament*, London, 1888.
3. *Hymns in Chwana*, by Father Temming, S. J., Marianhill, 1887.

### 62. Sources for the Nyambane cluster. — See Cust, pp. 302 (Gwamba), 303 (Hlengoe), 303 (Nyambane), and 308 (Siga = Nyambane).

1. Bleek's *Languages of Mozambique* (Lourenzo Marques, Inhambane), London, 1856.
2. Koelle's *Polyglotta Africana* (Nyamban = Nyambane).
3. *Leçons de Shigwamba*, par le Missionnaire P. Berthoud, Lausanne, 1883.

### 63. Sources for the Mozambique cluster. — See Cust, pp. 333 (Roro = Gunda (?) ), 333 (Kua).

1. Rankin's *Arab Tales*, mentioned above.
2. Chauncy Maples' *Collections for a Handbook of the Makua Language as spoken at Masasi*, London, 1879.
3. *Elementos para un Vocabulario do dialecto falado em Quelimane*, por Gustavo de Bivar Pinto Lopes, Moçambique, 1889.
4. *English-Tshigunda Vocabulary* (no title page).
5. Bleek's *Languages of Mozambique* (Quellimane, Mozambique).
6. Koelle's *Polyglotta Africana* (Meto, Kiriman, Matatan).
7. Last's *Polygl. Afr. Or.*, pp. 81-83. (Lomwe), 84-86 (Mozambique).

### 64. Sources for the Comoro cluster. — See Cust, p. 339.

1. Last's *Polygl. Afr. Or.*, pp. 179-182. (Anzuani, or Hinzua).
2. Bleek's *Languages of Mozambique* (Anjoane).
3. Dr. Steere's *Short specimens of three African Languages* (Angazidja).

### 65. Sources for the Tshagga cluster. — See Cust, p. 357 (Chagga).

1. *Wörterverzeichnis aus dem Kidshagga und Pare*, in the *Zeitschrift. f a. S.*, 1887-88, pp. 72-76.
2. H. H. Johnston's *Chagga and Gweno Vocabulary* in *The Kilimanjaro Expedition*.

### 66. Sources for Buma. — See Cust, p. 409.

H. H. Johnston's *Voc.* in *The River Congo*, 446-463.

### 67. Sources for the Mpongwe cluster. — See Cust, pp. 417 (Pongwe), and 420 (Shekiani).

1. *Dictionnaire Français-Pongoué*, par les missionnaires de la Congrégation du St-Esprit, Paris, 1877.
2. *Dictionnaire Pongoué-Français*, par le R. P. Gachon, de la Congrégation du St-Esprit, Paris, 1881.
3. *Grammaire de la Langue Pongouée*, par le R. P. Le Berre, de la Congrégation du St-Esprit, Paris, 1873.
4. *Mpongwe Gospels*, by American Missionaries at the Gaboon, 3d ed., New York, 1879.

### 68. Sources for the Dualla cluster. — See Cust, p. 426 (Dualla), 428 (Isubu), 420 (Benga), 415 (Kele).

1. Saker's *Grammatical elements of the Dualla Language* (incomplete), with Vocabulary and MSS. (in the British Museum), 1863.
2. C. Meinhof's *Ein Märchen aus Kamerun* in the *Zeitschrift f. a. S.*, 1889-90, pp. 241-246.
   Do. *Das Zeitwort in der Duallasprache, ibid.*, 1888-89, pp. 1-34.
   Do. *Benga und Dualla, ibid.*, pp. 190-208.
   Do. *Das Verbum in der Isubu-Sprache, ibid.*, 1889-90, pp. 206-234.
   Do. *Das Zeitwort in der Benga-Sprache, ibid.*, pp. 265-284.
3. Bleek's Notes on Dikele, Benga, Dualla, and Isubu, in the *Compar. Gr.*, pp. 231-240.

69. *Source for Fan.* — See Cust, p. 422.

*Vocabulary of the Fan Language*, by Señor Don Amado Osorio Zabala, S. P. C. K. 1887.

70. *Sources for the Fernandian cluster.* — See Cust, p. 426 (Ediya).

1. Bleek's Note on Fernandian in the *Compar. Gr.*, pp. 248-251.

2. Oscar Baumann's *Beiträge zur Kenntnis der Bube-Sprache auf Fernando Poo*, and *Vocabular des Banapa- (Sta Isabel) Dialektes*... von Padre Don José Martinez y Sanz, S. J., in the *Zeitschrift f. a. S.*, 1887-88, pp. 138-155.

It need scarcely be said that the materials thus placed at my disposal are more or less reliable. In this work my conclusions are generally drawn only from those which I thought could best be trusted.

## III. The Origin of the Bantu.

71. Before we begin to form a comprehensive view of the various Bantu languages, and their general and proper features, it may be good to put together a certain number of data regarding the origin of the various tribes that speak them. The sciences of ethnology and philology have so many points of contact that they must, as it were, go hand in hand. In a subject like this, in particular, the conclusions to which philology seems to lead may be right or wrong. It is therefore important to see what foundation history gives to them. A special reason for giving here some of the historical and ethnographical data which I have come across regarding the Bantu is that, if we may judge from various current and unfounded theories, they scarcely seem to be known to exist.

72. *First origin.* — The most probable account of the first origin of the Bantu seems to be the one found in Mas'oudi's " *Golden Meadows* ", a work written A. D. 943. Mas'oudi had crossed several times from Arabia to the east coast of Africa ([1]), and thus had been able to collect accurate information on the Bantu, or the Zindj, as he with the other Arab writers calls them. This is what he says : —

" When Noah's posterity began to spread itself over the earth, the children of Kush, the son of Kanaan (Cham), followed a westerly direction and crossed the Nile. There they formed two groups. Some of them, the Nubians, the Bedjah, and the Zindj, turned to the right, between east and west; the others, in great numbers, went westward in the direction of Zagawah, Kanem, Markah, Ghanah, and other parts of the land of the Blacks and the Dendemeh. Those who had taken the right, going between east and west, soon separated again, thus forming several tribes of the Zindj, such as the Makir (*alias* Mex, Meska), the Maskar (*alias* Miktar, Meshku, Mashku, Saka, Seka), the Marira, and others ([2]). "

A little further in the same work ([3]), Mas'oudi adds the following details : —

1. Maçoudi, " *Les Prairies d'Or* ". Texte et traduction par Barbier de Meynard et Pavet de Courteille. Paris, 1861-1877, vol. I, p. 233.
2. *Ibid.*, vol. III, p. 2.
3. *Ibid.*, p. 5.

"As we have said above, the Zindj with other Abyssinian tribes spread themselves to the right of the Nile, down to the extremity of the sea of Abyssinia. Of all the Abyssinian tribes the Zindj were the only ones who crossed the canal which comes out of the Upper Nile (Juba River?). They established themselves in this country and spread themselves as far as Sofala, which is on the sea of the Zindj the furthest limit whither ships sail from Oman and Siraf. For, as the Chinese sea ends at the land of Sila (Japan or Corea), so the limits of the sea of the Zindj are near the land of Sofala and that of the Wakwak (Hottentots and Bushmen), a country which yields gold in abundance with other marvels. There the Zindj built their chief-town. Then they elected a king whom they called *Falime* (or *Wafalime*) (1). This has been at all times the name of their paramount chief.

.... The Falime has in his dependency all the other Zindjan kings, and commands 300,000 mounted men. The Zindj use the ox as their beast of burden (2); for their country has neither horses, nor mules, nor camels; they do not even know these beasts. There are among them tribes which have very sharp teeth (3) and are cannibals (4). The territory of the Zindj begins at the canal derived from the Upper Nile, and extends to the land of Sofala and that of the Wakwak."

73. These are interesting assertions in the light of modern discoveries. A great empire in South-Africa with its chief-town in the land of Sofala, — nothing could tally better with the descriptions given of South-Africa by the latest explorers. For this country is now found to possess remarkable remnants of an ancient civilization.

Let us remark here that the land formerly called Sofala by the Arabs was not limited to the coast which has retained this name, but comprised all that part of South-Africa which lies between the Limpopo and the River Rovuma. Even in the times of the Portuguese Livius, de Barros, Sofala, or Cefala, as he spells it, was a synonym for "the empire of the Monomotapa" (5). This therefore is the land where we must most expect to find the first seat of the Zindjan Empire.

What was more exactly its situation? If we believe Abulfeda and Edrisi,

---

1. I have explained in the Grammar, nn. 365(²) and 344, that Mas'oudi's word *Falime*, plural of dignity *Wa-falime*, — which may also be read *Falimo*, *Wa-falimo*, etc. — must be identified with the Swahili *M-falme*, or *M-falume*, "a king", pl. *Wa-falme*, and with the Mozambique *Mu-limu* "a chief", lit. "a man of learning (?)". It seems that the original pronunciation of this word must have been *mf'a limo* = *m-fo u-a limo*, "a man of *limo*", whatever the exact meaning of *limo* may be. Certain it is that the Bantu stem which is pronounced *-zimo* in the main group, and *-limo*, or *-dimo*, or *-rimo*, in the Kua group, forms immediately the word *Mi-zimo* (Chwana *Ba-limo*, or *Ba-dimo*) "the spirits of the kings of old, " "the departed chiefs". See n. 365 (6). As to the word *m-fo*, it is often heard in Kafir, and means "an elderly man".

2. So the Kafirs only a few years ago still had their pack-oxen. Now they have horses.

3. See the note to n. 50. See also the *Proceedings of the R. G. S.*, 1887, p. 775, and Bateman's *First ascent of the Kasai*, p. 46.

4. The Nyuema are not the only Bantu tribe accused of cannibalism. The Yao themselves, east of Lake Nyassa, sometimes indulge in feasts on human flesh (*Proceedings of the R. G. S.*, 1887, p. 468). Ancient traditions say that Senna itself was a mart for human flesh before the advent of the Portuguese.

5. *Da Asia*, dec. I, lib. X, c. 1, quoted in the *Études Religieuses*, 1878, vol. I, p. 388.

in their time (before the 14th century) the chief-town of Sofala was *Siyuna*, which I think must be identified with the chief-town of *Ma-shona-land*, or the country of *Senna* ([1]). Is not the natural inference from this that Mas'oudi's seat of the first kings of the Zindj was somewhere in Mashonaland ? If the answer must be affirmative, the ruins of Zimbabye, or Zimbaze, which, discovered by Mauch a few years ago, have lately amazed the pioneers of the Chartered Company, seem to point out the exact spot for which we are looking.

The descriptions given of these ruins well corroborate this conclusion. Their features which most struck the Correspondent of the *Times* ([2]) are : —

1º A series of circular walls within one another, the outermost of which is 4 feet high, and may be over 500 yards in diameter ;

2º One of the inner walls "from 30 ft. to 35 ft. high, 80 yards in diameter, about 10 ft. in thickness at the base, and tapering to about 7 ft. or 8 ft. at the top, built of small granite blocks, about twice the size of an ordinary brick, beautifully hewn and dressed, laid in perfectly even courses, and put together without the use of a single atom of either mortar or cement " ;

3º On the eastern side of this enclosure, a narrow entrance, and close to it, at a place where the wall is 30 ft. high, " a conical shaped tower, or turret, 35 ft. in height and 18 ft. in diameter at the base, built of the same granite blocks, and consisting of solid masonry " ;

4º " On the south-east front of the wall and 20 ft. from its base a double zigzag scroll, one third of the distance round, composed of the samesized granite blocks placed in diagonal positions ".

According to the newspapers, indeed, an expert sent to study these ruins is inclined to think them to be of Phœnician origin. But, from the description given, I rather suspect that they are, on the whole, of purely native, or Zindjan, origin. In our own days the Gcaleka Kafirs, with whom I lived some time, never, when they can afford it, build for their cattle any but round stone kraals, which, though they cannot be compared with the ruins of Zimbabye, seem to belong essentially to the same style of building ; and with many Bantu tribes zigzag-shaped drawings are the usual pattern for all kinds of attempt at anything like artistic designs.

Finally, another good reason for identifying Zimbabye with both the Siyuna of Abulfeda and the seat of the first kings of the Zindj is, that the actual occupiers of the country round it, variously called *Zindja, Ba-nyai, Ma-shona*, etc., are properly part of the *Karanga*, who certainly have been for centuries the paramount tribe of the vast empire of the Monomotapa.

74. If, however, it were replied that, notwithstanding these evidences, Zimbabye may yet be found to have been the work of foreign gold-seekers,

---

1. See note to p. 25 in this work.
2. *The Times* of Oct. 7, 1890. Cf. Anderson's *Twenty-five Years in a Waggon*, London, 1887, vol. II, p. 202.

and that the first chief-town of the Zindj must be sought for not in Mashonaland, but somewhere near the Victoria Falls, I should not deny a certain probability to this opinion. It would readily explain why they are considered by the natives as being not only God's abode, but also the town of the ancient kings *(munzi ua Leza, munzi ua Mizimo)*. See Appendix I.

75. But whatever may be thought of this question, I see no reason to doubt of Mas'oudi's trustworthiness when exposing the traditions he had either picked up on the spot, or found in previous Hebrew, Christian, or Mohammedan writers, regarding the first origin of the Zindj. His veracity seems to be warranted by his exactitude in details of minor importance, such as the filed teeth and the cannibalism of certain tribes, the Bantu name of the king, the use of pack-oxen, the want of horses and camels, the goldmines of the country, the exact extent of the Bantu field on the east coast, the location of the Hottentots south of the Zindj, etc. etc. It may be added that Mas'oudi agrees with universal tradition, and with the most ancient Egyptian inscriptions, in considering the Blacks as children of Kush. He is mistaken only in calling Kush the son of Kanaan.

Writing of the language of the Zindj, Mas'oudi says that " they express themselves with elegance, and are not wanting in orators " [1]. This is another evidence of his veracity.

76. There is in Mas'oudi's narrative one detail which deserves particular attention. According to him the Zindj at first occupied only the eastern parts of South-Africa between the Upper Nile and the Ocean, and further south the land of Sofala. The black tribes which originally occupied the western parts would like the Zindj have descended of Kush, but from the earliest times they would also have constituted a quite distinct group. This, I think, is a valuable clue to the study of South-Western Africa. It is mostly in the west that we find non-Bantu tribes. In the south they are met with either isolated, or mixed up with the Bantu, as far north as the upper streams of the Kwanza. Perhaps some of them may still be discovered living in the mysterious caves of the Katanga. Then going further to the north-west, we meet with them in the Congo forest, and still more to the north they occupy the country all to themselves.

Then, if we look at the physical features of those tribes in the west which speak Bantu languages, we find that they belong to at least two distinct types, the one very similar to the most refined Bantu of the east, the other approaching more to the Bushman. Further, the ruling tribes of the greater part of the Congo basin and the Kwanza seem to have belonged until quite recently to what was called the Jinga nation.

All these considerations lead me to form a view of the south-western nations of Africa which agrees entirely with Mas'oudi's account. The original occupants of the Damaraland, Benguela, Angola, the Congo, and in general of nearly all that part of South-Africa which is to the west of the meridian

---

1. Vol. III, p. 30.

of the Victoria Falls, were not Bantu. It is only in comparatively recent times, probably not before the Christian Era, that Zindj invaders from the east, called Jinga (= Zinga), overran their country, and imposed upon them both their rule and their language.

77. What was the origin of those non-Bantu tribes? This is a difficult question to answer owing to the want of positive documents. General tradition, handed down to us mostly by the earliest Fathers of the Church, considers Phuth, the third son of Cham, as the father of the original occupants of Western Africa. If therefore his name meant " west " as the word *Mbunda*, or *Pouda*, or *Puta*, or *Mbundu*, I should suspect that the Ma-mbunda are children of Phuth. If we must allow with Mas'oudi that they are descended from Kush, and this I think is the most correct opinion, it may be that, being originally Kush's children, they had to submit, even before the earliest Jinga invasions, to the yoke of people descended from Phuth, and that they borrowed from these first rulers the name of Mbunda, which most of them have kept to this day.

What is certain is, that several of the Bantu languages of South-Western Africa, or the so-called Mbunda languages, have a certain number of words in common with those of the Bushmen, as if these were the true aborigines of those parts.

78. In any case, at least one of the above conclusions seems to be safe, and may serve as a good starting point, viz. that the original Bantu, or Zindj, were of Kush's race. How much foreign blood has filtered into theirs, and transformed it in the course of ages, even in the land which was theirs from the earliest times, is another question, the solution of which would shed light on the history of South-Africa, its modern inhabitants, and its languages. But a thick veil of mystery hangs over it. South-Africa has long been the *terra incognita* of classical writers. Sparse data may however be picked up here and there regarding the relation of its occupants to the outer world, which, if brought together, may at least shew that the land which was unknown to some civilized nations was not necessarily so to all.

79. *Relations of the Bantu to northern nations in Central Africa.* — It appears certain that there has existed continued intercourse in ancient times between the eastern Bantu and the tribes to the north of them, but I find no evidence that such relations, generally hostile or strictly commercial, have ever produced any mixtures of races in the Bantu field. The manner of acting of the Masai with respect to the Bantu in our own times may perhaps be regarded as the type of what has been going on for centuries. These warlike tribes have penetrated from the north into the Bantu field as far as the 5$^{th}$ parallel of south latitude, forcing their way through the Kamba, the Sagara, the Rangi, and other Bantu tribes, all of which are agricultural; but, instead of amalgamating with their enemies, they have kept their own language and customs, entirely distinct from those of their neighbours. There is nothing to show that the same hostile spirit between

the two races has not been going on for centuries, or that it has ever produced other effects than it does now.

*So.* Even the nearest approach I can find to friendly relations between the Bantu and the northern nations in ancient times was not of a nature to create a mixture of blood and languages. I read it in the "*Christian Topography*" of the Egyptian monk Cosmas Indicopleustes, a work written about A. D. 547. It is a typical description of the manner in which trade used to be carried on in Central Africa in his time. This is what he writes ([1]): —

"Beyond Barbaria (also called Troglodytica, i. e. the actual Somali-land), there stretches the Ocean, which has there the name of Ζίγγιον (*Zingi*, the sea of the *Zindj* of the Arabs, whence *Zanzi*-bar). Bordering on the same sea, there is the land called Sasos (South-Eastern Africa), which possesses abundant gold-mines, μέταλλα πολλά χρυσίου ἔχουσα. Every second year the king of Axum (on the Red Sea), through the intermediary of his prefects at Agau (in Abyssinia), sends men thither for the gold-trade. These go accompanied by a large number of merchants, so as to be, taken all together, over 500. They take with them for barter oxen, salt, and iron.

"When they come close to that land, they fix themselves in a certain spot, make a large bush-fence, and live in it. Then they kill the oxen, and expose the meat in pieces on the bushes, together with the salt and the iron. Thereupon natives come up bringing gold in the shape of θέρμια (lupine-beans), which they call *tankhara*, and each puts down one, two, or more θέρμια, as he likes; and goes aside. Then he to whom the ox belonged comes, and, if he be satisfied with the price, takes the gold, while the native comes back to take the meat, or the salt, or the iron. If the trader be not satisfied, he leaves the gold, and the native, seeing this, either adds something, or takes his gold back, and goes off. The trade is carried on in this manner because the language of the two parties is different, and no interpreters can be procured.

"The traders spend thus about five days, more or less according as their business proceeds, until they have sold everything. On their return they all march together under arms, because on the way they are attacked by hostile tribes, that would rob them of their gold. The whole of the expedition, coming and going, takes six months. The march is somewhat slower in coming, principally on account of the cattle : the traders hasten faster on their way back for fear they should be caught on the road by winter and by heavy rains. For the sources of the Nile are near those lands, and in winter many rivers caused by the heavy rains come to obstruct the road. Besides this, the winter of those regions coincides with summer amongst us...

"All this I have written, having partly seen it with my own eyes, partly heard it from the very men who had been trading there".

Whoever has been in Africa will readily give credit to such a description. The bush-fences, the salt-trade, the storms of the rainy season, the

---

1. Migne, *Patr. Gr.*, v. 89, col. 98.

three-months' distance from central Abyssinia, etc., are all details which cannot have been drawn from imagination.

*81.* What gives a peculiar interest to Cosmas' narrative is, that the manner of trading which he describes, when compared with other data, seems to have been going on in Bantu territory from time immemorial. Herodotus, writing of the remotest parts of Eastern Africa, mentions in one place (¹) its abundant gold (χρυσόν τε φέρει πολλόν), its large elephants (ἐλέφαντας ἀμφιλαφέας), its ivory (ἔβενον), its remarkably tall, fine, and long-lived inhabitants — something like the Zulu (?) — (ἄνδρας μεγίστους καὶ καλλίστους καὶ μακροβιωτάτους), and in another place (²), calling these people Μακροβίοι, he speaks of a certain plateau found in their land, which they call "the Sun's Table", and on which the chiefs expose cooked meat at night, that the natives may feast on it at will during the day. Pomponius Mela (³) and other writers mention the same marvel. Now, Heeren has shown that this mysterious flat is no other than the golden mart of the Macrobians, where meat, salt, iron, and other articles of trade, used to be exchanged for gold in the manner described by Cosmas (⁴). Might it not be added that it is also the place where Homer's gods meet to rest from their battles, and enjoy feasts and hecatombs among the pious blacks (⁵)?

*82.* If it be asked what is the exact situation of this plateau, I should say that, in my opinion, it is somewhere in Sagaraland, taking this to include, as it probably did formerly (⁶), the country comprised between longit. 34°-37° and south lat. 4°-8°. The word *Sagara*, or *Sagala*, seems even to mean "the Sun's flats", exactly as *Nyamwezi* means "the mountains of the Moon"; for I notice that *i gala* is the word used for "Sun" by Kafir women, and the prefix *sa*, derived from the elements *se* "ground" [502, and 581 (¹)] and *-a* "of", very likely means "the ground of..., the flats of...". The same word may also well be compared with Cosmas' *tankhara*, "θέρμα". Then, if this opinion be correct, we understand how the traders, on their way back to Abyssinia, had to cross several of the streams which go to make up the Victoria Nyanza, or Upper Nile, and that the whole journey took up six months. No doubt, to those who have little experience of travelling in South-Africa, three months may seem to be a short time to go from Central Abyssinia to Sagaraland. But they should consider that even heavy oxen-waggons often go in less than two months from Colesberg in the Cape colony to Gubuluwayo, a distance nearly equal to that between Southern Abyssinia and Sagaraland, and that formerly three months was the time usually spent by slave caravans in crossing from Benguela to Mozambique (⁷). The remarkably long strip of land occupied in the Bantu field by

---
1. Third Book, n. 114.
2. *Ibid.*, nn. 23 and 20.
3. Second Book, n. 9.
4. *Nouveau Journal Asiatique*, tome III, Paris, 1829, p. 363.
5. *Odyss.*, I, 26; *Iliad*, I, 423, etc.
6. Last's *Polygl. Afr. Or.*, p. 11.
7. Koelle's *Polygl. Afr.*, p. 15.

the non-Bantu Masai may perhaps show the track followed by these ancient traders from the north. As to how gold used to be brought to Sagaraland, there may have been a trade route thence to Lake Nyassa, whence canoes could go to Senna and Mashonaland. This might even explain why the Senna, Nyassa, and Sagara languages are so closely related to each other. Strange to say, I am told by Mr. André, S. J., who spent several years at Kilimane, that when the Portuguese first reached Senna, the trade for gold used still to be carried on there in a manner similar to that described by Cosmas.

But, whatever may have been the exact spot to which the Abyssinian traders used to resort for their dealings with the Bantu, the intercourse between the two races does not seem to have been calculated to produce a mixture of blood, or language.

*83. Ancient relations of the Bantu with the Sabæans and other traders from the Red Sea.* — If we turn to seafaring nations, we may have a better chance of finding some that have infused foreign blood into the original Bantu. The author of the *Periplus of the Erythræan Sea*, who probably wrote about A. D. 85, tells us that in his time the coast of Mombasa (Ἀζανία, the modern Tana, or Sania (?), River) was part of the possessions of Charibael, the king of the Sabæans, and this through some ancient right (κατά τι δίκαιον ἀρχαῖον). He adds that Charibael([1]), who resided in the town of Saphar (the modern Dhafar or Zafar), had entrusted it to his vassal Cholæbos, the tyrant of the Mopharitic region, who resided at Sawe, or Save, (the modern Taaes), and that Cholæbos in his turn left it in return for a tribute in the hands of the inhabitants of Muza [the modern Musa, or Mauschid (?)], who used " to send thither transport ships with Arab pilots and sailors..., *who knew the places and the language of the natives well* ([2]). " He says also that these traders knew how to win over the natives by presents of wine, corn, spears, knives, axes, and various sorts of beads.

This opens a new horizon to us. Knowledge of the languages and friendly relations soon bring about a fusion of races. We can easily understand that the Sabæan traders left children in the land, and that many of these, being more enterprising than the pure natives, may for centuries have furnished petty chiefs to various Bantu tribes, as often happens in our own times all over the east coast of Africa with men born of Arab, Banyan, and European parentage.

*84.* When did such relations between the Sabæans and South-Africa first commence? The author of the *Periplus* only says " from ancient times. " I strongly suspect that they existed before the time of Moses, when Egyptian fleets, going along the east coast of Africa to the land of Pun, met here men of two different types ; the one brown, armed, wearing a long beard, and evidently the ruling race, who, it seems, must be identified with the descend-

---

1. This king was known to the ancient Arab writers, who called him *K'harah'bil*.
2. *Geographi Graeci Minores*, Didot, Paris, 1855, pp. 271 and 274.

ants of Jectan, at that time rulers of the Sabæan Empire; the other painted red, short-nosed, thick-lipped, without beard, carrying no weapon, and forcibly reminding me of the Tonga I have seen. From them they received *a)* piles of a precious gum, which, perhaps, was no other than the gum copal of Eastern Africa, the most precious gum known to trade in our own days; *b)* giraffes, quadrupeds which are found nowhere but in South-Africa, *c)* a live leopard " from the south, " and many leopardskins ; *d)* heaps of copper-rings, like those which are common throughout all South-Africa, native gold, ivory, ebony, and other " southern products for Ammon "; etc. etc. (¹).

It matters little here whether the Egyptians did, or did not, go as far as the equator on the east coast of Africa. All I say is that the circumstances of their first expeditions to the land of Pun seem to imply that in those ancient times there existed a regular intercourse between the Sabæans and the Bantu. It may be mentioned, by the way, that the Ma-tabele, and several other Bantu tribes of the east coast of Africa were included by my Tonga informants under the name of *Ma-punu*, which cannot fail to remind one of the *Pun*, or *Punt*, of the hieroglyphic inscriptions.

I also think it probable that the same sort of relations between the Sabæans and the Bantu are implied by those chapters of the third Book of Kings and the first of Paralipomena, in which the coming of the Queen of Saba to Jerusalem is coupled with the narrative of the expedition to Ophir. For, however much may have been written to the contrary, we may still be allowed to think that the first Arab traders whom the Portuguese met at Sofala with ships laden with gold were correct in saying that this was the place where Salomon's ships used to come to get the precious metal, if not the other curiosities mentioned in the Bible. Some have even long since thought that they had shown on other evidence that the lands of Ophir, Paz, Upaz, and Parua-im, whence the Hebrews and Tyrians used to export treasures are in the neighbourhood of Cosmas' Sasos and Herodotus' Table of the Sun (²). I think that Solomon's Ophir, called Σωφίρ by the Septuagint, is properly the golden Sofala, or Sofara, of the ancient Arab writers, stretching from Delagoa Bay to the River Rovuma, a country which is still called *Ku-piri* in several Bantu languages, and in which numbers of tribes still go by the names of *A-mpire*, *A-mbiri*, *Ba-peri*, *Ma-fia* = *Ma-fira*, *Ma-via* = *Ma-vira*, etc. (³). Paz and Upaz may be

---

1. Cf. *Deir-el-Bahari*, par A. Mariette-Bey, Leipzig, 1877, principally pp. 14, 15, 18, 19, 20, 26. Mariette says that one of the inscriptions mentions a *horse* next to an elephant. Should it not be a zebra ? A horse would have been nothing new for Egyptians in the time of Moses, or even in that of Jacob. Cf. *Gen.* XVII 17 ; 49, 17 ; *Exod.* IX, 3 ; XV, 1 and 21 ; etc. Cosmas (*Patr. Gr.*, T. 88, col. 107) shows that Ptolemy II conquered the land of Sasos. Was not this conquest the result of Ptolemy's expedition " to the land of Pun " of the hieroglyphic inscriptions?

2. *Nouveau Journal Asiatique*, t. III, Paris, 1829, p. 364.

3. The name of Ophir is found among both the descendants of Kush and those of Jectan. It may have been given to various tribes of Arabia, India, and Africa. Solomon's Ophir must be the most famed for its gold among the traders of the Red Sea, which is tantamount to saying that it is in South-Africa.

either Mo-mbasa, which seems to have been the seat of the ancient Sabæan governors, or, more probably, the island of Patta, whose chief town, formerly renowned for its trade in gold, was still called *A-mpaza* in the seventeenth century. The *Parua-im* are no other than the modern *Ba-roa* or *Ba-tua* " Hottentots and Bushmen ", also called *Tu-roa* on account of their small size, or by the Arabs Wakwak, in whose land are the diamond-fields, and whose gold-fields on the Limpopo and its affluents have long been considered as the richest to be found in South-Africa. Cosmas says positively that not only the gold, but also the precious wood, and the monkeys, received by Salomon from the queen of Saba, or brought to Asion-gaber by his fleet, came from South-Africa ([1]).

*85.* If such identifications are correct, the natural conclusion from them must be that much of the treasures accumulated during centuries in the Yemen by Sabæans ([2]) came from South-Africa, a fact which implies intimate relations between them and the Bantu. Did these relations modify considerably the language of these people? Probably they did, but perhaps no more than Arabic and the language of the Banyans do in our own days. It may even be remarked that the author of the *Periplus* says that certain Arabs were employed by the Sabæans because they had a knowledge of the language of Azania. This supposes that the traders did not speak Himyaric, or Arabic, but Bantu, in their dealings with the natives.

*86.* Among the various traces to be found in East-Africa of these ancient relations with the traders from the Red Sea, I notice particularly the word *Mulungu*, for " God " in Nika, Swahili, Mozambique, etc. (323*). The existence of a God who is One is well known to all the Bantu tribes, even to those which show no sign of having been directly influenced by foreign intercourse. But, through some reverential fear of the supreme Being, they seldom address prayers to Him directly. They prefer to ask the *Mi-zimo*, or " spirits of the deceased chiefs " to pay homage to God for them, to scrape the ground before Him in token of submission, as they themselves are wont to do before their chiefs and before white people, thus to propitiate Him who gives and refuses rain to whom He pleases ([3]). But the name by which they know God is not *Mulungu*, except among the eastern tribes. Hence I consider it to be highly probable that this word, pronounced *Muluku*, or *Moloko*, in the vicinity of Mozambique, originally represented the *Molokh* of the neighbours of the Jews ([4]).

Circumcision, which is common to several Bantu tribes, may also have been borrowed by some of them from the Sabæans, or the other nations that shared in their trade. It is not in use among those Bantu tribes which seem to be the most primitive.

---

1. Migne, *Patr. Gr.*, T. 88, col. 98. Sandal-wood, which is probably the *al-gum-im* of the Bible, is called *li-gumi* in the language of Senna and of Lake Nyassa.
2. *Ezechiel*, XXVII, 22.
3. Cf. Appendix I.
4. See n. 363 (1 and 6) in this work, with the note to n. 110.

*87. Relations of the Bantu with the Arabs since the advent of Islam.* — The traders of the Red Sea appear to have abandoned the east coast of Africa in the time of the Roman Empire. Cosmas Indicopleustes, who before joining the monks in Egypt had gone trading all along the coast of Arabia, says that in his time the sailors of those parts did not dare to trust themselves to the sea of the Zindj (¹). But whatever may be thought of this assertion, it is certain that the East-African trade received a vigorous impulse soon after the spread of Islamism.

*88.* In the 8th century of the Christian era, some Arabs, separating themselves from Mahomet's successors, went under the leadership of Zaïd, Ali's grandson, to seek freedom from religious persecution on the northern part of the east coast of Africa. Men of other dissident sects soon followed their example, and thus were founded, among others, the towns of Brava and Magadoxo. Starting from this place they occupied by degrees all the small islands along the east coast as far as Delagoa Bay.

*89.* Mas'oudi says that they established themselves in the island of Kambalu (probably Comoro, some think Madagascar) at the time of the conquest of Crete by the Musulmans (about A. D. 730). They reduced into slavery all its Zindjan inhabitants, but adopted their language (²). He further says that in his time (A. D. 900-945) the trade on the East-African coast was in the hands of the Sirafians from Persia, and of Arabs from Oman of the tribe of Azd ; that the term of their voyages on the sea of the Zindj was the land of Sofala and that of the Wakwak in the southernmost parts of this sea ; that he himself crossed several times from Sendjar, the chief-town of Oman, to the island of Kambalu, and that such a voyage generally took up from one to three months (³).

*90.* In the Book of the Marvels of India, written about A. D. 960, we find that ships continued to go regularly for gold from Oman to Sofala, and that the king of the country, though the Arabs had once strangely abused his hospitality to make him a slave, had embraced Islamism, and on his return to his country continued to show himself very kind to the traders (⁴).

*91.* Edrisi, writing A. D. 1154, describes at length the dealings of the Arabs with the Zindj. We may notice particularly what he writes of the ruler of Keish, an island situated in the Persian Gulf, facing Muscat. This man, he says, had a large fleet numbering 50 ships, each of which, made of a single piece of wood, could carry about 200 persons, and besides these a great number of other ships. With these he used to cross over from the Persian Gulf to the coast of Zanzibar, to devastate it, and carry off numbers

---

1. Migne, *Patr. gr.*, t. 88, col. 87.
2. Vol. I, p. 205.
3. Vol. I, pp. 232-233 and 331-332. Ibn Batoutah, who crossed from Zhafar to Kiloa, says that this voyage used to last only one month. *Voyages*, traduits par C. Defrémery et Sanguinetti, Paris, 1851, tome II, p. 196.
4. Marcel Devic, *Les merveilles de l'Inde*, Paris, 1873, pp. 43-52, and 150.

of slaves (¹). The same author says that the Zindj had great respect and veneration for the Arabs, and that they easily allowed them to take their children off to distant lands (²).

*92.* From all this it may be easily deduced that at this date the influence of the Arabs had already extended far and wide in South-Africa. No wonder therefore that when Vasco de Gama discovered this country in the year 1498 he found them settled all over the east coast. They had even spread far inland. For, when Father Gonçalo da Sylveira went to the court of the Monomotapa in 1569, he found the place already occupied by preachers of the Koran, the very men who, soon after he had converted this emperor to the faith, and baptized him together with a number of the *inkosi* (³), managed by dint of calumnies, and by exciting superstitious fears, to have him put to death.

This is enough to explain how Arabic influence may now be felt in more than one Bantu language. For, though Mas'oudi says that the Mohammedan conquerors adopted the Zindj language, it can hardly be conceived that they spoke it in its purity.

*93. Ancient relations between the Bantu and the Persians.* — Mas'oudi relates that in his time the Arabs were not the only traders to be found in East Africa. He says that the inhabitants of Siraf (⁴) in Persia also used to cross over to the Zindj, and even to Sofala as far as the land of the Wakwak. This assertion, I think, throws a certain amount of light on the peculiar customs of certain Bantu tribes. The Sirafians, like other Persians, were fire-worshippers (⁵). Now, a kind of fire-worship exists among certain Bantu tribes, yet certainly it was not known to the primitive Bantu. Execrable fire-ordeals in use in the vicinity of Zanzibar have been mentioned by various writers. Those customary among the Rotse on the Upper Zambezi have often been described to me as being of daily occurrence. The Tonga know the Rotse only as fire-worshippers, *ba-yanda mu-lilo* (⁶).

Though I find no absolute evidence of dealings between South-Africa and Persia anterior to those mentioned by Mas'oudi, I should by no means be astonished if some were soon found to have existed, even in the most ancient times. The regularity of the monsoons of the Indian Ocean make the passage from the one country to the other so easy that it would be a marvel if the eastern traders had waited till the tenth century of the Christian era to discover, with or without the intention of doing so, this natural link between those two parts of the world.

*94. Ancient relations between the Bantu and the Chinese.* — Edrisi, de-

---

1. Amédée Joubert, *Géographie d'Edrisi*. Paris, 1836, tome I, pp. 59 and 152.
2. *Géographie d'Edrisi*, tome I, p. 58.
3. This word is used by Maffei in his account of Father Sylveira's death. It means " king ".
4. Siraf was the principal harbour of the province of the Fars, whose chief-town was Shiraz. Remnants of the Persian colonization on the east coast are described in the *Missions Catholiques*, 1889, p. 44.
5. *Géographie d'Edrisi*, tome I, p. 413.
6. See Appendix I, first section.

scribing certain islands which face the coast of the Zindj, and which he calls Zaledj, or Zanedj, says that, according to tradition, at the time when great troubles arose in China, the Chinese transferred their trade to these islands, and by their equity, good behaviour, mild ways, and accommodating spirit, soon came to very intimate relations with their inhabitants ([1]). Is this the origin of another tradition handed down to us by Ibn-Sayd ([2]), that the Zindj are the brothers of the Chinese? Whatever may be thought of these traditions, certain it is that the Chinese have been brought at one time or another into relation with the people of Eastern Africa. The chinese money, chinaware, etc., lately mentioned by Father Le Roy in the interesting account of his voyage from Zanzibar to Lamu ([3]) leave no doubt on this point.

Edrisi also says that in his time the Chinese used to come occasionally to the land of the Wakwak, in the southernmost parts of Africa ([4]). Not a little weight is added to this assertion by a similar one of Marco Polo saying that in his time (before A. D. 1295) the great Kaan of the Tartars sent ships to that part of Africa which is further south than Madagascar ([5]).

If it be true that the Japanese are called Wakwak, exactly as the Hottentots, by some Arab writers, it would appear from a passage in the *Book of the Marvels of India* that, A. D. 945, they sent a fleet numbering 1000 ships to conquer that island of Kambalu in which the Arabs had established themselves two centuries earlier, with the intention of procuring for themselves and the Chinese ivory, tortoise shells, leopard skins, amber, and slaves. They would not have succeeded in the main object of their enterprise, but, by way of consolation, they would have carried fire and sword into many towns of the land of Sofala. It must be added, however, that the author of the *Book of the Marvels* seems not to have believed altogether the man who gave him this information ([6]).

Considering these data with a few others, I have thought it legitimate in another part of this work to see traces of ancient relations with the Chinese in certain Kafir traditions, and in the name of the Gogo tribe ([7]).

*95. Relations between the Bantu and the Malays, the Javanese, etc.* — There existed once to the east of the Indian Ocean a powerful and very extensive empire, with the seat of its government probably at Java ([8]). Edrisi calls it the empire of the Mihradj, and says that its traders used to come to Sofala, were well received by the inhabitants, and had many dealings with them ([9]). Must we not connect this fact with Bleek's remark regarding the relationship of Bantu to the Malay, the Polynesian, and the

---

1. *Géographie d'Edrisi*, tome I, p. 60.
2. *Géographie d'Aboulféda*, traduite par M. Reinaud, t. II, p. 205.
3. *Missions Catholiques*, 1889, pp. 44 et 67.
4. *Géographie d'Edrisi*, t. I, p. 92.
5. Pauthier. *Le livre de Marco Polo*, 1re partie, Paris, 1865, p. 683.
6. Van der Lith. *Livre des Merveilles de l'Inde*, Leide, 1883-1886, pp. 175 and 301.
7. Appendix II, Second Tale, note *a*).
8. *Géographie d'Aboulféda*, Introduction, p. CCCXXXIX.
9. *Géographie d'Edrisi*, t. I, p. 78.

Melanesian languages? After having mentioned how he discovered " a trace of the common origin of the Fiji and the Bantu languages, " he writes as follows : " This probability was confirmed by so many other evidences, particularly those met with in the Papuan languages, that no doubt could any longer remain as to the fact that the Papuan, Polynesian, and Malay languages are related to the Bantu languages, and that thus the Prefix-Pronominal Class forms almost one continuous belt of languages on both sides of the equator, from the mouth of the Senegal to the Sandwich Islands (¹). " I also notice that, according to Edrisi, the place mostly frequented in South-Africa by the traders from the land of the Mihradj was the southernmost part of Sofala (probably Delagoa Bay), close to what he calls the island of Djalous or Djulus (²). Now, considering that the Zulu in their habits greatly resemble the inhabitants of Borneo ; that those among them who have gone up to Lake Nyassa and the Upper Ru-fiji, are there known by the name of *Ma-viti*, while *Viti* is the proper pronunciation of what we call the *Fiji* Islands ; and that their very name of *Zulu*, which I render elsewhere by " the children of the deep " or " of the sky ", strangely reminds one of the Sulu Sea and the Sulu Archipelago to the north of Borneo ; I am led to suspect that the rulers who first organised the Zulu nation were men who had come from the eastern empire of the Mihradj, perhaps brothers to those who in their erratic voyages were carried off to the Fiji Islands.

This no doubt would not sufficiently account for the distant relationship noticeable between the Bantu and the Malay, Papuan, and Polynesian languages. But, if South-Africa has long been frequented by those eastern traders, who can tell how many slaves have been exported by them from Sofala at various times, and in what proportion their blood flows in the veins of the occupants of the islands to the east of South-Africa ?

*96. Relations with India.* — Strange to say, the author of the *Periplus of the Erythræan Sea*, when describing accurately the trade of various ports of India, does not make any explicit mention of relations existing between them and South-Africa. But Cosmas Indicopleustes, in his description of the famous Taprobana Island (he certainly means Ceylon), says that it receives from Æthiopia many ships, which among other things bring emeralds and ivory (³). Which part of Africa does he mean by Æthiopia ? It seems legitimate to think of places south of the equator : for several authors anterior to him mention that Taprobana is reached in about 20 days by sea from Cape Prasos in South-Africa (Cape Delgado ?) (⁴), an assertion which could not be explained, if South-Africa had not been frequented at that time by the traders of this island. I do not know whether it has ever

---

1. *Comparative Gr.*, foot-note to p. 142.
2. *Géographie d'Edrisi*, t. I, p. 79.
3. Migne, *Patr. Gr.*, t. 88, col. 450.
4. See the foot-note in *Geogr. Graeci Minores*, Didot, 1855, t. II, p. 362.

been noticed in connection with this that in Marco Polo's time precisely 20 days was the normal duration of voyages from Southern India to Madagascar (¹).

97. It is a fact beyond all doubt that since the Mohammedans have occupied the islands and the shores of the Indian Ocean, a vigorous trade has never ceased to be carried on between India and South-Africa. It probably attained its greatest proportions after these countries were discovered by the Portuguese. Without going any further, there is sufficient evidence for it in the number of African tribal and other names derived from that of the seat of the Portuguese Indian empire. The word *Makua* or *Ma-goa*, which has puzzled more than one scholar and myself for a long time (²), means nothing else than " people from Goa ". The *Wa-ngwana* of Zanzibar, the *Be-chwana* of the Limpopo and adjacent countries, the *Ma-kuana* or *Ma-kuane* of Mozambique, probably unconsciously call themselves " *Goanese* " or " people from *Goa* ", evidently because their lords have long been Indians, indiscriminately included by them together with the whites under the name of *Goanese*. I have not yet properly examined how much the Goanese-Portuguese influence and the relations which it involves have affected the Bantu languages. Certain it is that the languages of most of these tribes which go by the name of *Ma-nkua*, *Ma-kuana*, or the like, differ considerably from the main group, as may be seen throughout the whole of this work.

98. *Relations with foreigners on the west coast.* — Not a single show of evidence exists that the western Bantu from the Cameroons to Damaraland have had commercial intercourse with foreigners in ancient times. I need not treat of their relations with the Portuguese and other European nations ever since the 15$^{th}$ century. I should only remark that such dealings have had a considerable influence on the language of Lower Congo, as it appears much purer in ancient than in modern works. Their influence on the languages of Benguela and the coast to the north of the Congo has probably been even greater, as they are much more remote than most others from what seems to be the original Bantu. But Angola has been wonderfully preserved. It may be conjectured that the people of Angola, having adopted Christianity soon after the discovery of the country by the Portuguese, have been for this reason comparatively free from the evils and disturbances which accompany slave-trade, and that this has saved the purity of their language. It may be also that Father de Coucto's catechism having long been classical in Angola has fixed the language better than any other agency would have done.

99. *Our own times.* — The Bantu seem to be slower than any other people to adopt European languages. They have a high opinion of their own, and excepting only their clumsy mode of reckoning, they think it as good a

---
1. Pauthier. *Le livre de Marco Polo*, p. 680.
2. See n. 246 of this work.

vehicle as any other for the necessities of trade, and for the knowledge which is brought to them by Europeans. A large number of foreign words, however, are one after another introduced into several languages. Kafir, Senna, and Swahili, in particular are respectively borrowing many from Dutch, Portuguese, and Arabic. But the construction of the sentences remains purely Bantu. As long as this is the case, it cannot be said that these languages are properly transformed.

100. On the whole, my opinion is that the Bantu race is more mixed than it is thought to be. But its languages may rank among the most primitive ([1]).

---

[1]. While going for the last time over the last proofsheet of this introduction, I noticed in the *Times* the following cablegram, which, perhaps, may indirectly throw further light on the origin of the Bantu and their language:

" Cape Town, Aug. 10. The Zimbabye ruins, which are being explored by Mr. Bent, are reported to be the most unique in the world. The walled enclosure, 260 yards round, containing many phallic emblems, is regarded as being a phallic temple. The walls in some places are 16ft. thick and 40ft. high. Two attempts have been made to open the large tower, which is solid and shows no opening at the top. There are ruins on a hill close by of the same age and style. These consist of numerous walls and steps, arches, and walled-up caves. There are indications that three persons occupied these caves. The original builders were probably Phœnician Arabs. The natives have found a phallic altar sculptured with birds and large bowls, and with a frieze representing a hunting scene. There are four quaggas at which a man is throwing a dart while holding a dog in a leash. Behind are two elephants. Some blue and green Persian pottery and a copper blade plated with gold have also been found, but no inscriptions. Mr. Bent remains a few weeks longer, hoping to discover who built the ruins. "

# A COMPARATIVE GRAMMAR

OF THE

# SOUTH-AFRICAN BANTU LANGUAGES.

## Chapter I.

### GENERAL PRINCIPLES

AND

### PHONETICS.

1. — What makes it possible to embrace in one work the numerous languages which are heard from Angola to the Comoro islands and from Kafirland to Fernando Po, is that, however manifold they may seem to be in point of vocabulary, they are none the less essentially one and the same in point of grammatical structure, and that, by elucidating certain phonetic laws, we may even bring out the identical origin in different languages of a large number of words which, at first sight, might have been thought to have nothing but their meaning in common.

2. — In this variety of languages, it was necessary, in order to avoid confusion, to select one as our standard, so as to borrow examples from it for all general laws throughout the work. Our choice has fallen on Tonga, which is the predominant language of that peninsula which is formed by the Chambezi, the Zambezi and the Loangwe. The plain reason of this determination is, that, of all those languages on which a fair amount of materials has been available to us, Tonga is the one which, on the whole, best represents the peculiar features of the whole group. And, as it is also the most central, it is only natural it should be so. It might be asked whether Tonga has also the advantage of being more primitive than the better known coast languages, such as Kafir, Swahili, Herero, Angola, Mozambique, Mpongwe, etc. But this is a question we prefer to leave to the judgment of the reader.

# I. — Alphabet.

**3.** — Unfortunately the various scholars who have dealt with Bantu languages have adopted different alphabets, thus giving in many instances to the same letter widely different powers. Hence it was no easy task, in a work like this, to keep uniformity without creating confusion. In this difficulty, no better plan has suggested itself than to attribute to every letter the value which is now attached to it by the larger number of Bantu scholars, without taking divergencies on the part of the others into consideration.

**4.** — *N. B.* 1. In a few cases this work so far yields to deeply rooted customs, as to follow them when they attribute to a letter or to a combination of letters, in one particular dialect, a value different from that which it has in most of the others. Thus, in Zulu and Xosa, the letters *c* and *x* are used to represent *clicks* or peculiar sounds proper to these dialects, though these same letters have a different value in the other languages. Again, in certain Eastern languages, we represent by *ch* a sound which differs little from that of *ch* in *church*, though in the other languages the same sound is represented by the simple *c*.

**5.** — 2. In certain cases, where it was necessary to distinguish slight varieties of sound proper to particular dialects from the more common pronunciation, confusion is avoided by giving a Gothic shape to certain letters.

Hence the following are the values of the letters used in this work :

**6.** — **a** = *a* in *father*. Ex. *ta*ta, my father.

**7.** — **b** = *b* in *bone*. Ex. **ba**ma, my mother.

Exception. — In Tonga and several other languages, *b* before *u* and *o* sounds nearly like the Dutch *w* in *wijn*. Thus *mu-bua*, " a dog ", is pronounced nearly like *mu-wua*.

**8.** — **c** or **ch** = *ch* in *church* (approximately). Ex. **ci**-*ntu*, a thing.

*N. B.* To be more exact, this sound comes between that of *ch* in *church* and that of *t* in *tune*.

Exceptions. — 1. In Chwana it is necessary to distinguish the two sounds *c* and *ch*. The simple *c* sounds nearly exactly like *ch* in church, while *ch* adds an aspiration to the same sound.

2. In Kafir (Zulu and Xosa), *c* represents a click-sound (cf. n. 36). See also n. 25.

**9.** — **d** = *d* in *done*. Ex. *in-de*zu, beard.

Exception. — In Chwana *d* represents a sound which stands halfway between *d* and *r*, as in *mo-sadi* " a woman ". It is even written *r* by Livingstone and some other authors. Others represent the same sound by *l*.

*N. B.* We represent by 𝔡 a sound similar to that of *th* in *this, that* (82).

**10.** — **e** = *ai* in *chair*. Ex. *im-be*le*le*, sheep.

Exception. — In Kafir, when *e* is followed immediately by a syllable which contains *i* or *u*, it sounds like the French *é* in *bonté*. Ex. *usahleli*, he lives still ; *wetu*, my dear. Pronounce : *usahléli, wétu*. In Chwana also, the letter *e* represents slightly different sounds in different positions, but the laws which regulate these differences have not yet been brought to light.

**11.** — **f** = *f* in *fall*. Ex. *ku-*fua, to die.

Exception. — In Chwana, *f* sounds nearly like the Dutch *v* in *vader*. In certain dialects of this same language, it sounds more like a sort of labial *h*. Ex. *le-fatshe* " the ground " (also spelt *le-hatshe*).

**12.** — g = *g* in *gone*. Ex. *i*-**g**olezia, evening.

*N. B.* We represent by ɡ the sound of *g* in *bring*. Ex. *in*-ɡombe, cattle.

Exception. — In Chwana, when *g* is not immediately preceded by *n*, it sounds like the Dutch *g* in *goed* (Arabic *ghain*). Ex. -a-gago, thine.

**13.** — h = *h* in *home*. We never use this letter in Tonga proper. Ex. in Kafir : *i*-**h**obe, a dove.

*N. B.* 1. Of course *h* has not this value in those instances in which the sound of *ch* in *church* and that of *sh* in *shall* are represented by *ch* and *sh* (8,29).

2. In Chwana, the singular custom has prevailed of rendering by *sh* the sound of *sh* in *shall*, though in this same language *tsh* is used to represent the sound *ts* followed by an aspiration.

**14.** — i = *i* both in *ravine* and in *tin*. Ex. *ku*-s**i**ka, to arrive ; *ci*-*tonga*, the Tonga language.

*N. B.* The sound of *i* in *tin* and in the Tonga word *ci-tonga* is rendered in this work by *i* in a few instances where it was necessary to call the attention of the reader to its susceptibility of being changed to *e* or of being elided (Cf. n. 270).

**15.** — j = *j* in *juice* (approximately). Ex. *i*-j**u**lu, the sky.

*N. B.* 1. To be more exact, *j* is the counterpart of *c*, representing a sound which holds the middle between *j* in *juice* and *d* in *due*. Exception must be made for Kafir and apparently for a few Swahili words, where *j* has almost exactly the sound of *j* in *juice*. Ex. *u ku*-j**i**ka, to turn round, (in Kafir).

2. The sound of the French *j* in *jour* is represented by ɟ (without the dot). This sound does not exist in Tonga nor in most of the interior dialects. It is heard in Angola, Karanga, Chwana, etc. Ex. *go-ɟa*, to eat, (in Chwana).

**16.** — k = *k* in *key*. Ex. *ku*-k**a**la, to sit.

*N. B.* We represent by ƙ a sound similar to that of the German *ch* in *buch*. Ex. *wu*-ƙ**u**a grass, (in Karanga).

**17.** — l = *l* in *lamb* (approximately). Ex. l**a**la, lie down.

*N. B.* 1. To be more exact, *l* represents in most dialects a sound which is midway between that of *l* and that of *r*. After the vowels *a*, *e* and *o*, it sounds more like *l*, while after the vowels *i* and *u* it sounds more like *r*, as if these vowels *i* and *r* as well as *u* and *r* had some sort of affinity. In some cases it sounds more like *d*. In fact, in most Bantu languages, *l*, *d*, and *r* are essentially one and the same letter, the pronunciation of which varies slightly according to position. In Chwana *l* and *d* are to *r* proper what *d* is to *t* in the other languages.

2. In Kafir, *l* is pronounced entirely as in English.

**18.** — m = *m* in *mine*, *embers*. Ex. m**u**-l**o**mbe, a boy.

**19.** — n = *n* in *nail*, *stand*. Ex. *in*-j**i**na, lice.

*N. B.* We represent by ŋ a Mpongwe sound which stands halfway between *n* and *l*. Some authors render the same sound simply by *n*, others by *nl*. Ex. *o-nome*, a husband, (alias *o-nome, o-nlome*).

**20.** — o = *o* in *boy*. Ex. m**u**-**o**yo, the heart.

Exception. — In Kafir, when *o* is followed immediately by a syllable which contains *u*, it sounds like *o* in *rope*. Ex. *i n-dlovu*, an elephant. In Chwana also, the letter *o* represents slightly different sounds in different positions, but, here again, the laws which regulate these differences have not yet been brought to light.

*N. B.* We represent by o a sound which is midway between *a* and *o*. Bleek renders the same sound by å. Some Mpongwe scholars render it by *â*, and others by *o*.

**21.** — p = *p* in *pass*. Ex. *ku*-p*ia*, to burn.

**22.** — q = a click sound (cf. 37).

**23.** — r = *r* in *rude*. This sound, in Tonga, is merely a phonetic modification of *l* (n. 17). It exists as a sound plainly distinct from that of this letter in Chwana, Karanga, Mozambique, etc. Ex. *go*-r*ala*, to love (in Chwana).

Exception. — In Kafir, we represent by *r* a sound similar to that of the German *ch* in *Nacht*, though somewhat more guttural. Ex. *u ku-razula*, to tear ; *i roti*, a great man.

**24.** — s = *s* in *see*. Ex. *ku*-s*amba*, to wash.

*N. B.* We represent by ŝ a sound which stands halfway between *th* in *think* and *s* in *see*. It is not heard in Tonga. It exists in Karanga, Kamba, Herero, etc. Ex. *u*-ŝ*wika*, to arrive, (in Karanga).

**25.** — t = *t* in *tin*. Ex. -t*atu*, three.

*N. B.* In Kafir *tsh* is used to render the sound of *ch* in *church*. Ex. *u ku-tsha*, to burn. (Cf. nn. 8 and 4.)

**26.** — u = *u* in *rude*. Ex. *mi-b*uy*u*, baobab-trees.

**27.** — v = *v* in *over*. Ex. *im*-v*ula*, rain.

*N. B.* We represent by b a Mpongue sound which is said to approximate to *hu* in the French *huître*.

**28.** — w represents a sound not quite so full as our English *w*. Generally it is a remnant of a weakened labial sound. Ex. *a*wo, there (=*apo*, n. 693, tables).

*N. B. U* between a consonant and a vowel has been written *w* by various authors in many cases where probably it should not be so, and vice versa. Thus the word for " child " should probably be written *mw-ana*, not *mu-ana* in Swahili, because here the semi-vowel sound *u* is more consonantal than vocal, as we see that in this language the substantives of the same class as *mw-ana* generally drop the vowel *u* of their prefix *mu*, as in *m-tu*, a person, *m-ji*, a village, etc. (= *mu-tu*, *mu-zi*, cf. 366) ; while the same word should be written *mu-ana* in Shambala, because in this language the *u* of the prefix is generally kept, as in *mu-ntu*, a person, *mu-tue*, a head, etc..

**29.** — x or sh = *sh* in *shall*. This sound is not heard in Tonga. It exists in Chwana, Karanga, Angola, etc. Ex. *xe* " the chief " (in Karanga) ; *go-sha* " to die ", (in Chwana).

Exception. — In Kafir *x* represents a click-sound (cf. 38).

**30.** — y = *y* in *year*. Ex. *ku*-y*oya*, to breathe.

*N. B.* 1. When *y* is preceded by *n, d* or *t*, the two sounds are combined into one. We thus obtain the three compound sounds *ny, dy*, and *ty*, which have no exact equivalents in English. The nearest approaches to them are *ni* in *onion, d* in *duty* and *t* in *tune*. Of these three sounds *ny* alone is heard in Tonga, as in *inyati*, a buffalo. *Dy* and *ty* are used mostly in Kafir, as in *u ku-dyoba*, to bemire, *u ku-tya*, food, etc..

2. *Ty* in Herero sounds apparently like *c* in Tonga, (n. 8).

**31.** — z = *z* in *zone*. Ex. *ku-zala*, to become full.

*N. B.* We represent by ӡ a sound which is to *z* what ʂ is to *s*. Ex. *u-ӡwara*, " to beget, " (in Karanga).

### ADDITIONAL SOUNDS IN CHWANA.
(Suto, Tlhaping, Rolong, Kololo, etc.)

**32.** — **tl,** in Chwana, approximates to *tl* in bottle. Ex. *tlala*, hunger.

**tlh** sounds more strongly aspirated than *tl*. Ex. *tlhapi*, a fish.

### ADDITIONAL SOUNDS IN KAFIR.
(Xosa, Zulu and Tebele.)

**33.** — **hl** approximates to the Greek combination χλ. Ex. *u ku-hlala*, to sit. This sound has also been spelt *kl* and *sl* by various writers.

**tl**, in Kafir, represents a sound similar to that of *hl*, but preceded by *t*. In fact, it is a mere modification of *hl*, caused by the presence of *n* before it. Ex. *in-tlalo*, a sitting.

**34.** — **dl** represents the two soft sounds corresponding to *hl* and *tl*. When not preceded by *n*, it approximates to *gl* in the Dutch *glorie*. Ex. *u-ku-dleka*, to be spent. When preceded by *n*, it sounds more exactly as it is spelt. Ex. *in-dleko*, expenses.

**35.** — The above sounds are not yet what have been termed clicks. These are still less easy to describe, being produced, as they are, rather by *drawing in* than by *expressing* sound. They have some analogy to *k* and *g*. They are six in number, viz. :

**36.** — **c**, produced by drawing a hard sound as if from the front teeth inwards. Ex. *u-ku-canda*, to split.

**gc**, a soft sound corresponding to *c*. Ex. *ingca*, grass.

**37.** — **q**, produced by drawing a hard sound as if from the palate downwards. Ex. *i qaqa*, a muir-cat (musk cat).

*N. B.* This click-sound is sometimes heard in Suto.

**gq**, a soft sound corresponding to *q*. Ex. *in-gqwelo*, a wagon.

**38.** — **x**, produced by drawing a hard sound as if from the side-teeth inwards. Ex. *u ku-xoxa*, to converse.

**gx**, a soft sound corresponding to *x*. Ex. *in-gxoxo*, a debate.

## II. — Characteristic Features
### of the
### Bantu Family of Languages.

**39.** — 1rst PRINCIPLE. — In these languages, concord is established by means, not of suffixes, but of prefixes, which being, as a rule, expressed first before the substantive, are then repeated, under a form sometimes identical and sometimes modified, before every expression which has to agree with it.

**40.** — These prefixes are, in the best favoured dialects, eighteen in number, some of them importing generally a plural, the others a singular meaning.

**41.** — The same stem, by assuming different prefixes, obtains various meanings, sometimes quite opposite.

Ex. 1) **Mu**-*tonga*, a Tonga.
3) **Mu**-*samo*, a tree, a medicine.
5) **I**-*samo* (or li-*samo*), a beam.
7) **Bu**-*tonga*, the Tonga territory.
8) **Ku**-*tui*, an ear.
9) **In**-*samo*, a whipstick.
11) **Ci**-*samo*, a stump of wood.
13) **Ka**-*samo*, a stick.
15) **Lu**-*limi*, the tongue.

2) **Ba**-*tonga*, Tonga people.
4) **Mi**-*samo*, trees.
6) **Ma**-*samo*, beams.
... ... ... ... ...
6) **Ma**-*tui*, ears.
10) **In**-*samo* (or **zin**-*samo*) whipsticks.
12) **Zi**-*samo*, stumps.
14) **Tu**-*samo*, sticks.
10) **In**-*dimi*, tongues.

16) **A**-*nsi* (or-**pa**-*nsi*), down.
17) **Ku**-*nsi*, below.
18) **Mu**-*nsi*, underneath.

**42.** — Examples illustrating the general principle of concord :

1. **Mu**-*ana*    **u**-*ako*    **u**-*afua ;*    *nda*-**mu**-*zika*.
The-child    he-yours    he is dead;    I have him buried.
Your child is dead ; I have buried him.

2. **Ba**-*ana*    **ba**-*ako*    **ba**-*afua ;*    *nda*-**ba**-*zika*.
The-children    they-yours    they are dead;    I have them buried.
Your children are dead ; I have buried them.

3. **Mu**-*samo*    **u**-*ako*    **u**-*afua ;*    *nda*-**u**-*tema*.
The-tree    it-yours    it is dead;    I have it cut down.
Your tree is dead ; I have cut it down.

4. **Mi**-*samo*    **i**-*ako*    **i**-*afua ;*    *nda*-**i**-*tema*.
The-trees    they-yours    they are dead;    I have them cut down.
Your trees are dead ; I have cut them down.

5. **Li**-*mue*    *sekua ( = li-sekua )*    **li**-*ako*    *nda*-**li**-*jana*    *ka*-**li**-*fuide*.
It-one    duck    it-yours    I have it found    when-it-dead.
I have found one of your ducks dead.

6. **Ma**-*sekua*    a-*ako*    **ma**-*ingi*    *nda*-**a**-*jana*    *ka*-**a**-*fuide.*
    The-ducks    they-yours    they-many    I have them found    when-they-dead.
    I have found several of your ducks dead.

7. **Bu**-*ci*    **bu**-*ako*    **bo**-*onse*    **bu**-*amana,*    *tu-a-***bu**-*lia.*
    The-honey    it-yours    all    it is finished    we have it eaten.
    All your honey is finished, we have eaten it.

8. **Ku**-*mue*    **ku**-*tui*    **ku**-*ako*    *n-***ku***-bi,*    *u-***ku***-sambe.*
    It-one    ear    it-yours    is dirty,    you it wash.
    One of your ears is dirty, wash it.

9. **I**-*mue*    **n**-*gombe* ( = **in**-*gombe* )    **i**-*ako*    **i**-*afua,*    *tua-***i**-*sinza.*
    It-one    cow    it-yours    it is dead,    we have it skinned.
    One of your cows is dead, we have skinned it.

10. **In**-*gombe*    **zi**-*ako*    **zi**-*ingi*    **zi**-*afua,*    *tua-***zi**-*sinza.*
    Cows    they-yours    they-many    they are dead,    we have them skinned.
    Several cows of yours are dead, we have skinned them.

11. **E***ci*    **ci**-*ntu*    **ci**-*ako*    *n-***ci***-bi,*    *u-***ci***-sambe.*
    This    thing    it-yours    is it dirty,    you it wash.
    This thing of yours is dirty, wash it.

12. **E***zi*    **zi**-*ntu*    **zi**-*ako*    *n-***zi***-bi,*    *u-***zi***-sambe.*
    These    things    they-yours    are they dirty,    you them wash.
    These things of yours are dirty, wash them.

13. **Ka**-*mue*    **ka**-*cece*    **ka**-*angu*    **ka**-*afua,*    *nda-***ka**-*zika.*
    It-one    baby    it-mine    it is dead,    I have it buried
    A baby of mine is dead, I have buried it.

14. **Tu**-*cece*    **tu**-*etu*    **tu**-*mue*    **tu**-*afua,*    **tu**-*mue*    **tu**-*ci-fua.*
    Babies    they-ours    they-some    they are dead,    they-some    they still are-sick.
    Some of our babies are dead, others are still sick.

15. **Lu**-*sabira*    **lu**-*angu*    **lu**-*afua,*    *nda-***lu**-*zika.*
    The-little-baby    it-mine    it is dead,    I have it buried.
    My little baby is dead, I have buried it.

16. **A**-*fuefui* ( = **pa**-*fuefui* )    *a Mpande,*    **pa**-*li a mu-longa.*
    Close    to Mpande,    there is with a-river.
    There is a river near Mpande.

17. **Ku**-*nsi* (**ku**) *-a*    *bu-sanza*    **ku***-a-bikua*    *mu-lilo.*
    Underneath (it) of    the-table    there was placed    fire.
    Under the table was placed fire.

18. **Mu**-*nganda* (**mu**)*-ako*    *mu-la-sia :*    *tinsi ndi-la-***mu**-*njira.*
    In the-house (in) yours    therein is dark :    t'is not I will therein enter.
    It is dark in your house : I will not enter therein (¹).

---

1. A series of Zulu and Herero sentences, similar to the above, all based upon the theme : " Our handsome So-and-so appears, we love him ", may be seen in Bleek's excellent " Comparative Grammar of the South-African Languages ", pp. 96-100. Unfortunately it is necessary to warn the reader that the Zulu sentences in that series are not quite correct in the sense in which they are intended. For the expressions *si-m-tanda, si-ba-tanda*, etc., which Bleek renders by " we love him, we love them, etc. ", are never used by natives with this meaning without being determined by some other expression. (Cf. nn. 844, 846, 915, etc.)

**43.** — It may be noticed already here that locatives and locative expressions, such as those in the last three sentences may serve as what are subjects from our point of view, so that even verbs, adjectives and other determinatives are made to agree with them. This is the cause of very great difficulties to the student of these languages, because it is the source of an incredible variety of constructions which are entirely unknown in our own languages (cf. nn. 530-568 ; 693-704, etc.).

**44.** — II$^d$ PRINCIPLE. — Monosyllabic stems of verbs and nouns (substantives, adjectives, and pronouns) are in nearly all the Bantu languages subjected to special laws tending to give them prefixes or suffixes in cases where other stems have none, as if, in polite Bantu, there were, or at least had been, a general aversion to monosyllables, or, more exactly, to pronouncing an accented sound without its being accompanied by a weaker one.

Thus, in those dialects which do not express in nouns the prefix *li*, this same prefix is found to be expressed or replaced by something else before monosyllabic stems (cf. 413, 414).

Again, in nearly all the dialects, though the imperative exhibits generally the bare stem of the word, the law is found to change when there is question of monosyllables (cf. 837-841). Cf. also nn. 283, 325, 368, 389, 472, 611, 661, 765, 808, etc.

This principle may be termed " the law of avoiding monosyllables or single sounds ". It may be compared with triliterality in the Semitic languages.

**45.** — The chief difficulty connected with the application of this principle is to know when a stem is really monosyllabic and when it is not so, because the accent is not always sufficiently marked to exclude all doubt, but principally because, in some cases, the very same stem, apparently identical in two different languages, may however happen to be perfectly *monosyllabic* in the one and yet to consist really of two sounds in the other, so that in these cases analogy is often misleading to the inattentive. Thus the principal element of the pronoun which means " we, us, " is in Tonga *sue*, in two inflections of the voice, the first *(su-)* on a lower, the second *(-e)* on a higher tone, while, in Swahili, it is *swi*, a single voice-inflection, variously written *sui* and *si*.

**46.** — *N. B.* 1. Hence, when monosyllables are met with in Bantu authors, they must generally be considered as enclitics or as proclitics, or they are onomatopoetic words (n. 596).

2. The stems which begin with vowels are generally governed by principles which have much analogy with the applications of the law of avoiding monosyllables.

3. There are many instances of stems which are monosyllabic in certain languages, while in others they begin with a vowel. For instance, the Tonga stems *-iza* " come " and *-ba* " steal " have in Swahili the forms *-ja* and *-iba*. Possibly, in such stems as *-iza* and *-iba*, the initial vowel is not radical, but is a mere application of the law of avoiding monosyllables.

**47.** — III$^d$ PRINCIPLE. — Phonetic changes being, as might be expected, one of the main sources of differences between the various Bantu languages, it is to be noted :

**48.** — 1) That, on the whole, they affect consonants more than vowels. This principle, though apparently new in philology, can be so readily verified that it needs no proof here.

**49.** — 2) That those among these changes which affect vowels bear mostly : a) On vowels which begin a stem, as *i* in *-injila* or *-njila*, enter. b) On the weaker of two vowels which are next to one another, as *u* (alias *w*) in *-fua*, *-fwa*, or *-fa*, die. — Other instances will be mentioned in their proper place (cf. 200, 213, 237, etc.).

**50.** — 3) That those among these changes which affect consonants may be traced, in a large proportion, to different conformations of lips and nose, with the well-known additions or absence of lip-rings, nose-rings, the various sorts of artificial gaps in the teeth, etc. (¹).

---

1. A large proportion of the Bantu tribes have such marks which necessarily modify the pronunciation of certain consonants. Thus the Tonga knock out their upper incisors, when they come to the age of puberty. My informants used to say that the gap thus produced is their national mark, exactly as circumcision is the national mark of the Kafirs. It is noticeable that the *Lea* people, who are a Tonga tribe living near the Victoria Falls have given up this practice, since they have yielded their liberty to the *Rotse*. Livingstone says that " when questioned respecting the origin of the same practice, the Tonga reply that their object is to be like oxen, " and that " those who retain their teeth they consider to resemble zebras. " (*Missionary Travels*, London 1857, p. 532.)

The *Nyamwezi* are also mentioned as knocking out their upper incisors (Giraud, *Les lacs de l'Afrique équatoriale*, 1890, p. 303).

My informants added that the tribes which inhabit the country near the Loangwe, or, as they used to call them, the *Mbara*, have the custom of filing their front teeth to a point, this being likewise their national mark. It is well known that this custom is more general, as it is common to a large number of tribes near Mozambique and on what used to be called formerly by the Portuguese, " the Senna Rivers, (rios de Senna) ". — The *Hehe* have also filed teeth (Giraud, *Les lacs de l'Afrique équatoriale*, p. 141). Cf. W. Montagu Kerr's *The Far interior*, p. 116, regarding the Mashona.

The *Kumbi*, on the Kunene river, knock out the two middle incisors of the lower jaw and file the two corresponding teeth of the upper jaw to the shape of an inverted V (.*Missions catholiques*, 1888, p. 269). A similar custom has been noticed by Dr. Hahn among the Herero, (*Ibid.*, p. 270).

According to Johnston (*The River Congo*, 1884, p. 402), the two front teeth of the upper jaw are occasionally chipped among the Congo tribe of Pallaballa, and further up the river, this custom is regular.

The same writer mentions that " among the Ba-bwende of Ma-nyanga and the surrounding district large nose-rings are passed through the septum of the nose " *(Ibid.)*. — The lip-rings of the women on the Mozambique coast are too well-known to require description.

**51.** — 4) That the nasals *n* and *m* have in many cases the beneficial effect of retaining consonants which, according to the general laws, should have been weakened or dropped altogether (nn. 93, 95, 192 compared with 172, 116, 126, 148, etc.), though in other cases those same nasals *n* and *m* have the apparently contrary effect of modifying the consonants which they precede (cf. 73, 74, 77, 69, 99 note, etc.). — This note is very important.

**52.** — The explanation of this 3ᵈ principle alone with its various exceptions and particular applications would require a whole volume. It will form the basis of the next article. Meanwhile a few of its applications may be seen in the examples given below(*). A large supply of more striking examples may be seen in the chapters on substantives and adjectives.

### * SPECIMENS OF PHONETIC CHANGES.

|  | to shape | steal | see | recover (*intr.*) | burn (*intr.*) | hear | die |
|---|---|---|---|---|---|---|---|
| Tonga | ku-bumba | -ba | -bona | -pona | -pia | -nvua | -fua |
| Subia | ku-bumba | -eba | -bona | ... | ... | -ijuba | -fua |
| Yao | ku-gumba | -iwa | -wona | -pola | -pia | ... | -uwa |
| Sagara | ku-umba | -hidja | ... | -hona | ... | ... | -fua |
| Shambala | ku-umba | -uya | -ona | -hona | ... | -wa | -fa |
| Boondei | ku-umba | -bawa | -ona | -hona | -ya | ... | -fa |
| Taita | ku-umba | -iva | -ona | -bona (?) | -iya | ... | -fwa |
| Nyamwezi | ... | -iwa | -wona | ... | -pia | ... | -cha |
| Kamba | ku-umba | -uya | -ona | -wona | ... | -iwa | -gwa |
| Swahili | ku-umba | -iba | -ona | -pona | ... | ... | -fa |
| Pokomo | ku-umba | -iva | -ona | -bfona | -bfia | ... | -fwa |
| Nika | ku-umba | -ia | -ona | -vona | -via | ... | -fua |
| Senna | ku-umba | -ba | -ona | ... | -psa | -bva | -fa |
| Karanga | u-wumba | -iba | -wona | ... | -psa | -wua | -fa |
| Yeye | ... | -iba | -mona | ... | -pia | -iva | -fa |
| Ganda | ku-umba | -ba | ... | -wona | ... | ... | -fa |
| Xosa-Kafir | ku-bumba | -ba | -bona | -pola | -tsha | -va | -fa |
| Zulu-Kafir | ku-bumba | -eba | -bona | -pola | -tsha | -zwa | -fa |
| Herero | ku-ungura | -vaka | -muna | ... | -pia | -zuva | -ta(128) |
| Bihe | ... | -iva | -mona | -pola | -pia | -yeva | -fa |
| Kwengo | ... | -eba | -mona | ... | ... | ... | ... |
| Lojazi | ... | ... | ... | ... | ... | ... | -sa |
| Rotse | ... | -ija | -mona | -bola (?) | -bia | -yopa | -fa |
| Nyengo | ... | ... | -mona | ... | ... | -yuba | -fa |
| Rua | ... | ... | -bona (?) | ... | ... | -va | ... |
| Angola | ... | -iya | -mona | ... | -bia | -ivua | -fua |
| Mbamba | ... | ... | ... | ... | -hia | ... | ... |
| Lower Congo | wumba | -yiya | -mona | -vula | -via | -wa | -fua |
| Mozambique | w-upa | -iya | -ona | -vona | ... | -iwa | -kwa |
| Kilimane | ... | -iba (?) | -ona | -vola | -pia (?) | -iwa | -ukwa |
| Chwana { weak | go-bopa | -ucwa | -bona | -fola | -sha | -utlwa | -shwa |
| Chwana { strong | -popa | do. | -pona | -phola | do. | do. | do. |
| Mpongwe { weak | goma | -yufa | -yena | -vona | -via | -yogo | -yuwa |
| Mpongwe { strong | do. | -dyufa | -dyena | -pona | -pia | -dyogo | -dyuwa |
| Dualla | ... | -iba | -jena | ... | ... | -bwa | -wo |

**53.** — *N. B.* 1. For many dialects, viz. for Subia, Lojazi, Angola, etc., the scantiness of materials at our disposal is the only cause of the blanks left in the subjoined tables. With more knowledge, most of these might probably be filled up with the exact words required.

**54.** — 2. In the same tables we give in every column only such words as seem to have been originally identical in form or nearly so. However, as may be readily observed, some words contain in certain languages one element more than in the others. For instance, in the Herero word *-vaka* " to steal, " the first element (*va*) is essentially the same as the Tonga *-ba* in the same column, but the element *-ka* is superadded. Likewise in the Shambala word *-itanga* " to call ", the element *nga* is superadded to the Tonga *-ita*, etc., etc.

**55.** — IVth PRINCIPLE. — The preceding principle causes a great many words to appear in the very same dialect under two or even three different forms, according as they are connected or not with a nasal sound, *n* or *m*.

### SPECIMENS OF PHONETIC CHANGES. (Continued.)

|  | dawn | leave | arrive | come | dress (*intr.*) | become full | beget |
|---|---|---|---|---|---|---|---|
| Tonga | -cia | -sia | -sika | -iza | -zuata | -zala | -ziala |
| Subia | ... | ... | ... | -iza | ... | ... | -tala (?) |
| Yao | -cha | ... | -ika | -isa | -wala | -gumbala | ... |
| Sagara | -cha | ... | ... | -ija | -vala | ... | ... |
| Shambala | ... | ... | -xika | -iza | -vala | ... | ... |
| Boondei | -cha | -sia | ... | -eza | ... | ... | -vyala |
| Taita | -cha | ... | -fika | -ja | -ruara | ... | -vala |
| Nyamwezi | ... | ... | -xika | -iza | -zuala | -okala | -wyala |
| Kamba | -cha (?) | -bia (?) | -vika | ... | -iwatoa(?) | ... | -chaa |
| Swahili | -cha | ... | -fika | -ja | -vaa | -jaa | -zaa |
| Pokomo | ... | -yadsa | -fika | -dza | ... | -dzaa | -wyaa |
| Nika | -cha | -sia | -fika (?) | -dza | -fuala | -dzala | -vyala |
| Senna | -cia | -sia | -fika | -dza | -bvara | -dzara | -bala |
| Karanga | ... | ... | -swika | -ja | -mbara | -jara | -twara |
| Yeye | ... | ... | ... | -ya | ... | ... | ... |
| Ganda | -kia | ... | -tuka | -ja | -ambala | -jula | -zala |
| Xosa-Kafir | -sa | -shiya | -fika | -za | -ambata | -zala | -zala |
| Zulu-Kafir | -sa | -shiya | -fika | -za | -ambata | -zala | -zala |
| Herero | -tya | -sia | ... | -ya | ... | ... | -koata |
| Bihe | ... | -sia | ... | -iya | -wala | ... | ... |
| Kwengo | ... | ... | ... | -iya | ... | ... | ... |
| Lojazi | ... | ... | ... | -sa (?) | ... | ... | ... |
| Rotse | ... | -dia | ... | -ya | ... | ... | ... |
| Nyengo | ... | ... | ... | -iya | ... | ... | -zala |
| Rua | ... | ... | -fika | ... | -vala | ... | ... |
| Angola | ... | -xia | -bixila | -iza | -zuata | -vala | -vuala |
| Mbamba | ... | ... | ... | ... | -zuala | ... | ... |
| Lower Congo | -kia | -xisa | -nyeka | -iza | -vuata | -zala | -uta |
| Mozambique | ... | -hia | -pia | — | -wara | -chara | -yara |
| Kilimane | ... | -tia | fia | — | -ambala | ... | -bala |
| Chwana {weak | -sa (S) | -sia | -fitlha | -tla | -apara | -tlala | -tsala |
| {strong | do. | do. | -phitlha | -tlha (?) | do. | -tlhala (?) | do. |
| Mpongwe {weak | ... | ... | -wia | ... | -wora | ... | -yana |
| {strong | ... | ... | -bia | ... | -bora | ... | -dyana |
| Dualla. | -sa | -dia | ... | -ya | -boto (?) | ... | -yaa (?) |

**56.** — Thus, in Tonga, the word for "sun," is in most cases pronounced *i-zuba*. Now this is a *weakened* form equivalent to *li-zuba*, which is heard only when emphasis is laid on the first syllable (411). And, if the copula *n* (cf. 582) be placed before it, the same word changes to *di-zuba*. Hence we may hear three different forms of the same word, viz, *i-zuba*, *li-zuba* and *di-zuba*, or, to be more exact, three distinct forms of the same grammatical prefix to the word, viz. *i*, *li* and *di*.

**57.** — Again, in Tonga, the word for "down" is in most cases pronounced **a**-*nsi*. But this apparently is a weakened form of **pa**-*nsi*, which reappears after *n*, with the effect of changing this *n* to *m*. Hence two forms for the same element, viz, *a* and *pa*.

**58.** — Again, if a dialect changes *t* to *h* in the generality of cases

SPECIMENS OF PHONETIC CHANGES. (Continued.)

| | cook | buy | go in | sit, remain | drink | eat | lie down |
|---|---|---|---|---|---|---|---|
| Tonga | -jika | -(g)ula | -(i)njila | -kala | -nyua | -lia | -lala |
| Subia | -kika | -gula | ... | -ikara | ... | -ria | -lala |
| Yao | ... | ... | -jinjila | ... | -ngwa | -lia | ... |
| Sagara | -ambika | -gula | -ingila | -kara | -nyua | -dia | ... |
| Shambala | -dika | -gula | -engila | -kala | -nua | -ja | ... |
| Boondei | -ambika | -gula | -irgila | -ekala | -nwa | -da | ... |
| Taita | ... | -gula | -ngila | -kala | -nwa | ... | ... |
| Nyamwezi | -deka | -gula | -ingila | -ikala | -ngua | -lia | -lala |
| Kamba | -wia | -ua | -ikia | -kaa | -nioa | -iya | -mama |
| Swahili | -pika | ... | -ingia | -kaa | -nywa | -la | -lala |
| Pokomo | -mbika | -guya | -ntyia | -kaa | -nwa | -tya | -hara |
| Nika | -jita (?) | -gula | -ingira | -kala | -noa | -ria | -lala |
| Senna | -pika | -gula | ... | -kala | -mwa | -dya | ... |
| Karanga | -bika | ... | -nguina | -gara | -nua | -ria | -rara |
| Yeye | ... | -wora | -njena | ... | ... | ... | -rankara |
| Ganda | -sika | -gula | -ingila | ... | -nyua | -lia | ... |
| Xosa-Kafir | -peka | ... | -ngena | -hlala | ... | -tya | -lala |
| Zulu-Kafir | -peka | ... | -ngena | -hlala | ... | -dla | -lala |
| Herero | ... | ... | ... | -kara | -nua | -ria | -rara |
| Bihe | ... | ... | ... | ... | -nua | -lia | -lala |
| Kwengo | ... | ... | -bela | -kara | ... | -ria | -lala |
| Lojazi | ... | ... | -twena | -ikara | ... | ... | ... |
| Rotse | ... | -ola | -ingena | -ikara | -nua | -riya | -rankana |
| Nyengo | ... | -ola | -ingena | -kala | ... | ... | ... |
| Rua | -ipika | -ota(?) | -twela | ... | ... | -shia | -lala |
| Angola | -bika (?) | ... | ... | -kala | -nua | -ria | -lambarala |
| Mbamba | ... | ... | ... | ... | -nua | -dia | ... |
| Lower Congo | ... | ... | ... | -kala | -nua | -dia | -lavalala |
| Mozambique | -apea | ... | -kela | -kala | ... | -lia | -thala |
| Kilimane | ... | -gula | -vira | -kala | -umua | -oja | ... |
| Chwana {weak | -apaea | ... | -tsena | ... | -nwa | -ja | -lala |
| {strong | do. | ... | do. | ... | do. | do. | -tala |
| Mpongwe{weak | ... | -gola | -yingin | ... | -yonga | -nya | -nana |
| {strong | ... | -kola | -dyingina | ... | -dyonga | do. | do. |
| Dualla | ... | ... | -ingea | -ja | -nyo | da | -nanga |

as in Nika, then the word for "*three*" which is "*tatu*" in the larger number of the Bantu languages, will, in this particular dialect, appear generally under the form *hahu*, as in *Vi-tu vi-hahu*, three things (= Tonga *zi-ntu zi-tatu*); but it will recover at least partly its proper form when influenced by *n*, expressed or even understood, as in *n-ŋombe tahu*, three cows (= Tonga *in-ŋombe* **n**-*tatu*). Cf. nn. 479, 608, 73, 83, etc.

**59.** — The applications of this principle are chiefly remarkable in *Chwana* and *Mpongwe*. And this is the real cause why, in the subjoined table it has been necessary to distinguish in these dialects between *weaker* and *stronger* forms, the latter being in most cases *nasal*, as will be shown later (cf. 183-197 and 214).

Cf. also the table of adjectives, n. 601.

### SPECIMENS OF PHONETIC CHANGES. (Continued.)

|  | cry | hoe | bite | bring | walk | send | call |
|---|---|---|---|---|---|---|---|
| Tonga | -lila | -lima | -luma | -leta | -enda | -tuma | -ita |
| Subia | -rira | ... | ... | ... | -enda | -tuma | ... |
| Yao | -lila | -lima | -luma | ... | -enda | -tuma | -wilanga |
| Sagara | -lila | -lima | -luma (?) | ... | -genda | ... | ... |
| Shambala | -lila | -lima | -luma | -leta | -genda | -tuma | -itanga |
| Boondei | -lila | -lima | -luma | -leta | -genda | -tuma | -itanga |
| Taita | -lila | -lima | -luma | -leta | ... | -tuma | -ita |
| Nyamwezi | -lila | -lima | -luma | ... | ... | ... | -ita |
| Kamba | -iya (?) | -ima | -uma | -ette | -enda | -tuma | -ita |
| Swahili | -lia | -lima | -uma | -leta | -enda | -tuma | -ita |
| Pokomo | ... | ... | -muma | -yeha | -enda | -huma | ... |
| Nika | -rira | -rima | -luma | -reha | -enda | -huma | -iha |
| Senna | -lira | -lima | -ruma | ... | -enda | -tuma | -itana |
| Karanga | -lira | -lima | -luma | -reta | -enda | -tuma | ... |
| Yeye | -rira | ... | ... | ... | -enda | -toma | .... |
| Ganda | -lira | -lima | -ruma | -leta | -genda | -tuma | -ita |
| Xosa-Kafir | -lila | -lima | -luma | ... | ... | -tuma | -biza |
| Zulu-Kafir | -lila | -lima | -luma | ... | ... | -tuma | -biza |
| Herero | -rira | ... | -rumata | -eta | -enda | -tuma | -isana |
| Bihe | -lila | -lima | -lumana | -nena | -enda | -tuma | ... |
| Kwengo | -lila | ... | ... | ... | -enda | -tuma | -zana(?) |
| Lojazi | -lila | ... | ... | ... | -enda | -tuma | -zana(?) |
| Rotse | -lila | -lima | -moma | -leta | -enda | -tuma | -izana |
| Nyengo | -lila | ... | ... | ... | -enda | ... | -isana |
| Rua | -jila (?) | -jima (?) | -suma | ... | -enda | ... | -ita |
| Angola | -rila | ... | -lumata | ... | -enda | -tuma | -ixana |
| Mbamba | ... | ... | -suma | -neha | ... | ... | ... |
| Lower Congo | -dila | ... | ... | ... | -enda | -tuma | ... |
| Mozambique | -unla | -lima | -luma | -lela | -eta | -ruma | -ihana |
| Kilimane | -lila | ... | -luma | ... | -enda (?) | -rruma | ... |
| Chwana { weak | -lela | -lema | -loma | -lere | -eta | -roma | -bitsa |
| Chwana { strong | -tela | -tema | -toma | -tere | *do.* | -toma | -pitsa |
| Mpongwe { weak | -lena | ... | -noma | -yira | -genda | -roma | -vwelia |
| Mpongwe { strong | -dena | ... | *do.* | -dyira | -kenda | -toma | -fwelia |
| Duala | -eya | ... | ... | ... | ... | -loma | -bela |

# III. — Comparative Phonetics

## of the

## Principal Bantu Languages.

**60.** — The Bantu languages interpenetrate each other so much that the principles which find application in one of them *exclusively* are very few indeed. This article will therefore be a mere attempt to classify some notes of greater or less import, according to the languages in which their application seems to predominate.

**61.** — *N. B.* 1. Those phonetic laws which are common to the larger number of the Bantu languages, such as the change of *n* to *m* before *b* and *p*, will not be mentioned here, but only in the next article.

2. Concerning our sources for the various languages which are dealt with in this article, and the locality where they are spoken, cf. Introduction.

## TONGA.

(Spoken between the Victoria Falls and Lake Bangweolo.)

**62.** — Tonga, which is taken in this work as the standard language for the reasons given above (cf. 2 and 52 table), may be said to represent fairly well, on the whole, the generality of the Bantu languages. Its most striking feature is, perhaps, to have regularly *ji* and *ci* where a large proportion of the others have the sharper sounds *gi* and *ki* (cf. 8 and 15), as in the word *-injila* or *-njila*, which, in most of the other languages, sounds rather like *-ingila* (cf. 52 table). However this latter form is heard in Tonga also, a fact which shows that the difference is not very important. With regard to *ci* and *ki*, cf. n. 492.

**63.** — It may be added that the plain sharp sounds *z* and *s* appear to be more common in Tonga than in any of the other Bantu languages, Kafir itself not excepted. This again may be seen exemplified in the above table of verbs, in the columns of the words *-sia*, leave, *-sika*, arrive, *-iza*, come, *-zuata*, dress, *-zala*, become full, *-ziala*, beget.

**64.** — It may be well also to notice that *p* is not heard in Tonga, or is replaced by *w*, in some cases in which many dialects have it, unless it be after *n*. Thus *im-pewo* " wind ", is pronounced *mpepo* in Senna and several other languages, and *ansi* " down " *(pansi* after *m)* is always pronounced *pansi* in Kafir and several other languages (cf. 57 and 534-540).

**65.** — Tonga may be considered as forming one language with *Subia* (spoken on the Zambezi, above the Victoria Falls), *Bisa* (¹) (spoken East of Lake Bangweolo), and *Bemba* (²) (spoken North of Lake Bangweolo.) A particular dialect of Tonga is spoken near Lake Nyassa. It differs considerably from that which is described in this work. Judging from the scanty documents at hand (³), it looks very much like a mixture of the Tonga and Senna or Shire language.

## YAO.

(Spoken on the tableland between Lake Nyassa and the coast.)

**66.** — 1° Of those words which are common to Tonga and Yao many are greatly reduced in form in the latter language, mostly through the fall of *z, v* or *f*. Perhaps it might be more correct to say that *z, v* and *f* are then changed into a mere aspiration.

| Ex. | Tonga | Yao | Tonga | Yao |
|---|---|---|---|---|
| | *im-vula*, rain | *ula* ('*ula?*) | *zi-ntu*, things | *i-ndu* ('*i-ndu*) |
| | *ma-futa*, fat, oil | *ma-uta* (*ma-'uta?*) | *in-dezu* beard | *n-deu* (*n-dé'u?*) |
| | *i-zuba*, sun | *li-ua* (*li-'ua*) | *ma-zina*, names | *mena* ( = *maina*) |

*N. B. Nz* is in a few cases changed to *s*. Ex. *sala*, hunger (Tonga *in-zala*).

**67.** — 2° On the contrary, those stems which in Tonga are monosyllabic or begin with a vowel or *n* nasal, and a few others, are found to have richer forms in Yao.

| Ex. | Tonga | Yao | Tonga | Yao |
|---|---|---|---|---|
| | *-ba*, (to) steal | *-jiwa* | *-injila* or *-njila*, (to) enter | *-jinjila* |
| | *i-ji*, an egg | *li-jele* | *-umi*, healthy | *-jumi* (*-yumi* after *n*) |
| | *-ita*, (to) call | *-wilanga* | *-ingi* or *-nji*, numerous | *-jinji* (*-yinji* after *n*) |
| | *-kulu*, aged | *-chekulu* | *-zala*, (to) become full | *-gumbala* |

**68.** — *N. B.* 1. From these examples it may be seen, among other things, that *j* is in favour in Yao before the initial *i* and *u* of the other languages. Cf. the use of *g* in Sagara, n. 77.

2. Some stems which begin with *y* or *z* in Tonga, have *j* instead in Yao.

Ex.   *li-joka*, a snake (Tonga *in-zoka*).
      *li-juni*, a bird (Tonga *i-yuni*).

---

1. Concerning Bisa, cf. Stanley's Vocabulary in " The Dark Continent ", and Last's collection in " Polyglotta Africana Orientalis ", pp. 135-138.
2. Concerning Bemba, cf. Last's " Polyglotta, " pp. 131-134.
3. In fact I have seen no other specimen of this language than a small primer which has been kindly presented to me by M. Cust. I suspect that the Tonga of Lake Nyassa are of those who are mentioned by Livingstone as having gone to the *Ba-mbala*, and having never returned, " because they liked tha country better than theirs. " (Liv. Miss. Travels, p. 532). If so, it must be said that they have adopted, partially at least, the *Mbara* language which is a dialect of the Senna group (cf. 98).

**69.** — 4° Some peculiar changes are caused by the sound *n* when it combines with other consonants, viz. :

| | | | | | |
|---|---|---|---|---|---|
| NP is changed to MB. | | Ex. *mbachile*, | I have painted, | for | *n-pachile* |
| NW | „ { MB or MBW | „ *ku-m-bona*, „ *a-m-bweni*, | to see me, he has seen me, | „ „ | *ku-n-wona a-n-weni* |
| NT | „ ND | „ *n-dawile*, | I have bound, | „ | *n-tawile* |
| NK | „ NG | „ *n ganile*, | I have refused, | „ | *n-kanile* |
| NJ | „ NY | „ *n-yigele*, | I have carried, | „ | *n-jigele* |
| NCH | „ NJ | „ *n-japile*, | I have washed, | „ | *n-chapile* |
| NL | „ N | „ *nindani*, | wait for me, | „ | *n-lindani* |

This law of Yao explains why we have the following correspondences of words between Yao and Tonga, which is not subject to such changes.

| Ex. : | Tonga | Yao | | Tonga | Yao |
|---|---|---|---|---|---|
| | *im-pewo*, wind | *m-bepo* | | *in-yati*, a buffalo | *n-jati* |
| | *mu-ntu*, a person | *mu-ndu* | | *in-kani*, a story | *n-gani* |
| | etc., etc.. | | | | |

**70.** — 5° It will be seen further on (861) that in all the Bantu languages, verbs undergo certain phonetic changes of consonants in the perfect form. But Yao distinguishes itself among them all in this respect.

| Ex. | *ku-tama*, | to sit | Perfect. | *a-teme*, | he is seated. |
|---|---|---|---|---|---|
| | *ku-kola*, | to get | | *a-kwete* | he possesses. |
| | *ku-kwela*, | to climb | | *a-kwesile*, | he has climbed. |
| | *ku-taga*, | to put | | *a-tasile*, | he has put, etc.. |

**71.** — The Rev. Alexander Hetherwick, in his " Handbook of the Yao Language, " p. XIII, observes rightly that from this cause combined with the phonetic changes previously described, " words in Yao are so modified in the process of grammatical construction as to be almost unrecognizable by a beginner. Thus from *ku-leka* " to leave, " we have *n-desile* " I have left "... And from *ku-pa*, " to give, " we have *a-m-bele* " he gave me ", where not a single letter of the original has been retained. "

**72.** — *N. B.* A large number of common Yao words differ radically from those of similar meaning in the other languages, or at least seem to do so.

| Ex. | Tonga and other languages | Yao |
|---|---|---|
| | *-bi*, bad (cf. adjectives, 601*) ... ... ... ... | *-chimwa* |
| | *mu-oya*, breath (cf. class MU-MI, 377) ... ... | *bu-musi* |
| | *mu-alumi*, husband (cf. class, MU-BA, 322*)... | *asono* |
| | *bu-ta*, bow (cf. class BU-MA, 453)... ... ... | *u-kunje* |
| | *ku-tui*, ear (cf. class KU-MA, 462*). ... ... | *li-pilikanyilo* |
| | *in-zila*, road (cf. class IN-ZIN, 385*) ... ... | *li-tala* |
| | *i-bue*, stone (cf. LI-MA, 410*)... ... ... ... | *li-ganga* |

2. Interesting comparisons might be established between Yao and Chwana. It may even be said that most of the peculiar features of Yao have their counterpart in the languages of the Chwana-Mozambique-Mpongwe group (169).

## NYA-MWEZI.

**73.** — The two Nya-mwezi dialects on which we have most information, viz. Nya-nyembe and Sukuma, differ from the generality of the Bantu languages : —

1º By a peculiar tendency to weaken certain consonants after nasals. In this they go even further than Yao.

| Ex. : | | | Tonga | Nyanyembe | Sukuma |
|---|---|---|---|---|---|
| NY changed to | N : | | *inyama*, meat | *inama* | *nama* |
| NT | ” | NH : | *mu-ntu*, person | *mu-nhu* | *munhu* |
| NK | ” | NH : | *in-kuni*, wood | *n-hui* | ? |
| ” | ” | NG : | *in-kuku*, hen | *n-goko* | *n-goko* |
| ND | ” | NH : | *-endela*, go to fetch | *-enhela* | ? |
| ” | ” | N : | *ndi*, I | *ni* | *ni* |
| MP | ” | MB : | *im-pewo*, cold | *m-beho* | *m-beho* |
| ” | ” | MH : | *im-pande*, pieces | *m-hande* | ? |
| MV | ” | MB : | *im-vula*, rain | *m-bula* | *m-bula* |

**74.** — *N. B.* What renders particularly interesting this tendency in Nyamwezi, Yao, and, as we shall see further on, in Sagara and Gogo, to weaken consonants after nasals, is that, in many of the other Bantu languages, the same nasals produce the very opposite effect, and that consequently those stems which in grammar are subject to changes of form, such as *-pia* " new ", *-bi* " bad ", etc., are found to be used in their weaker form in Nyamwezi, Yao, etc., precisely in those instances in which they have their stronger form in Ganda, Chwana, Herero, Nika, Mozambique, etc., and *vice versa*.

| Ex. | Nyamwezi | Ganda | Tonga |
|---|---|---|---|
| | *wu-su wu-*pia, new flour | *o bu-ta o bu-*gia | *bu-su bu-*pia |
| | *n-goma m-*hia, a new drum | *e n-goma e m-*pia | *in-goma m-*pia |

**75.** — 2º By having often *g* where Tonga has *f*.

| Ex. Tonga : | *ma-futa*, oil, fat | Nyanyembe : | *ma-guta* | Sukuma : | ? |
|---|---|---|---|---|---|
| ” | *i-fua*, a bone | ” | *i-guha* | ” | ? |
| ” | *-fuefui*, short | ” | *-guhi* | ” | *-guhi* |

**76.** — 3º By eliding, in many cases, certain vowels which, in the other languages, are at most contracted or assimilated with those which follow them.

| Ex. Tonga : | *meso*, eyes (for *ma-iso*) | Nyanyembe : | *m'iso* | Sukuma : | *m'inso* |
|---|---|---|---|---|---|
| ” | *meno*, teeth (for *ma-ino*) | ” | *m'ino* | ” | *m'ino* |
| ” | *in-goma zi-esu*, our drums (for *zi-a-isu*). | ” | *ngoma z'isu* | ” | ? |

## SAGARA AND GOGO.

**77.** — The documents available for these languages are so unreliable ([1]) that I cannot make out any of their characteristic features with certainty. Apparently they are nearer to Tonga than the Nyamwezi language. The nasal seems to weaken the following consonant in some cases, as in Nyamwezi, and to be itself dropped in others, principally before *s*. *H* replaces the Tonga *p*, though not after *m*. *G* is apparently a favourite, at least in Kaguru, as it is found replacing not only the Tonga *f*, but also *v*, *j*, and even *l*.

| | TONGA | KAGURU | GOGO |
|---|---|---|---|
| Ex. | *im-pewo*, cold | *m-behu* | *beho* (?) |
| | *a-nsi*, down | *ha-si* | *ha-si* |
| | *ku-pona*, to heal (intr.) | *ku-ona* or *ku-hona* | ? |
| | *i-fua*, a bone | *i-guha* | ? |
| | *ku-vuna*, to gather (harvest) | *ku-gola* | ? |
| | *ij-anza*, a hand | *i-ganza* | *i-ganya* |
| | *li-nso*, an eye. | *i-giso* | *ziso* |

## SHAMBALA AND BOONDEI.

(Spoken inland facing the Pemba island.)

**78.** — These languages differ but little from one another, and both of them are closely allied to Sagara.

Their most remarkable phonetic features are the following : —

1° The consonants which follow *n* nasal are firmer in Shambala and Boondei than in Sagara.

2° *N* nasal falls before a larger number of consonants in Shambala and Boondei than in Sagara, and generally it strengthens those before which it falls.

3° In Shambala and Boondei there is no preference for *g* as in Sagara.

4° *S* of the other languages is sounded *x* (english *sh*) in Shambala, though not in Boondei, so that this seems to be the most palpable difference between these two languages.

---

1. The Kaguru grammar published under Last's name is full of evident misprints. Thus, for example, the word for " man " is spelt *mu-ntu* (p. 14, etc.), *mu-nhu* (p. 21, etc.), *mu-nku* (p. 124, etc.), *mu-nbu* (p. 15), *mu-nha* (p. 129).

## Comparative Phonetics.

**79.** — Ex.:

| Tonga | | Shambala | Boondei | Sagara |
|---|---|---|---|---|
| *mu-ntu,* | a person | *mu-ntu* | *mu-ntu* | *mu-nhu* (77 note.) |
| *in-soni,* | shame | *xoni* | *soni* | *soni* |
| *im-pewo,* | cold | *peho* | *pcho* | *m-behu* |
| *im-vula,* | rain | *fula* | *fula* | *m-vula* |
| *li-nso,* | an eye | *zi-xo* | *zi-so* | *gi-so* |
| *i-fua,* | a bone | *mu-vuha* | *mu-vuha* | *i-guha* |

*N. B.* On the whole, Shambala, Sagara, and Gogo, look more like Tonga than most of the other East African languages.

## TAITA.

(Spoken on the hills between Mombasa and Kilima-njaro.)

**80.** — Taita has a great number of words which are not heard in the more Southern Bantu languages. As to those words which it has in common with them, when putting them together, we find no very regular transitions of sounds. We may observe however a tendency to weaken hard consonants after nasals, e. g. in *n-gano* " a story " (Tonga *in-kani*), *n-guni* " firewood " (Tonga *in-kuni*), *ki-ndu* " a thing " (Tonga *ci-ntu*), etc. Possibly also it is a general law of Taita to change in certain cases into *chu*, and in others into *vu*, the sound *su* or *fu* of the generality of the Bantu languages, as in *ma-vuta* " fat " (Tonga *ma-futa*), *i-chumu* " a spear " (Tonga *i-sumo*, Swahili *fumo*), *ku-chuila* " to spit " (Tonga *ku-suila*), etc.

## KAMBA.

(Spoken west from Mombasa to Mount Kenia.)

**81.** — 1° Not only *b*, but also *l, z,* and *j,* are generally dropped in Kamba or weakened, this, with other contractions, causing many stems to be reduced to very short forms.

| Ex. | Tonga | Kamba | | Tonga | |
|---|---|---|---|---|---|
| | *ku-gula,* to buy | *ku-ua* | | *ku-ulu,* a foot | *ku-u* |
| | *mu-bili,* the body | *mu-i* | | *ku-jaya,* to kill | *ku-aa* |
| | *mu-ezi,* the moon | *mu-e* | | *ku-boko,* an arm | *k-oko* |

**82.** — 2° The Tonga *s* is sounded ꞗ in Kamba. Last says in his *Polyglotta,* p. 3, that this sound is similar to that of *th* in *this, that.*

| Ex. | Tonga | Kamba | | Tonga | Kamba |
|---|---|---|---|---|---|
| | *bu-sio,* face | *u-ꞗio* | | *in-soni,* shame | *n-ꞗonni* |
| | *bu-su,* flour | *mu-ꞗu* | | *ku-seka,* to laugh | *ku-ꞗeka* |

**83.** — 3° Among the changes produced by the nasal *n* on a following consonant, there is not only that of *l* to *d* as in Tonga and most of the other dialects, and that of *w* and *v* to *b*, but also that of *t* to *z*.

Ex.   *u-lembua*, guttapercha, pl. *n-dembua*
      *u-wau*, a side    » *m-bau*
      *u-tuka*, night    » *n-zuka* (cf. Tonga *bu-siku* " night ", and n. 51)

## SWAHILI.

**84.** — This is said to be the most arabized of all the Bantu languages. However this assertion, though probably correct on the whole, might lead to false conceptions. For, arabized as it is, Swahili remains without some Semitic features which are noticeable in several Bantu languages. Thus it has no article, and it has many words beginning with vowels. Again, Swahili proper, when not spoken by a man who knows Arabic, rejects hiatus less than several other Bantu languages. Those Arabic guttural sounds which are heard in a limited number of these same languages have not penetrated into Swahili proper, etc., etc..

**85.** — But Swahili is arabized in this sense that Arabic words often intrude bluntly into it, without even putting on a Bantu dress. Thus, in a single tale of 9 lines, the first of Steere's and Rankin's Swahili and Makua tales, I notice no less than 7 words which have no Bantu color at all, viz. *ilmu*, doctrine; *hasira*, anger; *hatta*, until; *sababu*, cause; *killa*, each; *-rudi*, to return; *shekh*, a chief.

**86.** — And again, Arabic influence must probably be seen in some of the following peculiarities : —

1° The classifying elements of those words which are in most frequent use (cf. 42) are much weakened by elisions and contractions, some of them being reduced to mere nasals, others being dropped altogether. Examples may be seen further throughout the whole of the chapter on substantives. Here are some others : —

Ex.   TONGA                                                  SWAHILI
      mu-*nzi* u-*a* mu-*ame*, the king's residence,        m-*ji* w-*a* m-*falme*.
      i-*zina* li-*a* mu *zike*, the name of a slave,       *jina* l-*a* m-*tumua*.
      lu-*limi* lu-*e* in-*yati*, the tongue of a buffalo,  u-*limi* w-*a* n-*yati*.

**87.** — 2° Though Swahili has many words beginning with vowels, it prefixes *h* to many others as if purposely to avoid beginning with them, or, more probably, to change them into perfect dissyllables. Thus the Tonga demonstrative pronouns *oyu*, *eli*, *eci*, etc., are in Swahili *huyu*, *hili*, *hichi*, etc.

**88.** — 3° Swahili drops the Tonga *l*, though not so often as Kamba (cf. 81).

| Ex. | TONGA | SWAHILI | TONGA | SWAHILI |
|---|---|---|---|---|
| | *ku-ziala*, to beget | *ku-zaa* | *in-zila*, a road | *n-jia* |
| | *in-zala*, hunger | *-njaa* | *ku-lila*, to cry | *ku-lia* |
| | *ku-ulu*, a foot | *m-guu* | cf. *ku-lala*, to lie down | *ku-lala* |

**89.** — 4° There are some other remarkable phonetic differences between Swahili and the generality of the Bantu languages, but general laws cannot be laid down.

| Ex. | TONGA | SWAHILI | TONGA | SWAHILI |
|---|---|---|---|---|
| | *-onse*, all | *-ote* (812) | *mu-kazi*, female, | *m-ke* (cf. 81) |
| | *li-nso*, an eye | *ji-cho* or *ji-to* (413) | *mu-se*, earth | *n-chi* or *n-ti* |
| | *-jika*, to cook | *-pika* (52 examples) | *ma-nzi*, water | *ma-ji* (440 ex.) |
| | | (Cf. *jiko* = fire-place) | *-sano*, five | *-tano* (792) |

**90.** — *N. B.* 1. Some of these examples show at least traces of permutation between *s* and *t* or *ch* (cf. 63). Such double forms as *jicho* or *jito*, *nchi* or *nti*, properly belong to different dialects, viz. — *jicho* and *nchi* belong to the dialect of Zanzibar, while *jito* and *nti* belong to that of Mombasa.

**91.** — 2. Likewise it may be added that *z* is less in favour in Swahili than in Tonga as the former replaces in many words the *z* of the latter by *v* or *j*. The same may be said of many other languages (cf. 63).

## NYIKA AND POKOMO.

**92.** — *N. B.* Nyika is spoken inland from Mombasa, and Pokomo on the banks of the Pokomo river. Unfortunately, nearly all that we know on these languages has come to us through Germans who seem to have mistaken in many instances hard for soft consonants, and *vice versa*, for instance, *f* for *v*, *v* for *f*, *s* for *z*, *z* for *s*, etc..

**93.** — 1° These two languages, though differing considerably from each other, have this remarkable feature in common that they have generally the consonant *h* where the main group of the Bantu languages has a *t*. However this letter reappears regularly, according to n. 51, under the influence of *n*, expressed or dropped.

| Ex. | TONGA |  | NIKA | POKOMO |
|---|---|---|---|---|
|  | *ku-tuma,* | to send | *ku-huma* | *ku-huma* |
|  | *iny-ati,* | a buffalo | *nyahi* | *nyahi* |
|  | *ma-futa,* | fat | *ma-fuha* | *ma-fuha* |
|  | *bu-ato,* | a canoe | *w-aho* | *w-aho* |
|  | *ku-leta,* | to bring up | *ku-reha* | *ku-yeha* |
|  | *mu-ntu,* | a person | *mu-tu* | *mu-ntu* |
|  | *-tatu,* | three | { *-hahu* (without *n*)<br>{ *-tahu* (with *n*) | *-hahu* (without *n*)<br>*-tahu* (with *n*) |

**94.** — 2° They have also this in common that, like Senna (99) they have the compound sound *dz* (alias *ds*) where Tonga has the simple sound *z*. Pokomo has also in common with Senna the compound sound *bv* (alias *bf*) and probably *pf*. In Nika the sound *vu* (alias *fu*), and perhaps in Pokomo the sound *bvu*, become *pfu* under the influence of nasals. Under the same influence the Nika sound *vi* seems to become only *pi*.

| Ex. | TONGA |  | NIKA | POKOMO | SENNA |
|---|---|---|---|---|---|
|  | *ku-za,* | to come | *ku-dza* | *ku-dza* | *ku-dza* |
|  | *ku-zala,* | to become full | *ku-dzala* | *ku-dzaa* | *ku-dzala* |
|  | *i-zuba,* | the sun | *dzua* | *dzua* | *dzua* |
|  | *-fuide,* | dead | { *-vu* (without *n*)<br>{ *-fu* (with *n*) | ?<br>? | } cf. *pfuba*, a bone (or *pfupa*.) |
|  | *-pia,* | new | { *-via* (without nasal)<br>{ *-pia* (with nasal) | *-bfia* [*-bvia* (?)]<br>*-bfia* [*-pfia* (?)] |  |

**95.** — 3° As many other languages, Nika and Pokomo drop out or weaken the consonant *b*, when it is not preceded by *m* (cf. n. 52 examples), but this letter reappears regularly under the influence of nasals.

| | TONGA | | NIKA | POKOMO |
|---|---|---|---|---|
| Ex | *-bi,* | bad | { *-i* (without nasal)<br>{ *-mbi* (with nasal) | *-wi*<br>*-mbi* (?) |

**96.** — 4° Pokomo differs from Nika principally in this, that, like Kamba and Swahili, it weakens the *l* or *r* of the other languages in many cases, and drops it in others.

| Ex. | TONGA |  | NIKA | POKOMO | KAMBA | SWAHILI |
|---|---|---|---|---|---|---|
|  | *in-zala,* | hunger | *n-dzala* | *n-dzaa* | *n-sa (n-dzaa?)* | *n-jaa* |
|  | *ku-ziala,* | to beget | *ku-ziala* | *ku-wyaa* | *ku-dzia (ku-dziaa?)* | *ku-zaa* |
|  | *mu-bili,* | the body | *mu-iri* | *mu-i* | *mu-i* | *mw-ili* |
|  | *ku-le* or *ku-re* | far | *ku-re* | *ku-ye* | ... | *ku-le* |
|  | *mu-liango,* | doorway | *mu-riango* | *mu-yango* | ... | *mw-ango* |
|  | *mu-alume,* | a husband | *mu-lume* | *mu-yume* | *m-ume* | *m-ume* |
|  | *mu-cila,* | a tail | *mu-chira* | *mu-tyiu* |  | *m-kia* |

**97.** — *N. B.* The Gunda language, which is a mixture of that of Senna and of that of Kilimane, is, as it were, the connecting link between Senna and Pokomo. For, like the latter language, it drops *l* in many words, and changes it to *y* in several others, as in *be*, a woman's breast (Tonga *i-bele*), *n-sia*, a path (Tonga *n-zila*), *n-taya*, hunger (Tonga *n-zala*), *ku-kaya*, to be (Tonga *ku-kala*), etc.

## SENNA (INCLUDING TETTE AND NYASSA).

**98.** — *N. B.* This language, though known to the Portuguese as the " Kafreal de Senna, " is not so well spoken at Senna itself as at Tette and in the neighbourhood of the Nyassa Lake, this being probably a result of the greater contact of the natives with Europeans at Senna than in those other places. It is considered by the natives of the Lower Zambezi as being much more primitive than the language of Kilimane and far superior to it. Rebman also speaks of its Nyassa dialect in the following enthusiastic terms : " My study of the Ki-niassa was to me a continual feast. ... No sooner had I got an insight into it, than the dialects with which I had previously made myself more or less acquainted, appeared to me rather as so many rays of one and the same light (¹). " However, lest Rebman's enthusiasm should convey a false notion to the reader, it should be remembered that his terms of comparison were principally coast languages, viz. Swahili, Kamba and the various Nika dialects, all of which have certainly undergone more foreign influence than Senna.

**99.** — The most prominent phonetic feature of this language as compared with the others is that, where most of these have a sharp *z* or *v* or *f*, it has, in many instances, compound sounds, some entirely labial, others entirely dental, others partly labial and partly dental, variously pronounced in the various dialects. Most of these compound sounds are the result of a suppressed *i* or a suppressed nasal.

| Ex. | TONGA | | TETTE | SENNA | NYASSA (Blantyre spelling) | NYASSA (Rebman's spelling) |
|---|---|---|---|---|---|---|
| | *i-fua,* | a bone | *pfupa (?)* | *pfupa* | *fupa* | *pfuba* |
| | *mu-nvui,* | an arrow | *mu-bvi* | *mu-bvi* | *mu-bvi* | *mu-pfi* |
| | *im-vuvu,* | a hippopotamus | *m-bvu* | *m-bu* | ? | *m-pfu* |
| | *ku-zuata,* | to put on dress | *ku-bvara(?)* | *ku-bvala* | *ku-bvara* | *ku-pfara* |
| | *ku-zala,* | to be filled | *ku-dzala* | *ku-dzala* | *ku-dzala* | *ku-dsara* |
| | *i-zina,* | a name | *dzina* | *dzina* | *dzina* | *dsina* |
| | *zi-kowe,* | eyelids | *bzi-kope* | *bzi-kope* | ... | *psi-kope* |

**100.** — As in Nika, Taita, Swahili, and several other languages, the Tonga *b* is generally weakened or dropped altogether in Senna, as in *ku-ona*, to see (Tonga *ku-bona*), *dzua*, the sun (Tonga *i-zuba*), *ku-ziwa*, to know (Tonga *ku-ziba*), *a-ntu*, people (Tonga *ba-ntu*).

**101.** — In Senna the classifier MU of the classes MU-BA and MU-MI is reduced to N, though not before monosyllables nor before labial sounds (cf. 323 and 367).

---

1. *Dictionary of the Kiniassa Language*, 1877, p. VII.

N. B. However, it must be noted that Rebman in his Ki-nyassa dictionary reduces it only to M. But it may be that in this he is no more reliable than in spelling the above examples *mu-pfi, m-pfu, ku-pfara*, etc., whereas the correct spelling is probably *mu-bvi, m-bvu, ku-bvara*, etc..

**102.** — Tette and Nyassa are not the only varieties of the language of Senna. Others are that of Zumbo, the Mbara language of the Loangwe, and even the dialect of Sofala which is described in Bleek's " *Languages of Mozambique* ".

**103.** — We may probably add to these the Gindo language, very little of which is known. Dr. Steere, who supplies a short vocabulary of it, says that " the Gindos are a tribe lying between the coast Swahili from near the north of Monfia to Kilwa ".

Thus it may be seen that the Senna language is one of the most extensively spoken in South Africa.

## KARANGA (*alias* KALAKA).

**104.** — This, the language of the famous Monomotapa empire, is, on the whole, closely related to Senna. In fact, the three principal features of Senna, which have just been mentioned, are also features of Karanga, though the applications are somewhat different. However, on the other hand, Karanga has several remarkable features which distinguish it plainly from Senna, so that it deserves to be treated as a separate language. Hence : —

**105.** — 1° Double consonants of a peculiar kind are met with in Karanga as in Senna, but with some variety of pronunciation. Hence they are written ʂw, ʒw, pʂ, (cf. Alphabet). To these may be added *j* where Senna has *dz*.

| Ex. | TONGA | | KARANGA |
|---|---|---|---|
| | *ku-sika,* | to arrive | *u-ʂwika* |
| | *zi-ntu,* | things | *ʒwi-ntu* |
| | *ku-ziala,* | to beget | *u-ʒwara* |
| | *-pia* | new | *-pʂa* |
| | *ku-za,* | to come | *u-ja* (cf. Senna *ku-dza*) |

**106.** — 2° We hear in Karanga the sounds *j* (French *j*) and *x* (English *sh*), unknown in most Bantu languages. We hear also two peculiar guttural sounds, viz. ɠ and ƙ (cf. 12 and 16).

| Ex. | Tonga | | Karanga | Tonga | | Karanga |
|---|---|---|---|---|---|---|
| | ku-samba, | to wash | u-xamba | ci-fua, | the breast | foɡa |
| | i-saku, | a devil | xaku | mu-bua, | a dog | im-buɡa |
| | Leza, | God | Reja | bu-izu, | grass | wu-hua |
| | mu-sozi, | a tear | un-xoji | a--like, | itself | -oɡa |

**107.** — 3° Not only is the classifier MU of the classes MU-BA and MU-MI generally reduced to N as in Senna, (or to UN, when the word is not isolated), but also that classifier which in the other languages is N or IN, is in Karanga reduced to I, as in Mozambique (385), and the classifier which in the other languages has the form KU, is in Karanga reduced to U, as also happens in Mozambique (cf. 175).

Ex. Tonga     Karanga

 mu-kazi, a woman { isolated form :  un-kaji (Senna un-kazi)
           { connected form : n-kaji (Senna n-kazi)

 im-vula, rain   i-vura (Mozambique i-pula)
 ku-iata to seize  u-pata (Mozambique u-vara)

**108.** — 4° Karanga is full of contractions and elisions which are unknown in Tonga, and such that it cannot be termed an agglutinative language. This renders its study far more difficult than that of Tonga which is, on the whole, much more purely agglutinative.

Ex.   Tonga       Karanga

Leza u-a-ka-tuma m-vula, God sent rain. | Reja-ka-tume-vura ( = Reja u-a-ka-tuma i-vura).

U-a-ka mu-tuma mu mu-lilo u-ta-mani, he sent him to the fire without end. | U-a-kō-n-tuma mu motō-si-nō-pera ( = U-a-ka mu-tuma mu mu-oto u-si-na-ku-pera).

**109.** — In Livingstone's Mss. Comparative Vocabulary previously mentioned, there is a vocabulary of *Yeye*, or the language of Lake Ngami and the River Zouga. (Cf. *Livingstone's Miss. Trav.*, pp. 63-72). There can be no doubt that it is a variety of the Karanga language.

**110.** — The language of Mashonaland is also a dialect of Karanga. Perhaps it is one step nearer to Senna than Karanga proper ([1]).

---

[1]. The word *Ma-shonaland*, which has come so often before the public during these last months, is rather interesting. *Shona* is nothing else than the Karanga pronunciation of the word Senna (*Syona* or *Si-yuna* of the ancient Arab geographers). Hence the word *Ma-shona* is properly the name of the ancient " Senna Rivers " (50, note), which included large tracts of country South of the Lower Zambezi. As a great portion of this country is called *Ma-nica*, and the Senna language closely resembles Nika (99-100), should we not identify the ancient *Manica* gold-diggers with the *Manica* of Mombasa, and both with the *Amalika* of ancient Arabia? Concerning the *Syona* or *Siyuna* of the Arabs, cf. " *Géographie d'Abulfeda*", traduite par M. Reinaud, tome II, 1re partie, Paris, 1848, p. 208, and " *Géographie d'Edrisi*", traduite par P. Amédée Jaubert, Paris, 1836, tome I, p. 66.

## GANDA.

(Spoken on the shores of the Victoria Nyanza.)

**111.** — If Ganda be compared to the languages which have been reviewed before this, the first thing which will strike us is the repeated use of the vowel article *a, e,* or *o,* before substantives, and of the conjunction *na* " and ", before those verbs which are in a historic tense. The use of these particles in Ganda points perhaps to Semitic influence. In any case, it is more phonetic than grammatical. For such particles seem to be heard exclusively after a pause, long or short, as if to introduce verbs and substantives more gently.

**112.** — Ex.

| TONGA | GANDA |
|---|---|
| *Bu-ganda obu mu-bu-lie,* lit. this Ganda realm, eat it. | O *Bu-ganda buno mu-bu-lie.* (Grammaire Ruganda, p. 83.) |
| *U-a-njila mu bu-ato,* lit. he entered the boat, *u-a-zubuka,* he crossed (the lake), *u-eza ku mu-nzi.* he came to town. | **Na***-a-sabala,* lit. *and* he entered the boat, **na***-a-wunguka,* *and* he crossed, **na***-a-tuka mu kialo, and* he came to town. (Mat. 9, 1.) |

**113.** — Among other features of Ganda we may notice : —

1º A phonetic insertion of *g,* sometimes *b,* between vowels, as if to avoid a hiatus.

| TONGA | GANDA |
|---|---|
| Ex. *mu-tue u-angu,* my head. | *mu-tue gwange.* |
| *ku-amba,* to speak. | *o ku-gamba.* |
| *ku-enda,* to go (cf. 52*). | *o ku-genda.* |

**114.** — *N. B.* The love of this euphonic connexion manifests itself particularly in the stem *-pia* " new, " and in the word *e n-kuba,* " rain ". For the stem *-pia,* after having dropped the *p* according to nº 117, replaces it by *g,* as in *e bi-gia,* new things (Mat. 13, 32), the *p* reappearing regularly after *n,* which it changes into *m,* as in *e n-sao em-pia,* new bags. (Mat. 9, 17.) (Cf. 608.) And the word *e-nkuba,* rain, which is in Tonga *im-vula* (cf. 385), has passed probably through the Swahili form *m-vua,* or the Kamba *m-bua,* the *b* of the last syllable *-ba,* having been inserted afterwards, as if to replace the lost *l* of the primitive form *im-vula.*

**115.** — 2º Phonetic permutations of consonants, which show on the whole a tendency to labial and palatal sounds in opposition to the more dental and principally to the sibilant sounds of Tonga. Ganda has also a few double consonantal sounds which remind us of those which we have observed in Senna, and in general it has more in common with Senna and Karanga than with Tonga.

| Ex.: | Tonga | Ganda | Senna |
|---|---|---|---|
| Z to V : | *ku-zua*, to come out | *ku-va* or *ku-vwa* | *u-va* (Karanga) |
| » to W : | *ku-zubuka*, to cross a river | *ku-wunguka* | *u-vubuka*, (Karanga) |
| »dropped: | *ku-zika*, to bury | *ku-ika* | *ku-ika* |
| NZ» to NJ : | *in-zala*, hunger | *e n-jala* | *n-jala* |
| » to DZ : | *ma-nzi*, water | *ma-dzi* | *ma-dzi* |
| S to F : | *sue*, we | *fwe* or *fe* | *i-fe* |
| » to J : | *-sano*, five | *-jano* | *-sano* |
| J to G : | *ij-ulu*, the sky | *e gulu* | ... |
| N to NY : | *i-zina*, a name | *e ri-nya* | *dzina* |

**116.** — *N. B.* There are a few remarkable transitions from labial to palatal sounds.

Ex. Tonga : *im-vula*, rain       Ganda : *e n-*k*uba*
 „    *ku-zubuka*, to cross a river   „   *ku-wunguka*.

**117.** — 3° *P* is dropped or weakened to *w*, when not preceded by *n*, as in Tonga and several other languages. Ex. *o ku-ba-*w*a*, to give them; *o ku-m-*p*a*, to give me (cf. n° 114).

*N. B.* Other phonetic changes caused in Ganda by nasals may be seen described in the French Ganda Grammar, p. 2.

**118.** — A remarkable fact is that a certain number of common substantives are of a different class in Ganda from that to which they belong in nearly all the other Bantu languages.

Ex.: *e n-juba*, the sun (cl. IN-ZIN). Cf. cl. LI-MA, concerning the other languages, n. 410
  *e li-ato*, a canoe (cl. LI-MA).   „   BU-MA   „       „   n. 440
  *mu-bisi*, honey   (cl. MU-MI).„   BU-MA   „       „   n. 455

**119.** — Apparently *Nya-mbu*, which is spoken south-west of the Victoria-Nyanza, differs so little from Ganda that it may be considered as a dialect of it. If we judge from Last's collections on Nyambu in his " *Polyglotta Africana* ", we must say that the Nyambu article has the peculiarly interesting form *a* even in those classes of nouns where in Ganda it has the form *e* or *o*, as in *a mu-twe* " a head " (Ganda *o mu-twe*), *a mi-twe* " heads " (Ganda *e mi-twe*).

## KAFIR (Xosa, Zulu and Tebele).

**120.** — The prominent phonetic features of this language are : —
 1° The use of the click-sounds which have been described in nn. 38-41, and which are probably borrowed from Hottentot. Among the Kafir words which contain clicks, there are few which have equivalents radically identical with them in other Bantu languages.

**121.** — 2° The use of the compound liquid dentals *hl*, *tl*, and *dl* (cf. 35-37), which however is more remarkable in Chwana and is probably derived from it. Examples will be given in the article on Chwana (174, 194, 195). It is remarkable that these sounds, like the clicks, have not penetrated into the grammatical elements of Kafir (prefixes and suffixes), but merely into the verbal roots.

**122.** — 3° A marked tendency to elide vowels before vowels (249), or to combine them in some manner with other sounds. Hence, more particularly, the following phonetic changes, which, though met with occasionally in other languages, and even in Tonga, are more noticeable in Kafir, viz. : —

| Tonga | Kafir | Tonga | | Kafir |
|---|---|---|---|---|
| MU- before a vowel | = NY- | *mue*, | one | *-nye* |
| | | *mu-ana*, | a child | *nyana* |
| BU- and BI- ,, | = TY- or TYW- | *(l)i-bue*, | a stone | *i li-tye* |
| | | *bu-alua*, | beer | *u tyw-ala* |
| | | *ku-biala*, | to plant | *u ku-tyala* |
| BU- ,, (after *n*) | = J | *mu-bua*, | a dog | *i n-ja* |
| PU- and PI- | = TSH | *ku-puaya*, | to compress | *u ku-tshaya* (Zulu) |
| | | *ku-pia*, | to burn | *u ku-tsha* |
| | | *ku-(p)iayila*, | to sweep | *u ku-tshayela* (Xosa) |

The tendency to these changes is the cause of several remarkable phenomena in the Kafir Grammar, (cf. 595, 554, 1053).

**123.** — *N. B.* 1. Though this feature of Kafir, as well as that which has been described in n. 121, have their parallel in Chwana, nevertheless Kafir and Chwana cannot be coupled as belonging to the same group of languages, any more than Kilimàne can be coupled with Senna. Kafir belongs distinctly to the same group as Senna and Swahili, while Chwana with some other languages form a quite different group. Cf. 169 and sqq..

**124.** — 2. The most noticeable differences between the two best known dialects of Kafir, viz. Xosa and Zulu, are the following : —

a) The pronoun equivalent to our " I ", is pronounced *ndi* in Xosa, and in Zulu *ngi*.

b) The consonant *l* is prefixed to more demonstrative pronouns in Zulu than in Xosa (cf. 696, 697).

c) The construction of substantives after passive verbs is different in the two dialects, (cf. 589).

d) A few words in both dialects have either a slightly different meaning, or a slightly different form.

## HERERO.
(Spoken in Damaraland.)

**125.** — Herero is said to be very primitive. This is an opinion which we shall not discuss. However I venture to think that the following features of this language might lead us to a different conclusion : —

**126.** — 1° Herero has a very marked tendency to weaken several consonants, principally *s*, *z*, *k*, and *l*. Even where there is a nasal sound, the consonant which follows it is not always spared.

|  | Tonga | Herero |  | Tonga | Herero |
|---|---|---|---|---|---|
| S and NS | *u-ise*, his father | *ihe* | L and ND | *ku-leta*, to bring | *o ku-eta* |
| | *mu-sozi*, a tear | *o ru-hoʒi* | | *in-dezu* (= *in-lezu*), beard | *o ru-yeʒu* |
| | *in-soni*, shame | *o honi* | | *ku-yanda*, to wish | *o ku-vanga* |
| | *li-nso*, an eye | *e-ho* | | *ci-lundu*, a hill | *o tyi-hungu* |
| Z and NZ | *ku-za*, to come | *ku-ya* | N | *li-no*, a tooth | *e-yo* |
| | *mu-ezi*, the moon | *o mu-eʒe* | | *nyina*, his mother | *ina* |
| | *ku-buzia*, to ask | *ku-pura* | B | *i-bue*, a stone | *e-oe* |
| | *in-zila*, a road | *o n-dyira* | | *ku-bona*, to see | *ku-muna* |
| | *in-zala*, hunger | *o n-dyara* | V | *in-zovu*, an elephant | *o n-dyou* |
| K | *ku-kala*, to remain | *ku-hara* | | *im-vula*, rain | *o m-bura* |
| NK | *in-kuku*, a hen | *o n-dyuhua* | J | *ij-ulu*, the sky | *ey-uru* |

**127.** — *N. B.* 1. However *P* is apparently more firmly pronounced in Herero than in Tonga, though not after *n*, as in this case Herero weakens *p* to *b*.

Ex. :
| Tonga | Herero |
|---|---|
| *i-zuba li-pia*, a new day | *e-yuva e-pe* |
| *in-gubo im-pia*, a new dress | *o m-banda o m-be* |

**128.** — 2. *T* is apparently a favorite letter with Herero, at least before *u*, not however after *n*.

Ex.:
| Tonga | Herero | Tonga | Herero |
|---|---|---|---|
| *ku-fua*, to die | *ku-ta* (= *ku-tua*) | *ku-sabila*, to answer | *o ku-itavera* |
| *i-fu(w)a*, a bone | *e-tupa* | *i-sue*, we | *e-te* (= *e-tue*) |
| *-pofu*, blind | *potu* | *s-untue*, a hyaena | *o tyi-ungu* |
| *bu-siku*, night | *o u-tuku* | *mu-ntu*, a person | *mu-ndu* |

**129.** — 2° The fact that several consonants are more or less weakened in Herero, according as they are coupled or not with a nasal sound, is the cause of several stems having two forms, according to n. 55.

Ex. :
| Tonga | Herero | |
|---|---|---|
| *-pia*, new | *-pe*, without nasal | |
| | *-be*, with | ,, |
| *-bi*, bad | *-vi*, without | ,, |
| | *-bi*, with | ,, |
| *-iza*, come | *-ya*, without | ,, |
| | *-dya*, with | ,, Ex. : Imperative *in-dyo*, " come ". |
| | *o ka-ʒera*, a little bird | |
| | *o n-ᴅera*, a bird | |

**130.** — *N. B.* 1. The Herero article, with its only form *o*, is very noticeable in reading this language (319).

2. Analogies are not wanting between *Herero, Mozambique*, and *Mpongwe* (cf. 169-218 and the note to n. 50).

3. Certain features which are going to be described as being particularly remarkable in Bihe are shared in by Herero.

## BIHE.

(Spoken on the Upper Kwanza.)

**131.** — As described in the Grammar and Vocabulary published by the A. B. C. F. M., Bihe seems to be an amalgamation of several other languages. In some respects it reminds us of Tekeza of the East Coast. In others it reminds us more of Herero. Like the latter, it drops or weakens several consonants. Its other most remarkable features are : 1° to change in many words the syllable *mu* of the other languages to *u*, and *mi* to *vi* or to *i* ; 2° to change the Tonga sound *b* in some cases to *m*, in others to *v*; 3° to change the Tonga *z* to *l* (cf. 209).

Ex. :
| Tonga | Bihe | Tonga | Bihe |
|---|---|---|---|
| *mu-tue*, a head | *u-twi* | *ba-ntu*, people | *ma-nu* |
| *mi-tue*, heads | *vi-twi* | *soba* (Angola *sova*), chieftain | *soma* |
| *i-kumi*, ten | *e-kwi* | *-bi*, bad | *-mi* or *-vi* |
| *ci-lezu*, chin | *o ci-yeli* | *-bari*, two | *-vali* |
| *(z)i-ngombe*, cows | *o lon-gombe* | (Herero *o zon-gombe*). | |

## MBUNDA (¹), LOJAZI, NANO AND NDONGA.

(Spoken from Benguella to the Upper Zambezi.)

**132.** — These languages, though differing materially from one another, may be joined together, until they are better known. They are purer than Bihe. They stand halfway between Herero and Karanga. However, on the whole, they seem to be nearer to Herero. The materials at hand are not sufficient to allow of more explicit statements.

---

1. *Mbunda* is properly a generic name which is applied to many different tribes. With my native informants, Livingstone, Holub, and other travellers, I use it exclusively when speaking of the *Mbunda* proper, viz that nation whose proper seat is on the Mababe, the Ku-ando, and the western bank of the Zambezi. Livingstone, according to Chwana fashion, calls them the *Maponda*. Holub, who calls them correctly the *Ma-mbunda*, is mistaken when he locates them on the eastern side of the Upper Zambezi. *Mbunda* is also pronounced *Mbundu*, according to n. 272. In the Portuguese possessions of the West, this word has become a synonym for " black ". This is the reason why *Angola, Bihe* and other Western languages are variously termed *Ki-mbundu, Lu-mbundu, Bonda*, etc. Cf. Introduction. My native informants used to call the principal Mbunda tribe *Ma-kwengo*.

## 133. — Ex.:

| Mbunda (Kwengo) | Lojazi | Nano | Ndonga | Herero | Karanga |
|---|---|---|---|---|---|
| tisi, a bird | ka-ɓela | oka-ndyila | o n-ɓira | o ka-ʒera | i-nyuni |
| mema, water | mema | o v-ova | ...... | o meva | i-vura |
| ma-ze, fat | ma-ɓe | u-lela | ...... | o ma-ze | ma-futa |
| le-yolo, the nose | li-yolo | ...... | ...... | e-uru | ci-miro |
| lo-lime, the tongue | n-daka | e-laka | ...... | e-raka | ru-rimi |
| li-xo, the eye | li-xo | i-sso | e-xo | e-ho | ji-xo |
| me-nye, fingers | mi-nye | ...... | ...... | o mi-nue | mi-nue |
| ma-nki, stones | ma-ue | ...... | o ma-we | o ma-oe | ma-wue |
| n-golo, a zebra | n-golo | ...... | o n-goro | o n-goro | ...... |
| ko-gola, to laugh | ko-gola | ...... | ...... | o ku-yora | u-yola |
| ko-ti (?), to die | ko-ta | ...... | o ku-ta | o ku-ta | u-fa |
| mo-no, a person | mo-nu | o mu no | u m-tu | o mu-ndu | un-tu, pl. ba-nu |
| kho-ilo, above | kho-ilo, | ...... | ...... | ko tyi-uru | ie-juru |
| ko-yopa, to hear | ko-ɓeba | ...... | ...... | o ku-ʒuva | u-wua |
| n-jobo, a hut | n-jobo | o ka-ndyu | ...... | o n-dyuo | i-mumba |
| ko-landa, to buy | ko-landa | ...... | ...... | o ku-randa | ...... |
| yamba, an elephant | yamba | ...... | o-ndyamba | o n-dyamba | joo |

134. — *N. B.* We may notice in these examples the Lojazi and Ndonga form *ku-ta* or *ko-ta* " to die " for the Tonga *ku-fua*. We find likewise in Lojazi *ko-toma* (= Rotse *ku-fuma*) " to possess ", and *ki-tea* (= Tonga *ci-fua*) " a bone ". Hence it is probable that in these languages, as in Herero (128), we have the transition from *f* to *t* or *t*, at least before *u*.

## ROTSE.

(Spoken on the Upper Zambezi.)

135. — More information is wanted in order to make out how far the grammatical system of Rotse differs from that of Tonga. Some of the regular phonetic permutations between the two languages may however be safely traced already, and *they are well worth notice.* Thus: —

136. — 1° { Tonga z = Rotse t generally, (d after n), = y in a few words, or is suppressed.
Tonga s = „ d in some words, x in others (or j after n), or is suppressed.

| Ex. | Tonga | Rotse | Tonga | Rotse |
|---|---|---|---|---|
| | in-zi, flies | ndi | ku-sia, to leave alone | ko-dia |
| | mu-nzi, village | mo-nde | in-sui, fish | n-di |
| | -zima, destroy | -tima | in-singo, neck | n-dingo |
| | mu-ezi, moon | mo-eti | (l)i-sikati, midday | le-sekate |
| | mu-kazi, female | mo-kati | ku seka, to laugh | ko-seka. |
| | (p)a-nze, outside | ba-nde | -onse, all | -onje |
| | ku-za, to come | ko-ya | (p)a-nsi, down | ba-nje |
| | (l)i-zuba, sun | li-yoa | meso, eyes | meo |
| | ma-nzi, water | mei | mi-sozi, tears | mi-oti |

*N. B.* Apparently *s* in Tonga remains *s* in Rotse in *suffixes*. Ex. : *ko-tim-isa*, to destroy utterly (Tonga *ku-zim-isia*).

**137.** — 2° { Tonga $v$ = Rotse $p$.
{ Tonga $p$ (both clear and weakened or suppressed) = Rotse $b$.

Ex. | TONGA | ROTSE | TONGA | ROTSE.
---|---|---|---|---
| in-devu, beard | mo-lepo | -pia, a) new, b) burn | -bia
| -vula, breed, be multiplied, | -pula | im-pewo, winter | mo-bebo
| -invua, hear, (Her.-ʒuva) | -yopa | (p)e-junza, to morrow | be-yonda

**138.** — 3° The Tonga particle $ci$ is pronounced $si$ or $se$ in Rotse as in Kafir and Chwana (cf. 492). This is of some importance.

**139.** — 4° $B$ and $T$ of Tonga are suppressed in Rotse in some cases, and changed in others to various sounds.

Ex. | TONGA | ROTSE | TONGA | ROTSE
---|---|---|---|---
| bu-oya, hair of animal | oya | (p)ı-kati, in the middle | ba-kaci
| -bi, bad | -i (-bi after n, cf. 54) | (o mu-tima, heart, in Herero) | mo-cima
| (b)i-bue, stone | li-yoe | ku-ita, to call loud | ko-izana
| ku-ba, to steal | ko-iʒa (?) | -tatu, three | -atu

**140.** — 5° Consonants coupled with nasals are apparently weakened. Examples of this may have been observed above (136). Here are a few others.

Ex. | TONGA | ROTSE | TONGA | ROTSE | TONGA | ROTSE
---|---|---|---|---|---|---
| in-kuku, a hen | ngoku | in-ganga, a doctor | ngangа | mu-ntu, a person | mo-nu
| in-kulu, an old man | ngulu | im-pongo, a goat | mbongo | suntue, a hyaena | zondo (?)

**141.** — N. B. 1. The sound which we spell $ng$ is spelt by Livingstone variously: ñ, ñk, ñg. Sometimes the very same word occurs in Livingstone's manuscripts with all three different modes of spelling.

2. We cannot warrant the correctness of the vowels in all the examples given in this work for Rotse. Livingstone who is our only authority and who was principally a Chwana scholar, does not seem to have cared much for the differences between $o$ and $u$, $e$ and $i$ (cf. n. 200). Likewise we cannot certify that $y$ in some of preceding words is pronounced like $y$ in *year*. Possibly Livingstone meant to express by it the sound of the French $j$ (our $j$, 15).

3. At the end of Capello and Ivens' " *From Benguella to the territory of Yacca* ", there is a short collection of words which are said to represent the Ca-luiana language. As the Rotse call themselves *Ba-loi* or *Ba-luiana*, we should expect these to be Rotse words, but they are not so, or, if they are, we must say that they are considerably metamorphosed. The authors say that probably they belong to the Kololo language. Certainly they belong to nothing of the kind. But what approaches to Kololo are some twenty words given in the same work under the heading of " Njenji ". Concerning Kololo, see n. 169.

**142.** — Next to Rotse is the *Nyengo* language, which is described in Livingstone's Comparative Vocabulary MSS. It is spoken on the River Nyengo, which is an affluent of the Upper Zambezi.

Ex. 1°) *mo-kathi*, a woman; *dingo*, the neck; *monde*, a town; *inḃera*, a path, etc. cf. 136.
2°) *m-bebo* or *m'ebo*, wind, winter; *pe-onda*, to-morrow; *se-labo*, a paddle (Rotse, *selabo;* Tonga, *ci-lawo*), cf. 137.
3°) *m-bongo*, a goat; *nganga*, a doctor; *mo-no*, a person, etc. cf. 140.

## RUNDA or LUNDA, and LUBA.

*N. B.* Runda is spoken on the Upper, Luba on the Lower Kasai. Both these languages are closely connected with Rotse.

**143.** — If we judge from Koelle's specimens of Runda, its most remarkable phonetic feature is that the final vowels of its words are scarcely heard, while some others are broadened or weakened. This however is much less perceptible in Carvalho's Lunda Grammar and in Capello and Ivens' specimens of the same language. Traces of a tendency to the same effect in Luba may be seen in the short notes on this language which have been given by Dr. Büttner in the " *Zeitschrift für afrikanische Sprachen*, 1888-89 ", pp. 220-233.

| Ex. Tonga | Lunda | | | Luba |
|---|---|---|---|---|
| | Koelle | Carvalho | Capello and Ivens | |
| *ku-tui*, an ear | *di-dsh* | *di-tui* | *di-to* | *di-chu* |
| *i-fua*, a bone | *di-fup* | *di-fupa* | ...... | ...... |
| *mu-kazi*, a woman | ...... | *mu-kaje* | *mu-kaje* | *mu-kax* |
| *mu-zike*, a slave | *mo-ror* | *mu-roro* | ...... | ...... |
| *i-bele*, woman's breast | *di-yel* | *di-yele* | ...... | *chi-adi* |
| *im-vula*, rain | *um-fal* | *lu-nvula* | ...... | ...... |
| *lu-limi*, the tongue | *ar-dim* | *lu-dimi* | ...... | *lu-dimi* |
| *ma-nzi*, water | *menyi* | ...... | *meme* | *meii* |
| *ka-bua*, a little dog | *ka-b* | *ka-bua* | *ka-bo* | ...... |
| *li-no*, (Kafir *i-zi-nyo*), a tooth | *di-zeu* | *di-zeu* | ...... | *di-no* |
| *li-nso*, an eye | *di-z* | ...... | *di-ce* | ...... |

**144.** — 2° There is also every appearance that the Tonga *zi* is sounded *ji* or *ci* in Lunda.

Ex.  Tonga                   Lunda
*mu-lozi*, a wizard         *mu-laji* (?) or *u-rotchi*
*mu-kazi*, a woman          *mu-kaje*

*N. B.* Possibly also the Tonga sound *tu-* before a vowel is, in Lunda, changed to *tsh* or *dsh*, as in *di-dsh* (K), an ear, (Tonga *ku-tui*); *umo-dsh* (K), a head, (Tonga *di-dsh*), etc.. Cf. parallel changes in Chwana and Kafir for the sounds *bu*, *pu*, *mu*, etc., before vowels, nn. 122 and 202-207.

## RUA.

(Spoken on the Lualaba, South of Nyangwe).

**145.** — If we may rely upon Mr. Last's collections in his " *Polyglotta Africana* ", the most remarkable phonetic feature of Rua is the transition from LI to JI. There is however no trace of this in Cameron's Rua vocabulary at the end of his " *Across Africa* ".

|     | Ex. | Tonga | Rua | |
|---|---|---|---|---|
|     |     |     | Last | Cameron |
|     |     | -*bili*, two | -*biji* | -*wili* |
|     |     | *lu limi*, tongue | *lu-jimi* | *lu-vimi* |
|     |     | *li-no*, tooth | *ji-no* | *li-no* |

*N. B.* Guha, which is spoken West of Lake Tanganyika, is closely allied to Rua. However it shows no trace of the transition from LI to JI.

## ANGOLA, MBAMBA, AND FIOTE OR LOWER CONGO.

**146.** — In many respects these languages differ considerably from each other, but they practically agree in most of the points in which they differ from Tonga. The only regular permutations of consonants which are worth notice in them are the following : —

**147.** — 1° The Tonga *z* before *i* and *e* = generally *j* (French *j*) in the three of them.

The Tonga *s* before *i* and *e* = generally *x* (English *sh*).

| Ex. Tonga | Angola | Mbamba | Congo |
|---|---|---|---|
| *mu-nzi*, village | *mu-iji*, family | *mu-iji*, family | ...... |
| -*zima*, put out a light | -*jima* | ? | -*jima* |
| *in-zila*, road | *n-jila* | ? | *jila* |
| (*l*)*i-zina*, name | *ri-jina* | ? | *e jina* |
| *bu-si*, smoke | *ri-xi* | *mu-ixi*, | *mw-ixi* |
| *mu-se*, earth | *oxi* | ? | *n-xi* |

**148.** — 2° The Tonga *p* (both expressed and suppressed or weakened) = Angola *b* = Mbamba *h* (or *b* suppressed) = Congo *v* (sometimes *m*).

| Ex. Tonga | Angola | Mbamba | Congo |
|---|---|---|---|
| -*pia*, a) burn; b) new | -*bia* | -*hia* | -*via* |
| *ci-fu(w)a*, bone, chest | *ki-fuba*, bone | *ki-fúa* | ...... |
| (*p*)*a-nsi*, down | *b'o xi* | ? | (*o*)*va-nxi* |
| -*pa*, give | -*ba* | -*ha* | *vana* |

**149.** — *N. B.* In Congo, those stems which have generally *v* where Tonga has *p* recover this consonant after nasals. Ex. *m-pemo* " wind " (Tonga *im-pewo*).

**150.** — 3° Tonga *c* = Angola *g* (?) or *k* = Congo *k* (cf. 258).

| Ex. | Tonga | Angola | Congo |
|---|---|---|---|
|     | *ku-cia*, dawn of day | *ku-gia* | *ku-kia* |
|     | *mu-cila*, tail | *mu-kila* | *n-kila* |

**151.** — Though agreeing thus in many points, the language of Angola and that of Lower Congo seem to differ considerably on some others. Thus : —

1º In Angola, *n* or *m* is dropped before *s*, *x*, *p*. Not so in Congo. On this point Mbamba is apparently like Angola. The same phenomenon takes place in Swahili, Sagara, etc., cf. 282, 283.

| Ex. Tonga | Angola | Mbamba | Congo |
|---|---|---|---|
| in-soni, shame | sonye | ? | n-soni |
| ku-nsi, below | koxi | ? | ku-nxi |
| in-ziba (?), swallow | piapia, (of class IN) | pieha (of class IN?) | venga-m-punza |

**152.** — *N. B.* I find there are in Angola a few words in which the Tonga *n* is replaced by *i* before a consonant. Ex. *ku-ivua* " to hear " (Tonga *ku-nvua*), *mu-iji* " a family " (Tonga *mu-nzi*), etc..

**153.** — 2º In Congo, the classifier MU of the classes MU-BA and MU-MI is generally reduced to N (M before labials), as in Karanga and Senna (107, 101).

| Ex. | Tonga | Congo | Karanga |
|---|---|---|---|
| | mu-kulu, elder | n-kulu | (u)n-kuru |
| | mu-samo, a tree | n-ti | (u)n-ti |
| | mu-cila, a tail | n-kila | (u)n-cira |

**154.** — 3º Congo weakens also, or drops, the classifiers BU and KU of the classes BU-MA and KU-MA. Cf. 465 and 447-450.

*N. B.* In this again, Congo reminds one of Karanga. Are these merely accidental connexions between the principal language of the ancient Congo kingdom and that of ancient Monomotapa?

**155.** — 4º In general, in the classification of nouns, Congo recedes further from Tonga and from the generality of the Bantu languages than Angola does, as will appear from the chapter on substantives. Mbamba seems to be nearer to Tonga than either Angola or Congo.

**156.** — *N. B.* 1. The Congo dialects which are described in the old Grammar of the Capuchin Father Brusciotto a Vetralla and in the Mss. French-Congo Dictionary in the British Museum, were more perfect than the modern San-Salvador dialect described in Rev. W. Holman Bentley's " *Dictionary and Grammar of the Congo Language* " (London, 1887).

**157.** — 2. The Bangala language, of which Mr. Héli Chatelain has given us specimens in the " *Zeitschrift für afrikanische Sprachen* ", 1888-1889, pp. 136-146, is probably the same as that which is called *Kasands* or *Kasandshi* in Koelle's *Polyglotta*. It differs but little from Mbamba.

**158.** — 3. The old Angola dialect, which has been preserved to us in the Grammar of Father Pedro Diaz, S. J., and in the catechism of Father de Coucto, S. J., had fewer contractions and was consequently nearer to Tonga than the modern dialect.

## MIDDLE CONGO LANGUAGES.

**159.** — H. H. Johnston, in his "*Journey up the River Congo*", gives us precious, though short, vocabularies of three languages of Middle Congo, viz. Teke, Buma and Yansi. They are sufficient to show that these languages differ considerably from one another, comparatively speaking, and yet perhaps more from any other known Bantu language. But they are neither sufficiently accurate, nor complete enough, to allow us to bring out any of their phonetic features with certainty.

**160.** — *N. B.* A few words in Buma and Teke have the consonant *r* where Tonga has *t*. This, as we shall see further on, is characteristic of the Mozambique-Chwana-Mpongwe group of languages. The Buma language in particular has certainly a great deal in common with Mozambique.

**161.** — Here are, for the sake of comparison, a few of the words in which these languages agree best with Tonga, and consequently with the main Bantu group : —

| Ex. Tonga | Teke | Buma | Yansi |
|---|---|---|---|
| *ma-bele*, woman's breast | *ma-biela* | *ma-biela* | *ma-biela* |
| *bu-ato*, a canoe | *bw-atu* | *bw-aro* | *bw-engo* |
| *mu-ana*, a child | *mw-ana* | *mw-ana* | *mw-ana* |
| *mu-se*, country | *n-chi* | *ki-se* | *n-chi* |
| *ku-fua*, death | *a-fi* (the dead?) | *saa-fwa* (?) | *a-gui* (the dead?) |
| *mu-bua*, a dog | *m-bwa* | *m-bwa* | *m-bwa* |
| *in-goma*, a drum | *n-goma* | *n-goma* | *n-goma* |
| *ku-tui*, an ear | ... | *i-tui* | *i-tui* |
| *ma-tui*, the ears | *ma-chui* (144) | ... | ... |
| *mu-tue*, the head | *mu-chwi* | *mu-tu* | *mu-tu* |
| *i-ji*, an egg | *i-ke* | ... | *i-ke* |
| *li-nso*, an eye | *i-shu* | *di-u* | *li-shuu* |
| *in-sui*, a fish | *n-chwi* | *n-tu* | *n-chui* |
| *im-vuvu*, a hippopotamus | *m-vubu* | ... | *n-gubu* |
| *in-ganga*, a doctor | *n-gā* | *n-gā* | ... |
| *ma-fua*, a skeleton | *ma-fwa* | ... | *li-pfuba* (99) |
| *-bi*, bad | *-bi* | *-bi* | *-bi* |
| *-tatu*, three | *-tatu* | *-saru* | *-satu* |

**162.** — Here are also a few words in which, as far as we may rely on these small vocabularies, these languages differ widely from the main Bantu group.

| Ex. Tonga | Teke | Buma | Yansi |
|---|---|---|---|
| *mu-lilo* (Senna *m-oto*), fire | *m-ba* or *m-baa* | *m-bô* | *me-a* or *me-ya* |
| *m-pongo* (Swahili *m-buzi*), a goat | *n-taba* | *n-taba* | *n-taba* |
| *in-gubo*, cloth | *w-iko* | *ki-piu* | *bi-lamba* |
| *in-zoka*, a snake | *n-tare* | *m-pili* | *mu-shwema* |
| *i-suba*, the sun | *ma-tere* | *i-tere* | *n-dembe* |

# NYWEMA.

(Spoken North of the River Lukuga).

**163.** — The materials available regarding the language of the cannibal Nywema are not yet sufficient to allow us to pass a judgment on the features proper to it. However it may already be said that it has much in common with the language of the Bihe, while, in some respects, it reminds one more of Mpongwe (cf. 213 and sqq.).

**164.** — 1° The classifiers of the class MU-MI (366), are reduced in Nywema to *o* or *u* in the singular (Mpongwe *o*, Bihe *u*), and to *e* or *i* in the plural (Mpongwe *i*, Bihe *vi*).

| Ex. Tonga | Nywema | | Mpongwe | Bihe |
|---|---|---|---|---|
| | Bamba dialect | Kusu dialect | | |
| *mu-lomo*, the mouth | *o-lomo* | *u-lomo*, | *o-lumbu* | ... |
| *mi-lomo*, mouths | *e-lomo* | *e-lomo* | *i-lumbu* | ... |
| *mu-tue*, the head | *o-twe* | *o-twe* | ... | *u-twi* |
| *mi-tue*, heads | *e-twe* | *e-twe* | ... | *o vi-twi* |
| [*mu-ti* (Senna), a tree] | *o-ti* | *o-ti* | *o-tindi* | *u-ti* |

**165.** — 2° The Tonga *z* before *i* is replaced in Nywema, at least in some words, by *l*, (Mpongwe *l* or *n*, Bihe *l* expressed or suppressed, 131).

| Ex. Tonga | Nywema | Mpongwe | Bihe |
|---|---|---|---|
| *mu-ezi*, the moon | *w-eli* | *o-gweli* | ... |
| *mu-kazi*, a female | *w-ali* | ... | *u-kai* |
| *im-buzi*, a kind of goat | *m-buli* | *m-buni* | ... |

**166.** — 3° The sound which in Nywema is *v* when not influenced by a nasal, changes to *p* when influenced by one, as in Mpongwe, Congo, and several other languages. Ex. *lu-vita*, a finger, pl. *pita* (= *m-pita*, of class LU-IN).

**167.** — *N. B.* 1. Nywema differs from Mpongwe, among other things, by not having *r* where Mpongwe has it for the Tonga *t* (cf. 214). Otherwise the word for "head" should not be in Nywema *o-twe*, but *o-rue;* that for "belly" should not be *o-tima*, but *o-rima*, etc.

**168.** — 2. All these conclusions concerning Nywema are drawn from Last's precious collections in his "*Polyglotta Africana*", pp. 183-187 and 232-233. Mr. Stanley's collections in his "*Dark continent*" would lead to different conclusions. Probably they represent different dialects from those which have been studied by Last.

## KUA or MOZAMBIQUE, and CHWANA.

**169.** — The association of Chwana with the language of Mozambique may appear astonishing on account of its novelty. The fact is that we are passing to a class of languages which differ on important points from those reviewed until now, and that, precisely where such differences occur, these languages happen to have similar features. This part of our study is particularly interesting, because after having passed from Mozambique and the Comoro islands to Basutoland and the Kalahari, thus touching the very southernmost parts of Africa, we find ourselves obliged to retrace our steps towards Kilimanjaro, then to pass over to the Ogowe under the equator, across the whole African continent.

*N. B.* Nearly everything that will be said on Chwana in this article is true not only of Chwana proper, but also of its numerous dialects (Suto, Tlhaping, Kololo, etc.).

**170.** — To understand the language of Mozambique and Chwana, it is necessary to distinguish with a very peculiar attention between those consonantal *sounds which include a nasal* and *those which contain none*. Hence : —

**171.** — 1° Considering those *sounds which contain no nasal*, we have to notice a set of permutations which differs considerably from most of what we have seen until now. The correspondence of $r$ and $t$ is particularly remarkable. The general tendency is to guttural sounds.

**172.** —

| Tonga | Moz. | Chwana | Ex. Tonga | Mozambique Masasi | Mozambique Kilimane | Chwana |
|---|---|---|---|---|---|---|
| T | = r, rr = | r | -*tatu*, three | -*raru* | -*raro* | -*raru* |
| ,, | ,, ,, ,, | ,, | *ku-jata*, to hold | *u-vara* | *u-varra* | *go-chwara* |
| ,, | ,, ,, ,, | ,, | *ku-tuma*, to send | *u-ruma* | -*u-rruma* | *go-roma* |
| ,, | ,, ,, ,, | s, r | (*l*)*i-tama*, a cheek | *n-rama* | *ni-rrama* | *le-sama* pl. *ma-rama* |

**173.** —

| | | | | | | |
|---|---|---|---|---|---|---|
| Z | = r, rr = | d, r | *mu kazi*, a wife | *mw-ari* (isl. of Moz.) | *mu-arri*(?) | *mo-sadi* (or *mo-sari*, cf. 9) |
| ,, | ,, ,, ,, | ,, | *ma-nguzu*, strength | *i-kuru* | ... | ... |
| ,, | ,, ,, ,, | ,, | *mu-ezi*, moon | *mw-eri* | *mu-erre* | *kgwedi* (or *kgweri*) |
| ,, | ,, r, l ,, | ,, | *in-dezu*, beard | *i-reru* (isl. of Moz.) | *e-rrelo* | *tedu* |

| Tonga | Moz. | Chwana | Ex. Tonga | Mozambique | | Chwana |
|---|---|---|---|---|---|---|
| | | | | Masasi | Kilimane | |
| ,, | ,, ch, z | ,, dropped | (l)i-zina, a name | n-china | ni-zina(?) | le-ina |
| ,, | ,, ,, | ,, tl | ku-zala, to become full | u-chara | ... | go-tlala |
| si | ,, y, b | ,, ts | ku-ziala, to beget | u-yara | u-bala | go-tsala |
| | | | | | | (Suto tsuala) |
| zu | ,, u | ,, cw | ku-zua, to come out | u-ua | | go-cwa |

### 174. —

| | | | | | | |
|---|---|---|---|---|---|---|
| S | = t | = tlh | meso, eyes | me-to | ma-to | ma-itlho |
| | | | | | | (Kafir a mehlo) |
| ,, | ,, ,, | ,, ,, | mu-sana, back | m-tana | mu-tana | mo-thlana |
| | | | | | | (Kafir u m-hlana) |
| ,, | ,, ,, | ,, h | ,, ,, | ku-samba, to wash | u-hapa | u-haba | go-tlhapa |
| | | | | | | (Kafir u-ku-hlamba) |
| ,, | ,, ,, | ,, t | ,, r | mu-sisi, hair | ... | n-tite | mo-riri |
| si | ,, hi | ,, si | ku-sia, to leave behind | u-hia | ... | go-sia |
| ,, | ,, ,, | ,, ,, | bu-siku, night | u-hiu | u-tio | bo-sigo |
| ,, | ,, ,, | ,, x | ,, s | ku-busia, to rouse | u-wuxa | ... | go-cosa |
| ,, | ,, thi, ti | ,, dropped | ku-simba, to dig | u-thipa | u-timba | go-epa |
| se | ,, the, te | ,, tshe | ku-seka, to laugh | u-thea | u-tea | go-tshega |

### 175. —

| K | =dropped= | g | -ako, thine | -ao | -au | -ago |
|---|---|---|---|---|---|---|
| ,, | ,, ,, | ,, ,, | in-zoka, a snake | i-noa | noa | noga |
| ,, | ,, w | ,, ,, | ku-buka, to awake | w-uwa | u-uwa | go-coga |
| ,, | ,, k | ,, sh | i-kumi, ten | ni-kumi | kume | le-shome |
| ,, | ,, ,, | ,, ,, | ku-kuwa, to shout | u-kuwa | u-kuwa | go-shua |

### 176. —

| C | = dropped = | s | ci-ntu, a thing | i-tu | e-lo | se-lo |
|---|---|---|---|---|---|---|
| ,, | ,, ,, | ... | mu cila, tail | mw-ila | mu-ila | ... |
| ,, | ,, ,, | ,, ,, | cia-ku-lia, food | y-olia | ... | se-jo |
| | | | (= i-a-u-lia) | | | |

### 177. —

| F | = k | = sh | ku-fua, to die | u-kwa | u-kua | go-shwa |
|---|---|---|---|---|---|---|
| ,, | ,, ,, | ,, f, h | ma-futa, oil, fat | ma-kura | ma-kurra | ma-fura (or ma-hura cf. 11.) |

### 178. —

| LI | = li, j | = j | ku-lia, to eat | u-lia | u-oja | go-ja (205) |
|---|---|---|---|---|---|---|
| ,, | ,, l | ,, ,, | mu-liango, door-way | m-lako | ... | mo-jako |

### 179. —

| B | =dropped= | b | ku-bona, to see | w-ona, | u-ona | go-bona |
|---|---|---|---|---|---|---|
| ,, | ,, ... | ,, c, b | ku-boko, an arm | ... | ... | le-cogo, pl. ma-bogo (414). |
| ,, | ,, ,, | ,, c | ku-buka, to awake (intr.) | u-uwa | u-uwa | go-coga |
| bi | ,, ,, | ,, j | -biala, to sow | w-ala | ... | go-jala (202) |

**180. —**

| Tonga | Moz. | Chwana | Ex. Tonga | Mozambique | | Chwana |
|---|---|---|---|---|---|---|
| | | | | Masasi | Kilimane | |
| P = | „ | = f | (11) mu-ini(=mu-pini), handle | m'ini (pl. mi-vini) | | mo-fiŋa |
| „ | „ | „ | „ | (p)a-kati, between | v-ari | v-ari | fa-gare |
| „ | „ | „ | „ | i-fua (= i-fupa), bone | ni-kuva | ... | ... |
| „ | „ | „ | „ | (p)a-nsi, down | va-thi | va-ti | le-fatshe, earth |

**181. —** *N. B.* 1. This last permutation, viz. *p = v = f*, should be compared with what has been noticed in Congo (148, 149), Rotse (137), etc.

**182. —** 2. The fact of *b* being suppressed, as in Mozambique, though mentioned more particularly in this place, is common to many other Bantu languages, as may have been remarked throughout the whole of this article. Cf. class BU-MA, in the chapter on substantives.

**183. —** 2° Considering those consonantal sounds *which contain a nasal*, we meet here with an entirely new application of the general principles mentioned in nn. 55-59, viz. — the nasal is apparently suppressed, except before monosyllabic stems, and then, in Chwana, the consonant which remains is either hardened or strengthened, or, if possible, dentalized, while in most of the dialects of Mozambique there is a marked tendency to the same effect. Hence : —

**184. —**

| Tonga | Moz. | Chwana | Ex. Tonga | Mozambique | | Chwana |
|---|---|---|---|---|---|---|
| | | | | Masasi | Kilimane | |
| MP= | p | = ph | im-pewo, wind | i-pio. | pevo | phefo |

**185. —**

| MB= | p, b | = p | ku-bumba, to form | w-upa | u-uba | go-bopa |
| „ | „ | „ | im-buzi, goats | e-puri | bure | podi |
| „ | „ mb(?) | „ | im-bezu, seeds | m-beyu (?) | beu | peu |

**186. —**

| NVorMV= | p = | p | in-vula, rain | i-pula | | pula |
| „ | „ „ | „ | mi-nvui, arrows | ... | | me-cui |
| „ | „ iw „ | tl | ku-nvua, to hear | w-iwa | | go-utlwa |

**187. —**

| NF= | ...... | kh | in-zila n-fuefui, a short | ... | | tsela e khutshane |

**188. —** [road

| NK= | k | = kg | in-kuku, a hen | ... | -ku | kgogu |
| „ | „ | „ | (z)in-kuni, firewood | i-kuni | ... | di-kgoŋa |

**189. —**

| NG= | ŋg | = kg | in-ŋombe, a cow | i-ŋope | | kgomo |

**190. —**

| NG= | k | = k | in-goma, drum | i-koma | i-goma(?) | koma(= war song) |
| „ | „ | „ | mu-liango, the doorway | m-lako | ... | mo-jako |

| Tonga | Moz. | Chwana | Ex. Tonga | Mozambique | | Chwana |
|---|---|---|---|---|---|---|
| | | | | Masasi | Kilimane | |

**191.** —

| NJ = | k = | k, ts | *ku-njila*, to enter | *u-kena* | | *go-kena* or *go-tsena* |
|---|---|---|---|---|---|---|

**192.** —

| NT = | t = | th | *mu-ntu*, a person | *m-tu* | *mu-to* | *mo-thu* |
|---|---|---|---|---|---|---|
| „ | „ | „ | *in-tibi*, a shield | ... | ... | *thepe* |

**193.** —

| ND = | t, th = | t | *mu-lindi*, a pit | *n-liti*, | ... | *mo-lete* |
|---|---|---|---|---|---|---|
| „ | „ | „ | *ku-enda*, to go | *w-etha*, | *u-enda*(?) | *go-eta*(=to travel) |
| „ | „ | „ | *ku-linda*, to watch over | *u-lita*, | ... | *go-leta* |

**194.** —

| NS = | t, th = | tlh | *-onse*, all | *-othe* | *-ote-ne* | *-otlhe* |
|---|---|---|---|---|---|---|
| „ | „ | „ | *li-nso*, an eye | *ni-tho* | *ni-to* | *le-itlho* |
| „ | „ | x | *in-soni*, shame | *i-xoni* | | *di-tlhong* (Kafir *i n tloni*) |
| „ | „ | ... | *in-sangu*, a hoof, a shoe | ... | | *tlhaku* (Kafir *i n-tlangu*) |
| „ | „ | h | *mu-nsi*, within | *m-hi-na* | *mo-ti-n* | *mo-teng* |

**195.** —

| NZ = | th, d = | tl | *(p)a-nze*, outside | *va-the* | *va-nje*(?) | *kwa-ntle* |
|---|---|---|---|---|---|---|
| „ | „ | „ | *in-zala*, hunger | *i-thala* | *dala* | *tlala* |
| „ | „ | ts | *in-zila*, a road | ... | *dila* | *tsela* |
| „ | „ | x | *ma-nzi*, water | *ma-xi* | *ma-ije* | *metse* |
| „ | „ | n | *in-zoka*, a snake | *i-noa* | *noa* | *noga* |

**196.** —

| NY = | n = | n | *i-nyama*, meat | *i-nama* | *nyama* | *nama* |
|---|---|---|---|---|---|---|
| „ | „ | „ | *i-nyati*, a buffalo | *i-nari* | *narre* | *nare* |

**197.** — *N. B.* It is evident from this last permutation *(ny = n)* that the Mozambique word *noa*, snake, and the Chwana *noga* interchange *immediately*, not with the Tonga form *in-zoka*, but with the Kafir form *i nyoka*. And in general it may be said of many words both in Chwana and in Mozambique, that they are in more immediate connexion with their Kafir than with their Tonga equivalents.

**198.** — This influence — open or concealed — of nasals upon other consonants, in Chwana and Mozambique, causes a great many words to have in these languages two forms each, these forms being sometimes widely different (cf. 52-59).

| Ex. | Tonga | Mozambique | Chwana |
|---|---|---|---|
| | *ba-ntu ba-***tatu**, three persons | *a-tu a-*raru | *ba-tho ba ba-*raro |
| | *in-gombe (z)in-***tatu**, three cows | *i-gope (di)*taru | *di-kgomo tse (di)*taru |

N. B. I have not however sufficient evidence to trace with certainty to the influence of nasals the fact that verbs in Chwana adopt a stronger form after the reflexive pronoun *i* (655), as if *n* were suppressed. Possibly this fact might also be explained by saying that the vowel *i* produces in given cases the same effect as *n*, as if *i* and *n* were two cognate sounds in Bantu (cf. 152, 285, 412, 414). But this explanation does not seem to hold so well as the first in presence of the fact that the classifier DI of the class SE-DI (Tonga CI-ZI) does not cause the stems which follow it to adopt strong forms. (Compare n. 496 with n. 395.)

**199.** — Though Chwana and Mozambique agree very nearly in the remarkable features just mentioned, they can in no wise be considered as mere dialects of one and the same language. For they diverge in many other respects, principally in this, that, through contractions, elisions, and probably owing to European intercourse, the grammatical system of proclitics, enclitics, prefixes, and suffixes, is in Mozambique reduced to a mere skeleton, while its richness is extraordinary in Chwana.

**200.** — Again, Chwana, contrary to Mozambique, often changes to *o* the *u* of the other languages, and their *i* to *e*, as may be seen in the above examples. Likewise the syllable *ni* at the end of Bantu words is regularly changed to *nġ* in Chwana, though there is no evidence that the same is done in Mozambique (194).

**201.** — Again, a remarkable feature of Chwana, apparently not shared in by Mozambique, is a series of combinations of consonants and vowels which occur before such suffixes as begin with a vowel. They are for the most part similar to those which have been described in the note on Kafir (122-123) as affecting the consonants *m*, *b*, and *p*. A few others are new, affecting the consonants *l*, *r*, and *ts*. They are well described in Rev. William Crisp's " *Secoana Gr.* ", pp. 103-104, from which the following examples are drawn:—

**202.** —
1° *Be-* (vowel) = *j-*.   Ex. *thebe*, a shield; diminutive *thejana*, a small shield.
   *Bo-* (vowel) = *jw-* or *j-*. Ex. *tlhaba*, pierce; passive voice *-thlajwa*, be pierced.

**203.** —  *bo-gobe* ja *me* jo = (*bo-gobe* bo-a *me* bo-o), this is my bread.
2° *Po-* (vowel) = *cw-*.   Ex. *mo-lapo*, a river; dimin. *mo-lacwana*.
   *Phe-*(vowel) = *chw-*.   Ex. *tshephe*, a springbok; dimin. *tshechwana*.

**204.** —
3° *Mo-* (vowel) = *ngw-*.   Ex. *kgomo*, an ox; dimin. *kgongwana*.

**205.** —
1° *Le-* (vowel) = *j-*.   Ex. *le-itlho* ja *me* je (= *le-itlho* le-a *me* le-e), this is my eye
   *Lu-* (vowel) = *cw-*.   Ex. *khulu*, a tortoise; dimin. *khucwana*.   [(cf. 178).
   *Di-* (vowel) = *ts-*.   Ex. *podi*, a goat; dimin. *potsane*.

**206.** —

5° *Re-*(vowel)=*tsh-* Ex. *se-tlhare*, a tree; dimin. *setlhatshana*.
*Ts-* before *a* and *e* becomes *c* before *o*. Ex. *-botsa*, ask; *poco*, a question.

**207.** — *N. B.* 1. Through some sort of extension of the principle which causes the preceding permutations, those syllables which are liable to them, viz. *mo, bo, po*, etc., are sometimes found to interchange in the manner just described after a suppressed nasal.
Ex. *lo-mocana*, a small gulley, pl. *di-ngocana* (= *di(n)-mocana*, cf. 470).

2. All this naturally throws a good deal of light on some of the phenomena mentioned in nn. 172-180. From the examples given in these same numbers for Mozambique, I suspect that the transitions of sounds just described are not altogether foreign to the latter language, though far less numerous than in Chwana.

**208.** — Here we must come back to another point which is common to Kafir and Chwana. This is the use of the peculiar sounds *hl, tl, dl,* etc. It has just been seen (174) that the Chwana *tlh* corresponds to the Tonga *s*. So is it with the Kafir *hl* and *tl;* only *tl* is used exclusively after *n, hl* in the other cases. The Kafir *dl* is used without *n* only in a few words where it replaces the Tonga *zi-* before a vowel, as in *u-ku-dlala* " to play " (Tonga *ku-ziana*), *u ku-dla* " to eat " (Tonga *ku-lia*, Chwana *go-ja*), and its numerous derivatives. After *n*, the Kafir *dl* = Chwana *tl* = Tonga *z*.

| Ex. Kafir | Chwana | Kafir | Chwana |
|---|---|---|---|
| *a mehlo*, the eyes | *ma-itlho*, (174) | *i n-tlangu*, a shoe | *tlhaku* (194) |
| *u m-hlana*, the back | *mo-tlhana* (174) | *pa-ndle*, outside | *kwa-ntle* (195) |
| *u ku-hlamba*, to wash | *go-tlhapa* (174) | *i n-dlala*, hunger | *tlala* (195) |
| *i n-tloni*, shame | *di-tlhong* (194) | *i n-dlovu*, an elephant | *tlou* |

**209.** — *N. B.* 1. There are so many analogies between Mozambique and Karanga that it is impossible to doubt of their very intimate connexion (cf. 107, 921). Likewise it strikes me that Herero resembles Mozambique not only in those permutations of consonants which may be traced to the peculiar cut of the teeth of either tribe (50 note), but also in the use of certain words which are met with only in a few Bantu Languages.

| Ex. | Tonga | Mozambique | Herero |
|---|---|---|---|
| | *mu-bili*, body | *i-rutu* | *o rutu* (366*) |
| | *mu-oyo*, heart | *m-rima* | *o mu-tima*, etc. |

**210.** — 2. Several coast languages which are heard from Mozambique to Delagoa Bay are intermediary between Chwana and Mozambique on the one hand, and Zulu and Senna on the other. This is true to a certain extent of Kilimane, examples of which have been given above, as also of Gunda which has been mentioned in a previous article. But it applies more particularly to Tekeza (Delagoa Bay), Nyambane, and Gwamba (East of the Lower Limpopo). However all such languages have on the whole more in common with Chwana and Mozambique than with Zulu and Senna. Kafirs both in Natal and at Senna have a supreme contempt for all of them. I have even known a man born at Kilimane who considered his own native language as a mean brogue, while he used to extol Senna as a refined language. In fact, everything combines to make us believe that the peculiar features of the language of Mozambique and the like were originally the result of lip-rings and filed teeth. Lip-rings must have modified considerably the pronunciation of nasal and labial sounds, and filed teeth that of dental sounds, and the combined result of both must have been a tendency to gutturals, and to aspirates, or to half-suppressed sounds.

| Ex. Tonga | Tekeza, | Nyambane | Gwamba, | Chwana | Mozamb. | Senna | Zulu |
|---|---|---|---|---|---|---|---|
| *mu-ana*, a child | *w-ana* | *nyan* (?) | *ngwana* | *ngwana* (204) | *mw-ana* | *mw-ana* | *u nyana* |
| *ba-ntu*, people | *va-no* | *wa-no* (?) | *ba-nhu* | *ba-thu* (192) | *a-tu* | *a-ntu* | *a ba-ntu* |
| (*mi-samo*, trees) | *mi-re* | *mi-tanda* | *me-ri* | (*di-tlhare*)(172) | *mi-iri* | *mi-ti* | *i mi-ti* |
| *ma-nzi*, water | ... | *ma-ti* | *ma-ti* | *me-tse* (195) | *ma-xi* | *ma-nzi* | *ama-nzi* |
| *-tatu*, three | ... | { *-raro* <br> { ? (with *n*) | *-raru* <br> *naru* | *-raru* (172) <br> *tharu* (192) | *-raru* <br> *taru* } | *-tatu* | *-tatu* |
| *in-gombe*, a cow | *omo* | *ngombe* (?) | *homo* | *kgomo* (189) | *i-ngope* | *ngombe* | *i n-komo* |

## TSHAGGA AND HINZUA.

**211.** — *N. B.* Tshagga is one of the languages spoken near Kilima-njaro, Hinzua is one of those of the Comoro islands.

The short specimens we have of these two languages are evidently insufficient to judge of their proper features. However they show plainly that both of them have some of the features of Mozambique, principally with respect to dental and liquid sounds.

| Ex. | Tonga | Tshagga | Hinzua | Mozambique |
|---|---|---|---|---|
| T— | *-tatu* three | *-raru* | *-taru* [with *n* (?)] | *-raru* (*-taru* with nasal |
|  | *mu-ti*, a tree (Senna) | *mu-ri* | *mw-iri* | *mw-iri*  [influence] |
|  | *ma-tui*, ears | *ma-ru* | *ma-ki-yo* | *ma-ru* |
|  | *mu-tue*, the head | *mu-rue* | *xi-tswa* (cf. 206) | *mu-ru* |
|  | *mu-tumua*, a servant | ... | *m-ruma*(*m-rumia?*) | *ka-rumia* |
|  | *m-oto*, fire (Senna) | *m-oro* | *m-oro* | *m-oro* |
| Z— | *mu-kazi*, a female | *mu-ali* | *m-she* | *mw-ari* |
|  | *ma-nzi*, water | ... | *ma-zdi* (?) | *ma-xi* |
|  | *i-zuba*, the sun | *e-ruva* | *i-dzua* | *n-chuwa* |
| K— | *-ako*, thine | ... | *-aho* | *-ao* |
|  | *-akue*, his | ... | *-ahe* | *-awe* |
| P— | *ano* (= *pano*), here | ... | *vanu* | *vano* |
|  | *-ngai?* (= *-ngapi?*), how many?... |  | *-ngavi?* | *-chani?* or *-ngavi?* |

**212.** — *N. B.* 1. The Gweno language, of which Johnston gives us short specimens in his " *Kilima-njaro Expedition* ", is closely allied to Tshagga.

2. The short specimens of Angazidja which were published by Steere in 1869 represent a language of the Comoro Islands which seems to differ considerably from Hinzua. If these specimens may be relied upon, Angazidja is a mixture of Hinzua and Swahili.

## MPONGWE.

(Spoken on the Lower Ogowe.)

**213.** — Strange as it may appear, it is none the less true that Mpongwe is more closely allied to Chwana and Mozambique than to the languages of the Lake region. For : —

1° Here again the most noticeable permutations are from *t* to *r*, and from *z* to *l* (Chwana *l*, *d*, or *r*).

2° The influence of the nasal on consonants combined with it is in many respects similar to what has been noticed in Kua and Chwana, though it is to be noted that in Mpongwe, contrary to what occurs in Chwana and in some Mozambique dialects, the nasal is retained before consonants in given cases with the effect of changing *k*, *s*, and *t* to *ty*, *z* to *dy*, etc.

3° In many words the vowels *i* and *u* are changed respectively to *e* and *o*, as in Chwana (200).

**214.** — Ex.

|  | Tonga | Mpongwe | Chwana | Mozambique |
|---|---|---|---|---|
| T | -*tatu*, three | -*raro* | -*raro* | -*raru* |
| NT | -*ntatu*, do. (class IN) | -*ntyaro* | -*tharo* | -*taru* |
| Z | *mu-ezi*, the moon | *o-gweli* | *khwedi* | ... |
| NZ | *in-zovu*, an elephant | *n-dyogu* | *tlou* | ... |
| S | *i*-sue, we | *a*-zue | *ro-na* | *hi-yo* |
| NS | *in-soni*, shame | *n-tyoni* | *di-tlhong* | *i-xoni* |
| B | -*bi*, bad | -*we* | -*shwe* |  |
| MP | -*mbi*, do. (class IN) | -*mbe* | " |  |
| K / NK | *in-kuku*, a hen | *n-dyogoni* | *kgogu* | ... |
| L | *mu-alumi*, a husband / -*lanfo*, long | *o-nome* / -*la* | (cf. *mo-nona*) / -*lele* | (cf. *m-amna*) / ... |
| ND | *n-danfo*, do. (class IN) | -*nda* | -*telele* | ... |

**215.** — It may be added that in Mpongwe, as in Mozambique, *v* and *p* correspond to each other as weak and strong letters, e. g. *owaro ovolu*, " a large canoe," *nyare m-polu*, " a large ox." On this particular point, Mpongwe resembles the language of Lower Congo (cf. 149).

**216.** — A remarkable feature of Mpongwe, in the same line as those just described, and noticeable principally in verbs, is that these have double forms such as -*toma* and -*roma*, " send " (Tonga -*tuma*, Chwana -*toma* and -*roma*), -*dyonga* and -*yonga*, " drink " (Tonga *nyua*), etc. Probably the more dental, or stronger, of such forms is due to an occult influence of the nasal.

**217.** — A phonetic feature proper to Mpongwe is the use of the consonant ñ *(alias* nl) in many instances in which most other languages have *l*. Ex. *o-*ñ*ome*, " a husband " (Tonga *mu-alumi*), -*ba*ñ*i*, " two " (Herero -*bari*, Tonga -*bili*), *i-we*ñ*e*, " a woman's breast " (Tonga *i-bele*).

**218.** — *N. B.* The principal feature of Mpongwe, as compared with the other Bantu languages, is the partial obliteration and disappearance from it both of the classifying elements of nouns, and of the connective elements of other words, viz. those elements which refer verbs, adjectives, and pronouns to their proper noun (cf. 42). However it must be added that the richness of Mpongwe is saved by the introduction of a great many constructions apparently foreign to Bantu. The practical consequence of such a fact with respect to this work is that less will be said on Mpongwe than on the other great Bantu languages, because our aim is not so much to dwell on the features proper to particular languages as to bring out those that are proper to the main group.

## DUALLA.

**219.** — Dualla, the principal language of the Cameroons, has a great deal in common with Mpongwe, or scarcely differing from it. Thus : —

**220.** — 1° { The Tonga *t* not preceded by *n* (= Mpongwe *r*) = Dualla *l*.
{ The Tonga *z* before *i* (= Mpongwe *l* or *n*) = » *d*.

Ex.: TONGA   DUALLA   MPONGWE         TONGA              DUALLA   MPONGWE
*bu-ato*, canoe  *bolo*   *ow-aro*         *i-zina*, name         *dina*   *ina*
*ma-futa*, fat  *m-ula* (Chwana: *ma-fura*)  *im-buzi*, a kind of goat  *m-bodi*  *m-boni*
*-tatu*, three  *-lalu*  *-raru*          *loozi*, straight, good  *-lodi*   ...
*-tuma*, send  *-loma*  *-roma*          *mi-sozi*, tears        *mi-sodi*  *an-tyoni*

**221.** — 2° Dualla has, like Mpongwe, verbs with two forms, the one stronger, the other weaker (216).

Ex.: TONGA        DUALLA   MPONGWE    TONGA          DUALLA      MPONGWE
*-buena* (or) *-bona*, { stronger *-jene*  *-dyena*   *-njila*, enter { stronger *-gingea*  *-dyingina*
(cf. 264) { weaker   *-ene*   *-yena*                  { weaker: *-ingea*   *-yingina*

**222.** — *N. B.* 1. The change of the Tonga *-buena* or *-bona* into the Dualla *-jene* and the Mpongwe *-dyena* should be particularly noted, as it reveals another link which connects these languages with Chwana and Mozambique. Cf. 202 where *bo-* before a vowel is found to change regularly to *j* in most Chwana dialects.

2. Vowels are weakened in Dualla as in Mpongwe (213).

**223.** — Strange to say, if we consider Dualla from another point of view, we shall find that on the whole the Bantu grammatical elements are better preserved in it than in Mpongwe. Thus in particular the classifiers of the classes MU-BA and MU-MI are not reduced to O-A and O-I, as in Mpongwe, but they keep their consonants *m* and *b*.

Ex. :    TONGA                            DUALLA              MPONGWE
        *mu-ntu*, a person, pl. *ba-*     *mo-tu*, pl. *ba-*    *o-ma*
        *mu-alumi*, a husband, pl. *ba-*  *m-omi*, pl. *b'-*    *o-nome*, pl. *a-*
        *mu-lomo*, mouth, beak, pl. *mi-* *mo-lumbu*, pl. *mi-* *o-lumbu*, pl. *i-*
        (Herero: *mu-tima*) heart         *mo-lema*, pl. *mi-*  *o-rema*, pl. *i-*

**224.** — And, if we place ourselves in a third point of view, we may notice in Dualla a feature which reminds one of Swahili and Kamba of the East Coast, viz. *l* is often dropped (81, 88).

| Ex.: | TONGA | DUALLA | SWAHILI | KAMBA |
|---|---|---|---|---|
| | *im-vula*, rain | *m-bua* | *m-vua* | *m-bua* |
| | *in-zila*, a road | *n-gia* | *n-jia* | *n-sia* |
| | *-lila*, cry | *-eya* | *-lia* | *-iya* |

**225.** — Other consonants are dropped in some cases in Dualla, but apparently the laws cannot be generalized.

| Ex.: | TONGA | DUALLA | | TONGA | DUALLA |
|---|---|---|---|---|---|
| K | *i-kumi* (= *li-kumi*), ten | *d'-um* | *Z* before *a* | *-iza*, come | *-ya* or *-wa* |
| F | *ma-futa*, fat | *m'-ula* | *N* nasal | *mu ntu*, a man | *mo-tu* |

**226.** — *N. B.* Saker says in his Dualla grammar, " that the present Dualla are a very mixed people, greatly the result of the slave trade ". Their language is indoubtedly quite as mixed, and consequently cannot be said to be a good representative of pure Bantu.

**227.** — The same must be said of Benga, Isubu, and Kele, all three of which are languages closely allied to Dualla. Benga is spoken on the islands of Corisco Bay, Isubu north of the Dualla, and Kele principally along the Bembo River.

**228.** — The most remarkable phonetic difference between Benga and Dualla is the transition from *s* to *h*. Thus the Dualla words *sango* " father ", *di-so* " an eye ", *bo-so* " the face ", *esadu* " small " are respectively pronounced in Benga *hango*, *diho*, *boho*, *eholi* (*Zeitschrift*, 1888-89, p. 195).

**229.** — Between Isubu and Dualla the most remarkable phonetic differences are the transition from *p* to *f*, and the use of *k* in many instances in which it is dropped in Dualla (Saker's Grammar, pp. 12 and 18). Thus the Dualla words *mo-lopo* " the head ", *m-boa* " a town ", *ma-iya* " blood ", *mo-utu* " a child ", etc., are respectively in Isubu *mo-lofo*, *m-boka*, *ma-kia*, *mo-kutu*, etc.

**230.** — Kele differs more from Dualla, Benga, and Isubu, than these latter differ from one another. Its most characteristic feature seems to be to weaken vowels more than any of the languages we have hitherto reviewed.

| Ex.: | TONGA | KELE | DUALLA | MPONGWE |
|---|---|---|---|---|
| | *mu-ntu*, a person | *mu-tyī* | *mo-tu* | ... |
| | *ma-boko*, arms | *ma-bŏ* | ... | *a-go* |
| | *li-nso*, an eye | *dishī* | *d-iso* | *i-ntyo* |
| | *mi-nue*, the fingers | *mi-na* | *mi-ne* | *i-meno* |
| | *bu-ato*, a canoe | *bi-ali* | *b-olo* | *ow-aro* |
| | *bu-sio*, the face | *bo-she* | *bo-so* | *o-jo* |

## FAN.

(Spoken on the upper stream of the River Gabún.)

**231.** — Judging from Don Amado Osorio Zabala's Fan Vocabulary lately published by Mr. Cust (1887), there can be no doubt that this is a Bantu language. It is closely allied to Mpongwe perhaps more closely related to Kele, and again forcibly reminding one of Chwana, and even more of Mozambique. This is plain from the following permutations, several of which may be considered as being regular.

**232.** — Ex.:

| Tonga | Fan | Tonga | Fan | Mpongwe | Mozamb. | Chwana |
|---|---|---|---|---|---|---|
| *l* | = | *l* | -*tumigue*, sent | -*lomigue* -*romio* | | -*romelie*(?) -*romilwe* |
| | | | -*tatu*, three | -*lãa* | -*raro* | -*raru* -*raro* |
| | | | *ku-tue*, ear | *a-lõ*, | *o-roi*, | *nya-ru*, ... |
| | | | pl. *ma-tue* | pl. *molõ* | pl. *a-roi* | pl. *ma-ru* ... |
| „ | =*n* after *n* | *mu-tue*, head | *n-nũ* | ... | *mu-ru* | ... |
| *Z* = | | *l* | *in-dezu*, beard | *n-sel* | *e-lelu* | *e-reru* *tedu* |
| | | | *mu-zimo*, soul, spirit | *a-linã* | *i-nina* | *mu-rimo*(?) *mo-dimo* |
| „ | = | *n* final | *mu-ezi*, moon | *gõn* | *o-gweli* | *mw-eri* *kgwedi* |
| *B* | dropped before | and after *o, u* | *ma-zuba*, days | *me-lu* | ... | *ma-chuwa* ... |
| | | | *lu-boko*, arm | *u-õ* | *o-go* | ... *le-cogo* (cf. 179) |
| „ | = | *b* before *i, e, a* | *ba-ntu*, people | *b-oru* or [*b-ur* | ... | *a-tu* *ba-tho* |
| | | | { *ka-bia*, a flame (Guha) } { *ka-bã* | ... | | ... |
| | | | ( pl. *tu-bia*, fire ) ) pl. *do-a* | ... | | ... |

**233.** —

| | | | | | | |
|---|---|---|---|---|---|---|
| *L* | dropped | *ma-bele*, breasts | *ma-bī* | *am-bene* | *ma-pele*(?) | *mabele* |
| | | -*bili*, two | -*be* | -*bani* | -*ili* | -*bedi* |
| | | *in-gulube*, a pig | *n-giii* | *n-gowa* | *i-kuluwe* | *kolobe* |
| | | *ku-ulu*, a foot | *e-kõ* | *o-golo* | ... | ... |
| „ | =*s* (?) | *mu-lomo*, the beak | *en-soon* | *o-jumbu* | ... | *mo-lomo* |
| | | *li-no*, a tooth | *as-õn* | *i-no* | *n-ino* | *le-ino* |
| *F*=*k*, or dropped | | *u-fua*, a dying man | *e-gu*(*e-ku*(?)) or *e-u* | -*yuwa*, to die | -*kwa*, to die | -*shwa*, to die |
| | | *ku-fuma*, to be rich | *kuma*, riches | ... | | -*fuma* |
| *V*=*g* or *k*, etc. | | *in-zovu*, an elephant | *en-sok* | *n-dyogu* | | *tlou* |
| | | *im-vuvu*, a hippopotamus | *n-sogo-usui* | *n-guu* | | *kubu* |
| *K* | dropped | *i nyoka*, a snake | *ño* | ... | *i-noa* | *noga* |
| | | *in-kuku*, a fowl | *kũ* | *n-dyogoni* | ... | *koku* |

**234.** — Evidently this is not a complete list of the phonetic permutations of consonants between Fan and other Bantu languages. I exclude particularly all reference to the influence of *n* nasal, because I cannot trace its law in Fan as we have traced it in Chwana and Mpongwe. However, the extent of this influence may be conjectured from the fact mentioned by several travellers that " the nasalization of the language is very marked " (Cust's " *Languages of Africa* ", vol. II, p. 422).

**235.** — A very remarkable feature of Fan is the negligence with which the vowels are pronounced (230). For not only do we find here many words dropping their final vowel, principally after *n*, such as *engan*, "a doctor" (Tonga *in-ganga*); *asōn*, "a tooth" (Tonga *li-no*); *n-bom*, "a boa" (Tonga *im-booma*); *n-suur* or *n-suut*, "a black man" (Tonga *mu-sundu*, Kafir *on-tsundu*, Chwana *mo-sutu*, etc.); but also several accented vowels themselves have an uncertain pronunciation, as is evidenced from the fact that the author of the Fan Vocabulary writes the same words with different vowels in different places, e. g. *enōm* or *enām* or *enom*, "husband" (Mpongwe o\\ome); *em-borre* and *-vora* = one (Senna *-bozi*), etc.

**236.** — This furnishes probably the correct explanation of another remarkable feature of Fan, viz. that in many Fan words the vowel *a* = Tonga *o* or *u*; likewise Fan *e* = sometimes the Tonga *o* or *a*, and the Fan *o* = often the Tonga *u*, etc.

| Ex.: Tonga | Fan | Tonga | Fan |
|---|---|---|---|
| *meso*, the eyes | *mise* | *-kulu*, ancient | *-koā* |
| *mu-yuni*, a bird | *un-ōn* | *-a-palua*, filed (teeth) | *e-bōl*, etc. cf. examples above. |

**237.** — *N. B.* These, with the phenomena described in nn. 230, 213, 200, and 122, seem to be the most important exceptions to the general principle of the relative stability of the vowels in Bantu (48).

## FERNANDIAN (Fernando Po).

**238.** — Strange to say, Fernandian differs from Mpongwe and Dualla by using the *t* in the same cases as Tonga, Kafir, etc., instead of the *r* of *l* which we have just seen used in several other languages.

| Ex. Tonga | Fernandian | | | Mpongwe |
|---|---|---|---|---|
| | Banapa dialect | Banni dialect | Ureka dialect | |
| *bu-ato*, a canoe | *bu-ato* | *b-ato* | *b-ato* | *ow-aro* |
| *ku-tue*, an ear | *ba-ttu* | *b-ato* | *b-ato* | *o-roi* |
| *mu-tue*, the head | *e-tue* | *e-chue* | *e-chue* | (Kua *mu-ru*) |
| *-tatu*, three | *-tta* | *-ta* | *-ta* | *-raro* |

**239.** — Fernandian seems even to be fond of *t*'s as it replaces often by *t* the Tonga *z*, as in *n-tele*, "a road" (Tonga *n-zila*), *n-tohi*, "the sun" (Tonga *i-zuba*), etc.

However, in other words we find the *t* of the other Bantu languages replaced by *s* in Fernandian. Ex. *bw-aiso*, "a woman" (cf. Kamba *mw-aito*, "a mother"), *b-osso*, "fire" (*m-oto* in Senna, Swahili, etc.).

**240.** — Another remarkable feature of Fernandian, at least of its principal dialects, is the one noticed by Bleek, p. 248, viz. the frequent use of *b* where the other languages have *m*.

Ex.
| TONGA | BANNI DIALECT |
|---|---|
| *mu-ntu*, person | *bo-cho* |
| *mu-alume*, husband | *b-ube* (Dualla *m-omi*) |

**241.** — *N. B.* As for the rest, the documents at hand are insufficient to allow of any important conclusions being drawn safely from them. However I may say that in reading these same documents I am strongly reminded of the languages of the Lower Congo (nn. 146-158), and of Bihe (131).

## LANGUAGES OF THE CONGO FOREST.

**242.** — We are indebted to Stanley for giving us in his "*Darkest Africa*" words belonging to the languages of the dwarfs that inhabit the great Congo forest. Unfortunately no one can tell us whether these words belong to the original language of those tribes, or whether they have been borrowed by them from the agricultural tribes in whose neighbourhood they live. I take this latter view to be the correct one, principally because we know that the more southern dwarf tribes of the Kalahari desert readily adopt the languages of their neighbours. (Cf. Introduction). But, whatever view we take, the fact is that a large number of the words given by Mr. Stanley as belonging to the languages of his dwarfs are unmistakably Bantu in origin. Such are not only the numbers *-bari* " two ", *-saro* and *-karo* " three, " *-nna* " four ", *-tano* " five ", but also a certain number of substantives, e. g. : —

**243.** —

| KU-MBUTTI (Ba-kwa forest) | BA-KIOKWA (Ba-Kumu forest) | CF. IN BANTU : |
|---|---|---|
| *ba-kwa*, dwarfs | ... | *ba-tua*, (Tonga, Kafir, etc.) |
| *mo-ku*, a person | *mo-go* | *mu-ntu* (Tonga, etc., n. 322\*) |
| *kali*, woman | *kali* | *mu-kazi* (Tonga, Ganda, etc. n. 322\*) |
| *i-bu*, a dog | *i-bu* | *mu-bua* (Tonga, etc.) |
| *i-tindi*, a foot | *i-tindi* | *mu-lindi* (Senna, Gindo, etc.) |
| ... | *ma-bongo*, head | *ma-bongo*, brains (Tonga, etc. n. 440\*) |
| *in-du*, a house | ... | *in-du* (several Tonga dialects, n. 385\*) |
| *kupa*, the sun | ... | *i-zuba* (Tonga, etc. n. 410\*) |
| *m-bua*, rain | *m-bu* | *m-bua* (Kamba, etc. 385\*) |
| *i-tari*, a stone | ... | *ri-tari* (Angola, etc. n. 410\*) |
| *mi-nyo*, teeth | *mi-nyo* | *ma-nyo* (Ganda, etc. n. 410\*) |
| *ki-tu*, the ears | *ki-toi* | *ku-tui*, an ear (Tonga, etc. n. 462\*) |
| *i-dakka*, the tongue etc., etc. | *i-dakka* | *e-raka* (Herero, etc. n. 133). |

**244.** — Of course, the materials furnished by Stanley are not sufficient for fixing any of the laws which regulate the transitions of consonants in these languages. There are however at least three examples which tend to show that the Tonga *t* is more or less regularly sounded *k* or *g* by the dwarfs of the Congo forest. These examples are -*karo* "three", (Tonga -*tatu*, Chwana -*tharo* and -*raro*), *ba-kwa* "dwarfs" (Tonga *ba-tua*, Chwana *ba-rwa* or *ba-roa*) and *mo-ku* "a person" (Tonga *mu-ntu*, Chwana *mo-tho*). On the whole, these languages seem to have more in common with the Chwana-Mozambique-Mpongwe than with the main group of the Bantu languages.

## SEMI-BANTU.

**245.** — We leave it to others to compare with the Bantu languages which we study in this work several of those of the Soudan, Lower Niger, Liberia, Sierra Leone, Senegambia, and other parts of Western Africa. I believe that interesting affinities might be brought to light by such a comparison. Koelle's "*Polyglotta Africana*" and Christaller's collections in the "*Zeitschrift für afrikanische Sprachen*" will be found invaluable in this connexion. Most of these so-called negro languages are in fact semi-Bantu, and I do not think that a thorough investigation of their proper features can be made without some knowledge of the more primitive and less contracted Southern Bantu languages. Cf. nn. 598 and 830.

## CONCLUSION.

**246.** — This cursory glance at the most striking phonetic differences between the best known Bantu languages, while forcing upon our minds many unexpected conclusions, naturally gives rise to a number of highly interesting problems.

We see that this family of languages, if it be confined to the limits we have assigned to it after the example of other scholars, has been very improperly compared by certain philologists to the Aryan family. So far from finding any such distance between the most remote members of the Bantu family as between English and Sanscrit, we perceive that the greatest discrepancies between those members of the group which are furthest apart can scarcely be said to be equal on the whole to the difference between French and Italian.

This being so, what is simply amazing is that untold millions of so-called savages, inhabiting a country much larger than Europe, and devoid of political connexions, even in these days probably so remote from the time of their original separation, should still be found to have languages so closely related together.

Again, we see that in this Bantu family a whole group is separated from the rest by a peculiar set of phonetic features, such as the transition from *t* to *r*, *z* to *l*, and *k* to *g* or *h*, when it is not dropped entirely, together with changes due to an extraordinary influence of half-suppressed nasals. And then, if we look at a map of Africa, we are struck by a sight no less amazing than the first. For the tribes which speak the languages of this group live by no means in the neighbourhood of one another, but they are rather at the opposite extremities of the Bantu field. They are the Bechwana and the Ba-suto near the southern end of Africa, with the most eastern tribes of Mozambique and the Comoro islands, the Tshagga nation of Kilima-njaro, and the north-western tribes of the Ogowe, Cape Lopez, and the Gabún River. We understand that the ancient Oriental race which South-African natives call *Kua (Ma-nkua* or *Ma-kua* or *Ba-koa*, whence the diminutives *Ma-kuana*, *Ba-kuana*, *Wa-ngwana*, and *Be-chwana)*, after having occupied the Comoro islands and Mozambique, may have gone down along the coast of Sofala, then ascended the Limpopo and its tributaries in quest of gold. We may even understand that the same race may have gone to seek precious stones in the direction of Kilima-njaro to those mysterious caves at Elgon which have been described by Thompson in his " *Through Masai-land* ", pp. 300-302. But we should not have expected to find the same race settled at Cape Lopez, and we fail to see which way they followed in those emigrations of a past deeply veiled in mystery ([1]).

---

1. Since this went to the press it has struck me that the word *K'ua*, pronounced *Goa* or *Gua* at Kilimane, is no other than the name of *Goa* in India, and that the Oriental race called *Ma-nkua* are no others than the Moors, Parsis, Banyans, Battias, etc., indiscriminately included by the natives of several parts of Eastern Africa under the name of *Goanese*, probably because most of them come from Goa, and the Portuguese colonies of the same parts have long been a dependency of Goa. Now, as the harbours of Mozambique have been for the last three centuries the most noted places for shipping slaves, I much suspect that the linguistic and ethnological affinities existing between the tribes of Mozambique and those of the Gabún are the result of nothing else than an interchange of slaves.

I also notice that for the Tonga the word *Ma-nkua* is a synonym of *ba-kuala* " people who can write ".

## IV. — More General Phonetic Changes.

**247.** — The phonetic changes which have been described in the preceding article are for the most part so peculiar to this or that language as to form one of its prominent features. Here we shall turn our attention to a few other changes which are more generally met with. They occur mostly in the combination of the different elements of the words.

§ 1. We may include them under two heads, viz. 1° Changes of sounds caused by the collision of two vowels. 2° Changes caused by the concurrence of certain consonants with other sounds.

### § 1. Changes caused by the Collision of two Vowels.

**248.** — The general principle of these changes may be laid down as follows, with all reserve regarding its particular applications, as these are somewhat different in the different languages : —

**249.** — 1° *A*, when occurring before another vowel, is scarcely ever elided, except in Nyamwezi (cf. 76), but generally either there is a sort of assimilation of both vowels, each of them changing its sound into one which is intermediary between them, so that *a-i* and *a-e* become *e-e*, while *a-u* and *a-o* become *o-o;* or a contraction proper takes place, viz. *a-i* and *a-e* become *ē*, *a-u* and *a-o* become *ō;* *a-a* becomes *ā*. In some languages, e. g. in Tonga, assimilation is the rule, contraction proper is the exception. In others, e. g. in Kafir, contraction proper is the rule. When through assimilation the same vowel should be repeated three times, two of the vowels are contracted into one.

| Ex. : | Tonga (assimilation) | Kafir (contraction) |
|---|---|---|
| A-I = *ee* = *e* | *meeso* or *mēso* ( = *ma-iso*), the eyes. | *a mehlo* ( = *a ma-ihlo*) |
| A-E = *ee* = *e* | *ba-ntu beeza* ( = *ba-iza* = *ba-a-iza*), the people came. | *a ba-ntu beza* ( = *ba-eza, ba-a-iza*) |
| A-U = *oo* = *o* | *u-zoo-nvua* ( = *u-za-u-nvua* = *u-za-ku-nvua*), he will hear (cf. 948). | *u-o-va* ( = *u-a-u-va* = *u-ya-ku-va*) |
| A-O = *oo* = *o* | *ma-tanga oonse* ( = *a-onse*), all the pumpkins. | *a ma-tanga onke* ( = *a-onke*) |

**250.** — *N. B.* 1. I have heard in Tonga both *ba-ntu bo-onse* and *ba-ntu be-ense*, all the people, as if *a-o* could change not only to *oo*, but also to *ee;* unless the form *beense* may be explained by saying that the Tonga stem *-onse* ( = all) has also the form *-ense*, just as we have in Kafir *-odwa* or *edwa*, alone (815).

2. In Tonga as it is spoken, the initial *i* of the verb *-inka* " to go ", which is very frequently used, assimilates to itself entirely the final *a* of preceding words. Thus we may hear *tu-a-ki*

*inka* " we went " for *tu-a-ka inka, uli inka* " he is going off " for *ula inka*, etc. This may be explained by saying that the syllable *ka* being particularly accented in the verb-*inka* causes the preceding syllable to prefer the weaker sound *i* to the stronger sound *e*. No account is taken of this phenomenon in the written language (253).

On the contrary the verbs -*injila* " to go in ", -*invua* " to hear ", etc., and in many cases the substantives which begin with *in* lose their initial *i* after *a*.

**251.** — 2° The weak *I* or *i*, when occurring before another vowel, is generally assimilated with it, as in *ce-elo* ( = *ci-elo*), " a ceelo " (¹), and in *ca-a mu-luma* ( = *ci-a mu-luma)*, " it has bitten him. "

**252.** — *N. B.* 1. In Chwana, when a week *è* (= Tonga i) is immediately followed by a vowel, it is generally entirely assimilated with it. Ex. : *o-no o-reka* (= *o-nè o-reka*), " you were buying "; *o*-na *a-reka* = *o*-ne *a-reka*, " he was buying," etc. (Cf. Crisp's Gr., p. 31.)

**253.** — 2. The principles of assimilation and contraction thus laid down both for the vowel *a* and for the vowel *i* (or a weak *e*) are applied principally when prefixes or suffixes are joined to other elements of the same grammatical word. In this case it is better that the spelling should agree with the pronunciation, as in the above examples. But the same principles have other applications in the rapid pronunciation of such words as are immediately joined to one another. It will be sufficient to warn the reader of these once for all, without confusing the written language with them : otherwise we should have two different spellings of the same clauses, the one for slow, the other for rapid pronunciation.

Ex. Slow pronunciation and written language : *ndabona izuba*, " I saw the sun " *ma-kumi a-ta-balui* " a large number ", lit. " tens which are not counted, " = *ndabone izuba, ma-kuma a-ta-balui*, in rapid pronunciation.

When the first of the two words which meet in this way is a mere particle, such as the preposition -*a* " of ", its sound in Tonga and the like languages is always modified before a vowel, even in writing ; in Kafir, Ganda, Herero, etc., a contraction proper takes place.

Ex. Tonga : *ma-futa e in-zovu* (= ... a *in zovu*) " fat of elephant " (Kafir *ma-futa* e *ndlovu* = ... ai *ndlovu*).

**254.** — The impossibility of writing certain expressions as they are usually pronounced is particularly felt in Karanga, which, having a special horror of hiatus, always contracts or elides in ordinary pronunciation whatever vowels happen to succeed each other. Thus the Karanga would pronounce as a single word the whole sentence : " They saw a small house, " *bakabonemumbeccana*. Which evidently must be spelt so as to separate the different words, *bakabona imumba icecana* (cf. 108).

**255.** — 3° *I* proper, when occurring before another vowel, keeps very nearly its proper sound in Tonga and apparently in the greater number of the Bantu languages, such as Yao, Shambala, etc., though a beginning of assimilation is sometimes noticeable.

In Kafir, Herero, etc., *i* before another vowel becomes entirely consonantal, and is consequently spelt *y* when it is not immediately preceded by a consonant ; but it is dropped when immediately preceded by a consonant.

---

1. A sort of evil spirit which is supposed to fly about like a bird, and to bite people's heart, thus causing their death.

In Swahili, Senna, etc., the law is the same as in Kafir, except for the plural classifier of the class CI-ZI. This keeps the *i* or changes it to *y*.

| Ex. Tonga | Kafir | Swahili |
|---|---|---|
| *In-ganda i-angu*, my house | *i ndlu yam* | *nyumba yangu* |
| *i-zina li-ako*, thy name | *i gama lako* | *jina lako* |
| *in-ŋombe zi-esu*, our cattle | *i nkomo zetu* | *ŋombe zetu* |
| *zi-bula zi-enu*, your chairs | *i zitulo zenu* | *viti vyenu* (alias *vienu*) |

**256.** — *N. B. I* before a vowel is elided in Congo after *z*, and in Angola after *j*, e. g. in Congo : *nzo zanene* (= *zi-anene*), "large houses" (Vetralla).

in Angola : *jinzo ja mundele* (= *ji-a mundele*), "houses of a white man" (Héli Chatelain, p. 14.)

In the other cases *i* before a vowel keeps its proper sound in these languages, as in Tonga.

**257.** — Exceptions. — In some cases, *i* before a vowel combines into one sound with the consonant before it. Examples of this in Chwana have already been noticed in words in which the phonetic permutation is double, viz. first *i* is replaced by *e* according to n. 200, and then *be-*, *le-*, *re-*, etc. are changed respectively before vowels to *j-*, *tsh-*, etc. (cf. 202-206). Likewise in Tonga *li-* before a vowel (= Chwana *le*) changes in some cases to *j*, e. g. *janza*, "hand" = *li-anza* (plural *ma-anza*). This very natural phenomenon is common to many languages.

**258.** — Again, in Swahili and several other Eastern languages *ki-* before a vowel changes to *c* or *ch* (8). Ex. in Swahili : *ki-devu ch-ako* = "thy chin" (= *ki-devu ki-ako*).

**259.** — In Senna the same phenomenon takes place not only before *i*, but also before *e*. Ex. *u-fumu bu-anu bu-fice*, "thy (lit. your) kingdom come" (= *u-fumu bu-anu bu-fike*).

**260.** — *N. B.* It is interesting to notice that the Swahili sound *ki*, even before a consonant, is equivalent to the Tonga *ci*, Herero *tyi*, Kafir *si*, Chwana *se*, etc. (cf. class CI-ZI, 491.)

**261.** — 4° *U*, when occurring before another vowel, keeps its proper sound in the larger number of cases, and causes no change. In Kafir and several other languages it becomes more consonantal than in the others, and is consequently written *w*.

| Ex. Tonga | Kafir | Swahili | Lower Congo |
|---|---|---|---|
| *lu-limi lu-ako*, thy tongue | *u lw-imi lw-ako* | *u-limi w-ako* | *lu-bini lw-aku* |
| *ku-fua ku-ake*, his death | *u-ku-fa kw-ake* | *ku-fa kw-ake* | *fwa kw-andi* |
| *mu-nzi u-enu*, your town | *u m-zi w-enu* | *m-ji w-enu* | |

**262.** — *N. B. Ua* and *wa* often sound almost like *oa*, by a partial assimilation of *u* or *w* with *a*.

**263.** — Exceptions. — 1. *U* before *o* is changed to *o*, or these two vowels coalesce to *ô*, according as the languages prefer simple assimilation or contraction.

Ex. Tonga : *bu-siku bo-onse*, the whole night = Kafir *u bu-suku bonke*.

**264.** — 2. *U* before a vowel is dropped in a few cases to be mentioned further on. (Cf. 656 * *passim*, etc.) The most important case is *in Kafir* after the labial consonants *b* and *f*. Ex. *u bu-so bako*, " thy face, " (= *u bu-so* b*u-ako*).

**265.** — 3. *Ue* or *we* and *o* are convertible in some cases.
Ex. Tonga : *-buena* or *-bona*, " see. " Kafir : *i ngwenyama* or *i ngonyama*, " lion. "
*N. B.* Hence it is that in Kafir and Chwana stems of nouns ending with *o* are treated in composition with suffixes as if they ended with *-we* (cf. 202, 203, etc.).

**266.** — 4. Examples may also be found in some languages in which *we* or *ue* is convertible with *u*, as in *mw-eli* or *mu-li* " the moon ", in Mozambique. Hence the word *Na-muli*, which is the name of certain remarkable peaks East of Lake Shirua, is etymologically nothing else than a Mozambique transformation of *Nya-mwezi*, and consequently means as well as this word " Mountains of the Moon ".

**267.** — 5. *U* before *i* sometimes causes this latter vowel to be suppressed, e. g. *ku-za*, " to come "*,* = *ku-iza*, as if in such cases *u* were a more important vowel than *i*.

**268.** — 6. *U* before a vowel coalesces sometimes with its consonant, at least in several Bantu languages, viz. Chwana, Kafir, Senna, etc. (cf. 122 and 202-204).
Ex. In Senna : *nya-ku-sasamba* (= *mu-a ku-sasamba*), " a merchant. "

**269.** — *N. B.* It should be remembered that in grammatical elements (classifiers and collective pronouns, 637) and in some other instances, the Chwana *o* = *u* of the other Bantu languages. Before a vowel the same Chwana *o* is generally written *w*, when it does not coalesce with the preceding consonant (202-204).

**270.** — In the other Bantu languages *o* as well as *e*, not being found in any grammatical element, occur before vowels only at the end of words. Then *o* is sometimes decomposed into *ue* or *we*, according to n. 265, while in the other cases no change takes place at least in writing, according to the principle which has been laid down in nn. 253 and 254.

### § 2. Various Phonetic Changes.

**271.** — 1° In Tonga and several other languages we find a letter which, though sounded *e* when accented and in the middle of a word, becomes *i* when not accented at the end of a word. This is the sound which we represent in some instances by í to remind the reader of this very principle. Cf. 14.

Ex. *a-fue* = near.    Derivative : *a-fue-fui*, very near
    *-mue* = one           „         *mue-mui*, few
    *i-kumi* = ten          „         *ma-kume-kumi*, hundred
    *mu-sé* = earth        „         *a-nsi*, on the ground ; *mu-nsi*, in the ground, etc.

**272.** — *N. B.* 1. Probably it is due to some phenomenon of the same kind that authors often hesitate between *i* and *e* at the end of a word. Thus Livingstone in his Tette vocabulary writes *madze* " water " and *panse* " down " in one place, while in another he spells the same words *madzi* and *pansi*.

**273.** — 2. The penult often drags the last vowel of a word to its own sound. Thus we may hear *Zulu* or *Zula* (proper name), *Ba-lunda* or *Ba-lundu*, "the Lunda people, " etc.

**274.** — 2° *A* changes to *e* before certain sounds, though only in given cases, principally before *ci-*, *nyi-*, *ji-*, or similar sounds, and in Kafir before certain verbal stems, etc., as if in such cases there were a contraction of *a* with an obscured *i-* sound, or, more probably, a peculiar phenomenon of assimilation.

Ex. Tonga : B*e-ciseke*, the people of Sesheke [sing. *Mu-ciseke* = *Muiciseke (?)* n. 266] ;
    B*e-cikudu*, the people of Cikudu (sing. *Mu-cikudu); Me-ja*, horns (sing. *i-ja*).
Chwana : B*e-cwana,* B*e-suto,* the Chwana people, the Suto people (sing. *Mo-cwana Mo-suto*).
Congo : E-*sikongo* or E-*xikongo*, the Congo people (sing. *Mu-sikongo).*
Kafir : W*enyuka*, he went up ; W*esuka*, he went off ; W*egqita*, etc., he passed by, (where we should expect regularly *wa-nyuka, wa-suka, wa-gqita*, etc.).

**275.** — 3° *U* when occurring before *y* changes to *i*, if preceded by a dental consonant, provided there be no danger of a double meaning.

Ex. *ti-yuni (*=*tu-yuni)*, little birds.

**276.** — *N. B.* 1. *U* and *i* seem to be interchanged easily in pronunciation when the change partially *assimilates* two consecutive syllables. Thus among Kafirs the common people will generally say *ndu-ku-fumene* for *ndi-ku-fumene* " I have found thee ", *u mfundisu wati* for *u mfundisi wati*... " the master said... " *i kofu* for *i kofi* " coffee ", etc.

**277.** — 2. Through some assimilation of the same sort, the auxiliary forms *ye* and *ze* change in Kafir to *yo* and *zo* before *ku*. Ex. : *Hamba u-yo ku-ndi-ketela e mlanjeni*, " go to fetch water for me in the river " (916, 948).

**278.** — 3. In the *Xosa-Kafir* dialect *u* after *m* is half suppressed, and consequently is left out in writing ; but this is not done in the *Zulu-Kafir* dialect. Thus the Xosa word *u mntu*, " a person ", = *u muntu* in Zulu. The Kafir word *wemka*, "he went away" = *wemuka* in Zulu, etc. Likewise in Kafir I have often heard distinctly *e bsuku*, " at night, " for *e busuku :* however in this case the *u* after *b*, though suppressed in pronunciation, is kept in writing.

**279.** — 4° The syllable *mu* (or *mo* in Chwana) causes various changes when occurring before labials, principally before *m* and *b*. Thus in Tonga what should be regularly *mu manzi*, " in the water, " is often sounded *u-manzi*, and, on the contrary, what should be *mu mulilo*, " in the fire, " is sounded *mu-ndido*. Likewise in Chwana what should be *mo-b-* is regularly changed to '*m,* and *mo-f-* is changed to *m-f*. Ex. '*mele*, for *mo-bele*, " body " (Tonga *mu-bili); go- mfeta* = *go- mofeta*, " to pass him. "

**280.** — *N. B.* 1. Phenomena of the same kind as this are met with in *Angola.*
2. In Tonga and several other languages, when a syllable which contains *m* should be regularly followed by *l*, this in most cases is changed to *n*. Ex. *ku-fugamena*, " to kneel down " for... (= *ku-fugamela*, cf. 1065, 1072).

**281.** — 5° *N* is changed into *m* before *b, p, w, v,* and *f,* in nearly all the Bantu languages. However, before *v* and *f* the change is not so perceptible, principally in Tonga and Senna.

Ex.  *in-zila (i)*m*-bi*, a bad road *(in-zila* in*-bi)*
*i*m*-vula*, or in*-vula*, rain; *i*m*-pongo*, goats (= in*-pongo*).

*N. B.* We may compare with this the fact that *m* seems to change into *n* before dentals in Karanga, Senna, and Congo. (107, 101, 153.)

**282.** — 6° *N* and *m* before the consonants *s, f, p, k, t*, are scarcely audible to us Europeans when they are not immediately preceded by a vowel. However, it seems that natives are conscious of their presence in such cases. Thus *Mpande!* in the vocative, sounds almost like *Pande!*, but the *m* would be heard distinctly in the body of a sentence such as : *Ndabona Mpande*, " I have seen Mpande. "

**283.** — *N. B.* 1. It is probably owing to an extension of this principle that *n* and *m* are regularly suppressed in several languages before hard consonants, principally before *s* and *f* (cf. 78, 151, 389, etc.). It should be noticed however that the *law of avoiding single sounds* (principle II, nn. 44, 45) intervenes here when *monosyllables* are in question. Thus in Swahili we have n*-cha* " top-end, " n*-chi* " country, " n*-ta* " wax, " n*-so* " kidneys " (Père Delaunay's Grammaire Kiswahili, p. 5), though in the same language we have regularly *chui* for *nchui* " tiger, " *pepo* for *mpepo*, " winds, " etc. Cf. 389.

**284.** — 2. In these instances, where *n* is suppressed before hard consonants, its influence is felt, at least in Swahili, in this, that the consonant it should precede has a particular strong explosive sound. Hence, for instance, the Swahili words *pepo* and *chui* might be spelt more correctly *phepo* and *chhui*, or perhaps even better *hpepo, hchui* (cf. Steere's " *Handbook of the Swahili Language*, " p., 12).

**285.** — 7° *N* nasal and *i* after a vowel are interchanged in some cases. Ex. *li*-nso, " eye, " plural *meeso (* = *ma-iso)*. (Cf. Tonga *ku-nvua*, " to hear " = Angola *ku-ivua)*. And there are examples in which the *i* is transposed after the consonant it might be expected to precede. Ex. *bu-*sio " the face ", from *li*-nso " an eye ". (Cf. 152, and 198 note).

*N. B.* This may explain how the Tonga word *li-nso* " an eye " has come to be pronounced *di-shi* in Kele (230). For this word is evidently derived directly, not from *li-nso* or *di-nso*, but from *di-sio*.

**286.** — 8° After *n* nasal *l* changes to *d*. Ex. *in-zila n-danfo*, " a long road " (= *in-zila n-lanfo*).

**287.** — *N. B.* 1. It may be remembered that the vowel *i* has also the power of partly changing *l* to *d* (cf. 17). In fact, in the Bantu languages *l* and *d* seem to be essentially the same letter modified in sound *merely* through its position. In some instances I suspect that *d* has somewhat the value of a double *l*, or perhaps of *il*. Thus in Tonga *i-da* " belly ", seems to be for *i-ila* (cf. *bu-la* = *bu-ila* ?, " bowels.) "

**288.** — 2. Several other consonants when they follow the nasal sound *n* are adapted to it, more or less according to the different languages. Thus *z* and *s* generally become more dental, sounding in some cases like *dz, ts*, as in *manzi* or *mandzi* " water. " This principle finds application even in cases where the nasal sound *n* is suppressed according to n. 283. Hence, for instance, we find in Senna the word *tsamba* " a leaf " (= *n-tsamba* = *n-samba*) pl. *ma-samba* (Father Courtoi's " *Tete Grammar*," n. 20). Likewise in Kafir the sounds *hl, c, q, x*, after *n* are generally changed respectively to *tl, gc, gq, gx* (cf. 33-38). (Concerning other languages, cf. 79, 77, 72, 83, etc.).

**289.** — 3. In Kafir the verbal forms *-enza, -enze*, " make ", are changed into *enje* before *nja* and *nje*. Ex. *wenje nje*, he did so = *wenze nje*.

**290.** — 9° *K* is sometimes dropped between *a* and *u*, thus causing the contraction or assimilation of these two vowels, and likewise between *e* and *u*.

Ex. *ndi-zoo-bona*, I will see = *ndi-za ku-bona* or *ndize ku-bona* (cf. 948 and 956).

**291.** — 10° Several particles which as a rule begin with a *vowel* when they are not immediately joined to a preceding word take a *consonantal* sound before the same vowel in the contrary case, as if the consonant were then introduced to strengthen the vowel-sound, and thus to prevent an assimilation, or contraction, or elision, which would interfere with clearness. The consonants thus apparently added are *m, k, g, h, j, w,* or *y*, according to the different cases and the different languages.

Ex. *U* and *-ku* = thou, thee, e. g. u-*a bona*, you saw; *nda-*ku*-bona*, I saw thee.
*U* and *-mu* = he, him (in class MU-BA) e. g. *mu-lozui* u-*a-fua*, the sorcerer is dead; *nda-*mu*-jaya*, I have killed him.

**292.** — To be a little more explicit on this important principle, we must distinguish different cases, viz. : —

1° In some cases the consonant apparently superadded is probably primitive in reality, or regularly derived from a primitive consonant. Such are *p* in *m-*pa*-nsi* = " it is down, " from *a-nsi*, " down " (cf. 64), *k* in the above example *nda-*ku*-bona*, " I have seen you " (290), *m* in the above example *nda-*mu*-jaya* " I have killed him " and *w* (= *p*) in the Tonga demonstrative pronouns *awa* " here ", *awo* " there ", etc. (= *apa, apo,* etc.)

**293.** — 2° In other cases, more particularly where a consonant occupies the place of *m* or *n* in those pronouns which correspond to the classifiers MU, MI, MA, and IN, (cf. 640), the said consonant differs according as it is coupled or not with *n* nasal, and again according as it is coupled with such or such vowel. Thus : —

**294.** — A) After a nasal, the said consonant is generally *g* before *u* and *a*, and *j* or *dy* before *i*.

Ex. *mu-ntu ngu mue*, a single man; *in-gombe nji-mue*, a single cow.
*ma-tanga nga-tatu*, there are three pumpkins.

**295.** — B) Where there is no nasal influence, if a consonant be required to occupy the place of a dropped *m* or *n*, it will generally be *y* in Tonga. In several other languages, e. g. in Ganda, Sagara, etc., it will be *g* in most cases, and *y* in others. In Kafir it is generally a weak *y* before *i* and after *e*, and a weak *w* in other cases, etc..

| Ex. Tonga | | Ganda | Kafir |
|---|---|---|---|
| *mu-ntu oyo*, that man | | *mu-ntu oyo* | *u m-ntu lowo* |
| *mu-samo oyo*, that tree | | *m-ti oguo* | *u m-ti lowo* |
| *tu u-tole*, let us carry it (the tree) | | *tu gu-tuale* | *si-wu-twale* |
| *ma-nzi ayo*, that water | | *ma-dzi ago* | *a manzi lawo* |
| *tu-a-lie (ma-tanga)*, let us eat them (the pumpkins) | | *tu-ga-lie* | *si-wa-lye* |
| *in-zovu eyo*, that elephant | | *n-jovu eyo* | *i ndlovu leyo* |
| *tu i-jaye*, let us kill it (the elephant). | | *tu-gi-tie* | *si-yi-bulale* |

**296.** — *N. B.* 1. Divergencies from this general rule may be seen principally in nn. 639 and 694*, where the student may notice particularly the use of *j* as a euphonic letter in Yao.

**297.** — 2. The phenomena just described render it probable that *g* initial is not primitive in the Ganda, Shambala, and Sagara forms *-genda*, " go, " *-gamba*, " say " (= Tonga *-enda*, *-amba*), etc. (cf. 52 examples, 77, and 113).

**298.** — Hence the various applications of this principle read as if consonants, when they are dropped, generally leave behind as a trace of themselves some sort of aspiration which is re-strengthened when it happens to occur between two vowels, and principally after nasals, according to nn. 51-59.

Cf. 64, 113, 117, 67, 66, 81, 129, 93, 608, 639, 656, etc..

**299.** — Conclusion. On taking a general view of these phonetic changes, it is evident that assimilation is the most dominant note. It is owing to assimilation that *a-i* changes to *ee* or *e*, *au* to *oo* or *o*, *ki* to *ci*, etc. Hence diphthongs proper, such as the sound of our *i* in fire, or *au* in the German *Auge*, are not known in pure Bantu, or are even opposed to it.

**300.** — The importance of these simple laws will be sufficiently apparent throughout the whole of this work, so that there is no necessity to dwell upon it in this place. Were it not for them, the whole of the Bantu Grammar could be comprised in a few pages. But they graft so many apparent irregularities upon a grammatical system otherwise remarkably simple that whole treatises might be written upon their various applications.

# V. — On Accentuation in Bantu.

**301.** — We have first to distinguish between monosyllabic and polysyllabic stems. Hence : —

1° Concerning polysyllabic stems, the law in the generality of the Bantu languages seems to be to lay a light stress on the penultimate of what I should call *narrative or expositive words*, and to raise the voice on the last syllable of such words as are used in *calling out*, such as imperatives and vocatives. Hence I have often heard in Kafir such expressions as *a bantu a banīnzi*, " very many people ", *i nkosi e nkūlu* " a very great chief ", and also such expressions as *Tatà, velà!* " Father, come out ", *Nxamà, wetù!* " Make haste, my dear ", etc..

**302.** — *N. B.* 1. That accent which consists in laying a light stress on the penult is generally less marked in Tonga than in Kafir. When the Tonga wish to lay a particular stress on a stem, they prefer to reduplicate it entirely rather than merely lengthen its principal vowel. The larger number of the Bantu languages seem to agree with Tonga in this respect. (632, 705, 1079).

**303.** — 2. *Karanga* and *Kamba* prove a remarkable exception to the general law by throwing the accent as close as possible to the beginning of such words. This, combined with the fact that these languages have, in common with only a few others probably influenced by them, such sounds as ɉ or ɖ, ʂ or ʈ, together with several other analogies, makes me suspect strongly that the *Karanga* rulers of old Monopotapa came from the Kamba, or *vice versa*. And, as *Kāmba* is probably for *Kalamba* (cf. 81), I further suspect that this word is essentially the same as *Karanga* or *Kalanga*.

**304.** — 3. Herero is said to throw the accent generally on the last syllable of the word, but there are many instances in which it throws it on the penultimate. (Rev. F. W. Kolbe, " *Herero Dict.*, " p. XXXVI).

**305.** — 4. In Chwana, when words replace their final vowel by ŋ according to n. 200, the accent remains on what should be otherwise the penultimate. The same rule applies probably to Fan (cf. 235).

**306.** — 2° Monosyllabic stems follow a great variety of rules, all of which cannot yet be fixed with certainty. Here however are some of them : —

**307.** — 1° Two consecutive monosyllabic elements or particles are never equally accented.

**308.** — 2° I do not know of any case where a clearly marked accent rests on those pronominal elements which refer verbs and possessive expressions to their substantives, unless they be strengthened by a nasal consonant or otherwise (294).

**309.** — 3° The particle *-a*, when a sign of the past tense, as in *uáfua* (from *ku-fua*, " to die ) ", " he died ", is generally accented ; the same may be said of it, when used as a sign of a possessive expression (572), as in *in-gombe zi-a-ngu*, " my cattle. "

**310.** — 4° Monosyllabic stems of substantives and adjectives are clearly accented in Tonga, Kafir, Karanga, and probably in most of the other languages, after the classifier MU (of classes MU-BA and MU-MI), IN, and LI. Ex. in Tonga *mu-sé*, " the earth, " in Kafir *i-li-só*, " an eye. " They are not so accented after the other classifiers.

**311.** — 5° The locative classifiers *mu*, *ku*, and *(p)a* are accented in Tonga and in most other languages. Ex. *(p)a-nsi*, " down. "

**312.** — 6° The demonstrative pronouns and adverbs ending with -*a* have generally a very marked accent on this vowel. Ex. in Kafir : *payā*, " there. "

# Chapter II.

## ON SUBSTANTIVES.

**313.** — In the Bantu languages we find no genders based on sex, but instead other *genders* or *classes* of substantives, *based principally*, as I hope will appear in this chapter, *on the degree of unity and consistency* of those things of which they are the names, as determined by their natural position and shape, their proper motions, effects, relative strength, etc.

**314.** — The class of most substantives is generally marked by a peculiar prefix which we term the " classifying element " or " classifier " ([1]). There are a few substantives to which no such classifier is prefixed. The proper class of such can however be made out from the sort of concord they require.

These classifiers are, as has been already noticed, 18 in number, but some of them correspond unmistakably as plural to others, and thus the number of classes is found to be reducible to twelve, viz.: —

1º Class with prefix *mu-* in the sing., *ba-* in the pl., or Class MU-BA. Ex. *mu-ntu*, person, pl. *ba-ntu*.
2º ,, ,, *mu-* ,, *mi-* ,, ,, Class MU-MI. ,, *mu-bili*, body, pl. *mi-bili*.
3º ,, ,, *in-* ,, *(z)in* ,, ,, Class IN-(Z)IN. ,, *in-gombe*, cow, pl. *(z)in-gombe*.
4º ,, ,, *(l)i-* ,, *ma-* ,, ,, Class (L)I-MA. ,, *(l)i-zuba*, sun, pl. *ma-zuba*.
5º ,, ,, *bu-* ,, *ma-* ,, ,, Class BU-MA. ,, *bu-ato*, canoe, pl. *ma-ato*.
6º ,, ,, *ku-* ,, *ma-* ,, ,, Class KU-MA. ,, *ku-tui*, ear, pl. *ma-tui*.
7º ,, ,, *ci-* ,, *zi-* ,, ,, Class CI-ZI. ,, *ci-bula*, chair, pl. *zi-bula*.
8º ,, ,, *ka-* ,, *tu-* ,, ,, Class KA-TU. ,, *ka-cece*, baby, pl. *tu-cece*.
9º ,, ,, *lu-* ,, *(z)in* ,, ,, Class LU-(Z)IN. ,, *lu-limi*, tongue, pl. *in-dimi*.
10º Locative class with prefix ... ... *(p)a* or Class (P)A. ,, *(p)a-nsi*, down, (no plural).
11º ,, ,, ,, ... ... *ku* or Class KU. ,, *ku-nsi*, below, (no plural).
12º ,, ,, ,, ... ... *mu* or Class MU. ,, *mu-nsi*, underneath (no plural).

**315.** — Some substantives are found to depart from the general rule in the choice of their plural prefix. We shall treat them as forming *sub-classes*. Thus —

with cl. MU-BA we connect a *sub-class* MU-MA. Ex. *Mu-karanga*, a Karanga, pl. *Ma-karanga*
,, KA-TU ,, ,, KA-BU. ,, *ka-ntabua*, flea, pl. *bu-ntabua*
,, LU-ZIN ,, ,, LU-TU. ,, *lu-sabila*, baby, pl. *tu-sabila* or *in-sabila*
etc. etc.

---

1. In my " *Outline of a Xosa-Kafir Grammar* Grahamstown, 1887 ", I term these classifying elements " characteristic prefixes ", or simply " characteristics ". I now think that the term " classifier ", proposed by the Rev. F. W. Kolbe, ought to be preferred.

**316.** — In Angola, Yao, Mozambique, and Senna, we find substantives which have two classifiers in the singular number, both of which change regularly in the plural. Ex. in Angola : **ka**-mu-*xi* " a shrub ", plur. **tu**-mi-*xi*, **ka**-ri-*tari* " a small stone ", plur. **tu**-ma-*tari*, etc. In point of the concord required all such nouns are practically considered as having their first classifier only. Hence, for instance, **ka**-mu-*xi*, plur. **tu**-mi-*xi*, belongs to the class KA-TU.

## I. — On Articles.

**317.** — Before we begin to study each class separately, it is necessary to forewarn the reader against a mistake which has often been made, viz. that of confusing with the classifiers a different kind of prefix, or rather a proclitic, which is usually met with before nouns (substantive and adjective) in several Bantu languages, corresponding in some of them both to our definite and to our indefinite article, and in others to the definite article only.

In those languages which have some sort of such article before nouns its ordinary form is a mere vowel. Thus in Kafir the article, both definite and indefinite, is *u*, *i*, or *a*, according as the classifier following it, expressed or understood, somehow or other contains *u*, *i*, or *a*. Ex. *u mti* " a tree " or " the tree ", *i li-so* " an eye " or " the eye ", *a bantu*, " people " or " the people ". In Herero the article, also definite and indefinite, is always *o*, except before nouns of the class *li-ma* in the singular, where it is *e*. Ex. *o ma-yuru*, " the nostrils ", *e yuru*, " a nostril " or " the nostril ". In Kafir and Herero, the article, being both definite and indefinite, is generally expressed before substantives when they are pronounced or written by themselves.

In Angola the article, only definite, is always *o*. In Fiote or Lower Congo, where likewise it is probably definite only, its form is *o*, *e*, or *a*, according as the classifier, expressed or understood, which follows it, contains *u*, *i*, or *a*. As an exception, the article is *o*, or *e*, not *a*, before the classifiers MA and VA [= Tonga (P)A].

In Ganda its form is also *o*, *e*, or *a*, according as the following classifier contains *u*, *i*, or *a*. But, as far as we may judge from available materials, it seems to be both definite and indefinite. Probably it is heard only after a pause or breath, and even then not always (111).

## On Articles.

As a rule, no article is used in vocatives, nor after negative particles. In Kafir it is omitted also after demonstrative pronouns, and in a few other cases. On this subject of the use and omission of the article there are between the different languages considerable divergencies which we shall not dilate upon in this work.

*N. B.* In Kafir proper names themselves take an article in the same cases as other substantives. On the contrary in Herero proper names, and some other substantives which are equivalent to proper names, such as *mama* " my mother ", *ina* " his mother ", *tate* " my father ", *ihe* " his father ", *Ka-tyiungu* " Mr. Wolf " (cf. o *m-bungu* " a wolf "), *Kaha-Vandye* " Reynard " (cf. o *m-bandye* " a fox "), etc., are oftener used without the article than with it. Ex. : —

**318.** — KAFIR:

With article : *Ndi-tanda* **a** *ma-hashe*, I am fond of horses.
*Aye nga pina* **a** *ma-hashe?* In which direction have the horses gone?
*Ndabona* **u** *Langa-li-balele*, I saw Langa-li-balele (a Zulu chief).

Without article : *Yopula, ma* (not **u** *ma*), Mother, take the meat out of the pot.
*La ma-hashe...* (not *la* **a** *ma-hashe*), these horses...
*A ndi na nto* (not... *na* **i** *nto*), I have nothing.
*Ufuna n-to nina* (not **i** *n-to*) ? lit. What thing do you want?

**319.** — HERERO:

Without article : *Vanatye vandye, ke ndyi-pahere...* (not **o** *vanatye...*), My children, get for me... (" *Zeitschrift* ", 1887-1888, p. 191).
*Muatye uandye, ue ndyi-esa* (not **o** *mu-atye*) ? My child, dost thou forsake me ? (do. p. 202).

*N. B.* We however find in the same work, p. 199, the following sentence : O *mu-ndu, o zondu ze pi ?* Man, where are the sheep?
*Kahavandye atya...*, Reynard said... (do. p. 200).
*Ihe ua zepere...* (not **o** *ihe*), his father slaughtered...

With article : M'**o** *u-tuku...*, **o** *vanatye arire tyi ve-kutura* **o** *n-dyatu, n'arire tyi va-isa mo* **o** *muatye*. At night the children loosened the bag, and took the child out of it. (do. p. 192).

**320.** — GANDA:

*Daura n'azala bana* (not **a** *bana*)...,
*n'agamba bana-be* (not **a** *bana-be*)...:
" *Bana bange* (not **a**-*bana*),
O *Bu-ganda buno mu-bu-lie...* "
*Bana ne bagamba* (why not **a** *bana ?*) :
" *Kitafe, lero fe* **a** *bana bato,*
*fe tu-na lia Bu-ganda* (not **o** *Bu-ganda*) ? "

Daura begot children,
and he said to his children .
" My children,
this Ganda kingdom eat it you. "
And the children said :
" Our father, we little children, to-day
shall we eat the Ganda kingdom ? "

(" *French Ganda Grammar,* " p. 83).

**321.**—OLD ANGOLA: | MODERN ANGOLA: |
*Tat' etu, uekala ko maulu akondeke* **o** *rijina riae, heze ko tuekala* **o** *kifuci kiae, ...tubangele bo mu kiaiba.*
(Father de Coucto's "*Catechism*", 1661, p. 1. The spelling is adapted to our alphabet).

*Tat' etu, uala ku maulu axile* **o** *rijina rie, kize ko tuala* **o** *kifuxi kie, ...tubangelè mu kiaiiba.*
(Heli Chatelain's "*Kimbundu Grammar*", p. XX).

Our Father, who art in Heaven, hallowed be Thy Name, Thy kingdom come, ...deliver us from evil.

CONGO:

With article: *Ke lwalu* **o** *lu-kata*, there is the box (Father Visseq's *Gr.*, p. 9).
*Te kiaki* **e** *ki-kila*, there is the papaw (do.).
**E** *di-vula di-andi diabiza*, his house is beautiful (do.).
**E** *mi-nsenga mi-etu miavia*, our sugar-canes are ripe (do.). [p. 49].
Without art.: *Ki-nkutu ovene Npetelo* (not **e** *ki-nkutu*), he has given a book to Peter (do.

*N. B.* 1. Though Father Alexandre Visseq seems to have on the whole understood the Congo article better than the Rev. W. Holman Bentley, it is necessary to warn the reader that he has mistaken the classifier DI (= Tonga LI) for the article corresponding to it, and *vice versa*. What has given occasion to this mistake is that in Congo the classifier DI is generally reduced to E when there is no article before it.

If we had to judge of the value of the article in Congo from the remarkably sparse sentences which we find in Rev. W. Holman Bentley's *Grammar*, we could no more say whether it is definite or indefinite than when it is and when it is not used. Ex. *N-ti wau wambote* (why not o *n-ti*), " this tree is good "'(Bentley's *Gr.*, p. 556). Cf. o *matadi mama... i mau mama twamwene ezono*, these stones are those which we saw yesterday (do. p. 526).

2. Articles are found in a few languages which have not been mentioned above, such as Bihe, Nano, and other dialects of Benguella, as also in Nyambu (119), etc. But from available materials it is impossible to make out after what laws they are used.

3. If Mpongwe be compared with the language of the Bihe, it looks very probable that several of the Mpongwe classifiers were originally articles. The classifiers proper having been dropped through contractions in many cases, the articles have remained instead, and their original notion has probably been lost.

4. Strange to say, articles used often to make their appearance in Tonga, when with the help of my informants I would try to render English sentences into this language, but I do not find a single article in the stories and sentences which I wrote under their *immediate* dictation (Cf. *Appendix I*). In these the nearest approach to articles are substantive pronouns occasionnally placed before nouns where we should use definite articles in English. Ex. **Ue** *muana uangu wafua* " my child is dead ", lit. " *he*, child of me, is dead ". Hence, until further researches on this point, I consider Tonga as having no article. At the same time I conclude from these facts that probably the articles of the other languages were originally contracted substantive pronouns (830).

## II. — The MU-BA Class

### and the

### Sub-classes connected with it.

**322.** — The substantives which belong to the MU-BA class, including the sub-classes connected with it, are those which require in the singular number the same sort of concord as the word **mu-ntu** " a person ", plur. **ba-**ntu*.

These sub-classes connected with the class MU-BA are: —
1° the sub-class — BA, or those substantives which, though requiring in the plural the classifier BA, have none in the singular, as *tata* " my father ", plur. **ba-***tata;* — 2° the sub-class MU-MA,

*.EXAMPLES.

|  | a person | | a man *(vir)*, husband | | a child, son | |
|---|---|---|---|---|---|---|
|  | *Sing.* | *Plur.* | *Sing.* | *Plur.* | *Sing.* | *Plur.* |
| Tonga | mu-ntu, | ba- | mu-alume, | ba- | mu-ana, | ba- |
| Bisa | mu-ntu, | wa- | mu-analume, | wa- | mu-ana, | wa- |
| Gogo | mu-nhu, | wa- | m-lume, | wa- | mw-ana, | wa- |
| Sagara | mu-nhu (?), | wa- | m-lume, | wa- | mw-ana, | wa- |
| Shambala | mu-ntu, | wa- | m-goxi, | wa- | mw-ana- | wa- |
| Boondei | mu-ntu, | wa- | m-gosi, | wa- | mw-ana, | wa- |
| Taita | mu-ndu, | ... | m-lume, | ... | mw-ana, | ... |
| Nyanyembe | mu-nhu, | wa- | m-goxi, | wa- | mw-ana, | wa- |
| Sukuma | mu-nhu, | wa- | m-goxi, | wa- | mw-ana, | wa- |
| Kamba | mu-du, | a- | m-ume, | a- | mw-ana, | a- |
| Swahili | m-tu, | wa- | m-ume, | wa- | mw-ana, | wa- |
| Pokomo | mu-ntu, | wa- | mu-yume, | wa- | m-ana, | wa- |
| Nika | mu-tu, | a- | mu-lume, | a- | mw-ana, | āna |
| Senna | mu-ntu, | (w)a- | m-amuna, | wa- | mw-ana, | wa- |
| Karanga | (u)n-tu, | ba-nu | norume, | ba- | nona, | ba- |
| Ganda | mu-ntu, | ba- | m-saja, | ba- | mw-ana, | ba- |
| Zulu-Kafir | u mu-ntu, | a ba- | ... | ... | u nyana, | o nyana |
| Xosa-Kafir | u m-ntu, | aba- | ... | ... | u nyana, | o nyana |
| Herero | o mu-ndu, | o va- | o mu-rumendu, | o va- | o mu-na, | o vanatye |
| Bihe | o mu-nu, | o ma- | u-lume, | a- | o mōna, | ... |
| Mbunda | mo-no, | ba- | ... | ... | ngw-aneke, | ba- |
| Rotse | mo-nu, | a- | ... | ... | mu-ana, | a- |
| Guha | mu-ntu, | ba- | ... | ... | mu-ana, | ba- |
| Rua | mu-ntu, | ba- | mu-lume, | ba- | mu-ana, | ba- |
| Angola | mu-tu, | a- | mu-lume, | a- | mōna, | āna |
| Lower Congo | mu-ntu, | a- | n-kaza, | a-kaji | mw-ana, | āna |
| Nywema | o-ntu, | a- | ume (o-ume?) | ... | ōna, | āna |
| Yao | mu-ndu, | wa- | a-sono, | a-ch'a- | mw-ana, | a-chi w- |
| Kilimane | mu-to, | a- | m-amna, | ... | mw-ana, | āna |
| Mozambique | m-tu, | a- | mw-amna, | a- | mw-ana mwane, | āna-āne |
| Chwana proper | mo-thu, | ba- | mo-nona, | ba- | ngw-ana, | bāna |
| Suto | mo-tho, | ba- | mo-nna, | ba- | ngw-ana, | bāna |
| Mpongwe | o-ma, | a-naga | o-nome, | a- | onw-ana, | aw- |
| Fan | e-fâm, | ba- | e-nôm, | ... | môn, | ... |
| Dualla | mo-tu, | ba- | m-omi, | b- | mūna, | bāna |
| Fernandian (Banni dialect) | bo-cho, | be- | b-ube, | ba- | bo-lai, (Banapa dialect) | ba- |

or those substantives which, though requiring in the singular the classifier MU-, have in the plural the classifier MA-, as **Mu-***nkua* " a white man ", pl. **Ma-***nkua*.

## § 1. Transformations of the Classifier MU.

**323.** — This particle may be said to have in the different Bantu languages all the intermediate sounds between *mu* and *n*, as well as between *mo* and *o*. Even in those languages in which it is most reduced traces are preserved either of its labial nasal element, or of its *u*-sound. Hence more particularly the following forms: —

EXAMPLES. (Continued.)

|  | a woman, wife | | a chief | | a servant | | God |
|---|---|---|---|---|---|---|---|
|  | *Sing.* | *Plur.* | *Sing.* | *Plur.* | *Sing.* | *Plur.* |  |
| Tonga | mu-anakazi, | ba- | mu-ame, | ba- | mu-zike, | ba- | Leza |
| Bisa | mu-anakazi, | wa- | ... | ... | mu-sia, | wa- | Lesa |
| Gogo | m-chekulu, | wa- | ... | ... | mu-lelwa, | wa- | Mu-lungu |
| Sagara | m-ke, | wa- | m-ndewa, | wa- | m-fugwa, | wa- | Mu-lungu |
| Shambala | m-kaza, | wa- | ... | ... | m-xumba, | wa- | Mu-lungu |
| Boondei | m-kaza, | wa- | ... | ... | m-lugoja, | wa- | Mu-lungu |
| Taita | mu-ke, | ... | m-gosi | ... | m-tumu | ... | Mu-lungu |
| Nyanyembe | m-kema, | wa- | m-temi, | wa- | m-deki, | wa- | Mu-lungu |
| Sukuma | mu-kima (?), | wa- | ... | ... | m-sese, | wa- | Mu-lungu |
| Kamba | mu-ndu mu-ka, a-ndu a-ka | | ... | ... | mu-dedia, | a- | Mu-lungu |
| Swahili | mw-ana m-ke, wa-ana a-ke | | m-falme, | wa- | m-tumwa, | wa- | Mu-ungu |
| Pokomo | mu-ke, | wa- | ... | ... | ... | ... | Mu-ungu |
| Nika | mu-che, | a- | mu-vieri, | a- | mu-humiki, | a- | Mu-lungu |
| Senna | (u)n-kazi, | a- | (u)-mbuya, | a- | mu-lece, | a- | Mu-lungu |
| Karanga | nokaji, | ba- | xe, | ba- | (u)n-ja (?), | ba- | Reja |
| Ganda | m-kazi, | ba- | kabaka, | ba- | mu-ddu, | ba- | Katonda |
| Zulu-Kafir | u mu-fazi, | a ba- | ... | ... | u mu-ntu, | a ba- | u Tixo |
| Xosa-Kafir | u m-fazi, | a ba- | ... | ... | u m-ntu, | a ba- | u Tixo |
| Herero | o mu-kajendu, | o va- | o mu-hona, | o va- | o mu-karere, | o va- | Mu-kuru |
| Bihe | u-kai, | a- | ... | ... | ... | ... | Suku |
| Mbunda | mo-nokazi, | ba- | mw-ene | ... | mu-hikana, | ba- | Redza |
| Rotse | mo-kati, | a- | mo-yoande, | a- | mo-bika, | a- | Nyambi |
| Guha | m-kazi, | ba- | ... | ... | m-jia, | ba- | Kabeja (?) |
| Rua | mu-kazi, | ba- | m-lohhe | ... | mu-hika, | ba- | Virie |
| Angola | mu-kaji, | a- | ... | ... | mu-bika, | a- | Nzambi |
| Lower Congo | n-kaza, | a-kaji | ... | ... | n-leke, | a- | Nzambi |
| Nywema | o-azeni, | a- | o-lowe, | a- | o-hombo, | a- | o Kixi |
| Yao | a-sono, | a-ch'a- | m-chi-mw-ene, | wa- | kapolo, | a- | Mu-lungu |
| Kilimane | mu-yana, | a- | mu-enye | ... | ... | ... | Mu-lugo |
| Mozambique | mw-ari, | āri | mw-ene, ma-mwene | | karumia, | a- | M-luku |
| Chwana proper | mo-sadi, | ba- | mo-rena, | ba- | mo-tlhanka, | ba- | Mo-dimo |
| Suto | mo-sali, | ba- | mo-rena, | ba- | mo-tlhanka, | ba- | Mo-limo |
| Mpongwe | onw-anto, | ānto | o-ga, | a- | o-xaka, | a- | Anyambe |
| Fan | ... | | ... | | en-saga | ... | Añame |
| Dualla | mu-'tu, | b'-itu | mo-anedi, | ba- | mo-kum, | ba- | Loba |
| Fernandian | bo-adi, | ba- | bo-tukwe, | ba- | bo-taki | ... | Kadupe |
| (Banni dialect), | (Clarence dialect) | | | | (Banapa dial.) | | |

## The MU-BA Class.

**324.** — *MU-* generally, in Tonga, Bisa, Mbunda, Herero, Angola, Nika, etc.

*M-* with an affection to the vowel *u*, in Swahili, Mozambique, Shambala, Kamba, etc.

**325.** — *N. B.* 1. In most of these languages, if not in all, the law is evidently *to pronounce the vowel* u- *distinctly, when otherwise the word would be sounded like a monosyllable.* Hence in Ganda *mu-ntu*, "a person", not *m-ntu*; *mu-ddu*, "a slave", not *m-ddu*. Do. in Kamba, Nyamwezi, Shambala, etc. It is somewhat strange that Swahili and Mozambique should prove an exception to this law (cf. 44).

**326.** — 2. In these same languages the *u*-sound of this classifier is partly preserved before such stems as begin with a vowel. Hence *m*w-*ana*, "a child", etc.

**327.** — *N-* with an affection to *u*, in Senna, Karanga, and Lower Congo.

*N. B.* In Senna and Karanga the *u* is heard distinctly when the word begins the sentence, but then it precedes the nasal instead of following it, as if the sole reason of its

### EXAMPLES. (Continued.)

|  | (names of nations) |  | my father | | my mother | |
|---|---|---|---|---|---|---|
|  |  |  | *Sing.* | *Plur.* | *Sing.* | *Plur.* |
| Tonga | *Mu-tonga*, a Tonga, | *Ba-* | tata, | ba- | (ma), | ba-ma |
| Bisa | *Mu-bisa*, a Bisa, | *Wa-* | tata, | wa- | ma (?) | ... |
| Gogo | ... | ... | ... | tata | ... | yaya | ... |
| Sagara | *M-sagara*, a Sagara, | *Wa-* | baba | ... | mau | ... |
| Shambala | *M-xambala*, a Shambala, | *Wa-* | baba | ... | mlala | ... |
| Boondei | *M-boondei*, a Boondei, | *Wa-* | tate | ... | mlale | ... |
| Taita | ... | ... | aba | ... | mawe (?) | ... |
| Nyanyembe | *M-nyamwezi*, a Nyamwezi, | *Wa-* | tata, | wa- | mayu, | wa- |
| Sukuma | *M-sukuma*, a Sukuma, | *Wa-* | baba, | wa- | mayu, | wa- |
| Kamba | *M-kamba*, a Kamba, | *A-* | —,a-chakwa | | mw-aito, | a- |
| Swahili | *M-jomba*, a man of the Zanzibar coast, | *Wa-* | baba | ... | mamangu | ... |
| Pokomo | ... | ... | baba | ... | ... | ... |
| Nika | *Mu-nyika* a man of the desert, | *A-* | baba | ... | mayo(wangu) | ... |
| Senna | *Mu-zungu*, a Christian, a lord, | *Wa-* | —, | a-tatu | —,a mai anga | |
| Karanga | (*u*)*N-karanga*, a Karanga, | *Ma-* | tate, | ma- | ma | ... |
| Ganda | *Mu-Ganda*, a Ganda, | *Ba-* | kitangi | ... | nyabu | ... |
| Zulu-Kafir | u *Mu-tshaka*, a Zulu, | a *Ma-* | u baba, | o- | umame | ... |
| Xosa-Kafir | u *M-xosa*, a frontier Kafir, | a *Ma-* | tata(bawo), | o- | u ma | ... |
| Herero | o *Mu-herero*, a Herero, | o *Va-* | tate, | o tate | mama | ... |
| Bihe | ... | ... | tate | ... | mai | ... |
| Mbunda | *Mu-mbunda*, a Mbunda, | *Ma-* | n-tate | ... | ... | ... |
| Rotse | *Mu-loi*, a Rotse, | *Ma-* | xangoe (?) | ... | 'me | ... |
| Guha | ... | ... | tata, | ba- | maju | ... |
| Rua | *Mu-rua*, a Rua, | *Ba-* | tata | ... | lolo | ... |
| Angola | *Mu-mbundu*, a black, | *A-* | — | ... | ... | ... |
| Lower Congo | *Mu-sikongo*, a man of the Congo, | *e-* (273) | tata | ... | mama | ... |
| Nywema | ... | ... | yoni | ... | mboni | ... |
| Yao | *M-yao*, a Yao, | *Wa-* | a-tati,*a-ch'*a- | | a mawo | |
| Kilimane | *Mu-goa*, an Indian Portuguese, | *Ma-* | baba | ... | n-ma | ... |
| Mozambique | *M-kua*, do. (= Tonga *mu-nkua*), | *Ma-* | —, | a-thithi | mama | ... |
| Chwana proper | *Mo-chwana*, a Chwana, | *Be-* (273) | rara | ... | mme | ... |
| Suto | *Mo-sotho*, a Suto, | *Ba-* | n-tate | ... | 'me | ... |
| Mpongwe | ... | ... | rere | ... | ngi yami | ... |
| Fan | *N-suut* or *N-suur*, a black, | | ... | ... | naa (?) | ... |
| Dualla | ... | ... | tite | ... | ... | ... |
| Fernandian (Banni dialect) | ... | ... | obu-lieo (?) | | o berim (?) | |

pronunciation were to support the nasal. In such cases, as also before monosyllables, some people pronounce *mu*-rather than *un*-.

**328.** — *MO*- in Chwana and Dualla. *Bo*- in some Fernandian dialects (240).

**329.** — *U*- (seldom *MU*-) in Bihe.

**330.** — *O*- in Mpongwe and Nywema, with traces of the nasal in some nouns.

**331.** — *O*-, or *E*-(?), in Fan, also with traces of the nasal in some words.

**332.** — *N. B.* 1. As may be seen in the subjoined examples, the word *mu-ana* " a child ", changes variously to *mōna* or *mūna* (cf. 265), *nguana* (204), *nyana*, (122), *nōna* (265 and 328), etc.

**333.** — 2. There is no trace of this classifier being naturally long *(mū)* in any Bantu language. If so pronounced in some words, it is owing to some sort of contraction or to position before a nasal. Bleek mentions that it is marked long in Thlaping, a dialect of Chwana. It would be more correct to say that in Thlaping, though it is written *mo*- as in Suto, yet properly its sound is an intermediate one between *mu*- and *mo*-.

## § 2. Transformations of the Classifier BA-.

**334.** — This classifier has its consonant more or less weakened in the different languages, probably according to the shape of people's lips. Hence the various forms : —

**335.** — *BA*- in Tonga, Kafir, Ganda, Guha, Chwana, Karanga, Dualla, Fan, etc.
*N. B.* Properly speaking, in Tonga *Ba*- has a sound intermediate between *Ba*- and *Wa*-.

**336.** — *WA*- in Swahili, Shambala, Nyamwezi, Yao, etc.

**337.** — *A*- in Mozambique, Senna, Angola, Congo, Mpongwe, Kamba, Nika.
*N. B.* In Senna a slight labial aspiration is still perceptible in this classifier. Hence in some cases it is even spelt *wa*-.

**338.** — *VA*- in Herero and Nano.
*VA*- or *MA*- in Bihe (Cf. " *Observations upon... Umbundu* ", by the Rev. Wesley M. Stover, Boston 1885, pp. 13, 16 and 17).

**339.** — *N. B.* 1. *Be*- replaces *BA*- before *ci* and in some other cases, according to n. 274, as if *be*- were then a contraction for *ba-i*. The presence of *be*-, as if for *ba*-, is particularly remarkable in the Kafir word *a* Be*lungu* " white people " (sing. *u* M-*lungu* " a white man, a lord "). This phenomenon probably is due to the fact that this word is of foreign importation. (Cf. the Phenician and Hebrew word *melekh*, or *molokh* in the possessive expression *a-molokh*). It may be observed by the way in the preceding table of examples that the Bantu word *Mu-lungu* or *Mu-luku* " God " is probably no other than the Phenician *Moloch*.

**340.** — 2. In *Kele* (Di-kele) the plural *botyi*, " people ", is probably for *ba-utyi*, just as in Fernandian *buchu* " people " is for *ba-uchu*, and in Isubu *bomi* " men " for *ba-umi*.

**341.** — 3. Other phonetic changes produced by the concurrence of *ba*-, *wa*-, *a*- with vowels, are easily explained according to nn. 249 sqq.

## § 3. The Sub-class — -BA.

**342.** — There is a large proportion of those substantives which require the same sort of concord as the word *mu-ntu*, " a person ", though they have no classifier in the singular.

Such are 1°) the words, in nearly all these languages, for "father" and "mother", viz. (in Tonga) *tata*, "my father", *uso*, "thy father", *uise*, "his father", *usokulu*, "thy grandfather", etc. (Cf. 748).

**343.** — *N. B.* 1. In Tonga the words for "mother" are through politeness used in the plural instead of the singular. Hence *ba-ma*, "my mother", *ba-nyoko*, "thy mother", *ba-nyena*, "his mother", etc. (cf. 748).

**344.** — 2. In some other languages a similar law is extended to names of parents in general. It appears that in Yao it is even extended to some other substantives, as we find that the substantives " husband, master, brother, friend ", etc. are respectively rendered by the plural forms *a-sono*, *a-mbuje*, *a-kulu*, *a-mwene*, etc. (cf. 354). The Yao word *a-chi-mwene* " a chief ", which is sometimes used for *m-chi-mwene*, is likewise a plural of dignity or respect which contains the classifier *chi-* (502) besides the classifier *a-*. The fact that in this word *chi-* is in the singular number, while *a-* is a plural of dignity, shows that the Yao themselves must have practically lost this notion that *a-* is in the plural number.

**345.** — 3. In Senna, many substantives of this sub-class are formed with the prefix *nya-* (= *mu-a*, 122). Ex. nya-*ku-fula* " a smith ", pl. a-nya-*ku-fula*. Substantives of the same sort have in Mozambique the prefix *ka*. Ex. ka-*rumia* " an apostle ", pl. a-ka-*rumia*. Cf. 517.

**346.** — Such are 2°) all proper names of persons, as *Monze*, " the chief Monze ".

**347.** — *N. B.* Many proper names of persons begin with a prefix which means " Father " or " Father of... ", " Mother " or " Mother of ". Hence in Tonga *Si-meja*, lit. " Father Tusks ", *Sia-pi*, lit. " Father of where? ", *Na-simbi*, " Mother of iron ", etc. Hence also in Kafir *Sa-Rili*, lit. " Father Kreli ", *So-ndawo*, lit. " Father of the place ", *No-nto* " Mother of a thing ", etc. Hence also in various languages those names of God which begin with *Ka*, as *Ka-zova* (in Nyambu), *Ka-tonga* (in Ganda), etc.

**348.** — Such are 3° several names of animals, e. g. *su-ntue*, " a hyena ", *se-kale*, " a muircat ", etc.

**349.** — *N. B.* 1. Like proper names of persons, many such substantives may be decomposed into two parts, the first of which is a prefix which seems to mean " father ", or " mother ", or " son ". Such are in Tonga the words just mentioned, and in Kafir *u nomadudwane*, " a scorpion ", lit. " a mother of little dances ", *u no-meva*, " a wasp ", lit. " a mother of stings ", etc. Such are in Senna *s-ulo*, " a hare " (Tonga *s-ulue*), *nya-rugue*, " a tiger ", lit. " son of a tiger " (= Tonga *si-lugue*, lit. " Father tiger "), etc. etc.

**350.** — 2. In the language of Mozambique some names of inanimate things, principally of fruits, belong to this sub-class. They have *na-* or *ka-* as a prefix. Ex. *na-kuo*, " a cob of maize ", pl. *a-nakuo*; *ka-raka*, " a sweet potato ", pl. *a-karaka*.

**351.** — The plural of all such nouns is formed in the generality of the Bantu languages by prefixing the classifier BA- to the form of the singular number. Ex. *ba-suntue*, " hyaenas " (sing. *su-ntue*), *ba-sokue*, " baboons " (sing. *so-kue*).

**352.** — *N. B.* 1. In Kafir such substantives take *o* as a sort of plural article in the nominative, and *bo* in the vocative. Ex. *o dade*, " my sisters ", *o nomeva*, " wasps " (sing. *u no-meva*), voc. *Bo dade!* " sisters !, " etc. Plurals of this kind may be formed in Kafir with every proper name, e. g. *o Ngwe*, " Ngwe and his companion ", *o Saliwe*, " Saliwe and his companions ". But these are used in the singular in the vocative case, and consequently do not usually receive the prefix *bo-*. Hence *Ngwe !* may be used to call *Ngwe* alone, or *Ngwe with his companions*. Ex. *Ngwe, yiz' apa* " Ngwe, come here ", *Ngwe, yizan' apa* " Ngwe, come here with our companions. "

**353.** — 2. In Herero the substantives of this sub-class seem to admit the prefix *o* regularly in the plural, besides the article which has also the same form *o*. Hence *o o-tate* " my fathers " (sing. *o tate* or *tate* " my father " 319). Cf. Kolbe's *Dict.*, p. 201.

**354.** — 3. Those Yao words which have in the singular number a seemingly plural orm, as *a-sono* " a husband ", *a-mwene* " a friend " (344) form their real plural by means of the adjective *chi* " many ". Ex. *A-ch'a-sono* " husbands " (= *a-chi a-sono*). The real plural corresponding to the plural of dignity *a-chi-mwene* (344) seems to be likewise a-ch' *a-chi-mwene* (Steere's " *Yao Language* " p. 13), while the more regular singular *m-chi-mwene* (316), which means also " a chief ", changes in the plural to *wa-i-mwene* (Heterwick's " *Yao Language* ", pp. 13 and 88).

### § 4. THE SUB-CLASS MU-MA.

**355.** — Those substantives which, though agreeing in the singular with the word *mu-ntu* " a person ", borrow nevertheless the classifier MA- of cl. LI-MA in the plural, are found in nearly all the Bantu languages. They are mostly the names of warlike and dreaded tribes. Such are, for instance, in Tonga : —

*Ma-nkua*, " the white people ", or more particularly " the Portuguese ", or, in a still more limited sense, " the Indian Portuguese " (sing. *Mu-nkua*).

*Ma-punu* " the Boers ", including " the Ma-tebele " and whatever tribes are thought by the Tonga to depend on the Boers (sing. *Mu-punu*).

*Ma-kalanga* " the Karanga " (*alias* " Ma-kalaka "), who before the advent of the Ma-tebele were the ruling tribe of the whole Bu-nyai, or the Monomotapa of our ancient maps (sing. *Mu-kalanga*).

**356.** — *N. B.* This sub-class includes also in Kafir some titles of dignity, as *a ma-pakati* " councillors " (sing. *u m-pakati*).

### § 5. SUBSTANTIVES WHICH BELONG TO THE MU-BA CLASS AND THE SUB-CLASSES CONNECTED WITH IT.

**357.** — The substantives belonging to this category in the generality of the Bantu languages are exclusively the names of persons that are sufficiently grown up to be able to stand on their legs.

*N. B.* It does not follow from this that *all* names of persons are of this class.

**358.** — To this class belong also in Tonga, Lojazi, Mozambique, etc., several names of animals, principally, as it seems, of such as are distinguished by their relative power to take half-erect postures, as in Tonga *mu-aba*, "a jackal"; *mu-lavu*, "a lion" (Nika *munyambo*, Mozambique *ka-ramu*, pl. *a-karamu*, etc.); *mu-bua*, "a dog" (Lojazi *mu-bua*, Mozambique *mw-ala-pua*, Shire or Nyanja *garu*, pl. *a-garu*, etc.); *mu-yuni*, "a bird" in general; *mu-kubi*, "a vulture"; *mu-cyeta*, "a monkey"; *mu-kuku*, "a coq" (in opposition to *in-kuku*, which means more properly "a hen"); *mu-zohu*, "an eland", etc.

**359.** — *N. B.* 1. With regard to things which have no life, it seems that they are not brought into this class in any language, except in Mozambique (cf. *supra*, 350, some names of fruits with the prefixes *na* and *ka*).

**360.** — 2. Names of animals and others are often personified, and then are treated as being of this class. This is the case principally in Swahili with such words as *ngombe* "a cow", *mbuzi* "a goat", etc. (Cf. Father Delaunay's "*Grammaire Kiswahili*", p. 20).

## § 6. Etymologies. — Varia.

**361.** — The Rev. F. W. Kolbe has expressed the opinion (¹) that the primitive form of the classifier MU- was *ku-mu*. This opinion seems to me unwarranted. But the same author is probably nearer to the truth when seeing in the same particle the notion of something "upright." For it is very probable that the classifier MU- is radically identical with the adjective *-umi*, alive (cf. 601 Table) which is itself originally the perfect form of the verb *ma* or *ima* "to stand up", and which is still retained in nearly all the Bantu languages under the various forms *-gumi*, *-gima*, *ima*, etc. (Kafir *u b-omi* = life). Both the classifier MU- and the adjective *-umi* "alive", seem to be related to *-mue* "one" (792).

**362.** — *N. B.* I was made sensible of the relation of the classifier MU to the adjective *-umi* when I chanced once with a motion of the hand to connect a *horizontal* notion with the general notion of person. For this greatly astonished my Tonga informants, as it was new to them that man in his characteristic position should be represented lying flat on the ground like a stone, instead of standing upright. Their own motion corresponding to the notion of "person" was invariably the vertical position of the lower arm with the hand up.

---

1. "*A Language Study based on Bantu,*" by the Rev. F. W. Kolbe, London, Trübner, 1888, pp. 59-70.

**363.** — No etymology of the classifier BA- satisfies me altogether. What I consider as most probable is that it is essentially identical with the Senna verb *-bala* " to beget " (Tonga *-ziala*, cf. 52\*). The absence of the *l* will not astonish any one, if we remember that it is regularly dropped in Kamba, Swahili, and Dualla. At the same time it will explain why this classifier is long (*bā*). Hence BA- would mean properly " progeny ", as well as the classifier ZIN-, and the only difference between these two classifiers would be that BA- from *-bala* conveys more decent notions than ZIN- from *-ziala*. For *-bala* and *-ziala* are not quite identical in meaning : *-ziala* is rather applied to animals, *-bala* to persons, as also to trees with regard to their bearing fruits.

**364.** — *N. B.* This view may be confirmed by considering that BA- and *-bala* have every appearance of being etymologically one with the Semitic word *ben*, or *bar*, " son ". It is also a remarkable fact that in several Bantu languages we find the word *mu-ene*, plur. *b-ene*, replacing in many expressions the semitic *ben*.

**365.** — The readers who are fond of etymologies will find interesting matter for study in the examples which have been given under n. 322. Let us go rapidly through these tables.

1. *Mu-ntu* " a person ", means literally " one who is like us. ". For *-ntu*, which in the rigour of phonetic principles is equivalent to *-itu* (285), means " we, us ", in nearly all the Bantu languages (656 table, and 639 table). This word is very seldom used by the natives with reference to white people. These they call variously *Be-iungu* or *Ba-zungu* " the children of God ", *Ma-nkua* " the people from the East ", etc. Likewise chiefs are seldom called *ba-ntu*, because they are considered to be white and children of God by law, even if they be as black as charcoal. This explains the origin of the scientific word *Bantu* as distinctive of these African tribes. For Bleek, who was the first who used it in this sense, was led to do so because he found it employed several times with a special reference to black people in certain Zulu tales (¹).

2. The etymologies of *mu-alume* " a husband ", *mu-ame* " a chief " and *mu-zike* " a slave, a servant ", are not plain. We shall not suggest any, as they might only be misleading. It is interesting to find the Mozambique word *m-alimu* " a chief ", lit. " a man of learning " (Swahili *m-falme*, plur. *wa-falme*) in Masudi's " *Golden Meadows* ", a work written in the year 332 of the Hegira. But the copists, as they are wont to do with foreign words and proper names, have variously metamorphosed it into *falime* or *folima* or *felima*, *wa-flimo*, *wa-klima*, *wafiha*, *nufalla* (?), etc. Cf. Maçoudi, " *Les Prairies d'or* ". Texte et traduction par Barbier de Meynard et Pavet de Courteille, Paris, 1861-1877, vol. III, p. 445.

3. In *mu-ana* the element *-ana* means literally " with the self ", thus conveying the notion of close union and dependency. We shall see further on (1084) that the same element forms reciprocal verbs by expressing that an action is terminated within the limits of the subject, as in *ba-la-ya-sa*na, " they are fighting ", lit. " they thrust (spears or arrows) *between themselves* ". The element *na*, which is part of *-ana*, will be found likewise signifying " self " (661, 689).

4. In *mu-ana-kazi*, *mu-kaṭe-ndu*, *mu-no-kaji*, etc., we have two elements besides the classifier. The one is *-ana* or *-ntu (-no)* from *mu-ana* or *mu-ntu (mo-no)*. The other is

---

1. Mss. 214 of the Grey Library, Capetown, entitled " *Thirty chapters of Zulu tradition* " chapter V.

*-kazi* which conveys the notion of " bringing to existence ", from *ka*, notion of " sitting down ", hence of " existing ", and *-zi* " notion of fecundity. " The verb corresponding to *-kazi* is *kazia*, or *kazika*, " to cause to sit ", hence " to cause to exist ", from *-kala* " to sit, to exist " (1075).

5. The names of the South-African tribes are derived from various notions, some from that of a region, as *Wa-nya-mwezi*, from *nya-mwezi* " the mountain of the Moon ", others from that of the origin of the tribe, true or pretended, as *a Ma-zulu* " the children of Zulu " or " of heaven ", perhaps " of the deep, of the sea ", others probably from that of colour, as *Ba-suto* and *A-suut* or *A-suur*, probably from *-nsundu* (in the Chwana group *-sutu* or *-sotho*), which conveys the notion of " olive brown colour ", etc. etc.

6. We have as yet nothing certain to say concerning the etymology of the word *Leza* or *Reja* " God ". As to its synonym *Mu-lungu* or *Mu-luku*, we have already seen that probably it is no other than *Molokh* (339). It may be observed that this word is used only by Eastern tribes, that is precisely by those which have had undoubted relations with Sabæans in olden times. *Mo-dimo*, of the Bechwana, means " spirit ". In Tonga, Senna, etc. the word which corresponds to it etymologically is *mu-zimo* " soul, spirit ", from *-zimua* or *-zimoa*, which is the passive form of *-zima* " to efface, to render invisible ". The Tonga and most other Bantu tribes, when they have their sacrifices and prayers for rain, address them to God generally through the spirits of their former chiefs *(mi-zimo)*, instead of going to him directly. Cf. Appendix I.

7. *Tata* " father ", and *ma* or *mama* " mother ", are not words proper to Bantu languages. *Ma* or *mama* is the first consonantal sound which a babe utters before, and *tata* the first it pronounces after it has begun to cut its teeth.

## III. — The MU-MI Class.

**366.** — The substantives which belong to the MU-MI class are those which require the same sort of concord as **mu**-*bili* " a body ", plur. **mi**-*bili*.

### § 1. Transformations of the Classifier MU-.

**367.** — The classifier MU- of this MU-MI class varies in the different languages exactly as MU- of the class MU-BA, though, as will be seen further, it requires a different sort of concord.

*N. B.* It was an error on the part of Bleek to think that MU- of this MU-MI class is essentially long *(mū)*.

**368.** — Here again the Bantu tendency to avoid words which

### * EXAMPLES.

|  | the body | | the tail | | the head | | the mouth, lips, beak | |
|---|---|---|---|---|---|---|---|---|
|  | *Sing.* | *Plur.* | *Sing.* | *Plur.* | *Sing.* | *Plur.* | *Sing.* | *Plur.* |
| Tonga | mu-bili, | mi- | mu-cila, | mi- | mu-tue, | mi- | mu-lomo, | mi- |
| Bisa | mu-bili, | mi- | ... | ... | mu-tue, | mi- | mu-lomo, | mi- |
| Gogo | ... | ... | ... | ... | mu-twe, | mi- | m-lomo, | mi- |
| Sagara | m-tufi, | mi- | mu-se, | mi- | mu-twe, | mi- | m-lomo, | mi- |
| Shambala | mu-ili, | mi- | mu-kila, | mi- | mu-tui, | mi- | mu-lomo, | mi- |
| Boondei | mu-ili, | mi- | mu-kila, | mi- | mu-tui, | mi- | m-lomo, | mi- |
| Taita | mu-li | ... | m-koba | ... | ... | ... | m-lomo, | mi- |
| Nyanyembe | m-wili, | mi- | m-kila, | mi- | mu-twe, | mi- | m-lomo, | mi- |
| Sukuma | ... | ... | m-kila, | mi- | mu-twe, | mi- | m-lomo, | mi- |
| Kamba | mu-i (81), | mi- | mu-idi, | mi- | mu-tue, | mi- | m-omo, | mi- |
| Swahili | m-wili, | mi- | m-kia, | mi- | ... | ... | m-domo, | mi- |
| Pokomo | mu-i, | mi- | mu-tyia, | mi- | ... | ... | ... | ... |
| Nika | mu-iri, | mi- | mu-cira, | mi- | ... | ... | mu-lomo, | mi- |
| Senna | ... | ... | (u)n-cira, | mi- | (u)n-solo, | mi- | (u)n-domo, | mi-l... |
| Karanga | (u)m-biri, | mi- | (u)n-cira, | mi- | (u)n-xoro, | mi- | (u)n-domo, | mi-l... |
| Ganda | mu-bili, | mi- | m-kila, | mi- | m-tue, | mi- | mu-mua, | mi- |
| Zulu-Kafir | u mu-zimba, | i mi- | u mu-sila, | i mi- | ... | ... | u mu-lomo, | i mi- |
| Xosa-Kafir | u mu-zimba, | i mi- | u m-sila, | i mi- | ... | ... | u m-lomo, | i mi- |
| Herero | ... | ... | o mu-tyira, | o mi- | ... | ... | o mu-na, | o mi- |
| Bihe | ... | ... | u-sese, | o vi- | u-tui, | o vi- | ... | ... |
| Mbunda | ... | ... | ... | ... | mu-tue, | mi- | ... | ... |
| Rotse | ... | ... | mu-sila, | mi- | ... | ... | ... | ... |
| Guha | ... | ... | ... | ... | ... | ... | mu-lomo, | mi- |
| Rua | m-vilivili (?) | ... | ... | ... | ... | ... | ... | ... |
| Angola | mu-kutu, | mi- | mu-kila, | mi- | mu-tue, | mi- | mu-zumbu, | mi- |
| Lower Congo | ... | ... | n-kila, | mi- | n-tu, | mi- | ... | ... |
| Nywema | ... | ... | ... | ... | o-tue, | e- | o-lomo, | e- |
| Yao | ... | ... | m-cila, | mi- | m-tue, | mi- | ... | ... |
| Kilimane | ... | ... | mw-ila, | mi- | mu-soro, | mi- | mu-lomo, | mi- |
| Mozambique | mw-ili, | mi- | mw-ila, | mi- | mu-ru, | mi- | m-lomo, | mi- |
| Chwana proper | 'mele(278), | me-bele | mo-gatla, | me- | ... | ... | mo-lomo, | me- |
| Suto | 'mele, | me-bele | mo-gatla, | me- | ... | ... | mo-lomo, | me- |
| Mpongwe | o-kuwa, | i- | o-kwende | ... | ... | ... | o-lumbu, | i- |
| Fan | ... | ... | ... | ... | n-nu | ... | en-sôon | ... |
| Dualla | ... | ... | mo-undu, | mi- | mo-lopo, | mi- | mo-lumbu, | mi- |
| Fernandian | ... | ... | ... | ... | ... | ... | bu-ee, | bi- |

might sound like monosyllables is felt in those substantives which have monosyllabic stems. Hence in Ganda, for instance, we see *mu-mua* " the lips ", *mu-tue* " the head ", *mu-ddo* " grass ", etc. next to *m-lambo* " a dead body ", *m-kono* " an arm ", etc.

*N. B.* In the otherwise excellent "*Essai de Grammaire Ruganda*" the word for " tree " is spelt *m-ti*, not *mu-ti*. I wonder whether this spelling is correct. There is against it the fact that Stanley spells the same word *mu-tti*, while the translator of St Matthew's Gospel spells it *mu-ti*, and the Rev. C. F. Wilson hesitates between *m-ti* and *mu-ti*.

## § 2. Transformations of the Classifier MI-.

**369.** — This classifier seems to be regularly pronounced VI- in Nano and Bihe when the singular classifier corresponding to it

### EXAMPLES. (Continued.)

| | the back | | the heart | | a tree | | a baobab-tree | |
|---|---|---|---|---|---|---|---|---|
| | *Sing.* | *Plur.* | *Sing.* | *Plur.* | *Sing.* | *Plur.* | *Sing.* | *Plur.* |
| Tonga | mu-sana, | mi- | mu-oyo, | mi- | mu-samo, | mi- | mu-buyu, | mi- |
| Bisa | mu-sana, | mi- | ... | ... | mu-ti, | mi- | ... | ... |
| Gogo | m-gongo, | mi- | ... | ... | ... | ... | ... | ... |
| Sagara | m-gongo, | mi- | m-oyo, | mi- | mu-ti, | ni- | m-pera, | mi- |
| Shambala | mu-gongo, | mi- | m-oyo, | mi- | mu-ti, | mi- | m-uyu, | mi- |
| Boondei | mu-gongo, | mi- | m-oyo, | mi- | mu-ti, | mi- | m-buyu, | mi- |
| Taita | mu-gongo, | mi- | ... | ... | mw-iti, | mi- | ... | ... |
| Nyanyembe | m-gongo, | mi- | m-oyo, | mi- | mu-ti, | mi- | m-pela, | mi- |
| Sukuma | m-gongo, | mi- | m-oyo, | mi- | mu-ti, | mi- | m-pera, | mi- |
| Kamba | m-mongo, | mi- | ... | ... | m-ti, | mi- | mw-amba, | mi- |
| Swahili | m-gongo, | mi- | m-oyo, | mi- | m-ti, | mi- | m-buyu, | mi- |
| Pokomo | m-ongo, | mi- | m-otyo, | mi- | mu-hi, | mi- | ... | ... |
| Nika | m-ongo, | mi- | m-oyo, | mi- | mu-hi, | mi- | m-uyu, | mi- |
| Senna | (u)n-sana, | mi- | m-oyo, | mi- | (u)n-tengo, | mi- | (u)m-buyu, | mi- |
| Karanga | (u)n-xana, | mi- | m-oyo, | mi- | (u)n-ti, | mi- | u m-buyu, | mi- |
| Ganda | mu-bega, | mi- | m-oyo, | mi- | mu-ti, | mi- | ... | ... |
| Zulu-Kafir | u m-hlana, | i mi- | ... | ... | u mu-ti, | i mi- | ... | ... |
| Xosa-Kafir | u m-hlana, | i mi- | ... | ... | u m-ti, | i mi- | ... | ... |
| Herero | ... | ... | o mu-tima, | o mi- | o mu-ti, | o mi- | ... | ... |
| Bihe | ... | ... | u-tima, | o vi- | u-ti, | o vi- | ... | ... |
| Mbunda | m-ongo | ... | ... | ... | ... | ... | ... | ... |
| Rotse | m-ongo = end of spine | | mu-jima, | mi- | mu-sito, | mi- | ... | ... |
| Guha | m-gongo, | mi- | ... | ... | mu-ti, | mi- | ... | ... |
| Rua | mw-ongo, | mi- | mu-ula (?) | | mu-ti (?) | | ... | ... |
| Angola | ... | ... | mu-xima, | mi- | mu-xi, | mi- | m-bondo (?) | ... |
| Lower Congo | ... | ... | m-oyo, | mi- | n-ti, | mi- | n-kondo, | mi- |
| Nywema | o-vuna, | e- | o-tima = belly | | o-ti, | i- | ... | ... |
| Yao | m-gongo, | mi- | m-tima, | mi- | m-tela, | mi- | m-lonji, | mi- |
| Kilimane | ... | ... | ... | ... | mu-rre, | mi- | m-laba, | mi- |
| Mozambique | m-thana, | mi- | m-rima, | mi- | m-tali, | mi- | m-lapa, | mi- |
| Chwana proper | mo-tlana, | me- | ... | ... | ... | ... | mo-wana, | me- |
| Suto | mo-tlana, | me- | ... | ... | ... | ... | mo-wana, | me- |
| Mpongwe | o-kongo, | i- | o-rema, | i- | ... | ... | ... | ... |
| Fan | ... | ... | ... | ... | e-li | | ... | ... |
| Dualla | ... | ... | mo-lema, | mi- | ... | ... | ... | ... |
| Fernandian | ... | ... | bu-ila, | bi- | ba-ti (?) bo-ti | | ... | ... |

has the contracted form U-. It is pronounced ME- in Chwana according to n. 200, and BI- in some Fernandian dialects according to n. 240. In Mpongwe and Nywema its form is I- or E-. In most of the other Bantu languages its proper form is MI-.

**370.** — *N. B.* 1. In Tonga I often thought I heard it pronounced like *mu* in the French *mur*. This inclines me to think that its original form was MUI.

2. These two classifiers MU- and MI- correspond to one another as singular and plural in all the Bantu languages. Bleek has it that MI- corresponds regularly as plural in Nika to the classifier U- (= Tonga BU-), and he gives as an example the word *u-miro*, " voice ", to which he ascribes *mi-miro* as plural. But it is now plain from Rebmann's "*Nika Dictionary*" that the whole idea is incorrect, for properly speaking the word in Nika for " voice ", or more exactly for " word ", " speech ", is *m-oro*, pl. *mi-oro*, and certainly *m-oro* is regularly of cl. MU-MI, as in the Nika proverb : M-*oro* mu-*dzo ka*-u-*lavia dzua*, " a good word does not bring out (?) the sun. " (Rebmann's " *Nika Dict.*, " word *moro*).

## EXAMPLES. (Continued.)

| | fire | a river (muddy) | | a moon, month | | a year | |
|---|---|---|---|---|---|---|---|
| | *Sing.* | *Sing.* | *Plur.* | *Sing.* | *Plur.* | *Sing.* | *Plur.* |
| Tonga | mu-lilo | mu-longa, | mi- | mu-ezi, | mi- | mu-aka, | mi- |
| Bisa | mu-lilo | ... | ... | mu-ezi, | mi- | mu-aka, | mi- |
| Gogo | m-oto | m-ongo, | mi- | m-lenge, | mi- | mw-aka, | mi- |
| Sagara | m-oto | m-korongo, | mi- | m-lenge, | mi- | mw-aka, | mi- |
| Shambala | mu-oto | mu-to, | mi- | mu-ezi, | mi- | mu-aka, | mi- |
| Boondei | mu-oto | m-to, | mi- | mw-ezi, | mi- | mw-aka, | mi- |
| Taita | m-oto | mw-ita, | mi- | mw-ezi, | mi- | m-aka (?), | mi- (?) |
| Nyanyembe | mu-lilo | m-ongo, | mi- | mw-ezi, | mi- | mw-aka, | mi- |
| Sukuma | n-oto | m-ongo, | mi- | mw-ezi, | mi- | mw-aka, | mi- |
| Kamba | mw-aki | ... | ... | mw-ei, | mi- | mw-aka, | mi- |
| Swahili | m-oto | m-to, | mi- | mw-ezi, | mi- | mw-aka, | mi- |
| Pokomo | m-oho | ... | ... | mw-esi, | mi- | mw-aka, | mi- |
| Nika | m-oho | mu-ho, | mi- | mu-ezi, | mi- | mu-aka, | mi- |
| Senna | m-oto | (u)n-tsinje, | mi- | mw-ezi, | mi- | ... | ... |
| Karanga | m-oto | ... | ... | mw-eji, | mi- | mw-aka, | mi- |
| Ganda | mu-lilo | mu-gga, | mi- | mw-ezi, | mi- | mw-aka, | mi- |
| Zulu-Kafir | u mu-lilo | u mu-lambo, | mi- | ... | ... | u nyaka, i mi-nyaka | |
| Xosa-Kafir | u m-lilo | u m-lambo, | i mi- | ... | ... | u nyaka, i mi-nyaka | |
| Herero | o mu-riro | o mu-ramba = torrent | | o mu-eje, | o mi- | | |
| Bihe | ... | ... | ... | ... | ... | u-nyamo, | o vi- |
| Mbunda | (o)n-diro | (o)n-donga, mi-l.. | | (o)n-gonde (?) | | mw-akwari, | mi- |
| Rotse | mu-lilo | mu-lońka, | mi- | mu-eti, | mi- | mu-aka, | mi- |
| Guha | ... | mu-fito, | mi- | mw-ezi, | mi- | ... | ... |
| Rua | mu-jilo, mi- | ... | ... | ... | ... | ... | ... |
| Angola | mu-lengu = flame | ... | ... | ... | ... | mu-vu, | mi- |
| Lower Congo | n-laku = flame | n-koko, | mi- | —, mi-eji = moonlight | | m-vu, | mi- |
| Nywema | ... | ... | ... | o-eli, | ... | ... | ... |
| Yao | m-oto | m-lusulo, | mi- | mw-esi, | mi- | ... | ... |
| Kilimane | m-oto (?) | ... | ... | mw-erre, | mi- | ... | ... |
| Mozambique | m-oro | m-oloko, | mi- | mw-eri, | mi- | mw-aka, | mi- |
| Chwana proper | mo-lelo | ... | ... | ... | ... | ngwaga | ... |
| Suto | mo-lelo | ... | ... | ... | ... | ngwaga | ... |
| Mpongwe | o-goni | o-lovi, | i- | o-gweli, | i- | o-mpuma, | i- |
| Fan | ... | ... | ... | { o gon = moon  —; mi-el = moonlight } | | ... | ... |
| Dualla | ... | mo-opi, | ... | ... | ... | m-bu, | mi- |
| Fernandian | bo-sso | ... | | ... | | ... | |

## § 3. SUBSTANTIVES WHICH BELONG TO THE MU-MI CLASS.

**371.** — In Tonga, and, as it seems, in the generality of the Bantu languages, the substantives which belong to this class are principally : —

1° The names of such complete trees and plants as stand up without support, as in Tonga *mu-samo*, " a tree " in general; *mu-nga*, " a mimosa-tree "; *mu-konka*, " a cocoa-tree ", *mu-buyu*, " a baobab-tree ".

*N. B.* We shall see further on that the names for the fruits of such trees are generally of class LI-MA.

**372.** — 2° The names of such tools or artificial objects as remind one of the form of a tree by having branches or bushy parts, as *mu-ini (alias mu-pini)*, " a handle, " *mu-iaezio (alias mu-piaezio)*, " a broom ", *mu-nvui*, " an arrow " (bearded), *mu-zuete*, " clothes ", *mu-panda*, " a cross ", etc.

**373.** — 3° The human and animal body, *mu-bili*, as also such of its parts as branch off in some manner, growing out into accessory parts, or move up and down, as *mu-oyo*, " the heart ", *mu-nue*, " a finger ", *mu-limba*, " a feather ", etc. The same may be said of the similar parts of trees, as *mu-yanda*, " a root ", etc.

**374.** — 4° All beneficent elements and producers of animal or vegetable life, such as *mu-ezi*, " the moon ", which in Africa is thought to be the great source of rain, while rain is thought to be the greatest benefit which men can receive from God (cf. the specimens of Tonga at the end of this work) ; *mu-longa*, " a river " ; *mu-ezi*, " a pool of water " ; *mu-tulu*, " a fertile plain " ; *mu-nda*, " a garden " ; *mu-se*, " the soil " ; *mu-lilo*, " the fire ", which naturally reminds these people of the food it cooks, and of the warmth in which it keeps the body during cold nights ; *mu-nzi*, " a living-place ".

**375.** — 5° The soul, a shadow, and several objects noticeable either for their instability or their variety of design, as *mu-zimo*, " the soul ", the plural *mi-zimo* being used principally with reference to the departed souls (Kafir *i mi-nyanga* or *i mi-nyanya*) ; *mu-zimuemue*, " a shadow " ; *mu-mpini-ciongue*, " the rain-bow, " *mu-bala*, " a variety of colours, " etc.

**376.** — *N. B.* In a few languages, e. g. in Kafir, three or four personal substantives or tribal names belong to this class MU-MI. This seems to be due to their including some reference to the word for " spirit ", *mu-zimo*.

**377.** — 6° The breath, the air, and empty spaces, as *mu-oya*, " the breath, air, breeze " ; *mu-lindi*, " a pit in the ground " ; *mu-liango*, " the door-way ", etc.

**378.** — 7° Medicines, unfermented beverages, and some other products with beneficent or marvellous effects, as *mu-samo*, " a medicine", viz. anything belonging to that which to a primitive mind forms the genus " physics ", such as even secret sciences; *mu-ade*, a certain supposed judicious poison, which kills sorcerers, while it exculpates the innocent (cf. appendix I) ; *mu-bonobono*, " castor oil " ; *mu-sili*, " powder "; *mu-sinza*, " soup " ; *mu-kande*, " very light Kafir beer ", opposed to *bu-kande*, properly " fermented beer " (cf. 440*) etc.

**379.** — 8° A few names of immaterial things which occupy a fixed time, or come round at regular times, as *mu-aka*, " a year " ; *milia*, " feasts with sacrifice " (a word apparently not used in the singular) ; *mu-sebenzo*, " a work ", etc.

**380.** — *N. B.* In Senna the nearly total loss of the classifiers LI- and LU- has caused many words to be brought into this class MU-MI, which in the other Bantu languages do not belong to it. Ex. *mw-ala*, " a column, a stone " (= Tonga *lu-ala*, a column, *i-bue*, a stone). This remark extends partially to several other languages.

## § 4. Etymologies. — Varia.

**381.** — Judging from the sort of substantives thus admitted into the MU-MI class, it seems pretty evident that the predominant notion in this class is that of " objects which are light, move, change, grow, produce, or, in general, which contain some *principle of life and production*, a notion intimately connected with that of " *power of growing up* " like a tree. Hence I should think that the classifier MU- of this class is, like MU of the class MU-BA, radically identical with the adjective *-umi*, alive, from the verb *-ma* or *-ima*, " to stand ". Bleek connects it with the preposition *mu* which means " in ". Perhaps the correct thing is to unite both opinions by saying that the classifier MU- is directly connected in some words with the preposition *mu*, and in others with *-umi*. It may also be that in a few words its immediate connexion is with the verb *-nyua* (Karanga *-mua*) " to drink, " h. e. " to take light food " (Cf. 430).

**382.** — As to the classifier MI-, we should see in it the fundamental element of the verb *-mila* or *-mena* " to grow " (cf. 280(2) ), exactly as we connect BA- with *-bala* (363).

**383.** — *N. B.* The verb *-mila* or *-mena* " to grow " is the applicative form of *-ma* or *-ima* " to stand " (1065). This may be another reason to say that the singular classifier MU- is related to the latter verb.

**384.** — The examples given under n. 366 probably must be explained etymologically as follows :

1. *Mu-bili* " the body " = the upright thing which has its parts two by two. From *-bili* " two, double " (792).

2. *Mu-cila* " the tail " = the hanging thing, or sort of branch, which sits upon (the body). From *ka*, notion of " sitting ", which changes to *c* before *i* (cf. 257-259), and *-ila*, notion of " stretching along, or upon, something " (1065).

3. For *mu-tue* " the head ", and *mu-buyu* " a baobab (tree) ", we have only doubtful etymologies.

4. *Mu-lomo* " the lips " = that which is drawn inwards. From *lo*, notion of " being drawn " (cf. *-lala* " to lie down ", *i-lo* " a bed ", *-yala* " to stretch ", etc.), and *mo* " inside " (530, 656 Tables).

5. *Mu-sana* " the spine, the back ", lit. " that upright member which sends its own shoots through the body ". From *sa*, notion of " thrusting something through a body " (cf. *-yasa* " to thrust a spear, to shoot "), and *na* or *ana*, notion of " close union " (cf. 363(3)).

6. *Mu-oyo* " the heart ", lit. " the part of the body which beats, going up and down ". Cf. *mu-oya*, " the air, the wind ", *ku-yoya* " to breathe ", etc.

7. *Mu-samo* " a tree ", lit. " the standing thing which thrusts roots within (the ground) ". From *sa*, notion of " thrusting something through a body " (*supra* 384(5)), and *mo* " within, inside " (*supra*, 384(4)). Many languages replace *mu-samo* by *mu-ti*, which means lit. " a thing standing in the ground ", from *ti*, notion of " ground " (Swahili *n-ti* " ground "). In Chwana the usual word for " tree " is *se-tlhare* (cl. CI-ZI), in which *tlha* = Tonga *sa* (174) and *re* = *ti* of *mu-ti* (172,200). Hence *se-tlhare* means also lit. " the thing which thrusts roots through the ground ", but, as it is of cl. CI-ZI, it does not include the notion of something standing, like mu-*samo*.

8. *Mu-lilo* " fire, flame ", means lit. " the thing which goes up eating its own bed ". From *li*, notion of " eating " (cf. *-lia* " to eat "), and *lo*, notion of " something drawn out " or of " a bed " (*supra*, 384(4)).

9. *Mu-longa* " a river ", lit. " the thing moving down, being drawn through gaps ". From *lo*, notion of " bed " (*supra* 384(8)) and *nga*, notion of " going through a gap."

10. *Mu-ezi* " the moon ", lit. " the mother of water and fertility ". *Mu-ezi* = *mu-a-izi*, and *-izi* is the same element which appears in *lu-izi* " a river ", *mu-nzi* " dwelling-place ", lit. " birth-place ", *ma-nzi* " water ", etc. (cf. 284). This element *-izi* or *-nzi* conveys the notion of production, fecundity. The moon is considered by nearly all the Bantu tribes as the great fertilizing power in the world.

11. *Mu-aka* " a year ", lit. " one station ". Connected with *ku-yaka* " to build ". The Bantu are in the habit of renewing the thatch of their huts every year.

## IV. — The IN-(Z)IN Class.

**385.** — The IN-(Z)IN class includes the substantives which admit the same sort of concord as **in**-*zila* " a path ", pl. **(z)in**-*zila*\*.

*N. B.* In Kafir there is a sub-class IN-MA. Ex. i n-*doda* " a man, a husband ", pl. a ma-*doda*.

### § 1. Transformations of the Singular Classifier IN-.

**386.** — This classifier stands in nearly the same relations to the letters *N* and *I* as the classifier MU- to the letters *M* and *U*. Hence the following forms : —

**387.** — *NI*- or *NY*- before vowels in several languages, viz. in Tonga, Ganda, Kafir, etc.

**388.** — *(I)N*- before consonants [*IM*- before *b*, *p*, *v*, *f*, (n. 280)] in Tonga, Bisa, and Bemba, with a sound often approaching that of *en*. When this classifier is

### \* EXAMPLES.

|  | a native doctor | | the beard | | flesh, meat | a head of cattle | |
|---|---|---|---|---|---|---|---|
|  | *Sing.* | *Plur.* | *Sing.* | *Plur.* | *Sing.* | *Sing.* | *Plur.* |
| Tonga | in-ganga, | (zi)n- | in-dezu, | (zi)n- | iny-ama | in-gombe, | (zi)n- |
| Bisa | ... | ... | ... | ... | in-ama | n-gombe, | n- |
| Gogo | ... | ... | ... | ... | ny-ama | n-gombe, | n- |
| Sagara | n-ganga (?) | ... | ... | ... | ny-ama | n-gombe, | n- |
| Shambala | n-ganga (?) | ... | n-dezu, | n- | ny-ama | n-gombe, | n- |
| Boondei | ... | ... | n-dezu, | n- | ny-ama | n-gombe, | n- |
| Taita | ... | ... | gafa (?) | ... | ny-ama | n-gombe, | n- |
| Nyanyembe | ... | ... | ... | ... | n-ama | n-gombe, | n- |
| Sukuma | ... | ... | ... | ... | n-ama | n-gombe, | n- |
| Kamba | ... | ... | jeu | ... | ny-ama | n-gombe, | n- |
| Swahili | ... | ... | n-defu, | n- | ny-ama | n-gombe, | n- |
| Pokomo | ... | ... | ... | ... | ... | ... | ... |
| Nika | ... | ... | n-defu = hair | | ny-ama | n-gombe, | n- |
| Senna | n-ganga, | (zi)n- | n-debzu, | (zi)n- | ny-ama | n-gombe, | n- |
| Karanga | i-ganga, | i- | i-devu, | i- | i-nyama | i-ngombe (?), | i- |
| Ganda | n-ganga=a sacred bird | | ... | ... | ny-ama | n-te, | n- |
| Zulu-Kafir | i ny-anga, i ziny- | | i n-devu, | i (zi)n- | i ny-ama | i n-komo, | i(zi)n- |
| Xosa-Kafir | ... | ... | in-devu, | i (zi)n- | i ny-ama | i n-komo, | i(zi)n- |
| Herero | o n-ganga, o zon- | | ... | ... | o ny-ama | o n-gombe, ozon- | |
| Bihe | o n-ganga, o lon- | | (o n-jele), | o lon- | o situ | o n-gombe, o lon- | |
| Mbunda | n-ganga, | n- | n-jezu (?), | ... | situ | n-gombe, | n- |
| Rotse | n-ganga, | n- | ... | ... | ny-ama | n-gombe, (ti)n-(?) | |
| Guha | ... | ... | ... | ... | ny-ama | n-gombe, | n- |
| Rua | n-ganga (?) | | ... | ... | ... | n-gombe, | n- |
| Angola | n-ganga, | (ji)n- | ... | ... | xitu | n-gombe, | (ji)n- |
| Lower Congo | n-ganga, | (zi)n- | n-zevo, | ... | m-biji | n-gombe, | (zi)n- |
| Nywema | ... | ... | ... | ... | ... | ... | ... |
| Yao | ... | ... | n-deu, | (si)n- | ny-ama | n-gombe, | (si)n- |
| Kilimane | n-ganga, | n- | e-rrelo, | e- | ny-ama (?) | gombe, | di- |
| Mozambique | ... | ... | i-reru, | i- | i-nama | i-ngope, | di- |
| Chwana proper | ngaka, | di- | tedu, | di- | nama | kgomo, | di- |
| Suto | ngaka, | li- | telu, | li- | nama | kgomo, | li- |
| Mpongwe | ... | ... | ... | ... | ... | ny-are, | (si)ny- |
| Fan | en-găn | ... | n-sel | ... | en-dsôm | ... | ... |
| Dualla | ... | ... | n-sedu (?) | ... | nyama = animal | ny-akka | |
| Fernandian | ... | ... | e-sedu | ... | n-kelapi | n-gopo, or kopo (Banapa dial.) | |

## The IN-(Z)IN Class.

very intimately connected with a preceding word, no trace at all of its vowel *i* or *e* is perceptible, so that we may hear, for instance, *tu-a-komba* m-*vula*, " we have asked for rain " next to *tua-lapela Leza* im-*vula* " we have prayed God for rain. " The presence of the *i* in this form is particularly felt in possessive expressions, where it produces, together with the possessive particle *a*, the sound *ee*, which we write *e i* (249, 253), as in *mu-tue* ue-*ngombe*, " the head of a cow" (= ... *u*ain-*gombe*).

N. B. Before monosyllabic stems the classifier IN- sounds almost like *een* (*eem* before *b*, *p*, etc.). Ex. *eem-pie* " an ostrich ".

**389.** — *N* before consonants *(M-* before *b*, *p*, *v*, *f)* regularly in most of the other languages, if we may trust to our authorities. But several of these languages, viz. Swahili, Angola, Herero, Yao, Shambala, Mpongwe, etc., regularly drop this *n* before the hard consonants *s*, *f*, *x*, *h*, *k*, *p*, *t*, according to n. 283, as also before *m* and *n*. Here again however the tendency to avoid monosyllables comes in to prevent the *n* from being dropped before monosyllabic stems (nn. 283, 44, 325, 368, etc.).

### EXAMPLES. (Continued.)

| | a goat | | a fowl | | a snake | | an elephant | |
|---|---|---|---|---|---|---|---|---|
| | *Sing.* | *Plur.* | *Sing.* | *Plur.* | *Sing.* | *Plur.* | *Sing.* | *Plur.* |
| Tonga | im-pongo, | (zi)m- | in-kuku, | (zi)n- | in-zoka | (zi)n- | in-zovu | (zi)n- |
| Bisa | m-buzi, | m- | n-kuku, | n- | ... | ... | ... | ... |
| Gogo | m-peni, | m- | n-khukhu, | n- | ... | ... | n-zofu, | n- |
| Sagara | m-buzi, | m- | n-khukhu, | n- | n-joka, | n- | n-tembo, | n- |
| Shambala | m-buzi, | m- | n-guku, | n- | ny-oka, | ny- | tembo | |
| Boondel | m-buzi, | m- | n-guku, | n- | ny-oka, | ny- | n-tembo, | n- |
| Taita | m-buzi, | m- | n-guku, | n- | ny-oka, | ny- | n-jovu, | n- |
| Nyanyembe | m-buli, | m- | n-goko, | n- | n-zoka, | n- | n-zovu, | n- |
| Sukuma | m-buli, | m- | n-goko, | n- | ... | ... | ... | ... |
| Kamba | m-bui, | m- | n-guku, | n- | n-soka, | n- | n-zou, | n- |
| Swahili | m-buzi, | m- | kuku, | n- | ny-oka, | ny- | n-dovu, | n- |
| Pokomo | ... | ... | ... | ... | paa (?) | ... | n-dzofu, | n- |
| Nika | m-buzi, | m- | kuku | | ny-oka, | ny- | n-dzovu, | n- |
| Senna | m-buzi, | (zi)m- | n-kuku, | (zi)n- | ny-oka, | (zi)ny- | n-jou, | (zi)n- |
| Karanga | ... | ... | i-uko, | i- | i-nyoka, | i- | i-joo, | i- |
| Ganda | m-buzi, | m- | n-koko, | n- | n-joka, | n- | n-jovu, | n- |
| Zulu-Kafir | ... | ... | i n-kuku, i | (zi)n- | i ny-oka, | i(zi)ny- | i n-dlovu, | i(zi)n- |
| Xosa-Kafir | i-bokue, | i(zi)- | i n-kuku, i | (zi)n- | i ny-oka, | i(zi)ny- | i n-dlovu, | i(zi)n- |
| Herero | o n-gombo, | ozon- | o n-dyuhua, | ozon- | o ny-oka, | o zony- | o n-dyou, | o zon- |
| Bihe | o hombo, | o lo- | o sanje, | o lo- | o ny-oha, | o lo- | o n-jamba, | o lon-yamba |
| Mbunda | m-pembe, | m- | ... | ... | ... | ... | | |
| Rotse | m-pongo, | (tim-(?) | n-goku, | (ti)n- (?) | ny-oka, | (ti)ny- | n-dopo (?) | ... |
| Guha | m-busi, | m- | n-kuku | n- | ... | ... | ... | ... |
| Rua | m-buzi, | m- | n-zolo | n- | ny-oka, | ny- | holo | |
| Angola | hombo, | (ji)- | sanji, | (ji)- | ni-oka, | (ji)ni- | n-zamba, | (ji)n- |
| Lower Congo | n-kombo, | (zi)n- | n-susu | (zi)n- | ni-oka, | (zi)ni- | n-zamba, | (zi)n- |
| Nywema | m-buli | | ... | ... | ... | ... | ... | ... |
| Yao | m-busi, | (si)m- | n-guku | (si)n- | ... | ... | n-dembo, | (si)n- |
| Kilimane | buze(?) | ... | ku, | di-ku | noa, | di- | doo, | di- |
| Mozambique | i-puri, | i- | i-laku | i- | i-noa, | i- | i-tepo, | i- |
| Chwana proper | pudi, | di- | kgogo (?) | di- | noga, | di- | tlou, | di- |
| Suto | puli, | li- | khogo | di- | noga, | oli- | tlou, | li- |
| Mpongwe | m-boni, | (si)m- | n-dyogoni, | (si)n- | m-peüe, | (s)in- | n-dyogu, | (s)in- |
| Fan | ... | ... | kü | | ... | ... | en-sôk | ... |
| Dualla | m-bodi, | m- | ... | ... | m-bamba, | m- | n-dsou | ... |
| Fernandian | m-pori | ... | n-ko, or in-ko | | mapa | ... | ... | ... |

## 84    South-African Bantu Languages.

Hence in Swahili the words *n-so*, " loins "; *n-si*, " a gnat "; *n-xi*, " the eye-brow "; *n-ti* or *n-chi*, " land "; *n-ta* or *n-cha*, " a point "; *n-fi*, " the sting of a bee, " etc.

**390.** — *I-* or *E-* in Mozambique, with strengthening of the initial consonant of the stem, according to n. 183, sqq.

*I-* in Karanga, though without any such strengthening of the initial consonant of the stem.

*Dropped* in Chwana, but with strengthening of the initial consonant of the stem, according to n. 183 sqq. Here again the tendency to avoid monosyllables preserves the *n* before them, e. g. in *n-tlu* or *en-tlu*, " a house "; *n-ku* or *en-ku*, " a sheep "; *n-tlha*, " a point "; *n-tsi*, " a fly "; *n-ca*, " a dog "; *n-che*, " an ostrich "; etc.

### § 2. Transformations of the Plural Classifier ZIN-.

**391.** — Though the substantives of this class require a different

### EXAMPLES. (Continued.)

|  | shame | | rain | a house | | a path | |
|---|---|---|---|---|---|---|---|
|  | *Sing.* | *Plur.* | *Sing.* | *Sing.* | *Plur.* | *Sing.* | *Plur.* |
| Tonga | in-soni | | im-vula | in-ganda, | (zi)n- | in-zila, | (zi)n- |
| Bisa | ... | | in-fula | in-ganda, | in- | in-zira, | in- |
| Gogo | ... | | m-vula | n-ganda, | n- | n-jira, | n- |
| Sagara | soni | | m-vula | n-umba, | n- | n-gila, | n- |
| Shambala | soni | | fula | ny-umba, | ny- | sila | |
| Boondei | soni | | fula | ny-umba, | ny- | sila | |
| Taita | ... | | m-vula | ny-umba, | ny- | n-gila, | n- |
| Nyanyembe | n-soni | | m-bula | n-umba, | n- | n-zila, | n- |
| Sukuma | ... | | m-bula | n-umba, | n- | n-zira, | n- |
| Kamba | n-ɓoni (?) | | m-bua | n-umba, | n- | n-jia, | n- |
| Swahili | soni = abuse | | m-vua | ny-umba, | ny- | n-jia, | n- |
| Pokomo | ... | | ... | ny-umba, | ny- | ... | ... |
| Nika | ... | | m-fula | ny-umba, | ny- | n-jira, | n- |
| Senna | ... | | m-vula | ny-umba, | (zi)ny- | n-jira, | (zi)n- |
| Karanga | i xoni | | i vura | i-mumba, | i- | i zira, | i- |
| Ganda | n-sonzi | | n-kuba (114) | ny-umba, | ny- | ... | |
| Zulu-Kafir | i n-tloni | | i m-vula | i n-dlu, i zin-dlu | | i n-dlela, i (zi)n- | |
| Xosa-Kafir | i n-tloni | | i m-vula | i n-dlu, i zin-dlu | | i n-dlela, i (zi)n- | |
| Herero | o honi | | o m-bura | o n-dyuo, o zon- | | o n-dyira, o zon- | |
| Bihe | ... | | o m-bela | o n-jo, | o lon- | o n-jila, | o lon- |
| Mbunda | ... | | n-fera | n-jolo, | n- | n-gela, | n- |
| Rotse | ... | | n-fula | n-do, | tin-(?) | n-dela, | (ti)n-(?) |
| Guha | ... | | m-vula | n-sese, | n- | n-jila, | |
| Rua | ... | | m-vula | ... | ... | ... | ... |
| Angola | ... | | m-vula | in-zo, | (ji)n- | n-jila, | (ji)n- |
| Lower Congo | n-soni | | m-vula | n-zo, | zin- | n-jila | (zi)n- |
| Nywema | ... | | vula (m-vula ?) | m-vulu, | m- | ... | ... |
| Yao | soni | | ula ('ula ?, 66) | ny-umba, (si)ny- | | ... | ... |
| Kilimane | ... | | ... | ny-umba, | diny- | dila, | di- |
| Mozambique | i-xoni | | i-pula | i-nupa | i- | i-piro | i- |
| Chwanaproper | (tlhong), | di- | pula | (e)n-tlu, | ma- | tsela, | di- |
| Suto | (tlhong), | li- | pula | (e)n-thlo, | ... | tsela, | di- |
| Mpongwe | n-tyoni, | | ... | n-ago, | (s)in- | m-pono, | (s)im- |
| Fan | en-sãn = offence | | ... | en-dã | ... | en-kon-elê (?) ... | |
| Dualla | ... | | m-bua | n-dabo | ... | n-gia | ... |
| Fernandian | ... | | n-kola<br>(Ureka di | n-chibo, or n-jobo | | n-tele | ... |

concord when used in the singular and when used in the plural, yet practically they themselves generally have the same form in both numbers, viz. *in-*, *n-* or *i-*, as above. The following forms are therefore the exception rather than the rule : —

**392.** — *ZIN-* in Tonga, and probably, in Bisa, Nyamwezi, etc., when special attention is called to the plurality of the thing spoken of.

**393.** — *ZIN-* in Kafir in the same case, and besides — a) in vocatives, as in zin-*kosi!* " My chiefs!", — b) regularly before monosyllabic stems, as in *i* zin-*dlu* " houses", — c) regularly after the locative particle *e*, as in *e* zin-*dleleni* " in the roads"

**394.** — *JIN-* (*JI-* before hard consonants, 389) in Angola, when attention is called to plurality, and regularly before monosyllabic stems, as in jim-*bua* " dogs " (Chatelain's *Gram.*, p. 140), perhaps also regularly when substantives are preceded by the article *o*, as in *o* jim-*bongo* " riches ". Cf. n-*gulu* " pigs " (*Ibid.*, p. 133), n *dende*, " palm-nuts " (*Ibid.* pp. 142, 143).

*N. B.* Probably similar principles are applied in several other languages.

**395.** — *DI-* (alias *LI-*) regularly in Chwana, with a hardening of the following consonant ; *DIN-* before monosyllabic stems (390).

**396.** — *SIN-* (*SI-* before hard consonants) regularly in Mpongwe, *IN-*in given cases (Cf. Mgr Le Berre's *Gram.*, pp. 4, 5).

**397.** — *ZON-* regularly in Herero. A very extraordinary form, when compared with the others, on account of the vowel *o* which it contains (cf. 230).

*N. B.* I suspect that its true origin is to be sought for in some kind of imitation of the Portuguese article *os*.

**398.** — *LON-* in Bihe. A regular modification of the Herero *ZON-* (131).

### § 3. Substantives which belong to the IN- (Z)IN Class.

**399.** In the generality of the Bantu languages, we find in this class apparently all sorts of substantives, more particularly :

**400.** — 1° A few names of persons, as *in-ganga* " a native doctor ", etc.

**401.** — 2° A great many names of animals, principally of the milder type as *im-bizi* "a zebra, a horse ", *im-belele* " a sheep ", *im-booma* " a boa ", *eem-pie* (388 Note) " an ostrich ", *in-jina* " lice ", etc. Many of these substantives are often treated as belonging to cl. MU-BA (360).

**402.** — The flesh and a few parts of the body, as *iny-ama* " flesh, meat ", *in-dezu* " beard ", *in-kumu* " the forehead " (including the nose), *im-pemo* " the nose ", *in-go* " an ankle ", *in-singa* "a vein ", etc.

**403.** — 4° A few objects and phenomena in nature, as *inyenyezi* " a star ", *in-simbi* " metal ", more especially " iron ", *im-vula* " rain ", *i-nyika* " a place ", more especially " an empty place, a desert. "

**404.** — 5° A great many artificial objects, principally, as it seems, such as are curved, or yield to pressure, or are produced by smelting, as *in-samo* " a flexible rod ", *in-celua* " a pipe ", *in-juzio* " a key ", *in-kaba* " a die ", *in-goma* " a musical instrument ", more particularly " a drum ", *in-kando* " a hammer ", *in-gubo* " a piece of cloth, a blanket ", *im-pete* " a ring ", *in-sangu* " a shoe ", *in-tibi* " a shield ", *in-tiba* " a knife ", *in-tobolo* " a gun ", *in-sima* " porridge ", etc.

**405.** — 6° Uncomfortable sensations, as *im-peho* " cold ", more particularly " cold wind, winter ", *in-soni* " shame " ; *inyaezia* " danger ", etc.

**406.** — *N. B.* In Kafir nearly all foreign names of things are brought into this class, as *i kofu*, " coffee ", unless they begin with *s*, for these are generally brought under class SI-ZI (= Tonga CI-ZI).

### § 4. ETYMOLOGIES. — VARIA.

**407.** — In this great variety of substantives which are brought under the IN-ZIN class, it appears very probable that this is the proper class for all the substantives which there is no special reason for bringing under any of the others. The classifier IN or N may originally have been no other than the indefinite adjective *-nue* (Kafir *-nye*) " one, another, some " (792, 828). Cf. 122, 204, 327, 517, 559, etc.

**408.** — As to the classifier ZIN-, it seems to be connected with the verb *-ziala* " to bring forth young ", so that it would signify primarily " the progeny of beasts ", according to what has been said in n. 363. This further brings it into connection with the element *nzi* or *izi* " notion of fecundity ", which we have already met with in *mu-ezi* " the moon ", *ma-nzi* " water ", *mu-nzi* " village ", lit. " birth-place ", etc. (384(10)), and which probably furnishes the adjective *-nji* " many " (Kafir *ni*-**nzi** or *ni*-**nji**, etc. (601, Ex.)).

**409.** — The examples given under n. 385 probably must be explained etymologically as follows :

1. *In-ganga* " a doctor ", lit. " one who sees through and through ". From *nga*, the notion of " going through a gap " (384(9)).

## The IN-(Z)IN Class.                                     87

2. *In-dezu* (= *in-lezu*) " the beard ", lit. " what comes out long ". From *-le*, notion of " length " and *zu*, notion of " coming out ". The proper meaning of the elements *le* and *zu* in Bantu is perfectly plain. We find *le* in *ku*-le " far " (533, Ex.), and in nearly all the transformations of the adjective which means " long " (601, Ex.). The element *zu* gives us the verb *ku-zua* " to come out ". It may even be remarked that the last element of the word *in-dezu* varies in the different languages exactly as the verb *-zua*. Thus *Ganda, Karanga, Kafir*, etc. which replace *zua* by *vwa* or *va* (whence, in Kafir, the applicative verb *-vela* = *-vwela*, cf. 1069)), replace also *in-dezu* by *in-de*vu, *ki-le*vu, *i-de*vu, etc. In like manner Chwana which replaces *zua* by *cwa* (= *dwa* or *lwa*, whence the perfect *du-le* or *lu-le*, cf. 205), replaces also *in-dezu* by *tedu* (193, 173), etc.

3. For the words *inyama* " meat ", *in-gombe* " cattle ", *im-pongo* and *m-buzi* " a goat ", *in-zoka* " a snake ", *in-zovu* " an elephant ", we have only doubtful etymologies.

4. *In-kuku* " a fowl ". An onomatopoetic word, derived from the cry of this bird.

5. *In-soni* " shame ". This word includes unmistakably a reference to the eyes, *li-nso*, plur. *meso*. But I do not see exactly what notion is conveyed by the element *ni* unless it be the locative suffix described in nn. 553-555.

6. *Im-vula* " rain ", lit. " what opens out (the earth) ". Related to *-jula* (Kafir *-vula*) " to open ", from *zua* or *va* " to come out ".

7. *In-ganda* " a house ", lit. " a protection ". Related to *-yanda* " to love, to protect. "

8. *In-zila* " a path ", lit. " what goes to a definite place ". From *za* " to come " and *ila*, applicative suffix (1065).

## V. — The LI-MA Class.

**410.** — The class LI-MA includes the substantives which require the same sort of concord as (1)i-*bue* "a stone", pl. **ma-***bue* \*.

### § 1. Transformations of the Classifier LI-.

Here it becomes particularly important to distinguish the substantives which have monosyllabic stems from the generality of the others. Then we must also set aside such as have stems beginning with a vowel. Hence: —

#### I. Polysyllabic stems which begin with a consonant.

**411.** — Before the polysyllabic stems which begin with a con-

\* EXAMPLES.

|  | the devil, a pernicious spirit | | the sun, a day | | a duck | | an eye | |
|---|---|---|---|---|---|---|---|---|
|  | *Sing.* | *Plur.* | *Sing.* | *Plur.* | *Sing.* | *Plur.* | *Sing.* | *Plur.* |
| Tonga | li-saku, | ma- | (l)i-zuba, | ma- | (l)i-sekua, | ma- | li-nso, | mĕso |
| Bisa | ... | ... | ... | ... | i-dyoni, | ma- | l-inso, | mĕnso |
| Gogo | ... | ... | i-zuwa, | ma- | nyamwala, | ma- | z-iso, | mĕso |
| Sagara | i-zimu, | ma- | i-jua, | ma- | i-wata, | ma- | d-iso, | mĕso |
| Shambala | ... | ... | zua, | ma- | wata, | ma- | z-ixo, | mĕxo |
| Boondei | loho (?), | ... | zua, | ma- | wata, | ma- | z-iso, | mĕso |
| Taita | pepo(?), | ... | i-jua, | ma- | bata, | ma- | iz-izo | ... |
| Nyanyembe | li-gunhu, | ma- | li-uwa, | ma- | i-mbata, | ma. | l-iso, | m-iso |
| Sukuma | i-beho, | ma- | le-emi | ... | li-mbata (?), | ma- | d-iso | ... |
| Kamba | ... | ... | i-jua, | ma- | i-kuanyungu, | ma- | ito, | mĕnto |
| Swahili | zimui, | ma- | jua, | ma- | bata, | ma- | ji-cho, | ma- |
| Pokomo | ... | ... | dsua, | ma- | kaza, | ma- | dsi-tso, | ma- |
| Nika | pepo | ... | dzua, | ma- | bata, | ma- | dzi-tso, | ma- |
| Senna | saku (?), | ma- | dzua, | ma- | ... | ... | di-so, | ma- |
| Karanga | xaku, | ma- | juba, | ma- | ... | ... | j-ixo, | mĕxo |
| Ganda | mandwa (?) | | ... | ... | bata, | ma- | li-so, | ma- |
| Zulu-Kafir | i zimo«cannibal» | | i langa, | ma- | i dada, | a ma- | i lĭso, | a mĕhlo |
| Xosa-Kafir | i zim « cannibal » | | i langn, | ma- | i dada, | a ma- | i lĭso, | a mehlo |
| Herero | ... | ... | e yuva, | o ma- | ... | ... | ĕho, | o mĕho |
| Bihe | e li-abu | ... | e kumbi, | o va- | ... | ... | i-so, | o va- |
| Mbunda | ... | ... | li-tangwa, | ma- | ... | ... | l-ixo, | mĕxo |
| Rotse | ... | ... | li-yoba, | ma- | ... | ... | l-io (?), | mĕo |
| Guha | ... | ... | juwa, | ma- | ... | ... | l-iso, | mĕso |
| Rua | ... | ... | juva, | ma- | ... | ... | j-iso, | mĕso |
| Angola | ri-abu, | ma- | ... | ... | ... | ... | r-isu, | mĕsu |
| Lower Congo | e tombola, | ma- | ... | ... | ... | ... | d-isu, | mĕso |
| Nywema | ... | ... | yani | | ... | ... | i-so, | wa- |
| Yao | li-soka, | ma- | li-ua, | ma- | li-wata, | ma- | l-iso, | mĕso |
| Kilimane | ... | ... | n-zua, | ma- | ni-bata, | ma- | ni-to, | ma- |
| Mozambique | n-xoka, | ma- | n-chuwa, | ma- | n-rata, | ma- | n-itho, | mĕtho |
| Chwana proper | ... | ... | le-tsatsi, | ma-latsi | ... | ... | le-itlho, | ma-tlho |
| Suto | ... | ... | le-tsatsi, | ma- | ... | ... | le-itlo, | ma-tlo |
| Mpongwe | i-nini (?) | ... | ... | ... | i-zage, | a- | i-ntyɵ, | a- |
| Fan | ... | ... | yŏ | | ... | ... | d-iso, | misé |
| Dualla | i sangu = idol | | i-ve | ... | ... | ... | d-iso, | miso |
| Fernandian | ... | ... | i-tohi | ... | e-mipoto (?) | ... | j-oko | ... |
| | | | (Banapa dial.) | | | | (Ureka dial.) | |

sonant, the classifier of the singular number in this class is : —

*I-* generally, in Tonga, Bisa, Sagara, Kamba, Mpongwe, Dualla, etc.
*LI-* in Tonga, only when emphasis calls for it.
*DI-* in Tonga, after the copula *n*, according to nn. 286, 291 and 583.
*LI-* generally in Yao.
*RI-* in Angola and *DI-* in Congo. It is omitted in these languages when emphasis does not require it (321 (1)).
*LE-* generally in Chwana.
*NI-* generally in Mozambique. The vowel *i* is apparently very weak and, in some cases, omitted altogether.
*E-* in Herero. Apparently this vowel contains the article together with the classifier (317, 319).
*Omitted* generally in Kafir, Swahili, Ganda, Shambala, Nika, Senna, etc.

## EXAMPLES. (Continued.)

|  | a tooth | | a spear | | a bone | | a pumpkin | |
|---|---|---|---|---|---|---|---|---|
|  | *Sing.* | *Plur.* | *Sing.* | *Plur.* | *Sing.* | *Plur.* | *Sing.* | *Plur.* |
| Tonga | l-ino, | mēno | (l)i-sumo, | ma- | (l)i-fua, | ma- | (l)i-tanga, | ma- |
| Bisa | l-ino, | mēno | i-fumo, | ma- | ... | ... | ... | ... |
| Gogo | idz-ino, | mēno | ... | ... | ... | ... | ... | ... |
| Sagara | gego, | ma- | ... | ... | i-guha, | ma- | lengi, | ma- |
| Shambala | z-ino, | mēno | guha, | ma- | vuha (?), | ma- | tango (?), | ma- |
| Boondei | z-ino, | mēno | guha, | ma- | vuha (?), | ma- | koko, | ma- |
| Taita | i-jego, | ma- | i-chumu, | ma- | ... | ... | ... | ... |
| Nyanyembe | l-ino, | m-ino | i-cimu, | ma- | i-guha, | ma- | li-ungu, | m- |
| Sukuma | l-ino | ... | kimo | ... | ... | ... | ... | ... |
| Kamba | i-yeo, | ma- | i-tumo (?), | ma- | i-windi, | ma- | i-beki, | ma- |
| Swahili | j-ino, | mēno | fumo, | ma- | fupa (large bone) | | boga, | ma- |
| Pokomo | ... | ... | ... | ... | ... | ... | ... | ... |
| Nika | dz-ino, | mēno | fumo, | ma- | ... | ... | renge, | ma- |
| Senna | dzi-no, | ma- | dipa, | ma- | fupa, | ma- | tanga, | ma- |
| Karanga | j-ino, | meno | fumo, | ma- | fupa, | ma- | puji, | ma- |
| Ganda | li-nyo, | ma- | fumo, | ma- | gumba, | ma- | boga, | ma- |
| Zulu-Kafir | i zinyo, | a menyo | ... | ... | i tambo, | a ma- | i tanga, | a ma- |
| Xosa-Kafir | i zinyo, | a menyo | ... | ... | i tambo, | a ma- | i tanga, | a ma- |
| Herero | e yo, | o ma-yo | e nga, | o ma- | e tupa, | o ma- | ... | ... |
| Bihe | e yu, | o va- | ... | ... | e kepa, | o va- | ... | ... |
| Mbunda | ... | ... | li-onga, | ma- | ... | ... | li-mputo, | ma- |
| Rotse | li-yeo, | ma- | pinje, | ma-(?) | ... | ... | ... | ... |
| Guha | l-ino, | mēno | fumu, | ma- | ... | ... | ... | ... |
| Rua | j-ino, | meno | ... | ... | i-kupa (?), | ma- | ... | ... |
| Angola | ri-ju, | ma- | ... | ... | ... | ... | ... | ... |
| Lower Congo | d-inu, | mēno | e di-onga, | ma-di- | ... | ... | e-lenge, | ma- |
| Nywema | li-nyu, | wa- | li-konga | | ... | ... | ... | ... |
| Yao | l-ino, | nīcno | li-panga, | ma- | li-upa, | ma- | li-ungu, | ma- |
| Kilimane | l-ino, | mēno | ... | ... | ... | ... | ... | ... |
| Mozambique | n-ino, | meno | ni-vaka, | ma- | ni-kuva, | ma- | n-chuchu, | ma- |
| Chwana proper | le-ino, | mēno | le-rumo, | ma- | le-sapo, | ma-rapo | le-phutse, | ma- |
| Suto | le-ino, | mēno | le-rumo, | ma- | le-sapo, | ma- | le-phutse, | ma- |
| Mpongwe | i-no, | a- | i-gonga, | a- | ... | ... | i-loge, | a- |
| Fan | a-sŏn, | mesŏn | a-kŏn, | ma- | ... | ... | ... | ... |
| Dualla | i-sunga, | ma- | ... | ... | ... | ... | ... | ... |
| Fernandian | ?, | bĕlo | ... | ... | ... | ... | ... | ... |

**412.** — 1. In Kafir the article *i*, and in Congo the article *e*, before substantives of this class must not be mistaken for the classifier.

2. In Nika we find the word *domo* " a large lip ", of cl. LI-MA, derived from *mu-lomo* " a lip ". The dental *d* in this word points to the influence of a suppressed *n* before it. Several links connecting Nika with Mozambique may have been observed in the previous chapter. This is another. Likewise in Senna some substantives of this class LI-MA begin in the singular by double consonantal sounds which are simplified in the plural, as if the presence of these sounds in the singular were the result of a suppressed *n*. Ex. tsamba " a leaf ", pl. *ma-samba* (Father Courtois' " *Grammatica Tetense*, " p. 28). Cf. 99, N. B.

### II. Monosyllabic stems.

**413.** — In the words which have monosyllabic stems the law of avoiding single sounds (44) causes all sorts of irregularities, as may be noticed in the subjoined tables of examples under the words *eye, tooth,* and *stone*.

### EXAMPLES. (Continued.)

| | a stone | | the sky | | a hoe | | a name | |
|---|---|---|---|---|---|---|---|---|
| | *Sing.* | *Plur.* | *Sing.* | *Plur.* | *Sing.* | *Plur.* | *Sing.* | *Plur.* |
| Tonga | (l)i-bue, | ma- | (l)ij-ulu, | ma- | (l)ij-amba, | ma- | (l)i-zina, | ma- |
| Bisa | i ri-bue, | ma- | i-vimbi, | ma- | ... | ... | i-sina, | ma- |
| Gogo | i-bue, | ma- | vunde (?), | ma- | i-sile, | ma- | i-tagwa, | ma- |
| Sagara | i-bue, | ma- | ... | ... | i-sire, | ma- | i-sina (?), | ma- |
| Shambala | iwe, | ma-iwe | ... | ... | gembe, | ma- | zina, | ma- |
| Boondei | i-we, | ma- | ... | ... | gembe, | ma- | zina, | ma- |
| Taita | i-we, | ma- | ... | ... | i-gembe, | ma- | i-zina, | ma- |
| Nyanyembe | i-we, | ma- | i-lunde, | ma- | i-gembe, | ma- | i-gina, | ma- |
| Sukuma | i-we, | ma- | i-lunde, | ... | ... | ... | l-ina | ... |
| Kamba | i-ɓia, | ma- | ... | ... | i-zembe, | ma- | dz-itwa | ... |
| Swahili | ji-we, | ma- | ... | ... | jembe, | ma- | dzina, | ma- |
| Pokomo | dzi-we, | ma- | ... | ... | ... | ... | zari, | ma- |
| Nika | i-we, | ma- | ... | ... | jembe, | ma- | dzina, | ma- |
| Senna | ... | ... | ... | ... | paze, | ma- | dzina, | ma- |
| Karanga | ji-bwe, | ma- | ... | ... | ... | ... | zina, | ma- |
| Ganda | j-inja, | ma- | gulu, | ma- | ... | ... | li-nya | ... |
| Zulu-Kafir | i li-tye, | a ma- | i zulu, | a ma- | i kuba, | a ma- | i gama, | a ma- |
| Xosa-Kafir | i li-tye, | a ma- | i zulu, | a ma- | i kuba, | a ma- | i gama, | a ma- |
| Herero | e oe, | o ma- | e yuru, | o ma- | ... | ... | e na, | o ma- |
| Bihe | e-we, | o va- | ... | ... | e-temo, | o va- | ... | ... |
| Mbunda | le-manya, | ma-nki (?) | li-elo (?) | ... | li-tema, | ma- | ... | ... |
| Rotse | li-yoe, | ma- | li-uilo, | ma- | le-kao, | ma- | ... | ... |
| Guha | di-bue, | ma- | i-ulu | ... | ... | ... | sina (?) | |
| Rua | ji-ve (?), | ma- | ... | ... | ... | ... | i-sina (?) | |
| Angola | ri-tari, | ma- | rilu, | maulu | ri-temu, | ma- | ri-jina, | ma- |
| Lower Congo | e-tadi, | ma- | e-zulu, | ma- | ... | ... | e-jina, | ma- |
| Nywema | ... | ... | ... | ... | ... | ... | ... | ... |
| Yao | li-ganga, | ma- | li-unde, | ma- | li-jela, | ma- | l-ina, | mēna |
| Kilimane | ... | ... | ... | ... | ... | ... | ni-zina (?), | ma- |
| Mozambique | n-luku, | ma- | ni-hute, | ma- | n-hipa (?) | ... | n-china, | ma- |
| Chwana proper | le-ncwe, | ma-je | le-godimo, | ma- | ... | ... | le-ina, | ma- |
| Suto | le-ncue, | ma-joe | le-golimo, | ma- | ... | ... | le-bitso, | ma- |
| Mpongwe | i-do, | a- | ... | ... | ... | ... | i-ni, | a- |
| Fan | a-kogk (?) | | ... | ... | ... | ... | dyĕ | ... |
| Dualla | i-dali, | ma- | d-oba (?) | | di-bau, | ma- | dina, | ma- |
| Fernandian | i-te, | ba- | ... | . | ... | ... | i-la, | ba- (?) |

**414.** — *N. B.* 1. In Chwana the word *le-n-cwe* " a stone ", pl. *ma-jwe*, when compared with *le-cogo* " an arm ", plur. *ma-bogo*, *le-sama* " a cheek ", pl. *ma-rama*, etc., leads me to suspect that Chwana has undergone here the influence of a language like Mozambique in which the regular form of the classifier LI is NI or N. I see no other way of explaining the presence of *n* in *le-n-cwe* " a stone " (= Tonga *i-bue*, cf. 185+203). I have little doubt that we must have recourse to the same influence to explain the changes of *b* to the dental *c* in *le-cogo*, and *r* to the more dental *s* in *le-sama* (Tonga *i-tama*).

2. The variety noticeable in the formation of the words which have monosyllabic stems may be attributed in part to that sort of affinity between *i* and *n* which causes them to interchange in certain cases (285). This, coupled with transposition of letters, would explain the presence of *n* in the Tonga word *li-nso* " an eye " (Subia *li-nso*, Kamba *me-nto*, Nyambu *me-nso*, etc.). For in these words the regular form of the stem is probably -*sio*, which we find retained in the Tonga *bu-sio* " the face ", lit. " the place of the eyes ".

### III. Stems which begin with a vowel.

**415.** — In the words which have stems beginning with a vowel-sound either the classifier LI- is somewhat transformed, as in the Tonga word *(i)j-anza* (256) " a hand ", (plur. *ma-anza*), or a euphonic consonant, generally *g*, is inserted between the classifier and the stem, as in the Kaguru word *i-ganja* " a hand "; or again in a few languages the classifier LI- is used without any change, as in the Nyamwezi word *li-ungu* " a pumpkin " (Steere).

*N. B.* In the Herero *e-oe* " a stone ", and the like, the vowel *o* must be considered as having a semi-vowel or consonantal value, or as being preceded by a sort of labial aspiration which replaces the Tonga *b* of *i-bue*. Otherwise the classifier *e* would probably undergo a change.

### § 2. Transformations of the classifier MA-.

**416.** — The regular form of this classifier is : —
*MA-* in almost all the Bantu languages.

*N. B.* The exceptional form *ME-* is easily explained according to the laws of contraction (249).
*A-* regularly, *AM-* before vowels, in Mpongwe.
*A-* or *WA-* in Nywema.
*VA-* in Nano and Bihe (131).

### § 3. Substantives which belong to the Class LI-MA.

**417.** — The substantives which are brought under this class are principally such as refer to the following : —

**418.** — 1° Such persons or animals as are unproductive, barren or only productive of harm, and such as have a naked body, or a sleek, rigid, and relatively flat appearance, as *i-saku* " the devil ", *i-buto* " a naked slave ", (such as those which are employed by the

Rotse to row), *i-panda* " a water tortoise ", *i-sekua* " a duck ", etc. Hence also in several languages the young of animals, as, in Kafir, *i-tole* " a calf, a young of animal ", *i-takane* " a kid ", *i-tokazi* " a heifer, a female lamb or kid ", *i-tshontsho* " a nestling ", etc.

**419.** — 2° Fruits and those parts of bodies which are relatively hard, or bare, or flat, as *i-ji* " an egg ", *i-buyu* " the fruit of the baobab ", *i-konka* " a cocoanut ", *i-ja* " a horn, a tusk of elephant ", *i-fua* " a bone ", *ij-anza* " a hand ", *li-nso* " an eye ", *li-no* " a tooth ", *i-tama* " a cheek ", *i-kanda* " the skin ", *i-bele* " a woman's breast ", which in Bantu proverbs is compared to a stone (cf. Héli Chatelain's *Kimbundu Gr.*, p. 145), *i-baba* " a wing ", etc.

**420.** — 3° Such things in nature as are hard or unproductive, as *i-bue* " a stone ", *i-zulu* " the sky ", which the ancients thought to be hard as brass (Job, XXXVII, 18), *i-yoba* " a cloud " (*Ibid.*, v. 21), *i-saka* " a sandy unproductive land ", *i-dose* " a drop of water ", *i-suko* " dust ", *i-tue* " ashes ", etc.

**421.** — 4° The " sun ", or " day ", **i-zuba**, and those relations of time and place which the Bantu associate with the day, or with the various positions of the sun, as *i-jilo* " yesterday ", *i-junza* " tomorrow ", *i-golezia* " evening ", *li-no* " now " ; *i-tale* " the side of a river, or of other things ", etc.

**422.** — 5° Those tools and artificial objects which are hard, or flat and smooth, as *ij-amba* " a hoe ", *i-jegeso* " a saw ", *i-hola* " a kind of knife ", *i-kuati* " a table ", *i-sumo* " a spear ", etc.

**423.** — 6° Words and distinct sounds, as *i-zina* " a name ", *i-jui* " a loud sound ", *i-ko* " coughing ", *i-zumo* " a thunderclap ", etc.

**424.** — 7° A few actions, as *i-jayo* " a murder ", *i-guyulo* " a wound ", etc.

**425.** — To these must be added in several Bantu languages, e. g. in Tonga, Shambala, Nika, Swahili, Karanga, etc., *augmentative nouns*, or names of such persons or things as are remarkably tall, or high, or long, or large, as *i-lundu* " a high mountain ", *i-yuni* " a large bird ", *i-samo* " a high tree ", or " a large piece of timber "; etc.

**426.** — *N. B.* 1. In such augmentative nouns the classifier of the singular number seems to be used regularly with its full form *li-*, e. g. *li-tui*, "a long ear", *li-bizi*, "a large horse, " etc.

## The LI-MA Class.

**427.** — 2. Some augmentative nouns have two forms, one which keeps the usual classifier together with the augmentative particle, another which drops the same classifier. Ex. *jen-zoka* (= *li-en-zoka*) or *li-zoka* (from the usual noun *in-zoka* " a snake ") " a large snake ".

**428.** — 3. Augmentative nouns are comparatively little used in Tonga, as if they were somewhat foreign to that language.

### § 4. Etymologies. — Varia.

**429.** — The Rev. F. W. Kolbe in his ' *'Language Study based on Bantu* ", p. 52, considers the particle *li* to be 1°) the proper prefix for names of dead things, and 2°) to signify " in ", this, he thinks, being the reason why it is applied to "the dead teeth *in* the mouth, the bones *in* the body, the stones and metals *in* the earth ". The first part of this opinion may be correct enough, but the second part is more than probably the very reverse. And, if any classifiers signify " in ", these are rather the particles MU- and IN- which, as we have seen, are principally applied to such things as are covered with hair, or vegetation, or something similar, thus recalling to mind the fact that in ancient Egyptian a hieroglyph representing " a skin " is often affixed to the names of quadrupeds.

**430.** — More probably the classifier LI- or RI-, in the generality of the substantives of this LI-MA class, is rather the naked form of the verb -*lia* or -*ria* " to eat ", the same exactly as that which we have in the following expressions taken from Kolbe's *Herero Dictionary : matu* ri, " we ate " ; *ze 'sa ze tokere aze* ri, " let them feed till sunset ". Hence the notion of strength which this particle contains. Hence likewise its augmentative power, because to a Kafir mind the notion of " king " and " lord " is convertible with that of " well fed ". Hence also its adaptation to the teeth, and to whatever has a crushing power, as stones ; and again to such things as are hard or resistant, as also to fruits, eggs, bones, breasts, or other parts of bodies which draw to themselves the best substance of these. Hence again its adaptation to the sun, which according to the manner of speaking of these people, *eats* all that the moon (**mu**-*ezi*) labours to bring out of the earth (384 (10)), thus filling people both with reverence and terror by its power to cause the fearful droughts. Hence finally, on the one side its application to the eye, which is to the body what the sun is to the world, and on the other side to sterile beings, as also to such as are the terror of weak and superstitious people.

**431.** — *N. B.* 1. This conclusion is of some importance, as I notice that several missionaries honour the devil with the classifier MU-, calling him *mu-diaboli*, or some similarly formed word, which evidently is calculated to convey to the minds the very opposite of the notion it is intended to express. More logical than ourselves, the natives of Angola have changed the Portuguese *diabo*, not into *mu-diabo* or *mu-diaboli*, but into *ri-abu* or *äi-abu*.

**432.** — 2. Both my Tonga and my Kafir informants used to say that the particle *li-*, sometimes replaced by *izi-* before monosyllables, forms " bad names ". And my Tonga informants added that this was the reason why a certain white man, whom they had heard of in the interior, and of whom the less said the better, had not been called *mu-nkua*, as other white men, but *izi-kua*.

**433.** — Probably in some substantives of this class LI-MA, as in *i-lo* " a bed ", *ij-ulu* " the sky ", etc., the particle LI- is etymologically connected, not with the verb *-lia*, but with the element *-le* (Kafir *-de*) " long, high, far ", which seems to be itself essentially a form of the reduplicative verb *-la-la* " to lie down, to be stretched ".

**434.** — And in some others, as in *i-jui* " a sound ", *i-ko* " sneezing, coughing ", *i-zina* " a name ", etc. the particle *-li-* rather reminds of the verb *-lila* " to produce a sound ".

**435.** — Another question is whether the three verbs *-lia* " to eat ", *-lala* " to be stretched ", *-lila* " to cry ", are themselves formed from one and the same root. But this is not the place to discuss it.

**436.** — With regard to the plural classifier MA-, there appears no serious reason to say with the Rev. J. Rath (Bleek's *Comp. Gr.*, p. 200), that it is mainly used when speaking of things which constantly go in pairs. More probably the classifier MA- expresses properly " the end of natural production or multiplication ", being radically identical with the verb *-mala* or *mana* (280, 1065) " to end, to cease to produce ", exactly as the plural classifiers BA-, MI-, ZIN- are radically connected with the verbs *bala*, *mila*, *ziala*, all of which express *production* or *plurality*.

**437.** — This opinion is corroborated by the fact that the classifiers MA-, BA-, MI-, ZIN- are always long and accented, which is not the case with the singular classifiers MU-, IN-, LI-. And further it well agrees with the fact that the classifier MA- is precisely the plural for fruits " the end of the production of trees ", for the young of animals, for extremities of the body, for stones, bones, and other such things apparently no more subject to transformations.

**438.** — *N. B.* All this of course leaves more or less room for exceptions in the different languages, according as they have been more or less modified by foreign influence or other causes. Then it should always be remembered that the same things may be viewed in different lights, and brought accordingly under different classes. Hence from such words as mw-*ala* " a stone " (in Senna), *e* n-*juba*, " the sun " (in Ganda), *i* si-*qamo*, " a fruit " (in Kafir), etc., nothing can be inferred against the above conclusions.

**439.** — As to the substantives which may be found under n. 410 : —

1. We have only doubtful etymologies to give for *i-saku* " a pernicious spirit ", *li-no* " a tooth ", *i-tanga* " a pumpkin ", *ij-amba* " a hoe ", and *i-zina* " a name ".

2. *I-zuba* " the sun ", lit. " that which comes out with light ". From -*zua* " to come out ", and -*uba* " notion of light ".

3. *I-sekua* " a duck " is an onomatopoetic word derived from the cry of this bird. When I asked my Tonga informants what they meant by an *i-sekua*, their first answer was " the bird which makes *kua-kua*... ". *Bata* " a duck ", of Swahili, Ganda, etc., reminds one of the Old Egyptian word *apt* " a goose ".

4. *Li-nso* " the eye ", lit " that part of the body which can be veiled" is connected with *ku-sia* " to be veiled, dark " (285).

5. *I-sumo* " a spear ", lit. " that which disappears within (the body) ". From *su* " notion of disappearing " which we find in *ku*-su*ana* " to disappear within one another ", and *mo* " inside " (384 (4 and 7)).

6. *I-fua* " a bone ", lit. " a dead member ". From *ku-fua* " to die ". The element *fu* (Herero *tu*) may be said to convey the meaning of " death " almost in every Bantu word in which it is found.

7. *I-bue* " a stone ", lit. " that which falls, is heavy " (in all probability). From *ku-ua* (Angola *ku-bua*) " to fall " (cf. 462*).

8. *Ij-ulu* " the sky " lit. " that which is stretched out ". Related to the passive form -*ulua* of the element -*ula* which forms expansive verbs (1080).

# VI. — The BU-MA Class

## and the

## Sub-classes connected with it.

**440.** — The class BU-MA contains the substantives which require the same sort of concord as **bu-**_ato_ " a canoe ", plur. **ma-**_ato_. We connect with it the sub-class MA without singular (Ex. **ma-**_nzi_ " water "), as well as the sub-class BU without plural (Ex. **bu-**_su_ " flour "), and the sub-class BU-ZIN (Ex. in Nyamwezi **w-**_ato_ " a canoe ", plur. **ny-**_ato_ *).

**441.** — The reason for connecting the sub-class MA without singular with the class BU-MA is that the same words which

### * EXAMPLES.

|  | the face |  | grass | fermented drink beer, wine | the brains | flour |
|---|---|---|---|---|---|---|
|  | Sing. | Plur. |  |  |  |  |
| Tonga | bu-sio, | ma- | bu-izu | bu-kande (?) | bu-ongo | bu-su |
| Bisa | ... | ... | ... | ... | ... | bu-nga |
| Gogo | u-su | ... | ... | ... | ... | u-sagi |
| Sagara | ... | ... | ma-nyari | u-gimbi | w-ongo (?) | u-sagi |
| Shambala | ... | ... | ... | ... | uw-ongo | ... |
| Boondei | ... | ... | m-ani | ... | uw-ongo | u-nga |
| Taita | u-xu | ... | ma-nyasi | ... | w-ongo | u-nga |
| Nyanyembe | w-ixu | ... | ma-swa | bw-alwa | w-ongo | wu-su |
| Sukuma | ... | ... | ... | ... | w-ongo (?) | u-su |
| Kamba | u-ɓio, | n-zio | ... | ... | ... | ... |
| Swahili | u-so, | nyu- | ma-jani | u-ji « gruel » | w-ongo | u-nga |
| Pokomo | u-so | ... | (w-idzi «green») | ... | ... | u-nga |
| Nika | u-so | ... | ... | u-ji | ongo | u-nga |
| Senna | ma-so | ... | ma-u-dzu | bu-adua | w-ongo (?) | u-fa |
| Karanga | ... | ... | wu-ƙua | wu-kube (?) | wu-rubi | .. |
| Ganda | ma-so | ... | bu-so | m-alua | bu-ongo | bu-ta |
| Zulu-Kafir | u bu-so | ... | u ty-ani | u tyw-ala | ... | ... |
| Xosa-Kafir | u bu-so | ... | u ty-ani | u tyw-ala | ... | ... |
| Herero | ... | ... | ... | ... | o u-ruvi | ... |
| Bihe | ... | ... | o w-ongu | u-tepa | o w-ongo | ... |
| Mbunda | ... | ... | bo-ambo | bo-ala | ... | ... |
| Rotse | ... | ... | mōpo (= ma-upo) | ma-lupo | o-loi | o-nga |
| Guha | ... | ... | ... | ... | ... | u-xie (?) |
| Rua | ... | ... | ... | ma-lovu | ... | ... |
| Angola | ... | ... | (u-isu«green») | u-alua | ... | ... |
| Lower Congo | ... | ... | ... | ... | ... | ... |
| Yao | ... | ... | ma-nyasi | u-tulua | u-tutu | u-tandi |
| Kilimane | ... | ... | ma-ane | u-alua | ... | u-to |
| Mozambique | w-ito | ... | ma-nyaxi | ... | u-koko | ... |
| Chwana proper | ma-itlho | ... | bo-jang | bo-jalwa | bo-koko | bu-pi |
| Suto | ma-tlo | ... | bo-jang | bo-jalwa | bo-koko | bu-pi |
| Mpongwe | o-ju, | a- | am-ani | ... | ... | ... |
| Dualla | b-oso, | mi- | bi-ulu (?) | ma-u | ... | ... |
| Fan | ... | ... | b-ut | ... | ... | ... |
| Fernandian | bu-so | ... | ... | ba-u | ... | ... |

require the classifier BU- in Tonga are found to require the classifier MA- in a certain number of the other languages.

§ 1. Forms in the Class BU-MA and the Sub-class MA-.

**442.** — The classifier MA-, both in those substantives which have no singular, and in those which require BU- in the singular number, is essentially identical with the MA- of class LI-MA. Hence the same variations of its forms, viz. *ma-, a-, me-, am-, va-*, etc.

**443.** — But in some languages we meet with this peculiar phenomenon, that between MA- and the stem of the substantive BU- is retained under one form or another. Hence the following plurals, apparently irregular : in Angola *mota* " bows " (= *ma-u-ta*,

EXAMPLES. (Continued.)

| | night | | a boat | | (names of countries) |
|---|---|---|---|---|---|
| | *Sing.* | *Plur.* | *Sing.* | *Plur.* | |
| Tonga | bu-siku | | bu-ato, | ma- | *Bu-tonga*, Tongaland |
| Bisa | bu-siku | | bu-ato, | ma- | ... ... |
| Gogo | ... | | ... | ... | *U-gogo*, Gogoland |
| Sagara | ... | | ... | ... | *U-sagara*, Sagaraland |
| Shambala | ... | | ... | ... | *U-xambala*, Sambaraland |
| Boondei | ... | | ... | ... | ... ... |
| Taita | ... | | ... | ... | ... ... |
| Nyanyembe | wu-ziku | | w-ato, | ny- | *U-nyamwezi*, the Nyamwezi country |
| Sukuma | u-ziku | | ... | ... | ... ... |
| Kamba | u-tuka, | n-z... | ... | ... | *U-kamba*, Kambaland |
| Swahili | u-siku | | ... | ... | *U-nguja*, Zanzibar |
| Pokomo | ... | | w-aho | ... | |
| Nika | u-siku | | ... | ... | |
| Senna | u-siku, | ma- | ... | ... | *U-sungu*, the Portuguese territory |
| Karanga | wu-siku | | wu-ato | ... | *Wu-karanga*, Karangaland. |
| Ganda | ... | | ... | ... | *Bu-ganda*, the Ganda Empire |
| Zulu-Kafir | u bu-suku | | ... | ... | ... ... |
| Xosa-Kafir | u bu-suku | | ... | ... | ... ... |
| Herero | o u-tuku | | ... | ... | ... ... |
| Bihe | u-teke | | o w-ato | ... | ... ... |
| Mbunda | bo-rike | | bo-ato | ... | ... ... |
| Rotse | o-siko | | w-ato | ... | *O-lumbu* (?), the Rotse Empire |
| Guha | u-fuku | | w-ato | ... | ... ... |
| Rua | u-sikua | | u-kula | ... | *U-rua*, the Rotse country |
| Angola | u-suku | | u-lungu (?), | ... | ... ... |
| Lower Congo | fuku, | ma- | lungu, | ma- | ... ... |
| Yao | ... | ... | w-ato, | ma- | ... ... |
| Kilimane | ma-tio | | b-ote(?),ma-b-ote | | ... ... |
| Mozambique | u-hiu | | ... | ... | ... ... |
| Chwana proper | bo-sigo | | ... | ... | *Bo-rwa*, the country of the Bushmen |
| Suto | bo-sigo | | ... | ... | ... ... |
| Mpongwe | o-gwera, | i- | ow-aro, | am- | ... ... |
| Dualla | b-ulu | | b-olo, | mi- | ... ... |
| Fan | ... | | bi-al | ... | ... ... |
| Fernandian | bo-chio (?) | | b-ato, | bi- (?) | ... ... |

sing. *u-ta*, in Herero *o ma-u-ta*, in Nyamwezi *ma-wu-ta*, etc.), in Senna *ma-u-dzu* " straw ", in Nyamwezi *ma-wu-ziku* (?) " nights " (sing. *wu-ziku*), etc.

**444.** — *N. B.* Were it not for this last example, in which the stem has two syllables, I should see a new application of the laws relative to monosyllables (44, 413, etc.) in this fact of the retention of the classifier BU- after MA-. But then it should be said that the classifier MA- (and the same might be said of the element ZI- in the classifier ZIN-) is not so intimately united with the stem which follows it as to have a *single* accent (44) and to form rigorously a *single* word with it. MA- should therefore rather be considered as a sort of adjective preceding its substantive.

**445.** — The classifier which has the form BU- in Tonga has the same form in Bisa, Bemba, Subia, Ganda, Kafir, Lojazi, etc. In Kafir this classifier changes to *ty-* or *tyw-* before vowels, according to n. 122, as in *u ty-ani* " grass " (= *u bu-ani*), and apparently to

### EXAMPLES. (Continued.)

|  | wool | clay | life | water | fat |
|---|---|---|---|---|---|
| Tonga | bu-oya | bu-longo | bu-umi | ma-nzi | ma-futa |
| Bisa | ... | ... | ... | mēnsi | ... |
| Gogo | ... | ... | ... | ma-renga | ... |
| Sagara | ... | u-longo | u-gima | mēji | ma-futa |
| Shambala | ... | u-longo | ... | ma-zi | ma-vuta |
| Boondei | ... | u-longo | u-gima | ma-zi | ma-vuta |
| Taita | ... | ... | u-zima | mēji | ma-vuta |
| Nyanyembe | w-oya | wu-lolo | wu-panga | m-inzi | ma-guta |
| Sukuma | ... | ... | ... | m-inzi | ma-guta |
| Kamba | u-wea | ... | u-ima | ma-nzi | ma-uta |
| Swahili | ... | u-dongo | u-zima | ma-ji | ma-futa |
| Pokomo | ... | ... | ... | ma-dzi | ma-fuha |
| Nika | ... | u-longo | u-zima | ma-dzi | ma-fuha |
| Senna | u-bwea | ... | ... | ma-dzi | ma-futa |
| Karanga | ... | ... | wu-penyo | ... | ma-futa |
| Ganda | bu-iza (?) | bu-mba | bu-lamu | ma-dzi | ma-savui |
| Zulu-Kafir | u b-oya | u bu-longo | u b-omi | a ma-nzi | a ma-futa |
| Xosa-Kafir | u b-oya | u bu-longo | u b-omi | a ma-nzi | a ma-futa |
| Herero | o ma-inya | ... | ... | o mēva | o ma-je |
| Bihe | ... | o-tuma (?) | ... | o va-va | o vēte |
| Mbunda | ... | ... | ... | mēma | ma-ze |
| Rotse | ōia | o-toko (?) | ... | me-i | ma-je |
| Guha | ... | ... | ... | ma-ji | ... |
| Rua | ... | ... | u-umi (?) | mēma | ma-ni |
| Angola | ... | ma-vunzu | ... | mēnia | ma-ji |
| Lower Congo | w-ika | ... | ... | ma-za | ma-ji |
| Yao | u-mbo (?) | u-tope | u-umi | mēsi | ma-uta |
| Kilimane | ... | ma-taka | ... | ma-ije | ma-kurra |
| Mozambique | ... | ... | u-kumi | ma-xi | ma-kura |
| Chwana proper | bo-boea | bo-raga | bo-tshelo | mētse | ma-fura |
| Suto | bo-ea | bo-raga | bo-tshelo | mētse | ma-fura |
| Mpongwe | o-mwa | o-mbona | ... | a-ningo | a-gali |
| Dualla | ... | ... | ... | ma-diba | m-ula |
| Fan | ... | b-oka | ... | ma-chi | ... |
| Fernandian | bi-riba (?) | ba-isopa (?) | ... | bo-opi | bi-ta |

*j-* in the plural form of the same word in the Swahili *ma-j-ani* (= *ma-wu-ani*), etc.

**446.** — Other forms are : —

*BO-* in Chwana, which changes to *bo-j-* (= *bo-bo-*, 202) before vowels, e. g. in *bo-jang* " grass " (Mpongwe *am-ani*), *bo-j-alwa* " beer " (Mbunda *bo-ala*, Nyamwezi, *bw-alwa*, etc.), as if, the origin of the *j* for *bo-* (n. 202) in such words having been forgotten by the Chwana, they had restored *bo-* before it, either for the sake of uniformity, or to prevent all doubt as to the proper class of the same words. For the same reasons such Kafirs as have only a half-knowledge of their language say sometimes *u bu-tyw-ala* " beer ", instead of *u-tyw-ala*.

**447.** — *WU-* regularly in Karanga, Nyamwezi, etc.

**448.** — *U-* (*w-* or *uw-* before vowels), with a sort of *spiritus asper*, in Herero, Swahili, Nika, Senna, Angola, etc.

**449.** — *O-* (*ow-* before vowels) in Mpongwe, also in Rotse and Nyengo, unless Livingstone's spelling was influenced by Chwana, when he wrote his notes on these languages.

**450.** — It is *dropped* in Congo, where however it is retained under the form *w-* before vowels.

**451.** — *N. B.* 1. Bleek's remark (*Comp. Gr.*, p. 273) that this particle is sometimes elided in Kafir and Chwana does not seem to be correct. The error comes from not noticing the change of *bu* or *bo-* to *ty*, *j*, etc., before vowels.

2. The proper form of this classifier in Dualla, Fan, and Fernandian, is not evident from the documents I have come across.

## § 2. THE SUB-CLASSES BU WITHOUT PLURAL AND BU-ZIN.

**452.** — Of the words which have the classifier BU- by far the larger number have no plural form, because they express properly a sort of collective or abstract notion. They form the sub-class BU without plural.

**453.** — The sub-class BU-ZIN exists only in Swahili and in a few other languages.

*N. B.* The origin of the class BU-ZIN in Swahili comes from the confusion of the class BU-MA with the class LU-ZIN, through the fall of *b* and *l* in LU- and BU- (86 and 100). Hence the word *u-ta* " a bow " is mentioned by Krapf as having two plurals, viz. : *ma-ta* and *ny-u-ta* (*za...*); *u-so* " face " is said to have no other plural form than *ny-u-so*, etc. However *u-siku* " night " has only its regular plural *ma-siku*. This reminds one that the expression " at night " is rendered in Tonga by *ma-n-siku*, and in Senna by *ma-siku*. Cf. 556.

## § 3. SUBSTANTIVES WHICH BELONG TO THE CLASS BU-MA AND THE SUB-CLASSES CONNECTED WITH IT.

**454.** — The substantives which have no other classifier than MA- are principally those of fluids or quasi-fluids, or again of things which melt naturally, as *ma-nzi* " water ", *ma-lidi* " sour milk ", *ma-tanana* " snow ", etc.

*N. B.* 1. In several languages, principally in Chwana, MA- is often used to express great number. Ex. *ma-bitse* " many horses " (cf. *di-pitse* (390, 395) " horses ").

2. In Senna the classifier MA- is regularly used to form names of actions from applicative verbs. Ex. *ma-limiro* " agriculture ", from *ku-lima* " to cultivate the ground " (applicative : *ku-limira* (1065)), *ma-fambiro* " a journey ", from *ku-famba* " to go ", (applicative : *ku-fambira*), etc.

**455.** — The nouns which have the classifier BU- are principally those of : —

1° Things which ferment, or generate bubbles, as *bu-kande* and *bu-koko* " beer, wine ", *bu-su* " flour ", *bu-longo* " wet cow-dung " and " pot-clay ", *bu-ongo* " the brains ", *bu-loa* " the blood ", *bu-ci* " honey ", which Kafirs make into a fermented beverage, *bu-tale* " iron ore ", *bu-la* " the bowels ", *bu-si* " smoke ", *bu-ele* " small pox ", etc.

**456.** — Things which come into being or grow to light collectively and by gentle heat, as *bu-ana buenkuku*, " chickens ", *bu-izu* " grass ", etc.

**457.** — 3° " The night, " *bu-siku;* " the face, " *bu-sio*, and those feelings of the soul which transfigure the face, as *bu-botu* " a good face ", i. e. " happiness " and " kindness ", *bu-bi* " an ugly face ", etc.

**458.** — 4° Authority or empire, *bu-ame;* whence the sphere itself of authority, as *Bu-ganda* " the Ganda Empire ", etc.

**459.** — 5° " A canoe, " *bu-ato;* " a bow, *bu-ta*, " etc.

## § 4. Etymologies. — Varia.

**460.** — The etymology of the classifier MA- has been sufficiently studied in the preceding article. With regard to the classifier BU-, it is pretty certain that it implies generally readiness to *reaction* and *transformation*, whether by fermentation, as in " beer ", " flour ", etc.; or by hatching, as in " a brood " ; or by smelting, as in " iron ore " ; or by a fresh start, as in " the grass " so easily refreshed, and in " night ", which to a Kafir mind is nothing else than the universal silent renewing of nature after " the fall of the sun " ; or by transfiguration, as in " the face ", the mirror of the soul, and in " authority"; or by plasticity, as in " clay ", and in " cow-dung", which is generally used by Kafirs for plastering their huts ; or again by elasticity, as in " a bow "; or even by readiness for a change of position (?), as in " a canoe ", etc. All this supplies plenty of suggestive materials for the study of the association of ideas.

This classifier BU- in many words is unmistakably related to the verb *-bumba* (= *bubua*, cf. 285) " to work clay, to shape " (cf. 52*). And it probably is to *-ua* (*-bua* or *-gua*) " to fall " (462*) what the classifier LI- is to *-lia* " to eat " (430). Hence it seems to mean primarily " that which falls, which cannot stand upright or firm ".

**461.** — Coming back to the examples under n. 440, we may make the following statements : —

1. In *bu-sio* " the face " the element *-sio* is unmistakably the same as that which gives us *li-nso* " the eye ", pl. *mēso* (439 (4)). Hence the proper meaning of *bu-sio* must be " the place of the eyes ", or more exactly " that which falls over the eyes ". In Senna, Chwana, etc., the word for " face " is no other than that which means " eyes ".

2. *Bu-izu* " grass ", lit. " that which comes out (of the ground) ". Cf. 409 (2).

3. *Bu-alua* " fermented liquor ", lit. " a thing for bewitching ". From *-lua* or *-loa* " to bewitch ". In *ma-luvu* (perhaps *m-aluvu*), which is the word for " palm-wine " in several dialects of Angola and the neighbouring countries, the element *-vu* seems to add to *bu-alua* the notion of " vomiting ", or that of " foam " produced by fermenting liquors.

4. In *bu-ongo* " the brains ", and *bu-longo* " clay, cow-dung ", etc., the element *ngo* conveys very probably the notion of " something soft "; but I do not see exactly what notion is conveyed by the elements *o* and *lo*. In *bu-longo*, however, the element *lo* means probably " that which is spread " (Cf. 384 (9, 8, and 4)).

5. In *bu-siku* " the night " the element *si* is related to the verb *ku-sia* " to be veiled, to be dark ", and the element *ku* to the adjective *-kulu* " great ". Hence this word means lit. " great darkness ". The first element *si* is replaced in some languages by the element *su*, notion of " disappearing ", in others by *fu* (Herero *tu*), notion of " death ". Hence the words *bu-suku*, *bu-fuku*, and *u-tuku*.

6. *Bu-su* " flour ", lit. " that which is pulverized and rendered almost invisible. " From the element *su*, notion of " disappearing ".

7. *Bu-ato* " a canoe ", lit. " a thing for ferrying across ". From *a* " of ", and *to*, notion of " carrying ". Cf. *ku-tola* " to carry ".

8. *Bu-tonga* " Tongaland " (cf. 365 (5)).

9. *Bu-umi* " life ". From the adjective *-umi* " alive ".

10. *Ma-nzi* " water ", lit. " that which fecundates " (384 (10)). Karanga renders " water " by *i-vura*, which properly means " rain ". Thus it is perhaps of all the Bantu languages the only one in which the word for " water " is not of cl. MA. This peculiar exception is probably due to the custom, common to several South-African tribes, of not pronouncing the names of revered persons nor any of their principal parts. For I notice that the Chwana word for " water ", *metsi*, enters into the composition of a quasi-sacred national name of the Karanga, viz. *Ma-tapa*-metsi, lit. " the Water-elephants (sea-cows) ", whence the well-known word *Monomatapa* (= *Mu-ene wa Matapa( metsi )*, lit. " the Lord of the Water-elephants ", which was the title of their King or so-called Emperor. In connexion with this it may be mentioned that the hippopotamus is a sacred animal with the Karanga even to this day, and that their reverence for it has passed to their conquerors the Ma-tebele, or Ma-tabele. See Kerr's " *Far Interior* ", p. 20.

11. *Ma-futa* " fat " lit. " that which melts and is sticky ". From the element *fu*, notion of " dying " and *ta*, notion of " adhering to..., sticking to... (?) ".

## VII. — The KU-MA Class.

**462.** — This class includes the infinitives of verbs used as substantives, as *ku-fua* " to die, death ", and also in many of these languages a few other substantives which require the same sort of concord as **ku**-*tui* " an ear ", plur. **ma**-*tui* *.

*N. B.* In the materials at my disposal there is no evident trace of the classifier KU-, not even before infinitives, in Dualla, Fernandian, and Nywema.

### § 1. Forms.

**463.** — In the words of this class the classifier MA- is identical with MA- of the preceding classes LI-MA and BU-MA.

**464.** — *N. B.* A few words in Herero, and a larger number in Ndonga, are mentioned by Bleek (*Compar. Gr.*, p. 207) as keeping the particle KU- in the plural together

### * EXAMPLES.

|  | an ear | | an arm | | a foot | | to fall, a fall |
|---|---|---|---|---|---|---|---|
|  | *Sing.* | *Plur.* | *Sing.* | *Plur.* | *Sing.* | *Plur.* |  |
| Tonga | ku-tui, | ma- | ku-boko, | ma- | ku-ulu, | ma- | ku-ua, or ku-gua |
| Bisa | ku-tui, | ma- | ku-boko, | ma- | ku-ulu, | ma- | ... |
| Gogo | ... | ... | ... | ... | ... | ... | ku-kagwa |
| Sagara | (467) | | ... | ... | ... | ... | ku-gwa |
| Shambala | ... | ... | ... | ... | ... | ... | ku-gwa |
| Boondei | (467) | | ku-lume « right hand » | | ... | ... | ku-gwa |
| Taita | ... | ... | ... | ... | ... | ... | ku-gwa |
| Nyanyembe | ku-tui, | ma- | ku-kono, | ma- | ku-gulu, | ma- | ku-gwa |
| Sukuma | ku-tui, | ma- | ku-kono, | ma- | ku-gulu, | ma- | ku-gwa |
| Kamba | ku-tu, | ma- | ku-boko, | ma- | ku-u, | ma- | ku-waluka |
| Swahili | ... | ... | ... | ... | ... | ... | kw-anguka |
| Pokomo. | ... | ... | ... | ... | ku-guu, | ma- | ... |
| Nika | ... | ... | ... | ... | ... | ... | ku-bwa |
| Senna | (467) | | ... | ... | ... | ... | ku-gwa |
| Karanga | ... | ... | ... | ... | ku-tabeso, | ma- | ... |
| Ganda | ku-tu, | ma- | ... | ... | ... | ... | ku-gwa |
| Zulu-Kafir | ... | ... | ... | ... | ... | ... | u ku-wa |
| Xosa-Kafir | ... | ... | ... | ... | ... | ... | u ku-wa |
| Herero | o ku-tui, | o ma- | o ku-oko, | o ma- | ... | ... | o ku-ua |
| Bihe | ... | ... | o kw-oko, | o va- | o ku-ulu « leg » | | o ku-wa |
| Mbunda | ku-tui, | ma- | ku-boko, | ma- | ... | ... | ... |
| Rotse | ku-toe | ma- | k-oko | ... | ... | ... | ku-koa (?) |
| Guha | ku-tue, | ma-(?) | ku-boko, | ma- | ku-gulu, | ma- | ... |
| Rua | ku-twe, | ma- | ku-woko, | ma- | ku-ulu, | ma- | ku-fiona (?) |
| Angola | (467) | | (lu-ku-aku), | māku | ... | ... | ku-bua |
| Lower Congo | ku-tu, | ma- | k-oko, | | ku-lu, | ma- | bwa |
| Yao | ... | ... | ... | ... | ... | ... | ku-gwa |
| Killmane | (ny-arro), | m-arro | ... | ... | ... | ... | u-ogua |
| Mozambique | (ny-aru), | m-aru | ... | ... | ... | ... | u-lua |
| Chwana proper | ... | ... | ... | ... | ... | ... | go-wa |
| Suto | ... | ... | ... | ... | ... | ... | go-wa |
| Mpongwe | o-roi, | a- | o-go, | a- | o-golo | a- | poxwa |
| Dualla | ... | ... | ... | ... | ... | ... | ko |
| Fan | a-lõ, | mõlõ | a-bõ | ... | e-ko (?) | | ... |
| Fernandian | —, | ba-to | —, | ba-kole | ... | | ... |

with MA, e. g. *o ku-ti*, "field", pl. *o ma-*ku-*ti*. Here again I notice that their stems either are monosyllabic, or begin with a vowel (cf. 44, 413, etc.)

**465.** — The forms of the classifier which is KU- in Tonga, Bisa, etc., are : —

*KU-* in Karanga before ordinary substantives only, *U-* before infinitives.

*KU-* in Congo before ordinary substantives only, *dropped* before such infinitives as begin with a consonant, though retained before the others under the form *kw-*.

*GO-* in Chwana, where it is found only in infinitives.

*O-* in Mpongwe before ordinary substantives. In this language infinitives are apparently not used as substantives.

*U-* (*W-* before vowels) in Mozambique and Kilimane, where it is used only before infinitives. It is replaced by *nya* (= *ni-a-*) in *nya-ru*, or *nya-rro*, " an ear ".

§ 2. Substantives which belong to the KU-MA Class.

**466.** — In the larger number of the Bantu languages the words which fall under this class are exclusively : *a)* Infinitives (used as substantives) ; *b)* the few parts of the body mentioned in the preceding examples (462*) ; *c)* the names of such rivers as are considered as being " the arms " or " shoulders " of others, or of the sea, as the rivers *Ku-bango*, *Ku-a* or *Ku-ba*, *Ku-anza*, *Ku-nene*, etc.

**467.** — *N. B.* Those languages which have lost the classifier KU- in ordinary substantives have however retained traces of it, at least most of them. Thus in Senna the word for " ear " is *kutu* of class LI-MA, pl. *ma-kutu*, where the syllable *ku-* is evidently the primitive classifier. Cf. in Angola *lu-*ku-*aku* " an arm ", plur. *māku*, not *ma-*ku-*aku*, and in Kaguru *ghutwe* " an ear ", pl. *ma-ghutwe*, in Boondei *gutwi*, pl. *ma-gutwi*, etc.

§ 3. Etymologies. — Varia.

**468.** — The etymology and exact power of the classifier KU- offers no difficulty. It is originally identical with the locative classifier KU- (542, 563), and essentially connected with the verb *kula* " to grow out ", as also with the corresponding adjective *kulu* (Kamba *kū*) " full grown ". Hence its adaptation to those parts of the body which grow out of the main trunk, as : —

1. *Ku-tui* " an ear ", lit. " a thing protruding from the head ". From *mu-tue* " the head ". The change of the final *e* to *i* is caused by the transposition of the accent (*mu-tué*, *kú-tu*), and this transposition is itself due to the fact that the classifier MU- is naturally short (*mŭ*), while the classifier KU- is naturally long (*kū*). Cf. 271.

2. *Ku-boko* " an arm, a shoulder ", lit. " a thing protruding downwards at the side ". From the elements *bu* " notion of falling " and *ko* " notion of side ".

3. *Ku-ulu* " a foot ", lit. " a thing protruding flatwise ". From the element *ulu* " notion of something stretched out ". Cf. 439 (8).

In the infinitives of verbs KU- properly refers to the notion of time or place (563). Hence *ku-ua* " to fall " means lit. " when (or) where one falls ".

# VIII. — The LU-(Z)IN Class

## and the
## Sub-classes connected with it.

**469.** — In these we classify together all that refers to the various categories of substantives which have in the singular number the classifier LU-. There is comparatively little agreement between the various Bantu languages in the use of this classifier. Some use it as a diminutive, others as an augmentative, others both as a diminutive and as an augmentative, etc. All this causes a great diversity in the formation of the plural *.

### § 1. Transformations of the Classifier LU-.

**470.** — The classifier which is pronounced LU- in Tonga, Bisa, Ganda, etc., is pronounced : —

*DU-* after *n* in the same languages and in Karanga (286).
*RU-* regularly in Karanga and Herero.

### * EXAMPLES.

|  | the tongue | | A rope or string | |
|---|---|---|---|---|
|  | *Sing.* *Plur.* | *Sing.* *Plur.* | *Sing.* *Plur.* |
| Tonga | lu-limi, {ma-limi or lu-dimi} | *Lu-izi*, the Middle Zambezi... | lu-ozi (?) in-gozi (?) |
| Bisa | lu-limi, in-dimi | ... ... | lu-sisi ... |
| Gogo | lu-limi, ma-limi | lu-enga « a river », ... | ... ... |
| Sagara | lu-limi, ... | lu-kolongo « a river », ma- | l-uzi, s-uzi |
| Shambala | lu-limi, n-dimi | ... ... | lu-gole, gole (?) |
| Boondei | u-limi, n-dimi | lu-kolongo « a river » ... | lu-zigi, zigi (?) |
| Taita | lu-mi ... | ... ... | ... ... |
| Nyanyembe | lu-limi, n-dimi | ... ... | lu-goye, n-goye |
| Sukuma | lu-limi, ma-limi | ... ... | lu-goye, n-goye |
| Kamba | ... ... | u-tsi « a river » ... | ... ... |
| Swahili | u-limi, n-dimi | ... ... | ... ... |
| Nika | lu-rimi, n-dimi | ... ... | lu-goe, n-goe |
| Karanga | ru-rimi, in-dimi | ru-izi « a river », nj-izi | ... ... |
| Ganda | lu-limi, n-dimi | ... ... | lu-goi ... |
| Zulu-Kafir | u lw-imi, i lw-imi | u lw-andle « the sea » ... | u-tambo « a snare »,in- |
| Xosa-Kafir | u lw-imi, i lw-imi | u lw-andle « the sea » ... | u-tambo « a net », in- |
| Herero | ... ... | o ru-rondo « a rivulet », o tu- | o ru-sepa « a thread » o tu- |
| Bihe | ... ... | o lu-wi « a river », o lon-dwi | o lu-ndovi, o lo- |
| Mbunda | lo-lime (?) ... | ... ... | l-ozi ... |
| Rotse | lo-leme (?) ... | ... ... | l-osi (?) ... |
| Guha | lu-limi, n-dimi | ... ... | ... ... |
| Rua | lu-jini, n-jimi | lu-wi « a river » ... | ... ... |
| Lower Congo | lu-bini, tu-bini | ... ... | lu-kamba ... |
| Yao | lu-limi, n-dimi | lu-sulo « a river », n-sulo | lu-goji, n-goji |
| Chwana proper | lo-leme, di-teme | lo-tsitsi, « a watercourse », di- | lo-tlwa « a net », di- |
| Suto | lo-leme, di-teme | ... ... | ... ... |
| Mpongwe | o-neme, i-neme | ol-obi « a river », il- | o-goli, i- |
| Dualla | i-yeme, lo-yeme | ... ... | ... ... |
| Fan | ... ... | u-dsui « a river » ... | ... ... |
| Fernandian | lo-belo ... | ... ... | ... ... |

*LO-* in Chwana (n. 200), as also in Rotse, Mbunda, Nyengo, and Lojazi, if here again Livingstone's spelling has not been influenced by Chwana. In Fernandian we find both LO- and LU-.

*O-* in Mpongwe.

*U-* (*W-* before vowel) in Kamba and Swahili, according to nn. 81 and 88; and likewise in Nywema.

**471.** — *N. B.* 1. According to Bleek (*Comp. Gr.*, p. 237) the form of this classifier is LA- or ZA- in Kele (*Di-kele*). The examples given are *la-ngoko* "head", pl. *ma-ngoko*; *la-paja* "hoof", pl. *ma-paja*; *la-nyui* "honey-bee", pl. *nyui*; *la-nyaja* "a flee"; *la-ndongo* "the end", pl. *ma-ndongo*.

Bleek adds (p. 271), that "in *Timneh* (a semi-Bantu language spoken near Sierra Leone) rope-like or creeping plants have commonly the prefix *ra-* in the singular."

**472.** — 2. This classifier is *dropped* commonly in Kafir; for, in such words as *u sana* "a baby", *u-siba* "a feather", etc., *u* is not the classifier, but the article. In the same language it is retained under the form LW- before such stems as begin with a vowel, and under its proper form LU- before monosyllabic stems (cf. nn. 44 and 325, 368, 389, 413).

**473.** — 3. This classifier LU- has almost entirely disappeared from Angola, Senna, Lojazi, etc., and apparently altogether from Mozambique and Kilimane. In Dualla it is regularly replaced by DI- or LI- of cl. LI-MA.

## § 2. Plural Classifiers corresponding to LU-.

**474.** — In the formation of the plural we meet with more variety in this class than in any other.

**475.** — Bleek thinks that the plural classifier which corresponds properly as plural to LU- is the classifier TU- (of class KA-TU). But this opinion is unwarranted, as we find such correspondence only in Herero, Ndonga, and Congo, to which may be added the Dualla group, that is, precisely in those languages which, having practically given up the classifier KA- as the regular diminutive classifier (cf. 509, 522), replace it in many cases by LU-, and which separate themselves on many other points from the generality of the Bantu languages.

**476.** — *N. B.* In Dualla, TU- changes regularly to LO-, according to n. 220. Ex. lo-*yeme* "tongues" (Congo tu-*bini*).

**477.** — In the other languages, the classifier corresponding as plural to LU- is commonly (ZI)N-, as in Tonga, Bisa, Nywema, Karanga, Ganda, Swahili, Nika, Kafir, Chwana, etc., with the variety of forms which has been described in nn. 393-398, and with those various effects upon the initial letter of the stems of substantives which are regularly produced by *n* nasal expressed or suppressed. (Cf. 51 and 73, 77, 83, 140, 93, 95, 184-196, 389, 395, 396, etc., etc.).

**478.** — *N. B.* 1. In some cases the particle *lu-* is kept partially or totally in the plural, and combined with the classifier (ZI)N-. This causes some remarkable phenomena. Thus, in Kafir we have *i lw-imi*, " tongues ", *i lw-andle* " seas ", etc., which require the same concord as if we had *i(zi)n-lw-andle*, *i (zi)n-lw-imi*, etc. Ex. *i lw-imi e* zim-*bini* " two tongues ". Likewise, in Kaguru we find the following plurals *su-gha* " plots of ground " (sing. *lu-gha*), *su-ti* " shafts " (sing. *lu-ti*), *s-uzi* or *ny-uzi* " strings " (sing. *l-uzi*), *s-umo* or *ny-umo* " razors " (sing. *lu-mo*), etc., all of which require the same concord as if they contained the classifier ZIN-. (Cf. Last's *Kaguru Grammar*, pp. 11 and 15, 17, etc.). It may be further remarked that in all the preceding examples the stem of the substantive either is monosyllabic or begins with a vowel. Hence these phenomena seem to be due to an extension of the general laws concerning monosyllables (cf. nn. 44 and 325, 368, 389, 413, 464, etc.). Cf. Père Delaunay's *Grammaire Kisuahili*, p. 11.

**479.** — 2. The effects of *n* nasal, expressed or suppressed, upon the initial consonants of the stems of the words are more easily studied in this class LU-(ZI)N than in the class IN-(ZI)N, because here we have no longer the nasal both in the singular and in the plural number, but only in the plural. Thus we see plainly how under the influence of *n* nasal expressed or suppressed —

a) in Chwana *l* changes to *t*  Ex. *lo-leme* " a tongue ", pl. *di-teme*
　　　　　　*g* 　„　„ *kg* or *k*  Ex. *lo-gong* " a piece of wood ", pl. *di-kong*
　　　　　　*sh* 　„　„ *ch*  Ex. *lo-chu* " death ", pl. *din-chu*
　　　　　　*b* 　„　„ *p*  Ex. *lo-badi* " a scar ", pl. *di-padi*, etc.
b) in Mpongwe *r* changes to *t*.  Ex. *o-rove* " desert ", pl. *si-tove*
　　　　　　*w* 　„　„ *fw*.  Ex. *o-wera* " a nail ", pl. *si-fwera*
　　　　　　*b* 　„　„ *b*.  Ex. *o-bega*, " a shoulder ", pl. *si-bega*, etc.
c) in Nika *h* 　„　„ *t*.  Ex. *lu-hunde* " a trifle ", pl. *tunde*, etc.

For similar changes in other languages cf. Père Delaunay's *Grammaire Kisuahili*, pp. 11, 12.
　　　　　　　　Dr. Steere's *Collections for Nyamwezi*, pp. 14, 15.
　　　　　　　　*Grammaire Ruganda*, p. 7.
　　　　　　　　Last's *Kamba Grammar*, p. 5, etc.

**480.** — In some languages the plural classifier corresponding regularly to LU- is not (ZI)N- or any equivalent for it, but MA-. This is principally the case in Kaguru, though not when the stem of the substantive begins with a vowel, or is monosyllabic. Ex. *lu-bavu* " a rib ", pl. *ma-bavu; lu-singa* " a log of wood ", pl. *ma-singa*, etc. Examples of this are also given in Kondoa, which, as well as Kaguru, is a dialect of Sagara, in Kami, which also is a language of the East coast, in Mozambique, in Gogo, etc. In Tonga there seems to be a choice between MA- and (ZI)N-.

### § 3. Substantives belonging to cl. LU-.

**481.** — The substantives which fall regularly under this class in Tonga and, as it seems, in the greater number of the Bantu languages, are principally : —

1°. The words for " a sucking baby ", *lu-sabila* (Kafir *u sana*, Rotse *lo-keke*, Chwana *lo-sea*) and for " the new moon " *lu-sele* (Herero *o ru-tana*, *o ru-tandati*).

**482.** — 2° The words for regular rows or successions of men or things, as *lu-zubo* " a race, family " (Kaf. *u-hlanga, u-sapo*), *lu-sa* (?), " a row " (Kaf. *u lu-hla*), *lu-belɑ* " an endless succession of days ", *lu-luli* " a roof ", *lu-kuni* " a raft ", *lu-sobela* " a copper armlet ", etc.

**483.** — 3° A few names of animals, as *lu-boko*, an animal described as remarkable for its " *long tail*, " *lu-bondue* or *lu-bondo*, an animal described as taking remarkably " *long jumps*. "

**484.** — 4° Lengthy parts of the body, as *lu-boko* " the whole arm, including the hand ", whence *lu-lio* " the right arm " ; *lu-ja* " a cock's comb " (cf. *i-ja* " a horn, a tusk ", of class LI-MA), *lu-limi* " the tongue ", whence the names of several languages, as *Lu-ganda* " the Ganda language ", *Lu-mbamba*, " Mbamba ", *Lu-mbundu* the " language of the Bihe ", etc. ; *lu-kululu* " the throat ", *lu-kanda* " the skin, when soft or just taken off the body ", (cf. *i-kanda* " the skin in its natural condition on the body "), etc.

**485.** — 5° The words for " a rope ", *lu-ozi* or *lu-lozi (?)*, and, as it seems, most of the things in nature which have, or seem to have, no consistency, as *lu-ala* " a cliff ", *lu-sese* " sand ", *lu-buebue* " gravel " (cf. *i-bue* " a stone "), *lu-suko* " dust ", etc.

**486.** — 7° " The sea ", *lu-anja*, and many rivers, as *Lu-izi* " the Zambesi below the Victoria falls ", the rivers *Lu-apula, Lu-kugu, Lu-angwe, Lu-ngwe*, etc.

**487.** — 8° Several actions of some persistency and uniformity, as *lu-ele* " a meal ", *lu-lapelo* " prayer ", *lu-seko* " enjoyment ", *lu-kualo* " writing ", etc.

**488.** — *N. B.* In Kafir, and much more in Herero, the classifier LU- is often used with a diminutive power. This may be attributed to the fact already mentioned that these languages have practically lost the regular diminutive classifier KA- (cf. 476). It may be further remarked that several substantives which take the classifier LU- in nearly all the Bantu languages fall under a different class in Herero. Ex. *e raka* " a tongue " of class LI-MA (cf. Tonga *lu-limi*); *o ku-vare* " the sea ", etc.

### § 4. Etymologies. — Varia.

**489.** — In this variety of substantives which take the classifier LU-, the notion which comes out prominently is that of looseness, want of consistency, and lengthy uniformity, or of something which projects loosely from a solid body. It is only natural that with this notion there should have been connected, on the one hand that of weakness, as in the name of " a baby " and, on the other, that of mobility, as in the name of " the sea ".

In point of meaning, the verb most intimately related to this classifier might be thought to be *-zua* " to come out " (Chwana *-cwa=dwa*, 205), but phonetic laws rather show a connexion with *-lua* " to bewitch, to be treacherous, to war with… " Hence the notion which was conveyed primarily by the classifier LU- should have been that of something treacherous in some respect or other, or unreliable. Possibly the correct thing is to say that this classifier is related to the element *-ulu* or *-ula* which conveys the notion of " something expanded " (439(8), 1080, 468(3)).

**490.** — If we consider the examples under n. 469 etymologically, it may be said that : —

1. In the word *lu-limi* " a tongue " (470*) the element *li* probably conveys the notion of " eating ", and the element *mi* that of " something which grows up (383) ". Hence this word probably means lit. " that which eats food ". However I would not guarantee this etymology.

2. In *lu-izi* " a river ", we meet once more with the element *izi* which conveys the notion of " fecundity " (461(10), 384(10), etc.).

3. As to the word *lu-ozi (lu-lozi?)* " a rope ", its etymology is still doubtful as well as its correct form in Tonga. Probably this word referred primarily to the bark of trees from which ropes used to be, and are still, made by the larger number of the native tribes.

## IX. — The CI-ZI Class.

**491.** — The CI-ZI class includes the substantives which require the same sort of concord as **ci**-*ntu* " a thing ", pl. **zi**-*ntu* \*.

### § 1. Transformations of the Classifier CI-.

**492.** — With regard to the classifier of the singular number in this class CI-ZI, it is somewhat difficult to define properly the manner in which it is pronounced in most of the languages of the interior. It is a sound somewhat between *tyi*- or *tye*-, and *chi*- or *che*-. It is variously spelt *chi*-, *tshi*-, *dshi*-, *shi*-, *tyi*-, *qui*-, *çi*-, *ci*-, etc. We spell it : —

*CI- (ci-)* in Tonga, Senna, Karanga, etc. (cf. 8 and 14).
*TYI-* in Herero, where this mode of spelling is too fixed to be upset.
*CHI-* in Yao (apparently pronounced as *CI-* in Tonga).

### \* EXAMPLES.

|  | a thing | | (names of languages) | a seat, a stool | |
|---|---|---|---|---|---|
|  | *Sing.* | *Plur.* | *Sing.* | *Sing.* | *Plur.* |
| Tonga | ci-ntu, | zi- | *Ci-tonga*, the Tonga language | ci-bula, | zi- |
| Bisa | ... | ... | *Ki-bisa*, Bisa | ki-puna | ... |
| Gogo | ... | ... | *Ki-gogo*, Gogo | ki-goda (?) | ... |
| Sagara | ki-ntu, | vi- | *Ki-sagara*, Sagara | ... | ... |
| Shambala | ki-ntu, | vi- | *Ki-xambala*, Shambala | ... | ... |
| Boondei | ki-ntu, | vi- | ... | ki-ti, | vi- |
| Taita | ki-ndu | | *Ki-taita*, Taita | ki-fumbi | ... |
| Nyanyembe | ki-nhu, | fi- | *Ki-namwezi*, Nyamwezi | ... | ... |
| Sukuma | ... | ... | ... | ... | ... |
| Kamba | ki-ndu, | i- | *Ki-kamba*, Kamba | ki-tumbi, | i- |
| Swahili | ki-tu, | vi- | *Ki-swahili*, Swahili | ki-ti, | vi- |
| Pokomo | ki-ntu, | vi- | *Ki-pokomo*, Pokomo | ... | ... |
| Nika | ki-tu, | vi- | *Ki-nika*, Nika | ... | ... |
| Senna | ci-ntu, | bzi- | *Ci-nyanja*, Nyassa | ... | ... |
| Karanga | ci-no, | ɉwi- | *Ci-karanga*, Karanga | ci-bura, | ɉwi- |
| Ganda | ki-ntu, | bi- | (484) | ki-tulu, | bi- |
| Zulu-Kafir | ... | ... | *i Si-zulu*, Zulu | i si-tulo, | i zi- |
| Xosa-Kafir | ... | ... | *i Si-xosa*, Xosa | i si-hlalo, | i zi- |
| Herero | o tyi-na, | o vi- | *o Tyi-herero*, Herero | o tyi-havero, | o vi- |
| Bihe | o ci-na, | o vi- | (484) | ... | ... |
| Mbunda | ... | ... | *Ci-kuango*, Kuango | ... | ... |
| Rotse | ... | ... | *Se-luiana*, Rotse | ... | ... |
| Guha | ... | ... | *Ki-guha*, Guha | ki-wala, | vi- |
| Rua | ki-ntu, | vi- | *Ki-rua*, Rua | ... | ... |
| Angola | ki-ma, | i- | *Ki-mbundu*, the language of the blacks | ki-alu, | i- |
| Lower Congo | ki-uma, | y- | *Ki-xikongo*, Congo | ki-andu, | y- |
| Nywema | ... | ... | ... | ki-wala, | (?) |
| Yao | chi-ndu, | i- | ... | chi-tengu, | i- |
| Kilimane | e-lo, | vi- | ... | ... | ... |
| Mozambique | i-tu, | pl. i-tu | ... | i-hiche, | i- |
| Chwana proper | se-lo, | pl. di- | *Se-cwana*, Chwana | se-tulo, | di- |
| Suto | se-lo, | li- | *Se-sutho*, Suto | se-tulo, | li- |
| Mpongwe | ej-oma, | y- | ... | e-pue, | pue |
| Fan | (?), | pl. bi-ŏm | ... | ... | ... |
| Dualla | (?), | pl. bi-ma | ... | ... | ... |
| Fernandian | ... | ... | ... | ... | ... |

110  *South-African Bantu Languages.*

*KI-* before consonants, *CH-* before vowels, in Swahili, Nika, Nyamwezi, Angola, etc.
*KI-* in Congo before monosyllabic stems and such as begin with a vowel (cf. nn. 44, 325, 368, 389, 413, etc.). In the same language it is entirely dropped in other nouns.
*SI-* before consonants, *S* before vowels, in Kafir, Rotse, and Nyengo.
*SE-* in Chwana. It is often omitted before vowels. Ex. *Atla sa gagwe* " his hand ". *Aparo sa gagwe* " his clothes " (= *se-atla, se-aparo*).
*EJ-* before vowels, *E-* before consonants, in Mpongwe.
*I-* or *E-* in Dualla, Benga, etc.

**493.** — *N. B.* 1. The proper form of this classifier in Fan is still doubtful. It seems to be ECH- before vowels, e. g. *ech-um*, " a young man ". Perhaps it is E- before consonants, as in Mpongwe.

**494.** — 2. Bleek mentions also the form VI- in Kele and Benga. But this seems

EXAMPLES. (Continued.)

|  | the chin | | the chest, (a bone) | | (a cob, a bunch, etc.) | |
|---|---|---|---|---|---|---|
|  | *Sing.* | *Plur.* | *Sing.* | *Plur.* | *Sing.* | *Plur.* |
| Tonga | ci-lezu, | zi- | ci-fua, | zi- | ci-popue, « a cob of maize », | zi- |
| Bisa | ... | ... | ... | ... | ... | ... |
| Gogo | ... | ... | ... | ... | ... | ... |
| Sagara | ki-levula, | vi- | ki-fa, | vi- | ... | ... |
| Shambala | ki-dezu, | vi- | ki-fua, | vi- | ... | ... |
| Boondei | ki-evu, | vi- | ki-fua, | vi- | ... | ... |
| Taita | ... | ... | ... | ... | ki-konzi « a cob of corn » | ... |
| Nyanyembe | ... | ... | ki-kuwa, | fi- | ... | ... |
| Sukuma | ... | ... | ... | ... | ... | ... |
| Kamba | ki-nyezwa, | i- | ki-sivi, | i- | ki-tsakwa « a cob of corn », | i- |
| wahili | ki-devu, | vi- | ki-fua, | vi- | ki-tawi « a bunch », | vi- |
| Pokomo | ki-yefu, | vi- | ... | ... | ... | ... |
| Nika | ki-refu, | vi- | ki-fua (?), | vi- | ki-guta « a cob of corn », | vi- |
| Senna | ci-debzu, | bzi- | ci-fua, | bzi- | ci-konje « a bunch », | bzi- |
| Karanga | ci-revo, | ¡wi- | ... | ... | ... | ... |
| Ganda | ki-levu, | bi- | ki-fuba, | bi- | ... | ... |
| Zulu-Kafir | i si-levu, | zi- | i si-fuba, | i zi- | i si-kwebu « a cob », | i zi- |
| Xosa-Kafir | i si-levu, | i zi- | i si-fuba, | i zi- | i si-kwebu « a cob », | i zi- |
| Herero | o tyi-hehemeno, | o vi- | o ty-ari, | o vi- | ... | ... |
| Bihe | o ci-yeli | ... | ... | ... | ... | ... |
| Mbunda | ... | ... | ci-tea (?) | ... | ... | ... |
| Rotse | ... | ... | se-foba (?) | ... | ... | ... |
| Guha | ... | ... | ... | ... | ... | ... |
| Rua | ... | ... | ci-kupa (?), | vi- | ... | ... |
| Angola | kēxu, | (?) | ki-fuba " bone ", | i- | ki-lende « a bunch », | i- |
| Lower Congo | bobo, | pl. bobo | vixi " bone ", | pl. vixi | kangi « a bunch », pl. kangi | |
| Nywema | ... | ... | ... | ... | ... | ... |
| Yao | chi-mbundi, | i- | ... | ... | chi-sonde « the core of a cob » | i- |
| Kilimane | ... | ... | e-kua «the chest»(?), | vi- | ... | ... |
| Mozambique | ... | ... | ... | ... | i-konyo, « a bunch », | i- |
| Chwana proper | se-ledu, | di- | se-fuba, | di- | se-gwere « a cob of maize », | di- |
| Suto | se-lelu, | di- | se-fuba (?), | li- | ... | ... |
| Mpongwe | ... | ... | e-pa « bone », | pl. pa | e-goro « a cob », | goro |
| Fan | ... | ... | n-kuk (?), | (?) | ... | ... |
| Dualla | ... | ... | e-isi « bone », | be- | e-sambu « beard of corn », | be- |
| Fernandian | ... | ... | e-aka, | bi- (?) | ... | ... |

## The CI-ZI Class.

to be an error, because properly speaking the Kele class VI-LA and the Benga class VI-L' correspond to the Tonga class KA-TU, not to CI-ZI. (Cf. 522).

**495.** — 3. In Mozambique this class of nouns seems to have melted into the same with class IN-(ZI)N. Hence in this language the form I- (Y- before vowels) in both numbers, as in *i-tu* " a thing, things ", *y-o-lia* (= *i-a-u-lia* = Senna *ci-a-ku-lia*) " food ", lit. " thing for eating ". This is a result of the phonetic laws(176).

### § 2. Transformations of the Classifier ZI-.

**496.** — The principal forms of the plural classifier of this same class are : —

*ZWI-* in Karanga, and Yeye of Lake Ngami (cf. 109).
*BZI-* in the Tette dialect of the Senna group (cf. 99).
*DZI-* or *BZI-* in the Shire dialect of the same language and in Senna proper (cf. 99).
*ZI-* in Tonga, Kafir, Mbunda, etc.

### EXAMPLES. (Continued.)

| | a stump | | a dried hide | | a detached hill or mountain | | an ant-hill | | a light-hole | |
|---|---|---|---|---|---|---|---|---|---|---|
| | Sing. | Plur. | Sing. | Plur. | Sing. | Plur. | Sing. | Plur. | Sing. | Plur. |
| Tonga | ci-samo, | zi- | ci-kanda, | zi- | ci-lundu, | zi- | ci-olu, | zi- | ci-bonebone, | zi- |
| Bisa | ... | ... | ki-kanda, | ... | ... | ... | ... | ... | ... | ... |
| Gogo | ... | ... | ... | ... | ki-gongo, | ... | ... | ... | ... | ... |
| Sagara | ... | ... | ... | ... | ki-rima, | vi- | ... | ... | ... | ... |
| Shambala | ... | ... | ... | ... | ki-lima, | vi- | ... | ... | ... | ... |
| Boondei | ki-zibi, | vi- | ki-ngo, | vi- | ki-lima, | vi- | ... | ... | ... | ... |
| Taita | ... | ... | ... | ... | ki-fumvu | | ... | ... | ... | ... |
| Nyanyembe | ... | ... | ... | ... | ki-gongo, | fi- | ki-bumbuswa, fi- | | ... | ... |
| Sukuma | ... | ... | ... | ... | ki-gongo, | fi- | ... | ... | ... | ... |
| Kamba | ... | ... | ... | ... | ki-ima, | i- | ki-umbi, | i- | ki-tonia, | i- |
| Swahili | ... | ... | ki-kanda ( a bag ) | | ki-lima, | vi- | ki-suguli, | vi- | ... | ... |
| Pokomo | ... | ... | ... | ... | ... | ... | ... | ... | ki-za, | vi- |
| Nika | ki-siki, | vi- | ki-chingo, | vi- | ki-rima, | vi- | ki-so, | vi- | ki-sa (?), | vi- |
| Senna | ci-banda,bzi- | | ci-kuruo, | bzi- | ci-dunda,bzi- | | ci-uru, | bz- | ... | ... |
| Karanga | ... | ... | ... | ... | ... | ... | ... | ... | ... | ... |
| Ganda | ki-kolo, | bi- | ... | ... | ... | ... | ki-wo, | bi- | ki-tuli, | bi- |
| Zulu-Kafir | ... | ... | i si-kumba,i zi- | | ... | ... | i si-duli, i zi- | | i si-roba, i zi- | |
| Xosa-Kafir | ... | ... | i si-kumbo,i zi- | | ... | ... | i si-duli, i zi- | | i si-roba,i zi- | |
| Herero | o tyi-pute, o vi- | | ... | ... | o tyi-hungo, o vi- | | o tyi-tundu, o vi- | | o tyi-tuo(?)... | |
| Bihe | ... | ... | ... | ... | o ci-lundu (?) | | o ci-mu, o vi- | | ... | ... |
| Mbunda | ... | ... | ci-kanda, | zi- | ... | ... | ... | ... | ... | ... |
| Rotse | ... | ... | se-tumba, | ... | ... | ... | se-bukomolo(?) | | ... | ... |
| Guha | ... | ... | ki-sewa, | vi- | ... | ... | ... | ... | ... | ... |
| Rua | ... | ... | ki-seva, | vi- | ... | ... | ... | ... | ... | ... |
| Angola | ki-xinji, | i- | ki-ba, | i- | ... | ... | ... | ... | ... | ... |
| Lower Congo | xinza, pl. xinza | | ... | ... | kundubulu | | ki-nsama, | i- | ... | ... |
| Nywema | ... | ... | ... | ... | ... | ... | ... | ... | ... | ... |
| Yao | che-singa, i- | | chi-kopa, | i- | chi-tundulima, i- | | chi-kula, | i- | ... | ... |
| Kilimane | ... | ... | ... | ... | ... | ... | ... | ... | ... | ... |
| Mozambique | i-kokolo, i- | | ... | ... | ... | ... | ... | ... | ... | ... |
| Chwana proper | se-sipi, | di- | ... | ... | se-tlhaba, di- | | se-olo, | di- | se-iponi, di- | |
| Suto | se-sipi, | li- | ... | ... | se-tlhala, | li- | se-tlhaga, li- | | se-iponi, li- | |
| Mpongwe | ... | ... | e-banda,banda | | ... | ... | ej-imba, y-(?) | | ... | ... |
| Fan | ... | ... | ... | ... | ... | ... | ... | ... | ... | ... |
| Dualla | e-tenge(?)be- | | ... | ... | ... | ... | ... | ... | ... | ... |
| Fernandian | si-udi, | bi- | ... | ... | ... | ... | ... | ... | ... | ... |

*Dl-* in Chwana, spelt *LI-* in Suto and in some other Chwana dialects (cf. 9 and 173).
*VI-* in Swahili, Shambala, Nika, Herero, Guha, etc.

*N. B.* In Yao it is also VI- according to Last, but Hetherwick spells it I-, while Steere spells it FI-. It is also spelt FI- in Nyamwezi. If this form be correct, it may be noted as being so far the only plural classifier which contains a *hard* consonant.

*BI-* in Ganda and Nyambu, *BI-* or *BE-* in Dualla and the neighbouring languages.
*I-* in Angola, Mbamba, Kamba, etc.
*Y-* before vowels, *suppressed* before consonants, in Mpongwe.

### § 3. Substantives which belong to the Class CI-ZI.

**497.** — The substantives which fall under this class in Tonga, and in the generality of the Bantu languages, are principally : —

1° The names of languages, as *Ci-tonga* " Tonga ". (Cf. 484.)

**498.** — 2° The word for " a thing " *ci-ntu*, and some substantives in which this word is understood, as *ci-tede* " such and such a thing ", *ci-fula-mabue* " a hailstorm ", lit. " that which forges stones, " *ci-indi* " the past ", lit. " that which is remote ", etc.

**499.** — 3° The words for any sort of limited break, or cut, on land or water, or on a body, as *ci-kule* " a national mark or cut " (such as circumcision for Kafirs, filing between the front teeth for the Herero, etc., cf. 50), *ci-bongo* " a small lake ", *ci-sua* " an island in a river ", *ci-to* " a ford in a river ", *ci-vukumba* " an opening in a rock, a cave ", *Ci-ongo* or *Ci-ongue* (in Chwana pronunciation *Si-ongo*) " the great Zambezi falls ", *ci-limo* " summer " lit. " the break in the work ", from *-lima* " to till the ground " (cf. 52*) *ci-liba* " a well ", *ci-bonebone* " a light-hole ", etc.

**500.** — 4° Whatever is what the Tonga call " *short* ", i. e. relatively thick in one part and small in another, or halved, or protruding with a thick basis and to a comparatively small height, etc., as *ci-kulukulu* " a man stooping by age ", *ci-embele* " an old person or animal ", *ci-yuni* " a bird with short legs ", *ci-binda* " a land tortoise ", *ci-pembele* " a rhinoceros " (short legs), *ci-tapile* " a potato " (from the Dutch *aard-appel*), *ci-lezu* " the chin " *ci-zui*, " a knee ", *cyi-ni* " the liver ", *ci-popue* " a cob of maize ", *ci-lala* " a young palm-leaf ", *ci-lundu* " a hill ", *ci-panzi* " a half ", *ci-kalo* " a saddle ", *ci-bula* " a seat ", *ci-kanda* " a hide, a shield ", *ci-longo* " a wide earthen pot ", *ci-tungu* " a low-hut ", *ci-zumbo* " a nest ", *ci-sanza* " a low table ", *ci-tale* " a candlestick ", *ci-lapo* or *ci-lao* " a paddle ", etc., etc.

**501.** — *N. B.* In Congo the class KI-I (= Tonga CI-ZI) is the regular diminutive class. (Cf. 521.)

## § 4. Etymologies. — Varia.

**502.** — The Tonga and the Karanga still bear in mind very distinctly the proper meaning of the classifier CI-. They render it invariably by the English word " short ", or by the Dutch " kort ", and say it is identical with the adjective *-ce* " short ". But when they explain their mind, it can be easily made out that they attach to it in some cases a *negative* or *privative*, and in the others an *intensive* power, and that in many words it might be rendered by the adjective " *thick* ", rather than by the adjective " *short* ". Thus, while it has a *negative* power in *ci-ntu* " a thing ", lit. " that which is no person " (cf. *mu-ntu*, " a person "), and a *privative* power in *ci-panzi* " a half ", *ci-tungu* " a low hut ", *ci-sanza* " a low table ", etc., it may be said to have rather an *intensive* or *enlarging* power, at least from our point of view, in such words as *ci-pembere* " a rhinoceros ", *ci-rombo* (Senna word) " a lord, a wild beast ", etc. This *intensive* power is further associated with a *productive* or *causative* notion, as in *ci-lezu* " the chin " lit. " that protruding part of the body which produces beard " (cf. *indezu = inlezu* " beard "). Father Pedro Diaz, S. J., has noticed the privative and the intensive meaning of this classifier in his *Angola Grammar*, p. 32 (Lisboa, 1697), and explained their connexion by saying that CI- (KE-, KI-) is essentially negative, but that negative expressions may convey both privative and superlative notions, as " no-man ", for instance, may signify both " less than man " and " more than man ". Cf. 634. More probably the classifier CI- has two different etymologies, and this is the true explanation of its different powers. The first CI- may originally have been identical with the word which means " ground " in nearly all the Bantu languages (Tonga *mu-se*, whence *n-si* in *pa-nsi*, *ku-nsi*, and *mu-nsi*, Swahili *n-chi* or *n-ti*, Angola *xi*, Congo *n-xi* or *n-ci*, Herero *e-hi*, etc., cf. 533\*), and it is from this meaning of " ground " that is has derived that of " something low, short, on the ground ", as also, on the one hand, that of privation and negation, and, on the other, that of production. The second CI- may originally have been identical with the Karanga word *xe* " chief, lord ", whence its augmentative power, principally in Karanga, Senna, and Yao, as in *ci-rombo* " a wild beast ", lit. "a wild lord " (¹).

Analogies and phonetic laws seem to point to a relation of the classifier CI- to the verb *-cia* " to dawn " (52*), but it seems hard to associate the notion of " something short " with that of " dawn ", unless it be said that a thing short is only a beginning or remnant of something, exactly as the dawn of day is a beginning of day and the end of night. Cf. 994.

The classifier ZI- (Karanga ʒwi-, Swahili *vi-*) is probably related to *-vula* ( = *-vuila* ?) " to multiply ", which is itself derived from *-zua, -vua* or *-va* " to come out " (409(2)). Hence it conveys the notion of number without including that of the manner in which multiplication is obtained. Cf. 408. Possibly the elements *vu* and *izi* are closely related to one another in Bantu, as they both convey the notion of fecundity or development. Bleek thought that the original form of this classifier was PI- (²). But this opinion cannot stand with the fact that its modern forms contain no such hard letter as P. Cf. 496.

**503.** — In the examples under n. 491 : —

1. *Ci-ntu* " a thing " seems to mean lit. " that which is no person ". Cf. *mu-ntu* " a person ".

2. *Ci-tonga* " the Tonga language ". It might be asked how we can find in such names of languages the notion of " ground " which we consider to have been conveyed originally by the classifier CI- (502). We answer that in such words the classifier CI- takes from the idea of " ground " only the notion of something which is the basis of all the rest, which always remains, which is characteristic, so that, for instance, *Ci-tonga* means lit. " that which is characteristic of the Tonga ". A less probable explanation of such words would be that which would refer them to *ci-kule* " a national mark ".

3. *Ci-lezu* " the chin ", lit. " the ground of the beard ". Cf. 409(2).

4. *Ci-bula* " a seat, a stool ", conveys the notion of something bent over itself. Cf. *ku-bola* (Kafir *u ku-buya*) " to return ". *Ki-ti*, in Swahili, means lit. " a stump of wood ". Cf. *m-ti* " a tree ".

5. *Ci-fua* " the chest ", or " a thick bone ", lit. " a ground of bones ", in opposition to the more fleshy and muscular parts of the body.

6. *Ci-samo* " a stump ". Cf. *mu-samo* " a tree ".

7. *Ci-kanda* " a dried hide ", in opposition to *i-kanda* and *lu-kanda* " the skin ". The element *-anda* conveys the notion of " covering, protecting ". Cf. 409(7).

8. *Ci-lundu* " a hill ". Cf. *i-lundu* " a mountain ". The element *lu*, here reduplicated, conveys the notion of " something stretched out ". Cf. 439(8), 468(3), 489.

9. *Ci-olu* " an anthill ". Here again the element *lu* conveys the notion of something raised, but I do not see what notion is conveyed by the *o* before it.

10. *Ci-bonebone* " a light-hole, a window ", lit. " a hole for seeing ". From *ku-bona* " to see ". Cf. 52*.

---

1. The natives of Senna consider wild beasts as the embodiments of their deceased chiefs, and consider themselves bound to feed them.

2. *Comparative Grammar*, p. 264.

# X. — The Diminutive Class KA-TU

## and the

## Sub-Classes connected with it.

**504.** — Though the privative class CI-ZI may in some respects be considered as diminutive, yet, properly speaking, in the larger proportion of the Bantu languages such things as are *small in every respect* are found to take in the singular number the classifier KA- and in the plural the classifier TU-, as **ka**-*bua* " a small dog ", plur. **tu**-*bua* *. Those languages which do not agree with Tonga on this point, do not agree any better among themselves, some of them having the classifier FI- or VI- in the singular, others on the contrary using VI- with a plural meaning, others forming their diminutives by suffixing or prefixing the word for " son ", *muana*, etc.

### § 1. Forms.

**505.** — A single glance at the subjoined tables will show that more information of a reliable kind is still wanted. However, here

### * EXAMPLES.

|  | a baby (a youth) |  | a stick, a branch |  | the opening of the mouth |
|---|---|---|---|---|---|
|  | *Sing.* | *Plur.* | *Sing.* | *Plur.* | *Sing.* |
| Tonga | ka-cece, | tu- | ka-samo, | tu- | ka-nua |
| Bisa | ka-ana, | tu- | ... | ... | ka-nua |
| Shambala | ka-zana (youth) | vi- | ... | ... | ... |
| Boondei | ka-zana (youth), | vi- | ... | ... | ka-nua |
| Nyanyembe | ... | ... | ka-tambi, | tu- | ka-nwa |
| Sukuma | ka-gosia, | tu- | ... | ... | ... |
| Kamba | ka-ana, | tu- | ka-munsa | .... | ka-nyoa |
| Swahili | ... | ... | ... | ... | (kanwa, cl. IN) |
| Nika | ka-dzana, | vi- | ... | ... | ka-nwa (?) |
| Senna | ka-*mw*-ana, | tu-*wā*na | ka-*mu*-ti, | tu-*mi*-ti | ... |
| Karanga | ka-ana, | tw- | ... | ... | ... |
| Ganda | ka-ana, | bu- | ka-ti, | bu- | ka-mwa |
| Nyambu | ka-ana, | tw- | ... | ... | ... |
| Herero | o ka-natye, | o u- | o ka-ti, | o -u | ... |
| Bihe | ... | ... | ... | ... | ... |
| Mbunda | ... | ... | ... | ... | ka-nwa |
| Rotse | ka-uzi (?) | ... | ... | ... | ka-nwa |
| Lojazi | ... | ... | ... | ... | ka-nwa |
| Guha | ... | ... | ... | ... | ka-nya, tu- |
| Rua | ... | ... | ... | ... | ka-nwa |
| Angola | ka-*mō*na, | tu-ana (?) | ka-*mu*-xi, | tu-*mi*-xi | ... |
| Lower Congo | ... | ... | ... | ... | ... |
| Nywema | ... | ... | ... | ... | ... |
| Yao | ka-anache, | tu- | ka-pichi, | tu- | ka-mwa |
| Kele | ... | ... | ... | ... | ... |
| Fan | ... | ... | ... | ... | ... |
| Fernandian | si-neneheh, | to-(?) | s-aka, | tw- | ... |

are a few conclusions which can be drawn pretty safely from the documents at hand, viz. : —

**506.** — 1º The regular diminutive classifiers are KA- in the singular, TU- in the plural, in the larger number of the Bantu languages, viz. in Tonga and all the dialects which may be grouped with it (Bisa, Subia, Bemba, Lea, etc., n. 65), in all the dialects of Nyamwezi (Nyanyembe, Sumbua, Sukuma, etc., cf. 73), in Yao, Kamba, Karanga, Guha, Regga (near the Mut'a-nzige), Luba, Lojazi, Angola, etc.

**507** — 2º A few Tonga words, instead of taking in the plural the classifier TU-, require, or at least admit, another collective classifier. Ex. *ka-ntabua* " flees ", pl. *bu-; ka-ana ke inkuku* " a little chicken ", pl. *tu-ana tue inkuku* or *bu-ana bue inkuku; ka-bue* " a pebble ", pl. *tu-bue* or *lu-buebue*, etc.

**508.** — *N. B.* 1º The use of BU- as plural to KA- seems to be the rule in Ganda (*Grammaire Ruganda*, p. 6). However it may be noticed in Last's " *Polyglotta* " (p. 160) that in Nyambu, which is a language closely akin to Ganda, the classifier used as plural to KA- is not BU- but TU-. Ex. *ka-lumbu* " sister ", pl. *tu-; ka-ana* " child ", *tw-*.

EXAMPLES. (Continued.)

|  | the middle, the centre | (a match, embers, a little fire) | | | an axe | |
|---|---|---|---|---|---|---|
|  | *Sing.* | *Sing.* | | *Plur.* | *Sing.* | *Plur.* |
| Tonga | ka-ti | ka-lilo " a match ", | | tu- | ka-ngone, | tu- |
| Bisa | ... | ... | ... | ... | ... | ... |
| Shambala | ... | ... | ... | ... | ... | ... |
| Boondei | ... | ... | ... | ... | ... | ... |
| Nyanyembe | (ga-ti?) | ka-lilo " embers " | | tu- | ka-wunana, | tu- |
| Sukuma | ... | ... | ... | ... | ... | ... |
| Kamba | ka-ti | ... | ... | ... | ka-joka, | tu- |
| Swahili | ka-ti (*ka* ...) | ... | ... | ... | ... | |
| Nika | ka-hi (?) | ka-dzoho " a little fire ", | | vi- | ka-dzoka, | vi- |
| Senna | ... | ... | ... | ... | ... | |
| Karanga | ka-ti | ... | ... | ... | ... | ... |
| Ganda | ka-ti | ... | ... | ... | ka-badzi, | bu- |
| Nyambu | ... | ... | ... | ... | ... | ... |
| Herero | (ka-ti (?) ) | o ka-parua " a match ", | | o u- | ... | ... |
| Bihe | o ka-ti | ... | ... | ... | ... | ... |
| Mbunda | ka-ti (?) | ... | | tu-ya " fire " | ... | ... |
| Rotse | ka-ci | ... | | tu-via " fire " | ... | ... |
| Lojazi | ... | ... | | tu-ya " fire " | ... | ... |
| Guha | ... | ka-hia " a little fire ", pl. tu-hia | | | ... | ... |
| Rua | ... | ... | ... | ... | ka-solo, tu- | (?) |
| Angola | (xaxi *ka* ...) | ... | | tu-bia " fire " | ... | ... |
| Lower Congo | ... | ... | | ti-ya " fire " | ... | ... |
| Nywema | ... | ... | ... | ... | ... | ... |
| Yao | ka-ti | ... | ... | ... | ka-wago, | tu- |
| Kele | ... | v-eya " firewood ", | | l-eya | vi-ondshi, | l- |
| Fan | ... | ka-ba " a flame ", | | do-a (do-ba?) | ... | ... |
| Fernandian | ... | si-so (?) " a flame " | ... | ... | ... | ... |

**509.** — 2° Again, in Herero the classifier U- (= Tonga BU-) is considered as the regular plural of KA-. But here two points are to be noticed : *a)* KA- is by no means in Herero the *regular* diminutive classifier. Any one who will peruse Dr. Büttner's " *Mährchen der Ova-Herero* " in the " *Zeitschrift für afrikanische Sprachen* " (1887-1888) will rather find that far more diminutives are formed in Herero with the classifier RU- than with KA-. *b)* Even such substantives as admit the classifier KA- are found to be treated as if they had another, names of things being treated as if they had RU-, and names of persons as if they had MU-. Ex. *O* ka-*ti o* ru-*horoti* " a long stick " ("*Zeitschrift*", p. 189), ka-*kurukaze ua pendukire* " the little old woman got up ", etc.

**510.** — 3° In Nika the classifier TU- is replaced by VI- of class CI-ZI, probably because according to Nika phonetics the plural classifier TU- should be pronounced HU- (cf. 93), which might create confusion with the singular classifier U- (= Tonga BU-). In Shambala also we find VI- instead of TU-. But more information is required on this language, as it seems that even in the singular number the Shambala classifier KA- is practically identified with KI- (= Tonga CI-). Ex. *ka-zana ka* ki-*goxi* " a son ", (Last's " *Polygl.*, " p. 41).

**511.** — 4° In the language of the Gabún River and the like, what we pronounce TU- in Tonga is regularly pronounced *LO-* or *lo-* (cf. 220-230).

**512.** — 5° In Senna and Angola the classifiers KA-TU have kept the regular form, but in most words they allow classifiers between themselves and the stems of their nouns. Ex. in Senna : *ka-m-beni* (= *ka-mu-beni*) " knife " pl. *tu-mi-beni;* in Angola, *ka-m-bika* (= *ka-mu-bika* cf. 279), pl. *tu-a-bika*, etc. In one case in the Shire dialect of the Senna

## EXAMPLES. (Continued.)

| | a little bird | | a small dog | | a pebble | | a second time |
|---|---|---|---|---|---|---|---|
| | Sing. | Plur. | Sing. | Plur. | Sing. | Plur. | Sing. |
| Tonga | ka-yuni, | tu- or bu- | ka-bua, | tu- | ka-bue, | tu- | ka-bili |
| Bisa | ... | ... | ... | ... | ... | ... | ka-wili (?) |
| Shambala | ka-ndege, | vi- | ... | ... | ka-iwe, | vi- | ka-ili (?) |
| Boondei | ... | ... | ka-kuli, | vi- | ... | ... | ka-idi |
| Nyanyembe | ka-noni, | tu- | ka-bwa, | tu- | ka-we, | tu- | ka-wili |
| Sukuma | ka-noni, | tu- | ... | ... | ... | ... | ka-wili (?) |
| Kamba | ka-nyuni | ... | ... | ... | ka-iwia | ... | k-ele |
| Swahili | ... | ... | ... | ... | (kawe, cl. IN) | ... | ... |
| Nika | ka-dzuni, | vi- | ka-dya | ... | ka-dziwe, | vi- | ... |
| Senna | ... | ... | ... | ... | ... | ... | ka-wiri |
| Karanga | ka-nyuni, | tu- | ka-ja (?) | ... | ka-bwe, | tu- | ka-biri |
| Ganda | ka-bwa, | bu- | ka-inja, | bu- | ... | ... | ka-bili (?) |
| Nyambu | ka-nyuni, | ... | ... | ... | ... | ... | ka-wili (?) |
| Herero | o ka-ʈera, | o u- | o ka-ua, | o u- | ... | ... | ... |
| Bihe | ... | ... | o ka-*m*bwa(?), | o tu- | o ka-we, | o tu- | ... |
| Mbunda | ... | ... | ka-tari | ... | ... | ... | ka-bari (?) |
| Rotse | ... | ... | ... | ... | ... | ... | ka-yeri (?) |
| Lojazi | ka-ʈela, | tu- | ka-tari | ... | ... | ... | ... |
| Guha | ... | ... | ... | ... | ... | ... | ...,tu-wiri(?) |
| Rua | ka-yuni (?), | tu- (?) | ... | ... | ... | ... | ka-biji (?) |
| Angola | ... | ... | ka-*m*bua, | tu- | ka-*ri*-tari,tu-*ma*-tari | | ka-yari |
| Lower Congo | ... | ... | ... | ... | ... | ... | ... |
| Nywema | fi-ulu, | tu- | ... | ... | ... | ... | ... |
| Yao | ka-juni, | tu- | ka-wa, | tu- | ... | ... | ka-wili |
| Kele | vi-noni, | lo- | ... | ... | ... | ... | ... |
| Fan | ... | ... | ... | ... | ... | ... | ... |
| Fernandian | si-nodi, | to- | ... | ... | ... | ... | ... |

group I find TU- changed to TI-, viz. *ti-ana* " children " (sing. *ka-mu-ana*) (Nyanja New Testament, Mat. II, 16). Cf. 517.

**513.** — 6° In Swahili I can find no evident traces of the plural classifier TU-, but I find traces of KA- used as a classifier. Ex. *Ka-jua ni* ka-*pi?* " Where is the little sun?" (Krapf's *Dict.*, p. 125); *ka-ndia* ka-*dogo* " a small path " (Krapf, p. 128). However, it seems that, when the particle KA- forms diminutives in Swahili, it is oftener used as a *mere prefix* than as a *classifier*, as in *ka-we*. Ex. *kawe* ya... " a little stone of... ", not *ka-we* ka... I give in the preceding tables the Swahili word *ka-nwa* " the mouth ", but I have no knowledge of its ever being used as a word of cl. KA. The same applies to the same word in Boondei and Nika.

**514.** — In Mozambique the prefix KA- is not a classifier. It forms substantives of the sub-class — -BA (346, 350 and 527, 517).

**515.** — 3° In Tonga many diminutives, principally names of animals, are formed with the compound expressions *ka-nga*... pl. *tu-nga*..., lit. " little son of.., little sons of... ", in which the syllable *nga* is either a contraction for *mu-ana* (cf. 332), or a particular form of its stem -*ana* and then the noun following *ka-nga* or *tu-nga* keeps its regular prefixes. Ex. *ka-nga sekale* " a little musk cat, " lit. " a little son of musk cat ", pl. *tu-nga ba-sekale*; *ka-nga sulue* " a little hare ", pl. *tu-nga ba-sulue*, etc.

**516.** — *N. B.* 1. Somewhat similar expressions are met with in Herero, with this difference, however, that *ka* in such Herero expressions acts as a mere prefix, not as a classifier (cf. 347, 509). Ex. *ka-ha-vandye* " a jackal ".

**517.** — 2. In Senna many diminutives are also formed by using as a sort of prefix either the word *mu-ana* " son " in its full form, or the particle *nga-* (alias *nya-*) which seems to be a contraction for it. Ex. *mu-ana-mbua* " a little dog ", pl. *ana-mbua; mu-ana-mpuru* " a calf ", pl. *ana-mpuru*; *mu-ana-mpeyo* " a little stone for grinding " (*mpeyo*, alias *pheyo* = a grinding-stone). Such words as take the prefix *nga* or *nya* seem to be rather diminutives of politeness than real diminutives. Ex. *nya-rugue* " a tiger ", etc. (cf. 349). This manner of forming diminutives and their particular use without any real diminutive meaning is common to several other languages, and is to all appearances borrowed from the Oriental languages, in which we continually meet with such expressions as " son of death, son of error, son of the house, son of Babel, son of a hundred years ", etc. Cf. in Mozambique the prefixes KA, NA (344, 349).

**518.** — 3. In Chwana and Kafir, as also in Rotse, diminutives are also formed by using the word for " son " under the various forms *-ana, -nyana*, etc., but here, instead of being used as prefixes, these forms are on the contrary used as suffixes. Ex. in Kafir : *u mf-ana* " a young man " (from *u m-fo* " a man "), *u m-ntw-ana* or *u m-nt-ana* " a child " (from *u m-ntu* " a person "); in Chwana : *ntlw-ana* " a little house " (from *n-tlo* " a house ") etc. Further, in the adaptation of such suffixes to the stems of the nouns we meet with all the various phenomena which have been previously described (nn. 202-206 and 127.)

**519.** — 4. In Herero and Yao the suffix *-tye* or *-che* (= Tonga *-ce*, cf. 593) is appended to some diminutives, or even forms them by itself. Ex. in Herero : *o mu-a-tye*, pl. *o va-natye*, or *o ka-na-tye*, pl. *o u-na-tye* " child, children "; in Yao *ka-ana-che*, pl. *tu-ana-che* " child, children ".

**520.** — 4° In Nywema we find the Tonga classifier KA- replaced by FI-, which evidently is radically identical with the

Tonga adjective *-fui* " short ", cf. 601. Ex. *fi-ulu* " a little bird ", pl. *tu-fulu* (Last's *Polygl.*, p. 186).

**521.** — *N. B.* 1. This classifier FI- is also found in Lower Congo, but apparently without a plural (Bentley, p. 536). In Congo the regular diminutive class is KI-I (= Tonga CI-ZI).

**522.** — 2. It is evidently the same classifier wich is found in Kele under the form VI-, in Dualla and Benga under the form VI- before vowels only, I- before consonants. Ex. in Kele *vi-noni* " a bird ", pl. *lo-noni* (cf. 494), *vi-ondshi* " a hatchet " pl. *l-ondshi*.

**523.** — 3. In Fernandian the same classifier has the form SI-, thus being identical with the singular classifier of the preceding class CI-ZI. Ex. *si-iuki* " a fly ", pl. *to-iuki*; *si-nodi* " a bird " pl. *tu-nodi*, etc.

### § 2. SUBSTANTIVES WHICH BELONG TO THE KA-TU CLASS AND THE SUB-CLASSES CONNECTED WITH IT.

**524.** — Unmistakably only such substantives fall under this class as express true diminutives from a Bantu point of view. Such are : —

1° Points of separation of various things, as *ka-ti* " the very centre or middle of a thing ", *ka-kokola* " the joint of the arm ", *ka-ango* " the centre of the breast ", etc.

**525.** — 2° Things which are not only low or short, but comparatively small in every dimension, as *ka-nyamankala* " a little animal ", *ka-pamba* " a little baby ", *ka-samo* " a branch, a stick, a quite young tree ", *ka-nvua* " a thorn ", *ka-nyenyezi* " a little star ", *ka-sua* " a small island ", (cf. *ci-sua*, " an ordinary island "), *ka-ciocio* " an ear-ring ", *ka-langulango* " an ear-ring ", *ka-lilo* " a match ", *ka-longo* " a cup ", (cf. *i-longo* " a high earthen pot ", *ci-longo* " a low earthen pot ", *bu-longo* " pot-clay ", *mu-longa* or *mu-longo* " a muddy river "), *ka-ngone* " a small axe ", *ka-sako* " a small poisoned arrow ", *ka-simbi* " a nail ", etc.

**526.** — We must also consider as belonging to the class KA- such words as *ka-mue* " once ", or " the first time ", *ka-bili* " a second time ", *ka-tatu* " a third time ", etc. For though, from a European point of view, we might consider them as adverbs, they are nevertheless true substantives from the Bantu point of view. In Kafir and a few other languages the classifier KA- has been retained exclusively for such words, and in these languages they may be said to have become adverbs proper.

## § 3. Etymologies. — Varia.

**527.** — The diminutive classifier KA- is probably the element from which is formed the verb *-inka* " to start " (Kafir *mka*). There is no need to explain how this notion of " mere determination or departure " is very naturally applied to the starting point of a thing, and to things that are in their first stage of formation. This etymology throws light on another fact, viz. the peculiar use of the prefix KA- in Mozambique, NKA- in Kafir and Senna, before several substantives of the class MU-BA or of the class IN-ZIN. For it may be noticed that such substantives, when they are not diminutives, are principally either those of animals remarkable for their " rapid starts ", or the like. Ex. in Mozambique : *ka-lamu* " a lion ", pl. *a-kalamu* (in Senna *nka-lamu*, pl. *(zi)n-kalamu*), *ka-pwiti* " a gun ", pl. *a-kapwiti*, *ka-rumia* " a messenger ", pl. *a-karumia*, *ka-mruxo* " sensation ", etc.

In some words the diminutive classifier KA- reminds rather of the verb *-kala* " to sit, not to move " than of the verb *-inka*.

**528.** — The plural classifier TU- is probably derived from the verb *-tula* or *-tola* " to take, to carry " (Kafir *-twala*), exactly as the other *plural* classifiers are respectively derived from the verbs *-bala*, *-ziala*, *-mala* or *-mana*, and *-vula (-zuila?)*. Hence it is that we find it used almost exclusively for such things as are taken up, and, as it were, pluralised by the hand, such as *tu-samo* " branches ", *tu-simbi* " nails ", etc. This may even be the reason why the word *ka-ntabua* " a flea ", pl. *bu-ntabua*, and the like, borrow another classifier than TU- in order to form their plural. It may be noticed that this is of all the plural classifiers the only one which has a hard letter in the generality of the Bantu languages.

**529.** — The examples given under n. 504 may be explained etymologically as follows : —

1. *Ka-cece* " a baby ". The reduplicated element *ce* means " short, small ". It is essentially identical with the classifier CI- (502).
2. *Ka-samo* " a branch, a stick ". Cf. *mu-samo* " a tree ", 384(7).
3. *Ka-nua* " the opening of the mouth ". I have never heard this word myself in Tonga, I take it from Livingstone's Mss. It seems to be related to the verb *-nyua* (Senna *-mwa*) " to drink ". Possibly it is related to *li-no* " a tooth ", pl. *meno*. It may therefore be that it means lit. " the opening through the teeth " or " the opening for drinking ".
4. *Ka-ti* " the centre, the middle ", lit. " a point in the very ground (of a thing) " Related to *mu-se* " the ground " (Swahili *n-ti* or *n-chi*). Cf. 384(7), and 502.
5. *Ka-lilo* " a match ", lit. " a small fire ". Cf. *mu-lilo* " fire ", 384(8). The Guha word

*ka-hia* " a flame ", plur. *tu-hia* " fire " (Angola *tu-bia*, Rotse *tu-via*, etc.) is derived from *-pia* " to burn " (52*).

6. *Ka-ngone* " an axe ". This again is a word which I take from Livingstone's Mss. It must be related to *in-kuni* " wood ", and therefore signify lit. " that which goes through wood. "

7. *Ka-yuni* " a small bird ". The stem *-yuni* probably means " in the air ", from *-ni* " in " (553-555), and *-yu*, which is related to the stem *-oya* of *mu-oya* " the air ".

8. *Ka-bua* " a small dog ". The stem *bua* is onomatopoetic, being derived from the barking of the dog.

9. *Ka-bue* " a pebble ". Cf. *i-bue* " a stone ", 439(7).

10. *Ka-bili* " a second time ". From *-bili* " two ", 792.

# XI. — Locative Classifiers

### and

### Prepositions

**530.** — This is a subject which we must consider apart from European views concerning the cases of substantives in general and locatives in particular, because they would be an obstacle to a correct perception of the Bantu mind. To explain myself, when we say, for instance, " it is dark in the house ", " he lives above me ", " he lives below me ", etc., we are accustomed to consider the expression " in the house " as a locative which has no influence at all on the verb " it is dark "; and likewise the words " above, below " are not substantives, but prepositions : otherwise we should say " above *of* me, below *of* me ", etc. On the contrary in the larger number of the Bantu languages such expressions as " in the house ", " above ", " below ", etc., are substantives of the same type as those we have examined in the preceding articles, and require after them the same constructions as if we had " the-inside-of-the-house ", " the-place-above ", " the-place-below ", etc. Thus we have in Tonga : —

**Mu**-*nga:da* **mu**-*la-sia*, lit. " the-inside-of-the-house *it*-is-dark ", i. e. " it is dark in the house ".

*U-kede* **ku**-*tala* **ku**-*angu*, lit. " he lives the-place-above *that*-of-me, " i. e. " he lives above me ".

*U-kede* **ku**-*nsi* **ku**-*angu*, lit. " he lives the-place-down *that*-of-me ", i. e. " he lives below me ".

In all such sentences it may be seen how the locative elements MU- and KU- act as ordinary classifiers, requiring the expressions governed by them (**mu**-*la-sia*, **ku**-*angu*) to be also determined by prefixes like themselves (MU- and KU-).

**531.** — It will, however, be seen further on that in some languages these locative elements deviate partially from the nature of classifiers. Thus in Kafir we shall find *pe-zulu kw-am* " over me ", instead of *pe-zulu pa-am*, etc.

**532.** — In the generality of the Bantu languages the locative classifiers are three in number. In Tonga their forms are MU-, KU-, (P)A-. In several of the Eastern languages the classifier MU-, instead of being prefixed, is on the contrary suffixed, and changed to -*ng* or -*ni* or -*ini* (cf. 553).

**533.** — A good number of stems are susceptible of receiving

# Locative Classifiers and Prepositions.

the three different locative classifiers; but then the change of classifier produces a change of meaning, which seems not to have been sufficiently attended to in some translations of the New Testament. Thus in Tonga, for instance, three locatives are derived from the noun *mu-se* " earth ", viz. (p)a-*n-si*, ku-*n-si* and mu-*n-si*; but the meaning of the three is different, viz. (p)a-*nsi* = " on the ground, at the surface... " ; ku-*nsi* = " below ", with a notion of comparison; mu-*nsi* = " inside " (of some solid substance, such as the earth) *.

## § 1. Transformations of the Locative Classifier PA-.

**534.** — The principal forms so far known of the first of these locative classifiers exhibit all the intermediary labial sounds between *A*- with a slight labial aspiration and *PA*-, viz. : —

\* EXAMPLES.

| | down | below | within (beneath) | upon | above | in the air |
|---|---|---|---|---|---|---|
| Tonga | (p)a-nsi | ku-nsi | mu-nsi | (p)e-julu | ko-julu | mo-julu |
| Bisa | pa-nsi | ... | ... | pe-ulu | ku-e-ulu | ... |
| Gogo | ha-si | ... | ... | ... | ku-chanya | ... |
| Sagara | ha-si | ku-nda-*ni* | ... | ... | ... | ... |
| Shambala | ha-xi | ... | ... | ... | ... | ... |
| Boondei | ha-si | i-si (?) | nda-*i* | ... | ... | ... |
| Nyanyembe | ha-si | ... | ... | ... | kw-igulia | ... |
| Sukuma | ha-nsi | ... | ... | ... | ... | ... |
| Kamba | wa-si (?) | ... | ndi-*ni* | ulu (*wa*...) | ku-ulu | ... |
| Swahili | ... | ... | chi-*ni*,ti-*ni* / nda-*ni* | ... | juu | m-bingu-*ni* |
| Nika | ... | ... | dzi-*ni* | ... | ... | ... |
| Senna | pa-nsi | ku-nsi | mu-nsi | ... | ku-zulu(?) | ... |
| Karanga | pa-si | ku-si | mu-si | pe-juru | ku-denga | ... |
| Ganda | wa-nsi | ... | mu-nda | wa-gulu | gulu | ... |
| Zulu | pa-ntsi | e za-ntsi | ... | pe-zulu | ... | e-zulu-*ini* |
| Xosa | pa-ntsi | e za-ntsi | ... | pe-zulu | ... | e-zulu-*ini* |
| Herero | p-e hi | k-e hi | m-o ukoto | ... | ... | ... |
| Bihe | ... | ... | ... | ... | k-ilu | ... |
| Mbunda | ka-zi (?) | ... | ... | ... | ko-elo | ... |
| Lojazi | ... | ... | ... | ... | ko-ilo | ... |
| Rotse | ba-nje | ku-inje | ... | ... | ko-ilo | ... |
| Guha | ha-nsi | ... | ... | he-gulu | ... | ... |
| Rua | ha-nsi | ku-nsi | ... | he-ulu (?) | ku-ulu (?) | ... |
| Angola | b-o xi | k-o xi | m-o xi | ... | ... | ... |
| Congo | va-nxi | ku-nanxi | mu-nxi | ... | ... | ... |
| Nywema | ha-xi... | la-xi | ... | ... | lu-ulu | ... |
| Yao | pa-si | ku-si | ... | pe-nani | ... | ... |
| Kilimane | (v)a-ti | ... | mo-ti*n* | va-dulo | ... | ... |
| Mozambique | (v)a-thi | ... | mu-hi*na* | va-chulu,va-zulu | ... | m-chulu |
| Chwana proper | te*ng* | fa-tla-se | mo-te*ng* | ... | go-dimo | ... |
| Suto | te*ng* | (ka tla-se) | mo-te*ng* | ... | go-limo | ... |
| Mpongwe | ... | gontye | ... | ... | gw-igonu | ... |
| Fan | e-dsi | ... | ... | e-yu (we-yu(?)) | ... | ... |
| Duala | o wa-si | ... | ... | ... | ... | ... |
| Fernandian | ua-tshe (?) | *lo*-she (?) | ... | ... | o bo-ko(?) | ... |

**535.** — *A-* commonly, *PA-* after *m* nasal, in Tonga.
*A-* commonly in Taita. Ex. **a-***ndu* " a place ", **a-***vuhi* " near ".
*HA-* in Subia, Nyamwezi, Mbamba, Nywema, etc. Possibly this is pronounced as *A-* in Tonga.

**536.** — *WA-* in Ganda, and in a few words in Kamba and Swahili. In a few other words in Swahili it has kept the form *PA*. Ex. **pa-***hali* **p-***ote* " in every place ", etc. In some other words both in Kamba and Swahili, as also in Nika and perhaps in Congo, this classifier is simply omitted.

**537.** — *HA-* in some Chwana dialects, the *H* being pronounced as a sort of hard labial aspirate.
*FA-* in the other Chwana dialects (cf. 11).
*BFA-* in Pokomo, according to the " *Zeitschrift für afrikanische Sprachen* ", 1888-1889, p. 164. The only example given for it is

## EXAMPLES. (Continued.)

|  | near (on the same level) | near (on different levels) | far, very far | outside | outside |
|---|---|---|---|---|---|
| Tonga | (p)a-fu(p)i | ku-fu(p)i | ku-le, kulekule | (p)a-nze | ku-nze |
| Bisa | ... | ... | ku-tali | ... | ... |
| Gogo | ... | ... | ku-tali | ... | ... |
| Sagara | b-ehi | ... | ku-tali (?) | ... | ku-nje |
| Shambala | h-ehi | ... | ... | ... | ... |
| Boondei | h-ehi | k-ehi (?) | ha-le | ... | ... |
| Nyanyembe | b-ihi (?) | ... | ku-le | ha-nze "place" | ku-nze |
| Sukuma | ... | ... | ku-le | ... | ... |
| Kamba | wa-guwe | ... | ku-acha *alia*sku-atsa | e-nsa (?) | nsa |
| Swahili | ka-ribu | ... | m-bali | wa-zi (?) | nje |
| Nika | v-evi | ... | ku-re | ... | ndze |
| Senna | pa-fupi | ku-fupi | ku-tali | ... | ku-nje |
| Karanga | pa-fupi | ku-fupi | ku-re | ... | ... |
| Ganda | wa-mpi | ku-mpi | wa-la | w-eru | ku-sa |
| Zulu | ... | ku-fupi | ku-de | pa-ndle | e-ndle |
| Xosa | ... | ku-fupi | ku-de, ku-de le | pa-ndle | e-ndle |
| Herero | ... | ... | ku-re (?) | p-e ndye | k-o si |
| Bihe | ... | ... | ... | ... | ... |
| Mbunda | ba-moheje(?) | ... | ko-lajalaja | ... | ku-ese |
| Lojazi | a-moyeye(?) | ... | ko-laja | ... | kua-lebu |
| Rotse | b-ebe | ... | ko-re, korekore | ba-nde | ... |
| Guha | ha-buiyi | ... | ku-le | ... | ... |
| Rua | h-epi | ... | ku-lele | ... | ... |
| Angola | ... | ku-mbambu | ... | bu-kanga | ... |
| Congo | va-na ndambu | ku-na ndambu | va-la | ? | ku-na mbaji |
| Nywema | h-eni (?) | ... | ... | ... | lan-za |
| Yao. | pa-ngulugulu | ... | ku-talika | pa-sa | ku-sa |
| Kilimane | ... | ... | ... | va-nje (?) | ... |
| Mozambique | va-tama | ... | u-tai (=u-tali) | va-the | ... |
| Chwana proper | ga-ufe | ... | ... | fa-ntle | ... |
| Suto | ga-ufi | ... | go-le | fa-ntle | (ka ntle) |
| Mpongwe | ba-raba | ... | gw-evungu (?) | ... | gw-igala |
| Fan | ... | ... | e-valê | ... | ... |
| Dualla | ... | ... | ... | ... | ... |
| Fernandian | bi-ho | ko-pie | o bu-sualo (?) | ... | ... |

*Locative Classifiers and Prepositions.* 125

*bfa-ntu* " a place " ( = Yao *pa-ndu*, Sagara *ha-ntu*, Kamba *va-ndu* or *wa-ndu*, Taita *a-ndu*, Nika *va-tu*, Chwana *felo = fa-elo*, etc.) *VA-* in Mozambique, Nika, and Congo.

*N. B.* 1. In Congo the preposition NA (cf. 579) is generally appended to *VA-*. Hence the compound classifier VA-NA.

2. Concerning the suffix *-ni* or *-ng*, which is appended to some words of this class in Chwana, Mozambique, etc., cf. 553, 554.

**538.** — *BA-* in Rotse, and probably in Nyengo, perhaps also in a few words in Mpongwe.

*N. B.* In Mpongwe the classifier PA- seems to be regularly replaced by GO-. Besides, in this language the mechanism of locatives has lost much of its regularity.

**539.** — *BUA-*, or simply *BU-*, in Angola.

**540.** — *PA-* commonly in Karanga, Senna, Yao, etc.

*N. B.* In Herero it seems that the regular form of this classifier should also be PA.

EXAMPLES. (Continued.)

| | between | inside | together (same time or place) | yesterday (last night) | to-morrow (in the morning) |
|---|---|---|---|---|---|
| Tonga | (p)a-kati | mu-kati | (p)a-mue | (p)e-jilo | (p)e-junza |
| Bisa | ... | ... | ... | ... | ... |
| Gogo | ha-li-gati | ... | ... | ... | ... |
| Sagara | ha-gati | ... | ha-mue | ... | ha-usiku (?) |
| Shambala | ... | ... | ... | ... | ... |
| Boondei | ... | ... | ha-mue | ... | kelo-*i* |
| Nyanyembe | ha-gati | m-gati | ha-mo | h-igolo | ... |
| Sukuma | ... | ... | ... | ... | ... |
| Kamba | wa-kati | kati *(ya...)* | wa-mue | io | ... |
| Swahili | wa-kati (?) | kati *(ya...)* | pa-moja | ... | ... |
| Nika | ... | nda-*ni* | va-menga | dzana | ... |
| Senna | pa-kati | m-kati | pa-modzi | ... | ... |
| Karanga | pa-kati | mu-kati | pa-mue mpera | pe-jiro (?) | ... |
| Ganda | wa-kati | ... | wa-mu | e-guro | ... |
| Zulu | pa-kati | ... | ka-nye | pe-zolo | ... |
| Xosa | pa-kati | ... | ka-nye | pe-zolo | ... |
| Herero | o p-o kati | m-o kati | pa-mue | ... | ... |
| Bihe | p-o kati | m-o kati | ... | ... | ... |
| Mbunda | ... | ... | ... | ba-sindele (?) | he-mene (?) |
| Lojazi | ... | ... | ... | ? | he-mene (?) |
| Rotse | ba-kaci | ... | ... | be-goro | be-onda |
| Guha | ... | ... | ... | ... | ... |
| Rua | ... | ... | ... | ... | ... |
| Angola | bu-a-xaxi | mu-a-xaxi | bu-a-moxi | ... | ... |
| Congo | va-na kati | mu-na kati | va-moxi | e zono (?) | ... |
| Nywema | ... | ... | ... | ... | ... |
| Yao | pa-kati | m-kati | pa-mpepe | ... | ... |
| Kilimane | v-arre | m-arre | ... | ... | ... |
| Mozambique | v-ari | e-ri-ari (ya) | va-moka | ... | ... |
| Chwana proper | fa-gare | mo-gare | ... | (ma-abane) | (ka moxo) |
| Suto | fa-gare | mo-gare | ... | ... | ... |
| Mpongwe | go gare | ... | ... | ... | ... |
| Fan | ... | ... | ... | ... | ... |
| Dualla | ... | . . ... | ... | ... | ... |
| Fernandian | ua-muela | ... | ... | m-padi | ... |

But in this language the articles *e*, *o*, are kept after locative classifiers. Hence the forms PE = PA-E, and PO = (PA-O).

**541.** — Concerning the mode of connecting this classifier with the stem, it may be remarked that in many words the non-locative classifier does not disappear altogether. Thus in Tonga we find *(p)a*-**nsi** " down " = *(p)a*-**mu**-*se*, from *mu-se* " the ground "; *(p)*ej-*ulu* " up " = *(p)a*-li-*julu*, or rather *pa*-ij-*ulu* (cf. 256), from *ij-ulu* " the sky ". Cf. 559. In fact the classifier *PA*- is joined immediately to the stem only when the same stem is that of an adjective, as in *(p)a-fu(p)i* " near ", from *-fu(p)i* " short " (cf. 601 \*), *(p)a-mue* " together " from *-mue* " one " (cf. 792).

### EXAMPLES. (Continued.)

|  | before, in front | behind | where? | whither? whence? | in the house |
|---|---|---|---|---|---|
| Tonga | ku-ne-mbo | mu-sule | (p)a-li? | ku-li? | mu nganda |
| Bisa | ku-menso | ku-numa | ... | ... | ... |
| Gogo | ku-mwando | ku-mgongo | ... | ... | ... |
| Sagara | ku-mwande | ku-nyuma | ho-ki? | ... | mu numba |
| Shambala | ... | ... | ... | ... | ... |
| Boondei | ... | nyuma-*i* | ha-i? | ku-i? | nyumba-*ni* |
| Nyanyembe | ku-mbele | ku-numa | ... | ... | mu numba |
| Sukuma | ku-mbele | ku-mpirimu | ... | ... | ... |
| Kamba | ku-longuisia (?) | ... | wa? | ... | ... |
| Swahili | ... | ... | wa-pi? | ... | nyumba-*ni* |
| Nika | mbele | nyuma | ... | ... | ... |
| Senna | pa tsogolo | ku mbuyu | ... | ku-pi? | m'nyumba |
| Karanga | ku-mbiri | ... | pi (?) | ku-pi? | mu mumba |
| Ganda | mbele | nyuma | wa? (=wa-pi) | ... | mu nyumba |
| Zulu | pa-mbili | e-mva | pi? | ... | e ndl-*ini* |
| Xosa | pa-mbili | e-mva | pi? | ... | e ndl-*ini* |
| Herero | k-o meho | k-o mbunda | pi? | ... | m-o ndyuo |
| Bihe | ... | ... | ... | ... | ... |
| Mbunda | ... | ... | ... | ku-i? | ... |
| Lojazi | ... | ... | ... | ... | ... |
| Rotse | ... | ... | ... | ko-fe? ko-bi(?) | mo mbata (?) |
| Guha | ... | ku-nimba | ... | ... | mu nsese |
| Rua | ku-mbele | ku-nimba | ... | kw-ehi? | ... |
| Angola | ku-polo | ku-rima | ... | ... | ... |
| Congo | ku-na mpuaxi | ku-na nima | v-eyi? | kw-eyi? | mu-na nzo |
| Nywema | lu-kavi | lu-kongo | ... | ... | ... |
| Yao | pa-ujo | ku-nyuma | pa-pi? | kw-api? | m nyumba |
| Kilimane | ... | ... | va-i (?) | ... | mo nyumba (?) |
| Mozambique | u-holu | u-thuli | va-i? | ... | }mwa-ngi }(or) va-nupa-ngi |
| Chwana proper | pele | mo-rago | ka-e? | ... | mo tlu-*ng* |
| Suto | pele | mo-rago | fa ka-e? | ... | tlu-*ng* |
| Mpongwe | go bosyo | go-nyuma | ... | gw-ee? | go nago |
| Fan | e-nsu | e-nvis (?) | ... | ... | ... |
| Dualla | o-boso | ... | ... | ... | ... |
| Fernandian | ... | ua-i (?) | ... | ... | ... |

## § 2. — Transformations of the Locative Classifier KU-.

**542.** — The principal forms of the second locative classifier (Tonga *KU-*) are : —

*KU-* in Tonga, Bisa, Gogo, Nyamwezi, Senna, Kaguru, Herero, etc.; and also in some words in Kafir, Swahili, and Nika.

*N. B.* 1. Here again Herero distinguishes itself by allowing an article to stand after the locative classifier. Hence the forms KE = KU-E, and KO=KU-O.

2. In Congo generally, and in a few words of some other languages, the preposition NA is appended to the locative classifier KU-. Hence in Tonga *ku-nembo* " in front of " *ku-na-imbo* " to the face ". It will be seen further on how LI is appended to KU- in several cases (579-581).

**543.** — *GO-* in Chwana, *KWA-* (= Kafir *e* or *se*) in certain cases (cf. 579).

*N. B.* The Chwana KWA- must have originally contained the preposition KA (Kafir NGA, which conveys the notion of " direction to or from... ". For, according to phonetic laws, the Chwana *k* always stands for *ng* of the other languages, unless it be followed by *h* (190, 175).

*GO-* in Mpongwe.
*U-* in Mozambique and in some languages of the Comoro islands.

**544.** — *KU-* in certain Kafir expressions, as *ku-bo* " near them ", *ku-tatu* " in three moves ", etc. Cf. *ku-a*, n. 784.

*E-* (*SE-*, when immediately preceded by a vowel) in certain other Kafir expressions as *entloko* " on the head ", etc.

*N. B.* 1. It should be noted that when the Kafir prefix E is equivalent to KU-, the locative it forms does not receive the suffix -INI, which it does when it corresponds to the Tonga locative classifier MU-. Thus the Kafir word *entloko* " on the head " is equivalent to the Tonga word *ku mutue*, while *e ntlokweni* (= *e ntloko-ini* (cf. 554) should be rendered in Tonga by *mu mu-tue* " in the head ".

2. E- is used also in Ganda and in Nyambu as a locative classifier corresponding to the Tonga KU-. This is another link connecting the language of the Upper Nile with the Kafir of the South. In Ganda *e-* is often replaced by *eri* (cf. 579).

**545.** — *LU-* or *LA-* in Nywema.

*N. B.* 1. In Last's " *Polyglotta* " we find only *LU-* in the Kusu dialect of Nywema, while in Nywema proper we find both *LU-* and *LA-*. Examples may be seen in the preceding comparative tables (533).

2. More information is wanted with regard to Fan, Dualla, and Fernandian.

**546.** — In Swahili and in Nika no locative classifier is prefixed to the equivalents of the Tonga words *ku-nze*, *ku-nsi*, etc., as may be seen above. However, in both these languages we find *KU-* locative often prefixed to the possessive particle *a*. Ex. in Swahili : *kw-a-mamae* " at his mother's place " *kw-a-ko* " at thy place ", etc. And in Swahili we find the expression *ku-wili* " the second time ", where *KU-* is properly the locative classifier (cf. 544).

## § 3. Transformations of the Classifier MU-.

**547.** — The 3$^d$ locative classifier distinguishes itself from all the other classifiers by the fact that in some languages, e. g. in Swahili, it is suffixed to the stem of the word instead of being prefixed, and in some others, e. g. in Kafir and Chwana, it is partly prefixed, partly suffixed.

**548.** — *N. B.* It will be explained further on (760, 761) how the suffix -*ni* or -*ini* is a real classifier. Meanwhile here is an example which makes it plain : in Kamba *nyumba* y-*ako* renders " thy house ", while *nyumba*-ni mu-*ako* renders " in thy house ", where the change of *y-ako* " thy " to *mu-ako* can be only explained by saying that the suffix -ni in the expression *nyumba*-ni " in thy house " is a *classifier* equivalent to MU-. (Cf. Bleek's *Gr.*, p. 179).

**549.** — The principal forms of this locative classifier are : —
   *MU-* in Tonga, Congo, Angola, Rotse, Karanga, etc.

*N. B.* 1. In Herero this classifier combines with the article. Hence MO = MUO.

2. In Congo the particle *na* " with " is generally added to MU-. Ex. *mu-nakati* " inside ". (Cf. 579).

**550.** — *MU-* commonly, *MW-* before vowels, in Ganda, Boondei, Nyamwezi, etc.

**551.** — *M-* in Senna.

*N. B.* In the manuscripts of my Senna informant M- is often changed to N- before dental sounds. In all probability it was also pronounced N- before it came to be dropped in Swahili, Nika, Kamba, Suto, etc. [552(1), 554, and 555.]

**552.** — *MO-* + suffix -*ing* or -*ng* in Chwana. Ex. m*o-tseleng* " in the road " (= mo-*tsela*-*ing*) cf. 201.

*N. B.* 1. In Suto and some other Chwana dialects the prefix *mo* is generally omitted. Ex. *tseleng* " in the road " [= *n-tseleng*(551) = *mo-tseleng*].

2. In these languages, the suffix -*ing* or -*ng* is appended to many locatives which do not seem to belong to this class. Cf. 568.

**553.** — *MU-* or *M-* + suffix -*ngi* or -*ni* in Mozambique. Ex. m-*piro*-ngi or m-*piro*-ni " in the road ".

*N. B.* 1. In this language, as in Chwana, this suffix -*ngi* or -*ni* is also found after the locative classifiers VA and U. Ex. *m-wa-ngi* or *u-wa-ngi* or *va-nupa-ni* " in the house "; *u-bingu-ni* " in the sky ", etc.

2. The suffix -*ni* is replaced by -*na* in the word *mu-hi-na*, or *m-hi-na*, " inside " (= Tonga *mu-nsi*, cf. 174).

**554.** — *E-* + suffix -*ini* in Kafir. Ex. e *ndlele*-ni " in the road " (= e *ndlela*-ini

*N. B.* In Kafir the suffixing of -*ini* or -*ing* causes the various changes of consonants described in n. 122. Ex.: *e mlonyeni* " in the mouth " (from *u mlomo* " the mouth "), *e mlanjeni* " in the river " (from *u mlambo* " a river "), *e ngutyeni* " in the blanket " (from *i ngubo* " a blanket "), *e zinsatsheni zam* " among my children " (from *i nsapo* " the children of... "), *e mahlwentsheni* " among the poor " (from *a mahlwempu* " the poor ").

**555.** — Suffix -*ni* without prefix in Swahili, Nika, and Kamba.

## § 4. Plural Locative Classifiers.

**556.** — Strange to say, we find some appearance of a plural locative classifier. Thus in Swahili we find the word for " place " rendered not only by *pa-hali*, but also by *ma-hali*. I cannot explain this otherwise than by saying that *ma-hali* was originally a sort of plural of *pa-hali*, unless the prefix *ma-* in *ma-hali* be considered as being of foreign importation. Again, in Tonga, Senna, and in some other languages, we find the expression " at night " rendered by *ma-n-siku* (= Kafir *e b-suku*), from *bu-siku* " night ". This is either a plural form, or a contraction for *mu-a-n-siku*, which is not probable.

**557.** — *N. B.* The Swahili word *ma-hali* is treated as if it had the classifier PA. Ex. Ma-*hali* p-*ote* " in every place ".

## § 5. Effects of the Locative Classifiers on the other Prefixes of the Substantives.

**558.** — There is a great variety in the effects produced by locative classifiers on the prefixes of the nouns to which they are prefixed or suffixed, or *vice versa*. Let us just notice the most important : —

**559.** — 1° In Tonga and in most other languages the locative classifiers in some cases weaken the classifier MU- of classes MU-BA and MU-MI, as well as the classifiers (L)I-, (I)N- and BU-, often causing them to be reduced to the mere nasal *n*, but seldom to disappear altogether. Ex. : —

From mu-*se* " the ground ": *A*-n-*sì*, *Ku*-n-*sì*, *Mu*-n-*sì*.
*N. B.* In this example the further change of *e* to *ì* is caused by the accent being displaced (cf. 271).
From mu-*lilo* " fire " : *mu*-n-*dido* " in the fire ".
*N. B.* With regard to the change of *l* to *d* cf. 285. *N* directly causes the change of the first *l* to *d*, while the second *l* is also changed to *d* by attraction.
From in-*ganda* " a house " : *ku*-nganda " towards the house " ; *mu*-nganda " in the house ".
From i-*tala* " a sloping ground " : *(p)e-tala* " on the side " ; *ku-tala* " above " ; *mu-tala* " on sloping ground ".
From ij-*ulu* " the sky " : *(p)*ej-*ulu* " upon " ; *koj-ulu* " on high " ; *moj-ulu* " in the air ".
From bu-*botu* " good land " : *(p)a*-u-*botu* " on good land ". Cf. *ma*-n-*siku* " at night " from bu-*siku*.
*N. B.* In Angola we find even *mu-a-lunga* " in the sea ", from *ka-lunga* " the sea ". Cf. Chatelain's *Gr.*, p. 87.

**560.** — 2° On the contrary, the locative classifier MU- is often weakened when occurring before the classifier MA-. Ex. *u-manzi* or *m'manzi* = in the water (cf. 279).

**561.** — 3° Something more remarkable is to be noticed in the application of the laws concerning monosyllables to which the use of the locative classifiers gives place. Thus it may be remembered how the law of avoiding monosyllables had given us in Swahili *n-so* " the loins ", *n-ta* or *n-cha* " a point ", *n-ti* or *n-chi* " land ", etc., (cf. 389); and in Chwana *n-tlu* or *en-tlu* " a house ", *n-ku* or *en-ku* " a sheep ", etc., (cf. 392), instead of the monosyllables *so, ta, cha, ti, chi, tlu, ku,* etc. Now, when locative classifiers are prefixed or suffixed to these words, the initial *n-* or *en-* is no longer required by the law of avoiding monosyllables. Hence the locative forms of the same words are in Swahili, not *n-so-ni* " in the loins ", but *so-ni;* not *n-chi-ni* or *n-ti-ni* " on the ground ", but *chi-ni* or *ti-ni;* etc.; and in Chwana, not *mo-n-tlu-nġ* " in the house ", but *mo-tlu-nġ* (in the Suto dialect *tlu-nġ*), etc.

### § 6. On the Use of the Locative Classifiers.

**562.** — 1° In Tonga, and in the larger number of the Bantu languages, the locative classifiers serve to form those locative substantives which correspond to most of our adverbs of time and place, such as " down, up, below, yesterday ", etc., etc., and to our compound prepositions, such as " be-fore, in-side, a-side, a-midst, with-in ", etc. Only, as has been mentioned above (530), and as will be more fully explained further on (755-764), it should be well kept in mind that from the Bantu point of view they are substantives, and that, consequently, when they are equivalent to such compound prepositions as the above, they generally require to be completed by various connective particles. The Tonga say, for instance : *u-a-kala kunsi* **kua** *manzi* " he remained under water ", not *u-a-kala kunsi manzi*.

**563.** — 2° The locative classifiers do duty for most of our simple prepositions ; then in most cases there is no objection to separating them from their noun.

In Tonga, and in the larger number of these languages, (P)A means " on, flat on, close to, etc. ", thus expressing properly a relation of close proximity, as of things which are face to face. PA is also used when mentioning the determined time of an action.

KU implies distance, or " receding from ", or again " coming from some distance to... " It may be rendered according to the cases by " to, from, among, over, compared to..., etc. ".

MU means properly " in ".

Ex. : —

**564.** — (P)A. *U-a-yala* a *bu-enga*, he went *along* the edge of the water.
*Ba-a-mu-bika* a *mu-lilo*, they put him *over* the fire.
*Ta ku-kondua* a *lu-sele*, no work is done *on* the day of the new moon.
*Ba-lia in-sima* e *junzajunza*, they eat porridge *in* the morning.
A *mi-lia*, *on* feast days.
*Ba-a-bika n-zoka mu-nkomo* a *mu-liango*, they put a snake in a bag *on* the doorway.
*Ba-a-bika n-zoka* a *mu-biri*, they put a snake *round* their body.

**565.** — KU. *Mu-oya ua Leza uza* ku *ba-ntu*, the spirit of God comes *to* men.
*Inyue-no mu-a-ka ya* ko *julu*..., you who have gone *to* heaven.
*Ba-a-ka tuba* ku *mu-tue*, they turned white *at* the head, i. e. their hair turned white.
*Ba-lavu ba* ku *ba-bua ba-akue*, lions are *among* his dogs.
*Ba-ana ba-la toligua* ku *Bu-rumbu*, the children are taken *to* the land of the Rotse.
*Ba-kede* ku *Kafuefue*, they live *on* the Kafuefue.

**566.** — MU. *Tu-njizie ma-anza* m'*manzi*, let us put the hands *into* the water.
*U-la njila* mu *nganda*, he enters *into* the house.
*Ba-sangu ta be-zi* m'*munzi*, the sangu (kind of spirit) do not come *into* the town.
*U-a-fua* mu *nganda i-a-kue*, he died *in* his house.
*U-kede* mu *cisua*, he lives *in* an island.
*Ba-la kala* mu *mabue*, they live *in* the rocks (in caves).

**567.** — *N. B.* 1. In Senna PA seems to be often used where the Tonga use KU. Likewise, in Ganda WA (= PA) and in Congo VA (= PA) are often used where the Tonga would prefer KU.

**568.** — 2. Of course all these principles concerning the proper use of the locative classifiers are not much applied in the languages where the mechanism of the locatives is considerably, or even altogether, disturbed, such as Swahili, Chwana, Mpongwe, etc.

### § 7. Prepositions which are not Classifiers.

**569.** — There remain to be noticed a few particles which, having nothing of the nature of classifiers, may be considered as prepositions proper. These are : —

**570.** — 1° A connective preposition which means properly " with ". Often it renders our " and " before substantives. Its principal forms are : —

| | | |
|---|---|---|
| *A* in Tonga (*E*, *O*, by assimilation) | Ex. | *ba-a-ka jana ka-cece* a *ba-nyena Maria.* |
| | ,, | They found the child *with* his mother Mary. (Mat. 2, 11). |
| *NA* in Karanga | ,, | *baka bona nona* na *mamae Maria. (do.)* |
| *do.* in Kafir | ,, | *babona u m-ntana* no *nina* (= na-*u nina*). *(do.)* |
| *do.* in Swahili, etc. | ,, | *waka m-wona m-toto* na *Maryamu mama yake. (do.)* |
| *NE* or *NA* in Ganda | ,, | *balaba o mwana* ne *Maryamu nyina. (do)* |
| *NDI* in Senna (Shire, Tette, etc.) | ,, | *naona kamwana* ndi *Maria amai ace. (do.)* |
| ΠE *(alias NLE)* in Mpongwe | ,, | *w'ayen' ongwana* ne *Maria yi ngi ye. (do.)* |
| *LE* in Chwana | ,, | *bafumana ngwana* le *mae Maria. (do).* |
| *YA* in Lower Congo | ,, | Yo *mwana aku* ye *lekwa...*, your child and his things (= ya *o mwana ...*ya *e lekua...*) |

**571.** — OTHER EXAMPLES :

TONGA

*Tu-a-li ba-sano* o *u-mue*, we were five *with* one, i.e. six.
*Ba-a-ka yasana* a *Nguaru*, they fought *with* Lobengula.
*Ba-ntu be-eza* e *in-tobolo*, the people came *with* guns.
*A-fu'* a *mi-liango ilia*, close *by* those holes.

KARANGA

*t-a-ri ba-xano ba-*na*-ntu mue.*
*ba-kabayana no Ngaru* (=na-*u Nguaru*).
*ba-nu be-ja* ne *noboro.*
*pa-fupi* na *mi-riango iria.*

**572.** — *N. B.* 1. In Tonga I find this preposition A sometimes replaced by ANE, as if this were a more emphatic form.

2. In Karanga, Angola, Herero, etc., NA or NI changes to NE, NO, when combined with I, E ; O, U. Likewise, in Lower Congo YA changes to YE, YO, in the same cases.

**573.** — 2° A preposition which marks properly the *instrument* and the *material cause*. It may be rendered variously in English by " with, through, by means of, by, " etc. In Tonga and several other languages this preposition does not differ from the preceding. It differs from it in Kafir, Chwana, Swahili, etc. Hence its principal forms are the following : —

*A* in Tonga(*E*,*O*, by assimil.) Ex. *be-ense ba-tula i-sumo, ba zo-o-fua* e *i-sumo.* (Mat. 26, 52).
Whosoever takes the sword, shall die of the sword.

| | | |
|---|---|---|
| *NA* in Karanga | ,, | *banu barire batura fumo, boofa* na *fumo. (do.)* |
| *NDI* in Senna | ,, | *onse awo omwe atenga mpeni..., adza mwazika* ndi *mpeni... (do.)* |
| ΠE *(NLE)* in Mpongwe | ,, | *waodu wi bang' okwara, wibe jono* n *'okwara. (do.)* |
| *NGA* in Kafir | ,, | *boonse a bapete u mkonto, baya kufa* ngo *mkonto* (=nga *u mkonto*). |
| *KA* in Chwana | ,, | *botle bacwereng sabole, batla bolawa* ka *sabole. (do.).* [*(do.)* |
| *NA* and *KWA* in Swahili | ,, | *uo wote watwaao upanga, wata kufa* kwa *upanga. (do.)* (Cf. *twa-fa* na *n-daa*, we are dying from hunger). |

**574.** — *N. B.* This preposition is frequently used before locative expressions in Chwana and Kafir. It seems then to convey the notion of " an interval " between two places, or that of " a certain direction " followed. Ex. in Kafir : *Uye* nga *pina ?* (Chwana : *Oile* ka *kae ?*) " Which way has he gone ? "

**575.** — OTHER EXAMPLES :

TONGA

*Ba-a-inka* e *in-zila im-pia* (= a *in-zila...*), they went *by* a [new road.
*U-a-fua* e *in-zala* (= a *inzala*), he died *from* hunger.
*Yaka* a *bu-longo*, build *with* mortar.

KAFIR

*ba-hamba* nge *ndlela entsha* =nga [*i ndlela*)
*wa-fa* nge *n-dlala* (= nga *indlala*)
*yaka* ngo *bulongo* (= nga-*u*...).

*N. B.* In Senna the instrumental preposition NDI is sometimes replaced by the locative classifier PA.

**576.** — 3° An equiparative preposition which means "as, like". Its principal forms are: —

*ANGA* in Tonga. Ex. *Mu-ade u-bede* **anga** *in-cefo* (or *ni-ncefo*, cf. 583), the *muade* is *like* arsenic.
*INGA* or *KALA* in Angola. Ex. ...**inga** *be-ulu* or **kala** *be-ulu, as* in heaven.
*NGA* or *NGA-NGA* in Kafir. Ex. *Lo m-fo u nganga lowo*, this man is *as big as* that.
*JAKA* in Chwana. Ex. *Obua jaka mogolwe*, he speaks *like* his brother.
*N. B.* These particles are also used as conjunctions before verbs with the same meaning as above.

**577.** — 4° A possessive preposition which is practically equivalent to our "of". Its proper form is *-A* in all the Bantu languages, excepting Mpongwe and other languages north of the Congo. Ex. in Tonga: **-a** *Leza* "of God", **-a** *mu-ntu* "of a man", **-a** *bu-longo* "of mud", etc.

This preposition changes to -E or -O, according to the general rules of contraction and assimilation, when it happens to be immediately followed by *i*, *e*, or by *u*, *o*. Ex. in Tonga: **-e** *in-ŋombe* "of -a cow" (= **-a** *in- gombe*, cf. 249), **-o** *uise*, "of his father" (= *a uise*, cf. 249). Ex. in Kafir: **-e** *n-komo* "of a cow" (= a͡i *nkomo*), **-o** *m-ntu* "of a person" (= a͡u *m-ntu*).

Besides this, the possessive expressions thus formed are treated as if they were a kind of *determinative adjectives*. Hence it will be seen further on that they are not immediately joined to the substantive which they determine, but are connected with it by a *connective pronoun*, such as *u* in the expression *mi-cila* **u**-*a mu-lavu*, " the tail of a lion ", or *i* in the expression *mi-cila* **i**-*a ba-lavu* " tails of lions ", etc., cf. 743.

**578.** — *N. B.* 1. In some Tonga proper names the possessive particle *-a* seems to be replaced by *-na*, as if this were a fuller or more primitive form. Ex. *Si*-na-*meja* " Man (or father, or son) of tusks ", *Si*-na-*mpondo* or *Si*-a-*mpondo* " Man (father, son) of horns ", etc. It may be that, etymologically speaking, the possessive particle *-a* is related to the connective particle *a* or *na* (570).

2. With regard to the use of the particles *kua, kwa, ka, ga*, etc., in possessive expressions, cf. 783.

## § 8. The Particles *-LI*, *-NA*, etc., in Locative Expressions.

**579.** — We often find in locative expressions such particles as *-li*, *-na*, etc., which might be thought to be prepositions, or parts of prepositions, but in reality are verbal forms equivalent to our " to be ", or " to have ". As they will be shown in their proper place (1040-1046) to have this value, it will suffice here to state the fact that, when the word which should immediately follow a locative classifier is a pronoun, or a substantive which has no classifier proper, such as *Leza* " God ", *tata* " my father ", *uso* " thy father ", *uise* " his father ", etc. (cf. cl. — -BA, 342), then in Tonga the copula *li* (1025) is inserted between this classifier and the following pronoun or substantive. The Karanga use in almost all the same cases the particle *na* " to have ". In the same cases the Chwana use the locative pronoun *go*, and understand the copula after it. In Senna and Ganda the copula *li* is used as in Tonga, but before a greater number of substantives. In Congo the particle *na* " to have " is used as in Karanga, but before all sorts of substantives; etc. etc.

**580.** — Ex.

| TONGA | KARANGA |
|---|---|
| *Uaka fugama ku*li *Leza*, he knelt down to God. | *Uakafugama ku*na *Reja*. |
| *Ukede ku*li *uise* (or *ku*li *nguise*), he lives with his father. | *Ugere pa*na *tate*. |
| *Uaka inka ku*li *imue nyika*, he went to another place. | *Uakeja ku*ne*mwe nyika*. |
| *Mu*li *Leza*..., in God... | *Mu*na *Reja*. |

KAFIR: *Mkulu ku*na*we*, he is taller than you.
SWAHILI: ...*ku*na*ye*, ...relating to him.
SENNA: *Pida ficei pa*li *sulo*..., when he came to the hare,...
CONGO: *Va*na *kati*, between ; *mu*na *kati*, inside, etc., etc., 1040-1046.

### § 9. ETYMOLOGIES. — VARIA.

**581.** — There is every reason to believe that the locative classifiers belong to the most primitive elements of the Bantu languages. PA- conveys the notion of " opposition between two things ", or " their facing each other ", or " the application of the one upon the other ", and consequently of " close proximity ". It seems to be related to the verb *-pa* " to give ". KU- conveys the notion of " receding from, going aside ". It is related to the verbal suffix *-uka*, which forms neuter expansive verbs (1080), to the adjective *-kulu* " great ", " ancient ", and to the corresponding verb *-kula* " to grow out ". Cf. 468. MU- conveys the notion of " intimate union ", of " things which are within one another ". It is related to the adjective *-mue* " one ". Cf. 725. Hence its change to *-ni* or *-ini*, which has its parallel in the change of *-mue* to *-nye* in Kafir (122).

The etymology of several of the examples which have been given under n. 553 has just been explained in nn. 541, 559. We may complete here the notions there given.

1. *Pa-nsi* " down ", lit. " on the ground ", *ku-nsi* " below ", etc. From *mu-se* " the ground ". It may be remarked that the word *(p)a-nsi* is generally used after the verb *-kala* " to sit " (Chwana *-nna* or *-dula*), just as we generally say " to sit down ", not simply " to sit ". Hence the mistake of several scholars who give us such verbs as *ku-kalansi, u-kalathi, u-kalati*, etc. " to sit down ",when they should decompose them into *ku-kal'ansi, u-kal'athi*, etc. In Chwana the word *te-ng*, which was originally identical with the Swahili *ti-ni* or *chi-ni* (= Tonga *mu-nsi*), has come to be used not only for the Tonga *pa-nsi* " on the ground ", as in *go-dula teng* " to sit down ", but also, as it seems, as a purely expletive particle, somewhat like our " down " in vulgar English. And in the expressions *koa teng, ka fa teng*, etc., it seems to mean " inside ", when we might rather expect it to be equivalent to the Tonga *pa-nsi* or rather to the Kafir *nga pa-ntsi* " downwards ". Perhaps this anomaly is only apparent, as it may be that in these expressions the word *teng* does not answer to the Swahili *tini* or *chini*, but to *ndani* " inside ", lit. " in the belly ", from *i-dda* or *n-da* " belly ". It may also be remarked that the Bantu *pa-nsi* has given to Chwana the word *le-fatshe* " the earth " (Senna *pa-nsi*), which at first sight might have been thought to have nothing in common with *teng*. This again shows what a mixed language Chwana is. Cf. 753.

The Kafir word *e zantsi* " below " means properly " where it comes down ", from *-za* " to come " and *n-tsi* (= *n-si* = Tonga *mu-se*) " the ground ". Its Chwana equivalent *ka tla-se* is formed in the same manner, as the Chwana verb *-tla* " to come " is the equivalent for the Kafir *-za* (173, 195). Here therefore the Chwana element which means " ground " is no longer *te* as in *te-ng*, nor *tshe* as in *le-fatshe*, but *se*.

2. In *pa-fu(p)i* " near " the element *fu* conveys originally the notion of " death, the end of a thing ". The meaning of the element *pi* is not clear. Considered in the light of the phonetic laws it should be related to *-pia* " to burn ". Cf. 541, 601.

3. In *(p)a-nze, ku-nze*, " outside ", the stem *nze* means properly " approaching ground ". It is related to *-za* " to come " and to *in-zila* " a way, a path ".

4. In *(p)ējulu, kōjulu* " above ", etc., the word *ij-ulu* " the sky " means lit. " the open expanse ". Cf. 468(3), 503(8), etc. The verb *-jula* means " to open ".

5. *(P)a-kati* " between ". From *ka-ti* " the centre ", 529(4). The Swahili *wa-kati*, which should be the equivalent for the Tonga *pa-kati*, seems to have come to mean exclusively " a time, the time of... "

6. *(P)a-mue* " together ". From *-mue* " one ".

7. *(P)ējilo* " yesterday ", more properly " last night ", lit. " at bed-time ", from *i-lo* " bed ". The Kafir *pe-zolo* means lit. " at the time of stretching oneself out ", from *ku-zola* " to stretch oneself out ".

8. *(P)ējunza* " to morrow ", more properly " to-morrow morning ". From the element *ju*, notion of " opening " (cf. *ku-jula* " to open "), and *-za* or *iza* " to come ", which implies the notion of " something future ".

9. *Ku ne-mbo* " in front ". From *im-bo* " the front side of the body ".

10. *Mu-sule* " behind ". The word *i-sule* " the back side " seems to be derived from the elements *su*, notion of " disappearing ", and *le*, notion of " length, distance". Cf. 439(5).

11. *(P)a-li?* " Where? " (whence probably *pi ?*) leaves the thought suspended, and probably contains the classifier LI- with a reference to orientation, i. e. to an indefinite position of the Sun. Cf. 421, and 800, 808.

Most of those prepositions which are not classifiers (569-578) seem to have been originally verbal forms related to the auxiliaries *ya* " to go " (911), *enda* " to go " (cf. 918 and 939), *kala* " to sit " (cf. 941 and 944), *nga* " to be inclined to... " (cf. 995), etc.

## XII. — Copulative Prefixes before Substantives.

**582.** — Among the numerous manners of expressing the copula in the Bantu languages, most of which will be studied together in another chapter, there is one which is to be noted here, because in some languages it is a mere modification of the prefixes of the substantives. Its proper effect seems to be that of verbalizing nouns, i. e. changing them into expressions which have more of the nature of verbs than of that of substantives, as if we should say in English " this *bleeds* ", instead of " this (is) *blood* ". Its proper form in Tonga, and some other languages of the interior, is a mere nasal sound, *m* or *n* nasal, prefixed to classifiers. In some cases it is a full nasal syllable, viz. *nga*, or *ngu*, or *ni*. In Kafir its form varies as the classifiers themselves. In Senna, Chwana, Swahili, etc., it has the same form before all sorts of nouns, etc.

**583.** — Ex. : —

| Cl. | | Tonga | Kafir | Senna | |
|---|---|---|---|---|---|
| Cl. | MU¹- | (m)-*mu-ntu* | ngu *m-ntu* | ndi *mu-ntu* | it is a man. |
| „ | — | ngu *Leza* | ngu *Tixo* | ndi *Mu-lungu* | it is God. |
| „ | BA- | m-*ba-ntu* | nga *ba-ntu* | ndi *a-ntu* | those are men. |
| „ | MU²- | (m)-*mu-cila* | ngu *m-sila* | ndi *n-cira* | it is a tail. |
| „ | MI- | (m)-*mi-cila* | yi *mi-sila* | ndi *mi-cira* | those are tails. |
| „ | IN- | ni-*n-gombe* | yi *n-komo* | ndi *ngombe* | it is a cow. |
| „ | (Z)IN- | nzi-*n-gombe* | zi *n-komo* | ndi *(zi)n-gombe* | those are cows. |
| „ | (L)I- | n-*di-tanga* | li *tanga* | ndi *tanga* | it is a pumpkin. |
| „ | MA- | (m)-*ma-tanga* (or)nga-*ma-tanga* | nga *ma-tanga* | ndi *ma-tanga* | those are pumpkins |
| „ | BU- | m-*bu-kande* | bu *tyw-ala* | ndi *bu-adua* | it is beer. |
| „ | KU- | (n)-*ku-lia* | ku *ku-tya* | … … | it is food. |
| „ | LU- | n-*du-anja* | lu *lw-andle* | … … | it is the sea. |
| „ | CI- | n-*ci-bula* | si *si-tulo* | ndi *ci-bura* | it is a seat. |
| „ | ZI- | n-*zi-bula* | zi *zi-tulo* | ndi *byi-bura* | those are seats. |
| „ | KA- | (n)-*ka-pamba* | … … | ndi *ka-mw-ana* | it is a baby. |
| „ | TU- | (n)-*tu-cece* | … … | … … | those are babies. |
| „ loc.(P)A- | | m-*pa-fui* | … … | ndi *pa-fupi* | it is near. |
| „ „ KU- | | (n)-*ku-le* | ku *ku-de* | ndi *ku-tali* | it is far. |
| „ „ MU- | | (m)-*mu nganda* | …se *ndli-ni* | ndi *m-nyumba* | it is in the house. |

**584.** — *N. B.* In general, mere nasals which precede hard consonants or *m* are practically not heard, unless they be immediately preceded by a vowel which supports them. Hence it is that in the above Tonga examples *n* or *m* are in some cases put between brackets, because at the beginning of a sentence, or after a pause, they would not be perceived.

**585.** — It is impossible to make out to what extent the copulative prefixes of Tonga are used in the languages of the interior, because nobody that I know of has even adverted to their existence. However it can be traced in Khutu, a language spoken inland from Zanzibar, in Bisa, in Guha, etc. Thus in Bisa (Last's *Polygl.*, p. 135) we find *u-limi* "a tongue", pl. **ni**-*n-dimi*, and **ni**-*mbua* "a dog", where it is pretty evident that *ni* is not a classifier, but the copulative prefix, so that **ni**-*m-bua* must be rendered literally by "it is a dog", and **ni**-*n-dimi* by "they are tongues". Likewise, in Guha, Stanley has the word **m**-*bu-ato*, which he renders by "boat, canoe", but the exact rendering must be "it is a canoe", since the proper word for "canoe" is simply *bu-ato*, etc.

*N. B.* It will be seen further on that the copulative prefixes of Tonga are used in Senna before pronouns (cf. 656* and 1035).

**586.** — Copulative prefixes of the same reduplicative sort as those of Kafir are met with in Kaguru, Gogo, Nyamwezi, etc. For Kaguru this is evident from Last's *Kaguru Grammar*, where we find, pp. 47 and 50, a complete series of reduplicated pronouns such as *zi-zo, lu-lo, li-lo, chi-cho*, etc., "it is it, it is they", answering exactly to their Kafir equivalents *zi-zo, lu-lo, li-lo, si-so*, etc. (= Tonga *nzi-zio ndu-luo, ndi-lio, nce-co*, etc., 662). Likewise in Last's *Polyglotta*, p. 222, we find the Kaguru expressions *di-kumi* "it is ten", *di-kunda* "it is nine", where we should have only *kumi, kunda*, if these meant simply "ten", "nine", etc.

**587.** — Invariable copulative prefixes similar to the Senna NDI are used in Chwana, Swahili, Karanga, etc. The Chwana form is KE. Ex. **Ke** *mo-tho* "it is a man", **ke** *ba-lotsana* "they are rascals", **ke** *ba-thaba-nchu* "they are people of Thaba-nchu", etc. (Crisp's *Gr.*, p. 52). The Swahili form is NI. Ex. *Ndugu yangu* **ni** *sultani*, "my brother is the Sultan".

*N. B.* We shall see later on that in Swahili NI is apparently replaced by NDI before pronouns.

In Karanga the regular form of the copulative prefix seems to be NDI, as in Senna.

**588.** — There is no evidence of any prefix which can be identified with the above in Herero, Angola, Congo, etc. In Mpongwe the particle NE is sometimes used with a copulative meaning. Ex. *Wao* **ne** *mande?* "Who are they?" (= Tonga *Boo* **m**·*bani?*)

## XIII. — The Particles which introduce Substantives after Passive Verbs.

**589.** — Bantu languages fall under three classes with regard to the manner of introducing the name of the agent after passive verbs. Some make use of the *instrumental* preposition (Tonga *A*, Karanga *NA*, etc., § 572). Such are Tonga, Karanga, Swahili, etc. Others make use of the copulative prefixes just described. Such are Kafir and Chwana. Swahili admits also of this construction. Others join such substantives to their verb without any particle. Such is Ganda. Such is also Zulu, which departs on this point from the Kafir construction.

> Ex. Tonga : *U-a-ka zialigua* **a** *Maria*, he was born of Mary, lit. he was begotten *by* Mary.
> Karanga : *U-a-ka-ywarwa* **na** Maria, do.
> Swahili : *Isa a-ka-ongozwa* **na** *Roho* (or ni *Roho*)... Jesus was led *by* the spirit... (Mat., 4, 1).
> Congo : *Idilu* **kwa** *ngandu*, it was eaten *by* a crocodile (Bentley's *Dict.* p. 29).
> Chwana : *Go-boletsweng* **ke** *Morena*, it was said *by* the Lord.
> Kafir : ...*kwa-tiwa* **yi** *nkosi*, do.
> Zulu : ...*kwa-tiwa* **i** *nkosi*, do.
> Ganda : ...*Isa na-a-twalibwa o Moyo mu dungu*, Jesus was led *by* the spirit into the desert (Mat., 4, 1).
> etc., etc.

## XIV. — The Suffixes of Substantives.

**590.** — In the Bantu languages the suffixes of substantives have very little importance from a grammatical point of view, because, unlike the suffixes of our classical languages, they have no influence on the construction of sentences. The only noticeable exception to this is that of the locative suffix -*ni* or -*ini*, which, according to what has been said, has in Swahili and some other languages the same ruling power as other locative classifiers, e. g. *nyumba*-**ni** mw-*ako* " in thy house " (= **mu**-*nyumba* **mw**-*ako*). However some stems may be noted which are more easily appended than others to substantives as suffixes. Such are : —

> **591.** — -**ana** or -**nyana**, which has already been described as forming the regular diminutives of some languages. Ex. in Tonga : *mu-kulu*-**ana** " an elder brother ", lit. " the elder child ". (517, 518).
> -**kulu** " great, elder ". Ex. in Tonga: *uise*-**kulu** " his grandfather ",

**592.** — -kazi (Rotse -kati or -ati, Mozambique -ari, Kafir -azi or -kazi, etc.) = " female ". Hence in Tonga *mu-ana*-kazi " wife ", lit. " child female ", or more exactly " female member-of-the-family ".

*N. B.* In Kafir when the substantive to which -*kazi* is suffixed has no distinction of sex, this denotes fecundity, beauty, or excellence. Ex. *u m-ti-*kazi " a fine tree ".

**593.** — -ike or -ke (Yao -che, Herero -tye, etc.) = " small ". Ex. *mu-an-*ike " a small brother " (519).

**594.** — Less important suffixes in Kafir are -ra " something like ", and -ndini, a sort of vocative suffix.

**595.** — *N. B.* In Kafir and Chwana the addition to a word of the suffixes which begin with a vowel causes the phonetic changes described in nn. 122 and 202-207. Ex. in Kafir : *u m-lanj*ana " a small river " (Chwana *mo-lac*wana), from *u mlambo* " a river " (Chwana *mo-lapo*), *inkony*ana " a calf " (Chwana *kgong*wana), from *i nkomo* " one head of cattle " (Chwana *kgomo*), etc.

## XV. — Onomatopoetic Substantives.

**596.** — We meet in these languages with a peculiar kind of onomatopoetic substantives, which, though having no classifiers, deserve special attention, were it only because they seem to give the key to the formation of a large number of other words. These onomatopoetic substantives are used principally : — a) by themselves, as exclamations ; — b) after the verb -*ti* " to say, to do ", as in *masekua alila ka a*ti **kuakuakua** " when ducks cry, they say *kuakuakua ;* — c) after a certain number of other verbs, as in *mulilo ulasarara* **piri-biri-biri** " fire gives a red *blazing flame* ". Some authors prefer to class this kind of word as adverbs. But, considering that they generally do duty as direct objects of verbs, they are substantives rather than anything else.

Examples in other languages : —

KAFIR : *Wati* **tu**, lit. he did *tu*, i. e. he kept silent.
*Umbona wati* **sa**, the maize did *sa*, i. e. was spread about.
SENNA : *Chiko charira* **chonchoncho**, a calabash sounds like *chonchoncho*, i. e. gives a hollow sound.
etc., etc.

*N. B.* A whole list of such onomatopoetic words may be seen in the Rev. Alexander Hetherwick's *Yao Grammar*, p. 77-79. Cf. also Rebmann's *Kinyassa Dictionary (passim)*.

## XVI. — Varia.

**597.** — The classifiers which have been described in this chapter are the very marrow of the Bantu languages, as may be judged from a single glance at n. 42. Adjectives, verbs, determinatives of all sorts, vary exactly as the classifiers of their nouns, thus giving to the sentences a clearness which has perhaps no parallel in any other language. Hence, for any one who wishes to study a Bantu language, the importance of learning first how to analyse substantives, that is, how to distinguish in them the classifier or determining element from the stem or determined element.

**598.** — We have already stated (245) that many languages of the Niger, the Guinea Coast, and even Senegambia, are semi-Bantu, and cannot be explained properly without some knowledge of the purer Bantu languages. This is particularly true in the matter of substantives.

It is no rash assertion to say, for instance, that such words in Ibo of Lower Niger as *n-ri* "food", *n-ti* "an ear", ɴwa "a child", *on-wu* "death", *u-ta* "a bow", *w-anyi* "a woman", *ma-du* "people", *e-kiti* "the middle", *e-lu* "above", etc., are closely related to the Tonga *ku-lia* or *ku-ria* "food", "to eat" (52*), *ku-tui* "an ear" (462*), *mu-ana* "a child" (322*), *ku-fua* "death", "to die" (52*), *bu-ta* "a bow" (453), *mu-kazi* "a woman" (322*), *ba-ntu* "people" (322*), *(p)a-kati* "in the middle" (533*), *(p)ejulu* "above" (533*), etc.; and that, consequently, the Ibo prefixes of substantives, *a, e, i, o, u, n,* are, like similar prefixes in Mpongwe, mere remnants of the old Bantu classifiers. (Cf. *Grammatical Elements of the Ibo language*, by the Rev. J. F. Schön, London, 1861).

Likewise, or rather *a fortiori*, when we find in the scanty available collections of the Avatime language of the middle Niger (?) such words as **o**-*no* "a person", **o**-*nyime* "a man *(vir)*, plur. **be-**; **o**-*dshe* "a woman", plur. **ba-**; **li**-*gume* "one head of cattle", plur. **e-**; **li**-*tu*kpo "the head", plur. **e-**; **ko**-*to*kpa "an ear", plur. **ba-**; **ki**-*nemi* "the tongue", plur. **bi-**; **li**-*we* "the sun", plur. **e-**; etc., it is not difficult to recognise in them transformations of the Bantu words *mu-ntu* "a person" (322*), *mu-alume* "a man" (322*), *mu-kazi* "a woman" (322*), *in-gombe* "one head of cattle" (385*), *mu-tue* (alias *li-tue*) "the head" (366*), *ku-tui* "an ear" (462*), *lu-limi* "the tongue" (469*), *i-zuba* (Dualla *i-we*) "the sun" (410*), etc. And it is even easier to see that the prefixes of such

Avatime words are radically identical with the Bantu classifiers. (Cf. *Zeitschrift für afrikanische Sprachen*, 1887-88, pp. 161-188, and 1889-90, pp. 107-132.)

What we say of Ibo and Avatime can be extended to many other so-called Negro languages. Cf. n. 830.

**599.** — This thought has also occurred to me sometimes, that, notwithstanding all prejudices to the contrary, several Semitic prefixes, such as *MA-* in the biblical names of tribes and men, *MA-*, *MI-*, *M-*, *I*, etc., in *ma-bbul* " deluge " (Chwana *ma-bula*), *ma-dda*, " knowledge ", *ma-tʿmon* " a treasure ", *ma-zon* " food ", *ma-kon*, *mᵉ-kunah* and *tᵉ-kunah* " a place ", *mi-kᵉloth* " perfections ", *ta-kᵉlith* " perfection ", *mi-kᵉthabh* " a writing ", *mᵉ-dan* " disputes ", *tᵉ-shubah* " the return ", *tᵉ-shurah* " a present ", etc., *A-* in *a-don* " a lord " (Zulu *in-duna*), *E-* in *e-sheth* " a married woman " (Chwana *mosadi*), etc., etc., and, in general, such prefixes as these to substantives, participles, and locatives, may be found to be distantly related to the Bantu classifiers. This, however, is a mere suggestion.

# Chapter III.

## ADJECTIVES.

**600.** — The student may have noticed above (nn. 39-43) that in Bantu every determinative of a substantive requires a prefix, which is no other than that of this substantive, or part, or a fuller form, of it. Hence it is, for instance, that in the examples under n. 42 we find the determinative " your " rendered by *u-ako* in *mu-ana u-ako* " your child ", by *ba-ako* in *ba-ana ba-ako* " your children ", by *i-ako* in *mi-samo i-ako* " your trees ", by *a-ako* in *ma-sekua a-ako* " your ducks ", by *ku-ako* in *ku-tui ku-ako* " your ear ", by *zi-ako* in *zi-ntu zi-ako* " your things ", etc. Hence also, the Tonga equivalent for our adjective " bad " is *mu-bi* in *mu-ana mu-bi* " a bad child ", *ba-bi* in *ba-ana ba-bi* " bad children ", *mi-bi* in *mi-samo mi-bi* " bad trees ", *ma-bi* in *ma-sumo ma-bi* " bad spears ", *ku-bi* in *ku-tui ku-bi* " a bad ear ", *zi-bi* in *zi-ntu zi-bi* " bad things ", etc., etc.

**601.** — Another most important principle is that — if however we do not consider all the Bantu languages, but only the larger number of them — these people must be said to be far from agreeing with us in the distribution of the various determinatives of substantives. Basing their own distribution of these on a principle of logic which we ourselves overlook, they have one kind of construction for the few determinatives which express nature, dimension, age, or in general the *quantitative, intrinsic*, and comparatively *permanent* properties of things, such as *old, young, big, thin, tall, short*, etc., and another kind of construction for all determinatives whatever which are expressive of colour, sensible qualities, position, relations, or in general of the *external* or *changeable* qualities and relations, such as *white, red, clean, dirty, near, far, mine, thine*, etc.

In other words, the Bantu treat differently the determinatives which properly express *being* (intrinsically), and those which express *being with (having* or *belonging to)*, or *being like*...

The former alone are adjectives proper. If we consider neither

Swahili nor Angola or Congo, but the generality of the Bantu languages, we may put nearly all such adjectives under the heading of *Quantitative adjectives* \*. The others may therefore be termed *Non-quantitative*.

**602.** — *N. B.* 1. In Swahili and a few other Coast languages, in which foreign influence is particularly felt, some adjectives which do not refer to anything like quantity are treated nevertheless as quantitative.

**603.** — 2. In Angola and Lower Congo the notion of quantitative adjectives seems to have been lost altogether. In these languages most adjectives pass as possessive expressions, and consequently we shall not treat of them in this chapter, but in the next. (n. 780).

### \* THE MOST USUAL QUANTITATIVE ADJECTIVES.

| | Good | nicely fat, pleasant, fine | lean, poor, bad | large, great | ancient, great | small |
|---|---|---|---|---|---|---|
| Tonga | -botu | -nono | -bi | -pati | -kulu | -nini |
| Bisa | ... | ... | ... | ... | ... | -nini (?) |
| Gogo | -swamu | ... | -bi | ... | -baha | -dodo |
| Kaguru | -swamu | -nogo (?) | -bi | -kulu | -kulu | -dodo |
| Shambala | -edi | -tana (?) | -wi | -kulu | -kulu (?) | -dodo |
| Boondei | -edi | -tana | -baya | -kulu | ... | -dodo |
| Nyamwezi | -iza | -soga | -wi | -kulu | -nikulu | -do |
| Taita | -rani | -rifu | -lagelage | -baa | ... | -chahe |
| Kamba | { -cheo / -tseo | -nene | -vii | -nene | -uu or kū | -nini |
| Swahili | -ema | -nono | -baya | -kubwa | -kuu | -dogo |
| Pokomo | ... | -nona | -wi (?) | ... | ... | -tyutyu |
| Nika 1. / 2. | -dzu / » | -nonu / » | -i / -(m)bi | -bahe / » | -kulu / » | -dide / -tide |
| Senna | ... | ... | ... | -kulu | ... | -ngono |
| Karanga | -buya | -naki | -bi | -urwana | -urwana | -cecana |
| Ganda | -lungi | -mene | -bi | -kulu | -kulu | -tono |
| Xosa-Kafir | ... | { -hle / -tle | -bi | -kulu | -kulu | -ncinci |
| Zulu-Kafir | ... | { -hle / -tle | -bi | -kulu | -kulu | -ncane |
| Herero | { -ua / -bua | -ua / -bua | -vi / -bi | -nene | -kuru | -titi |
| Bihe | -wa | -wa | -mi | -nene | -ale | -titu |
| Kwango | -bwa | -bwa | -bi | -kamakama | ... | -ndondo |
| Rotse | { -wawa / -bwa | -wawa / -bwa | -i / -bi | -nene | ... | -nini |
| Guha | ... | ... | ... | ... | ... | -ke (?) |
| Rua | -ampi | -nune | -bi | ... | ... | -sheshe |
| Yao | -bone | -koto | -chimwa | -kulungwa | -chekulu | -nandi |
| Mozambique | ... | ... | ... | -ulupale | -ulupale | ... |
| Chwana 1. / 2. | ... / ... | -ntle / » | -be, -shwe / -mpe | -golu / -kgolu | -golugolu / -kgolukgolu | -nyenyane / » |
| Mpongwe 1. / 2. | -bia / -bia | -bia / -bia | -be / -be | -volu / -polu | -lungu / -nungu | -ango / -yango |
| Fan | ... | ... | -be | -nene | ... | ... |
| Dualla | -lodi | ... | -bi | ... | -kuon | -sadi |
| Fernandian | -boke | -lile (?) | ... | -roterote | -boloolo | -koko (?) |

*N. B.* Concerning Angola and Lower Congo, cf. n. 603.

# I. — Quantitative Adjectives.

## § 1. Adaptation of the Quantitative Adjectives to the different Classes of Substantives.

**604.** — Quantitative adjectives, such as *-lanfo* " long ", *-pia* " new ", *-kulu* " ancient ", *-pati* " large ", and the like, incorporate, as a rule, the classifier of their substantive, expressed or understood.

Ex. in Tonga:
CL. MU-NTU: mu-*ntu* mu-*lanfo*, a tall man.   CL. BA-NTU: ba-*ntu* ba-*lanfo*, tall men.
   „   silantumbue mu-*lanfo*, a long cameleon.   „   ba-silantambue ba-*lanfo*, long cameleons.
   „   MU-CILA: mu-*cila* mu-*lanfo*, a long tail.   „   MI-CILA: mi-*cila* mi-*lanfo*, long tails.

### THE MOST USUAL QUANTITATIVE ADJECTIVES. (Continued.)

|  | long, tall | short, small | old | young, new | alive, whole | abundant, many |
|---|---|---|---|---|---|---|
| Tonga | -lanfo / -danfo | -fuefui | -nene | -pia | -umi | -ingi or -nji |
| Bisa | -tali | ... | ... | ... | ... | -ingi |
| Gogo | -tali | ... | ... | -pia (?) | ... | -ingi |
| Kaguru | -lefu | -guhi | -dala | -sia | -gima | -engi |
| Shambala | -tali | ... | ... | -hia | -gima | -ingi |
| Boondei | -le | -jihi | -dala | -hia | -gima | -ngi |
| Nyamwezi | -lihu | -guhi | -lala / -dala | -pia | -panga | -ingi |
| Taita | -lele | -vui | -kale | -ishi | ... | -engi |
| Kamba | -acha / -adza | -guwe | -tene | -via | -ma | -ingi |
| Swahili | -refu | -fupi | -kukuu | -pia | -zima | -ingi |
| Pokomo | -yeya | ... | ... | -bfya | ... | ... |
| Nika 1. | -re | -fuhi | -kare | -via | -zima | -ngi |
| Nika 2. | -(n)de | » | » | -pia | » | » |
| Senna | -tali | -fupi | ... | -pia | ... | -inji |
| Karanga | -refo | -fupi | ... | -psa | -penyo | -nji |
| Ganda | -wanvu / -panvu | -mpi | -daa | -gia / -pia | -lamu | -ngi |
| Xosa-Kafir | -de | -futshana | -dala | -tsha | ... | -ninzi / -ninji |
| Zulu-Kafir | -de | -fupi | -dala | -tsha | ... | -ningi |
| Herero | -re / -de | -supi | -nene | -pe / -be | ... | -ingi |
| Bihe | ... | ... | -ale | ... | ... | ... |
| Kwango | ... | ... | ... | ... | ... | ... |
| Rotse | ... | -canana | ... | -bia | ... | ... |
| Guha | -la | ... | ... | ... | ... | -ingi |
| Rua | -lampi | -ipi | -nunu | ... | -umi | ... |
| Yao | -leu | -jipi | -chekulu | -wisi | -jumi / -yumi | -jinji / -yinji |
| Mozambique | ... | -kani | ... | -kana | ... | -inchi or -injeni |
| Chwana 1. | -lele | -kutshane | ... | -sha | ... | -ntsi |
| Chwana 2. | -telele | -khutshane | ... | -ncha | ... | » |
| Mpongwe 1. | -la | -pe | -lungu | -ona | ... | -enge |
| Mpongwe 2. | -da | » | -nungu | -yona | ... | -yenge |
| Fan | ... | -chun | ... | ... | ... | ... |
| Dualla | ... | ... | ... | ... | ... | ... |
| Fernandian | ... | ... | -boloolo | ... | ... | -nkenke |

CL.(I)N-GOMBE:in-*gombe* n-*lanfo*(388) a long cow.   CL.(ZI)N-GOMBE:in-*gombe*(zi)n-*lanfo*, long cows.
„ (LI)I-BUE: i-*bue* (li-)*lanfo*, a long stone (411).   „ MA-BUE: ma-*bue* ma-*lanfo*, long stones.
„ BU-SIKU: bu-*siku* bu-*lanfo*, a long night.   ... ... ...
„ KU-TUI: ku-*tui* ku-*lanfo*, a long ear.   ... ... ...
„ LU-LIMI: lu-*limi* lu-*lanfo*, a long tongue.   ... ... ...
„ CI-NTU: ci-*ntu* ci-*lanfo*, a long thing.   „ ZI-NTU: zi-*ntu* zi-*lanfo*, long things.
„ KA-SAMO: ka-*samo* ka-*lanfo*, a long branch.   „ TU-SAMO: tu-*samo* tu-*lanfo*, long branches.

**605.** — I do not know that any such adjectives are regularly used in Tonga in the locative classes *(P)A-nsi, KU-nsi, MU-nsi*. However the locative expressions *pa-fui* and *ku-fui* " near ", *(p)a-fuefui* " very near ", etc., may be considered as adjectives which refer to certain notions of place understood. It seems that in a few languages, principally in Yao, quantitative adjectives can agree with locative expressions as well as with other substantives.

Ex. IN YAO: **Pa**-*akulima pa* **pa**-*kulungwa*, a large hoeing place. (*N. B.* The first *pa* after *pa-kulima* is a sort of relative particle, cf. 617.)

**Mu**-*akulima mua* **mu**-*kulungwa*, in a large hoeing place. (*N. B.* Here again, the first *mua* after *mu-akulima* is a sort of relative particle.)

### § 2. EFFECTS OF THE PHONETIC LAWS UPON THE FORMS OF QUANTITATIVE ADJECTIVES.

**606.** — The phonetic principles which have been described in the previous chapters are applicable to adjectives exactly as they are to substantives. Special attention should be paid to the following : —

**607.** — 1° The general law of changing *n* to *m* before labials (281), as in *in-zila* **m**-*pia* " a new road " (not *in-zila* **n**-*pia*) ; and that of dropping nasals before hard consonants in Swahili, Shambala, etc. (283). Ex. in Swahili : *nyumba kubwa* " a large house " (not *nyumba* **n**-*kubwa*).

**608.** — 2° The law, in certain languages, of restoring the original consonants after *n* and *m*, and the opposite law, in certain other languages, of modifying certain consonants after nasals, together with the more general law of changing *l* to *d* after *n*. Cf. 286, 51. Ex. : —

I CONSONANTS RESTORED.

GANDA : *e nsao e m-*pia, new bags, (not *e nsao e n-*gia, cf. *e bi-*gia, new things).
NIKA : *ngoma m-*bi, a bad drum, (not *ngoma ny-*i, cf. *lu-goe lu-*i, a bad string).
etc. etc.

II CONSONANTS MODIFIED.

TONGA : *inzila n-*danfo, a long way, (not *inzila n-*lanfo).
NYAMWEZI : *nshu m-*hia, new knives, (not *nshu m-*pia, cf. *lushu lu-*pia, a new knife).

**609.** — 3° The law of imbibing nasals into the next consonant in Chwana, Mozambique, etc. Ex. in Chwana : *Pitsa e kgolo* (not *pitsa e* n-*golo*) " a large pot ". Cf. *Mosadi eo mo-golo* " a great woman " (nn. 184-196).

**610.** — 4° The law of avoiding monosyllables, even in opposition to the preceding laws relative to *n* nasal. Ex. : —

SWAHILI : *njia* m-*pia*, a new road (not *njia pia*, 389, 607).
*jombo* ji-*pia*, a new vessel (not *jombo pia*, 413).
CHWANA : *tsela e* n-*cha*, a new road (not *tsela e cha*, 609, 390.)

**611.** — 5° Those laws relative to the stems beginning with vowels which cause certain classifiers to be retained before them under a modified form, though they are dropped in most other cases. Ex. in Swahili : *Buyu* j-*ema* " a good calabash ", (not *buyu ema* ; cf. *buyu kukuu*, not *buyu* ji-*kukuu* " an old calabash "). Cf. 415.

**612.** — 6° The laws for contracting, assimilating, or dropping vowels when they happen to meet. Ex. in Swahili : *ma-buyu mēma* (= *ma-ema*) " good calabashes ".

### § 3. ON THE USE OF QUANTITATIVE ADJECTIVES AS EPITHETS.

**613.** — 1° In the generality of the Bantu languages, when quantitative adjectives are used as epithets they are simply placed after their substantive, after having first incorporated the proper classifier.

Ex. IN TONGA : *Mu-ntu* mu-*bi*, a bad man ; *mu-samo* mu-*lanfo*, a high tree ; *mi-liango* mi-*pati*, large holes ; *zi-ntu* zi-*botu*, good things, etc.

**614.** — *N. B.* In Tonga, and several other languages, adjectives of cl. LI- very often drop this classifier, and adjectives of cl. IN- generally drop the initial *i* after their substantive. Ex. *i-bue pati* or *i-bue* li-*pati* " a large stone ", *in-zila* n-*danfo* " a long road " Sometimes also, adjectives of cl. ZIN- drop the initial syllable *zi*. Ex. *Ezi nganda* m-*botu*. (oftener *ezi nganda* zim-*botu*) " these good houses ".

**615.** — Other examples : —

SENNA : *Ma-dzi* ma-*kulu*, the great waters, i. e. the deluge. *Mba-ona somba* zi-*kulu*, ( = *(n)somba zin-kulu*, the *n* being dropped before the hard letter *k*), and he saw great fishes, etc.

NYAMWEZI : *Mu-nhu* m-*soga u-mo*, one fine man ; wa-*nhu* wa-*soga* w-*ingi*, many fine men, etc.

KARANGA : *Ma-puji* ma-*uruana*, large pumpkins ; ʂwi-*nu* ʂwi-*nji*, many things, etc.

| | |
|---|---|
| GANDA: | *O mu-sana* **mu**-*ngi*, much light ; *e mmere nungi* ( = **n** *nungi*), good food, etc. |
| KAMBA: | *Mu ndu* **mu**-*cheo*, a good man ; *a ndu* **a** *cheo*, good men, etc. |
| KAGURU: | *M-tomondo* **m**-*kulu*, a large hippopotamus ; *wa-ntu* **wa**-*swamu*, good men, etc. |
| BOONDEI: | *Mu-ti* **mu**-*tana*, a fine tree ; *mi-ti* **mi**-*tana*, fine trees, etc. |
| POKOMO: | *M-punga* **mu**-*bfya*, a new journey, etc. |
| SWAHILI: | *M-buyu* **m**-*kubwa*, a large baobab ; *siku* **ny**inji ( = *siku* **ziny**-*inji*), many days, etc. |
| ROTSE: | *Mo-jima* **mo**-*wawa*, a good heart ; *mo-jima* **mo**-*i*, a bad heart, etc. |
| MOZAMBIQUE: | *M-laba* **m**-*ulubale*, a large baobab ; *ma-juto* **m**olubale ( = **ma**-*ulubale*), large rivers, etc. |
| MPONGWE: | *O-londa* **om**-*polu*, **om**-*bia*, **onw**-*ona*, a large, good, fresh fruit. |
| | *Ej-a* **e**-*volu*, **e**-*bia*, **ej**-*ona*, a large, good, new thing, etc. (For particulars see Mgr. Le Berre's *Grammaire Pongouée*, pp. 13-15). etc., etc. |

**616.** — 2° In Kafir adjectives which are used as epithets require before themselves a relative particle (718) when their substantive has an article : on the contrary, they admit none when their substantive has no article. The forms of the relative particles in Kafir are *o, e*, or *a*, according as the classifiers of the nouns which are referred to contain *a, i*, or *u* (cf. 718, 719).

In Herero it seems that quantitative adjectives require before themselves a relative particle in every case, as if this had become an integrant part of the classifier. Its form is *e* for class LI-, *o* for all the other classes.

In Chwana and Yao the use of relative particles before quantitative adjectives seems also to be regular. The forms are various, viz. in Chwana : *eo, ba, o, e*, etc. (cf. 719) ; in Yao : *jua*, pl. *wa*, in cl. MU-BA ; *wa*, pl. *ja*, in cl. MU-MI ; *ja*, pl. *sia* in cl. IN-ZIN, etc. (cf. 720).

**617.** — Examples : —

KAFIR :   1° WITHOUT RELATIVE PARTICLE.

*Kangela la m-ntu m-hle*, look at that fine person.
*Asi m-ti m-kulu*, it is no(t a) large tree.

2° WITH A RELATIVE PARTICLE.

*Nda-bona u mntu* **o** *m-hle*, I saw a fine person.
*Ngu m-ti* **o** *m-kulu*, it is a large tree.

CHWANA : *Le-ina* **je** *le-sha*, a new name; *dithipa* **tse** *din-cha*, " new knives ";
*Mo-tho* **eo** *mo-ntle*, a good-looking person ; *di-lo* **tse** *di-potlana*, small things, etc. (Cf. Rev. W. Crisp's *Chwana Gr.*, pp. 22, 23).

YAO : *Mu-ndu* **jua** *m-kulungwa*, a great man ; *m-tela* **wo**-*kulungwa* (= **wa** *mu-kulungwa*), a great tree ; *mi-tela* **ja** *mi-kulungwe*, great trees, etc. (Cf. Rev. A. Hetherwick's *Gr.*, p. 17.)

HERERO : *O mu-ti o mu-re*, a long beam (Rev. F. W. Kolbe's *Dict.*) ; *o ndyira o n-de*, a long road ; *e horo e-pe*, a new pail ; *o m-banda o m-be*, a new dress, etc.

### § 4. ON THE USE OF QUANTITATIVE ADJECTIVES AS PREDICATES.

**618.** — 1º In Tonga and Karanga, when these adjectives are used as predicates with the copula, either the copula is expressed by *li* (cf. 1024), negative *sinsi*, *tinsi*, etc., and in this case they have the same forms as when used as epithets ; or oftener, at least when the clause is in the present tense, they admit the nasal copula with those various phonetic effects on their classifier which have been described in the chapter on substantives (582-585). Ex. : —

TONGA

*Oyu mu ntu u-li mu-pati*, or oftener, *oyu mu-ntu* '**m**-*pati*, this man is big.
*Izuba li-li pati* „ *izuba* **ndi**-*pati*, the sun is great.
*Ezi zintu zi-li zi-botu* „ *ezi zintu* **nzi**-*botu*, these things are good.
*Ei nyika i-li m-botu* „ *ei nyika* **nim**-*botu*, this ground is good.
*Ei nyika tinsi m-botu* „ *ei nyika tinsi* **nim**-*botu*, this ground is not good.
etc., etc.

KARANGA.

*U u-li* **n**-*juja* (= Tonga *ue u-li mu-embezi*), thou art young.
*Irie nyika tobe m-buyana na ?* (= Tonga *Inyika ilia tinsi m botu na ?*) Is not that ground good ? etc.

**619.** — 2º In Ganda, and in most of the other Eastern languages, the copula seems to be generally expressed by the particle *li* or its equivalent in affirmative clauses. Concerning negative clauses nothing certain is to be found.

Ex. IN GANDA : *Gwe o-kia-li mu-lamu*, (while) thou art still alive...

**620.** — 3º In Swahili and Mozambique the copula seems to be generally understood before adjectives of quantity when they are used as predicates. Ex. : —

| SWAHILI | MOZAMBIQUE |
|---|---|
| *Wè hu kufa*, **m**-*zima*. | *Weyo* **m**-*gumi*, *kukwali*, thou art not dead, but *alive*. |
| *Kana mimi* **m**-*zima*... | *Kana minyo gi* **m**-*gumi*..., if I am alive... |
| (Rankin's *Makua Tales*, p. 23.) | |

**621.** — 4º In Kafir generally neither copula nor relative prefix is expressed, at least in the present tense, and the predicate adjective is usually for clearness' sake placed at the head of the clause.

Ex. M-*ninji u mbona*, the maize is abundant ; **M**-*de lo mti kakulu*, this tree is very high ;
In-*dala le nkomo*, this cow is old ; *Si* ba-*tsha*, we are young ; etc.

**622.** — Likewise, in Chwana the copula is generally understood in the present tense, but its connective pronoun subject is expressed.

Ex. *Motse* o mo-*ntle*, lit. the town it (is) pretty ; *le-tseba* le le-*golo*, lit. the pigeon it (is) great, etc. (Cf. Rev. W. Crisp's *Gr*, p. 55).

**623.** — In Herero quantitative adjectives seem to require an article or relative particle before them, even when they are used as predicates. Ex. *Owami* o *mu-nene p'ove*, lit. " I am *one* older than you."

## II. — Non=quantitative Adjectives.

**624.** — Leaving aside possessive, demonstrative, and numeral adjectives, as well as certain others, all of which will be dealt with in the next chapter, we may mention here a particular kind of adjective which radically are or have been substantives and which are treated in a somewhat peculiar manner.

Such are for instance : —

In Kafir : *bomvu* " red ", *mhlope* " white ", *mnyama* " black ", and other adjectives expressive of colour, as well as several others, such as *nzulu* " deep ", *-banzi* " wide ", etc.
In Chwana : *molemo* " good ", *thata* " strong ", etc.

**625.** — *N. B.* 1. I am not certain that such adjectives exist in Tonga and in the generality of the Bantu languages. However it is probable that we should consider as such in Tonga the word *lu-lozi* " straight ".

**626.** — 2. In Kafir *bomvu* is properly the ancient substantive *bo-mvu*, or more probably *bu-omvu*, which means " red clay " (cf. the word for " red ground " *mo-mvu* in Nyengo, *m-bu* in Chwana, *mo-vu* in Yeye, *mo-pu* in Rotse, *li-bu* in Lojazi, etc.). The substantive *u m-hlope* still exists in Zulu, and means properly " the white of the eye ". *U m-nyama* means properly " an enclosure ", or " the rain-bow ". *N-zulu* (= *li-zulu* (cf. 414) means " the sky ", etc.

Likewise, in Chwana *mo-lemo* means properly " straightness, goodness "; *thata*, (= *n-tata*, cf. n. 390) means " strength ", etc.

3. Thus it may be noticed that in general such adjectives contain already in themselves a classifier.

**627.** — It is peculiar to this kind of adjective that they are immediately appended to the copula when this is expressed, or to the pronoun subject of the copula when this is understood, without first incorporating the classifier of their substantive. Ex. : —

KAFIR : *Si bomvu*, we are red (not *si ba bomvu*, cf. *supra*, n. 621, *si*-ba-*tsha*, we are young).
*U-ya ku-ba bomvu*, he will be red (not *u-ya ku ba* mu-*bomvu*).
*U-mntu obomvu*, a red man, lit., a man who (is) red (not *u mntu o* mu-*bomvu*).

CHWANA : *Ke thata*, I am strong (not *ke mo-thata*).
etc., etc.

**628.** — *N. B.* 1. In Bantu a great many of our adjectives are rendered by verbs.

Ex. TONGA : *Muntu u-a-ka* tuba *ku mu-tue*, a man who has white hair, lit. who has become white at the head, (from *ku-tuba*, to turn white).
*Muntu u-tede*, such a man, a certain man, lit. a man who has done so, who is so, (as pointed out by a motion of the hand). *Tede* is the perfect of *ku-ti*, to say so..., to do so...

KAFIR : *U mntwana o-lungile-yo*, a good child, lit. a child who has turned out straight, (from *ku-lunga*, to become straight). — *U-lungile*, he is good, is the perfect of *ku-lunga*.

2. In Angola and Congo nearly all adjectives are treated as possessive expressions, cf. 780.

## III. Comparatives and Superlatives.

**629.** — 1° In Bantu comparison causes no changes in the adjectives themselves, as if they were essentially comparative, but it is shown either by the context itself, or by some other means, for instance —

**630.** — *a)* By the use of a locative expression which may then be said to be comparative, as in the above Herero example : *O wami o mu-nene* p'ove, lit. " I am old with respect to you ", i. e. " I am older than you ". Ex. : —

TONGA : *Ei nzila nindanfo* kuli ndilia, this road is longer than that, lit. this road is long with respect to that.

KAFIR : *Ndi mde* ku-we, I am taller than you, lit. I am tall with respect to you.
*M-futshane lo mntu* kwa bakowabo, this woman is smaller than her relations.
*M-kulu lo* e milanjeni yonke, this (river) is larger than all the others.

**631.** — *b)* By the use of the verb *ku-pita* " to surpass ", or an equivalent for it (in Chwana *go-feta*, in Angola *ku-beta*, etc.).

Ex. In Chwana : *Pitse e ethata* **go-feta** *eeo*, this horse is stronger than that, lit... is strong *to surpass* that one.

**632.** — 2° Superlatives, or intensive adjectives, are generally obtained by repetitions or by laying a particular stress on the principal syllable of a word. Ex. : —

Tonga :  *Matanga* **maingi-maingi**, or oftener **maingiingi**, very many pumpkins.
Karanga : *Mapuji* **manji-manji**, very many pumpkins.
Kafir : *Imfene e zi-nīnji*, very many baboons. A particular stress is laid on the first *i* of *-nīnji*.

*N. B.* 1. The reduplicative adjectives *nini* " small ", *fuefui* " short ", etc., are applications of the same principle.

2. We find in Kafir reduplications of the stems of substantives which convey the same notion as our adjective " genuine ". Ex. *i-cubacuba* " genuine tobacco ", from *i cuba* " tobacco ".

**633.** — There are various other manners of expressing intensity, e. g. by the use of the adverbial adjective *ku-nene* " greatly ", or, in Kafir, *ka-kulu* " greatly ", or by the use of an intensive verb, such as *ku-botesia* " to be very good ", from *-botu* " good ", etc. (cf. 1079).

**634.** — A particularly interesting manner of expressing superlatives, at least in Kafir, consists in denying that a thing is what it is with respect to the quality which it possesses in a high degree. Ex. *A si mntu u kuba mhle*, lit. " he is not a man (with respect) to being beautiful ", i. e. " he is a marvel of beauty ".

# Chapter IV.

## PRONOUNS.

**635.** — Here again we must remember that there are in the generality of the Bantu languages eighteen categories of substantives distinguished from one another by classifiers expressed or understood, and that, consequently, there is a proportionate number of pronouns which cannot be used indifferently. Foreigners in general attend very little to this, and the immediate consequence of it is that natives, anxious to speak like the white man, often come by degrees to neglect entirely what constitutes the proper beauty and perfection of their own language. This effect is very noticeable in several coast languages. It goes to its extreme limit in certain Northern semi-Bantu languages. And perhaps in Bantu languages in general the disturbances in the pronominal system are the best criterion of the amount of foreign influence on them in past times.

**636.** — An element essential to every pronoun of the third person is a form *derived from the classifier of its substantive*. This element is what we shall term the *connective pronoun*, because its proper function is to connect verbs and determinatives with their substantive.

### I. — Connective Pronouns.

**637.** — The connective pronouns are a kind of proclitic particle prefixed to verbs and verbal expressions in order to point out their subject and their object. When we come to relative, possessive, and other determinative expressions, we shall see that most of them, from the Bantu point of view, are considered as verbal expressions, and consequently require also connective pronouns before them. In this article we consider only how these pronouns are formed, and how in their most ordinary use they are prefixed to verbs in absolute clauses.

To give a general notion of the essential difference which exists between them and substantive pronouns, it may be said that they are equivalent to the French *je, tu, il, ils ; me, te, le, les*, etc., while substantive pronouns rather answer to the French *moi, toi, lui, eux*, etc.

Ex. *(Mu-ntu)* u-*lede*, (the man) *he* is asleep, (French : *il* dort).
*(Ba-ntu)* ba-*lede*, (the people) *they* are asleep, (French : *ils* dorment).
*(Lu-sabila)* lu-*lede*, (the baby) *it* is asleep.
*(Ndi-ue)* u-*bonide*, (you) *you* have seen, (French : (toi) *tu* as vu).
*(Me)* ndi-ba-*bonide*, (I) *I* have seem them, (French : (moi) *je les* ai vus).

**638.** — Concerning the use of these connective pronouns the most important thing to be observed is that the fact of expressing the substantive subject of a verb does not dispense from expressing the connective pronoun before the same verb.

Ex. *Leza* u-*kede*, God lives, lit. God *he* lives.
*Ma-lozui* a-*la sisia*, the Rotse are very black, lit. the Rotse *they* are very black.
*Bu-izu ta* bu-*ci-two*, there is no more grass, lit. grass *it* is no more there.
*Ba-anike beesu ba a-fua*, our brothers are dead, lit. our brothers *they* are dead.

§ 1. FORMS.

**639.** — Below may be seen comparative tables of the various connective pronouns in the principal Bantu languages according to the different classes and persons \*. There are a few columns in

### \* COMPARATIVE TABLE OF CONNECTIVE PRONOUNS.

| | 1st person. | | 2d person. | | 3d person : Cl. MU-BA. | | |
|---|---|---|---|---|---|---|---|
| | Sing. | Plur. | Sing. Subj. Obj. | Plur. | Sing. Subj. | Obj. | Plur. |
| Tonga | ndi, n | tu | u, *ku* | mu | u, a, | *mu* | ba |
| Kaguru | ni ... | chi | u, *ku* | m(u) | yu, a, ka, | *mu* | wa |
| Boondei | ni, n | tu, ti | u, *ku* | m(u) | yu, a, | *m* | wa |
| Nyamwezi | ni, n | tu | u, *ku* | mu | u, a, | *mu* | wa |
| Kamba | ni ... | tu | u, *ku* | m(u) | yu, a, | *m(u)* | ma, *a* |
| Swahili | ni, n | tu | u, *ku* | m(u) | u, a, | *m(u)* | wa |
| Pokomo | ni ... | ha | ku, *ku* | mu | (ty)u, ka, | *mu* | wa |
| Senna | ndi ... | ti | u, *ku* | mu | u, a, | *m(u)*, *u* | (w)a |
| Karanga | ndi, n | ti | u, *ku* | mu | u, a, | *m(u)*, (*u*)*u* | ba |
| Ganda | nzi, nyi, n | tu, ti | o, *ku* | mu | u, a, | *mu* | ba |
| Kafir | ndi (ngi, z.) | si | u, *ku* | ni | u, a, e, | *m(u)* | ba, be |
| Herero | ndyi, mbi | tu | u, *ku* | mu | u, | *mu* | ve |
| Rotse | ni, i | tu | u, *ku* | mu | u, a, | ... | a |
| Angola | ngi ... | tu | u, *ku* | mu, nu | u, a, | *mu* | a |
| Congo | ngi, i, n | tu | u, o, — | nu, lu | o, a, e, | *m, n* | be |
| Yao | ni, n | tu | u, *ku* | m(u) | u, a, | *m(u)* | wa |
| Mozambique | ki | ni | u, *u* | m(u) | u, a, | *m(u)* | ya, a |
| Chwana | ke, n, *u* | re | o, *go* | lo, le | o, a, | *mo* | ba |
| Mpongwe | mi | azwe | o, ... | anwe | a, | ... | w(i) |
| Dualla | n(a) | di | o, ... | o | a, | ... | ba |

which it is important to distinguish objective from subjective forms. For clearness' sake such objective forms are printed in italics. In the other columns no such distinction is to be made, as the objective forms do not differ from the subjective.

*N. B.* The *Kafir* pronouns set in black letters are found only in participial expressions.

**640.** — As may be readily seen from these tables, most connective pronouns have almost the same form as the corresponding classifiers. A great exception to this principle is found in the pronouns which correspond to such classifiers as contain *m* or *n*, viz. MU, MI, MA, IN. For in most languages these classifiers commonly drop their *m* or *n* when they are converted into pronouns, keeping it almost exclusively in the objective pronoun MU of cl. MU-BA. Strange to say, Lower Congo, Mpongwe, Dualla, and some other western languages differ on this point from the others by keeping the *m* or the *n* in most of those same pronouns. This difference is all the more remarkable as we have seen in the chapter on substantives that in the Mpongwe classifiers the consonant *m* is generally dropped, and in the Congo classifiers it is often weakened to *n* nasal.

**641.** — *N. B.* 1. Modern Angola agrees in several instances with Lower Congo with regard to retaining the *m* in the connective pronouns *mu, ma, mi*.

## COMPARATIVE TABLE OF CONNECTIVE PRONOUNS. (Cont<sup>d</sup>.)

|  | Cl. MU-MI. | | Cl. IN-ZIN. | | Cl. LI-MA. | | Cl. BU. | Cl. KU. |
|---|---|---|---|---|---|---|---|---|
|  | Sing. | Plur. | Sing. | Plur. | Sing. | Plur. | Sing. | Sing. |
| Tonga | u | i | i | zi | li | a | bu | ku |
| Kaguru | u | i | i | zi | li | ga | bu | ku |
| Boondei | u | i | i | zi | di | ya | u | ku |
| Nyamwezi | gu | i | i | zi | li | ga | u | ku |
| Kamba | u | i | i | zi | i | ga | u | ku |
| Swahili | u | i | i | zi | li | ya | u | ku |
| Pokomo | u | i | i | zi | dji | ya | tyu (?) | ku |
| Senna | u | i | i | zi | ri | a | bu | ku |
| Karanga | u, *un* | i | i | ji | ri | a | bu | u |
| Ganda | gu | gi | i, *gi* | zi | li | ga | bu | ku |
| Kafir | u, *wu* | i, *yi* | i, *yi* | zi | li | a, e, *wa* | bu | ku |
| Herero | u | vi | i | zi | ri | (y)e, we | u | ku |
| Rotse | u | ... | ... | ... | li | a | u | ... |
| Angola | u, *mu* | i | i | ji | ri | ma | u | ku |
| Congo | mu | mi | i | ji | di | me, ma | u | ku |
| Yao | u | ji | ji | si | li | ya | u (?) | ku |
| Mozambique | u | chi (?) | i | chi (?) | ni | a | u | u |
| Chwana | o | e | e | di | le | a | bo | go |
| Mpongwe | w(i) | m(i) | y(i) | s(i) | ny(i) | m(i) | w(i) | w(i) |
| Dualla | mu | mi | ni, e | i | di, li | ma | bu, bo | ... |

2. The Herero pronoun *vi* corresponding to cl. MI is also interesting.

3. Probably in Ganda, Yao, Kafir, Mozambique, etc., the consonants *g, j, w, y*, etc., in the pronouns *gu, ji, wu, yi*, etc., are merely euphonic (295). The Rev. F. W. Kolbe thinks that some of them are vestiges of primitive consonants which have been weakened.

**642.** — The subjoined tables of pronouns exhibit only regular forms independent of phonetic laws. To complete it, it will suffice to apply the general principles of Bantu phonetics which have been laid down in the first chapter of this work. Thus the pronoun *ki* of Kaguru, Swahili, Ganda, etc., will be changed to *c* or *ch* before vowels according to n. 258; the pronouns *u, mu, ku, tu, bu, lu*, will be changed in many languages to *w, mw, kw, tw, bw, lw*, etc., before vowels; likewise, before vowels the pronouns *i, li, ri, zi*, etc., will in some languages be changed to *y, ly, ry, zy*, etc., and in others to *y, l, r, z*, etc., etc. Cf. principally nn. 247-298.

**643.** — *N. B.* In the same tables, it should be observed that in Kafir, Chwana, and Congo, the three locative classifiers are referred to by the pronoun *ku* (Chwana *go*), instead of *pa (va, fu), ku (go)* and *mu (mo)*. The same takes place sometimes in Tonga and several other languages.

### § 2. Connective Pronouns prefixed to Verbs as Subjects.

**644.** — As a rule every verb in an absolute clause requires a connective pronoun before it to point out the substantive subject.

**COMPARATIVE TABLE OF CONNECTIVE PRONOUNS. (Cont<sup>d</sup>.)**

|  | Cl. LU. | Cl. CI-ZI. |  | Cl. KA-TU. |  | Locative Classes. | | |
|---|---|---|---|---|---|---|---|---|
|  | Sing. | Sing. | Plur. | Sing. | Plur. | PA | KU | MU |
| Tonga | lu | ci | zi | ka | tu | pa | ku | mu |
| Kaguru | li (?) | ki | bi | ka | ... | wa | ... | ... |
| Boondei | lu | ki | vi | ka | ... | ha | ku | mu |
| Nyamwezi | lu | ki | fi (?) | ka | tu | ha | ku | ... |
| Kamba | u | ki | i | ka | tu | ... | ... | mu |
| Swahili | u | ki | vi | ka | ... | pa | ku, y- | mu, y- |
| Pokomo | tyu | ki | vi | ... | ... | bfa | .. | ... |
| Senna | ... | ci | pi (?), bzi | ka | ... | pa | ... | mu |
| Karanga | ru | ci | jwi | ka | tu | pa | ku | mu |
| Ganda | lu | ki | bi | ka | ... | wa | ku | ... |
| Kafir | lu | si | zi | ... | ... |  | ku |  |
| Herero | ru | tyi | vi | ke, (ru) | tu | pe | ku | mu |
| Rotse | ... | si | ... | ... | ... | ... | ku | ... |
| Angola | lu | ki | i | ka | tu | ... | ku | mu |
| Congo | lu | ki | i | fi | tu |  | ku |  |
| Yao | lu | chi | i | ka | tu | pa | ku | mu |
| Mozambique | u | i | chi (?) | ... | ... | va | u | m |
| Chwana | lo | se | di | ... | ... |  | go |  |
| Mpongwe | w(i) | j(i) | y(i) | ... | ... | ... | ... | ... |
| Dualla | ... | i, e | bi, be | ... | lo | ... | ... | ... |

| | Ex. | TONGA | KAFIR |
|---|---|---|---|
| 1rst pers. | | { *Me* ndi-*la yeya nawo*,<br>{ *Iswe a* tu-*lie to-onse*, | *Mna* ndi-*cinga njalo*..., As to me, *I* think so...<br>*Tina, ma* si-*tye sonke*, As to us, let *us* eat all together. |
| 2d pers. | | { *Iwe* u-*a-ka ba*, ......<br>{ *Inyue,* mu-*kede a li?* | *Wena* w-*eba,* You, *you* have stolen.<br>*Nina,* ni-*hleli pina?* You, where do *you* live? |
| Cl. MU-BA | | { *Leza* u-*kede m'manzi,*<br>{ *Ba-bue ta* ba-*zuati ngubo,* | *U Qamata* u-*hleli e manzini,* God *(he)* lives in the water..<br>*A Babue a* ba *ambati ngubo,* the Bue*(they)* wear no clothes. |
| Cl. MU-MI | | { *Mu-longa* u-*zuide,*<br>{ *Mi-longa* i-*zuide,* | *U mlambo* u-*zele,* the river *(it)* is full.<br>*I milambo* i-*zele,* the rivers *(they)* are full. |
| Cl. IN-ZIN | | { *In-gombe* i-*a-inka ku-li?*<br>{ *In-gombe* zi-*a-inka ku-li?* | *I nkomo* y-*emka pina?* Where did the cow go to?<br>*I nkomo* z-*emka pina?* Where did the cattle go to? |
| Cl. LI-MA | | { *I-suba* li-*a-salala,*<br>{ *Ma-tanga* a-*bolide,* | *I langa* li-*babele,* the sun *(it)* is scorching.<br>*A ma-tanga* a-*bolile,* the pumpkins *(they)* are rotten. |
| Cl. BU. | | *Bu-izu* bu-*la zua,* | *U tyani* bu-*ya vela,* the grass *(it)* is coming up. |
| Cl. KU. | | *Ku-fua* ku-*zoo-sika,* | *U ku-fa* ku-*ya ku-fika,* death *(it)* will come. |
| Cl. LU. | | *Lu-limi* lu-*la luma,* | *U lw-imi* lu-*ya luma,* the tongue *(it)* bites. |
| Cl. CI-ZI | | { *Ci-bula* ci-*a-ua,*<br>{ *Zi-bula* zi-*a-ua,* | *I si-tulo* si-*wile,* a chair *(it)* has fallen.<br>*I zi-tulo* z-*a-wa,* the chairs *(they)* fell. |
| Cl. KA-TU | | { *Ka-pambu* ka-*la lila,*<br>{ *Tu-pamba* tu-*la lila,* | .................. the baby *(it)* is crying.<br>..................... the babies *(they)* are crying. |
| Loc. PA. | | *Pa-la pia a-nsi* (rare), | Ku-*ya tsha* pa-*nsi,* it is warm on the ground. |
| Loc. KU. | | Ku-*la pia* ku-*nsi,* | Ku-*ya tsha ezantsi,* it is warm below. |
| Loc. MU. | | *Mu-nganda* mu-*la pia,* | Ku-*ya tsha e ndlini,* it is warm in the house. |

Similar examples might be given for all the other Bantu languages. But they would present no remarkable difference.

**645.** — Pronouns are often omitted before certain auxiliary forms of the verbs, as will be seen further on (nn. 873 and sqq.).

**646.** — Some peculiarities have to be noticed with regard to the pronouns of the first person singular and those of class MU-BA, viz. : —

1° In Chwana, Swahili, etc., the full form of the pronoun of the 1rst person singular is reduced to *n* before certain auxiliary forms of the verbs.

Ex. IN CHWANA : **N**-*ka reka* I may buy (= **ke**-*ka reka*).

IN SWAHILI : **N**-*ta rudi,* I shall come back (= **ni** *ta rudi*).

**647.** — *N. B.* 1. In Tonga the pronoun of the first person singular seems to be omitted in certain negative forms beginning with *si*. Ex. *si-yandi* " I do not like ".

**648.** — 2. In Lower Congo the law seems to be to replace the full form *ngi* or *ngy* by *i* or *y* before such auxiliary forms of the verbs as begin with a vowel, and by *n* before such auxiliary forms as begin with a consonant. Ex. : *ngi-enda* " I may go ", *y-a-yenda* " I went ", *n-kw-enda* " I go ". Cf. Bentley's *Congo Grammar.*

**649.** — Of course wherever the pronoun of the first person is thus reduced to *n* nasal, the immediate consequence of it is the application of all the phonetic laws relative to that sound. Thus in Nyamwezi we have *n*-di-*tula* " I strike ", *u-li-tula* " thou strikest ", etc., instead of *n*-li-*tula*, *u*-li-*tula*, etc. And in Yao, which softens consonants after *n* nasal, we have *n*-d**e**sile " I have done ", *u*-*tesile* " thou hast done ", etc., instead of *n*-*tesile*, *u*-*lesile*, etc., etc., (cf. 69, 73, 77, etc.).

**650.** — 2° In Tonga, Kafir, Chwana, Herero, etc., the connective pronoun of the singular number of cl. MU-BA (= " he ") is regularly *u* (Chwana *o*) in the affirmative forms of what may be called the *historical* or *indicative* mood of the verb, such as, in Tonga, *u*-*kede* " he is seated ", *u*-*a*-*kala* " he sat down ", *u zookala* " he will sit down " (cf. 948). But in the negative forms of the same mood, and in all the forms of what may be termed the *intentional mood*, the same pronoun has the form *a*. Ex. in Tonga : *ta* **a**-*kede* " he is not seated ", *ta* **a**-*kali* " he is not sitting down ", *ta* **a**-*zi ku-kala* " he will not sit down "; *a* **a**-*kale* " (I wish) he would sit down ", (let him) sit down ; **a**-*ta kali* " he must not sit down ", etc.

**651.** — In Swahili the regular form of the same pronoun is *a* in every absolute clause. Ex. **a**-*li ku-ja* " he came " ; **a**-*na ku-ja* " he is coming ", etc. Apparently the same must be said of Nyamwezi, Yao, Ganda, etc.

**652.** — *N. B.* Whatever the exact general formula of the law relative to monosyllables may be, the fact is that it causes this connective pronoun *a* to be replaced by yu before certain monosyllabic stems in Swahili and several other languages. Ex. in Swahili : yu-*mo* " he is therein ", yu-*ko* " he is there ", etc., (not a-*mo*, a-*ko*, etc.).

## § 3. CONNECTIVE PRONOUNS PREFIXED TO VERBS AS OBJECTS.

**653.** — Besides the connective pronoun subject, transitive verbs admit also *as prefix* a connective pronoun of the class of their direct object. They even require it when this direct object is not expressed after them. These objective pronouns correspond to the French *me, te, le, les*, etc.

| Ex. TONGA | KAFIR | | |
|---|---|---|---|
| *u*-**ndi**-*bonide*,............ | *u*-**ndi**-*bonile*, he has seen me. Cf. French : il *m*'a vu. | | |
| *tu*-*a*-**ku**-*bona*,............ | *s*-*a*-**ku**-*bona*, we saw thee, | ,, | nous *te* vîmes. |
| *tu*-*a*-**mu**-*bona*,............ | *s*-*a*-**m**-*bona*, we saw him, | ,, | nous *le* vîmes. |
| *u*-*a*-**si**-*bona*,............ | *w*-*a*-**tu**-*bona*, he saw us, | ,, | il *nous* vit. |
| *tu*-*a*-**mu**-*bona*,............ | *s*-*a*-**ni**-*bona*, we saw you, | ,, | nous *vous* vîmes. |
| *tu*-*a*-**ba**-*bona*,............ | *s*-*a*-**ba**-*bona*, we saw them, | ,, | nous *les* vîmes. |
| *tu*-*a*-**u**-*bona* (mu-*longa*), | *s*-*a*-**wu**-*boua* (*u m*-*lambo*), we saw it (the river). | | |
| *tu*-*a* **i**-*bona* (*mi*-*longa*), | *s*-*a*-**yi**-*bona* (*i mi*-*lambo*), we saw them (the rivers). | | |
| *tu*-*a*-**i** *bona* (*in*-ŋombe), | *s*-*a*-**yi**-*bona* (*i n*-*komo*), we saw it (the cow). | | |

*tu-a* **zi** *bona (in-gombe),* | *s-a-***zi**-*bona (i n-komo),* we saw them (the cows).
*tu-a-*li-*bona (i-sekua),* | *s-a-*li-*bona (i dada),* we saw it (the duck).
*tu-a-***a**-*bona (ma-sekua),* | *s-a-***wa**-*bona (a ma-dada),* we saw them (the ducks).
etc., etc.

**654.** — *N. B.* 1 In some languages even locative pronouns may be thus used as objects before verbs. Ex., in Tonga : *Ua-*mu-*lemba (mu-nganda),* "he painted it inside" (the interior of the house).

2. In those forms of the verbs which contain an auxiliary the objective pronoun is not prefixed to the auxiliary, but to the principal verb.

## § 4. Reflexive Pronoun.

**655.** — There is in nearly all, perhaps in all, the Bantu languages a reflexive pronoun of the same nature as those just described. Its form is : —

*Zi-* in Tonga and Kafir. Ex. *U-a-***zi**-*bona* " he saw himself".

*Dzi-* in Nika. Ex. *A-***dzi**-*endera* " he goes for himself ", (from *ku-endera* " to go for... ")

*Dsi-* (*dzi-* (?)) in Pokomo, (*Zeitschrift*, 1888-89, p. 172).

*Ji-*in Swahili and Karanga. Ex. in Swahili : *ku-***ji**-*penda* " to love oneself ".

*Ri-* in Herero and Angola. Ex. in Angola : *Eme ngi-***ri**-*zola* " I love myself ", (from *ku-zola* " to love ").

*Li-* in Yao. Ex. *ku-***li**-*gawa* " to wound oneself ", (from *ku-gawa* " to wound ").

*I-* with strengthening of the following consonant in Chwana. Ex. *O-a-***i**-*thaea* " he spoke to himself", (from *go-raea* " to speak to ") — This *i* becomes *ik-* before vowels. Ex. *go-***ik**-*ama* " to touch oneself ", (from *go-ama* " to touch ").

*I-* in Kaguru. Ex. *kw-***i**-*toa* " to strike oneself ", (from *ku-toa* " to strike ").

*E-* in Ganda. Ex. *kw-***e**-*tta* " to kill oneself ", (from *ku-tta* " to kill ").

## II. — Substantive Personal Pronouns.

**656.** — In most Bantu languages substantive personal pronouns appear under three different forms \*, viz. : —

1º A *self-standing* form, which is a complete word by itself, as *ime* in **ime** *ta ndi-pengi*, " *I*, I am not mad ".

2º An *enclitic* form, which, being generally monosyllabic, cannot form a whole word by itself, as *-ngu* in *mu-alume u a-***ngu** " my husband ", lit. " the husband of *me* ".

*N. B.* The enclitic forms which are set in italics in the subjoined tables are used exclusively in possessive expressions.

3º A *copula-containing* form, which, though derived from the others in a regular manner, appears at first sight to differ from them sufficiently to deserve to be considered separately, as *ndime* " It is *I* ", *ngue* " It is he ".

### \* SUBSTANTIVE PERSONAL PRONOUNS.

| | 1st Person. Singular. | | | 1st Person. Plural. | | |
|---|---|---|---|---|---|---|
| | Self-standing. | Enclitic. | Copula-containing. | Self-standing. | Enclitic. | Copula-containing. |
| Tonga | ime | me, -ngu / nje (?) | ndime | isue | sue, | -*isu* / ndisue |
| Kaguru | anye | nye, -*ngu* | ... | ase | se, | -*itu* |
| Boondei | mimi | mi, -*ngu* | ... | swiswi | swi, | -*itu* |
| Nyamwezi | nene | ne | ... | isu | tui, | -*isu* |
| Kamba | ninye | nye, -*kwa* | ... | nisi | si, | -*itu* |
| Swahili | mimi | mi, -*ngu* | ndimi | sisi | swi, si, | -*itu* / ndisi |
| Pokomo | mimi | mi | ... | swiswi | swi | ... |
| Nika | mimi | mi, -*ngu* | ndimi | suisui | sui, | -*ihu* / ndisui |
| Senna | ine | ne, {-*nga* / -*ngu*} | ndine | ife | fe, | -*tu* / ndife |
| Karanga | eme | me, -*ngu* | ndime | isu | su, | -*idu* / ndisu |
| Ganda | nze | nge | ... | fwe, fe | fe | ... |
| Kafir | mna | m (= mi) | ndim | tina | ti, | -*itu* / siti |
| Herero | oami | ami, -*ndye* | owami | ete | ete, | -*itu* / oete |
| Angola | eme | ami | ... | etu | etu | ... |
| Congo | mono | ... | me | yeto | ... | -*ito* |
| Yao | une | ne, -*ngu* | ... | uwe | we, | -*itu* |
| Mozambique | minyo | mi, -*ka* | {dimi / diminyo} | hiyano | hena, | -*ihu* |
| Chwana | nna | me, (-*ka*) | ke nna | {rona / chona} | {ro, / cho,} | (-echo) / ke rona |
| Mpongwe | mie | mie, -*mi* | ... | azwe | zwe, | -*jio* |
| Dualla | mba | ... | -*mi* | ... | biso | ... | -*su* |

## § 1. Forms.

### I. Enclitic forms.

**657.** — The enclitic forms of the substantive pronouns are the simplest of all. The principle of the formation of most of them is very plain from the subjoined tables, viz. : in most classes of nouns they consist of *a connective pronoun* and *the suffix* **o**, blended together with the usual contractions. Thus, in cl. MU-MI we find *u-o* or *w-o* in the singular, and *i-o* or *y-o* in the plural, where *u* or *w*, and *i* or *y*, are the connective pronouns of the same class, while *o* is the suffix proper to substantive pronouns.

**658.** — Important apparent exceptions to this principle may be observed in the enclitic pronouns of cl. MU-BA, and in those of the 1st and 2d person. For the ending *o* shows itself in a few of them only. But the divergency between the mode of formation of these pronouns and that of the others may not be so great in reality

**SUBSTANTIVE PERSONAL PRONOUNS. (Continued.)**

| | 2d Person. Singular. | | | 2d Person. Plural. | | |
|---|---|---|---|---|---|---|
| | Self-standing. | Enclitic. | Copula-containing. | Self-standing. | Enclitic. | Copula-containing. |
| Tonga | iue | ue, -*ko* | ndiue | imue | mue, -*ino* | ndinyue |
| Kaguru | agwegwe | gwe, -*ko* | ... | anye | nyie, -*inu* | ... |
| Boondei | wewe | we, -*ko* | ... | nwinwi | nwi, -*inu* | ... |
| Nyamwezi | wewe | we, -*ko* | ... | imue | mue, -*inu* | ... |
| Kamba | niwe | we, -*go* | ... | inywi | nywi, -*inyu* | ... |
| Swahili | wewe | we, -*ko* | ndiwe | nyinyi | nyi, -*inu* | ndinyi |
| Pokomo | wewe | we ... | ... | nywinywi | nywi ... | ... |
| Nika | ... | ... -*ko* | ... | muimui | mui, -*inu* | ... |
| Senna | iwe | we, -*ko* | ndiwe | imue | mue, -*nu* | ndimue |
| Karanga | ewe | we, -*o* | ndiwe | ... | ... -*ino* | ... |
| Ganda | gwe | o | ... | mwe | mwe | ... |
| Kafir | wena | we, -*ko* | nguwe | nina | ni, -*inu* | nini |
| Herero | ove | ... -*oye* | ... | ene | ene, -*inu* | oene |
| Angola | eye | e | ... | enu | enu | ... |
| Congo | ngeye | nge, -*ku* | ... | yeno | ... -*ino* | ... |
| Yao | ugwe | gwe, -*ko* | ... | umwemwe | mwe, -*inu* | ... |
| Mozambique | weyo | we, -*o* | diwe | nyenyu | nyenyo -*inyu* | ... |
| Chwana | wena | o, (*ga*)*go* | ke wena | { lona { nyena | lo, -*eno* | ke lona |
| Mpongwe | awe | o, we, -*o*, | ... | anwe | nwe, -*ni* | ... |
| Dualla | wa | ... *ongo* | ... | binyo | ... -*nyu* | ... |

as it seems to be at first sight, as the following considerations may show : —

**659.** — 1º The fullest and more primitive forms of the pronouns in cl. MU-BA, and in the 1ˢᵗ and 2ᵈ person, seem to be the following : —

| COMMON FORM. | AFTER THE POSSESSIVE PARTICLE. |
|---|---|
| 1ˢᵗ PERS. SING.: *mue* (perhaps *mbue*) whence *me, mi* *nye* (122) *ne* (73, etc.) | *-ngu* or *nge*. This with the poss. part. gives *-a-ngu* mine, whence *-a-nga*(273) etc. |
| 1ˢᵗ PERS. PLUR.: *sue* (or *tue, fue*, etc.) | *-isu* or *-itu*, ,, ,, *-esu* (=*a-isu*), ours. |
| 2ᵈ PERS. SING.: ,, *ue* (whence *we, o*, 265) | *-ko*. ,, ,, *-a-ko*, thine. |
| 2ᵈ PERS. PLUR.: ,, *mue* (whence *nywe*, 122) | *-ino, -inu*. ,, ,, *-enu*(=*a-inu*), yours. |
| Cl. MU-BA SING.: ,, *ue*(whence *ee,ye,yu*,etc.) | *-kue*(whence *-ke, -ce*),, ,, *-a-kue*, his. |
| Cl. MU-BA PLUR.:,, *bao*(whence *bo,wao*,etc.) | *-bo* ,, ,, *-a-bo*, theirs. |

2º Considering that almost all these forms end in *ue* or *o*, reduced in some cases to *u*, and comparing them with the substantive pronouns of the other classes, most of which take *o* as their suffix, it may be said that we have here nothing else than an

## SUBSTANTIVE PERSONAL PRONOUNS. (Continued.)

| | 3ᵈ person. Cl. MU-BA. | | | | | |
|---|---|---|---|---|---|---|
| | Singular. | | | Plural. | | |
| | Self-standing. | Enclitic. | Copula-containing. | Self-standing. | Enclitic. | Copula-containing. |
| Tonga | uwe | ue, | -kue | ngue | abo | bo | mbabo |
| Kaguru | yuyu | yu, | -kwe | ... | wao | o | ... |
| Boondei | yeye | ye, | -kwe | ... | wao | o | ... |
| Nyamwezi | uwe | ue, | -kue | ... | awo | wo | ... |
| Kamba | miya | ya, | -kwe | ... | acho | cho, -iyo | ... |
| Swahili | yeye | ye, | -ke | ndiye | wao | o | ndio |
| Pokomo | tyetye | tye | ... | ... | wao | ... | ... |
| Nika | ... | ... | -kwe | ... | ao | o | ... |
| Senna | iye | ye, | -che | ndiye | iwo | wo | ndiwo |
| Karanga | iye | ye, | -e | ndiye | iwo | wo | ndiwo |
| Ganda | ye | ye | ... | ... | be | bo | ... |
| Kafir | yena | ye, | -ke | nguye | bona | bo | ngabo |
| Herero | oye, eye | e, | -e | ... | owo, ovo | wo | ... |
| Angola | muene | ê | ... | ... | ene | â | ... |
| Congo | yandi | ... | -ndi | ... | yau | yau | ... |
| Yao | jue | jo (?), | -kwe | ... | wao | wao | ... |
| Mozambique | { yoyo { yena | { hio, { hiho, | -we | ... | yayo | yayo | ... |
| Chwana | ene | e, | (-ga)gwe | ke ene | bone | bo | ke bone |
| Mpongwe | aye | e, ye, | -ye | ... | wao | wao | ... |
| Dualla | mo | ... | -u | ... | babo | babo | ... |

application of the general phonetic principle of Bantu that *ue* and *o* are convertible in given cases (265).

**660.** — Hence the general law of the original formation of simple substantive pronouns in Bantu may be expressed by the following formula : —

*Connective pronoun* + *suffix* -ue or -o.

*N. B.* The presence of *k* in -*ko* " thee " and -*kue* " he " after the possessive particle *a* is perhaps merely euphonic, or, to be more exact, is intended to prevent contractions which might interfere with clearness of expression.

### II. Self-standing forms.

**661.** — Great dialectic divergencies are noticeable in the formation of the self-standing substantive pronouns. However they all seem to be applications of the one and same great principle of avoiding monosyllabic self-standing words (44).

For, admitting this to be the correct view of the subject, we find that in order to maintain this principle : —

**SUBSTANTIVE PERSONAL PRONOUNS. (Continued.)**

| | Cl. MU-MI | | | | | | Cl. IN-ZIN | | | | | |
|---|---|---|---|---|---|---|---|---|---|---|---|---|
| | Singular. | | | Plural. | | | Singular. | | | Plural. | | |
| | Self-standing. | Enclitic. | Copula-containing. | Self-standing. | Enclitic. | Copula-containing. | Self-standing. | Enclitic. | Copula-containing. | Self-standing. | Enclitic. | Copula-containing. |
| Tonga | ... | uo | nguo | ... | io | njio | ... | io | njio | ... | zio | nzio / nzizio |
| Kaguru | ... | wo | nwo(?) | ... | yo | iyo (?) | ... | yo | iyo (?) | ... | zo | zizo (?) |
| Boondei | ... | wo | ... | ... | yo | ... | ... | yo | ... | ... | zo | ... |
| Nyamwezi | ... | go(?) | ... | ... | yo | ... | ... | yo | ... | ... | zo | ... |
| Kamba | ... | ... | ... | ... | ... | ... | ... | ... | ... | ... | ... | ... |
| Swahili | ... | wo | ndio | ... | yo | ndiyo | ... | yo | ndiyo | ... | zo | ndizo |
| Pokomo | ... | o | ... | ... | yo | ... | ... | yo | ... | ... | zo | ... |
| Nika | ... | o | ... | ... | yo | ndiyo | ... | yo | ndiyo | ... | zo | ndizo |
| Senna | ... | wo | ndiwo | ... | yo | ndiyo | ... | yo | ndiyo | ... | zo | ndizo |
| Karanga | iwo | wo | ndiwo | iyu | yo | ndiyo | iyo | yo | ndiyo | ijo | jo | ndijo |
| Ganda | gwe | gwo | ... | gie | gio | ... | ye | yo | ... | ze | zo | ... |
| Kafir | wona | wo | nguwo | yona | yo | yiyo | yona | yo | yiyo | zona | zo | zizo |
| Herero | owo | wo | ... | ovio | vio | ... | oyo | yo | ... | ozo | zo | ... |
| Angola | ... | ... | ... | ... | ... | ... | ... | yo | ... | ... | jo | ... |
| Congo | wau | wo | ... | miau | mio | ... | yau | yo | ... | zau | zo | ... |
| Yao | we | o | ... | je | jo | ... | je | jo | ... | sie | sio | ... |
| Mozambique | ... | ... | ... | ... | ... | ... | ... | ... | ... | ... | zio(?) | ... |
| Chwana | one | o | ke one | eone | eo | ke cone | eone | eo | ke eone | cone | co | ke cone |
| Mpongwe | ... | ... | ... | ... | ... | ... | ... | ... | ... | ... | ... | ... |
| Dualla | ... | ... | ... | ... | ... | ... | ... | ... | ... | ... | ... | ... |

## Substantive Personal Pronouns.

a) Swahili, Nyamwezi, Nika, etc., make use of reduplications, e. g. *mi-mi* " I ", in Swahili.

b) Kafir, Chwana, etc., make use of the suffix *-na* or *-ne* " self ", e. g. *m(i)na* " I ", in Kafir.

c) Tonga, Senna, Kamba, etc., make use of some kind of article, e. g. *ni-nye* " I ", in Kamba.

*N. B.* Possibly the Kamba prefix *ni* means "self", exactly as the Chwana suffix *-ne* or *-na*.

d) Lower Congo, Mozambique, Mpongwe, etc., make use in some cases of prefixes, in others of suffixes.

*N. B.* 1. It is probable that the Ganda pronouns *nze, mwe, fwe,* etc., are monosyllabic (cf. 45). If so, they must be considered as being proclitic, not self-standing, pronouns.

2. I have not sufficiently reliable or abundant data on substantive pronouns in Nywema, Dualla, etc., to lay down the principle of their formation.

In Tonga, Senna, Swahili, etc., there are apparently no self-standing substantive pronouns out of cl. MU-BA, and the 1$^{rst}$ and 2$^{d}$ person. Demonstrative pronouns are used instead, or those forms of substantive pronouns which contain the copula, as will be seen further on.

### SUBSTANTIVE PERSONAL PRONOUNS. (Continued.)

| | Cl. LI-MA | | | | | | Cl. BU | | | Cl. KU | | |
|---|---|---|---|---|---|---|---|---|---|---|---|---|
| | Singular. | | | Plural. | | | Singular. | | | Singular. | | |
| | Self-standing. | Enclitic. | Copula-containing. | Self-standing. | Enclitic. | Copula-containing. | Self-standing. | Enclitic. | Copula-containing. | Self-standing. | Enclitic. | Copula-containing. |
| Tonga | ... | lio | ndilio | ... | o | ngao | ... | bo | mbubo | ... | ko | nkuko |
| Kaguru | ... | lo | dido(?) | ... | go | gago(?) | ... | wo | nwo(?) | ... | ko | ... |
| Boondei | ... | do | ... | ... | ... | ... | ... | ... | ... | ... | ... | ... |
| Nyamwezi | ... | lo | ... | ... | yo | ... | ... | ... | ... | ... | ... | ... |
| Kamba | ... | ... | ... | ... | ... | ... | ... | ... | ... | ... | ... | ... |
| Swahili | ... | lo | ndilo | ... | yo | ndiyo | ... | wo | ndio | ... | ko | ndiko |
| Pokomo | ... | djo | ... | ... | yo | ... | ... | djo | ... | ... | ... | ... |
| Nika | ... | lo | ndilo | ... | ... | ... | ... | ... | ... | ... | ... | ... |
| Senna | iro | ro | ndiro | ... | yo | ndiyo | iwo | wo | ndiwo | ... | kwo | ndikwo |
| Karanga | irio | rio | ndirio | ... | ... | ... | iwo | wo | ndiwo | ... | ... | ... |
| Ganda | rie | rio | ... | ge | go | ... | bwe | bwo | ... | ... | kwe | kwo |
| Kafir | lona | lo | lilo | wona | wo | ngawo | bona | bo | bubo | kona | ko | kuko |
| Herero | oro | ro | ... | oo | o | ... | owo | wo | ... | oko | kwo | ... |
| Angola | ... | ... | ... | ... | o | ... | ... | ... | ... | ... | ... | ... |
| Congo | diau | dio | ... | mau | mo | ... | wau | wo | ... | kwau | ko | ... |
| Yao | lie | lio | ... | ge | go | ... | we | o | ... | kwe | ko | ... |
| Mozambique | ... | no | ... | ... | ... | ... | ... | ... | ... | ... | ... | ... |
| Chwana | gone | jo | ke jone | one | o | ke one | jone | jo | ke jone | gone | go | ke gone |
| Mpongwe | ... | ... | ... | ... | ... | ... | ... | ... | ... | ... | ... | ... |
| Dualla | ... | ... | ... | ... | ... | ... | ... | ... | ... | ... | ... | ... |

### III. Copula-containing forms.

**662.** — If we consider the copula-containing forms of the substantive pronouns, we shall find that all of them contain an enclitic pronoun as one of their elements. Their other element is a sort of copula which is modified according to the classes or remains invariable, more or less according to the principles laid down above regarding the copula before ordinary substantives (582-588).

The formulas of such expressions are : —

IN TONGA : Copulative prefix varying with the class, viz. *ngu, mba, nji*, etc., + enclitic substantive pronoun.

IN KAFIR AND KAGURU (?) : Copulative prefix varying with the class, but without initial nasal in most cases, + enclitic substantive pronoun.

IN SWAHILI, KARANGA, SENNA, etc. : The copulative prefix *ndi* invariable, + enclitic substantive pronoun.

IN CHWANA : The copulative particle *ke* invariable, + enclitic substantive pronoun, + suffix -*ne* or -*na*.

*N. B.* 1. Expressions of the kind just described have as yet been observed in a few Bantu languages only.

### SUBSTANTIVE PERSONAL PRONOUNS. (Continued.)

| | Cl. CI-ZI. | | | | | | Cl. KA-TU. | | | | | |
|---|---|---|---|---|---|---|---|---|---|---|---|---|
| | Singular. | | | Plural. | | | Singular. | | | Plural. | | |
| | Self-standing. | Enclitic. | Copula-containing. | Self-standing. | Enclitic. | Copula-containing. | Self-standing. | Enclitic. | Copula-containing. | Self-standing. | Enclitic. | Copula-containing. |
| Tonga | ... | cio | ncecio | ... | zio | nzizio | ... | ko | nkako | ... | to | ntuto |
| Kaguru | ... | cho | kicho (?) | ... | vio | vivio (?) | ... | ... | ... | ... | ... | ... |
| Boondei | ... | cho | ... | ... | vio | ... | ... | ... | ... | ... | ... | ... |
| Nyamwezi | ... | cho | ... | ... | fo | ... | ... | ko | ... | ... | to | ... |
| Kamba | ... | ... | ... | ... | ... | ... | ... | ... | ... | ... | ... | ... |
| Swahili | ... | cho | ndicho | ... | vio | ndivio | ... | ... | ... | ... | ... | ... |
| Pokomo | ... | tyo | ... | ... | vio | ... | ... | ... | ... | ... | ... | ... |
| Nika | ... | cho | ndicho | ... | vio | ndivio | ... | ... | ... | ... | ... | ... |
| Senna | ... | cio | ndicio | ... | bjo | ndibjo | ... | ... | ... | ... | ... | ... |
| Karanga | icio | cio | ndicio | iju | jwo | ndijwo | ... | ... | ... | ... | ... | ... |
| Ganda | kie | kio | ... | bie | bio | ... | ke | ko | ... | ... | ... | ... |
| Kafir | sona | so | siso | zona | zo | zizo | ... | ... | ... | ... | ... | ... |
| Herero | otyo | tyo | ... | ovio | vio | ... | oko | ko | ... | otuo | tuo | ... |
| Angola | ... | ... | ... | ... | ... | ... | ... | ... | ... | ... | ... | ... |
| Congo | kiau | kio | ... | yau | yo | ... | fiau | fio | ... | twau | two | ... |
| Yao | che | cho | ... | ye | yo | ... | ke | ko | ... | tue | tuo | ... |
| Mozambique | ... | cho | chicho | ... | ... | ... | ... | ... | ... | ... | ... | ... |
| Chwana | shone | sho | ke shone | cone | co | ke cone | ... | ... | ... | ... | ... | ... |
| Mpongwe | ... | ... | ... | ... | ... | ... | ... | ... | ... | ... | ... | ... |
| Dualla | ... | ... | ... | ... | ... | ... | ... | ... | ... | ... | ... | ... |

*Substantive Personal Pronouns.* 165

2. In Herero I find *owami* " it is I ". *Oete* is also probably a copulative pronoun of the 1st person plural, and *oene* one of the 2d person plural, as if the article *o* had the same power as the copula.

## § 2. Use of the Different Forms.

### I. Self-standing forms.

**663.** — Substantive personal pronouns are used in their self-standing form principally to express contrast or emphasis (= French *moi, toi, lui, eux,* etc., before or after verbs). Ex. : —

Tonga :
Iue *mulozi,* lit. *thou,* thou art a sorcerer.
*Mu-zoo-jana baaka sika,* inyue *ka muli lede,* you will find that they came while *you,* you were asleep.
*Bo ba-la tuba,* iue *u-la sia,* they are white, (but) *he,* he is black.
Isue *tu-li ba-nini,* izio *(zi-pembele) n-zipati,* (as for) *us,* we are small, but *they* (the sea-cows) they are big.

**664.** — Senna :
Ene *ndi-na kala, I,* I remain ; iue *u-na kala, thou,* thou remainest ; iye *a-na kala,*

**SUBSTANTIVE PERSONAL PRONOUNS. (Continued.)**

| | Cl. LU. | | | LOCATIVE CLASSES. | | | | | | | | |
|---|---|---|---|---|---|---|---|---|---|---|---|---|
| | Singular. | | | Cl. PA. | | | Cl. KU. | | | Cl. MU. | | |
| | Self-standing. | Enclitic. | Copula-containing. | Self-standing. | Enclitic. | Copula-containing. | Self-standing. | Enclitic. | Copula-containing. | Self-standing. | Enclitic. | Copula-containing. |
| Tonga | ... | lo | ndulo | ... | wo | mpowo | oko | ko | nkuko | ... | mo | ... |
| Kaguru | ... | lo | lulo (?) | ... | ho | haho (?) | ... | ko | ... | ... | ... | ... |
| Boondei | ... | ... | ... | ... | ho | ... | ... | ... | ... | ... | ... | ... |
| Nyamwezi | ... | lo | ... | ... | ho | ... | ... | ko | ... | ... | mo | ... |
| Kamba | ... | ... | ... | ... | ... | ... | ... | ... | ... | ... | ... | ... |
| Swahili | ... | wo | ndio | papa | po | ndipo | ... | ko | ndiko | ... | mo | ndimo |
| Pokomo | ... | ... | ... | ... | bfo | ... | ... | ... | ... | ... | ... | ... |
| Nika | ... | ... | ... | ... | vo | ... | ... | ko | ... | ... | ... | ... |
| Senna | ... | ... | ... | ... | po | ndipo | ... | ko | ... | ... | mo | ... |
| Karanga | iro | ro | ndiro | ... | po | ndipo | ... | ... | ... | ... | ... | ... |
| Ganda | rwe | rwo | ... | we | wo | ... | gie | gio | ... | inwe | mu | ... |
| Kafir | lona | lo | lulo | ... | ... | ... | kona | ko | kuko | ... | ... | ... |
| Herero | oruo | ruo | ... | opo | po | ... | oko | ko | ... | omona | mo | ... |
| Angola | ... | ... | ... | ... | ... | ... | ... | ... | ... | ... | ... | ... |
| Congo | luau | lo | ... | vau | vo | ... | kwau | ko | ... | mwau | mo | ... |
| Yao | lu | luo | ... | pe | po | ... | kwe | ko | ... | mwe | mo | ... |
| Mozambique | ... | ... | ... | vavo | vo | ... | ... | ... | ... | ... | ... | ... |
| Chwana | lone | lo | ke lone | ... | ... | ... | gone | {eo/ko} | ke gone | ... | ... | ... |
| Mpongwe | ... | ... | ... | ... | ... | ... | ... | ... | ... | ... | ... | ... |
| Dualla | ... | ... | ... | ... | ... | ... | ... | ... | ... | ... | ... | ... |

*he*, he remains ; **ife** *ti-na kala, we*, we remain ; **imue** *mu-na kala, you*, you remain ; *iwo a-na kala, they*, they remain ; *kala-ni* **imue**, do ye remain, *you*, etc.

### 665. — KARANGA :

**Isu** *ti-ri ba-cecana*, **iṅu** *nṅu-kuruana; we*, we are small, *they* (e. g. sea-cows) they are big.
**Ibo** *bati pe, they* (e. g. the men), they said no.
*U-no-penga* **iue**, thou art mad, *thou*.
**Imue** *mu-a-fana Reja ; you*, you are like God.
**Iye,** *ua-ru-ba xe n-kuruana ; he*, he was a great king.

### 666. — OLD ANGOLA (from F. de Coucto's *Angola Catechism*, Rome, 1661) :

*Nga-ku-sawile* **iye** *ngana yami*, I have offended you, *you* my Lord (page 6).
**Bene**, *o kitatu kiao ; they*, the three of them (p. 11).
**Enue**, *ne atu ossololo, you* and all men (p. 17).
*Mu-ng-ijie* **:me** *ngana yenu*, do ye know me, *me* your Lord (p. 17).

### 667. — HERERO (from Dr. Büttner's *Märchen der Ova-Herero* in the *Zeitschrift für afrikanische Sprachen*, 1887-88) :

*Ku-tura* etc *k'o uvi*, to deliver *us* from evil (p. 294).
*Ka* **ove**, it is not *thee* (p. 190).

### 668. — SWAHILI (from Dr. Steere's *Swahili Tales*, London 1889) :

**Wewe** *ingia ndani*, go inside, *thou*.
**Wewe** *nani?* or **weye** *nani?* Who art *thou?* (p. 338).
*Wa-toka wapi*, **wee? Mimi** *natoka mjini kwetu*. Where dost thou come from, *thou? I*, I come from our town (p. 338).
*Ku-nywa* **wewe**, drink *thou* (p. 358).
*Wa-ka-enda* **vivio** *hivio*, thus they went, lit. they went *it*, that (manner), (p. 342).
**Papa (papo (?))** *hapa* = here, (lit. (at) *it*, this place).

### 669. — KAFIR :

*Ku-ya hamba* **mna**, lit. There will go *myself*, i. e. I will go myself.
*Nda ku-ku-bulala* **wena**, *ukuba utsho*, lit. *Thee* I shall kill, if thou sayst so.
*Kwaba njalo ukufa kwa lo mfo : bati ke* **bona**, *bapuma emanzini*, such was the death of that man ; as to *them*, they came out of the water.

### 670. — GANDA (from the *Grammaire Ruganda*) :

*Tu-na sika* **gue** *o-kia-li mulamu?* Lit. Shall we come into power when *thou*, thou art still alive?
**Nze** *bue ndia mmere, sikkuta, I*, when I eat porridge, I cannot be satiated.

### 671. — CHWANA :

**Nna**, *ka-re jalo*, lit. *I*, I said so (Crisp's *Gr.*, p. 13), etc., etc.

### 672. — *N. B.* 1. In some languages, viz. in Karanga, Herero, Chwana, Mozambique, etc., substantive pronouns are also used regularly in their self-standing form after the preposition which means " with, and, also ", viz. *na* or *ne* in Karanga and Herero *ni* in Mozambique, *le* in Chwana, etc. (570).

Ex.: KARANGA: **Ne-ebo**, *ba-ka-ba banji*, they also became numerous.
HERERO: **N'eye** *a kotoka*, and she came back; **n'owo** *va-ire*, and they went.
MOZAMBIQUE: **Ni-minyo** *gi-na hogoloa*, I too, I shall come back. **Ni-yena** *a-kala na mwaraui*, he too had a wife.
IN CHWANA: **Le-ene**, he too; **le-bone**, they too, etc...

**673.** — 2. In Chwana and Mozambique, substantive pronouns are used regularly in their self-standing form after several other prepositions or particles (cf. Crisp's *Chwana Gr.*, p. 13).

## II. Enclitic forms.

**674.** — The reader may remember first that all the other forms of substantive pronouns contain at least originally the enclitic form. This is found also doing duty regularly either as a noun or as a determinative in many other expressions which vary according to the different languages.

Thus, in Tonga, we find it: —
a) After the prep. *a* " and, with, also ".

Ex.: *Baainka a-***ue** *ku-nganga*, they went to the doctor with him, (lit. they went he-also to the doctor).

*N. B.* Concerning the forms of the pronouns after the other prepositions in Tonga, cf. 688 and 1040-1041.

b) Before or after verbal expressions without emphasis.

Ex.: **Ue** *u-ti*... He (the man already mentioned), he says...
*Ba-lapelela* **sue**, they pray for us.

c) Before locative expressions.

Ex.: *Ta mu-zoo-inki* **ko** *ku-lia*, do not go there, (it... to it, that (place).

d) In such expressions as *u-ci-li* **wo**, he is still there; *u-a-li* **ko** *lu-bela*, he was there from the beginning, etc.

**675.** — In Karanga, Swahili, Kafir, Senna, Angola, etc., we find these enclitic forms of pronouns in the same cases as in Tonga, though not so often before verbal expressions, and in several others, more particularly after prepositions in general, and often before numbers, as also before the words which render our " all ". Ex.: —

KARANGA:
*Ndoonda na-***yo** *(ijira)* lit. I shall go by *it* (the road).
*Banu beja ku-na-***su**, men came to *us*.

**676.** — ANGOLA:
*O ngana yekala na-***e**, the Lord is with *thee* (*Catechism*, p. 2).
*Ku-tunda na-***lo**, to stretch *it* (*lu-kuako*, the arm) (p. 23).

*O muenye uae uaile* **ko** *o ku-katula* **mo** *o miyenyo*... lit. his soul went *thither* to draw *from therein* the souls... (*ibid.*, p. 27).
*O mussa uetu tube* **o**, lit. our food give *it* (to) *us* (*ibid.*, p. 1).
*Ituxi ngiriela* **yo**, the sins I have committed *(them)* (p. 54).

### 677. — SWAHILI:
*Looo! simba u-***mo** *ndani*, Oho! lion, thou art *there* inside.
*Yu-***mo** *ndani*, he is *there* inside.
*Na-***mi**, and (or) with *me* ; *na-***we**, and (or) with *thee*, etc...
*Si-***mi**, it is not *I* ; *si-***ye**, it is not *he*, etc...
*Ki-su ni-li-***cho** *na-***cho**, the knife I have..., lit. the knife I am *it* with *it* (cf. 733).
**Zo** *zote (njia)*, all the roads, lit. *they* all (the roads).

### 678. — SENNA:
*Si-***ne**, it is not *I*.
*Mba-pita-***ye** *nkati*, and *he* entered inside.
*Mba-pita na-***yo** *(mbuzi) n-nyumba*, and he entered the house with *it* (the goat).

### 679. — KAFIR:
*Yiza-***ni**, come *ye*.
*U* **ko** *ku-***ni**, he is *there* near *you*.
*Yiza na-***m**, come with *me*.
*A-si-***ye**, it is not *he*.
*A-si-***lo** *hashe*, it is not a horse, lit. it (is) not *it*, horse.

### 680. — GANDA:
*Na-***nge**, and (or) with *me*.
*N'a-wangula* **wo** *e mpagi*, lit. and he drew out *there* a pole.

### 681. — 3° In Herero after prepositions and locative classifiers we do not as a rule find enclitic, but self-standing pronouns. Enclitic pronouns are found however in locative expressions of a different kind.

Ex. *N'u-i-***ko**, and he goes off *(there)*.
*A-rire ty'a-tua* **mo** *m'o ndyatu*, lit. and she put it in *therein* in the sack (*Zeitschrift*, 1887-88, p. 190).

### 682. — 4° In Chwana enclitic substantive pronouns are found almost exclusively after the preposition *na* " with ".

Ex. *Na-***bo** " with them ", *na-***o** " with thee ", etc. The locative pronoun *eo* is often used after a negative copula. Ex. *Ga a-***eo**, he is not there ( = Tonga *ta a-***ko**, Kafir *a ka-***ko**).

### 683. — 5° In Mozambique enclitic substantive pronouns are found principally after a negative copula.

Ex. *Ka-***vo**, he is not *there*, ( =Swahili *ha-***ko**).
*Minyo a-gi-***hio** *Amrani*, I am not *he*, Amran, (= Swahili *mimi si-***ye** *Amrani*).

N. B. Self-standing pronouns are used regularly in most other cases. Ex. *Ni-minyo gi-na hogoloa*, I too, I shall come back (Rankin's *Makua Tales*, p. 2) etc.

**684.** — From all this are excluded possessive expressions. For in these almost all the Bantu languages agree in regularly using enclitic pronouns.

Ex.: IN TONGA: *Ingombe zia*-ngu, *zie*tu, *zie*nu, *zia*-bo, etc. my, our, your, their cattle, etc., (cf. 659).

### III. Copula-containing forms.

**685.** — 1º These copula-containing forms are used generally before substantives, or independently, to assert identity with a *particular* and *determined* person or thing.

Ex.: TONGA, KARANGA, SENNA: *Iwe* ndi-ue *Marani*, *You* are Maran, lit. You, *it is you*, Maran.

| | | |
|---|---|---|
| SWAHILI: | *Wewe* ndi-we *Marani*, | do. |
| MOZAMBIQUE: | *Weyo* di-we *Marani*, | do. |
| KAFIR: | *Wena* ngu-we *Marani*, | do. |
| CHWANA: | *Wena* ke-wena *Marang*, | do. |

**686.** — *N. B.* 1. A similar construction in Herero is the following: Owami *Kaare*, I am Kaare, lit. It is I, Kaare. Cf. 662.

**687.** — 2. We may observe in Tonga the difference between such expressions as Iue *mu-lozi* and Ndiwe *mu-lozi*. The first means only: " You are a sorcerer "; the second means: " You are *the* sorcerer (I am looking for) ".

Tonga idiom: Nceco *ci nda-ta fuambana ku-za*, " *that is why* I have not hurried to come ". Ci-*ntu* " a thing " is here understood.

**688.** — 2º In Tonga these copula-containing pronouns are also used regularly after all prepositions and locative classifiers, though not always after the particle *a* when it means " and " (cf. 674), neither after the possessive particle *a* (684).

Ex.: *Tu-la kondua a-*ngue, *a-*mbabo, we shall rejoice with him, with them.

*U-a-inka ku-li* ndilio *(i-saku)*, he is gone to him (to the devil).

*N. B.* With regard to the insertion of *li* between *ku* and *ndilio*, cf. n. 1040.

*U-a-lapela a-*nzio *(in-gubo)*, he wears them (clothes) when praying, lit.: he *U-bed' anga* ndi-me, he is like me.  [prays with them.

*N. B.* I do not know that these peculiar constructions have been noticed as yet in other Bantu languages.

### § 3. VARIA.

**689.** — 1º In Tonga, the suffix -*nya* " self ", equivalent to the Kafir -*na*, Chwana -*na* or -*ne*, Ganda -*nna*, Mozambique -*nyo*, etc. (cf. 824), is often added to substantive pronouns for the sake of greater emphasis.

Ex.: *Tu-la kondua a-ngue-*nya, *( Leza )*, we shall rejoice with him himself (God).

*Ncecio-*nya *cio, (ci-ntu)*, that is the very thing.

**690.** — *N. B.* 1. In the last two expressions *ncecio* and *nzizio* are copula-containing pronouns, while *cio* and *zio* are enclitic pronouns.

2. Tonga idiom : **Mpawo-nya** *na aka amba*, immediately after he had spoken...

**691.** — 2° In Tonga the suffix *-bo* is generally appended to substantive pronouns of the 1rst and 2d person when they are preceded by the particle *a* " and, also ". Hence *a-sue-*bo, we also ; *a-nyue-*bo, you also ; *a-e-*bo (= *a-ue-*bo), thou also ; *a-mbe-*bo (= *a-me-*bo), I also. This suffix *-bo* is radically identical with *-mue* " one, another " (n. 792).

*N. B.* 1. Likewise in Karanga *na-su-*bo *tonda*, " we shall go, we also ", and in Senna *ine-*bve " I also ", *ife-*bve " we also ", etc.

2. Kafirs use in similar cases the prefix *kua-* " also ". Ex. *kua-mna* " I too " *kwa-wena* " thou also ", etc.

**692.** — 3° In Ganda we find a sort of dual formed in the same manner with the suffix *-mbi* " two (cf. 792) ". Ex. *fe-mbi* " both of us " ; *bo-mbi* " both of them " etc. (cf. 794).

### III. — Demonstrative Pronouns.

**693.** — The various forms of demonstrative pronouns are distributable into fundamental, emphatic, and copula-containing forms *.

### * FUNDAMENTAL DEMONSTRATIVE PRONOUNS.
#### Class MU-BA.

| | Singular : *MU-ntu* | | | | Plural : *BA-ntu* | | | |
|---|---|---|---|---|---|---|---|---|
| | 1rst Position | | 2d Pos. | 3d Pos. | 1rst Position | | 2d Pos. | 3d Pos. |
| Tonga | (o)yu | (o)uno | (o)yo | (o)ulia | aba | (a)bano | abo | (a)balia |
| Kaguru | ayu | ... | yuyo | yudia | wawa | ... | wawo | wadia |
| Nyamwezi | uyu | ... | uyo | ... | awa | ... | awo | ... |
| Boondei | uyu | ... | uyo | yuda | awa | ... | awo | wada |
| Kamba | ... | uya | uyu | uuyā | ... | aya | awu | aayā |
| Swahili | huyu | ... | huyo | yule | hawa | ... | hawo | wale |
| Pokomo | huyu | ... | huyo | huyude | hawa | ... | hao | hawade |
| Senna | uyu | ... | uyo | ule | awa | ... | awo | ale |
| Karanga | (i)oyu | ... | ... | (e)ondia | ... | ... | ... | ... |
| Ganda | uyu | ono | oyo | oli | ... | bano | abo | bali |
| Xosa-Kafir | lo | ... | lowo, lo | lowa, la | aba | ... | abo | abaya |
| Zulu-Kafir | lo | lona | lowo | loya | laba | ... | labo | labaya |
| Herero | (i)ngui | ... | ... | { nguini { nguinā | (i)mba | ... | ... | { mbeni { mbenā |
| Angola | iu | ... | (i)o | (i)una | awa | ... | oo | (i)ana |
| Lower Congo | oyu | ... | oyo | ona | aya | ... | owo | ana |
| Yao | (a)ju | (a)jino | (a)jojo | (a)jula | (a)wa | (a)wano | (a)wo | (a)wala |
| Mozambique | ... | ula, ola | uyo | ole | ... | ala | ayo | ale |
| Chwana | eo | { eono { eonā | eoo | eole | ba | { bano { banā | bao | bale |
| Mpongwe | ... | wino | wono | ... | ... | wino | wono | ... |

## Demonstrative Pronouns.

The student's attention is particularly called to the fact that our adverbs " here ", " there ", " yonder ", are rendered in Bantu by the demonstrative pronouns which correspond to the locative classes PA, KU, and MU.

### § 1. Fundamental Forms.

**694.** — In Bantu grammars the fundamental forms of demonstrative pronouns are generally distributed into pronouns expressive of proximity, pronouns expressive of things already mentioned, or of limited distance, and pronouns expressive of greater distance. This certainly is not a correct view of the subject, at least in those languages on which the greatest amount of reliable materials is available. My informants of various tribes all agreed in distributing these pronouns as follows : —

1º Pronouns expressive of proximity *to the person speaking*, or, as we may call them, demonstrative pronouns of the 1rst position. Ex. in Tonga : **eli** *sekua*, this duck (near *me*).

In some languages these pronouns have two forms, the one without any suffix, as *aba* in *aba bantu* " these people ", the second

**FUNDAMENTAL DEMONSTRATIVE PRONOUNS. (Continued.)**
Class **MU-MI.**

| | Singular : *MU-cila* | | | | Plural : *MI-cila* | | | |
|---|---|---|---|---|---|---|---|---|
| | 1rst Position | 2d Pos. | 3d Pos. | | 1rst Position | 2d Pos. | 3d Pos. | |
| Tonga | (o)yu | (o)uno | (o)yo | (o)ulia | ei | (e)ino | (e)yo | (e)ilia |
| Kaguru | au | ... | uo | udia | ni | ... | iya | idia |
| Nyamwezi | ugu | ... | ugo | ... | ii | ... | io | ... |
| Boondei | ... | unu | uwo | uda | ... | inu | iyo | ida |
| Kamba | ... | uya | uyu | uuyā | ... | iya | iyu | iiyā |
| Swahili | huu | ... | huo | ule | hii | ... | hiyo | ile |
| Pokomo | huu | ... | huo | huude | hii | ... | hiyo | hiide |
| Senna | uu | ... | ... | ule | ii | ... | iyo | ile |
| Karanga | oyu | ... | oyo | (e)ondia | ... | ... | iyo | ilia |
| Ganda | ... | guno | ogo | guli | ... | gino | egio | gili |
| Xosa-Kafir | lo | ... | lowo, lo | lowa, la | le | ... | leyo, lo | leya, la |
| Zulu-Kafir | lo | lona | lowo | lowa | le | lena | leyo | leya |
| Herero | (i)mbui | ... | ... | { mbuini<br>{ mbuina | (i)imbi | ... | ... | { mbini<br>{ mbina |
| Angola | iu | ... | (i)o | (i)una | eyi | ... | oyo | ina |
| Lower Congo | owu | ... | owo | owuna | emi | ... | emio | emina |
| Yao | (a)u | (a)uno | (a)oo | (a)ula | (a)ji | (a)iino | (a)jo | (a)jila |
| Mozambique | ... | { ula<br>{ una | uyo | ole | ... | chila | ... | chile |
| Chwana | o | { ono<br>{ ona | oo | ole | e | { eno<br>{ ena | eeo | ele |
| Mpongwe | ... | wino | wono | ... | ... | yino | yono | ... |

with the suffix *no (na, la)*, as *bano* in *bantu bano*, which means also " these people ".

2° Pronouns expressive of proximity *to the person spoken to*, whatever be the distance from the person speaking, or demonstrative pronouns of the 2$^d$ position. Ex. **Elio** *sekua*, that duck (near *you*). Almost all these pronouns end in -*o*.

3° Pronouns expressive of *distance from both* the person speaking and the person spoken to, or demonstrative pronouns of the 3$^d$ position. Ex. **Elilia** *sekua*, that duck (far both from me and from you).

**695.** — *N. B.* This then is the correct division of demonstrative pronouns, at least in Tonga, Karanga, Kafir, Chwana, and Senna. That the same may be said of Swahili and Angola can be safely established by considering that in the safest specimens of native literature in these languages the demonstrative pronouns ending with the suffix -*o* are used almost exclusively with reference to position near the person spoken to. There is no difficulty with regard to the pronouns of the first or the third position.

**696.** — Ex. IN SWAHILI (from Steere's *Swahili Tales*, London, 1889) :
Page 20. *Ume kwenda kwa harrako* hapo, You have gone in a hurry *thither* (where *you* are).
do.     *Nangojea* hiyo *tumbako*, I am waiting for *that* tobacco (which I say is near *you*).
do.     *Kitwa* kicho *kita kuuma, that* head (*of yours*) will ache.
Page 26.*Ah ! mume wangu,... maneno* yayo *kwa* yayo *siku zote !* Ah ! my husband, every day *those* words (*of yours*), *those* same words.

**FUNDAMENTAL DEMONSTRATIVE PRONOUNS. (Continued.)**
Class IN-ZIN.

|  | SINGULAR : *IN*-gombe. | | | PLURAL : (*Z*)*IN*-gombe. | | |
|---|---|---|---|---|---|---|
|  | 1$^{rst}$ Position. | 2$^d$ pos. | 3$^d$ pos. | 1$^{rst}$ Position. | 2$^d$ pos. | 3$^d$ pos. |
| Tonga | ei | (e)ino | eyo | (e)ilia | ezi | (e)zino | ezio | (e)zilin |
| Kaguru | ai | ... | iyo | idia | azi | ... | zizo (?) | zidia |
| Nyamwezi | ii | ... | io | ... | izi | ... | izo | azia |
| Boondei | ... | inu | iyo | ida | izi | ... | izo | zia |
| Kamba | ... | iya | iyu | iiyā | ... | ziya | ziyu | ziiyā |
| Swahili | hii | ... | iyo | ile | hizi | ... | hizo | zile |
| Pokomo | hii | ... | hiyo | hiide | hizi | ... | hizo | hizide |
| Senna | ii | ... | iyo | ile | izi | ... | izo | zile |
| Karanga | ei | ... | iyo | (e)ilia | (i)oji | ... | ijo | { (e)jilia  { eja |
| Ganda | ... | eno | eyo | eli | ... | zino | ezo | zili |
| Xosa-Kafir | le | ... | { leyo  { lo | { leya  { la | ezi | ... | ezo | { eziya  { eza |
| Zulu-Kafir | le | lena | leyo | leya | lezi | ... | lezo | leziya |
| Herero | (i)ndyi | ... | ... | { ndyini  { ndyina | (i)nDa | ... | ... | { (i)nDeni  { (i)nDena |
| Angola | eyi | ... | oyo | ina | eji | ... | ojo | jina |
| Lower Congo | eyi | ... | cyo | (ey)ina | eji | ... | ezo | ejina |
| Yao | (a)ji | (a)jino | (a)jo | (a)jila | (a)si | (a)sino | (a)sio | (a)sila |
| Mozambique | ... | ila | iyo (?) | ile | ... | chila | ... | chile |
| Chwana | e | { eno  { ena | eeo | ele | tse | { tseno  { tsena | tseo | tsele |
| Mpongwe | ... | yino | yono | ... | ... | ... | xino | xono | ... |

Cf. *ibidem*, page 26, line 12 ; p. 36, l. 7, 8 and 36; p. 40, l. 3, 9, 10, etc. *N. B.* At page 40, line 8, of the same work, the pronoun *hilo* in *nyumba hilo* " this house ", might be thought to create a difficulty ; but in reality it is a misprint for *hii*. *Nyumba* hilo is in no sense correct, because *nyumba* is a word of cl. IN, while *hilo* is of cl. LI.

**697.** — Ex. In Angola :
*O messo ae oo, those* eyes (*of yours*). From Father de Coucto's *Cat.*, p. 3.

## 1. Formation of these pronouns.

**698.** — As may be easily seen from the subjoined tables, the most general formula for the formation of these demonstrative pronouns is as follows : —

A kind of article + connect. pr. + suffix  $\begin{cases} \text{none, or } \textit{-no (-na,-la)}, \text{ for the 1}^{\text{st}} \text{ position.} \\ \textit{-o} \text{ for the 2}^{\text{d}} \text{ position.} \\ \textit{-lia (}\text{or } \textit{la, na, ya, le)} \text{ for the 3}^{\text{d}} \text{ position.} \end{cases}$

The article seems not to be used at all in Chwana, Mozambique, or Mpongwe. In the other languages it is left out only in given cases, which vary according to the different languages.

The forms of the same article are also various, viz. *a* in Yao ; *a, e,* or *o,* in Tonga, according to the class of the pronoun, etc. It may be noticed that we meet here one of the rare instances in which the Zulu language differs from Xosa. For the article of the demonstra-

**FUNDAMENTAL DEMONSTRATIVE PRONOUNS. (Continued.)**
Class LI-MA.

| | Singular : (L)I-sumo | | | Plural : MA-sumo | | |
|---|---|---|---|---|---|---|
| | 1st Position | 2d Pos. | 3d Pos. | 1st Position | 2d Pos. | 3d Pos. |
| Tonga | eli | (e)lino | elio | (e)lilia | aya | (a)ano | ayo | (a)alia |
| Kaguru | ali | ... | lilo (?) | lidia | aya | ... | ayo | yadia |
| Nyamwezi | ili | ... | ilo | ... | aya | ... | ayo | ... |
| Boondei | idi | ... | ido | dia | aya | ... | ayo | yada |
| Kamba | ii | ... | iyu | iiyā | ... | gaa | gau | gaiyā |
| Swahili | hili | ... | hilo | lile | haya | ... | hayo | yale |
| Pokomo | hidji | ... | hidjo | hidjide | haya | ... | hayo | hayade |
| Senna | iri (?) | ... | iro(?) | rile (?) | aa | ... | ... | nle |
| Karanga | eri | ... | ... | (i)riya | aa | ... | ... | ... |
| Ganda | ... | lino | erio | lili | ... | gano | ago | gali |
| Xosa-Kafir | eli | ... | elo | eliya | la | ... | { lawo { lo | { lawa { la |
| Zulu-Kafir | leli | ... | lelo | leliya | la | lana | lawo | lawa |
| Herero | (i)ndi | (i)ndino | ... | { (i)ndini { (i)ndina | (i)nga | ... | ... | { ngeni { ngena |
| Angola | eri | ... | orio | (e)rina | ama | ... | { omo { oo | (o)mana |
| Lower Congo | edi | ... | edio | (e)dina | oma | ... | omo | (o)mana |
| Yao | (a)li | (a)lino | (a)lio | (a)lila | (a)gn | (a)gano | (a)go | (a)gala |
| Mozambique | ... | nna | ... | nne | ... | ala | ... | ale |
| Chwana | je | { jeno { jena | jeo | jele | (w)a | { ano { ana | ao | ale |
| Mpongwe | ... | nyino | nyono | ... | ... | { mino { awano | mono | ... |

tive pronouns of Zulu always contains *l*, whereas in Xosa the *l* is only heard as a rule in such pronouns as have no other proper consonant.

**699.** — *N. B.* 1. In Angola the pronouns *baba*, *bobo* (of class PA), *kuku*, *koko* (of class KU), and *mumu*, *momo* (of class MU), are properly reduplicative pronouns (cf. 705). If the simple pronouns corresponding to these existed in Angola, they would be apparently *aba*, *obo; oku*, *oko; omu*, *omo*.

2. The demonstrative pronouns in Karanga seem to have two articles, the one ordinary, viz. *a*, *e*, or *o*, the other emphatic, viz. *i*. More information is wanted as to this language, one of the most interesting of the Bantu family.

3. The presence of *h* in the articles of the Swahili pronouns is probably due to Arabic influence. Possibly the presence of *l* in the corresponding Zulu articles is due to some ancient influence of the same sort.

4. I consider it as probable that the suffix -*o* for pronouns of the 2ᵈ position was originally identical with the pronoun *ue* or *ko* " you " of the 2ᵈ person singular. Perhaps the suffix -*no* for pronouns of the 1ʳˢᵗ position was also identical with the pronoun -*ngu*, the possessive form of the 1ʳˢᵗ person singular. The suffix -*le* for pronouns of the 3ᵈ position means " far ". The full form *lia* is probably a compound of *le* " far " + *a*, demonstrative in the distance.

### 2. Use and place of these pronouns.

**700.** — First, demonstrative pronouns can be used substantively as self-standing words. Ex. : —

TONGA :
Oyu *mu-lozi*, this (man) is a sorcerer.

**FUNDAMENTAL DEMONSTRATIVE PRONOUNS. (Continued.)**

|  | Class BU. *BU-siku*. | | | | Class LU. *LU-limi*. | | | |
|---|---|---|---|---|---|---|---|---|
|  | 1ʳˢᵗ Position. | 2ᵈ pos. | 3ᵈ Pos. | | 1ʳˢᵗ Position. | 2ᵈ Pos. | 3ᵈ Pos. | |
| Tonga | obu | (o)buno | obo | (o)bulia | olu | (o)luno | oluo | (o)lulia |
| Kaguru | au | ... | uo | udia | alu | ... | lulo (?) | ludia |
| Nyamwezi | uwu | ... | uwo | ... | ulu | ... | ulo | ... |
| Boondei | ... | unu | uno (?) | uda | ... | lunu | luno (?) | luda |
| Kamba | uu | ... | uyu | uuyā | uu | ... | uyu | uuyā |
| Swahili | huu | ... | huo | hule | huu | ... | huo | hule |
| Pokomo | hutyu | ... | hutyo | hutyude | ... | ... | ... | ... |
| Senna | uu | ... | uo | ule | ulu | ... | ulo | ... |
| Karanga | (i)obu | ... | ubo | ... | (i)oru | ... | ... | ... |
| Ganda | ... | buno | obwo | buli | ... | runo | orwo | ruli |
| Xosa-Kafir | obu | ... | obo | { obuya / oba | olu | ... | olo | { oluya / olwa |
| Zulu-Kafir | lobu | ... | lobo | lobuya | lolu | ... | lolo | loluya |
| Herero | (i)mbui | ... | ... | { mbuini / mbuina | (i)ndui | ... | ... | { (i)nduini / (i)nduina |
| Angola | iu | ... | o | (i)una | olu | ... | olo | luna |
| Lower Congo | owu | ... | owo | (o)wuna | olu | ... | olo | (o)luna |
| Yao | (a)ju | (a)juno | ao | (a)ula | (a)lu | (a)luno | (a)lo | (a)lula |
| Mozambique | uu | ula (?) | ... | ule | uu | ... | ... | ule |
| Chwana | jo | { jona / jono | joo | jole | lo | { lona / lonn | loo | lole |
| Mpongwe | ... | wono | wino | ... | ... | ... | wino | wono | ... |

**Aba** *mba kazoaxa bako*, these (men) are thy priests.
*Ba-yuni ba-a* **wano**, the birds of this place, lit. of here.
*Nda-ka inka* **okulia**, I went there.

    *N. B.* **Lino** or **elino**, demonstrative pronoun of cl. LI, and **ino** or **eino**, demonstrative pronoun of cl. IN, are often used independently to render our adverbs " then, now, immediately ". Ex. *Ndi-li-wo* **lino**, I shall be there *directly*.

    SWAHILI :
  *Una fanya nini* **hapo?** What are you doing there? (Rankin's *Makua and Swahili Tales*, p. 5).
**Huyu** *si kondoo*, this is not a sheep (*ibid.*, p. 5).
**Kule** *koondeni*, there among the sheep (*ibid.*, p. 7).
*Wakakaa* **kule**, they remained there (*ibid.*, p. 9).

    MOZAMBIQUE :
*Una vara sheni* **va?** What are you doing here? (*ibid.*, p. 4).
**Hoyo** *kahiyo ibwitibwiti*, that is not a sheep, (*ibid.*, p. 4).
**O**·*madani*, there among the sheep (*ibid.*, p. 6).
  etc., etc.

**701.** — Secondly, in the generality of the Bantu languages, when demonstrative pronouns are used adjectively, they seem to be placed somewhat indifferently before or after their substantive. In Chwana and Ganda they seem to be always placed after. Ex.: —

## FUNDAMENTAL DEMONSTRATIVE PRONOUNS. (Continued.)
### Class CI-ZI.

|  | SINGULAR : *CI-ntu* | | | | PLURAL : *ZI-ntu* | | | |
|---|---|---|---|---|---|---|---|---|
|  | 1st Position | 2d Pos. | 3d Pos. | | 1st Position | 2d Pos | 3d Pos. |
| Tonga | eci | (e)cino | ecio | (e)cilia | ezi | (e)zino | ezi | (e)zilia |
| Kaguru | achi | ... | chicho(?) | chidia | avi | ... | vivo (?) | vidia |
| Nyamwezi | iki | ... | icho | ... | ifi | ... | ifo | ... |
| Boondei | iki | ... | iko | kia | ivi | ... | ivio | via |
| Kamba | ... | kiya | kiyu | kiiyã | ... | iya | iyu | iiyã |
| Swahili | hichi | ... | hicho | kile | hivi | ... | hivio | vile |
| Pokomo | hityi | ... | hityo | hityide | hiwi | ... | hiwyo | hivide |
| Senna | ici | ... | icio | cire | { ibzi / ipi | ... | { ibzo / ipo | { bzire / pire |
| Karanga | (i)oci | (i)ocino | ... | ... | (i)o|wi | ... | i|wo | ... |
| Ganda | ... | kino | ekio | kili | ... | bino | ebio | bili |
| Xosa-Kafir | esi | ... | eso | { esiya / esa | ezi | ... | ezo | { eziya / eza |
| Zulu-Kafir | lesi | ... | leso | lesiya | lezi | ... | lezo | leziya |
| Herero | (i)hi | ... | ... | { hini / hina | (i)mbi | ... | ... | { mbini / mbina |
| Angola | eki | ... | okio | kina | eyi | ... | oyo | ina |
| Lower Congo | eki | ... | ekio | (e)kina | eyi | ... | eyo | (ey)ina |
| Yao | (a)chi | (a)chino | (a)cho | (a)cila | (a)i | (a)ino | (a)yo | (a)ila |
| Mozambique | ... | ila | ... | ile | ... | chila | ... | chile |
| Chwana | se | { seno / sena | seo | sele | tse | { tseno / tsena | tseo | tsele |
| Mpongwe | ... | jino | jono | ... | ... | yino | yono | ... |

| TONGA | KARANGA |
|---|---|
| *Baaka fua e inzala* **oyu** *muaka*, | *Bakafa nejara muaga* **oyu**, they died from hunger *this* year. |
| **Ilia** *nyika tiinsi mbotu na?* | **Irie**nyika *tobembuyanana na?* Is not *that* ground good? |
| *Mbuzie mukuarana angu* **oulia**, | *Mu-buje nkuru anga* **eondia**, Ask *that* brother of mine. |
| **Ei** *nkani iamana* | *Mawui* **aa** *apera*, This story is finished. |

**702.** — Examples taken from Rankin's *Arab Tales translated from Swahili :* —

| SWAHILI : | MOZAMBIQUE : |
|---|---|
| *Kila mmoja katika* **wale** *wezi* (p. 2) | *Moz' a v'***ale**... *weyi*......, Each one of those thieves... |
| ... *akatia* **zile** *dinari.* (p. 4), | ... *kuhela* **ole** *mzurugu,* ...and he put *those* pieces of money inside. |
| *Wakija* **hawa** *wezi*... (p. 6), | **Ala** *weyi yaroa*..., when *these* thieves shall come... |
| *Na paa* **huyu** *amekuja*. (p. 6), | *Na-nazoro* **ola** *ahoroa*, yet this gazelle has come. |
| *Tulize sisi paa* **huyu,** *na-ufito* **huu,** *na kisu* **hiki.** (p. 8). | *Ntumiheri nazoro* **ola,** *ni-mtali* **ola,** *ni-mwalu* **ola.** Sell us *this* gazelle, and *this* stick, and *this* knife. |

**703.** — Other examples : —

| GANDA : | *E kifananyi* **kino** *kia ani?* Whose is *this* likeness? (New Testament). |
|---|---|
| SWAHILI : | *Ya-nani sanamu* **hii?** do. |
| CHWANA (SUTO) : | *Secwanco* **sena** *ke sa-mang?* do. |
| MPONGWE : | *Edidi* **zinu** *za-mande?* do. |

## FUNDAMENTAL DEMONSTRATIVE PRONOUNS (Continued.)
### Class KA-TU.

| | SINGULAR : *KA-samo.* | | | PLURAL : *TU-samo.* | | |
|---|---|---|---|---|---|---|
| | 1st Position. | 2d Pos. | 3d Pos. | 1st Position. | 2d Pos. | 3d Pos. |
| Tonga | aka | (a)kano | ako | (a)kalia | otu | (o)tuno | otuo | otulia |
| Nyamwezi | aka | ... | ako | ... | utu | ... | uto | ... |
| Boondei | aka | ... | ako | kada | ... | ... | ... | ... |
| Kamba | ii (?) | ... | kayu | kaayā | twii (?) | ... | tuyu | tuuyā |
| Karanga | ... | ... | ako | ... | (i)otu | ... | ... | ... |
| Ganda | ... | kano | ako | kali | (Cf. Class BU) | | | |
| Herero | (i)nga | ... | ... | { ngeni { ngena | (i)sui (475) | ... | ... | { suini { suina |
| Angola | aka | ... | oko | kana | otu | ... | oto | tuna |
| Lower Congo | efi (521) | ... | efio | (e)fino | otu (475) | ... | oto | (o)tuna |
| Yao | (a)ka | (a)kano | (a)ko | (a)kala | (a)tu | (a)tuno | (a)tuo | (a)tula |

Angola :   *Mo kiluiji* **eki** *kia masoxi*, in *this* vale of tears (*Angola Cat.*, p. 2).
Senna :   *Ndoko kadzuke luku* **ii**, go and wash *this* spoon.
Kafir :   *Yopula i nyama* **le**, or *Yopula* **le** *nyama*, take *this* meat out of the pot.

### § 2. Emphatic forms.

**704.** — In the generality of the Bantu languages great stress is laid sometimes on the last vowel of the demonstrative pronouns of the 3ᵈ position in order to express great distance.

Ex. In Tonga :   *okuliā*, there (far); *muntu* **ouliā**, that man (far).
In Kafir :   *payā*, there (far); *u mntu* **lowā** or **lowaya**, that man (far).
In Kamba :   *mtu* **uuyā**, that man (far). (Last's *Kamba Gr.*, p. 28).
In Swahili :   *mti* **ulē**, that tree (yonder, far away). (Rev. P. Delaunay's *Swah. Gr.*, p. 31).

**705.** — In Swahili, Kamba, etc., another kind of emphatic demonstrative pronoun is formed by reduplicating their full forms. Such pronouns lay stress on the strict identity of a thing.

Ex. In Swahili :   *Akalala* **palepale**, and he slept at that very place.
*Mto* **uleule**, that very river yonder.
In Kamba :   *Umama* **paapae**, you may stand just here.

**706.** — In some other languages, as also in Swahili, emphatic

## FUNDAMENTAL DEMONSTRATIVE PRONOUNS. (Continued.)
The two classes KU (*non-locative* and *locative*).

| | Non-locative class : *KU-tui* | | | Locative class : *KU-nsi* | | | |
|---|---|---|---|---|---|---|---|
| | 1ʳˢᵗ Position | 2ᵈ Pos. | 3ᵈ Pos. | 1ʳˢᵗ Position | 2ᵈ Pos. | 3ᵈ Pos. | |
| Tonga | oku | (o)kuno | oko | (o)kulia | oku | (o)kuno | oko | (o)kulia |
| Kaguru | aku | ... | kuko(?) | kudia | ... | ... | ... | ... |
| Boondei | ... | kunu | kuno(?) | kuda | ... | kunu | kuno(?) | kuda |
| Nyamwezi | uku | ... | uko | ... | uku | ukunu | uko | ikudia(?) |
| Kamba | ... | kwaa | kuyu | kuuyā | ... | kwaa | kuyu | kuuyā |
| Swahili | huku | ... | huko | kule | huku | ... | huko | kule |
| Senna | uku | ... | uko | kure | uku | ... | uko | kure |
| Karanga | (i)oku | ... | ... | (i)okuya | (i)oku | okuno | oko | (i)okuya |
| Ganda | ... | kuno | okwo | kuli | ... | eno | eyo | ... |
| Xosa-Kafir | oku | ... | oko | okuya | (l)oku | ... | (l)oko | okuya |
| Zulu-Kafir | loku | ... | loko | lokuya | loku | ... | loko | lokuya |
| Herero | (i)ngui | ... | ... | { nguini<br>{ nguina | (i)ngui | nguno | ... | { (i)nguini<br>{ (i)nguina |
| Angola | oku | ... | oko | kuna | kuku | ... | koko | kuna |
| Lower Congo | oku | ... | oko | (o)kuna | oku | ... | oko | (o)kuna |
| Yao | (a)ku | (a)kuno | (a)ko | (a)kula | (a)ku | (a)kuno | (a)ko | (a)kula |
| Mozambique | uu | ... | ... | ule | ... | ... | o | ngwe |
| Chwana | ... | ... | ... | ... | koa | koano | koo | koale |
| Mpongwe | ... | ... | ... | ... | ... | guno | gogo | ... |

forms are often obtained by adding to the simple demonstrative pronoun a substantive pronoun of some kind or other.

Ex. In Kafir : **Yiyo-le** *i ndlela*, this is the very road (you are looking for).

### § 3. Copula-containing Forms.

**707.** — We find in Bantu two distinct kinds of demonstrative expressions which contain the copula. Those of the first kind render our " it is this, this is it, it is that, " etc. Those of the second kind render our " there he is, there she is, there it is, " etc.

#### First kind.

**708.** — Those of the first kind, which we find in Tonga, Kafir, Senna, Chwana, etc., are mostly formed according to the same principles as the copula-containing personal pronouns.

Ex. In Tonga :
**Ng**-*oyu*, **ng**-*oyo*, **ng**-*oulia mu-ntu*, it is this, that person.
**Nz**-*ezi*, **nz**-*ezio*, **nz**-*ezilia n-gombe*, it is these, those cows.
**Mp**-*awa* " it is here " ; **mp**-*awo* " it is there ", etc.

In Kafir :
**Ngu**-*lo*, **ngu**-*lowo*, **ngu**-*lowa m-ntu*, it is this, that person.
**L**-*eli*, l-*elo*, l-*ela dada*, it is this, that duck.
etc., etc.

### FUNDAMENTAL DEMONSTRATIVE PRONOUNS (Continued.)
#### The locative classes (P)A and MU.

|  | *PA-nsi.* | | | *MU-nsi.* | | |
|---|---|---|---|---|---|---|
|  | 1rst Position. | 2d Pos. | 3d Pos. | 1rst Position. | 2d Pos. | 3d Pos. |
| Tonga | awa | { (p)ano { awano | awo | (a)walia | omu | (o)muno | omo | (o)mulia |
| Kaguru | baha | ... | baho | hadia | ... | ... | ... |
| Nyamwezi | haha | ... | haho | ... | ... | ... | ... |
| Boondei | ... | hanu | aho | hada | umu | ... | umo | mda |
| Kamba | ... | waa | wayu | waayā | ... | ... | ... |
| Swahili | hapa | ... | hapo | pale | humu | ... | humo | mle |
| Pokomo | habfa | ... | habfo | habfade | ... | ... | ... |
| Senna | apa | pano | apo | pare | ... | muno | ... | ... |
| Karanga | (i)opa | opano | opo | (i)opaya | ... | omuno | ... | ... |
| Ganda | ... | wano | awo | wala | ... | ... | ... | ... |
| Xosa-Kafir | (l)apa | ... | apo | paya | ... | ... | ... | ... |
| Zulu-Kafir | lapa | ... | lapo | (la)paya | ... | ... | ... | ... |
| Herero | (i)mba | mbano | ... | ... | mui | ... | ... | omonamui |
| Angola | baba | ... | bobo | bana | mumu | ... | momo | muna |
| Lower Congo | ova | ... | ovo | (o)vana | omu | ... | omo | (o)muna |
| Yao | (a)pa | (a)pano | (a)po | (a)pala | (a)mu | (a)muno | (a)mo | (a)mula |
| Mozambique | va | vano | vao | vale | mui | ... | moo | mule |
| Chwana | fa | { fano { fana | foo | fale | mo | { mono { mona | moo | mole |
| Mpongwe | vava | veno | vovo | ... | ... | ... | ... | ... |

**709.** — *N. B.* Kafirs and Tongas often like to replace such expressions by simple demonstrative pronouns preceded by copula-containing personal pronouns : Ex. in Kafir: Yiyo le *i ndlela*, this is the road ; nguye lo *mntu*, it is this person ; lilo elı *dada*, it is this duck. Expressions of this kind are often used even in the first and second person. Ex. in Kafir : *Ndim lo*, it is I here present ; *siti aba*, it is we here present, etc.

**710.** — We must probably associate with this kind of pronoun various compound demonstrative forms which are found in Mozambique, Ganda, Herero, and Kaguru.

**711.** — In Mozambique these forms are the following : —

|  | Singular | Plural |
|---|---|---|
| Class M-A (= Tonga MU-BA) : | *Thiola, thiyola* | *Piyala, piayo* |
| Class M-MI (= Tonga MU-MI) : | *Puyola* | *Pichechi* |
| Class I (= Tonga IN-ZIN) : | *Piyela* | *Pichechi* |
| Class NI-MA (= Tonga LI-MA) : | *Pinena* | *Piyala* |
| Class U ...................................: | *Puwowu* |  |
| Loc. cl. VA (= Tonga PA) : | *Pivava* |  |
| Loc. cl. M (= Tonga MU) : | *Pumomu* |  |

Cf. Chauncy Maples " *Handbook of the Makua Language* ", p. 55.

**712.** — In Ganda, where these forms are found even in the 1rst and the 2d person, they are as follows : —

|  |  | SINGULAR. | | | PLURAL. | | |
|---|---|---|---|---|---|---|---|
|  |  | 1rst Pos. | 2d Pos. | 3d Pos. | 1rst Pos. | 2d Pos. | 3d Pos. |
| Cl. MU-BA | 1rst Pers. : | *nzuno* | *nzuyo* | ... | *tutuno* | *tutuo* | ... |
|  | 2d Pers. : | *uno* | *uyo* | ... | *mumuno* | *mumuo* |  |
|  | 3d Pers. : | *uno* | *uyo* | *uli* | *babano* | *babo* | *babali* |
| Cl. MU-MI : |  | *guguno* | *guguo* | *guguli* | *gigino* | *gigio* | *gigili* |
| Cl. N : |  | *iino* | *iiyo* | *iili* | *zizino* | *zizo* | *zizili* |
| Cl. LI-MA : |  | *ririno* | *ririo* | *ririli* | *gagano* | *gago* | *gagali* |
| Cl. KI-BI : |  | *kikino* | *kikio* | *kikili* | *bibino* | *bibio* | *bibili* |
| Cl. KA-BU (508) : |  | *kakano* | *kako* | *kakali* | *bubuno* | *bubwo* | *bubuli* |

etc. etc. Cf. " *Grammaire Ruganda* ", pp. 28, 29, where these forms are rendered by " here I am, here he is, there he is, " etc.

**713.** — Thus it may be seen that the copulative power of the connective pronoun repeated, which we have already observed in Kafir (708, 582, 586, 669), is not entirely foreign to Ganda.

The Ganda forms just described are often used in connection with substantive pronouns. This probably renders them more emphatic. Ex. *nze nzuno*, it is I here present ; *nze nzuyo*, it is I just mentioned to you ; *gue uno*, it is you here present, etc.. Such expressions seem to be parallel to those noticed above in Kafir,

e. g. *ndim lo*, it is I here present ; *nguwe lo*, it is you here present, etc. (709).

**714.** — The Kaguru forms which may be compared with the preceding are : —

1ʳˢᵗ Pers. : *Nhoneni anye*, it is I ; *nhosese ase*, it is we.
2ᵈ Pers. : *Nhogwegwe agwe*, it is thou ; *nhonyie anyie*, it is you.
Cl. MU-BA : *Nhoyuyu ayu*, it is he ; *nhoao wao*, it is they.
etc , etc. Cf. Last's " *Kaguru Grammar* ", p. 45.

**715.** — Expressions somewhat similar to these are in Herero : —
Cl. MU-VA : *Eye ingui*, it is he *or* there he is.
*Owo-mba*, it is they *or* there they are.
etc., etc. Cf. Kolbe's *Herero Dict.*, pp. xlviii and 497.

### Second kind.

**716.** — That kind of copula-containing demonstrative pronoun which renders properly our " here he is, there he is, here it is, there it is, here they are ", etc., has been noticed as yet in Kafir only, but it probably exists in several other languages. Its forms are particularly interesting, viz. : —

|  | SINGULAR. | | | PLURAL. | | |
|---|---|---|---|---|---|---|
|  | 1ʳˢᵗ Pos. | 2ᵈ Pos. | 3ᵈ Pos. | 1ʳˢᵗ Pos. | 2ᵈ Pos. | 3ᵈ Pos. |
| Cl. MU-BA : | *nanku* | *nanko* | *nankuya* | *naba* | *nabo* | *nabaya* |
| Cl. MU-MI : | *nanku* | *nanko* | *nankuya* | *nantsi* | *nantso* | *nantsiya* |
| Cl. N-ZIN : | *nantsi* | *nantso* | *nantsiya* | *nanzi* | *nanzo* | *nanziya* |
| Cl. LI-MA : | *nali* | *nalo* | *naliya* | *nanga* | *nango* | *nangaya* |
| Cl. BU : | *nabu* | *nabo* | *nabuya* | *nazi* | *nazo* | *naziya* |
| Cl. KU : | *naku* | *nako* | *nakuya* | | | |
| Cl. SI-ZI : | *nasi* | *naso* | *nasiya* | | | |
| Cl. LU : | *nalu* | *nalo* | *naluya* | | | |

## IV. — Relative Pronouns

### and

### Relative Particles.

**717.** — Properly speaking, *relative pronouns* are no other than the connective particles previously described. This principle is of capital importance for understanding this article.

Ex. In Tonga: *U-la busia ba-ntu* **ba-a-ka** *fua*, he can raise to life people *who* are dead.

In Kafir: *A si zo ngubo* **zi**-*lungele a ma-doda*, these are not clothes *that* are good for men.

etc., etc. Cf. n. 730.

**718.** — But in given cases, relative clauses require as a sort of antecedent certain *relative particles* \*, which correspond to our " *he, they,* or *the one* ", in such expressions as " the one who..., he who..., they who... ", or to the French " *celui, ceux* ", etc., in such expressions as " celui qui..., celui que..., ceux qui..., ceux que... ", etc.

Ex. In Kafir: *Lipina i hashe* a *bateta nga lo?* Where is the horse which they are speaking of? Lit. Where is the horse *the one* they are speaking of it? (Lit. in French : " Où est le cheval *celui* (qu')ils parlent de lui ? ")

### § 1. Forms of the Relative Particles.

**719.** — On this subject there are divergencies greater perhaps than on any other between the different Bantu languages, as may be judged from the subjoined tables.

### \* RELATIVE PARTICLES.

|  | Cl. MU-ntu | Cl. BA-ntu | Cl. MU-cila | Cl. MI-cila | Cl. IN-gombe | Cl. (ZI)N-gombe |
|---|---|---|---|---|---|---|
| Tonga | u, ngu | { ba; be { mba | u, ngu | i, nji | i, nji | zi, nzi |
| Kaguru | ano | wano | nwo (?) | iyo | iyo | zizo |
| Boondei | e... (-ye) | we... (-o) | we... (-o) | ye... (-yo) | ye... (-yo) | ze... (-zo) |
| Kamba | ... | a | u | i | i | zi |
| Swahili | ... -ye | ... -o | ... -o | ... -yo | ... -yo | ... -zo |
| Senna | o(mue) | wo(mue) | o(mue) | yo(mue) | yo(mue) | zo(mue) |
| Ganda | { y, a { ye | a be | o gwe | e gie | e ye | e ze |
| Kafir | { o... (-yo) ( oyena | a... (-yo) aboua | o... (-yo) owona | e... (-yo) eyona | e... (-yo) eyona | e... (-zo) ezona |
| Herero | ngu | mbu | mbu | mbi | ndyi | nbu |
| Angola | u | ... | mu | mi | i | ji |
| Lower Congo | ona | ana | una | mina | ina | jina |
| Yao | ju | wa | u | ji | ji | si |
| Mozambique | u | ya | u | chi | i | chi |
| Chwana | eo... (-ng) | ba... (ng) | o... (-ng) | e... (-ng) | e... (-ng) | tse... (-ng) |

**720.** — Thus 1º it may be seen that in Yao, Kamba, and probably Mozambique, relative pronouns do not differ essentially in their forms from the connective pronouns previously described.

*N. B.* In Yao relative particles take before adjectives, and in some other cases, the suffix *a*. Hence *jua* in cl. *MU-ntu*, *ja* in cl. *MI-cila*, etc. Cf. 617.

**721.** — 2º In Tonga relative particles have two sets of forms, the one which does not differ from connective pronouns, the other which is derived from it by prefixing to the same pronouns a nasal copula (582), whence the forms *ngu*, *mba*, *nji*, *ndi* (= *nli*), *ndu* (= *nlu*), etc. The simple forms *a*, *u*, and *i*, are seldom used, being generally replaced by the copula-containing forms, probably for clearness' sake, or to avoid a hiatus. In like manner, for no other apparent reason, those relative particles which contain a soft consonant, viz. *ba*, *li*, *lu*, etc., are often replaced by the nasalized forms *mba*, *ndi*, *ndu*, etc.

**722.** — 3º The Herero and Angola relative particles are also derived directly from connective pronouns, but with this peculiarity that their final vowel is generally *u* where it might be expected to be *a*, as in *mu* for *a* or *ma*, *ku* for *ka*, etc. Those Herero particles which contain no hard consonant take besides this an initial nasal, which originally must have been identical with the nasal copula in Tonga.

**723.** 4º Relative particles in Kafir are *a*, *e*, or *o*, in their simple forms, according as they are followed by a pronoun containing *a*, *i*,

| | Cl. (L)I-bue | Cl. MA-bue | Cl. BU-siku | Cl. KU-tui | Cl. CI-ntu | Cl. ZI-ntu |
|---|---|---|---|---|---|---|
| Tonga | li, ndi | a, nga | bu, mbu | ku | ci | zi, nzi |
| Kaguru | dido | gago | nwo (?) | kuko | kicho | vivio |
| Boondei | de... (-do) | ye... (-yo) | we... (-o) | kwe...(-ko) | che... (-cho) | vie... (-vio) |
| Kamba | i | ga | | u | ki | i |
| Swahili | ... -lo | ... -yo | ... -wo | ... -ko | ... -cho | ... -vio |
| Senna | lo(mue) | o(mue) | wo(mue) | ko(mue) | cio(mue) | -bzo(mue) |
| Ganda | { e, lie | a, ge | o, bue | o, kue | e, kie | e, bie |
| Kafir | { e.. (-yo), elona | a.. (-yo) awona | o.. (-yo) obona | o.. (-yo) okona | e.. (-yo) esona | e.. (-yo) ezona |
| Herero | ndi | ngu | mbu | ku | tyi | mbi |
| Angola | ri | ma, mu | bu | ku | ki | i |
| Lower Congo | dina | mana | wuna | kuna | kina | ina |
| Yao | li | ga | u | ku | chi | i |
| Mozambique | ni | a | u | ku | i | chi |
| Chwana | je... (-ng) | a... (-ng) | jo... (-ng) | ... | se... (-ng) | tse... (-ng) |

or *n*. They have besides these emphatic forms, such as *o-yena, a-bona*, etc., which contain the same particles *a*, *e*, or *o*, with a self-standing pronoun (661).

In the same language the particle *-yo*, which is a sort of locative pronoun corresponding to the classifier *-ini* (554), in relative clauses is appended to the verb when this is not *immediately* followed by another word.

With regard to copula-containing relative particles in Kafir, see n. 776.

**724.** — 5° In Ganda relative particles have the forms *a*, *e*, *o*, only when they refer to the *subject* of the verb of the relative clause. When they refer to its *object* they borrow the forms of those substantive pronouns which have the suffix *-e* (656). Cf. n. 777.

The Boondei relative particles ending with *-e* seem to have been originally the same as these Ganda pronouns. The others are ordinary substantive pronouns. More information is wanted on the relative particles of this language.

**725.** — 6° In Senna also the relative particles are no other than the ordinary substantive pronouns. But the particle *-mue* is generally suffixed to them.

*N. B.*.On the one hand, the form *-mue* means properly " one " (792). On the other hand, the same form when thus suffixed to relative particles is unmistakably a sort of pronoun corresponding to the locative class MU, and originally identical with the Chwana suffix *-ng* (727, cf. 204), as well as with the Kafir suffix *-yo* (723). These two facts when put together are particularly interesting, as they show distinctly that the locative elements

**RELATIVE PARTICLES. (Continued.)**

|  | Cl. KA-samo | Cl. TU-samo | Cl. LU-limi | Cl. (P)A-nsi | Cl. KU-nsi | Cl. MU-nsi |
|---|---|---|---|---|---|---|
| Tonga | ka | tu | lu, ndu | (p)a, mpa | ku | mu |
| Kaguru | ... | ... | lulo | haho | ... | ... |
| Boondei | ke... (-ko) | ... | o... (-we) | he... (-ho) | kwe...(-ko) | mwe... (-mo) |
| Kamba | ka | tu | u | ... | ... | ... |
| Swahili | ... | ... | ... -lo | ... -po | ... -ko | ... -mo |
| Senna | ... | ... | ro(mue) | po(mue) | ko(mue) | mo(mue) |
| Ganda | { a<br>{ ke | ... | e<br>rwe | · we | gie | mue |
| Kafir | ... | ... | { o... (-yo)<br>{ olona | ... | e... (-yo)<br>okona | ... |
| Herero | ku | tu | ndu | pu | ku | mu |
| Angola | ka, ku | tu | lu | bu | ku | mu |
| Lower Congo | kuna | tuna | luna | vana | kuna | muna |
| Yao | ka | tu | lu | pa | ku | mu |
| Mozambique | ... | ... | ... | va | ... | ... |
| Chwana | ... | ... | lo... (-ng) | fa | e (?) | ... |

*MU-*, *-ini*, *-ng*, *-ni*, (548-555), are closely related to the adjective *-mue* " one ", and must therefore be said to signify primarily " one, together with ".

**726.** — 7º In Swahili also the relative particles are identical with the substantive pronouns. But they have this peculiarity, that, instead of introducing the relative clauses, as in most other languages, they are suffixed to their first verbal form, even when this is a mere auxiliary. (See examples n. 733).

**727.** — 8º The relative particles in Chwana do not differ from the simplest forms of the demonstrative pronouns. But in this language the suffix *-ng* ( = Kafir *-yo*, 723, 725) is generally appended to the principal verb of a relative clause.

In Congo the relative particles look like demonstrative pronouns of the third position without their initial article (693*).

*N. B.* More information is wanted on the proper forms of the relative particles in the other languages.

## § 2. USE OF RELATIVE PARTICLES AND CONSTRUCTION OF RELATIVE CLAUSES IN GENERAL.

**728.** — The proper use of relative particles, and in general the construction of relative clauses, is the main difficulty in all Bantu languages. That of treating it here is considerably increased by the variety of the languages with which we are dealing, and by their divergencies on this very point.

For clearness' sake we may consider separately : 1º The relative clauses in which the antecedent is represented by the subject of the verb, as in *Mu-ntu u-a-fua*... or *u mu-ntu u-a-fua*..., " the man who is dead... " — 2º The relative clauses in which the antecedent is represented by an object of the verb, as in *Mu-ntu ngu nd-a-bona*, " the man whom I have seen. " Hence : —

**1. Relative clauses in which the antecedent is represented by the subject of the verb.**

**729.** — *First Construction* (without a relative particle).

In most Bantu languages, when the antecedent is represented in the relative clause by the pronoun subject of the verb, this pronoun alone generally does duty as relative pronoun, and no relative particle is used. This is the usual construction in Tonga, Karanga,

Angola, Mozambique, Kaguru, Kamba, Nyamwezi, Mpongwe, and the Suto dialect of Chwana. In Kafir these relative clauses without a relative particle are found only after antecedents which have themselves no article.

**730.** — Ex. : —

 Tonga : *Monze u-la busia bantu* **ba**-*a-ka fua*, Monze can raise to life people who are dead.
  *Ndi-ue u-a-ka- ndi-loela mu-ana* **u**-*a-ka fua ejilo*, it is you who had bewitched my child *who* died yesterday.
  *Ni-n-ganga mu-ntu u-sonda*, lit. it is a Nganga, a man *who* smells, i. e. a Nganga is a man *who* smells people.
  *Ue, tata uesu* **u**-*a-ka tu-bumba*, Thou, our Father, *who* didst form us.
  *Ba-la sondela ba-ntu* **ba**-*la fuide*, they come near, the persons *who* are not dead.
 Karanga : *Ji i-pone ixindi* **ji**-*no-psanga nda?* Where are the muircats *which* like to go?
 Old Angola : *Esue* **tu**-*ekala ko uze ou...*, We *who* live in this world... (Father de Coucto's *Cat.*, p. 34).
 Mozambique : *M-tu* **a**-*ruele*, the man *who* went. (Chauncy Maples' *Gr.*, p. 56).
 Kaguru : *Mu-ntu* **a**-*ny-enda*, the man *who* loves me. (Last's *Gr.*, p. 47).
 Kamba : *Mu-ndu* **a**-*ny-enda*, the man *who* loves me. (Last's *Gr.*, p. 28).
 Nyamwezi : *N-zwile* **z**-*a-za*, lit. hair *which* is red, i. e. red hair.
 Mpongwe : *Nyare* **yi**-*re veno, i-nyare* **si**-*re veno*, the ox *which* is here, the oxen *which* are here. (M^gr Le Berre's *Gr.*, p. 11).
 Suto : *Leseli* **le**-*leng go uena...* the light *that* is in thee. (Mat., 6, 23).
 Kafir : *A-si m-ntu* **u**-*tanda a ma-hashe* (not ...**o**-*tanda*), he is not (a) man *who* likes horses.
  *Ndi-teta la m-ntu* **u**-*hamba paya*, (not ...**o**-*hamba*), I mean that man *who* is walking yonder.
  *Kangela ela dada* **li**-*se m-lanjeni* (not ...**e** *li-se...*), look at that duck *which* is in the river.
  *Wena,* **u**-*hamba-ze* (not **o**-*hamba-ze*), you *who* walk naked.

**731.** — *Second Construction* (a relative particle before the relative clause).

This is the usual construction in Kafir, Chwana proper, Senna, Ganda, Yao, and Lower Congo. I find also examples of it in Tonga, but with this peculiarity, that the relative particle is placed before the antecedent itself, not after it as in these other languages. With regard to Kafir and Chwana we must remember that a suffix, viz. *yo* in Kafir, *ng* in Chwana, is in given cases appended to the verb (723, 727).

**732.** — Ex.

KAFIR : *Ngu m-ntu* o-*tanda a ma-hashe* ( = o *u-tanda...*) he is a man *who* likes horses.

*Ngu m-ntu* o-*ndi-tanda-*yo, he is a man *who* likes me.

*N. B.* Here the antecedent *m-ntu* being preceded by an article, the relative clause likewise requires a relative particle.

CHWANA PROPER : *Le-sedi* je *le-le*ng *mo go wena*. (Cf. Suto : *le-seli le-leng go uena, supra* n. 730.) the light *that* is in thee, lit. the light *that which* is in thee.

*Dinku* tse *di-timetse*ng, the sheep *that* have strayed.

*Monna* eo *o-na a-ka re-bolelela*, the man *who* could have told us. (Rev. William Crisp's *Gr.*, p. 52.)

GANDA : *A ba-ntu* a *ba-genze*, the people *who* have gone.

*O mu-ntu* y-*a-ja* ( = e-*y-a-ja*) the man *who* is coming. (Cf. French Ganda *Gr.*, p. 30).

SENNA : *Ku-unika* ko-mue *ku-li mw-a iwe*, the light *that* is in thee. (Mat., 6, 23).

*Mu-ana* o-mue *wa-sua n-diro u-a-tawa*, the child *which* was crying has gone off. (Rev. Father Courtois' *Tete Grammar*, p.47.)

YAO : *Nyumba* ji *j-a-gwile liso j-a-pile moto*, the house which fell yesterday has been burnt. (Rev. A. Hetherwick's *Gr.*, p. 34).

LOWER CONGO : *E n-taudi* in *'o-kuizanza*, the child *which* is coming. (Rev. Father Visseq's *Gr.*, p. 25).

TONGA : U *mu-ntu u-a-keza ejilo, the* man who came yesterday, lit. *he* the man who...

**733.** — *Third Construction* (a relative particle appended to the first verb of the relative clause).

This is the regular construction in Swahili and Boondei. It is also met with in some Senna dialects.

SWAHILI : *Ki-su ki-kata-*cho, the knife *which* cuts.

*Ki-su ki-na-*cho *anguka*, the knife *which* is falling.

*Ki-su ki-li-*cho *anguka*, the knife *which* has fallen.

*Ki-su ki-taka-*cho *anguka*, the knife *which* will fall.

*Ki-su ki-si-*cho *kata*, the knife which does not cut.

BOONDEI : *Mu-ntu e-za-*ye, the man who is coming.

*Mu-ntu enda-*ye *eze*, the man who will come.

**734.** — *N. B.* 1. In Boondei this construction is generally coupled with the second. Ex. *Muti* we *kugwa*-o, the tree which fell.

2. The Kafir construction with the suffix -*yo*, and the Chwana construction with the suffix -*ng*, may well be compared with this.

## 2. Relative clauses in which the antecedent is represented by an object of the verb.

**735.** — Here again we may distinguish two kinds of construction. In the first kind the antecedent is represented in the relative clause *by the relative particle alone*. In the second kind the antecedent is recalled either before the verbal stem by an objective pronoun (connective), or after the verb by a substantive pronoun.

**736.** — *First construction* (the antecedent represented in the relative clause by the relative particle alone placed at the very beginning of the clause).

This is the usual construction, at least for affirmative clauses, in Tonga, Karanga, Angola, Yao, Senna, Ganda, etc., when the relative particle represents the *direct* object of the verb of the relative clause.

> Ex. TONGA: *Ka mu-cita zi-ntu* zi *ndi-ya:da*, Do ye the things *which* I like.
> *Ka u-ndi-pe ci-ntu* ci *nd-a-amba*, Give me the thing *which* I have said (= *Ka u-ndi-p*a... cf. 274).
> *I-sekua* li *nd-a-ka bona ejilo*..., the duck *which* I saw yesterday...
> *Ndi ue na* u *nd-a-ka bona ejilo?* Is it you *whom* I saw yesterday?

*N. B.* In such clauses, whether for the sake of clearness or that of euphony, we often hear those nasalized forms of the relative particles which contain the copula, viz. *ngu, nga, ndi, nji, mba*, etc. (721), instead of *u, a, li, i, ba*, etc. Ex. *I-lili isekua* nd-*u-amba?* (= ...*li-u-amba*) Which is the duck *which* you mean?

> HERERO: *E purura* ndi *u-a-tora*, the purura *which* thou hast carried off.
> OLD ANGOLA: *O y-uma* y-*a-tu-tuma*, the things *which* they order us. (Father de Coucto's *Cat*.)
> MODERN ANGOLA: *O mbua* i *ng-a-jiba*..., the dog *which* I have killed. (Cf. Héli Chatelain's *Gr.*, p. 95).
> KARANGA: *I nyika* i *nd-a-ka lebereka*..., the ground *which* I have said.
> YAO: *Nyumba* ji *tw-a-weni liso*..., the house *which* we saw yesterday.
> GANDA: *A ba-ntu* be *tu-laba*, the men *whom* we see.
> SENNA: *Ma-u* o-mue *na-nena*, the words *which* he says.

*N. B.* In clauses of this kind in Senna the connective pronoun subject of the verb is generally understood, as in the preceding example, in which *na-nena* is for *u-na nena*.

**737.** — *Second construction* (the antecedent recalled by a second pronoun besides the relative particle).

This is the usual construction in Tonga, and the other languages just mentioned, when the relative particle represents an *indirect* object of the verb. I find it also in Tonga in negative clauses when the antecedent represents a *direct* object.

In Kafir, Chwana, Swahili, and Kamba, it is the usual construction for all kinds of relative clauses in which the antecedent is represented by an object of the verb. In Yao it seems to be as usual as the first construction (Rev. A. Hetherwick's *Gr.*, p. 34). Ex.: —

TONGA : *Ba-la loa mu-ntu* u *ba-ta* **mu**-*yandi,* they bewitch the man *whom* they do not like, lit. the man *him* they do not *him* like.
*In-gubo* zi *a-lapela a-***nzio**..., the clothes in which he prays, lit. the clothes *them* he prays with *them.*

*N. B.* In such clauses the connective pronoun *u* of class *MU-ntu* is changed to *a*, 650.

OLD ANGOLA : ... *ne pango* **y**-*a-tu-fuila na*-**yo**, ... and the manner in which he died for us, lit. ... and the manner *that* he died for us with *it.*

**738. —**

KAFIR : *Zi-ye pina i nkomo* e *ndi-***zi**-*tengile*-**yo** ? Where are the cows which I have bought ? lit. They have gone whither, the cows *that* I *them* bought ?

*In-gubo* **a** *ba-tandaza na-zo*, the clothes in which they pray, lit. the clothes *that* they pray with them. •

*N. B.* 1. Kafir idioms : *Ezi nqanawe* zi-*hamba a belungu* or ...zi-*hamba a belungu nga-zo*, lit. these ships (with) which go white people, i. e. which white people go by. — *Hamba u-yo ku-ba eza nkabi* zi-*lima aba bantu,* Go to steal those oxen which those men are ploughing with, lit. ...(with) *which* are ploughing those people. — In such constructions, where that which should be the object of the verb is apparently made the subject, there is a great deal of analogy with the Tonga construction, only the real subject is understood.

2. Kafirs say, for instance : *I nkomo* a-*zi-tengile-yo* (= *I nkomo* a-*a-zi-tengile-yo* = ...o-*a-zi-tengile-yo*), " the cows which he has bought " ; and likewise : *i nkomo* a-*wa-zi-tenga-yo* = " the cows which he bought ", thus replacing by *a* the relative particle *o* of class *MU-ntu.*

**739. —**

CHWANA : *Mo-lelo* o *re-*o-*tukisitse-*ng, the fire which we have kindled.

*Tlhobolo* e *ke-fudile-*ng *ka-***eone**, the gun with which I have shot, lit. the gun *that* I have shot with *it.* (Cf. Rev. W. Crisp's *Gr.*, p. 18.)

SWAHILI : *Neno gani a-li-***lo** *li-sema ?* What is it that he says ? Lit. Which (is) the word he is *it* saying *it* ?

KAMBA : *Ka-indo* **ka** *ni-na* **ka**-*onie iyo*, the insect which I saw yesterday, lit. the insect *that* I saw *it* yesterday. (Cf. Last's *Kamba Gr.*, p. 29.)

**740.** — To complete this matter, we must add a word on the possessive relative " whose ", and the like, viz. " of which " and " of whom ". As a general principle it may be said that in Bantu the clauses which contain such a particle have a construction similar to that just described. Ex. : —

TONGA : *Ba-li ku-li bantu* **ba** *n-zim-pongo zi-a-***bo** *ezi ?* Where are the people whose goats these are ? lit. ...the people *they* it is the goats of *them* these.

CHWANA : *Kgosi* e *le-fatshe e-le-*ng *ja-***eone**, the chief whose land this is, lit. the chief *that* the land is that of *him* (Rev. W. Crisp's *Gr.*, p. 18).

**741.** — The usual Kafir construction equivalent to this is somewhat idiomatical. Ex. : —

*Yi-nto* e *zandla zi mnyama*, he is a man *whose* hands are black, lit. he is a thing *which* (has) hands that are black.

**742.** — *N. B.* Though these are the main principles which preside over the construction of relative clauses in the Bantu languages, it remains true that this point requires further study. I have at hand several grammars in which these delicate questions seem to have been carefully avoided. I have others which in this matter are by no means reliable.

## V. — Pronouns in Possessive Expressions.

### § 1. General Principle.

**743.** — In most Bantu languages possessive expressions are formed by placing the particle *-a* before substantives and pronouns. Thus from *mu-ame* " a king " we obtain *-a mu-ame* " the king's " or " of the king ", and from *bo* " they " we obtain *-abo* " their ". Being thus formed, these expressions are treated as if they were a kind of relative clause, or, in other words, as if the possessive particle *-a* were properly a verb meaning " to belong to..., to appertain to... ". Hence they require connective pronouns as well as relative clauses.

Ex. in Tonga :
*Mu-anakaz'* **u**-*a mu-ame*, the king's wife, lit. the wife which (is) of the king.
*Ba-anakazi* **ba**-*a mu-ame*, the king's wives.
*Mu-cila* **u**-*a mu-lavu*, a lion's tail.
*Mi-cila* **i**-*a ba-lavu*, tails of lions.
*Im-bizi* **i**-*ako, (z)im-bizi* **zi**-*ako*, thy horse, thy horses.
etc., etc.

**744.** — In those languages however which require relative particles of various kinds in certain relative clauses (731), these particles are not generally required before possessive expressions.

Exceptions to these principles will be seen further on (761 and 774-778). Thus, in Kafir we have *u-mfazi w-ako*, thy wife (not *u mfazi* **o** *w-ako*, 732 and 775), and in Chwana we have *mo-sadi* **o**-*a gago*, thy wife, (not *mo-sadi* **eo** *o-a gago*, 732).

**745.** — *N. B.* 1. As may be seen from the examples just given, the principles relative to possessive expressions in general are applicable as well to the possessive adjectives *-angu* " my ", *-ako* " thy ", *-akue* " his ", *-esu* " our ", *-enu* " your ", *-abo* " their ", *-awo*, *-ayo*, *-alio*, *-alo*, etc. " its ", etc. (656\*, 658, 659).

**746.** — 2. In Mpongwe the possessive particle *-a* is not heard in ordinary possessive expressions. Ex. *Mboni yi ngowe* (not *mboni ya ngowe*), the chief's goat. But it is retained in possessive adjectives, as in *Mboni* ya-*mi*, my goat.

## § 2. CONNECTIVE PRONOUNS SUPPRESSED.

**747.** — Before possessive expressions such connective pronouns as consist of a mere vowel, viz. *u*, *i*, or *a*, are sometimes suppressed. Thus we may hear in Tonga *mu-ana a-ngu* " my child " for *mu-ana* **u**-*a-ngu*, *tat'esu* " our father " for *tata* **u**-*esu*, etc., in Kafir *i bokw' a-m* " my goat " for *i-bokwe* **y**-*a-m*, etc.

**748.** — This, combined with various other principles, has produced in several languages a remarkable series of nouns of relationship, as may be seen from the following table : —

|  | my father | thy father | his father | my mother | thy mother | his mother |
|---|---|---|---|---|---|---|
| Tonga | tata | uso | uise | ba-ma | ba-nyoko | ba-nyena |
| Shambala | tate | ixo | ixe | m-lala | nyokwe | nine |
| Guha | tata | so | se | maju | nyoko | nina |
| Kafir | { tata<br>{ bawo | u yihlo | u yise | u ma | u nyoko | u nina |
| Herero | tate | o iho | o ihe | o mama | o nyoko | o ina |
| Ganda | { sebo<br>{ kitange | kito (?) | kite (?) | { mange<br>{ nyabo | nyoko | nyina |
| Chwana | rre | rrago | rragwe | mme | mmago | mmagwe |
| Swahili | babangu | babako | babaye | mamangu | mamako | mamaye |
| Mpongwe | rere | ? | ? | ngi yami | ngi yo | ngue |

etc., etc.

**749.** — *N. B.* 1. Most of these words are easily analysed. Thus in Tonga *uso* = *u-si-a-o* = *u-isi a-ko; u-ise* = *u-isi a-e* = *u-isi a-kwe; ba-nyoko* = *ba-ma u-a-ko* (cf. 122), etc. In *tata*, *ba-ma*, the possessive pronoun is understood. The word for " his mother " in Tonga, Shambala, etc., seems to be derived from the element *anya*, notion of " giving the breast ", and *-ana* " child ".

**750.** — 2. As has been said in n. 143, in Tonga the words for " mother " are generally used in the plural number instead of the singular as a mark of respect. In some other languages on the contrary the words for " mother " may be used in the singular number, but not so the words for " father ". Thus in Mozambique the word *a-thithi* " my father " is a plural of class MU-BA, and in Kafir *tata* is generally used as a plural of class IN-ZIN. Hence we may hear sometimes *tata z-am* " my father ", *tata z-ako* " thy father " (= *u yihlo*), etc. In Senna both the word *a-tatu* " father " and *a-mai* " mother " seem to be used always as plurals of cl. MU-BA.

**751.** — 3. In some languages the words for " father " are oftener brought under cl. IN-ZIN than under cl. MU-BA. This is the case particularly in Angola, Nika, Swahili, etc.

**752.** — 4. *Baba* or *Bawo* is apparently borrowed from Arabic or from another Semitic language, and in some languages it is not used properly with the meaning of " father ", but with that of " sir, master ", or as an honorific title. The true Bantu word for " father " is *tata* or *rara* (*tate*, *n-tate*, etc.)

**753.** — 5. The Rev. W. Crisp (*Secoana Gr.*, p. 21) notices some contractions in various nouns of relationship in Chwana which show distinctly that this language is impregnated with words borrowed from several others. Thus the possessive expression -*eno* " your, yours ", is borrowed from Tonga, or Karanga, or Kafir, to form the words *rraeno* " your father ", *mmaeno* " your mother ", etc. *A-ke* (= *a-nge*) " mine ", is borrowed from Karanga to form the words *moro-ake* " my son ", *nnake* " my younger brother " (= Karanga *nonange*), *mo-gatsake* " my spouse " (= *mo-gadi-ake*, cf. 205), etc.

**754.** — 6. In Ganda, among other expressions similar to those above mentioned, we may notice *baze* " my husband ", *baro* " thy husband ", etc. (French *Ganda Grammar*, p. 26).

### § 3. Possessive Expressions after Locatives.

**755.** — Locative expressions give rise to a great variety of construction for the possessive expressions which depend on them. Thus : —

**756.** — 1° In Senna, Nyamwezi, Karanga, Mozambique, etc., possessive expressions which depend on locatives regularly admit the connective pronoun corresponding to the locative classifier of their noun.

Ex. Nyamwezi : *Ha-numba* **h**-*a wawa* " at the house of my father ".
*Ku-numba* **ku**-*a wawa* " towards the house of my father ".
*Mu-numba* **mu**-*a wawa* " in the house of my father ".

Karanga : *Ku-mberi* **ko** ʒ*winu* ʒ*wirire* " before all things ", *pe-juru pon-sece* (= *pa-un-sece*) " on the earth " ; *pa-kati* **pe**n*jizi m-biri* " between two rivers ", *mu-kati mu-e-mumba* " inside of the house ".

Senna : *Pa-kati pa akazi* " amidst women " ; *pa-maso pa-ace* " before his eyes " ; *apano pa-kati pa pili pa mi-sozi* " here in this vale of tears " ; *m-mimba mw-anu* " in your bosom " ; *ku-musa ku-a nzou* " at the abode of the elephant ".

Mozambique : *Va-zulu* **va**-*ia* " over it " ; **mu**-*hina* **m**-*a-ia* " inside of it ", etc.

**757.** — 2° In Tonga, Herero, Angola, Kongo, etc., the possessive expressions which depend on locatives admit only in a few cases the connective pronoun corresponding to the locative prefix : more commonly they require the connective pronoun corresponding to the proper classifier of their noun : in some cases they require no connective pronoun at all, principally when the locative expression is formed with an adjective.

**758.** — Ex. Tonga : With a *locative* pronoun : *Ba-lala* **ku**-*nsi* **ku**-*a-manzi* " they (the Mbunda) can sleep at the bottom of the water ". *Enda* **ku**-*nembo* **ku**-*angu* " walk before me ".

With a *non-locative* pronoun : *A* **ka**-*ti ka-a ma-cedo* " in the middle of night ". *Ku* **mi**-*nzi* **i**-*a-bo* " in their villages ". *Mu* **n**-*ganda* **i**-*a-ko* (or through assimilation *mu-*n**ga**n*da* **a**-*a-ko*) " in thy house ".

Without any connective pronoun : *Ba-la njila mu-kati a-manzi* " they go into the water ". *U-kede ku-tala a Si-ongo, ku-nsi a Mukuni* " he lives above *Siongo* (Victoria Falls), below Mu-kuni ". *Mu-nsi a mu-se* (or *mu-ns'a mu-se* " under the ground ").

**759.** — OTHER EXAMPLES :
HERERO : *Tua p'-e kuma r'o mu-vero* (Kolbe's *Dict.*) " put it down behind the door " ; *k'o* me*ho* y-*oye* " before your eyes " ; *k'o* mu-*rungu* u-*e* " before him " ; *m'o* ka-*ii* k'*o meva* " in the midst of the water ".

ANGOLA (from F. de Coucto's *Catechism*, 1661). *Mo kumbi* ri-*a kufua ku-etu* " in the hour of our death ". *Mo* ki-*luiji eki* ki-*a ma-soxi* " in this vale of tears ". *U-ekala ko* m-*bando* y-*a lu-kuako lu-a kuria* " he sits at the right hand... "

CONGO. *Muna* di-*ambu* di-*a*... " on account of... " ; *ku-na* lōse lu-*a*... " before the face of... " etc. (Cf. Bentley's *Dict.* p. 612).

*N. B.* It is worthy of notice that, the diminutive classifier *ka* having been lost in Congo, the ancient expressions formed with *ka-ti* " middle, centre " are now connected with following substantives by the pronoun *ku*, as in *mu-na* ka-*ti* ku-*a*... " in the centre of ". This connects Congo with Kafir, Chwana, etc.

**760.** — 3° In Swahili the possessive expressions which depend on locatives require different connective pronouns according to the meaning of the locative expression.

Ex. *Kati* y-*a njia* " in the middle of the road " ; *juu* y-*a-ke* " over it ", etc. (as if *kati* and *juu* were nouns of the class *IN* or *MA*).

*Kati* ka *ile jiwe* " in the middle of that stone " (as if *kati* were here a noun of class *KA*, a class nearly obliterated in Swahili).

*Nyumba*-ni kw-*a-ke* " at his house " ; *kanwa*-ni kw-*a Muungu* " from the mouth of God " (as if the locative suffix *ni* were here equivalent to *ku*).

*Mi-kono*-ni mw-*a-o* " in their arms " ; ...*uvuli*-ni mw-*a ma-uti* " in the region of darkness " (as if the locative suffix *ni* were here equivalent to *mu*).

*Ma-hali* pa *raha* " the place of rest " (as if *ma-hali* were a locative of class PA).

**761.** — 4° In Kafir and Chwana, where the mechanism of locatives is perhaps still more disturbed than in Swahili, the possessive expressions which depend on old locative expressions are in most cases connected with them by means of the pronoun *ku* (Chwana *go*). Other locative expressions require the connective pronoun corresponding to the proper classifier of the noun which they contain.

Ex. KAFIR. *Pezu* kw-*a-ko* " over thee ". *E-caleni* kw-*a-m* " at my side ". *Ezantsi* kw-*en-taba* " below the mountain ". — *E*-n-*dlini* y-*a-ko* " in thy house ".

CHWANA. *Kwa-ntle* ga *motse* (= go-*a motse*) " outside the town ". *Fa-gare* ga *ba-sadi* " amidst women " (= ...go-*a ba-sadi*). *Mo-teng* ga *lesaka* (= go-*a le-saka*) " inside of the kraal ". — *Mabogong* a *ona* " in their arms ".

**762.** — 5° In Mpongwe the locative particle *go* generally does duty for all the locative classifiers of the other Bantu languages, and it acts as *a mere preposition*. Hence in this language, when possessive expressions follow locative expressions, the connective pronoun which is required is, as a rule, that which corresponds to the classifier of the noun which is preceded by the locative particle.

Ex. *Go nyumi* y-*ani* " behind you ".

**763.** — *N. B.* In the same language some ready-made expressions remind one of the regular constructions of the other Bantu languages. Ex. *Ati* ga *impumi itani* " within five years " (cf. Swahili *kati* ka..., Tonga *a ka-ti* ka..., etc., n. 758) ; *m-pangini* ga *ndego* " in the quality of friend " (cf. Chwana *supra*), etc.

**764.** — Concerning the locative expressions which mean " near " and " far ", it must be noticed that in nearly all the Bantu languages they are generally followed by the preposition which means " with " (Tonga *a*, Karanga, Kafir, etc. *na*, Chwana *le*, etc.).

Ex. KARANGA : *pa-fupe* ne-*mumba* ( = na-*imumba*) " near the house ".
    KAFIR : *ku-fupi* na-*m* " near me "; *ku-de* no *mti* ( = *na-u mti*) " far from the tree ".
    CHWANA : *kgakala* le *rona* " far from us "; *ga-uchwane* le *motse* " very near the town " ; etc., etc.

**765.** — Finally, in this matter we again find applications of the principle of avoiding monosyllables. For, when possessive expressions should be reduced to mere monosyllables, this is avoided either by appending them as suffixes to the preceding word, or by prefixing a relative particle to the possessive expression. The first of these forms may be remarked principally in Ganda, the second in Karanga.

Ex. GANDA : *O Moyo*-gwe " his heart " ; *o mu-kono*-gwo " thy hand "; *e kanzu*-yo, " thy cloth ".
KARANGA : *Ba-nona* ba-*b-e* " their brothers " ; *zina* li-*ri-o* " thy name ".

**766.** — *N. B.* 1. In Karanga the possessive is expressed by a suffix when it contains no consonant proper. Ex. *Nona*-uo " thy son " (= *nona u-a-o*).

**767.** — 2. Following a somewhat similar principle, Kafirs generally say *u-m-ntan*, am " my child ", *i n-gubw'* am " my blanket ", etc., instead of *u m-ntana w-a-m*, *i ngubo y-a-m*, etc.

## VI. — Relative and Possessive Expressions used Substantively.

**768.** — Relative and possessive expressions may be used substantively, viz. as subjects or predicates. Supposing, for instance, that a Tonga had spoken of " feasts " *mi-lia*, he may say : *I-e impewo nji-a-ku-sanguna*, lit. " (those) of winter are (those) of the beginning, i. e., are the first ".

In order to understand the formation of such expressions in Bantu, we must distinguish between those languages which have articles and those which have none. Hence : —

**769.** — 1° *In those languages which have no article*, such as Tonga proper, Senna, Chwana, Swahili, etc., when such relative and possessive expressions are used substantively as subjects or objects, they appear to have commonly the same form as when used adjectively. When used as predicates they require before them a copula-containing relative particle. These laws however suffer exceptions, and may require to be modified when reliable materials are more abundant.

Ex. In Tonga :  *A. Relative clauses.*

Without a copulative prefix. · With a copulative prefix.

*U-a-ka sanguna, ngu Monze*, he who began was Monze. · *Monze* **ngu**-*a-ka sanguna*, lit., Monze it is he who began.

A-*luma bantu, nga-masaku* (or *m'masaku*), lit. they who bite men are the devils. · *Ma-saku,* **nga**-*luma ba-ntu*, the devils are they who bite men.

I-*la inka a bantu babi (in-zila)*, nji *li-a mu-lilo ;* i-*la inka a babotu,* nji *li-a ku-kondua*, lit. *that* (road) *which* goes with bad people, *that is it which* has fire; *that which* goes with good people, *that is it* which has happiness.

**770.** — *B. Possessive clauses.*

U-*a ku-sanguna mu-ntu, ngu-Adamo*, the man of the beginning (i. e. the first man), was Adam. · *Adamo* **ngu**-*a ku-sanguna*, Adam was the first man.

Zi-*enu (zintu) nzezi*, yours are these (things). · **Nzi**-*zienu, ezi zintu*, they are yours, these things.

Li *angu (isekua), ndeli*, mine is this (duck). · *Eli sekua* **ndi**-*li-angu*, this duck is mine.

Lu-*a Leza (lu-zubo), m-baame*, lit. that (the race) of God, they are the chiefs. · *Ba-ame,* **ndu**-*lu-a-Leza*, the chiefs are God's race.

Ci-*ako (cintu) nceci*, thine (thing) is this. · *Eci cintu* **nci**-*ako*, this thing is thine.

**771.** — *N. B.* 1. In Tonga, for clearness' sake relative and possessive clauses very often admit that form which begins with the copula-containing relative particle. We have seen above that this is done particularly when the relative pronoun is the object of the verb (736). It is also done regularly when the relative or possessive clause is of some length containing several distinct words. This may be considered as a sort of *bracket construction*. Ex. *Baa jaya mberere* nja *ku-pa-ila* " they have killed the sheep for the sacrifice " (lit... " it is that of the sacrifice ") ; *Ba-la lia nyama* nja *ku-sunsia insima* " they eat the meat which has been cooked with the porridge " (lit. " ... it is that of flavouring the porridge ".)

2. This kind of bracket construction seems to be particularly frequent in Herero.

**772.** — Examples in other languages : —

### A. Without copulative prefix.

#### Relative clauses.

SENNA : *Muka, u-gulitse ciomwe uli na-cio,* go, sell what thou hast (Mat., 19, 21.)
CHWANA : *Ea, o-bapatse tse o-nang na-co,* do.
SWAHILI : *Twaa i-li-yo yako,* take what is thine (Mat., 20, 14.)
etc. Cf. Mat., 5, 3-10, in the various translations of the New Testament.

#### Possessive clauses.

CHWANA : *Cula ea gago* or *cula eeo ea gago,* take what is thine (Mat. 20, 14.)
MPONGWE : *Wong' i-yo,* do.
SWAHILI : *Y-a nani sanamu hii...? ... Ya Kaisari.* Whose is this image...? Cesar's. (Mat., 22, 20) etc.

### B. With a copulative prefix.

CHWANA : *Pitsa e e-thubegileng* ke-*e mosetsana ona a-e-reka ngogola,* the pot which is smashed *is* that which the girl bought last year. (Rev. W. Crisp's *Gr.*, p. 18).
KARANGA : **Ndi**-*ru-a Wange (ru-jubo),* it is Wange's (family).
SWAHILI : *Ufalme wa mbingu* **ni** *wao,* theirs is the kingdom of heaven. (Mat., 5, 10).
SUTO : *Lengolo lena* **ke** *la mang? ...* **Ke** *la Kesare.* Whose inscription is this? Caesar's. (Mat., 22, 20).

**773.** — *N. B.* It is remarkable that in some Senna dialects, though the copula before substantives is generally *ndi* (587), nevertheless before possessive expressions it has forms similar to those of Tonga (721).

Ex. *N-kazi uyu* ngu-*ani ?* Ngu-*anga.* This woman, *whose* is she ? *Mine.*
*Mi-adia ii* nji-*ani ?* Nji-*anga.* These canoes, *whose* are they ? *Mine.*
*Ci-kazi ici* nci-*ani ?* Nci-*anga.* This bottle, *whose* is it ? *Mine.*

**774.** — 2° *Those languages which* in given cases *have an article* before substantives require a relative particle, or a simple article, in similar cases before possessive and relative expressions when these are used substantively. Thus : —

**775.** — A) In Kafir such expressions require the relative particle *o, e,* or *a* (723), where substantives would require the article *u, i,* or *a*.

Ex. O *wam u mfazi mtsha,* o *wako mkulu,* my wife is young, yours is old.
O *sebenza kakulu, ndim lo* ( = o *usebenza*...), lit. he who works much, it is myself.

Reciprocally, no relative particle is used where substantives require no article (317).

Ex. *Wetu, yiz'apa* (not o *wetu*...). Our (friend), come here.
*Yinina, betu* (not ...a *betu*)? What is it, our (friends)?
*Lo wam u mfazi* (not *lo* o *wam*), this wife of mine.
*A si wam u mfazi* (not *a si* o *wam*), it is not my wife.

Where substantives require to be preceded by a copulative prefix (582) the possessive and relative expressions are likewise preceded by a copula-containing relative particle, viz. *ngo* in cl. *MU*, *nga* in classes *BA* and *MA*, *ye* in classes *MI* and *IN*, *le* in cl. *LI*, *lo* in cl. *LU*, *bo* in cl. *BU*, *ko* in cl. *KU*, *ze* in classes *ZI* and *ZIN*, *se* in cl. *SI*.

Ex. *Lo mfazi* **ngo** *ka bani?*, This woman, whose is she?
*Eli cuba* **le** *li ka bani?* **Le** *lam.* This tobacco, whose is it? It is mine.
*La ma-hashe* **nga** *ka bani?* **Nga** *wetu.* These horses, whose are they? They are ours.

**776.** — B) In Herero, Angola, and Congo, the same sort of expressions require an article where substantives require one.

Ex. HERERO: *O ruvio* o *ruandye,* the knife is mine. Cf. *o ruvio ruandye,* my knife. (Kolbe's *Dict.*)
CONGO: **E** *yame mbele ivididi,* my knife is lost, lit. mine knife is lost, or it is my knife that is lost. (Bentley's *Gr.*, p. 523).
ANGOLA: **O** *yatuma Santa Ngeleja*..., that which Holy Church commands... (De Coucto's *Cat.*, p. 6).

*N. B.* This last example exhibits a relative clause. Possessive clauses used substantively have no article in Father de Coucto's *Catechism.*

**777.** — In Ganda expressions of the same sort, when not used as predicates, generally require a simple article; in a few cases they prefer a peculiar kind of relative particle which much resembles the demonstrative pronouns of the first position in several languages, viz. *oru, ebi, eyi,* etc.

Ex. *Mudu wange Muganda,* o *wo Musoga,* my slave is a Ganda, thine is a Soga (French *Ganda Gr.*, p. 25).
*Genda otunde* **ebi** *bio* (not simply **e** *bio*), go and sell what is thine (Mat., 19, 21).
*Twala* **eyi** *yo* (not simply **e** *yo*), take what is thine (Mat., 20, 14).

*Relative and Possess. Expressions used Substantively.* 197

When used as predicates, they remind us of the Kafir construction above noticed by requiring as a kind of copula that kind of substantive pronoun or relative particle which ends in *e* (724).

Ex. *O bwakabaka o bwo mu gulu* **bwe** *bwabwe* (Kafir *U bukumkani ba se zulwini* **bo** *babo*), the kingdom of heaven is theirs. Cf. 830.

## VII. — Relative and Possessive Expressions Equivalent to our Adjectives.

**778.** — It has been mentioned above that in Bantu adjectives proper are comparatively few in number, and that their apparent want is supplied principally by relative clauses and possessive expressions. I now add a few remarks for a better understanding of this principle. Thus : —

1° In Tonga the words which correspond to our adjectives expressive of colour, sensible qualities, exterior form, etc., are mostly verbs, such as *ku-tuba* " to be white ", or more exactly " to become white ", *ku-salala* " to be red ", *ku-sia* " to be black ", *ku-lulama* " to be straight ", *ku-pia* " to be hot ", etc. Hence the adjectives " white, black, hot, " etc., of our languages pass simply as verbs in Tonga.

Ex. Absolute clause : *Ma-nzi a-a-pia*, the water is hot , lit... has become hot.
Relative clause : *Ndi-yanda ma-nzi a-a-pia*, I want hot water, lit... water that has become hot.

Absolute clause : *Ei n-zila i-luleme* (*-luleme* = perfect of *-lulama*), this road is straight.
Relative clause : *Inka e in-zila i-luleme*, go by the direct road, lit... by the road that is straight.

*N. B.* Expressions of the same kind are found in all the Bantu languages.

**779.** — 2° In Angola and Congo most of the expressions which correspond to the quantitative adjectives of the other Bantu languages (601, 603) have the form of possessive expressions. Such are, for instance, *-a m-bote* (= *a mu-bote* or perhaps *-a bu-bote*) " good ", lit. " of goodness ", *-o-nene* (= *a u-nene* = *a bu-nene*) " great ", lit. " of greatness ", *-o-be* (= *a u-be*) " new ", lit. " of freshness ", *o-kulu* (= *a u-kulu*) " old " lit. " of growth ", etc.

Ex. *Eme ngi mu-tu* **u**-*a mbote*, I am a good man (= Tonga: *ndime mu-ntu* **mu**-*botu*).
*Eye* **u**-*o-nene*, thou art great (= Tonga : *iwe mu-nene*).

**780.** — *N. B.* Expressions similar to these, but for different kinds of adjectives, are found in nearly all the Bantu languages.

Ex. KAFIR : *I yeza l-e-nene* " a true, genuine medicine " ( = *i yeza l-a i-nene* "a medicine of a truthful man ", from *i-nene* " a gentleman, a man who does not cheat "). Hence in Kafir *ngo kwenene* " in true language, truly " ( = *ngo ku-teta kw-e-nene*, lit. " in the language of a gentleman ").

SWAHILI : *M-tu* w-*a choyo* " a greedy person ", (lit. " a man of small heart ", from *ch-oyo* = *ki-oyo* " small heart " ; cf. *m-oyo* " heart ").

etc., etc.

## VIII. — Pronouns referring to Substantives understood

### and

### Pronouns used as Conjunctions.

**781.** — Connective pronouns and others are often used with reference to substantives which are entirely understood, being not even expressed in preceding sentences. Their meaning must then be made out from the context. The number of the substantives which may be thus understood is however limited. In Tonga they are principally the following : —

In class LI : *i-zuba* " the sun, a day. " Ex. Li-*a ku-sanguna* li-*a in-sipi*, the first (day) of the week.

» MA : *ma-nzi* " water. " Ex. *U-a-yala a-bu-enga, pa* a-*ka selelela*, he went along the bank, where *it* (the water) rushes down.

» BU : *bu-siku* " night. " Ex. *A-ta*-bu-*ci*..., when *it* (night) has not yet cleared up...

» KU : notion of action, time or manner. Ex. *Ta*-ku-*kondua a lu-sele*, no work is done on the day of the new moon, (lit. *it* is not worked......)

» CI : ci-*ntu* " a thing. " Ex. *Nci-nyamanzi* co *o-yeya ?* ( = *ci u-eya*, 251). What is *it* that you are thinking about ?

*N. B.* 1. In Kafir the word *i n-to* " a thing, " being of class *IV*, the connective pronoun used with reference to this word, when it is understood, is *i*. Ex. : I-*mnandi u ku-ncokola na-we*, " it is pleasant to chat with you. "

2. In Tonga the plural *zi-ntu* " things " is seldom understood. But in Angola its equivalent *y-ima* " things " appears to be as often understood as the singular *ki-ima* " a thing ". Ex. I *ua-ngi-bele*, *nga-*1*-ria kia* " (the things) which you gave me, I have eaten them already ". (Héli Chatelain's *Ki-mbundu Gr.*, p. 143).

*Pronouns referring to Substantives understood.* 199

In class LU : *lu-zubo* " family, race. " Ex. *Ba-leya bala tulua* lu-*a-baana*, The Lea are deprived (by the Rotse) of their children, lit. of *that* (part of their family which is) children. — **Ndulo-ndulo** *ndu-lu-a Davide* (cf. 770), it is David's own (race).

*N. B.* In Kafir the connective pronoun *lu* is often used with reference to *u-suku* " day " understood, exactly as in Tonga *li* is used with reference to *i-zuba*. Ex. *O* lu-*e si-tatu*, *o* lu-*e sinne*, etc. " the 3$^d$ day (of the week), the 4$^{th}$ day ", etc.

**782.** — Hence some ready-made locative expressions which have the form of possessive expressions, such as **mu**-*a-kale* " to the bottom ", lit. " unto the (inside part) of the end " ; **ku**-*a-kale* " for ever ", lit. " to the (time) of the end " ; **ku**-*a-Mpande* " at Mpande's (place) ", etc. Of course in such locative expressions the connective pronoun cannot be understood as it often is when its antecedent is expressed (757).

Ex. *Ba-lapela Mpande ka be-enda a bu-botu* **ku**-*a-kale*, they pray to Mpande that they may go in happiness for ever.

*Mu-nari u-a-njila* **mu**-*a-kale*, Livingstone went in right to the bottom (of the water).

**783.** — Locative expressions of the same description as the preceding are commonly found in nearly all the Bantu languages.

Ex. KAFIR : *kw-etu*, at our place ; *kw-ake*, at his place ; *kw-a Gcaleka*, at Gcaleka's place ; etc.

SWAHILI : *kw-etu*, at our place; *mw-etu*, in our house; *kw-a mamae*, at his mother's place ; etc.

GANDA : *ew-ange*, at my place; *ew-o*, at thy place ; *ew-e*, at his place; etc. Cf. 546.

*N. B.* In Kafir and several other languages, when those substantives of cl. MU-BA which have no classifier in the singular, as *u-yise* " his father ", *u Sa-rili* " King Kreli ", etc. (342), have to come into possessive expressions, they are first made into possessive locative expressions of the kind just described. Ex. *i nkomo za* kwa *Rili* " Kreli's cattle ", lit. " the cattle of Kreli's place ". This particle *kwa* is in Kafir sometimes contracted to *ka*. Ex. *U mnt' a kwa Tixo* or *U mnt' a* ka *Tixo*, " the child of God ", lit. " the child of God's place ".

*Ga* (= *go-a*) is used in Chwana where Kafir has *kwa* or *ka*, and in a few other cases. The regular use of this particle before certain possessive pronouns is particularly remarkable, as in *batho ba* ga-*gwe* " his people " (Tonga *bantu baakue*) ; *pitse ea* ga-*go*, " thy horse " (Tonga *im-bizi iako*).

PRONOUNS USED AS CONJUNCTIONS.

**784.** — As a result of the principles just laid down, some relative particles have come to be regularly used as conjunctions.

They may then be considered as referring to certain notions of time, place, or manner of thought, understood. Ex. : —

LI (referring to *i-zuba*, the sun) = " when ", with reference to a determined moment of the day.

Ex. *Baamuzika* li *bu-cia*, they bury him *when* night is clearing up.

**785.** — (P)A = " when ", with reference to *successive* actions.

Ex. **Pa**-*a ka fua muntu, bala muzika*, when a man is dead, they bury him.

*N. B.* The Swahili relative clauses which correspond exactly to the preceding contain the relative particle -*po*, in accordance with the genius of this language (726). Ex. *Tu-li*-po *ku-ja*..., " when we had come "... (Tonga **Pa** *tu-eza*...)

(P)A = also " where ". The other locative particles, viz. *ku* and *mu*, may likewise be used as conjunctions.

Ex. **Pa**-*a-ka tuba*, (in the part of the body) *where* he is white.

**Mu** *nd-a-ka njira*, where I went in.

*N. B.* 1. Cf. in Mozambique : **Va** *no-kelaka*, wherein I am entering ; u (= **ku**) *no-kuma nchua*, where the Sun comes out.

2. Cf. in Herero : **Ku** *me-kara*, where I stay ; *o n-dyuo* mu *tu-rara*, the house wherein we sleep.

3. Cf. in Ganda : *To-manyi* **we** (or **gie**) *n-sula*, You do not know where I live ; *U-a-laba nyumba* **mwe** *n-sula ?* Have you seen the house wherein I live? — *We, gie, mwe* are relative particles corresponding respectively to the locative classifiers *wa, e, mu* (= *pa, ku, mu*). Cf. 719 and 540, 546, 552.

etc., etc.

**786.** — BU = " supposing that..., if... ".

Ex. **Bu** *tu-bona u-bereka nawo*..., *Suppose* we see you working thus...

*N. B.* 1. Cf. in Chwana *BO* = " as if ". Ex. *A o-lira jalo* bo *o ngoanyana ?* Do you act thus, as if you were a child? (Rev. W. Crisp's *Gr.*, n. 74).

2. Cf. in Ganda the relative particle *Bwe* " if ". Ex. **Bwe** *o-no-genda ruegulo, o-no-tuka kiro*, if you go this evening, you will arrive during night. *Ne* **bue** *ba-lia, ti ba-kkuta*, even if they eat, they will not be satisfied. (French *Ganda Gr.*, p. 40).

**787.** — CI = " while, if ".

Ex. **Ci** *tu-bereka*..., *while* we are working.

*N. B.* 1. Cf. in Herero : tyi *ma mu-tyiwa*, if ye know ; tyi *tu-a-kara koyenu*, when we were with you. (Rev. F. W. Kolbe's *Dict.*)

2. In Herero the relative particle *(i)ndu* (referring to *o ru-veze* " time ") is used in the same manner for " when, while ". Ex. ...ndu *ma tu-ya*, when we come.

**788.** — KA = " if, when, while, and ".

Ex. *Ba-lia* **ka** *ba-ti*..., they eat saying *at the same time*...

*Siabulongo u-a-toligua a Leza* **ka** *a-ci lu-sabila*, Siabulongo was taken up by God *while* he was still a baby.

*Ba-a-ka sika, inyue* **ka** *mu-li-lede,* they arrived *while* you were asleep.
**Ka** *a-li a-fuefui, uti...,* **ka** *a-li ku-le, uti...,* if he be near, he says..., if he be far, he says... Cf. 970.

## APPENDIX ON THE LUNDA LANGUAGE.

**788**bis. — While reading over the last proofsheets of this article I received Henrique Augusto Dias de Carvalho's " *Methodo pratico para fallar a lingua da Lunda* ([1])", a most valuable addition to Bantu literature. As I had till then only a few pages of this work, my conclusions on this important language were limited to the few remarks laid down above in nn. 143 and 144. Complete as the same work now is, it furnishes good materials for comparison with these pages.

*I. Phonetics.* — Lunda has a great deal in common with Angola, Lower Congo, and Mbamba, more particularly with the last. Its most remarkable feature seems to be the uncertain sound of certain vowels, and the transition of some others to *a*. Ex. *ku-mana* " to see " (Tonga *ku-bona*), *mu-lambo* " a lip " (Tonga *mu-lomo*, Angola *mu-zumbu*, Dualla *mo-lumbu*, cf. 360*), *n-zavo* " an elephant " (Tonga *inzovu*), etc.

The following verbs may be compared with the table of examples under n. 52 : *ku-hia* " to steal ", *ku-mana* " to see ", *k'ovua* " to hear ", *ku-fua* " to die ", *ku-cia* " to dawn ", *ku-fika* " to arrive ", *kw-eza* " to come ", *ku-jala* " to dress ", *ku-nvala* " to beget ", *ku-nua* " to drink ", *ku-dia* " to eat ", *ku-lala* " to lie down ", *ku-dila* " to cry ", *ku-dima* " to hoe ", *ku-suma* " to bite ", *ku-neta* or *ku-leta* " to bring ", *ku-enda* " to walk ", *ku-tuma* " to send ".

*II. Substantives.* — Lunda has the 12 classes of substantives described in a previous chapter. Ex. : —

Cl. MU-A (= MU-BA) : *Mu-ntu* " a person ", *a-* ; *mw-ana* or *mona* " a child ", *a-* ; *mu-kaje* " a woman ", *a-* ; *mu-ata* " a chief ", *a-* ; *mu-roro* " a servant ", *a-* ; *Nzambi* " God "; *Mu-kuarunda* " a Lunda ", *a-* ; *tatuko* " father "; *maku* " mother ".

Cl. MU-MI : *Mu-jimba* " the body ", *mi-* ; *mu-kila* " the tail ", *mi-* ; *mu-tue* " the head ", *mi-* ; *mu-lambo* " a lip ", *mi-* ; *mu-xima* " the heart ", *mi-* ; *mu-tondo* " a tree ", *mi-* ; *mu-pueji* " a stream ", *mi-* ; *mu-vo* " a year ", *mi-*.

Cl. N-JIN : *Mbiji* or *nama* " meat " ; *n-gombe* " one head of cattle ", *jin-* : *m-pembe* " a goat ", *jim-* ; *n-zolo* " a fowl ", *jin-* ; *n-naka* " a snake ", *jin-* ; *n-zavo* " an elephant " ; *jin-* ; *n-vula* " rain " ; *n-jila* " a path ", *jin-*.

Cl. (D)I-MA : *Di-ciko* " a day ", *ma-* ; *di-su* " an eye ", *mesu* ; *di-zeu* " a tooth ", *ma-* ; *di-fupa* " a bone ", *ma-* ; *di-yala* " a stone ", *ma-* ; *di-jina* " a name ", *ma-*.

Cl. (B)U-MA : *Ma-rufo* " wine " ; *u-nga* " flour " ; *u-ato* " a canoe " *ma-u-* ; *u-cuko* " night " ; *mema* " water ".

Cl. KU : *Ku-hua* " to fall ". Only infinitives of verbs seem to belong to this class.

Cl. LU-JI(N) : *Lu-dimi* or *Ru-dimi* " the tongue ". According to Carvalho the plural of this word is *ji-dimi*, and, in general, the plural classifier of this class is not *jin*, but *ji*. It seems scarcely possible that this should be correct. The plural classifier of *lu-dimi* must be *jin-dimi*, and, in general, if the *n* of the classifier *jin* is not heard in some words, it must be only before hard consonants, according to nn. 151 and 283.

---

1. Lisboa, Imprensa nacional, 1890.

Cl. CI-I ( = CI-ZI): *Ci-ouma* " a thing ", *i-* ; *ci-kanda* " a hide ", *i-* ; *ci-lalo* " a bridge ", *i-* ; *i-kumbo* " a hut ", *i-*.

Cl. KA-TU : *Ka-kungi* " a youth ", *tu-* ; *ka-swe* " fire ", *ka-bwa* " a dog ", *tu-*. Locative classes PA, KU, and MU : *Pa-xi* or *pa-nci* " down "; *mu-ixi*ni " within "; *pa-suipa* " near " ; *pa-lepa* " far "; *pola* " outside " ; *pa-kaxi* " between "; *pe-uro* " upon "; *ku-nyima* " behind "; *mu-cikumbo* " in the hut ".

The author gives also the locative classifier *BU*. But is not this again a mistake? *BU* is the Angola classifier corresponding to the Lunda *PA*. Hence, for instance, when he says, p. 159, that " down " is rendered into Lunda by *paxi* or *boxi*, must not his words be understood in this sense that *boxi* is the Angola equivalent for the Lunda *paxi?*

I find in Lunda the two interesting locatives *polo* and *kolo* ( = *pa-ulo* and *ko-ulo*), both of which mean " a place ". I have as yet noticed their exact equivalents only in Chwana in the words *felo* and *golo*. Cf. 537.

*III. Adjectives.* — The laws for the adjectives which I term quantitative, such as *wape* " good ", *-ipe* or *impe* " bad ", *-jima* " great ", *kiepe* " small ", *-lepa* " long ", *-ki* " new ", etc., are the same as in Tonga (596). Ex. *mu-tondo mu-jima* " a large tree ".

*Pronouns.* — The connective personal pronouns seem to be *ni* " I ", *u* " thou ", *u* " he ", *tu* " we ", *nu* or *mu* " you ", *a* " they ", *u, i, lu, di*, etc. The substantive personal pronouns seem to be *ami* " I ", *eye* " thou ", *endi* " he ", *ecu* " we ", *enu* " you ", *ene* " they ", etc. But in Carvalho's work I remark a certain inconsistency in the forms of those pronouns which correspond to classifiers containing *m* (cf. n. 649). Thus I find *ma-zui ama* a-*mi* " these words of mine " (p. 205) next to *ma-i* ma *nzolo* " eggs of fowls " (p. 51), *ma-ciko* ma-*oso* " all the days " (p. 227) next to *ma-ciko ama a-oso* " all these days " (p. 231), *mu-tue* mu-*a mona* " the head of the child " (p. 209) next to *mu-tue* u-*ei* " thy head " (p. 223), *mu-jikita* ou " this work " (p. 136) next to *mu-lambo* omu " this present " (p. 135), etc.

Other conclusions on Lunda will be introduced into the following pages. Strange to say, many words in Lunda remind one of the languages which are heard near Delagoa Bay.

# IX. — Numerals.

## § 1. Bantu Numeration.

**789.** — As far as I have been able to verify, counting among the Bantu is done principally with the aid of fingers. Old Kafirs, for instance, seldom express a number by the proper word, but they show it by a motion of the hand which they accompany with the expression *zi-nje* " they are so many... " or *ba-nje, mi-nje, ma-nje,* etc., according to the class of the things in question.

*N. B.* The following is in general the meaning of the principal signs : —

| | | | | |
|---|---|---|---|---|
| Raising one of the small fingers alone................. | | counts | 1 |
| » | » | with the next...... | » | 2 |
| » | » | with the next two | » | 3 |
| » | » | with the next three | » | 4 |
| » | the five fingers of a single hand............... | | » | 5 |
| » | the thumb alone or the thumb of one hand with the five fingers of the other | | » | 6 |
| » | the thumb with the index.................... | | » | 7 |
| » | » | with the next two fingers...... | » | 8 |
| » | » | with the next three fingers...... | » | 9 |
| Both hands laid flat against one another............ | | | » | 10 |

Ten is a *kumi;* two tens (20) are 2 *ma-kumi* or opening both hands twice ; three tens (30) are 3 *ma-kumi* or opening both hands three times, etc.
One hundred in Kafir is a *kulu*, i. e. " a large number ". In many languages it is a *gana*.

**790.** — There are however also for the different numbers the proper words or expressions, which may be used when required. These are partly adjectives of one kind or another, partly substantives. Thus among the Tonga and other tribes of the interior, there exist numeral adjectives up to five, but 6 is five-and-one, 7 is five-and-two, etc. Ten is expressed by the substantive *ikumi*, a hundred by *ma-kume-kumi*, which is a superlative of " ten ". Beyond that there are in Tonga only " tens without number ", *makumi a-ta balui*.

In most of the other languages there are numeral adjectives up to 6, and substantives or foreign words for the other numbers. In a few languages " a whole man " is " twenty ".

In general South-African natives will see at a glance that one of their goats or head of cattle is missing even in a very large flock or herd. Yet they are very slow at counting properly, until they have been taught our own methods, which, it may be remarked, they adopt readily.

**791.** — On the point of numeral adjectives the Bantu languages go two different ways. Most of them, like Tonga, usually treat them as pronouns, so that they incorporate *connective pronouns*, not classifiers. Others, like Kafir, treat them as quantitative adjectives, so that they incorporate *classifiers*, not connective pronouns.

792. — I subjoin comparative tables *, which exhibit in their bare form the numbers 1, 2, 3, 4, 5, 6, 10, and 100, in the principal Bantu languages. Where two forms are given for one number in the

### * COMPARATIVE TABLE OF NUMBERS.

|              | 1            | 2              | 3             | 4            |
|--------------|--------------|----------------|---------------|--------------|
| Tonga        | -mui (14)    | -bili          | -tatu         | -nne         |
| Bisa         | -mo          | -wili          | -tatu         | -ne          |
| Subia        | -moina       | -bere          | -tatue        | -ne          |
| Ungu         | -mwe         | -wili          | -tatu         | -ne          |
| Hehe         | -monga       | -wile          | -datu         | -tai         |
| Bunga        | -weka        | -sona (?)      | -lila(?)      | -dai         |
| Gogo         | -monga       | -bili (-yete)  | -datu         | -ne (-ena)   |
| Kaguru       | -mue         | -ili, -bili    | -datu         | -nne         |
| Kondoa       | -mosi        | -ili, -pili    | -tatu         | -ne          |
| Shambala     | -mwe         | -ili           | -tatu         | -nne         |
| Boondei      | -mwenga      | -idi           | -tatu         | -nne         |
| Zeguha       | -mwenga      | -idi           | -tatu         | -nne         |
| Kami         | -mosi        | -ili, pili     | -tatu         | -nne         |
| Taita        | -mojoeri     | -bili          | -datu         | -nne         |
| Nyamwezi     | -mo          | -wiri          | -datu, -yatu  | -nne         |
| Sukuma       | -mo          | -wiri, -bili   | -datu, -yatu  | -nne         |
| Nyambu       | -mwe         | -wili          | -datu         | -ne          |
| Ganda        | -mo          | -bili          | -satu         | -nya (-na)   |
| Kamba        | -mondi       | -eri           | -datu         | -na          |
| Swahili      | -moja        | -wili, pili    | -tatu         | -nne         |
| Pokomo       | -manda       | -wi, pili      | -hahu, -tahu  | -nne         |
| Nika         | -motsi       | -iri, -biri    | -hahu, tahu   | -ne          |
| Senna        | -bozi        | -wiri, piri    | -tatu         | -nai         |
| Karanga      | -muempera    | -biri          | -tatu         | -nna         |
| Xosa-Kafir   | -nye         | -bini          | -tatu         | -nne         |
| Zulu-Kafir   | -nye         | -bili          | -tatu         | -nne         |
| Herero       | -mue         | -vari          | -tatu         | -ne          |
| Bihe         | -mosi        | -vali          | -tatu         | -kwana       |
| Kwengo       | -morika      | -bari          | -tatu         | -nana        |
| Rotse        | -mue         | -yeri          | -atu          | -nne         |
| Nyengo       | -moya        | -bibi          | -ato          | -nne         |
| Guha         | -mo          | -wiri          | -sato         | -nna         |
| Rua          | -mo          | -biji          | -satu         | -nne         |
| Angola       | ...          | -yari          | -tatu         | -wana        |
| Lower Congo  | -moxi        | -ole           | -tatu         | -ya          |
| Nywema       | -mo          | -fi            | -satu         | -neng        |
| Yao          | -mo          | -wili          | -tatu         | m-cheche     |
| Komoro       | -monsi       | -bili          | ..., taru     | -nne         |
| Mozambique   | -moka        | -ili (-nli), pili | -raru, taru | -chexe       |
| Chwana       | -ngwe        | -bedi, pedi    | -raro, tharu  | -nne         |
| Mpongwe      | -mori        | -wani, -bani   | -raro, tyaro  | -nai         |
| Dualla       | -wo, po      | -ba            | -lalu         | -nei         |
| Fernandian   | -buli        | -iba           | -ita (?)      | -ela (-ele)  |
| Lunda        | -mue         | -adi           | -sato         | -nyi         |

## Numerals.

same language, they cannot be used indifferently, but the first-placed generally is the regular one, while the second is that used under a nasal influence (55-59). Where however the second is between brackets, it is merely a dialectical modification of the first.

*N. B.* The elements *-ka* or *-nga*, *-si* or *-zi*, etc. in the words of the column for the number "one" originally meant "only, exclusively, by itself" (814-818 and 824). The Bantu word for "one" is properly *-mue* (variously changed to *-mo*, *-ngwe*, *-nye*, *-bo*), etc.

### COMPARATIVE TABLE OF NUMBERS. (Continued.)

| | 5 | 6 | 10 | 100 |
|---|---|---|---|---|
| Tonga | -sano | -sano a-mue | i-kumí | ma-kumekumi |
| Bisa | -tano | -tano na-mo | i-kumi | i-gana |
| Subia | -ϑanue | -omoiana (?) | kume | ... |
| Ungu | -tanu | -kaga | kumi | ka-gana |
| Hehe | -hano | -tandatu | chumi | chi-gana |
| Bunga | -fundo | -mfu | li-hundu | ... |
| Gogo | -hano | -tandatu | i-kumi | i-gana |
| Kaguru | -sano | -tandatu | i-kumi | i-gana |
| Kondoa | -sano | -tanda | kumi | gana |
| Shambala | -xano | -tandatu | kumi | gana |
| Boondei | -xano | -tandatu | kumi | gana |
| Zeguha | -xano | -tandatu | kumi | gana |
| Kami | -thano | -tanda | i-kumi | i-gana |
| Taita | -sanu | -tandatu | i-kumi | i-gaona |
| Nyamwezi | -tanu, -hanu | mkaga | i-kumi | i-gana |
| Sukuma | -tano, -hano | -tandatu | i-kumi | i-gana |
| Nyambu | mxa | mkaga | i-kumi | i-xana |
| Ganda | -jano (-tano) | mkaga | kumi | ki-kumi |
| Kamba | -ϑano | -thandatu | i-kumi | i-yana |
| Swahili | -tano | sita (Arabic) | kumi | gana |
| Pokomo | -zano, -dsano | -handahu, -tandahu | kumi | gana |
| Nika | -dzano | -handahu, tandahu | kumi | gana |
| Senna | -sano (-canu) | -tandatu | kumi | dzana |
| Karanga | -xano | -xano na-mue | kumi | makume-makumi |
| Xosa-Kafir | -hlanu, -tlanu | -tandatu | i shumi | i kulu |
| Zulu-Kafir | -hlanu | -tandatu | i shumi | i kulu |
| Herero | -tanu | -hamboumue | o mu-rongo | e-sere |
| Bihe | -tanu | e pandu | e kwi | o cita |
| Kwengo | -tanu | -tanu na-mo | li-kumi | ... |
| Rotse | -tanu | aombomue | li-kume | ... |
| Nyengo | -tanu | -temoya (?) | ni-kume (?) | ... |
| Guha | -tano | -tanda | kumi | gana |
| Rua | -tanu | -samba | ki-kwi | ka-twa |
| Angola | -tanu | -samanu | (ri)-kuinyi | kama |
| Lower Congo | -tanu | -sambanu | e kumi | n-kama |
| Nywema | -tano | -samalo | vum | lu-kama |
| Yao | m-sanu | m-sanu na-mo | li-kumi | ma-kume li-kumi |
| Komoro | -sano | ... tandaru | kumi | i-jana |
| Mozambique | -thanu | -thanu na-moka | ni-kumi | ma-kumi (?) |
| Chwana | -tlanu | -rataro, thataro | le-shume | le-kgolo |
| Mpongwe | -tani, -tyani | o-rowa | i-gomi | n-kama |
| Dualla | -tanu | ... | d-um | ... |
| Fernandian | -ito | ito la buli | biu | ... |
| Lunda | -tano | -sambano | di-kumi | ci-tota |

### § 2. Formation and Use of the Numbers from "One" to "Six".

**793.** — 1º According to what has been previously noticed, the numbers from "one" to "six" in Tonga, Bisa, Herero, Kamba, Nyamwezi, Ganda, Nyambu, Guha, Rotse, etc., incorporate the connective pronoun corresponding to the classifier of their noun, and consequently their construction is essentially identical with that of possessive expressions. This however is remarkable, at least in Tonga, that such numbers often admit before themselves, merely, as it seems, for the sake of emphasis, a copula-containing relative particle, and then the connective pronoun which should follow them immediately is generally understood, so that we hear, for instance, *uli a ci-to nci-mue* " he possesses one ford " (not... *nci-ci-mue*). Ex. : —

TONGA:   A) Without a copula-containing relative particle :

*Baati ku muntu* u-*mue*..., they said to one man...
*Bali e ingoma* zi-*tatu*, they have three drums.
*Uaka cita (miezi)* i-*tatu*..., *(miaka)* i-*nne*, he remained there three months..., four years.

B) With a copula-containing relative particle ;

*Miezi ie jinza* nji-*sano a i-mue*, the months of the rainy season are *five* and one.
*Bakede kule, muezi* ngu *mue kuli Zuanga*, they live far, at one month's distance from Wange.

BISA: *Mabuzi* ga-*wili*, two fowls. (Last's *Polygl.*, p. 138).
HERERO: *O muhona yu-mue*, one Lord ; *o rutu* ru-*mue*, one body ; *o n-gamburiro* yi-*mue*, one faith, etc. (Rev. F. W. Kolbe's *Herero Dict.*, p. 349). *N. B.* Instead of *yu-mue, yi-mue*, we should expect regularly *u-mue, i-mue* (cf. 639*) ; the presence of the initial *y* is probably due to the fact of *-mue* being monosyllabic, and the consequent necessity of not exposing the whole adjective *umue* or *imue* to be sounded as a monosyllable through contractions or elisions (44).

KAMBA: *Mundu yu-mwe*, one man; *mti u-mwe (wu-mwe ?)*, one tree ; *mi-longo* i-*tatu*, three tens (i. e. 30), etc. *N. B.* Notice *yu-mue* for *u-mue*, as in Herero.

NYAMWEZI : *Ma-kumi* a-*wili* (not *ma-kumi* ma-*wili*, Steere's *Coll.*, p. 49), two tens (20).

GANDA : *Nagamba o mudu-we* o-*mu na bakazi-be* ba-*satu*..., and he said to *one* of his slaves and to three of his wives..., etc.

NYAMBU : *Ma-kumi* a-*wili*, two tens (= 20). Last's *Pol.*, p. 160.
etc., etc.

**794.** — 2° In Kafir, Chwana, Mozambique, Swahili, etc., the numbers from "one" to "six" are treated as quantitative adjectives, and consequently incorporate the classifiers of their nouns (cf. 604).

Ex. in Kafir.

A) **Numbers used as epithets (616).**

*Wa-tenga a mayeza a* ma*-tatu*, he bought three medicines.

*N. B.* The numeral *nye* or *nye-qa* " one only " causes its noun to be used without an article, and consequently does not admit itself any relative particle (616). Ex. *Una mfazi* m-*nye-qa*, he has a single wife.

B) **Numbers used as predicates (618).**

*Mangapina a mahashe apo?* **Ma***-tatu.* How many horses are there near you? Three. Other examples :

Chwana : *Ba-sadi ba* **ba-***raro batla sila*, the three women will grind ; cf. *Basadi* **ba-***raro*, the women are three. (Cf. Rev. W. Crisp's *Secoana Gr.*, page 27).

Swahili : *Meno yake* **ma-***wili*, his two teeth. *Dinari tatu* ( = ...*ntatu*, cf. 282), three coins.

Mozambique : *Meno awe ao* me*nli* ( = **ma-***inli*), his two teeth ; *atu* **a-***tanu* ne*nli* ( = ...*na-a-inli*) five and two men ( = 7 men), etc.

*N. B.* After substantive pronouns numerals are treated somewhat as suffixes in Kafir, Chwana, Swahili, etc. Ex. in Kafir : *bo-ba-bini*, both of them, lit. they both ; *zo-n-tatu (in-komo)*, the three of them (cattle), etc. (675).

Hence in Ganda that kind of dual formed with the suffix -*mbi* ( = -*bili*) " two ". (692).

### § 3. Formation and Use of the Numbers above " Six ".

**795.** — The numbers above " six ", when they are not complex (796), are generally substantives, and, as such, require various particles before them, according as they are self-standing, or predicates, or in apposition to other nouns. Ex. : —

Tonga : *I-kumi lie imberere* ( = *li-a-imberere*) or *Imberere kumi*, ten sheep ; *Imberere* ndi-*kumi* or *zi-li-ikumi*, the sheep are ten.

Kafir : *In-komo e zi li-shumi*, lit. cows they which (are) a ten, i. e. ten cows.

*In-komo zi li-shumi*, the cows are ten.

etc., etc.

### § 4. Complex Numbers.

**796.** — In complex numbers, such as " five and two (seven) ", " ten and one (eleven) ", " a hundred and three ", etc., care is always had to give to every number its *proper* prefix. Ex. : —

Tonga : *Ndabona* ing*ombe ziali* ma-*kumi* nga-*nne a* zi-*tatu*, I have seen cows which were 4 tens (40) + 3 (cows), where it may be noticed that *nga-nne* agrees with the tens *(ma-kumi)*, while *zi-tatu* has to agree with the cows *(zi)n-gombe*.

OLD ANGOLA : **Mi**-*vo* **ma**-*kuim* **a**-*tatu* nc-itatu, 33 years, lit. Years tens (which are) three + three (years) ; **a**-*tatu* agreeing with **ma**-*kuim* and **i**-*tatu* with **mi** *vo*, etc., etc.

### § 5. Ordinal Numbers, and Numerical Adverbs.

**797.** — In Bantu ordinal numbers are possessive expressions proper. " First " = " that of the beginning ", $2^d$ = " that of the second place (or order) "; $3^d$ = " that of the $3^d$ place (or order) ", etc.

Ex. *I-zuba li-a ku-sanguna*, the 1rst day, lit. the sun of the beginning.
*I-zuba lia bu-biri*, the $2^d$ day, lit. the sun of the second change.
etc., etc.

In several languages numbers are changed into quasi-adverbs by prefixing to them one of the classifiers KA- or KU-. Ex. in Tonga : *ka-mue* " once ", *ka-bili* " a second time ", *ka-tatu* " a third time " (526) ; *ku-bili* " in two parts ", *ku-tatu* " in three parts ", etc.

#### The negative particle before the number "one".

**798.** — In Kafir and Bihe I find here and there before the number " one " a peculiar negative particle which does not seem to be used in any other position. Its form is *na* in Kafir, *la* in Bihe. Apparently it means " not even ". Cf. 570. Ex. : —

BIHE : *La u-mue* " no one ", *la-kumwe* " nowhere ", *la ci-mwe* " nothing ", etc. Stover's *Umbundu Gr.*, pp. 40-41

KAFIR : *Ngu bani na ongatshoyo...?* Na *m-nye*. Who is the man who can say...? No one.

## X. — Interrogative Pronouns,

### and

### Various Determinatives.

**799.** — Interrogative pronouns, and most of those determinatives which we usually term " indefinite pronouns " in Bantu generally incorporate the connective pronoun of their class, exactly as demonstrative pronouns and possessive expressions. Only in a few languages some of them incorporate classifiers, not connective pronouns, being thus treated as quantitative adjectives. They also present in their use several peculiarities, varying according to the different languages. I shall touch on the most striking only.

## § 1. THE PRONOUN "HOW MANY?".

**800.** — The Bantu equivalent for our " How many ? " is *-nga-pi?* lit. " going where ? going how far? " from *-pi?* " where? " and *-nka* or *-nga* " go ". This is pronounced *-nga-pi* in Kafir, Herero, Karanga, Senna, etc. *nga-i* or *nga-hi* in Tonga, Bisa, Subia, Kaguru, Shambala, etc., *-nga (nga-i (?))* in Gogo, Nyamwezi, Guha, etc.; *-nga-vi (ka-vi (?))* in Mozambique, *ka-e* in Chwana. Its equivalent is *-lingwa* in Yao ; *-meka* in Ganda, *-mia* in Mpongwe, *-kwa* in Congo, *-anata* in Kamba, *ku-xi* in Angola, etc.

This pronoun is treated exactly as the numbers from " one " to " six " : hence it incorporates a connective pronoun in certain languages, a classifier in the others (791). Ex.: —

TONGA : *Mi-samo* i-*ngai?* how many trees ?
KAFIR : *Mi-ti* mi-*ngapi?*     »

*N. B.* In Angola *Ki-kuxi?* is used instead of *A-kuxi?* in class *A-ntu*. Ex. *A-ntu ki-kuxi?* How many persons ? (Héli Chatelain, *Zeitschrift*, 1889-90, p. 304).

## § 2. THE PRONOUN AND ADJECTIVE " WHAT ? WHAT SORT OF... ? "

**801.** *A).* — Originally the simple form corresponding to our " What? " was essentially, in the generality of Bantu languages, the bare classifier of the word which means " a thing ", or " things ", though a little modified in some cases, according to certain phonetic laws. Hence we still have the following : —

| Pronoun " What ? " | Cf. " Thing " or " things ". |
|---|---|
| TONGA : *nzi?* | „ zi-*ntu*, things. |
| HERERO : *tyi?* or *vi?* | „ *o* tyi-*na*, a thing ; *o* vi-*na*, things. |
| SWAHILI : *ki?* | „ ki-*tu*, a thing. |
| GANDA : *ki ?* | „ ki-*ntu*, a thing. |
| CONGO : *nki?* | „ ki-*ma*, a thing. |
| KAFIR : *ni?* | „ in-*to*, a thing. |
| LUNDA : *eci?* | „ ci-*ouma* a thing. |

Instead of the simple *nzi?* the Tonga prefer to use generally *nyama-nzi?* lit. " what sort of meat ? what sort of stuff ? " In like manner, instead of the simple *ni?* the Xosa-Kafirs prefer in most cases *nto-ni?* " what thing ? " Ex. : —

TONGA : *Ucita-*nzi ? or *ucita nyama*nzi ? What are you doing ?
HERERO : *Maungura* tyi ? What is he working at ? *Motya* vi ? What are you saying ? (Kolbe's *Dict.*)
KAFIR : *Wati-*ni ? What did he say ? *Uteta* ntoni ? What do you mean ?

An interrogative suffix, for instance -*na* in Kafir, -*ke* in Herero, is often added to such pronouns, as in general to other interrogative expressions. Ex. in Kafir: *Uti* **nina?** What does he say? *Uteta ntoni***na?** What do you mean?

In some other languages the original pronoun for " what? " is either more transformed than in the preceding or borrowed from a neighbouring language. Thus we have : —

CHWANA : -*ng* ( = Kafir -*ni*). Ex. *Obatla*-**ng**? What do you seek?
ANGOLA : -*nyi* ( = do.).
SENNA : -*dyi* (probably for *ci*). Ex. *Unafuna*-**dyi**? What do you want?

**802.** — Several of these particles have also a self-standing, originally a copula-containing form. Such are in Kafir *yini?* " What is it? " (sometimes *tyini?*), in Chwana *eng* (Ex. *ke eng*? " What is it? "), in Swahili *nini?*, in Ganda *kiki?*, in Tonga *ni-nyamanzi?*, etc.

**803.** *B)* — The pronouns which are used for " What? What sort of... ? " either as adjectives, or with reference to a determined class, generally incorporate the connective pronoun of their class. In Kafir they incorporate its classifier. In a few languages they are invariable. These pronouns are the following : —

TONGA : *nyamanzi?* with a connective pronoun. Ex. *Uyanda musamo* **u**-*nyamanzi?* What sort of tree do you want?
ANGOLA : -*anyi?* (lit. of what?), with a connective pronoun. Ex. *Ene ngi mutu* **u**-*anyi?* What sort of man am I? (Héli Chatelain, *Zeitschr.*, p. 304).

*N. B.* In Angola the pronouns of the locative classes are *bu-nyi?  ku-nyi?  mu-nyi?* not *bu-anyi?*, etc. (*ibid.*)

CHWANA : -*ang?* (lit. of what?) with a connective pronoun. Ex. *Selo se ke* **s**-*ang?* What sort of thing is this? (Crisp's *Gr.*, p. 19).
SENNA : -*ani?* with a connective pronoun. Ex. *Mu-adia* (**ng**)**u**-*ani?* What sort of canoe?

*N. B.* In Herero -*ani?* means " whose? ". Ex. *o muatye ingui o* u-*ani?* This bag, whose is it? (Rev. F. W. Kolbe's *Herero Dict.*, p. 547). In Senna -*ani* may also be used with the same meaning (Cf. 773.)

YAO : -*achi?* (lit. of what?). Ex. *M-kalo* **w**-*achi?* What kind of knife? (Rev. A. Hetherwick's *Yao Gr.*, p. 35).
KAFIR : -*ni?* with a classifier. Ex. *I zinti za mti* **m**-*ni?* Sticks of what sort of tree?

*N. B.* In Kafir this adjective -*ni* causes its substantive to be used without an article.

HERERO : -*ke?* or -*nge?* with a classifier. Cf. Rev. F. W. Kolbe's *Dict.*, p. 543.
SWAHILI : *gani?* invariable. Ex. *Mtu gani? Kitu gani?* What sort of man? What sort of thing?
POKOMO : *ga?* invariable.
CONGO : *nkia?* invariable, followed by its noun ; etc., etc.

## § 3. The Pronoun "Who?".

**804.** — The pronouns for "Who?" are the following: —

TONGA: *u-ani?*, pl. *ba-ani?*, or with the copula *ngu-ani?*, pl. *mba-ani?* Ex. **Ngu**-*ani izina liako?* What is thy name? lit. Who art thou (with regard to) thy name?

    Cf. IN NGURU: *Zina diako mbwani?* What is thy name? (Last's *Polyglotta*, p. 47).

KARANGA AND SENNA: Sing. *ani?*, or with the copula *ndi-ani?* Ex. in Karanga: *fina lirio ndi-ani?* What is thy name?

GANDA: *Ani?* pl. *bani?* Ex. *Ani adze?* Who has come?

HERERO: Sing. *ani?* or *yani*.

    *N. B.* Probably *yani?* = the Tonga copula-containing form *ngu-ani?*

MOZAMBIQUE: *U-pani?* pl. *a-pani?*

KAFIR: *U-bani?* pl. *o-bani?*, or with the copula *ngu-bani?* pl. *ngo-bani?* Ex. *Igama lake ngu-bani-na?* What is his name?

CHWANA: *Mang?* pl. *bo-mang?* Ex. *Ke bo-mang?* Who are they?

MPONGWE: *Mande?* pl. *wa-mande?* Ex. *Wa-mande mongi xino?* Who are these people?

ANGOLA AND LUNDA: *Nanyi?* pl. *a-kua-nyi?*

CONGO, SWAHILI, BOONDEI, etc.: *Nani?* Ex. in Congo: *Nkumbu andi nani?* What is his name?

**805.** — *N. B.* 1. "Whose?" is generally rendered by a possessive expression regularly formed from the above. Ex. in Kafir: *I gama li-ka bani?* "Whose name?" Here it may be remembered that in Kafir the prefix of possessive expressions before individual names is *ka*, not *-a*, as it is *ga* in Chwana (783, *N. B.*).

    2. It may be noticed that here again in the forms of these pronouns Mpongwe differs more from Congo than from Chwana and Mozambique. (Cf. 213).

## § 4. The Discriminative Pronoun "Which?"

**806.** — As far as we can judge, in the generality of the Bantu languages the discriminative pronoun "Which?" is rendered by an expression which means literally "the one which is where?", viz. *li* in Tonga, *ne* in Herero, *pi* in Kafir, etc., with a connective pronoun. Ex.: —

TONGA: -*li?* with a connective pronoun. Ex. *U-yanda ci-bula* **ci-li?** Which chair do you want? lit... the chair which is where?

    *N. B.* This particle -*li?* being a mere monosyllable generally requires its connective pronoun to be strengthened by a sort of relative particle when such a connective pronoun should be otherwise a mere vowel. Ex. *Mu-samo o-u-li?* "Which tree?" instead of *mu-samo u-li?* Probably for the same reason, when it is preceded by one of the copulative relative particles *ngu*, *mba*, *ndu*, etc., this does not cause the connective pronoun to be dropped. Ex. *Ngu-u-li (mu-samo)?* "Which is it (the tree)?" not simply *Ngu-li?* Cf. *Ngu-a-ka fua*, it is the one which is dead (769).

**807.** — Other languages : —

HERERO : -*ne?* with a connective pronoun, and a relative particle in some cases. The same in Karanga.

KAFIR : -*pi?* with a connective pronoun. Ex. *U-funa si-hlalo* **si-pi?** Which chair do you want?

*N. B.* When the connective pronoun is a mere vowel, it is strengthened by a semi-vowel placed before it. Ex. *U-funa m-ti* **wu-** pi? "Which tree do you want?" Hence, with the copula : *Ngu-*wu-pi *u-mti o-wu-funa-yɔ?* " Which is the tree you want?" Cf. My *Outline of a Xosa-Kafir Gr.*, p. 39.

SWAHILI : -*pi?* with a connective pronoun, **yu-pi?** in class *M-tu* (cf. 806).
CHWANA : -*fe?*     do.     Ex. *Motho* **o-fe?** Which man?
ANGOLA : -*ebi?*     do.     Ex. *Ki-fua* **ki-ebi?** Which manner?
CONGO : -*eyi?*     do.
MPONGWE : -*e?*     do.     Ex. *Nagu* **y-e?** Which house? *A-dombe* **m-e?** Which sheep?

KAGURU : -*ahoki* (lit. of where?), with a connective pronoun. Ex. *Wa-ntu* **wahoki?** Which men?

**808.** — In Tonga " When?" is rendered by *izuba* **li-li?** " Which sun?" or simply *li-li?*, the word *izuba* being then understood, (cf. 782), and in Herero by *ru-ne (o ru-veze)*, lit. Which time? This is probably the origin of the word for " when?" in several other Bantu languages (Kafir *nini?*, Ganda *di?* Swahili *lini?*, Chwana *leng?*) etc.

When our " When?" means " Which year? Which season? etc.," it is rendered in Bantu languages by a full expression, as in Tonga : *Mu-aka* **ouli?** Which year?

*N. B.* The Tonga self-standing form *a-li?* "where?" is also properly the discriminative interrogative pronoun of class PA (536).

### § 5. INTERROGATIVE PRONOUNS USED INDEFINITELY.

**809.** — In Kafir, and probably in several other languages, interrogative pronouns are often used with an indefinite meaning, such as " no matter who, no matter where, etc." Then they are generally reduplicated.

Ex. IN KAFIR : *Wena ka-***bani-bani**..., thou, (child) no matter of whom...
*Waya* **pipipi**..., he went, no matter where.

### § 6. THE PRONOUN AND ADJECTIVE "ALL, WHOLE ".

**810.** — In Tonga " all " is rendered by -*onse* (sometimes -*ense* after *a* or *e*, 250) preceded by a connective pronoun. Contrary to most other pronouns, it has forms proper to the 1ˢᵗ and 2ᵈ person, at least in the plural number. But in the 2ᵈ person plural *no-onse* is used instead of *mu-onse*.

Examples : *Iswe* **to**-*onse*, all of us; *Inywe* **no**-*onse*, all of you; *Bantu* **bo**-*onse* or **be**-*euse*, all men; *mu-samo* **u** *onse* (or through assimilation **o**-*onse*), the whole tree, etc.

*N. B.* 1. Ko-*onse* (= ku-*onse*), when self-standing, means " always, permanently ". Ex. *Nebombua u-la-kunka ko-onse*, the river Nebombua flows permanently.

2. In many instances the word -*onse* is not so well rendered by " all " as by " all together (I and you, you and they, etc.). "

**811.** — The construction of the word for " all " in most other languages is essentially the same as in Tonga. But its stem varies as follows : Kafir -*onke*, Senna -*onse*, or -*ense*, or -*onsene*, or -*ensene*, Chwana -*otlhe*, Congo -*onso* or -*nso*, Swahili -*ote*, Mozambique -*oteni*, Angola -*eselele* or *osololo* or -*ese*, Mpongwe -*odu*, Ganda -*onna* or -*enna*, etc. In several of these languages a substantive pronoun is often used as a sort of determinative before this adjective when already completed by its connective pronoun, principally when it means " whoever, whatever ". Ex. In Swahili : **Ye** *yote atakaye pita, mpige*, Whoever will pass by, strike him.

*N. B.* The stem of this adjective being a dissyllable beginning with a vowel, its form in class *Mu-ntu* has become somewhat irregular in some languages, for instance, in Swahili *y-ote*, not *w-ote*, in Ganda *y-enna*, not *w-onna* or *w-enna*, etc.

**812.** — In Herero and Karanga a particle is always required as a kind of determinative before this adjective, viz. *a-* in Herero, where the stem itself is *-he*, and *bu-* in Karanga, where the stem itself is -*rire*. Ex. : —

HERERO : *O vandu* **a** *ve-he*, all men ; *o-vina* **a**-*vi-he*, all things.
KARANGA : *Ixindi* **bu**-*ji-rire*, all the muircats ; *inyika* **bu**-*i-rire*, the whole earth.

**813.** — Some Bantu languages have a sort of superlative form of this adjective which means " whoever, whatever, any one ". Ex. in Angola : *Mutu u-ese u-ese*, any man (who...)

§ 7. THE PRONOUN *A-like* " ALONE, BY HIMSELF ".

**814.** — 1° In Tonga the following is the formula of the expression which renders " alone " : —

*a* + connective pronoun + *like*.

Ex. *Leza* **a**-*a*-*like*, God alone ; *Aba bantu* **a**-**ba**-*like*, these men alone.

*N. B.* In such expressions *a* is the kind of preposition described in n. 573. It is equivalent to our " by " in " by himself ".

We hear in the 1rst person singular *ndime e-ndike* ( = ...*a-(i)ndi-like*) " It is I alone ", and in the 2d *iue alike* ( =*a-u-like*) " thou alone "; the other persons are regular.

**815.** 2º In Ganda the stem of the word rendering " alone " is -*okka* or -*ekka*, in Karanga -*oka* or -*eka*, in Kafir -*edwa* or -*odwa*. These follow the same laws as the Tonga -*onke* " all " (-*onna* in Ganda, etc.), and have their proper forms even in the 1rst and 2d person of the singular number.

Ex. IN KAFIR: *mna* nd-*edwa*, I alone, = Ganda *nze* nz *ekka* = Karanga: *eme* nd *oka* ; *yena* y-*edwa*, he alone, = Ganda *ye* y-*ekka*.

N. B. As the Kafir stem -*edwa* " alone " seems to be foreign to Bantu, may it not be thought to be related to the word *edua* or *dua* " one " in Fiji? This reference to a Papuan language might seem out of place here, if it stood isolated. But it is warranted by several other signs of distant relationship between Bantu and several languages Oceania. (See Introduction, 3d section).

**816.** — 3º In Chwana the same word is -*osi* or -*esi*. In some cases it admits before itself the particle *ka* ( = Tonga *a*, 573). In others it follows the same laws as the Kafir -*edwa* or -*odwa*.

Ex. *Ke nna* ka-n-*osi*, It is I myself; *Ke-bone* b-*osi* it is they alone.

**817.** — *N. B.* In all these languages the same pronouns are sometimes used to render "himself, itself", etc.

**818.** — 4º In Herero " alone " is rendered in the first person singular by -*erike*, in the other cases by *peke* (invariable). Ex. *Mba-ende erike* " I went alone "; *ma-kara peke* " he stays alone ". It may also be rendered by *poru-* followed by a possessive expression varying according to the class. Ex. *Poru-andye*, " by myself "; *poru-oye* " by yourself "; *poru-e* " by himself ", etc.

**819.** — 5º In Swahili " alone " is rendered by *peke* (invariable) or by *peke y-* followed by a possessive expression. Ex. *peke y-angu* " by myself "; *peke y-ako* " by yourself ", etc. Cf. in Mozambique *yek-aga* " by myself ", *yek-ehu* " by ourselves ", etc.

### § 8. THE PRONOUNS *A-a-la-kue* " HE ALSO ", *A-ba-la-bo* " THEY ALSO ", ETC.

**820.** — In Tonga a series of expressions rendering " he also, they also ", etc. is formed according to a formula somewhat similar to that of the expressions for " alone ", viz. : —

*a* + connective pronoun + *la* + substantive pronoun.

Ex. *Leza* **a-a-la-kue,** God also ; *aba bantu* **a-ba-la-bo,** these people also.

**821.** — *N. B.* 1. Notice -*kue* instead of -*ue* in class *MU-ntu*. In the other classes we have *a-u-la-o (mu-cila)*, *a-i-la-io (mi-cila)*, *a-li-la-lio (i-zuba)*, etc. In the 1ˢᵗ and 2ᵈ person the expressions corresponding to these are *a-mbe-bo* (= *a-me-bo*) " I also ", *a-e-bo (a-ue-bo)* " thou also ", *a-sue-bo* " we also ", *a-nyue-bo* " you also ". (Cf. 691). I fail to see distinctly the exact value of the particles *a* and *la* in these expressions.

**822.** — 2° Possibly expressions of the same sort exist in Yao, as I read the following in Rev. A. Hetherwick's *Yao Grammar*, p. 37 : " -*alakwe*, with the characteristics (connective pronouns) of the first class (*Mu-ndu*), is frequently used in the sense of " this person ", " he ", " those persons ", " they ", and may be used as representing the third personal pronoun. Ex. *Ana-wani ajiwile, angati* jualakwe, " Who stole? Was is not he? "

**823.** — 3° In most other Bantu languages the expressions " he also, they also ", etc. are generally rendered by the preposition which means " with, and ", followed by a substantive pronoun. In Kafir the particle *kua* " also " is often used along with such expressions. Ex. Kwa *u mlambo wa-hamba* na-wo, or *U mlambo wa-hamba* kwa-na-wo, " the river also went along ".

### § 9. The Pronouns rendering " Self ".

**824.** — It has already been noticed (655) that in Bantu " himself, itself, themselves " after verbs are regularly rendered by a connective objective pronoun, such as *zi* in Tonga, *i* in Chwana, *ri* in Angola, etc. Again, it has been noticed that in certain languages the same expressions are rendered after nouns by the same pronouns which render " alone " (817). But there is also in Bantu a special particle for " self ", viz. -*nya* in Tonga, -*ene* in Angola, -*ini* in Herero, -*enyewe* in Swahili, etc.

In Tonga -*nya* is suffixed to substantive pronouns. Ex. *a-ngue-nya*, with him himself.

In more emphatic expressions the substantive pronoun is again repeated after -*nya*. Ex. *Ngue-nya-***ue**, it is he himself ; *nce-co-nya-***co**, it is the very thing, etc.

**825.** In Angola -*ene*, in Herero -*ini*, in Swahili -*enyewe*, etc., are preceded by connective pronouns. But in Angola *mu-ene* is used in class *MU-tu* instead of *u-ene*, and *mu-nne* in the locative class MU instead of *mu-ene*. In Herero all such pronouns require the article before them, e. g. *o veni* (cl. *VA-ndu*), *o zeni* (cl. *o ZO-ngombe*), etc., and, in class *MU-ndu*, *o mu-ini* is used instead of *o u-ini*. In Swahili *mw-enyewe* is used in the three classes *M-tu*, *M-ti*, and *U-siku*.

*N. B.* In Swahili similar expressions are formed with *-enyi* " one who has... ", followed by a determinative. Ex. *Mw-enyi ku-penda* " the same who loves "; *Ki-tu ch-enyi m-virongo* " a round thing ".

### § 10. The Pronoun *-mbi* " Other, Different, Foreign ".

**826.** — In Tonga and Kafir the word " different " is rendered by *-mbi*, preceded by the proper connective pronoun. But, because this stem is monosyllabic, the connective pronoun generally requires to be strengthened when it should be otherwise a mere vowel; is it not dropped after the copula. In Chwana the form of this pronoun is *-pe* (185). Ex. : —

    Tonga : *Tinsi ngue pe, ngu-u-mbi*, It is not he, no, it is another (man).
    Kafir : *Asi ye, hayi, ngu-wu-mbi* or *ngo wu-mbi*, do.
    Chwana : *Ga ke na se pe*, I have nothing else.

**827.** — The equivalent of this pronoun is in Herero *-arue* with a connective pronoun. Ex. *o va-ndu v-arue*, other people (foreigners, strangers). In Yao it is *-ine*, also with a connective pronoun.
    Ex. *mu-ndu ju ine*, another man, etc.

### § 11. The Pronouns " One... another ", " Some ... others ".

**828.** — In Tonga the expressions " one... another " " some... others " are rendered by the numeral adjective *-mue* " one " repeated.
    Ex. *U-mue uati..., u-mue u-ati*, the one said..., the other said...
    *Ba-mue baasiala, ba-mue baainka*, some remained behind, others went.
    *N. B.* Hence the repetitive expression *-muemui*, " few, scarce ". Ex. *Bantu bamuemui*, few men. (Cf. Superlatives, n. 632.)

**829.** — Likewise in Kafir they are rendered by *-nye* " one " with the proper classifier and an article. Ex. *O m-nye wasala, o mnye wemka*, one remained behind, the other went.

In Ganda they are rendered by the quantitative adjective *-lala*, repeated. Ex. *M-lala a-lia, m-lala talia*, the one eats, the other does not eat, etc., etc.

## Retrospect on the Article.

**830.** — We have seen in a previous chapter (321,4), that the nearest approach in pure Tonga to the article of Kafir, Angola, Congo, Herero, Ganda, etc., is a kind of relative particle occasionally placed before substantives as if to determine them. From this fact I there might have drawn the conclusion that Bleek had rightly considered the Kafir article as having originally been " a pronoun derived from the derivative prefix (classifier) which it precedes ". (*Compar. Gr.*, p. 153). But this conclusion I have reserved for this place, that I may the better show in what relation the various kinds of the Bantu particles now reviewed stand to one another.

The *classifiers*, which are essentially a kind of adjective or generic nouns, are the basis of the whole mechanism of Bantu with respect to nouns and pronouns. The most elementary of all the pronouns is the *connective pronoun*, which in the various classes of the $3^d$ person is itself nothing else than the classifier, weakened in some instances, strengthened in others, of the substantive which it represents (639). The connective pronoun, when emphasised and made into a word, no longer a mere particle, becomes a *substantive pronoun* (656). This substantive pronoun may be used in most Bantu languages as a *relative particle* (718) and then it becomes again a kind of enclitic or proclitic particle. It is properly from such relative particles that the *article* is derived in most of the languages in which it exists. And this is only natural, as articles are to substantives what relative particles are to relative clauses (774). Hence, for instance, the Kafir **u** *m-ntu* " *a* person " might originally have been rendered by " *he* person ", exactly as **o**-*telayo* is still exactly rendered by " *he* who speaks ". It is from the same relative particles, or directly from the connective pronouns, that *demonstrative pronouns* are derived (698).

Thus we find that the derivation of the various kinds of pronouns in Bantu agrees perfectly with what might be suggested by reason itself, and by their natural relation to each other.

In connection with this conclusion I notice that the Bantu demonstrative pronouns have become a kind of article in certain semi-Bantu languages. To borrow an instance from Wolof, a language of Senegambia, in this language an article consisting of a consonant and a vowel is generally appended to substantives. In the plural the consonant is always *y*, but in the singular it is in most cases the initial consonant of the substantive, exactly as the consonant of demonstrative pronouns in Bantu is regularly that of the corresponding classifier. The vowel is *i* for things which are near (1rst position), *u* for things which are at some distance (2d position), *a* for remote things. (Dard's " *Dictionnaire Français-Wolof,* 1825 ", p. XIX). It can hardly be doubted that such articles were originally identical with the Bantu demonstrative pronouns.

Ex.

| SINGULAR. | PLURAL. |
|---|---|
| *marre*-mi, the river (here) | *marre*-yi, the rivers (here) |
| *marre*-mu, the river (there) | *marre*-yu, the rivers (there) |
| *marre*-ma, the river (yonder) | *marre*-ya, the rivers (yonder) |
| *daaba*-di, the lion (here) | *daaba*-yi, the lions (here) |
| *daaba*-du, the lion (there) | *daaba*-yu, the lions (there) |
| *daaba*-da, the lion (yonder) | *daaba* ya, the lions (yonder) |
| *saigue*-si, the leopard (here) | *saigue*-yi, the leopards (here) |
| *saigue*-su, the leopard (there) | *saigue*-yu, the leopards (there) |
| *saigue*-sa, the leopard (yonder) | *saigue*-ya, the leopards (yonder) |

etc., etc.

In general, African natives, endowed as they are with keen senses, and little accustomed to consider abstract notions, are fond of vivid descriptions, in which motions of the hand coupled with demonstrative pronouns necessarily play a prominent part. For instance, a native will seldom be heard using a vague expression like this : " He lost one eye " ; but, as he noticed which eye was lost, he will say : " This eye of his died ", pointing at the same time to one or the other of his own. Likewise, instead of telling you that there is a three hours' distance between two places, he will say : " If you start when it (the sun) is there, you will arrive when it is there ", and he will show you at the same time different points of the sun's course.

The same remark accounts for the general use of motions of the hand and demonstrative pronouns to express numbers (789). When my native informants had to enumerate objects of the same kind, I never heard such expressions as " the first, the second, the third ", etc., but " the first " was expressed by " this " with the little finger pointed out, " the second " was also " this ", with the second finger pointed out, " the third " was again " this ", and so forth.

The same remark again may account for the variety of descriptive auxiliaries which will be dealt with in the next chapter.

# Chapter V.

## ON VERBS.

**831.** — It is no easy task to coordinate my materials on verbs. On the one hand, the peculiarly descriptive Bantu turn of mind has introduced into the conjugation so great a variety of particles ; on the other, it is so hard to obtain directly from natives proper information as to their exact value ; besides, the correspondence of these particles in the various languages is so far from being plain, that in matter like this one does not see how to avoid either confusion or misleading connections.

The plan which I have finally adopted is to consider : —
1º The fundamental forms of the simple verb.
2º The various auxiliary forms.
3º The copula.
4º The derivative verbs, including the passive voice, causative forms, etc.

## I. — Fundamental Forms of the Simple Verb.

### § 1. Principal Parts of the Verbs in Bantu.

**832.** — We have here to attend principally to five sources of modification in the verb, viz. : —

1º The form of the verbal stem itself, according as it is monosyllabic or polysyllabic, beginning with a vowel or with a consonant (837, 840, 843, etc.).

2º The class and person, as also in some cases the object, of the verb. This point has already been elucidated in the preceding chapter (637-655). For the convenience of the student in the following pages the connective pronouns are generally either set in different type from the rest, or separated from the verbal stem by a dash.

3° The difference of mood. Here we may distinguish four moods, viz. : —

a) The *indicative*, naturally expressive of an actual fact, as *tu-bona...*, " we see... "

b) The *subjunctive*, expressive of a fact still in the mind, as... *tu-bone,...* " that we may see ".

c) The *imperative*, which might also be referred to the one or the other of the previous two, according to its various forms, as the quasiindicative *bona*, and the subjunctive imperative *u-bone*, both of which mean " see thou ".

d) The *infinitive*, or *substantive* mood, as *ku-bona* " to see ".

4° Duration in the indicative mood. Here we distinguish two stages, viz. : —

a) The transient or non-permanent stage. Ex. *Tubona...*, " we see... "

b) The permanent or perfect stage. Ex. *Tu-bonide* " we have seen ".

5° The difference of actuality, according as the clause is affirmative or negative.

Ex. Affirmative form : *tu-bona...*, " we see ".

Negative form : *ta-tu-boni* " we do not see ".

**833.** — Thus, considering the variations which affect the verb in its endings, we are led to distinguish in most Bantu languages four principal parts, or different forms, of the verbs, viz. : —

1° An indicative, imperative, and participial form, ending in *-a*, as *bona* " see ", *tu-bona...* " we see ", *ku-bona* " to see ".

*N. B.* There may be coupled with this form in Angola and in most other Western languages a form ending with a sort of mute, or indifferent vowel, which varies as the vowelsound of the penultimate, as in Angola *-jimi*, from *-jima*, in *tu-a-jim*i (Tonga *tu-a-zim*a) " we have extinguished ", and *-nu* for *-nu*u, from *-nua*, in *tu-a-nu* (Tonga *tu-a-nyua*) " we have drunk ".

2° A negative form ending in i (*e* or *i*, 270), as *-bone* or *-boni* in *ta tu-bone...* or *ta tu-boni* " we do not see ".

3° A subjunctive form, which is also imperative, ending in *e*, as *-bone* in *a tu-bone* " let us see ".

4° A perfect form ending, in the larger number of the verbs, in *-ide* or *-ile*, as *-bonide* in *tu-bonide* " we have seen ".

In Kafir and several other languages there may be added to these a fifth, ending in *-anga*, as in Kafir *-bonanga* in *a si-bonanga* " we have not seen ".

Hence, for instance, if we were to recite the principal parts of the verb *ku-bona* " to see ", we should say : *bona, boni, bone, bonide*, and in Kafir we should add *bonanga*.

**834.** — *N. B.* 1. In Swahili there are many exceptional verbs borrowed from Arabic, or from other foreign languages, which have a form ending in *i* where it should end in *a*, as *ku-hinni* " to refuse to give ". In the other languages there are very few such verbs. We may however notice in nearly all of them the verb *ku-ti* " to say, to do " (perfect -*tede* in Tonga, -*te* and -*tile* in Kafir, etc.). The form of this verb in Chwana is *go-re* (172 and 200). We may notice also in Tonga and several other languages the verb -*kuzi* or *ku-azi* " to know " (without a perfect, as far as I know). Another remarkable verb in Kafir is *ku-tsho* " to say so " (with reference to something already said or done). Its perfect form is -*tshilo*. In Ganda this verb has the form -*tyo*.

2. In Swahili there is no such perfect form as -*bonide*.

### § 2. Fundamental Forms derived from BONA.

#### 1. Imperative form BONA " see ".

**835.** — In nearly all the Bantu languages there exists for the second person singular an imperative form which regularly is the bare form ending in *a*, as *bona* " see ". In most languages the addition to this form of a pronoun which means " you " (-*ni*, -*ini*, -*enu*, etc.) produces an imperative form for the 2$^d$ person plural.

| Ex. | See thou | See ye | | See thou | See ye |
|---|---|---|---|---|---|
| Tonga | bona | ... | Kafir | bona | bona*ni* |
| Kaguru | langa | lang*eni* | Herero | muna | ... |
| Boondei | ona | ona*ni* | Rotse | mona | ... |
| Kamba | ona | ona*i* | Angola | mona | mon*enu* |
| Swahili | ona | ona*ni* | Congo | mona | *nu*mona |
| Nika | ona | ... | Yao | wona | wona*ni* |
| Senna | ona | ona*ni* | Mozambique | ona | ona*ni* |
| Karanga | wona | wona*ni* | Chwana | bona | bona*ng* |
| Ganda | labba | ... | Mpongwe | yena | yena*ni* |

**836.** — *N. B.* In Nyamwezi the forms corresponding to these have generally the suffix -*ga* in the singular, -*ge* in the plural, as *wonaga* " see ", pl. *wonage*. In some verbs, principally in those which end in -*ia* in the infinitive, these suffixes are replaced respectively by -*ja* and -*je*, and then various phonetic changes often take place, as in *suma*ja " consent " (cf. *ku-sumia*, to consent), *oka*ja " bake " (cf. *ku-ocha*, to bake). Cf. Steere's *Collections for a Handbook of the Nyamwezi Language*, pp. 67 and 64.

**837.** — The effect on imperatives of the phonetic laws relative to monosyllabic stems, and to such as begin with a vowel (44 and 46, n. 2), is remarkable in most Bantu languages, principally in the verb " to come ". We may notice particularly the following forms : —

|  |  |  |  |
|---|---|---|---|
| GANDA : *jangu*, | from the stem -*ja*, | " come " |  |
| NYAMWEZI : *nzagu*, pl. *nzoji* | ,, | -*iza* | " come thou, come ye " |
| HERERO : *indyo*, pl. *indyoni* | ,, | -*ya* | ,, ,, |
| SWAHILI : *njoo*, pl. *njooni* | ,, | -*ja* | ,, ,, |
| BOONDEI : *soo* ( = *n-soo*), pl. *nsooni*, | ,, | -*eza* | ,, ,, |
| CHWANA PROPER : *eintlo*, pl. *tlang* | ,, | -*tla* | ,, ,, |
| SUTO : *tlho*, pl. *tlhong* | ,, | -*tlha* | ,, ,, |
| MPONGWE : *yogo*, pl. *yogoni* | ,, | -*ya* | ,, ,, |
| LOWER CONGO : *wiza*, pl. n**uiza** | ,, | -*iza* | ,, ,, |
| KAFIR : *yiza*, pl. *yizani* | ,, | -*za*, -*iza* | ,, ,, |

etc., etc.

**838.** — In Swahili the other monosyllabic verbs, and a few of those which begin with a vowel, take in the singular the prefix *ku-*, which is probably the pronoun which means " thou " (639\*). Ex. k**u***la* (from -*la*) "eat thou ". There is no plural form properly corresponding to this ; for such imperatives as *kuleni* " eat ye " must be referred to the subjunctive imperative form (855).

**839.** — In Lower Congo there are probably no monosyllabic verbs. Verbs which begin with a vowel take in the imperative singular (2ᵈ person) the prefix *w-* " thou ", as w-*enda* " go thou ". The plural is regular.

**840.** — In Kafir the verbs which begin with a vowel take the prefix *y-*, and monosyllabic verbs the prefix *yi*. Ex. y**i***ya* " go thou " (from -*ya*), y**enza** " do " (from -*enza*).

**841.** — In Senna *u* is prefixed to monosyllabic verbs. Ex. u*dya* " eat ", u*dyani* " eat ye ", u*mua* " drink ", u*muani* " drink ye ".

In the same language the verb *ku-enda* " to go " becomes in the imperative *ndoko* " go thou ". In Angola also we find this form *ndoko* next to *nde*, which has the same meaning (cf. 938).

### 2. Indicative form NDI-BONA " I see ".

**842.** — This form is obtained as a rule by prefixing the various connective pronouns (639) immediately to the form ending in -*a*. Ex. : —

## Fundamental Forms of the Simple Verb. 223

|         | I see    | thou seest | he sees | we see  | you see | they see, etc. |
|---------|----------|------------|---------|---------|---------|----------------|
| Tonga   | *ndi*bona | *u*bona   | *u*bona | *tu*bona | *mu*bona | *ba*bona, etc. |
| Kaguru  | *ni*langa | *u*langa  | *a*langa | *chi*langa | *mu*langa | *wa*langa, etc. |
| Ganda   | *n*dabba | *o*labba  | *a*labba | *tu*labba | *mu*labba | *ba*labba, etc. |
| Swahili | *ni*ona  | *wo*na    | *a*ona  | *tw*ona | *mw*ona | *wa*ona, etc. |
| Kafir   | *ndi*bona | *u*bona  | *u*bona | *si*bona | *ni*bona | *ba*bona, etc. |
| Congo   | 'mona    | *o*mona   | *o*mona | *tu*mona | *nu*mona | *be*mona, etc. |
| Chwana  | *ke*bona | *o*bona   | *o*bona | *re*bona | *lo*bona | *ba*bona, etc. |

etc., etc.

**843.** — *N. B.* In Congo and Angola monosyllabic and vowel verbs generally insert -*ku*- or -*kw*- between the connective pronoun and the verbal stem. Ex. in Congo: *n*kw*enda*, I go.

**844.** — This form **ndi***bona*, being indefinite, is not much used by itself, though it is frequently found in the compound forms which contain an auxiliary, as will be seen further on.

When used by itself it is generally expressive of an action either indefinite with respect to time, or properly present. Hence it is that in Tonga, Swahili, Chwana, Kafir, etc., we find it used principally in relative clauses to express one fact *concomitant* with another. In Swahili it seems to be never used except in relative clauses. In Tonga, Kafir, some Chwana dialects, etc., we find it sometimes in non-relative clauses, but then it is always followed by a determinative of some kind. In Lower Congo, Ganda, Kaguru, etc., it seems to be freely used even without being thus immediately followed by another word. etc., etc. Ex. : —

**845.** — TONGA :
*Ningoma zi-lila*, Those are the drums that are beaten, lit... that cry.
*Bantu ba-ba*, thieves, lit. people who steal.
*Ngue u-njila muakale Zuanga*, It is he, Wange, who goes inside.
*Zielo zi-zialua a balozi, zi-njila m'mubili, ta zi-bonigui a zi-njilila*, Evil spirits are begotten by sorcerers, they enter the body, they are not seen when they come in.
*Ba-amba nzi?* What do they mean?
*U-yanda a-funde*, He wishes to learn.
*Matezi u-tilila paa Ceezia*, The river Matezi joins (the Zambezi) at Ceezia's.
*Muntu u-teka manzi, intale i-mu-jata*, ... and while a person is drawing water, a crocodile gets hold of him.
*Tu-ku-kombelela*, We pay homage to thee.

**846.** — KAFIR :
*U-teta mti mni na?* What sort of tree do you mean?
*A ndi na nkomo i-tengwa-yo*, I have no cow for sale, lit... which is being sold.
*Yi nto ni na lo nto ni-za nayo?* What is that you are coming with?
*Ndi-vela kwa Sabalala, ndi-ya kwa Sikwebu*, I am coming from Sabalala's, I go to Sikwebu's.

**847.** — SWAHILI :
*Yeye a-ni fuata-ye*, He who follows me. ... (Mat., 3, 11.)
*Kwani baba yenu a-jua m-taka-yo*, ... because your Father knows what you want. (Mat., 6, 8.)

**848.** — CHWANA :
Chwana proper : *O-tshaba-ng?* What do you fear?
*Ke-bona motho eoo, eo o-tsamaea-ng ka-bonako*, I see that man, who walks quickly.
*Logadima lo-ewa kwa Isetem*, Lightning comes from the East. (Mat., 24, 27).
Suto : *Le-gopelela-ng bobe?* Why do you think evil?
*Gobane Ntat'a lona o-tseba seo le-se-tloka-ng*, ... because your Father knows what you want. (Mat., 6, 8).

**849.** — ANGOLA :
Old : *O ngana y-ekala nae*, The Lord is with thee. (*Cat.*, p. 2).
*Eye tu-ku-tenda..., eye tu-ku-andala*, To thee do we cry..., to thee do we send up our sighs. (*Ibid.*, p. 2).
*O mukutu u-bolel' a-xi*, The body rots in the ground. (*Ibid.*, p. 33).
*Esue tu-ekala ko uze ou*, We who live in this world. (*Ibid.*, p. 34).
Modern : *U-enda ni muzumbu k-a-jimbirile*, He who walks with a mouth (h. e. he who has a mouth) does not lose his way. (Chatelain's *Gr.*, p. 132).
*Henda, se y-a-vula, i-beka njinda*, Love, if immoderate, brings anger. (*Ibid.*)

**850.** — HERERO (Dr. Büttner's *Märchen der Ovaherero*, p. 190) :
*O mundu eingui... u-tua o vanatye m'o zondyatu, x u-i-ko*, This is the woman who puts children into bags, and goes off.

*N. B.* In Herero and some other Western languages the final vowel of this form is sometimes dropped, or weakened, or assimilated with the penultimate, as in the above example *nuiko* " and he goes off " (= *n'u i1-ko* = *n'u-ia-ko*). Cf. 833.

**851.** In Kafir we find in some cases, principally after auxiliaries, the form *e-bona* where we might expect *u-bona* (cl. *MU-ntu*) or *a-bona* (cl. *MA-tye*), and *be-bona* where we might expect *ba-bona* (cl. *BA-ntu*). We find likewise the perfect forms *e-bonile* and *be-bonile* for *u-bonile*, *a-bonile*, and *ba-bonile* (865). Probably all such forms must be considered as participles. Possibly also, as no such participles are found in the other languages, they are really indicatives, but their original vowel *a* has come to be changed to *e* through some sort of assimilation, because they are mostly used after auxiliaries ending with *e*, as in *ba-ye be-bonile*, they had seen.

When the verbal stem of these expressions and the like is monosyllabic, *-si-* is inserted between it and the connective pronoun ; *s* is likewise inserted before vowel stems.

**852.** — *N. B.* Out of their connection with auxiliaries, these forms are found mostly after the verbs *ku-bona* " to see ", *ku-mana* " to continue, to go on ", *ku-va* " to hear ", *ku-fika* " to arrive ", etc., and in certain clauses which express an action concomitant with another. Ex.: *Ndababona* be*siza* " I saw them coming ", *bendibone* u*siza* " I had seen you coming ", *wamana epeka ekaya* " she went on cooking at home ", *ndafika* e*ngeko* " I arrived when he was not a home ", lit. " ...he (being) not there ", *bahamba* be*buza* " they went on asking on the way ", *u kupupa elele* " to dream (when) sleeping ", *kwa' kuko u mfazi* e*ngahambi emini* " there was a woman who never went in the day-time ", *kudala* e*ngeko* " it is a long time since he went ", lit. " ...he (being) not there ", etc.

### 3. Infinitive form KU-BONA " to see ".

**853.** — The infinitive form *ku-bona* " to see " being in reality a substantive (of cl. *KU*), nothing concerning its formation need be added to what has been said about it in the chapter on substantives (462-468), except that in certain languages, when it is used in conjunction with auxiliaries, its classifier *KU*-, or *GO*-, is generally understood, as in the Chwana *Re-tla bona*, we shall see (= Tonga *tu-za* ku-*bona*). Apart from its use in conjunction with auxiliaries, it is used almost exclusively as a substantive proper.

Ex. IN Tonga : *Ta tuzi ku-yasana*, We cannot fight, lit. we do not know fighting.
*Milia ie impewo nja ku-sanguna*, The feasts of winter are the first, lit... are those of the beginning.

We find also, at least with auxiliaries, the locative form *mu ku-bona*, at seeing.

**854.** — In Tonga there is also an indicative form immediately derived from *ku-bona*, viz. *u-ku-bona* (= *ndi-ku-bona*) " I am to see ", *u-ku-bona* " thou art to see ", *u-ku-bona* " he is to see, he must see ", etc. Cf. 843.

In Swahili, Angola, Congo, and a few other languages, monosyllabic verbs, as in Swahili *ku-ja* " to come ", and those which begin with a vowel without an initial aspiration, as *kw-enda* " to go", require their classifier *ku* after most auxiliaries in those tenses in which other verbs do not take it. Ex. in Swahili : *nina kuja* " I am coming ", *nina kwenda* " I am going ". Cf. *nina penda* " I am loving ". This is an application of the general laws exposed in nn. 44 and 45.

### § 3. SUBJUNCTIVE FORM **NDI-BONE**.

**855.** — This form is regularly used in all the Bantu languages with an imperative power, as *tu-bone* " let us see ". In the 2$^d$ person singular its connective pronoun is sometimes understood, as may be seen in the subjoined examples. In the 2$^d$ person plural its connective pronoun is in some cases suffixed instead of being prefixed, as in Kafir : *Ba-kangele*-ni " look ye at them ".

**856.** — The same form is also used in all the Bantu languages to express one act which is *intended* to follow another, as in *mu-zue* **tu-mu-bone** " come out that we may see you ".

**857.** — EXAMPLES FOR THE CHANGES IN THE CONNECTIVE PRONOUNS :

|  | That I may see | that thou mayst see | that he may see | that we may see | that you may see | that they may see |
|---|---|---|---|---|---|---|
| Tonga | *ndi*bone | *u*bone | *a*bone | *tu*bone | *mu*bone | *ba*bone |
| Kaguru | *ni*lange | *u*lange | *a*lange | *chi*lange | *mu*lange | *wa*lange |
| Ganda | *n*dabbe | *o*labbe | *a*labbe | *tu*labbe | *mu*labbe | *ba*labbe |
| Swahili | *ni*one | *w*one | *a*one | *tw*one | *mw*one | *wa*one |
| Kafir | *ndi*bone | *u*bone | *a*bone | *si*bone | *ni*bone | *ba*bone |
| Lower Congo | 'mona | *o*mona | *o*mona | *tu*mona | *nu*mona | *ba*bona |
| Chwana | *ke*bone | *o*bone | *a*bone | *re*bone | *lo*bone | *ba*bone |
| Mozambique | *ki*wone | *u*wone | *a*wone | *ni*wone | *m*wone | *ya*wone |

etc., etc.

**858.** — Thus it may be seen that in this form the connective pronoun of cl. *MU-ntu* is generally *a*. Here again Congo differs from the generality of the Bantu languages in having *o* instead of *a*. And, singularly enough, in the same language the vowel-ending of this form is *a* instead of *e*.

**859.** — VARIOUS EXAMPLES :
TONGA : Mu*zubuke*, Cross (ye) the river.
U*ende e nzila ndanfo*, Go by the long way.
*Kwali kuba kubotu bamue* **bakale***, bamue* **bainke***,* It would be good that some should remain, and others go.
KARANGA : Mu*vubuke*, Cross (ye) the river.
U*nde nejira indefo*, Go by the long way.
ROTSE : Mu*lete kono uato*, Bring (ye) the canoe here.
U*ye kono*, Come here.
*Kokena mei* ni*noe*, Get (me) water, that I may drink.
NIKA : *Mutu hiye ni muivi*, u*abukane naye*, This man is a thief, separate yourself from him. (Rebmann's *Dict*.)
*Yudziamba "* a*pigue ",* He said he would be beaten (*ibid*.).
KAFIR : *M-bete or* u*-m-bete,* Beat (thou) him ; *M-bete*ni, Beat (ye) him.
N*dikutume na ?* Shall I send you ? Si*hambe ?* Must we go ?
*Imvula yona nini na si*lime *?* When will rain fall, that we may plough ?
SWAHILI : *L*eni " eat ye ", or *ku--l*eni (with prefix *ku* before monosyllabic stem, cf. 838 and 842).

|          |                                                                                                       |
|----------|-------------------------------------------------------------------------------------------------------|
|          | **Tu**-*mw-ambie*, Let us tell him ; *ngoje* (= **u***ngoje*), wait.                                  |
|          | **U***tulize sisi*, Sell it to us.                                                                    |
|          | *Nipe habari* (= **U**-*ni-pe*...) Give me the news.                                                  |
|          | **Ni***fanye shauri gani?* What plan am I to take?                                                    |
|          | (From Steere's *Swahili Tales*.)                                                                      |
| Lunda :  | *Eza ko...* **tu***londe*, come here that we may talk together. (Carvalho's *Gr.*, p. 89.)            |
|          | **Tu***kuete difanda*, let us take powder (*ibid.*, p. 100).                                          |

|           | Get up and walk. (Mat., 9, 5.) | Tie his hands. (Mat., 22, 13.) |
|-----------|--------------------------------|-------------------------------|
| Swahili : | *Simama* **u***tembee.*        | *M-fung***eni** *mikono.*     |
| Ganda :   | *Golokoka* **u***tambule.*     | **Mu**-*mu-sibe e mikono.*    |
| Kafir :   | *Suka* or *yima* **u***hambe.* | *M-bope*-**ni** *i zandla.*   |
| Chwana :  | *Tloga* **ueme** **u***tsamaee.* | *'Mofe*-**nŋ** *diatla.*    |
| etc., etc. |                               |                               |

## § 4. Perfect Form **NDI-BONIDE**.

**860.** — This form does not seem to exist in Swahili, nor in Pokomo. The general law for its formation in the other languages may be laid down as follows : —

*A* final of the form ending in -*a* is changed —

| In Tonga to -*ide*.    | Ex. -*fua*, die.   | Perfect : | *ndi-fuide*.       |
|------------------------|--------------------|-----------|--------------------|
| In Kaguru to -*ile*.   | Ex. -*tiga*, flee. | „         | *ni-tigile*.       |
| In Nyamwezi to -*ile*. | Ex. -*tula*, strike. | „       | *n-hulile* (73).   |
| In Yao to -*ile*.      | Ex. -*tawa*, bind. | „         | *n-dawile* (69).   |
| In Kafir to -*ile*.    | Ex. -*teta*, speak. | „        | *ndi-tetile*.      |
| In Chwana to -*ile*.   | Ex. -*reka*, buy.  | „         | *ke-rekile*.       |
| In Mozambique to -*ele*. | Ex. -*roa*, go. | „         | *ni-roele*.        |

In Herero  } to -*ire* (Angola -*ile*) after a short penult, viz. after *i* or *u*.
and Angola } to -*ere* (Angola -*ele*) after a long penult, viz. after *e*, *o*, or *ā*.

In Congo { to -*idi* after a short penult, viz. after *ă*, *i*, or *u*.
         { to -*ele* after a long penult, viz. after *a*, *e*, or *o*.

| In Kamba   to -*iti*. | Ex. -*thaima*, hunt. Perfect : *ni-thaimiti*. |
| In Ganda   to -*ie*.  | Ex. -*siba*, bind.  „   *n-sibie*.           |
| In Mpongwe to *i*.    | Ex. -*yena*, see.   „   *a-yeni*, he has seen. |
| etc., etc.            |                                               |

**861.** — Phonetic laws cause many deviations from this general principle, particularly when the final syllable of the form ending in -*a* is -*ma* (cf. 280), and when it contains a dental sound, such as *ia*, *da*, *la*, *na*, *ta*, etc. Thus in Tonga the perfect forms of -*kala* " sit ", -*lala* " lie down ", -*zuata* " dress ", etc., are -*kede*,

-*lede*, -*zuete*, etc. Here are a few specimens of such phonetic peculiarities : —

| -*a* endings | | -*ala* | -*ala* Chwana -*ara* | -*ana* | -*ona* | -*ama* | -*anya* | -*sia* or -*za* Chwana -*tsa* | -*sia* or -*sa* | -*ula* |
|---|---|---|---|---|---|---|---|---|---|---|
| Perfect endings. | Tonga | *ede* | *ele* | *ene* | *uene* | *eme* / *amine* | ... | ... | ... | ... |
| | Ganda | *adde* | *ase* | *anye* | *onye* | *amie* | *anye* | *ziza* | *sisa* | *udde* |
| | Kafir | *ele* | *ele* | *ene* | ... | *eme* | ... | ... | ... | *ule* |
| | L. Congo | *ele* | *ele* | *ene* | ... | ... | ... | *iji* | *ixi* / *ese* | *widi* |
| | Yao | *ele* / *asile* | *ele* | *ene* | *wene* | *eme* | *enye* | *sie* | *sisie* | *uile* |
| | Chwana | *etse* | *ere* | *anye* / *anne* | *onye* | *ame* | *antse* / *amule* | *ditse* | *sitse* | *utse* |
| | etc., etc. | | | | | | | | | |

Cf. *Grammaire Ruganda*, pp. 34 and 35.
Rev. A. Hetherwick's *Handbook of the Yao Language*, pp. 46-48.
Rev. W. Crisp's *Secoana Grammar*, pp. 39 and 40.
M<sup>gr</sup> Le Berre's *Grammaire Pongoué*, pp. 50 and 51.
Rev. H. Bentley's *Dict.* and *Gram. of the Congo Lang.*, pp. 642-644.

**862.** — Some verbs may be used both in the regular and in the modified form. Thus in Tonga we may hear both *ndi-buene* and *ndi-bonide*, from -*bona* " see ". In Kafir nearly all the perfects ending in -*ile* can change this to -*e*, when they are immediately followed by another word. Ex. *ndibon*e *i nkomo* (= *ndiboni*le...), I have seen the cattle.

**863.** — Properly speaking, the form *ndi-bonide* is expressive of distance or persistency with respect to time, as is sufficiently evidenced from the fact that the suffix -*le* or -*de* implies the notion of distance (cf. 533*). Practically it is used with somewhat different powers in the different languages. It may however be laid down as a general rule that, out of its use in connection with auxiliaries, it is mostly found expressing completed actions which have resulted in a present state or impression. Examples : —

**864.** — Tonga :
*U-zuete ngubo zinono*, He wears (lit. he has put on) fine clothes.
*Basukulumbui ba-kede ku Bulumbu*, The Shukulumbue live on Lumbu territory,
*U-lede*, He is asleep, (lit. he has lain down, from -*lala*, lie down).

**865.** — Kafir :
*Awu ! i-sitile le ngubo yako*, Dear me ! This coat of yours is warm.
*Lento i lungile*, This thing is good (lit. has become correct).

*Si-bulele u Mlonjalonjani*, We have killed Mlonjalonjani.
*Si-qelile u kudla a banye a bantu*, We are accustomed to eat other people.
*Ndi-gqibile u kwenza i ndlela*, I have finished making the road.
*U ma u-file*, My mother is dead.
*U-ye pina ?* Where is he gone to? ( *-ye* = *-yile*, from *-ya*, 862.)

*N. B.* In Kafir the form *ndi-bonile* may be used as a kind of participle, and then *e-bonile*, *be-bonile* are found instead of *u-bonile*, *a-bonile*, *ba-bonile*, 851.

### 866. — ROTSE :
*Ki-yopile*, I have heard (from *-yopa*, hear).
*Ku-fekile*, It is the same (from *-feka*, become alike).

### 867. — CHWANA :
*Motlanka oame o-letse*, My servant is lying down (from *-lala*).
*Dilo tse, ke-dibuile... ka dikao*, These things I have spoken (lit. said them) in parables. (John, 16, 25.)
*Me lo-dumetse gore ke-ewa kwa Modimong*, And you have believed that I come from God (John, 16, 27).

### 868. — GANDA (From the *Grammaire Ruganda*, pp. 83-91.) :
*O-sumise burungi*, He is well dressed (lit. he has tied well).
*We n-suze wabi*, Where I am lying down is not confortable (from *-sula*, lie down).
*Emmere e-m-puedde-ko*, My porridge is all gone (from *-wera* = *-pwera*, to come to an end).

### 869. — ANGOLA :
*U-owele k-a-kambie mavunzu*, He who has swum does not lack mud. (from *-owa* swim). Chatelain's *Kimbundu Gr.*, p. 138.

etc., etc.

## § 5. THE FORMS **NDI-BONANGA** AND **NDI-BONAGA**.

**870.** — I do not know that any of these two forms is used in Tonga, but —

1º In Kafir we find *ndi-bonanga* used regularly as a perfect form with a negative auxiliary. Ex. *A ndi-bonanga*, I have not seen.

2º In Mozambique the exact equivalent of this Kafir form takes the suffix *-ali*. Ex. *Ka ni-m-on*ali, I have not seen him.

3º Other forms occur which may be compared with, but are not equivalent to, these, in Mozambique with the suffix *-aka* or *-aga*, in Congo and Ganda with the suffix *-anga*, in Yao, Kaguru, Nyamwezi, and Mpongwe, with the suffix *-aga*. These suffixes *-anga*, *aka*, and *-aga*, seem to be properly expressive of continuity. In all these languages such forms are found both in affirmative and in negative clauses. In some of them they are used exclusively in connection with auxiliaries. Examples: —

**871.** —
LOWER CONGO: *N-tanganga*, I am reading.
YAO: *Ni* n-*dawaga* ( = *ni* n-*tawaga*), If I bind, when I bind...
NYAMWEZI: *Ne* n-*iwaga* ( = *ne n a-iwaga*, 76) *mwenda, w-a-n-hunga*, When I stole a piece of cloth, they bound me. Cf. Steere's *Nyamwezi Handbook*, p. 65.

*N. B.* The Nyamwezi suffix *-aga* changes to *-aja* in certain cases (cf. 836).

MOZAMBIQUE: *A-thiraka* or *a-thiraga* ( = Swahili *a-ki-pita*, 993), While he passes...
*Ya-gi-kohaga, wa-himerie*..., ( = Swahili *wa-ki ni-uliza, wa-ambie*...), When they ask for me, tell them...
(From Rankin's *Swahili and Makua Tales*, pp. 3 and 5).
MPONGWE (only with an auxiliary): *Mi a-dyenaga*, I was seeing.
GANDA (do.): *Edda tu-a-tulanga nyo*, Once we remained a long time.

## § 6. THE NEGATIVE FORM (TA) NDI-BONI.

**872.** — The proper ending of this form is i (*-i* or *-e*) in Tonga (271), *-i* in Kafir, Swahili, etc., *e* in Chwana and Angola. It does not seem to be negative by itself, as we commonly find it coupled with a negative auxiliary.

Ex. TONGA: *Ta* tu*boni*, or *ta* tu*bone*..., we do not see.
KAFIR: *A* si*boni*, do.
CHWANA: *Ga* re*bone*, do.
SWAHILI: *Ha* tw-*oni*, do.
ANGOLA: *Muene* ka-*ku-zole*, he does not love thee.
etc., etc.

In the section on negative auxiliaries (875-891) we shall see the principal peculiarities relative to the construction of this form.

In Ganda, Kamba, Yao, Kaguru, and Lower Congo, the positive forms of the verbs are also used in negative clauses, though with different auxiliaries. Hence in these languages the Tonga form *(ta) ndi-boni* is replaced respectively by *si-ona, n-di-ona*, etc. Cf. 876.

*N. B.* Various apparently locative particles are more or less regularly appended to the negative forms of the verbs in various languages. Notice particularly the use of *ko* in Lower Congo, as in *ke besumba* ko " they do not buy ", and that of *pe* in Tonga, as in *ta ndiboni* pe " I do not see at all. "

## II. — Auxiliaries.

### § 1. General Principles.

**873.** — I consider as auxiliaries all the verbal particles which have come to be used before principal verbs in order to determine time, mode of thought, and other such notions. Most of them are somewhat puzzling to the students of Bantu, both because they have no exact equivalents in our languages, and still more because they undergo, or cause, a great variety of contractions and elisions.

The auxiliaries which are in most frequent use seem to be all borrowed from the verbs which express the visible and best defined human acts, such as " to go, " " to go off, " " to come, " " to start, " " to get up, " " to stop, " " to sit ", etc. Hence no little attention is required principally on the part of Europeans, when they wish to use them in the proper time and place. In Kafir, for instance, we may hear six or seven forms of imperatives, all of them including different notions, e. g. : —

>**Ma** *unyuke e ntabeni*, lit. Stand to go up the hill.
>**Ka** *unyuke e ntabeni*, lit. Make one move to go up the hill.
>**Suka** *u nyuke e ntabeni*, lit. Wake up to go up the hill.
>**Hamb'o** *kunyuka* (= **hamba uye** *kunyuka*), lit. Walk to go to go up.
>**Uz'** *unyuke e ntabeni*, lit. Come to go up the hill.
>etc., etc.

I cannot say that all Kafirs are always accurate as to the proper use of such auxiliaries. Most of them however are so when they have not allowed their language to be corrupted by foreign influences, and, consequently, though all the above expressions may be rendered into English by " go up the hill ", yet properly **ma** *u-nyuke* supposes a change of occupation, **ka** *unyuke* may be used only of a momentary action, **suka** *unyuke* will best be said to one who is too slow to fulfil an order, **hamb'o** *kunyuka* will be said to one who has to go some way before beginning to go up the hill, **uz'***unyuke* conveys an order or prayer which allows delay in the execution etc., etc.

Hence it is that in many cases Bantu auxiliaries are expressive of the same notions as our adverbs or conjunctions, and may be rendered respectively by " at once, just, already, yet, not yet, never, when, until ", etc.

**874.** — When auxiliaries are used before verbs, the connective pronoun subject is expressed in some cases both before the auxiliary and before the principal verb, in other cases it is expressed only once. There are considerable divergencies on this point in the different languages.

*N. B.* As a rule, in Kafir (out of relative clauses) the connective pronouns are not expressed before monosyllabic auxiliaries when they are expressed before the principal verb, unless such connective pronouns consist of a mere vowel.

Ex. U*b'* u-*ye pina ?* (= u-*be* u-*ye pina ?*) Where hast thou been ?
*Be* ni-*ye pina ?* (= ni-*be* ni-*ye pina ?*) Where have you been ?

Auxiliaries are more exposed than verbs proper to have their final vowel modified or weakened. This is particularly noticeable in Kafir, where auxiliaries very often take the ending -*e* in tenses in which they might be expected to have -*a*, as in *way*e... for *waya*..., *waz*e... for *waza*... (917, 959), and the ending -*o* where they should have -*e*, as in *hamba uy*o *kulima* for *hamba uy*e *kulima* (916) " go to plough. "

## § 2. THE NEGATIVE AUXILIARIES.

### 1. Forms.

**875.** — One form of negative auxiliary in nearly all the Bantu languages is *si* (Chwana *se*, Kamba *di*, Mpongwe *re*, Herero and Mozambique *hi*). This seems to have been originally a form of the verb -*sia*, to leave, to avoid (52\*). Hence it is that in the infinitive several languages replace it by -*leka*, to leave (880).

Another form is *ta (ti* before *i)* in Tonga, *ta* or *ti* in Ganda. This is perhaps derived from the verb *tia*, to fear. The equivalent of this form is *nga* or *a* in Kafir, *nga* in Yao, *ga* and in some cases *sa* in Chwana, *ka* in Mozambique, *ke* or *ka* in Angola, *ha* in Swahili. I do not see to which verb these forms originally belonged, unless they are connected with the verb -*kaka* " to refuse ", or with -*leka* " to leave, to avoid. "

*N. B.* The Mpongwe negative particle *pa* has every appearance of being no other than the French *pas*.

When the negative clause is absolute and indicative, in most languages the negative auxiliary comes first without any connective pronoun before it, as in Tonga **ta** *ba-boni*, they do not see. When the negative clause is relative, or subjunctive, or infinitive, the connective pronoun in most languages is expressed before the negative auxiliary and is not repeated before the principal verb, as in Tonga *aba mbantu* ba*ta boni*, these are people who do not see. Ex. : —

## 876. — A. ABSOLUTE INDICATIVE CLAUSES.

|  | I do not see. | Thou dost not see. | He does not see. | We do not see. | You do not see. | They do not see. |
|---|---|---|---|---|---|---|
| Tonga | { (*n*)siboni <br> { ta *ndi*boni | ta *u*boni | ta *a*boni | ta *tu*boni | ta *mu*boni | ta *ba*boni |
| Ganda | si*l*abba | to*l*abba | ta*l*abba | ti *tu*labba | ti *mu*labba | ti *bu*labba |
| Boondei | k*i*ona | k*u*ona | k*a*ona | ka*ti*ona | ka *mw*ona | ka *wa*ona |
| Kamba | *n*diona | *u*di ona | *a*di ona | *tu*di ona | *mu*di ona | *ma*di ona |
| Swahili | sioni | h*u*oni | h*a*oni | ha *tw*oni | ha *mw*oni | ha *wa*oni |
| Pokomo | sioni | h*u*oni | k*a*oni | ta *hu*oni | ta *mu*oni | ta *wa*oni |
| Tette | si *ndi*ona | s*u*ona | s*a*ona | si *ti*ona | si *mu*ona | si *wa*ona |
| Kafir | a *ndi*boni | a k*u*boni | a k*a*boni | a *si*boni | a *mu*boni | a *ba*boni |
| Herero | { *hi na*... <br> { I have not | *ko na*... <br> thou hast not | *ke na*... <br> he has not | *ka* tu *na*... <br> we have not | *ka* mu *na*... <br> you have not | *ka* ve *na*... <br> they have not |
| Lower Congo | ke' mona... | k*u*mona... | k*e*mona... | ke *tu*mona... | ke *nu*mona.. | ke *be*mona |
| Chwana | ga *ke*bone | ga *o*bone | ga *a*bone | ga *re*bone | ga *lo*bone | ga *ba*bone |
| Mpongwe | { mi pa dyena <br> { mi re dyena | o pa dyena <br> o re dyena | e pa dyena <br> a re dyena | azwe pa dyena <br> azwe re dyena | anwe pa dyena <br> anwe re dyena | wi pa dyena <br> wi re dyena |
| etc., etc. |

**877.** — *N. B.* 1. The Yao and Kaguru forms equivalent to these have *ku-bona* instead of the simple -*bona*. Besides this, the vowel of the negative particle *nga* in Yao is assimilated to that of the following syllable. Ex. Yao : nge n-*gu-wona* (= *nga* ni-*ku-wona*, 69) " I do not see ", ngu u*kuwona* " thou... ", nga a*kuwona* " he... ", ngu tu *kuwona* " we... ", etc. Kaguru : n*isi kulanga* " I do not see ", *usi kulanga* " thou... ", a*si kulanga* " he... ", chi*si kulanga* " we... ", etc.

2. In Nyamwezi the present indicative negative is *ku-ona-ngo* for all persons and classes, but the perfect negative varies, as n*ha wine* (= n*ka wine*, 73) " I have not seen ", u*ka wine* " thou... ", a*ka wine* " he... ", etc.

3. In Mozambique the negative auxiliaries *a* and *ka*, and in Senna proper the negative auxiliaries *si* and n*ka*, do not seem to be ever used in the indicative unless accompanied by some other auxiliary, as in Senna si*na ona* " I do not see ", n*kuna ona* " thou... ", n*kana ona* " he... ", n*ka tina ona* " we... ", etc. The same remark appears to apply to the Karanga negative auxiliary *a*.

4. In Angola a substantive pronoun seems to be, as a rule, appended to the verb in indicative negative clauses, and the negative auxiliary *ki* is usually understood in certain cases, as (*ki*) ngi*mon*-ami " I do not see ", *ku*mon-e " thou... " *ka*mon-e " he... ", (*ki*)tu*mon*-etu " we... " *ki* nu*mon*-enu " you... " *ka*mon-a " they... ".

## 878. — B. RELATIVE CLAUSES.

|  | (I) who do not see. | (Thou) who dost not see. | (He) who does not see. | (We) who do not see. | (You) who do not see. | (They) who do not see. |
|---|---|---|---|---|---|---|
| Tonga | *ndi*ta boni | *u*ta boni | *u*ta boni | *tu*ta boni | *mu*ta boni | *ba*ta boni |
| Ganda | ... | *o*ta labba | *u*ta labba (?) | *tu*ta labba | *mu*ta labba | *ba*ta labba |
| Kaguru | *ni*si langa | *u*si langa | *a*si langa | *chi*si langa | *m*si langa | *wa*si langa |
| Boondei | ... | ... | *u*ka ona (?) | ... | ... | *wa*ka ona |
| Pokomo | *ni*so ona | *ku*so ona | *ka*so ona | *hu*so ona | *mi*uso ona | *wa*so ona |
| Yao | ... | ... | *ju*anga wona | ... | ... | *wa*nga wona |
| Kafir | *ndi*nga boni | *u*nga boni | *u*nga boni | *si*nga boni | *ni*nga boni | *ba*nga boni |
| Herero | *mbi*ha muni | *u*ha muni | *ngu*ha muni | *tu*ha muni | *mu*ha muni | *ve*ha muni |
| Chwana | *ke*sa bone | *o*sa bone | *a*sa bone | *re*sa bone | *lo*sa bone | *ba*sa bone |
| Mpongwe | *mie* ayena | *o*yena | *aye* ayena | *a*zwe ayena | *a*nwe ayena | *wa*yena |
| etc., etc. |

*N. B.* In Swahili a substantive pronoun is appended to the negative auxiliary according to n. 733. Ex. ni*si*ye *ona* " (I) who do not see ", u*si*ye *ona* " (thou) who... ", a*si*ye *ona* " (he) who... " tu*sio ona* " (we) who... ", m*sio ona* " (you) who... " wa*sio ona* " (they) who... " etc.

## 879. — C. SUBJUNCTIVE CLAUSES.

|  | (that) I may not see. | (that) thou mayst not see. | (that) he may not see. | (that) we may not see. | (that) you may not see. | (that) they may not see. |
|---|---|---|---|---|---|---|
| Tonga | *ndi*ta boni | *u*ta boni | ata boni | *tu*ta boni | *mu*ta boni | *ba*ta boni |
| Kaguru | *ni*si lange | *u*si lange | asi lange | *chi*si lange | *m*si lange | *wa*si lange |
| Boondei | *nese* kwona | *wese* kwona | ese kwona | *tese* kwona | *mwese* kwona | *wese* kwona |
| Nyamwezi | *nha* wone | *u*ka wone | aka wone | *tu*ka wone | *mu*ka wone | *wa*ka wone |
| Kamba | *ndi* one | *u*di one | adi one | *tu*di one | *mu*di one | *ma*di one |
| Swahili | *ni*si one | *u*si one | asi one | *tu*si one | *m*si one | *wa*si one |
| Pokomo | *ni*si one | *ku*si one | *ka*si one | *hu*si one | *mu*si one | *wa*si one |
| Senna | { si *ndi*one<br>{ *ndi*sa one | su *wo*ne<br>*u*sa one | sa*o*ne<br>a*sa* one | si *ti*one<br>*ti*si one | si *mu*one<br>*mu*sa one | sa *wa*one<br>a*sa* one |
| Karanga | *ndi*si wone | *u*si wone | asi wone | *ti*si wone | *mu*si wone | *wa*si wone |
| Ganda | si labbe | t*o*labbe | t*a*labbe | ti *tu*labbe (?) | ti *mu*labbe(?) | ti *ba*labbe (?) |
| Kafir | *ndi*ngaboni | *u*nga boni | *a*nga boni | *si*nga boni | *ni*nga boni | *ba*nga boni |
| Herero | emune (?) | *u*hi mune(?) | ahi mune | *tu*hi mune | *mu*hi mune | a*ve*muna(?) |
| Angola | ki *ngi*mone | *ku*mone | *ka*mone | ki *tu*mone | ki *nu*mone | *ka*mone |
| Lower Congo | ke'moni(?) | *ku*moni (?) | *ka*moni(?) | ke *tu*moni | ke *nu*moni | ke *ba*boni |
| Yao | *n*ga wona | *u*ka wona | aka wona | *tu*ka wona | *m*ka wona | aka wona |
| Mozambique | *ki*hi one | *u*hi one | *a*hi one | *ni*hi one | *u*hi one | *a*hi one |
| Chwana | *ke*se bone | *o*se bone | *a*se bone | *re*se bone | *lo*se bone | *ba*se bone |
| Mpongwe | *mi* ayena | *o* yena | *a* yena | a*we* ayena | a*nwe* ayena | *wa*yena |

etc., etc.

## 880. — D. IMPERATIVE CLAUSES, AND THE INFINITIVE.

|  | Imperative. | | | | Infinitive. |
|---|---|---|---|---|---|
|  | Do not see | Do ye not see | Let me not see | . | not to see |
| Tonga | { t*o*boni<br>{ *u*taboni | ta *mu*boni }<br>*mu*ta boni } | *ndi*ta boni | etc. | *ku*ta boni |
| Kanguru | *u*si lange | *mu*si lange | *ni*si lange | etc. | ... |
| Boondei | *kwe*se kwona | *mwe*se kwona | *ne*se kwona | etc. | *ku*leka *kwo*na |
| Nyamwezi | *u*ka wone | *mu*ka wone | *nha* wone (73) | etc. | ... |
| Kamba | di ona | di ona*i* | *ndi* one | etc. | ... |
| Swahili | { si ona<br>{ si one | si ona*ni* }<br>si onen*i* } | *ni*si one | etc. | *ku*toa *kwo*na |
| Senna | { si ona }<br>{ sia ona } | si ona*ni* | (ine) si *ndi*one | etc. | *ku*leka *kwo*na |
| Karanga | *u*si wone | *mu*si wone | *ndi*si one | etc. | *ku*leka *ku*wona |
| Ganda | { t*o*labba<br>{ *u*labbanga | ti *mu*labba<br>te *mu*labbanga } | si labbe | etc. | ... |
| Kafir | *u*nga boni | *ni*nga boni | *ndi*nga boni | etc. | *ku*nga boni |
| Herero | ... | a *mu*muna | emune (= n *i* mune) | etc. | ... |
| Angola | *ku*mone | ki *nu*mone | ki *ngi*mone | etc. | ... |
| Yao | *u*ka wona | *m*ka wona | ... | etc. | ... |
| Chwana | { se bone<br>{ *o* se bone | se bone*ng*<br>*lo*se bone | (n) *ke*se bone | etc. | *go*bisa *go*bona |
| Mpongwe | ayena | ayena*ni* |  |  |  |

etc., etc.

## Auxiliaries. 235

Out of the second person imperative do not differ from subjunctive clauses, but in the second person we find slightly different forms in most languages, as may be seen from the preceding examples.

In the infinitive, the negative auxiliary is in some languages placed between the principal stem and its classifier.

**881.** — *N. B.* Throughout the whole of this section we pass by certain auxiliaries which, though used mostly or exclusively in negative clauses, are not essentially negative. Such are, for instance, in Tonga : *kue*, as in *ta* ba*kue* baaka *bona* " they never saw " (964); in Karanga and Swahili : *ja*, as (in Karanga) *a* ba*ja ka bona* " they never saw (960). Cf. 976.

### 2. Examples showing the use of these forms.

**882.** — TONGA :
*Si-zi*, I don't know ; *si-yandi kuinka*, I don't wish to go.
*Ta ndi yandi buame buemu*, I do not wish to be your king.
*Aba bantu ta ba nunide*, These people are not fat.

**883.** — *Ta a-nvuide mulilo*, He has not felt the fire.
*Bantu babotu ta ba-fui a muade*, Good people do not die from the *muade* (poison).
*Makumi a-ta balui*, lit. Tens which are not counted, h. e. An unlimited number.
*Uanjila mu mulilo u-ta mani*, lit. He went into the fire which does not end.
*Ta mucite citede*, Do not do so ; *T-o-yowi*, Do not fear.

**884.** — GANDA (From the *Grammaire Ruganda*, pp. 83-91) :
*Bwe ndia mmere, si-kkuta*, When I eat porridge, I cannot eat my fill.
*Munnange, si-kkuse*, My friend, I have not eaten my fill.
*Nalia nga t-a-kkuta*, And he eats without getting satisfied.
*Mugenyi t-a-kkuse*, The stranger has not eaten his fill.
*T-o-n-dangir-anga a bantu*, Do not betray me to the people.
*T-o-n-dopa* or *t o-n-dop-anga*, Do not mention me.
*Ti-mugenda ku-nzi-tta*, lit. Do not go to kill me.
*Si-genda ku-ku-lopa*, I am not going to mention you.

**885.** — OLD ANGOLA (From Father de Coucto's *Catechism*, 1661) :
*Ke tu-ila " mo majina avula "*, We do not say : " In many names ". P. 25.
*Ke mu-iza kufua*, You are not going to die. P. 17.
*Ke mu-chile, ke mu-fu*, Do not fear, you will not die. P. 18.

MODERN ANGOLA (From Héli Chatelain's *Kimbundu Grammar*) :

*Muzueri wonene k-a-lungwe*, lit. A great talker is not right. P. 131.
*Hima k-a-tarie ku muxila ue*, A monkey does not see at its tail. P. 132.

*Nguba ka-bu* (= *ka-i-bu*) *boxi, mulonga ka-bue* (= *ka-u-bue*) *ku muxima,* A groundnut does not rot in the ground, a word does not vanish in the heart. P. 132.

**886.** — HERERO (From the *Zeitschrift für Afrikanische Sprachen,* 1887-88):
*Ne k-a-pendukire,* And she did not answer. P. 202.
*O mundu o musiona k-a-rara,* A poor man does not sleep. P. 202.
*A mu-rara,* Do not sleep. P. 202.
*A mu-mu-es'eye,* Do not leave him. P. 202.
*A ve-yaruka,* They must not return. P. 203.
*O wami ngu mbi-ha tyindi,* I, who do not remove. (Kolbe's *Dict.,* p. 341).

**887.** — KAFIR (From various native tales):
*A ndi-boni nto,* I do not see anything.
*I ndlovu a-yi-libali msinyane,* The elephant does not soon forget.
*A nd-azi,* I don't know; *Ndi-nga hambi?* Must not I go?
*U mquma ngu mti o-nga-boli e mhlabeni,* Wild olive is a tree which does not rot in the ground.
*Uz' uti, u-si-ya e bukweni, u-nga-wa-tyi a masi,* Take care, when going to look for a wife, not to take sour milk.
*U-nga-fi,* lit. Do not die, i. e. Beware!

**888.** — SWAHILI (From Steere's *Swahili Tales,* 1089):
*Si-ku-taki,* I do not want you. P. 206.
*Baba yake h-a-m-pendi,* His father did not like him. P. 199.
*Amenena naye sana, h-a-sikii,* He talked to him a good deal, but he paid no heed. P. 199.
*... yule nunda a-si-inuke,...* (so that) the *nunda* did not raise himself. P. 274.
*Tw-ende-ni m-si-ogope,* Let us go, and do not be afraid. P. 274.
*Mwanangu, u-si-ende,* My child, do not go. P. 260.
*Tu-si-chukwe viombo vietu,* Dont let us carry our things. P. 272.

**889.** — MOZAMBIQUE (From Rankin's *Arab Tales*):
*Ka-ni-m-on-ali* (= Swahili *ha-tu ku-mw-ona*), We have not seen him. P. 8.
*Weyo k-u-kw-ali* (= Swah. *wee k-u ku-fa*), You are not dead. P. 23.
*Kana mimi a-ki-kw-ali* (= Swah. *kana mimi si ku-fa*), If I am not dead... P. 23.
*K-a-pwany-ali etu* (= Swah. *hawa kw-ona kitu*), They did not see anything. P. 5.
*Ku-soma... ku-hi zuela kabisa* (= Swah. *Aka soma... a-si jue kabisa*), He read without understanding at all. P. 4.

**890.** — CHWANA (From the *New Testament*):
*Eo o-sa n-thate-ng, ga a-tshegetse mafuku ame,* He who does not love me, does not keep my words *(John,* 14, 23.)
*Ga a-kake a-tsena mo bogosing ja ga Modimo,* He cannot enter into the kingdom of God *(John,* 3, 5).
*Gone ba-sa tlhape diatla,* Because they don't wash their hands *(Mat.,* 15, 2).
*Fa motho a sa tsalwe...,* If a man be not born... *(John,* 3, 5).

*Lo-se bwabwele*, Do not talk much (*Mat.*, 6, 7).
*O-se gakgamale*, Be not astonished (*John*, 3, 7).

**891.** — NIKA (From Rebmann's *Nika Dict.*) :
*Nazi hino ka i-hendeka kaha*, This cocoa-nut cannot be made into a *kaha* (calabash?)
*Madzi gano ka ga-lasa kala*, This water contains no crab.
   etc., etc.

### § 3. THE AUXILIARY A.

**892.** — The auxiliary *-a* furnishes several compound forms of the verbs. The first, which may be termed the form *nd-a-bona* " I have seen, I saw, I see ", is one of the most frequently used in all the Bantu languages, excepting perhaps Mozambique and Yao. But its power is not the same in them all. In most of them it may be considered as a past tense. In the others, such as Swahili, Karanga, and some Chwana dialects, it looks rather like a present tense. In general, it seems to express properly a motion or actuation which is already past, at least in the thought, without any reference to its duration.

In Yao we find the auxiliary *-a* principally in a form derived from the perfect, as *n-a-wene* " I have seen ", *w-a-wene* " thou hast seen ", etc. In Mozambique we find it principally in a form composed of the same elements as the Tonga *nd-a-bona*, but which means " when I saw, when he saw ", etc., as *k-a-pia* or *y-a-pia* (= Swahili *ni-ki-fika*) " when I came ", *w-a-pia* (= Swahili *w-a-li-po fika*) " when you came ", *w-a-pia* or *a-pia* (= Swahili *a-li-po-fika*) " when he came ", etc. Cf. Rankin's *Arab Tales, passim*.

In Angola, Herero, and several other Western languages, the auxiliary *-a* furnishes three indicative forms expressive of the past, viz. *ng-a-mona*, *ng-a-mono* (form with weakened final vowel. 833), and *ng-a-monene* (in which *monene* is the perfect of *-mona*). Cf. 904 and 905.

Unmistakably the auxiliary *-a* was originally identical with the verb *-ya* " to go ", and was expressive of the past exactly as *za* " to come " was expressive of the future. Cf. 911.

*N. B.* It might be questioned which is more correct in point of orthography, whether to join this auxiliary *-a* to its verb, as *ndabona*, or to separate it, as *nda bona*. It seems to me that, in general, when no contraction takes place, auxiliaries must be separated from their verb in writing; and those languages which have a special aversion to monosyllabic sounds plainly show that they are so separated in the native mind. Thus I do no see why in Swahili, Angola, etc., *ku* should be inserted between monosyllabic verbs and their auxiliary, as in the Swahili *nina ku ja* (not simply *nina-ja*) " I am coming " (854), if both together were a single grammatical word *(ninakuja)*. Likewise in Swahili and Boondei, if most auxiliaries were not separable from their verb, relative particles should be suffixed to the latter, not to the auxiliary. Thus, for instance, the Swahili should say *mtu a-na-kw-enda-*ye " the man who is going ", instead of saying *mtu a-na-*ye *kwenda* (733). But these, and all such reasons, tending to show that most auxiliaries must in writing be separated from the principal verb do not exist for the auxiliary *-a* in the form *nd-a-bona*. Consequently, I consider it as forming a single grammatical word with its verb.

## 893. —

### EXAMPLES SHOWING THE FORMS OF THE PRONOUNS BEFORE -A BONA.

|  | I saw, see have seen, etc. | thou... | he... | we... | you... | they... |
|---|---|---|---|---|---|---|
| Tonga | *nd*a-bona | *u*a-bona | *u*a-bona | *tu*a-bona | *mu*a-bona | *ba*a-bona |
| Kaguru | *na*-langa | *wa*-langa | *ya*-langa | *cha*-langa | *mwa*-langa | *wa*-langa |
| Boondei | *na*-ona | *wa*-ona | a-ona | *ta*-ona | *mwa*-ona | *wa*-ona |
| Nyamwezi | *na*-ona | *wa*-ona | *ya*-ona | *twa*-ona | *mwa*-ona | *wa*-ona |
| Kamba | *na*-ona | *wa*-ona | *ya*-ona | *twa*-ona | *mwa*-ona | *ma*-ona |
| Swahili | *na*-ona | *wa*-ona | a-ona | *twa*-ona | *mwa*-ona | *wa*-ona |
| Senna | *nd*a-ona | *u*a-ona | a-ona | *ta*-ona | *mua*-ona | a-ona |
| Karanga | *nd*a-wona | *wa*-wona | *wa*-wona | *ta*-wona | *mwa*-wona | *wa*-wona |
| Ganda | *na*-labba | *ua*-labba | *ya*-labba | *tua*-labba | *mua*-labba | *ba*-labba |
| Kafir | *nd*a-bona | *wa*-bona | *wa*-bona | *sa*-bona | *na*-bona | *ba*-bona |
| Herero | *mba*-muna | *wa*-muna | (*u*)a-muna | *tua*-muna | *mua*-muna | *va*-muna |
| Rotse | *ka*-mona | *ua*-mona | *ua*-mona | *tua*-mona | *mua*-mona | *a*-mona |
| Angola | *nga*-mona | *ua*-mona | *ua*-mona | *tua*-mona | *nua*-mona | *a*-mona |
| Congo | *ya*-mona | *wa*-mona | *wa*-mona | *twa*-mona | *nwa*-mona | *ba*-mona |
| Yao | *na*-wene | *wa*-wene | a-wene | *twa*-wene | *mwa*-wene | *wa*-wene |
| Mozambique | *ka*-ona | *wa*-ona | a-ona | *na*-ona | *mwa*-ona | *ya*-ona |
| Chwana | *ka*-bona | *ua*-bona | a-bona | *ra*-bona | *loa*-bona | *ba*-bona |
| Mpongwe | *mi* a-yeni | *o*-yeni | a-yeni | *azwe* a-yeni | *anwe* a-yeni | *wa*-yeni |

etc., etc.

*N. B.* It should always be remembered that connective pronouns are changed, not only according to the person of the verb, but also according to the class, as *kacece* ka-*a bona* " the child saw ", *tucece* tu-*a bona* " the children saw ", etc. (644).

### Examples showing the use of the form nd-a-bona
### AND THE LIKE.

**894.** — Tonga : *U-a-tu-itila nyamanzi?* What have you called us for?
*Mbuzie kana nd-a-beja*, Ask him whether I have told a lie.
*U-a-njila, tokue ua kuzua pe*, If you go in, you will never come out (lit. have you gone in... *U-a-njila* is here expressive of a relative past, or future perfect).

**895.** — Ganda (From the *Grammaire Ruganda*) :
*Kababa y-a-dda wa? Y-a-bula?* Where is the king gone to? He has disappeared. P. 84.

*Bwe w-a-ja ewange, w-a-lia e mmere nyingi*, When you came to my place, you ate much porridge.

**896.** — NYAMWEZI (From Steere's *Collections for Nyamwezi*):
*Linze li-a-m-galula*, The world has overturned him, h. e. times are changed. P. 100.
*Twi tw-a-misaja tw-a-wuka*, We awoke and got up. P. 65.
*Ne n-iwaga mwenda, w-a-n-hunga*, While I was stealing some cloth, they bound me. P. 65.

**897.** — BOONDEI (From Woodward's *Collections*):
*W-a-amba se?* What do you say? (Lit. What have you just said?). P. 30.
*W-a-hita hahi? W-a-lawa kuhi?* Where are you going to? Where do you come from? P. 29.

**898.** — SWAHILI (From Steere's *Swahili Tales* and Rankin's *Arab Tales*):
*W-a-taka nini?* What do you want? (St., p. 202.)
*Sasa tw-a-taka ngombe zetu*, To-day we want our cattle. (Rankin, p. 7.)
*W-enda wapi?* (= *W-a-enda...*) Where are you going to? (*Ibid.*, p. 14.)
*Tw-a-ku-pa wasio wetu*, We give you our advice. (*Ibid.*, p. 11.)

**899.** — KARANGA (Cf. Tonga examples, 894.)
*U-a-ti-xobera ni?* What have you called us for?
*U-m-buje kana nd-a-nyepa*, Ask him whether I have told a lie.
*U-a-nguina, utonova pe*, If you go in, you will never come out.

**900.** — ROTSE (From Livingstone's MSS.)
*K-a-komba*, I pray.
*U-a-lingoa*, (The wind) blows.
*Liyoa (lijoa?) li-a-cwa*, The sun comes out.

**901.** — SENNA (From private sources):
*Lelo kw-a-balwa mwana*, To-day a child has been born.
*Nd-a-tambira cakudya*, I have received food.
*Pida ficei, w-a-kwira mu nteme*, When he arrived, he climbed up a tree.

**902.** — KAFIR (From private sources):
*A ndise mntu wa nto, kuba nd-a-citakala*, I am nobody now, because I am ruined.
*Ndibone i mpunzi ete, ya kundibona, y-a-baleka*, I have seen a duiker, which, on seeing me, ran away.
*Kw-a-ti nge nye i mini, kwa Gcaleka kw-a-bizwa i nqina. Kw-a-puma i Qolora ne Qoboqaba, kw-a-yiwa e Cata, kw-a-zingelwa...*, Once upon a time, at Gcaleka's, the hunting pack was called out. There came out the dogs Qolora and Qoboqaba, (the hunters) went to Cata, the hunt was carried on...
*N. B.* In Kafir the form *nd-a-bona* is thus regularly used in historical narratives to express consecutive actions. Cf. 972, 939, etc.
*Kw-a-ti, kw-a kuzingelwa, kw-a-lakwa apo*, and when the hunt was over, the people slept there.
*N. B.* The auxiliary -*a*, thus followed by the infinitive, as in *kw-a ku-zingelwa*, is used in Kafir to render a past tense after " when ". Then in class *MU-ntu* we have *a-ku-bona* instead of *wa-ku-bona*.

**903.** — CHWANA (From Crisp's *Buka ea Merapelo*):
*Morago ga tse k-a-leba...*, After this I beheld... P. 131.
*'Me (bontsi) j-a-gowa ka lencwe je legolo, j-a-re...*, And (the multitude) cried with a loud voice, and said... P. 131.
*'Me Pilato a-kwala lokwalo...*, And Pilate wrote a title... P. 70.
*Baperiseta b-a-araba b-a-re...* The priests answered, and said... P. 70.

*N. B.* The Chwana form *k-a-bona* (= Kafir and Tonga *nd-a-bona*) is distinct from the form *ke-a-bona* (= Kafir *ndi-ya-bona* = Tonga *ndi-la-bona*). Cf. 914, 922, etc.

**904.** — ANGOLA (From Father de Coucto's *Catechism*).
1. Form **ng-a-mona**. *Ko atu ayari awa tu-a-tunda esue*, From these two persons we draw (lit. have drawn) our origin. P. 17.
*Nzambi u-a-ijia kiwa...* God knows that... P. 18.
*A-mu-betele ibeto y-a-vula*, They gave him many blows (lit. blows which are multiplied, 778). P. 22.
*Kia ingin'eki Pontio Pilato u-a-batula uchi...*, When Pontius Pilate had said that... P. 22.
*Iye u-a-tumbula...*, You have just told us...

*N. B.* Thus it may be seen that in Angola the form *ng-a-mona* (= Tonga *nd-a-bona*) is expressive, sometimes of an immediate past, sometimes of an indefinite past, principally in relative clauses.

2. Form **ng-a-mono**. *Kambexi u-a-mi-be o kijilla eki*, That is why he has given you this commandment. P. 18.

*N. B.* According to Father Pedro Dias, S. J., *Angola Gr.*, 1697, p. 24, the form *ng-a-mono* is expressive of a somewhat more remote past than the form *ng-a-mona*.

3. Form **ng-a-monene**. *Nzambi u-a-a-bakele Adam ne Eva mo xi imoxi, u-a-a-kutule anae...*, God placed Adam and Eve in a certain land, he made them his children... ( = Tonga: *Leza u-a-ka ba-beka Adamo a Eva m'muse umue, u-a-ka be-enza baana bakue*).

*N. B.* Hence the Angola form *ng-a-monene* is equivalent to the Tonga *nd-a-ka bona* (916), or, as Father Pedro Dias puts it (*Gr.*, p. 25), is expressive of a more remote past than either *ng-a-mona* or *ng-a-mono*. Cf. 908.

**905.** — HERERO (From Dr. Büttner's *Zeitschrift*, 1887-88):
*O mukajendu ingui e ingui o kakurukaze ngu-a-zepa o vanatye nu ngu-a-tua mo o muatye uetu mo ndyatu*, This woman is that old hag that killed our children, and put our child into a bag. P. 191.
*Tyi ty-a-piti nu tyi ty-a-tara*, When he went out and looked. P. 295.
*E purura ndi u-a-tora*, lit. The *purura* which thou hast carried off. P. 190.
*Ty-(a-)a-munine...*, When he saw... P. 199.

*N. B.* 1. The use of the auxiliary *-a* seems to be nearly, though not quite, the same in Herero as in Angola. In particular, no difference of meaning is noticeable between the form *-a-muna* and the form *a-munu*.

2. In Herero the auxiliary *-a* is in some cases replaced by *-e*, which seems to be its perfect form. Ex. *U-e-ndyi-esa?* Hast thou forsaken me? (p. 202). *A-rire ty-e-mu-tono...*, and when he struck him... P. 199.

## Auxiliaries. 241

**906.** — The auxiliary -*a* is also used in some languages to form, or to introduce, various tenses, principally : —

1° In Tonga and Zulu, to introduce the imperative *ndi-bone*. Ex. : —

TONGA : *A tu-lie toonse*, Let us all eat together.
*A tu-ende* (= Swahili *Na tu-ende*, 924), Let us go.
ZULU : *A bantu a ba-fe*, Men must die.
*N. B.* Such a use of the auxiliary -*a* is unknown in Xosa.

**907.** — 2° In Tonga, Karanga, and Kafir, to form one kind of future with the infinitive *ku-bona*. Then, in Karanga and Kafir the auxiliary *a* nearly always coalesces into *oo* or *o* with the following classifier *ku* or *u*, e. g. *nd-o-bona* = *nd-a u-bona* = *nd-a ku-bona*. Ex. : —

TONGA : *U-a-njila, tokue u-a kuzua pe*, If you go in, you will never come out.
KARANGA : *B-oo-psanda*, They will love (= Tonga *ba-zoo-yanda*, 948).
*Bati " t-oo-nda "* They said : " We shall go ".
KAFIR : *Kwela, wena, nd-o-ku-beta*, lit. climb up, you, or I shall beat you.
*B-o-hluzwa nini u tywala ?* When will the Kafir beer be strained?

**908.** — 3° In Modern Angola, to form one kind of future with the form -*mona*. Ex. *ng-a-mona*, I shall see.

*N. B.* According to Héli Chatelain (*Zeitschrift*, 1890, p. 177), this form differs from the past form *ng-a-mona* (904) only by a slight difference of intonation. The future form *ng-a-mona* is not mentioned in the old *Angola Grammar* of Father Pedro Dias. But we find there instead of it the form *ngi-ka-mona* (975).

**909.** — 4° In Kafir, to form with the participle *ndi-bona* (851) one kind of continuative past, as : —

*Nd-a ndi-bona*, lit. I was seeing.
*B-a be-nga-sebenzi*, They were not working.
*Kw-a kuko u mfazi...*, There was a woman.

**910.** — 5° In Herero, to form a kind of continuative past tense, and also a kind of participle. In this case no connective pronoun is used before the auxiliary -*a*, and the pronoun which follows it takes the ending *e* when we might have expected *a*, as : —

*A pe-kara o mbungu no mbandye*, There was a wolf, and a jackal. (*Zeitschrift*, 1887-88, p. 198.)
*A-rire tyi va-raerere ku ihe a ve-tya...*, And they spoke to their father, saying... (*Ibid.*, p. 191.)
... *u-ka-ende, a mo-ri mo ndyira...*, lit... and go, eating on the road. (*Ibid.*, p. 201.)

## § 4. THE AUXILIARY YA " TO GO ".

**911.** — Though this auxiliary was originally identical with the auxiliary *a* just described, it has become practically different from it in several languages. It is used mostly in Tonga, Kafir, and Chwana.

**912.** — In Tonga it gives one form of remote future tense, as *u-yoo-bona* (= *u-ya u-bona* = *u-ya ku-bona*), he will see. This form of the future is less frequently used than the form *u-zoo-bona* (948).

**913.** — In Kafir it furnishes the continuative present *ndi-ya bona* (= Tonga *ndi-la bona*, 920) " I am seeing ". Ex. *U-ya lila u mnt' a ka Sihamba-nge-nyanga* " he is crying, the child of Sihamba-nge-nyanga." When the verb is immediately followed by a determinative, this form *ndi-ya-bona* is replaced by the simple *ndi-bona* (844).

**914.** — Chwana possesses likewise the form *ke-a-bona* (= *ke-ea bona* " I am seeing ", which is exactly equivalent to the Kafir *ndi-ya-bona*, just as the Chwana verb *go-ea* " to go " is no other than the Kafir *ku-ya*.

**915.** — In Kafir the most usual form expressive of the future indicative is obtained by means of the auxiliary *ya* followed by the infinitive *ku-bona*, as *ndi-ya ku-bona* " I shall see ", lit. " I go to see ", *a ndi-yi ku-bona* " I shall not see ". In the negative form *yi* is sometimes understood, as *a ndi ku-bona* = *a ndi-yi ku-bona*.

**916.** — In the same languages the subjunctive form *-ye* forms in the same manner a subjunctive future, as : *Hamba u-ye ku-bona* " Go to see ", lit. " Go that you may go to see ". Through partial assimilation, *ye* before *ku* in such expressions is generally changed to *yo*, and very often *u-yo* is further contracted to *o*. Hence *hamb'o ku-bona* = *hamba uyo kubona* = *hamba uye kubona*.

**917.** — In Kafir again, the form *nd-a-ya* or *nd-a-ye* (874) followed by a participle forms one kind of continuative past, and a variety of other continuative forms. Cf. 909.

Ex. *Nd-a-ye ndibona, w-a-ye ubona, w-a-ye ebona*, I was seeing, thou wast seeing, he was seeing, etc.

*Nd-a-ye ndi-nga-boni*, I was not seeing.
*Nd-a-ye ndiya kubona*, I would have seen, lit. I was going to see (915).
*Nd-a-ye ndibonile*, I had seen, lit. I was having seen (865).

## § 5. The Auxiliary **ENDA** "to Go", and various Continuative Auxiliaries.

**918.** — In this section I put together several auxiliary forms which have every appearance of being all derived from the one and same verb, though there is no evidence as to which is precisely the independent (non-auxiliary) form of this verb. These are the forms *la*, *na*; *li*, *ne*; *da*; *nda*, *enda*. They are essentially expressive of *continuation*, and most of them are the exact equivalents of the Kafir forms *ya* and *ye* which have just been described. Hence I am led to connect them all with the verb *ku-enda* "to go onwards", which is itself the common Bantu equivalent for the Kafir verb *ku-ya* "to go, to go on". There are however also reasons to connect some of them with the verb *-kala* "to sit". Cf. 942 and 1033.

**919.** — *N. B.* We shall see further on that most of these forms are also used for the copula (1022, 1033, etc.), and that, in such use, their fuller form is in some cases *ila*, *ina*, *ine*, *ele*, etc. Hence, to define more exactly their probable connection with the verbs *ku-enda* "to go", and *ku-kala* "to sit", I should think that the stem *-la* or *-na*, following the general laws concerning monosyllabic stems, becomes an independent verb under the double form *n-da* (or *en-da* = *en-la*) and *i-la* or *i-na* (cf. 284), while it has been kept as an auxiliary under the monosyllabic form *la* or *na* (perfect *li* or *ne*) as also under the strengthened forms *da*, *de*. I should add that the same stem *la* is the second element of the verb *ku-kala* "to sit".

**920.** — The auxiliary which has in Tonga the form *la*, and in several other languages the form *na*, furnishes a tense which is at the same time both *a continuative present* equivalent to our "I am seeing", and *a near future* equivalent to our "I am going to see". It is followed variously by the simple *bona* or by the infinitive *ku-bona*. Its nearest equivalent is *ya* in Kafir (913), *-olo* in Angola (942), the suffix *-nga* in Lower Congo (870), the suffix *-ga* in Kaguru (870), etc.

## 921. — Examples : —

| | I am seeing<br>I am going to see | thou art seeing<br>thou art going to see | he is seeing<br>he is going to see | we are seeing<br>we are going to see | you are seeing<br>you are going to see | they are seeing<br>they are going to see |
|---|---|---|---|---|---|---|
| **Tonga** | *ndi*la bona | *u*la bona | *u*la bona | *tu*la bona | *mu*la bona | *ba*la bona |
| **Swahili** Common | *ni*na ona | *u*na ona | *a*na ona | *tu*na ona | *m*na ona | *wa*na ona |
| **Swahili** {Monosyl. stem} | *ni*na ku-ja<br>I am coming | *u*na ku-ja<br>thou art coming | *a*na ku-ja<br>he is coming | *tu*na ku-ja<br>we are coming | *m*na ku-ja<br>you are coming | *a*na ku-ja<br>they are coming |
| **Ganda** | *u*na labba | *o*no-labba<br>(= ona ku-labba) | *a*na labba | *tu*na labba | *mu*na labba | *ba*na labba |
| **Senna** | *ndi*na ona | *u*na ona | *a*na ona | *ti*na ona | *mu*na ona | *a*na ona |
| **Karanga** { | *ndi*no-wona<br>(= *ndi*nau-wona) | *u*no-wona<br>(= *u*na u-wona) | *u*no-wona<br>(= *u*na u-wona) | *ti*no-wona<br>(= *ti*na u-wona) | *mu*no-wona<br>(= *mu*na u-wona) | *wa*no-wona<br>(= *wa*nau-wona) |
| **Mozambique** { | *ki*no-ona<br>or *gi*na ona | *u*no-ona<br>or *u*na ona | *a*no-ona<br>or *a*na ona | *ni*no-ona<br>or *ni*na ona | *mi*no-ona<br>or *mi*na ona | *ya*no-ona<br>or *ya*na ona |

etc., etc.

### 922. —

**TONGA:**
*U-la ambisia, muame*, You speak well, sir.
*Ue u-la penga*, You are a fool, you.
*Okulia mu-la bona ingombe*, You are going to see cattle there.
*Baati " tu-la inka "*, They said : " We go directly ".

**KARANGA:**
*U-no-lebesa, xe.*
*U-no-penga ewe.*
*Iokuya mu-no-bona ingombe.*
*Bati " ti-no-nda ".*

*N. B.* In Tonga the form *ndi-la bona* sometimes means " we can go ". Ex. *Leza u-la cita zintu zionse*, God can do all things.

### 923. —

**SWAHILI** (Rankin's *Arab Tales):*
*A-ka-jua kana wale wezi wa-na kuja*, And he knew that the thieves were coming.
*N-na kwenda kutafuta paa*, I am going to look for a gazelle.
*Watu a-na kuja leo*, Men will be coming to-day.
*A-ka mw-ona... a-me kaa... a-na lia*, He saw him sitting and weeping.

**MOZAMBIQUE** *(ibid.):*
*Kuzuela wera ale eyi a-na 'roa.* P. 7.
*Gi-na roa u-m-pavela nazoro.* P. 7.
*Atu a-na roa ilelo.* P. 7.
*Ku-m-ona... o-kal'athi... o-na unla.* P. 15.

### 924. — *N. B.* In Swahili the auxiliary *na* is also used to introduce certain imperative clauses, and then it is rendered into Mozambique by *nroa* " to go ". This shows distinctly that the Swahili auxiliary *na* was originally the same as the verb *enda* " to go ". Ex. *Na tu-tume paa wetu* = Moz. *Nroa-ni ni-m-rume nazoro ehu*, let us send our gazelle. Rankin, p. 9.

### 925. — SENNA :
*U-n-enda kupi?* Where are you going to?
*Ndi-n-enda ku musa*, I am going home.
*Ndi-na funa ku-mua*, I want to drink.
*Ndi-na guisa nyumba ya Mulungu*, I can bring down God's House.

### 926. — *N. B.* In the dialect of the Shire the auxiliary *na* seems to be expressive of the past. Ex. *Eliya a-na ku-dza kali*, Elias has already come (Mat., 17, 12). In Senna

*Auxiliaries.* 245

proper we find in similar clauses the auxiliary *da*, which probably is also derived from the verb *enda* " to go ". Ex. *A-da tambila mimba, mb-a-bala mwana*, she conceived and bore a child. See 929.

**927.** — POKOMO (*Zeitschrift*, 1888-89, p. 177):
*Keso ni-na kwenda Wito*, To-morrow I shall go to Witu.
*Ni-na dsakka*, lit. " I am loving " or " I am going to love. "

**928.** — NIKA (Rebmann's *Dictionnary*):
*Moho u-na aka*, the fire is blazing.
*Dzua ri-na ala*, The sun shines.

**929.** — With the auxiliary just described we may connect the Rotse auxiliary *na*, expressive of an action just completed (cf. 926), the Ganda auxiliary *nna*, which, coupled with a negative particle, means " not yet ", and the Kafir auxiliary *da*, expressive of an action *finally* completed, or to be completed. Ex. : —

ROTSE (From Livingstone's Mss.) :
*E-na mana k-a-joaka (?)*, I have finished building.
*A-na kela*, They have come.
*Tu-na tenda* ( = Chwana *re-rihile*), We have done.
GANDA (From the *Grammaire Ruganda*) :
*Si-nna genda*, I have not yet gone. P. 42.
*Ti tu-nna genda*, We have not yet gone. P. 42.
*Kabaka t-a-nna genda*, The king is not yet gone.
KAFIR :
*U-de w-a-teta*, He has spoken at last.
*W-a-da w-a-teta* or *w-a-de w-a-tete* (874), He spoke at last.
*W-o-de a-tete na?* Will he speak at last?
*U-nga-de u-tete*, Take care not to be led to speak.

**930.** — In Tonga, Karanga, Swahili, etc., we find an auxiliary which seems to be to *la* or *na* exactly what *ye* is to *ya* in Kafir, viz. a sort of perfect form. This auxiliary is *li* in Tonga, Swahili, etc., *ne* in Chwana, etc. In most languages it is used exclusively in the formation of present and past tenses, but in Ganda, by a very remarkable exception, it forms a kind of remote future.

**931.** — EXAMPLES :
TONGA : *ndi-li mu ku-bona*, I am seeing, lit. I am in seeing.
   *nd-a-li ku-bona* ( = Kafir *nd-a-ye ndi-bona*, 917) I was seeing.
KARANGA : *nd-a-ru-bona* (contr. for *nd-a-ri u-bona*)   do.
SWAHILI : *ni-li bona* ( = *ni-li ku-bona*)   do.
MOZAMBIQUE : *gi-nu-ona* ( = Karanga *nd-a-ru-ona*)   do.
CHWANA : *ke-ne ke-bona* ( = Kafir *nd-a-ye ndi-bona*)   do.

*ke-ne k-a-bona*, I saw.
GANDA : *n-di labba* ( = *n-li labba*), I shall see.
*n-a-li labba*, I was seeing.
NYAMWEZI : *n-di wona* ( = *n-li wona*), I am seeing.
MPONGWE : *mi a-re dyena-pa*, I have seen.

OTHER EXAMPLES :

**932.** — TONGA
*Ba-la bona bantu ba-li mu kuendenda*, They will see people walking about.
*Mu-zoo-jana bantu ka ba-li ba-a-cabuka*, lit. You will meet the people when they have just risen from the dead.
*Ba-céta ba-a-li kusamba*, Monkeys were swimming.

*N. B.* In Tonga the form *nd-a-li ku-bona* is also expressive of a kind of conditional tense. Ex. *Ta tu-no-inki okulia, tu-a-li ku-fuida 'u-manzi*, let us not go there, we should die in the water.

**933.** — KARANGA :
*Inkao ja-ru-ba ji-xamba*, Monkeys were swimming.
*T-a-ru-fira mu vura*, We should die in the water ( = Tonga *tu-a-li ku-fuida 'u manzi*).

**934.** — SWAHILI :
*Wewe u-li nena...*, You were saying...
*Pa-li ku-wa na-mtu*, There was a man. (Cf. 1044).
*Kondoo zi-li-zo potea*, The sheep which have perished.

**935.** — GANDA :
*Ba-a-li ba-lia*, They were eating (= Tonga *ba-ali ku-lia*).
*Y-a-li y-a-genda edda*, He had gone long before.

**936.** — CHWANA :
*Ke-ne k-a-reka pitse, k-a-e-isa kwagae*, I had bought a horse, then I took it home. (Crisp's *Gr.*, p. 40).
*Dilo cothle di-ne ts-a-dirwa ka ene* (John, 1, 3), All things were made by him.

**937.** — Auxiliary forms more certainly borrowed from *enda* than the preceding are *-enda* in Boondei, *-ondo* in Modern Angola. These form a kind of future. Ex. : —
BOONDEI : *N-enda ni-kunde*, I shall love (Woodward's *Gr.*, p. 33).
ANGOLA : *Ng-ondo beta, ng-ondo kw-iza*, I shall beat, I shall come.

*N. B.* Héli Chatelain thinks that *-ondo* is derived from *andala* " to wish " (*Zeitschrift*, 1889-90, p. 170). Perhaps it would be more correct to say that *-andala* itself is derived from *-enda* " to go ".

**938.** — The verb *-enda* may also be considered as an auxiliary in certain other expressions in which it causes slight irregularities, though without losing its proper and independent meaning. Ex.:—

ANGOLA : *Nde ka bange* ( = *nda-e u-ka bange*), Go and do. Cf. Chat. *Kimb. Gr.*, p. 72.
SENNA : *Ndoko ka-lale* ( = *nda ko u-ka lale*) Go and sleep.
*Ndoko-ni muka lale* (for *nda-ni ko muka lale*), Go(ye) and sleep.
SWAHILI : *Enende ka-lala* or *enende ka-lale* ( = *enda u-ka-lala* or *enda u-ka lale*), Go and sleep.
*Ni-ta kw-enda lala* ( = *nita kwenda ku-lala*), I shall go to sleep.
etc., etc.

**939.** — Various auxiliary forms probably derived from those described in this section may now be considered practically as conjunctions, some of them rendering our " and ", the others our " when ". They are used to connect *consecutive actions*, principally in the past. Such are : —

*NI* in Tonga : Ex. Ni *tu-a-ke-za, tu-a-li basano*, When we came, we were five.
*NLE* or ᴺE in Mpongwe. Ex. *Abraham a-ya*ñi *Isak*, n'a-*ya*ñi *Isak a-ya*ñi *Yakob*, lit. Abraham begat Isaac, and Isaac begat begetting Jacob. (Mat., 1, 2.)
*NA* in Ganda (cf. 111.) Ex. *Daura* n'a-*zala bana*, n'a-*kula* n'a-*kaddiwa*, lit. Daura and begat children, and grew up, and grew old. *(Grammaire Ruganda*, p. 83.) etc., etc.

**940.** — Perhaps we must recognise here the origin of some of the particles which mean " and, with ", such as *na* in Kafir, *ne* in Herero, *le* in Chwana, *ndi* in Senna, etc. (569). We shall see further on that the conjunction '*me* in Chwana, and the like in other languages, are derived from the auxiliary *ma* " to stand " (985).

### § 6. THE AUXILIARIES **KALA** AND **NNA** " TO SIT, TO REMAIN ".

**941.** — In nearly all the Bantu languages we find the verb *ku-kala*, which means properly " to sit ", hence " to remain ", hence in some languages " to be " (56 and 1031). Chwana is one of the rare languages in which this verb does not exist. In most of its dialects it is replaced by *go-nna* (perfect *-ntse*), which has exactly the same meaning.

We may consider the following auxiliary forms as being derived from the one or the other of these verbs : —

**942.** — 1º *Olo* ( = *ala mu*... = *kala mu*...) in Angola, where it forms a kind of continuative present (920). Ex. *Ng-olo banga* ( = *ng-ala mu banga* = *ngi-kala mu ku-banga* = Tonga *ndi-la cita* or *ndi-li mu ku-cita*, 931) " I am doing "; *ng-olo kw-iza* (854) " I am coming ".

Cf. Héli Chatelain's *Kimbundu Gr.* in the *Zeitschrift*, 1889-90, p. 180.

**943.** — 2° *Kaza* (= *kala*) in Tonga and Swahili. This is used to introduce eventualities, and may be rendered practically by " if ", so that, if we looked at it from a European point of view, it might be said to be a mere conjunction. Ex. in Tonga : *Kana n-ku-fua, ndi-la-fua*, If I am to die, I shall die ; in Swahili : *A-ka enda ku-tazama kana pa-na maji anwe*, And he went to see if there was water to drink (Rankin's *Arab Tales*, p. 3).

**944.** — *N. B.* In Swahili *kana* is also used as a true conjunction with various other meanings, such as " like, as ", etc. We find equally in Angola the quasi-conjunction *kala* " as ". Ex. *Eye u-eri o maju kala matemu*, Your teeth are like hoes, lit. Thou art (as to) the teeth like hoes. (Héli Chatelain's *Kimbundu Gr.*, p. 108).

**945.** — 3° *Nna* (perfect *-ntse*) in Chwana, expressive of a formally continuative tense. Ex. *Ke-ntse ke-bona* " I am seeing ", *ke-tla nna ke-bona* " I shall continue to see ", lit. " I shall remain seeing ".

**946.** — 4° *Na* in Tonga. In positive clauses it implies a repetition of the same action in the future. With a negative auxiliary it answers to our " never " in imperative clauses. Ex. *Ba-noo-bona* (= *ba-na ku-bona*, cf. 948) " they will see repeatedly ", *ta tu-noo-jayi* (= *ta tu-ne ku-jayi*), let us never kill.

**947.** — 5° *Enyo* (= *ene ku*) in Angola, expressive of habit. Ex. *Ng-enyo-beta* (= *ng-ene ku-beta*), I am accustomed to beat. (Héli Chatelain, in the *Zeitschrift*, 1889-90, p. 179). Cf. n. 825.

### § 7. The Auxiliary ZA or IZA " to Come ".

**948.** — In a large number of Bantu languages the auxiliary *za* " to come ", variously transformed to *dza, dsa, tlha*, etc., forms a remote indicative future. Cf. 920. It is then followed in some languages by the infinitive *ku-bona*, in others by the simple *bona*. Ex. : —

| | | | | | |
|---|---|---|---|---|---|
| Tonga : | *ndi-zoo-bona,* | | I shall see ; | *u-zoo-bona,* | he will see ; etc. |
| | (= *ndi-za ku-bona*, (249) | | | | |
| Kafir : | *ndi-za ku-bona* | ,, | | *u-za ku-bona* | ,, ,, |
| Old Angola : | *ng-iza ku-mona* | ,, | | *u-iza ku-mona* | ,, ,, |
| Lunda : | *ni-eza ku-mana* | ,, | | *u-eza ku-mana* | ,, ,, |
| Ganda : | *n-ja ku-labba* | ,, | | *a-ja ku-labba* | ,, ,, |
| Pokomo : | *ni-dsa ona* | ,, | | *ka-dsa ona* | ,, ,, |
| Suto : | *ke-tlha bona* | ,, | | *o-tlha bona* | ,, ,, |

## Auxiliaries. 249

CHWANA PROPER : *ke-tla bona*        I shall see ; *o-tla bona*    he wil see; etc.
SWAHILI :        *(ni)-ta ona*            „    *a-ta ona*        „        „
 do. (monos.)    *ni-ta ku-la*,        I shall eat ; *a-ta ku-la*, he will eat; etc.
etc., etc.

**949.** — *N. B.* 1. In Modern Angola the old form *ng-iza ku-mona* is replaced by *ng-ondo-mona* (937). But the perfect of *-iza*, which is *-eji(le)*, furnishes the modern conditional form *ng-ojo-mona* = *ng-eji ku-mona*, I would see, etc. Cf. 947, 942, 937, and 995.

2. It might be questioned whether the auxiliary *ta* in Swahili originally meant " to come ", because we find in the same language the auxiliary *ja*, which certainly has this meaning (963), as also because in Karanga, which is closely related to Swahili, the verb *ta* means " to do ". However, considering that the Swahili *-ote* " all ", *tanu* " five ", etc., were originally the same words as the Chwana *-otlhe*, *-tlhanu*, etc., I am led to think that the Swahili *ta* is also etymologically identical to the Chwana *-tlha* or *-tla*, which certainly means " to come ". In relative clauses in Swahili, the auxiliary *ta* is replaced by *-taka* " to want ".

3. In Kafir the form *ndi-za ku-bona* is little used. The ordinary future is *nd-o-bona* (907) or *ndi-ya ku-bona* (915).

### Various examples :

**950.** — TONGA :
*Tu-zoo-inka ejunza* (= ...*a ijunza*), We shall go to- morrow.
*Bantu babotu ba-zoo-ya ku-li Leza*, The good people will go to God.

**951.** — GANDA *(New Testament)*:
*O mwana-we bw'a-mu-saba e mmere, a-ja ku-mu-wa ejinja? Oba bw'a-saba e kyenyanja, a-ja ku-mu-wa o musota?* If his son shall ask him bread, will he reach him a stone? Or if he shall ask him a fish, will he reach him a serpent ? (Mat., 7, 9-10).

**952.** — OLD ANGOLA (Father de Coucto's *Catechism*) :
*Ke mu-iza ku-fua*, You will not die. P. 17.
*Ng-iza ku-mi-beka ko eulu*, I shall place you in heaven. P. 17.
*He mu-a-somboka o kijilla kiami, mu iza ku-fua, ke mu-iza kuya ko eulu*, If you break my commandment, you shall die, you shall not go to heaven. P. 18.

**953.** — SWAHILI (Steere's *Swahili Tales*) :
*Baba yangu kesho a-ta ku-la tende*, To-morrow my father will eat dates. P. 208.
*A-taka-o pona a-ta-pona, na a-taka-o ku-fa, a-ta ku-fa*, He that will escape will escape, and he that will die will die. P. 264.

**954.** — SUTO (New Testament) :
*U-thla bona tse-kholo go tseo*, Greater things than these shalt thou see. (John, 1, 50).
*U-tlha bitsoa Kefase*, Thou shalt be called Cephas. (John, 1, 42).

**955.** — In Tonga, and still more in Kafir and Suto, the same auxiliary is often used in its subjunctive form *-ze* (Suto *-tlhe*) to supply a future subjunctive. Then in Tonga the verb which follows it generally admits the ending *-e*. Then also in Kafir, Chwana proper, and Suto, the regular connective pronoun of *-ze* or *-tlhe* is often either replaced by the indefinite pronoun *i* (Chwana *e*), or understood. Ex. : —

**956.** — TONGA :
*Tu-zoo-za tu-zoo mu-suaye* ( = ...*tu-ze ku-mu-saye*), We shall come to pay you a visit.

**957.** — KAFIR :
*Ndi-kulule-ni, i-ze ndi-fe,* Untie me before I die.
*Yi nto nina le iti, nxa kuna i mvula, i-hlokome i-ze i kanyise?* What is that which, when it rains, (first) thunders, *then* flashes?
*Ze si baleke ngo mso,* let us race to-morrow. Cf. *ma si-baleke* (978), let us run (some time or other). Cf. 874.
*U-z' u-nga-ti, w-a ku-kontwa zi zinja, u-kale,* Take care, if you are barked at by dogs, not to utter any cry.

**958.** — SUTO (New Testament) :
*'Me le-rapelle... le-tlhe le-be bana ba Ntat' alona...* (Mat., 5, 44-45), And pray... that you may be the children of your Father...
*...tlama e-tlhe e-kokomoge kaofela* (Mat. 13, 33), ...until the whole was leavened.
*N. B.* Hence, perhaps, in Swahili, the conjunction *ha-ta* or *ha-tta* " until ", = Suto *etlhe* = Kafir *i-ze*. Ex. *Bassi i-ka-wa hali hiyo, hatta tu-ka-fika,* and so things were, till we came (Steere's *Swah. Tales,* p. 162).

**959.** — In Kafir the same auxiliary is variously used to connect *consecutive* actions. Ex. *W-a-hamba w-a-za w-a-fika,* he went, until he arrived ( = Swahili... *hatta a-ka fika) ; u-nxamele u ku-ze ndi-hambe,* he wishes me to go.
*N. B.* In the last example, *u ku-ze* is the infinitive form, but *za* is changed to *ze* by the vowel-attraction of *ndi-hambe*.

**960.** — The same auxiliary is often used in conjunction with a negative auxiliary, in Kafir and Karanga with the same meaning as our " never ", in Swahili with the meaning of our " not yet ". Then in Swahili its form is *ja*. Ex. : —

**961.** — KARANGA :
*A ndi-ja ka bona* ( = Tonga *sikue ndaka bona,* 964), I never saw.
*A ba-ja ru-n-tuma* ( = Tonga *ta bakue baali kumutuma,* 964 and 931), they never would send him.

**962.** — KAFIR :
*A ndi-zange ndi-bone* ( = *a ndi-za-nga...,* 874 and 870).
*A ka-zang 'a-bone,* he never saw.
*Az 'a-nga-ze a-kangele,* he must never look.
Notice the use of the subjunctive form *ndi-bone* after *zange*.

**963.** — SWAHILI (Steere's *Swahili Tales*):

*A-ka m-kuta h-a-ja amka*, he found him not yet awake. P. 216.

*Nao ha-wa-ja amka, na mvua ha-i-ja anuka*, and they were not yet awake, and the rain had not yet held up. P. 222.

*Ni-ta kwenda mimi kabla h-a-ja m-leta mtu hapa*, I will go myself before he sends any one here, lit... when he has not yet sent...

*U-ta m-pata a-si-je lala*, you will seize him before he goes to sleep. (Krapf's *Dict.*, p. XXIX.)

*N. B.* 1. In Swahili the same auxiliary is found sometimes in relative clauses, as expressive of something hypothetical. Ex. *ni-ja-po penda*, if I happen to love, in case I should love. *Ni-ja-po ku-ja*, in case I should come.

2. In Pokomo the auxiliary *dsa* together with a negative particle means " not yet " as *ja* in Swahili. Ex. *Ta hu-dsa ku-dsa*, we have not yet come. (*Zeitschrift*, 1888-89, p. 183.)

### § 8. THE AUXILIARY **KUJ**.

**964.** — In Tonga we find in negative clauses the auxiliary *kui* — probably a negative form of a defective verb *kua* —, which with negative particles answers to our " never " or " not at all ", exactly as *ja* in Karanga and *zange* in Kafir (960-962). Ex. : —

*Si-kue nd-a-ka bona*, I never saw.
*To-kue* ( = *ta u-kue*) *u-a-ka bona*, Thou didst never see.
*Ta a-kue u-a-ka bona*, He never saw.
*Ta tu-kue tu-a-ka bona*, We never saw, etc.

I should be inclined to trace to this construction the origin of the Swahili and Pokomo past negative tense, which is as follows : —

SWAHILI : *Si kw-ona*, I have not seen ; *h-u kw-ona*, thou hast not seen ; *h-a kw-ona*, he has not seen ; *ha tu kw-ona*, we have not seen ; etc.

POKOMO : *Si kw-ona*, I have not seen ; *k-u kw-ona*, thou hast not seen ; *k-a kw-ona*, he has not seen ; *ta hu kw-ona*, we have not seen ; etc.

*N. B.* We shall see further on that *kui* is used in Tonga to render our " to have " in negative clauses, as in *si-kue ngubo* " I have no clothes ", *ta ba-kue ngubo* " they have no clothes." Hence there is no doubt that it means properly " to have ", though it be used exclusively in negative clauses ; but, as I find nothing like it in the other languages, I am still at a loss as to its original meaning.

### § 9. THE AUXILIARY **KA**.

**965.** — The auxiliary *ka*, which probably stands to the verb *-inka* " to start, to step, to go off " in the same relation as the auxiliary *la* or *na* to the verb *-enda* " to go forward, to walk ", seems to be essentially expressive of a change of action, or state, or position. But its exact value is somewhat different in the different languages. Hence we had better study it first in one language, then in another.

## Tonga.

**966.** — 1° *A-ka* or the auxiliary *ka* preceded by the auxiliary *a* is expressive of a comparatively remote past, or more exactly of something done formerly or completely. Ex. : —

*Monze ula busia bantu ba-a-ka fua ciindi*, Monze can raise to life people who died formerly.
*Bakalanga ba-a-ka zua ku Bunyai*, The Karanga came *in former times* from the Bunyai.
*Muanaena ngu-a-ka yasana a Bambala*, Muanaena is the man who fought once with the Bambala.
*Tu-a-ka jana i nyika i-a-ka anzua*, We found the earth already made.
*Sue tu-a-ka zoo-jana i nyika i-a-ka anzua* ( = ... *tu-a-ka za ku-jana* ..., n. 948), We came to find the earth already made.
*Inyue no mu-a-ka fua, mu-a-ka ba kuli Leza*..., You who are dead, and have gone to live with God...
*Zikua u-a-ka kede mu Matezi*, Mr. N. lived formerly in the Matezi valley.

**967.** — 2° *Ka* is also the proper auxiliary of the negative future. Ex. *ta ndi-koo-bona* ( = *ta-ndi-ke ku-bona*, cf. 948), I shall not see.

**968.** — 3° *Ka* at the beginning of a clause before the form *ndi-bona* has an imperative or precative power. Ex. : —

*Ka mu-ndi-lapela kutede*, Pray to me in this manner.
*Ka mu-tu-kombelela kuli Leza*, Pay homage to God for us.
*Ko-tu-pa mvula* ( = *ka u-tu-pa*..., 249), Give us rain.
*Balapelela baana baabo ka beenda* ( = *ba-enda*, 249) *bubotu*, They pray for their children that they may walk in the way of happiness.
*Kenziana na ?* ( = *Ka ndi-ziana na ?*), Must I dance ?

**969.** — 4° *Ka* followed by the subjunctive form *-bone* implies distinctly motion to some distance. Ex. : —

*Inka ka-lume ndaba muntu* ( = ...*u-ka-lume*), Go and bite So-and-So.
*Me ndinka ndi-ka-tole ngombe na ?* Must I go to fetch the cows ?

**970.** — *N. B.* We have considered in a previous chapter the use of the relative particle *ka* to render our " if, when, while, and ". In many instances a doubt might arise as to whether *ka* is such a relative particle, or an auxiliary of the kind just described. In most of these doubtful cases I would take it to be the relative particle. But, even as such, I consider it to be related to the auxiliary *ka*. Cf. 527.

## Swahili.

**971.** — The auxiliary *ka* before the form *-bona* seems to express generally the transition to a new act, and in a few cases the perfect completion of an act. Before the subjunctive form *-bone* it supposes motion to some distance, as in Tonga. In all its positions it acts as a prefix inseparable from the verb, as if it were not properly an auxiliary, but an objective connective pronoun referring to a notion of time. Cf. 970. Hence it admits no *ku* between itself and monosyllabic or vowel verbs, and in the second person plural of the imperative it supplies the form *ka-bone-ni* " see ", instead of *m-ka-bone*. Examples (from Steere's *Swahili Tales*) : —

*Wali kuwa wapi hatta mtenge wangu u-ka-liwa?* Where were you all the time till my date-tree was *all* eaten ? P. 204.

*A-ona-cho chote kati ka mji hu-kamata a-ka-la,* Whatever he sees in the town, he catches it, and *straightway* eats it. P. 248.

*A-ka-sangaa, akili zake zi-me potea, mashikio yake ya-me ziba, miguu yake i-ka-tetemeka, ulimi u-ki-wa mzito, a-ka-tekwa,* And he stared, and his wits forsook him, and his ears were stopped, and his legs trembled, and his tongue was heavy, and he was all bewildered. P. 208.

*Ondoka u-ka-tazame,* Get up and look. P. 203.

*Enenda wewe u-ka-tazame,* Go thou and look. P. 228.

*Enenda ka-zoe* (= ...*u-ka-zoe*), Go and gather the dates. P. 203.

*Ni-ka-tazame,* Let me go and look. P. 240.

*Ka-tazame-ni,* Look ye. P. 240.

**972.** — *N. B.* The third of these examples shows that *ka* before *-bona* expresses rather *transitory* or *completed* facts, and the other auxiliaries *me* and *ki* *continued* situations or *incomplete* facts. It does not seem correct to say, as is found everywhere, that *ka* simply means " and ", because several other auxiliaries might be rendered by " and " just as well.

## Herero.

**973.** — The auxiliary *ka* seems to imply in every case motion to some distance. Examples (from Dr. Büttner's *Märchen der Ovaherero, Zeitschrift,* 1887-88).

*Kahavandye, ka-teka,* Jackal, go and fetch water. P. 201.

*Ka-teke* (= *u-ka-teke*), Go and fetch water. P. 202.

*Ka-tore,* Go and take. P. 204.

*Me aruka me ka-pura e purura randye,* I am going back to ask for my *purura*. P. 190.

*Me ka-eta e purura ra mama,* I shall bring the *purura* of my mother. P. 190.

*Ndino me ka-teka,* To-day I go to fetch water. P. 201.

*Ke-ndyi-pahere o rukune,* Go and fetch firewood for me. P. 191.

*A-i a-ka-teka*, And he went and fetched water. P. 201.
*Kahavandye u-a-tuarere ina ye, a-ka-tua m'o muina*, The fox took his mother, and went to put her into a hole. P. 200.

### Kafir.

**974.** — With a negative particle the auxiliary *ka* means " not yet ". In the other cases it seems to be expressive of a *momentary* act, or an *accidental* event. Ex. : —

*A ndi-ka boni*, I do not yet see, or I have not yet seen.
*Ka u-kangele*, Just have a look.
*Ke ndi-kangele* (= *ndi-ke ndi-kangele*, 874), Let me just have a look.
*U-ke w-a-bona na ?* Did he see at all? *U kuba u-ke w-a-bona*, If he ever saw.
*W-a-ke w-a bona* (= *w-a-ka w-a-bona*, 874), He once saw.
*Kw-a-ka kw-a-ko i nkosi ngapa y-a-ti...* Once upon a time there was a king in this neighbourhood who said...
*... a-nga-ke a-bone*, ... lest he should happen to see.

*N. B.* In my " *Outline of a Xosa-Kafir Grammar* ", p. 64, I have, with several other scholars, considered the auxiliary *ka* as being immediately related to the verb *ku-ka* " to dip ". This view is not correct.

### Other Languages.

**975.** — In most of the other languages, the auxiliary *ka* seems to have more or less the same power as in Tonga, or in Herero. In Chwana this auxiliary is pronounced *nka*. Ex. : —

GANDA :    *Ka n-dabbe* ( = Tonga *ke m-bona)*, Let me see; *Ka tu-labbe* (= Tonga *ka tu-labba )*, Let us see.
ROTSE :    *Ko-kela mo mondi* (= Tonga *ko-njila m'munzi* = *ka u-njila...*), come into the town.
OLD ANGOLA :    *Ngi-ka-zola* (= Herero *me ka-hora ?)* I shall love (Father Dias' Gr., p. 121, cf. 908).
MODERN ANGOLA :    *Ng-a-ka-beta* (= Old Angola *ngi-ka-beta)*, I shall beat (Chatelain, *Zeitschrift*, 1889-90, p. 178).
LUNDA :    *N-a ka dima*, I shall plough.
CHWANA :    *Ga nka ke-bona, ga o-nka o bona* (= Tonga *ta ndi-koo-bona, ta u-koo-bona )*, I shall not see, thou shalt not see.

*N. B.* I have no evidence of this auxiliary being used in other tenses in Chwana. The Chwana auxiliary *ka* is quite different from this : it corresponds to the Kafir *nga* (1000).

### § 10. THE AUXILIARY **INSI**.

**976.** — *Insi* is a verbal form which we shall find further on regularly used in Tonga as the copula in negative clauses. In the same language it is also frequently used as an auxiliary after negative particles. Ex. *T-insi ndi-la bona*, I cannot see ; *t-insi ba-la mu-njila* or *ta ba-insi ba-la mu-njira*, they cannot enter therein. Considering this form in the light of phonetic laws, I do not feel authorized to see in it anything else than the *-boni* form of the verb *ku-insia* " to cause to go off ", whence " to be able (?) ", which is the causative of *ku-inka* " to go off ". It is probably related to the Ganda *ku-inza* " to be able ", e. g. in *si kia-inza* " I am no longer able ". Cf. *Grammaire Ruganda*, p. 83.

§ 11. THE AUXILIARIES **MA** AND **BA** " TO STAND, TO STOP ".

**977.** — As the Kafir auxiliary *be* is the nearest equivalent of the Swahili *me*, it is probable that *ma* and *ba* are essentially one and the same auxiliary. I have as yet no evident example of the use of this auxiliary in Tonga, but it is one of those most frequently used in Kafir, Swahili, and Herero. It helps principally to the formation of continuative tenses, and thus generally is the opposite of *ka*. In Kafir it also implies in many cases a *causal* notion. It is remarkable that in this language its consonant in past tenses is *b*, while before imperatives it is *m*, and that its infinitive form is *ku-ba* in the Xosa, though it is *(k)u-ma* in the Zulu dialect of the Kafir language. Ex. : —

**978.** — KAFIR :
*Be ndi-bone u-si-za* (= *ndi-be ndi-bonile u-si-za*), It is because I saw you coming.
*Kwela*. — *Hayi, e-b' e-te u bawo ze ndi-nga kweli*, Climb up. — No, because my father has said that I should not climb up.
*U yise no nina* **be** *be-nga vumi u ku-ba*... His father and mother would not allow him to...
*U ku-ba* (Zulu *u-ma*) *u-b' u-nga ngweni, nge u-ya*..., If you were not lazy, you would go...
*Kw-a-tiwa* " *u nwaba ma lu-yo ku-ti : A bantu ma ba-nga fi* ", lit. There was said : " Let the chameleon go to say : Men must not die ". (Callaway's *Unkulunkulu*, p. 3).
*Vuma u ku-ba ma ndi-ye* (Zulu *vuma u-ma ma ndi-ye*), lit. Allow that I go, i. e. allow me to go.

**979.** SWAHILI :
*A-ka-mw-ona mtu a-me-kaa*, he saw a man sitting (Rankin, p. 15).
*Tende zi-me-liwa na ndege zote*, the dates have all been eaten by birds (Steere's *Swah. Tales*, p. 203). Cf. 972.

**980.** — HERERO (*Zeitschrift*, 1887-88) :
*O ngurova, tyi ma mu-aruk' o kurara*, In the evening, when you begin to sleep. P. 191.

*Nu tyi m-a-riri...*, And while he cried... P. 191.
*Ne a-ende a-me-utuka*, And she went on walking. P. 190.

**981.** — Pokomo and Rotse :
Pokomo . *Ni-ma dsakka*, I have loved (*Zeitschrift*, 1888-89, p. 178).
Rotse : *Mo-ma tenda* (= Chwana *Lo-rihile*), You have done.

**982.** — *N. B.* 1. From this same auxiliary are derived in Kafir the particles *ku-ba* and *u ku-ba* " if, because ". Ex. *U ku-ba u-tsho*, if you say so, because you say so. — We find likewise in Ganda *oba* " because, since ". Ex. *Oba o-maze*, since you have finished. — The Chwana particle *go-bane* " because " seems rather to be derived from *-mana* " to finish " (1011), which is itself a derivative of the verb *-ma* " to stop ".

**983.** — 2. We shall see further on (1012) that the auxiliary *buya* " to return " is in some cases reduced to *ba* or *be*. This makes it difficult in some instances to make out the proper meaning of these forms.

**984.** — 3. In Senna there is an auxiliary *mba* which is probably related to those described in this section. Its use is twofold. First it introduces imperative clauses, exactly as the Kafir auxiliary *ma*. Ex. *Mba ti-cite nyumba iatu*, Let us make our house. Secondly it is used to connect historical facts, somewhat in the same manner as the Ganda conjunction *na* (939). Ex. *Yesu u-a-lamuka pa meza, mb-a-kuata madzi, mb-a-gogoma pansi, mb-a-suka miendo ia disipura*, Jesus rose up from table, and took water, and knelt down, and washed the feet of the disciples.

**985.** — 4. The Chwana conjunction *'me* or *mi* " and " was probably not different originally from the Swahili and Herero *me*. It is used to join sentences, not substantives, together. Ex. *Abraham a-tsala Isaka, 'me Isaka a-tsala Yakobo*, Abraham begat Isaac, and Isaac begat Jacob. Cf. 940.

## § 12. The Auxiliaries CI, KI, SI, SA, etc.

**986.** — There is in most Bantu languages an auxiliary which more formally than any other expresses *duration* or *non-achievement*. Its form undergoes nearly the same phonetic changes as the classifier *ci* (492\*), to which it is etymologically related.

**987.** — In Tonga its form is *ci*. It may be rendered variously. However, in most cases its nearest English equivalent is the adverb *still*. Ex. : —

Still :    *Liwanika u-ci li wo*, Liwanika is still there.
        *U-ci-li muumi*, He is still alive.
Just :    *Mu-a-zua anze ka mu-ci buka, mu-a-zoo-jana ba a-ka sika*, If you come out just when you awake, you will find that they have come.
Already :  *U-la cisa, u-ci zezela, u-ci ua*, He suffers atrociously, he already staggers, finally he falls.
Not yet (with negation) : *Ta a-ci fui pe, u-a-luka, u-a-pona*, he shall not die yet, he vomits and recovers.

**No longer, no more** (with negation): *Bo ba-a-ka buka ta ba-ci fui pe*, those who have risen will die no more, will not die again.

**988.** — *N. B.* The particle *ci* at the beginning of a clause means " while ". In this case I consider it to be a relative particle (787) rather than an auxiliary. Ex. *Mbuli ci tu-bereka ci tu-zuete ezi ngubo, umue muntu u-a-tu-bona...* " Suppose that, while we work wearing these clothes, another man sees us... " This is one more of those instances which show the close relation between classifiers and auxiliaries. Cf. 970, 971.

**989.** — In Ganda the form of the same auxiliary is *kia*. It may also be rendered variously. Ex. : —

**Still** : *Tu-kia li balamu*, We are still alive, (= Tonga *tu-ci li baumi*).
**While** : *Tula wano, tu-kia genda Mbuga*, Remain here while we go to Mbuga.
**Not at all** (with negation): *Si-kia lia*, I do not eat at all (I no longer eat ?)
Cf. *Grammaire Ruganda*, p. 46.

**990.** — In Rotse its form is *si*. It equals " still ". Ex. : —
*O-si tenda*, he still does (= Chwana *o-sa dira*).

**991.** — In Kafir it has one form *sa*, which properly means " still, yet ", and another form *se*, which properly means " already ". The latter form is used principally to introduce participles. Ex. : —
**Still** : *Ndi-sa ba-bona*, I see them yet.
*Ba-sa pilile*, They are still in good health.
**No longer** (with negation) : *A ndi-sa ba-boni*, I no longer see them.
**Already** : *Se be-qala u ku-lima*, Already they begin to plough.
*Ms' u ku-gibilisa le nja nga matye, uya ku-yi-bona se yi kufupi, se yi-kwela kuwe*. Never throw stones at this dog, you would soon see it close to you, already coming up to you.
*Kw-a-yiwa kw-a-fikwa se be-m-bulele*, The people went and came up to them, when they had already killed him.

**992.** — In Chwana the same auxiliary has the double form *sa*, which means " still ", and *kile* (Kafir and Suto *se*), which means " already ". To these may be added the form *ese*, which with a negative particle means " not yet ". Ex. : —

**Still** : *O-sa-bona* or *o-sa ntse a-bona*, he still sees. (With regard to *ntse*, see n. 945).
**Already** (in Chwana proper) : *N-kile k-a-bona, o-kile o-a-bona*. I have already seen, thou hast already seen (= Kafir *se ndi-bonile*).
**Already** (in Suto) : *Selepe se-se se-beiloe*... The axe has already been put...
**Not yet** : *Ga ke-ese ke-bona*, I have not yet seen.

**993.** — In Swahili the same auxiliary is pronounced *ki*. It seems to be, like the auxiliary *ka* (971), a prefix inseparable from the principal verb, and to form exclusively a kind of participial expression. Ex. : —

*Paka a-ka-hama njia nyingine, a-ki-kamata*, The cat removed to another road, continuing to prey in the same way. (St. *Swah. Tales*, p. 248).

*Ni-me ambiwe ni-ku-pe khati, u-ki-ishe soma tu-fanye safari*, I have been told to give you the letter, and that, *when* you have finished reading it, we should start on our journey. (*Ibid.*, p. 152.)

*Jua li-ki-chwa wa-ka-fanya khema zao, wa-ka-lala*, When the sun set they got their tents ready, and slept. (*Ibid.*, p. 158.)

*A-ki-pita mtu hu-m-la*, *Whenever* a person passes, he eats him.

**994.** — I cannot make out with certainty to which verbs these auxiliaries originally belonged. The Tonga form *ci*, as well as the Ganda *-kia*, and the Kafir and Chwana *-sa*, seem to belong to the verb *-cia* " to dawn "(Ganda *-kia*, Kafir *-sa*, etc., cf. 52*), but this, while explaining the meaning " already ", would give no reason for the meaning " still ". On the other hand the Tonga *ci* may well be also a contracted form of *-kede*, which is the perfect of *-kala* " to sit, to remain ", and I suspect that, if a Tonga, for instance, were asked to develop the notions implied in the sentence *u-ci bona* " he is still seeing ", he would render it by *u-kede u-bona* " he remains seeing. " Again, the Kafir *se* " already " is sometimes replaced by *sele*, which is the perfect of *-sala* " to remain behind " (= Tonga *-siala*), and, consequently, may well be derived from this verb, or from the Tonga *-sia* " to leave behind ", a simpler verb from which *-siala* itself is derived.

Hence, finally, I am of opinion that the auxiliaries *ci, ki, kia, sa, se,* etc., are in fact related to the various verbs *-cia, -siala, -kede,* etc., and that in some cases they have more of the meaning of one, in other cases of another, viz. where they mean " already ", or " to begin ", they originally were no other than the verb *-cia* " to dawn ", and where they mean " still ", or " to continue ", they are more directly connected with *-sia* " to leave behind ", or with *-kede*, the perfect of *-kala*. Cf. 502.

## § 13. The Auxiliary **NGA**.

**995.** — I do not yet know whether this auxiliary is used in Tonga. It is found in Kafir, Swahili, Pokomo, Herero, Ganda, etc., where it generally forms a kind of *hypothetical* or *conditional* tense. It is derived from *-nga* " to wish " [originally " to bend the body, as when entering a Kafir hut (?) "]. Its perfect and subjunctive form is *-nge*. Ex. : —

**996.** — Kafir :
*U-nga ya na? Ndi-nga ya.* Do you feel inclined to go? I do.
*Nge ndi-si-za, ndixakekile,* I wished to come, but I could not do so.
*Ezo ntaka zi-ku-fumene e matoleni azo, a ku-nge tandi u kupinda uye apo zizalele kona,* If these birds found you near their young, you *would* not like to go again where they have their nest.
*U-ya z-azi na i nkomo? Ewe, ndi-nga z-azi.* Can you manage cattle? I think I can.
*A maxalanga u-nga-ti, u kuba ute waya e-si-tya, aza a-ku-bona, a-nga ku-tya,* lit. Vultures, you would say, if you went (near them) while eating and they saw you, that they *have a mind* to eat you.

N. B. In cl. *MU-ntu* Kafirs say in affirmative clauses *a-nga-bona* " he may see, he would see ", not *u-nga-bona*, but in relative clauses they say *o-nga-bona* " who may see ". Ex. *Nanku u mntu o-nga-ya,* Here is a man who may go.

**997.** — SWAHILI (from Steere's *Handbook*, p. 139):
*A-nga-wa*, " though he be " or " he would be ".
*Ni-nga-li penda*, " I should have loved " or " had I loved... " Cf. 1002.
*Si-nga-li penda*, " I should not have loved " or " had I not loved... "
*Kama u-nga-li ku-wa po hapa, ndugu yangu a-nga-li pona*, If you had been here, my brother would have got well.
*Ni-nge penda*, " I should love " or " if I did love ".
*Si-nge penda, ha tu-nge penda*, " I should not, we should not, love " or " if I did, if we did not, love ".
*Kama u-nge ku-wa na akili, mali yako u-nge dumu nayo*, lit. If you were with wits, your property you would continue with it, i. e. if you were a man of sense, your property would still be yours.

*N. B. Nga* is used only before monosyllabic verbs, the others require *nge*.

**998.** — POKOMO *(Zeitschrift,* 1888-89, p. 180):
*Ni-nge dsakka*, I should have loved.
*Ta hu-nge dsakka*, We should not have loved.
*Yeo ni-nge ku-dsa mudsina, luka muntu tywangu ka-na-weza*, To day I should have gone to town, but my man could not (go).

**999.** — HERERO *(Zeitschrift,* 1887-88):
*Nga tu-tyite vi?* [= *U-nga tu-tyite vi?* (?)], What do you wish us to do? P. 191.
*Nga tu-zepere mumue*, Let us kill together. P. 200.
*Nu nga tu-zepe o mama*, And let us kill our mothers. P. 200.

**1000.** — CHWANA:
*N-ka reka, o-ka reka, o-ka reka*, I am, thou art, he is, inclined to buy.
*Ke-ne n-ka reka*, I would have bought, etc.

**1001.** — An auxiliary like to the above, though perhaps more expressive of wish, is *singa* in Ganda, *sinka* in Rotse. Ex. : —

GANDA *(Grammaire Ruganda)*:
*Singa n-dia* (= *n-singa n-lia*), I should like to eat. P. 38.
*Singa tu-a-genze*, We should have gone. P. 38.
*Singa nina e mmere, singa n-dia kakano*, If I had food, I would eat now. P. 39.
*Singa w-a-genda edda, w-a-ndi-tuse kakano*, If you had gone before, you would already have arrived. P. 39.
ROTSE (Livingstone's Mss.):
*U-sinka ko-i-ba* (= Chwana *o-batla go-i-polaea* or *o-ka i-polaea*), He is nearly killing himself.

**1002.** — *N. B.* 1. The fact that in Swahili the auxiliary *nga*, and in Ganda the auxiliary *sinka*, is used not only in the apodosis, but also in the protasis of conditional sentences, must probably be explained by considering that in fact both may include the notion of some sort of wish ; so that, for instance, the Ganda sentence *singa nina e mmere, singa ndia kakano* might be rendered literally by " I wish I had food, (because) I should like to eat now ".

**1003.** — 2. In Karanga the verb *da* " to wish " may in some instances be considered as an auxiliary nearly equivalent to the Kafir *nga*. Ex. *u-no-da gara* (= *u-no-da (k)u-gara*), he wishes to remain.

## § 14. THE AUXILIARY TI " TO SAY ".

**1004.** — 1° In most Bantu languages the verbs which mean " to speak ", as *-ambola* in Tonga, are seldom used without being followed, and, as it were, completed by the verb *-ti* " to say " (Angola *-ixi*, Chwana *re*, 172), as if such verbs did not mean properly " to utter sounds ", but only " to open the mouth ". This principle is generally extended to other verbs which express an act of the mind or the will.

It may also be noted that generally there is no pause in Bantu after the verb *-ti*, but it is joined immediately to the sentence which is to it what a direct object is to a transitive verb.

**1005.** — Examples : —

TONGA :
*Muame u-a-ka ambola u-a-ti* " *A mu-inke* ". The king spoke and said : " Go away ".
  (Lit. the king opened the mouth (?) and said...)
*Ba-a-ka amba ku-ti* " *Tu-la inka* ". They spoke to say : " We go ".
*Ba-la nwika ku-tua*..., they are heard saying... (*N. B. Ku-tua* " to be said " is the passive form of *ku-ti*, 1047).
*Ndi-yanda ku-ti* " *tu-li ba-ingi* ", I am glad we are numerous.

SENNA :
*Amakabuzi a-longa okaoka ku-ti* " *Mba t-ende* ". The shepherds said one to another: " Let us go ".

ANGOLA (Chatelain's *Kimbundu Gr.*, p. 147) :
*U-ambela o muhatu u-ixi*..., He spoke to the woman, saying...

CHWANA :
*Ke-a-itse go-re o motho*, I know that you are a man.
  etc., etc.

**1006.** — *N. B.* 1. The translator of S<sup>t</sup> Matthew's Gospel into Ganda has at every page the expression *na agamba nti*... " and he spoke saying... " I do not see how this can be correct, because *nti* is a form of the 1<sup>st</sup> person singular, and means " I say ", not " he said ". It seems that the connective pronoun should vary according to class and person, as *n-ti* " I say ", *o-ti* " thou sayest ", *a-ti* " he says ", *tu-ti* " we say ", etc. Cf. *Grammaire Ruganda*, p. 21.

**1007.** — 2. In Kafir some verbs prefer to be followed by *u ku-ba* or *u-ba* (Zulu *u-ma*, 978), rather than by *u ku-ti*. Ex. *Babuza u ku-ba* " *u na mahashe na?* ", lit. They asked to say (more literally " to stand ") : " Have you got horses? " *Babuza u kuti*... would also be correct. In Chwana *go-re* is likewise replaced after some verbs by *fa* (= Zulu *uma* = Kafir *u-ba*).

## Auxiliaries.

**1008.** — In Tonga, and still more in Kafir and Chwana, the verb *ti* (Chwana *re*, perfect *rile*) is much used as an auxiliary to introduce conjunctive clauses. Then in most cases it is practically equivalent to our conjunction " when ", or it completes some particle or expression which has this meaning. Literally it means " to do so (as follows...) ". Cf. 834. Ex. : —

**1009.** — TONGA :
*Umue muezi a-ti u-ze, oyu u-fue, ba-cite milia* (=... *u-a-ti u-ze*...), lit. When the next moon comes, and this is dead, they will make feasts.
*Na a-ka ti a-fue, mulilo ula pia, ba-a-mu-tenta,* When he is quite dead, the fire begins to flame, and they burn him.

**1010.** — KAFIR:
*Yi nyamakazi u mvundla e-ti, y-a ku-vuka, i-papateke,* The hare is an animal which, when it awakes, is all nervous from fear. (Lit. which does so, when it awakes...)
*I mbovane zi-hlala e sidulini, a-*ti *u mntu u kuba u-*te *w-a-hlala, zi-me zonke,* Ants live in an ant-hill, so that if a man happens to sit upon it, they all come up. Lit... so that *he* does so, a man, if he has done so he sat, they all will stand up.

*N. B.* In this sentence it would be equally correct to say... zi-*ti, u mntu u kuba u-te w-a-hlala...,* lit. ... so that *they* do so, if a man... However, through some sort of attraction, Kafirs generally prefer to give to the auxiliary *ti* the connective pronoun of the verb of the *incident* clause which follows it closely rather than that of the principal verb which is more distant. The same may be noticed in the following examples : —

*U mfazi w-a-landela i ndoda, w-a-*ti *a ku-fika, y-a-ti i ndoda u kuba " U-funa nto nina?".* The woman followed the man, and when she came up to him, he said : " What do you want ? "
*Ba-ti, ba ku-gqiba, y-a-buza i nkosi...* When they had finished, the king asked...
The following, on the contrary, is an example in which the connective pronoun of *ti* is necessarily that of the principal verb.
*Ze ni-ti nd-a ku-biza, ni-pume...* lit. Do ye so, when I call, do come out.

**1011.** — CHWANA (Rev. W. Crisp's *Secoana Grammar*, n. 68) :
*E-tla re* (or *ke-tla re*) *ke-tsamaea ke-go-bitse,* When I go I will call you.
*E-a-re* (or *e-rile,* or *ke-a-re,* or *ke-rile*) *ke-fitlha kwa molacwaneng, k-a-timela,* When I got to the brook, I lost my way.

### § 15. THE AUXILIARY **BUYA** " TO COME BACK ".

**1012.** — In Tonga I can find no evident example of the verb *-bola* " to come back " used as an auxiliary proper. But its Kafir equivalent *-buya* is often used as such under various forms, such as *buya, buye, ba, be, bi.* In like manner, its Chwana equivalent *boea* or *boa* often appears under the forms *ba, bo,* and *bile.* We find the same auxiliary in Mpongwe under the forms *fo* and *vo*. This auxiliary may be rendered practically into English in some cases by " back ", in others by " again ". Ex. : —

**1013.** — KAFIR:
*W-a-puma e manzini, w-a-be w-a-ngena* (or ...*w-a-buye w-a-ngena*, or *w-a-buya w-a-ngena*, 874), He went out of the water, and went in again.
*W-o-puma a-be a-ngene* (or *a-b' a-ngene*), He will come out and go in again.
*U-b' u-ye pina ?* (= *U-be u-ye pina ?*), Where do you come back from? Lit. You come back, having gone whither?

N. B. In the last example, and in the like, there is no evident sign that this auxiliary *be* (= *buye*) is essentially different from the other auxiliary *be*, which has been described in n. 978. Hence, though it be more probable that the latter is related to the verb -*ma* " to stand ", it may also be correct to derive it from *buya*.

**1014.** — CHWANA (Rev. W. Crisp's *Secoana Grammar*, p. 38 and *sqq*.):
*Ke-bile ke-a-reka*, I buy again, lit. I have come back (and) I buy.
*Ke-tla ba ke-reka*, I shall buy again.
*Ke-a-bo ke-reka*, I am buying again. (Crisp renders it : " I am buying as usual. ")
*N-tla bo ke-reka*, I shall buy again. (Crisp : " I shall be buying. ")
*N-ka bo ke-reka*, I would buy again (Crisp : " I would (or should) buy. ")

**1015.** — MPONGWE (Mgr Le Berre's *Mpong. Gr.*, p. 134 and *sqq*.)
*Mi fo dyena*, I see again.
*Mi a-fo dyenaga*, I was seeing again.
*N-a-vo dyeni mie*, and I saw again.
etc., etc.

## § 16. THE AUXILIARY **MANA** OR **MALA** " TO COME TO AN END ".

**1016.** — The verb -*mana* or -*mala* (52* and 280) is derived from *ma* " to stand " and the suffix -*ala* = *kala* " to sit, to remain ". Hence etymologically it properly means " to stop, to stand at the end ". From this are derived some idiomatic uses and meanings of it in various languages. Thus we find : —

IN TONGA : *mane* " until ". Ex. *U-a-li ku-tua inseke, mane zi-a-mana*, he was grinding corn, until it came to an end.

IN GANDA : *maze* (perfect of *mala*) " already ", " finally ". Ex. *Y-a-maze ku-genda*, he was already gone ; *oba o-maze o-n-dagira*, since you have finally betrayed me.

IN SENNA : *mala* " afterwards, then ". Ex. *A-mala a-famba, a-famba*, Then he went and went.

IN KAFIR: *mana* " to continue to ". Ex. *Man 'u ku-ndi-nceda*, continue to help me ; *u-man 'u ku-gqita...*, he is passing continually...
etc., etc.

**1017.** — *N. B.* In Swahili the same idiomatic use is noticeable in the verb -*isha* " to finish ". Ex. *Tende zi-me kw-isha liwa na ndege* (= *zi-me kw-isha ku-liwa*...), The dates are *already* eaten by birds (Steere's *Swah. Tales*, p. 220).

## § 17. Various Auxiliaries.

**1018.** — A good number of other verbs might be mentioned as being often used idiomatically in various languages. But this is not the place to dilate on them, because in their idiomatic use nothing is common to any large number of languages. It will suffice to say that many of our adverbs are rendered into Bantu by such verbs. Thus, in certain cases " soon " will be rendered into Kafir by -*hlalela* " to sit upon ", e. g. *u hlalel 'u kufika* " he will soon arrive ", lit. " he sits upon arriving "; and into Congo by -*vita* " to pass by " (= Swahili -*pita*), e. g. *oyandi wa-vita kw-iza* " he will soon come " (Bentley's *Gr.*, p. 693). In like manner some Kafirs continually use the verb -*suka* " to get off " with the meaning of our " then, straightway ", or simply to express a change of idea or determination, etc., etc.

### III. — 𝔗𝔥𝔢 𝔙𝔢𝔯𝔟𝔰 " 𝔗𝔬 𝔅𝔢 " 𝔞𝔫𝔡 " 𝔗𝔬 𝔥𝔞𝔳𝔢 ".

**1019.** — It was necessary in the chapter on substantives (582) to mention some peculiar forms of the Bantu copula. We now go on to state what remains to be said on this matter. I think that originally there was no verb in Bantu which expressed simply the act of *being*, and which consequently could be termed properly a *copula*, or *substantive verb*. Hence it is that in the present stage of development of these languages : — 1° In many cases in which we make use of the verb " to be " nothing of the kind is expressed in Bantu, and the predicate is joined immediately to the subject. — 2° In other cases we find in Bantu verbs or particles which correspond to our " to be ", but these vary according to the facts expressed, and they always include some peculiar *mode of being*, such as position, or situation, in addition to the fact of being. These verbs and particles are in fact no other than those which we have seen used as auxiliaries in the preceding article. Hence : —

## § 1. Copula Understood.

**1020.** — In Kafir, Chwana, and Karanga, the copula is generally understood in absolute clauses of the present tense, except in those cases in which it is rendered by one of the particles mentioned in nn. 582-588. In nearly all the Bantu languages the most noticeable case in which the copula is understood is when it would be followed by one of the locative pronouns *ko, po, mo*, or their equivalents. Ex. : —

KAFIR :   *Mninji u mbona*, the maize is abundant. Cf. 621.
          *U ko e ndlini* or *u se ndlini*, he is in the house.
CHWANA :  *O motho*, thou art a man ; *o montle*, he is good-looking.
          *O mo tlung*, he is in the house.
KARANGA : *E-t-o-be nyika i-li kule, i pafupi*, the ground is not far, it is near. (Lit. it is not a ground which is far, *it is near*).
          *Irie nyika i mbuya*, that ground is good.
SWAHILI : *Bwana yu-ko wapi? Yu-ko koondeni*. Where is the master of the house? He is with the sheep.
BOONDEI : *Yu-ko kwangu*, he is at my house.
          etc., etc.

**1021.** — In Herero an article often acts as the copula. Ex. *Owami o muhona*, I am a king ; *Ka ove?* Is it not thou ?

## § 2. The verbal Forms *LI, LE, ELE, IRI*, etc., used as the Copula.

**1022.** — The most usual form of the copula is *li* or *ri* in most Bantu languages, *di* in Lunda, *ji* in Rua, *iri* in Angola, *le* or *ele* in Chwana, *la* in Nyambu, etc. This is in fact no other than the form which we have found used as an auxiliary in n. 929.

Considered etymologically, this form is to *ila* what in Tonga *kede* " seated " is to *-kala* " to sit down ", viz. a sort of perfect form. Hence it is that in some languages it admits in certain cases the perfect suffix *-le*, or an equivalent for it, as *rire* in Herero, *irile* in Angola, *liji* in Yao, etc. Nevertheless, there are difficulties as to its original meaning, because there is no such verb as *-ila* in the generality of the Bantu languages. We find this verb regularly used in Angola only, and even in this language its exact meaning is not quite plain. Héli Chatelain in his *Kimbundu (Angola) Grammar* renders it by " to do, to say ", which sheds very little light on the

matter, as it may be used only in a few given cases to render
" to do " and " to say ". My opinion is that the original Bantu *ku-ila*
was the applicative form (1065) of *ku-ya* or *ku-a*, " to go, to act ",
and meant properly " to act towards obtaining a certain effect ".
We have explained above (919) its probable connection with *ku-enda*
" to go ". What seems to confirm this view is that the perfect of
*kw-enda* " to go " is given as being *-ele* in Lower Congo (Bentley's
*Gr.*, p. 642).

**1023.** — *N. B.* 1. In Old Angola *okuila* is often used to render " that is to say "
(= *ku ku-ti* in Tonga, *oku ku-ti* in Kafir, cf. 1004).
2. In Kafir the nearest equivalent to the Tonga copula *li* is *ye*, which is a perfect form
of the verb *ku ya* " to go " (cf. 913-917). Likewise in Herero *-rire* and *-ri* are often replaced
by *-e*, which seems to be originally identical with the Kafir *ye*.

**1024.** — Whatever be the etymology and the original value of
the copula *li* or *ri*, the fact is that it is treated as if it were a sort
of perfect form, and consequently it is never used in future nor in
imperative clauses. In Tonga, Karanga, Senna, Yao, etc., it may
generally be used to render the copula in affirmative present and
past clauses. In Chwana, Angola, Herero, and Swahili, its use is
more limited. The use of *ye* as the copula in Kafir is also limited.
Ex. : —

**1025.** — TONGA :
*Ndi-li muumi*, I am in good health ; *tu-li basano*, we are five ; *u-li mu nganda*, he
is in the house.
*Nd-a-li munini*, I was small ; *ba-a-li wo*, they were there ; *tu-a-ka li basano*, once
we were five ; *ndi-ci li muumi*, I am still in good health, etc.
YAO : *ndi-li...* I am ; *n-a-liji...*, I was...
SENNA : *Muzungu a-li ku musa*, the master is at home.
KARANGA : *U u-li njuja*, thou, thou art young ; *t-a-ri baxano*, we were five ; *e-t-o-he
nyika i-li kule*, the ground is not far. (Lit. it is not a ground which is far.)

**1026.** — HERERO :
*U-ri pi?* Where art thou ? *U-a-ri pi?* Where have you been ?
*Ve-ri pi?* Where are they ?
*A-rire tyi mb-a-i* or *a-e tyi mb-a-i*, and then I went, lit (it was that I went).
*N. B.* I suspect that the same *e* acting as the copula must be seen in such examples as
the following : *O zondu ze pi* (= Kafir *i gusha zi-*ye *pi na ?*) " Where are the sheep ? ",
*O maje ye pi?* (= Kafir *a ma futa a-*ye *pi na ?*) " Where is the fat ? ", etc.

MODERN ANGOLA :
*Eye u-eri* (= *u-a-iri*) *maju kala matemu*, lit. thou art (as to) the teeth like hoes,
i. e. thy teeth are like hoes, or *O maju ma-ku-iri kala matemu*, lit. the teeth are
(to) thee like hoes. Cf. Héli Chatelain's *Kimbundu Gr.*, p. 108.

MPONGWE :
*Mi-are-veno.* I am here, etc., etc.

**1027.** — LANGUAGES IN WHICH THE USE OF THIS COPULA IS MORE LIMITED:
SWAHILI : Relative clauses, as *Kanzu zi-li-zo ndefu,* shirts which are long.
CHWANA : Past clauses, as *Ba-ne ba-le mo tlung,* they were in the house.
KAFIR : Before locative expressions, as *I n-komo si-*ye *pi na?* Where are the cattle? — Past clauses, as *z-a-ye zinkulu,* they were large.

*N. B.* In such Kafir clauses the copula may as well be understood.

## § 3. THE VERB *KU-BA* " TO BECOME, TO COME TO BE ", USED AS THE COPULA.

**1028.** — In the article on auxiliaries, considering that the auxiliary *ba* interchanges with *ma,* we treated them as having been originally one and the same verb. Here it matters little whether this view is correct or not. The fact is that the verb *-ba (-wa* in Swahili, and some other languages) is one of those most frequently used to render our " to be ". Particular attention however has to be paid to this, that properly speaking the form *ba* is expressive of an act which is still in progress, not of an act already accomplished. Hence, generally, *ba* will be more exactly rendered by " to become, to come to be " than by " to be ". Hence also, as a mere consequence of this, the present " I am, thou art ", etc. is not rendered by *ndi-ba, u-ba,* etc., but by past or perfect forms, such as *nd-a-ba, u-a-ba,* etc., *ndi-bede, u-bede,* etc.

The principal parts of this verb are in Tonga : *ba, bi, be, bede.*
                      "                         "    in Ganda : *ba, be, badde.*
etc., etc. Cf. 833.

Examples : —

**1029.** — TONGA :
**Nd-a-ba.** *Tu-a-ba basano,* now we are five, lit. we have come to be five.
**Nd-a-ka ba.** *Bo ba-a-ka fua, ba-a-ka ba kuli Leza, ba-a-ka ba a baana baakue,* Those who are dead are now with God, they are among his children, lit... they have gone to be with God, they have gone to be with his children.
**Ndi-zoo-ba.** *Tu-zoo-ba bakazoasa baako,* we shall be your priests.
**Ndi-be.** *U-be mubotu,* be good, lit. become good.
**Ndi-bede.** *Muade u-bed 'anga ncefo, muade* is (a poison) like arsenic.

**1030.** — *N. B.* In most of these languages the construction of this verb presents nothing essentially different from Tonga. In Swahili, and a few other languages, the fact of its being monosyllabic causes it in certain cases to take the prefix *ku,* according to

n. 853. In Xosa-Kafir the substantives which follow the verb *-ba* require that kind of copulative prefix which has been described in n. 583. Ex. : —

SWAHILI : *Maneno-ye ya-me ku-wa uwongo*, his words are false.
KAFIR :   *U-ya ku-ba yi nkosi*, you shall be king.

### § 4. The Verbs *-KALA* and *-NNA* or *-INA* " to sit ", used as the Copula.

**1031.** — The verb *-kala* (Old Angola *-ekala*), which means properly " to sit " (52\*), hence " to remain ", is used as the copula in several languages, principally in Angola, Lower Congo, and Mozambique. But, besides the copulative notion, it always implies a determined local meaning. Cf. Héli Chatelain, *Zeitschrift*, 1889-90, p. 164.

There is nothing very peculiar in its forms except in Modern Angola, where *ng-ala*, *u-ala*, *tu-ala*, etc. mean " I am, thou art, we are ", etc., while *ngi-kala*, *u-kala*, *tu-kala*, etc. mean " I shall be, thou wilt be, we shall be ", etc. (908, 975). The perfect form is *kedi* in Congo, *kexi* or *kexile* in Angola. Ex. : —

OLD ANGOLA :   *Nzambi y-ekala mo atu atatu* (*Cat.*, p. 8) lit. God is in three persons.
MODERN ANGOLA : *Kize ku tu-ala o kifuxi kie*, lit. Let thy kingdom come where we are. Chat. *Kimb. Gr.*, p. XX.
LOWER CONGO :  *E nsusu kwa ji-kalanga mo?* How many fowls are here? Rev. H. Bentley's *Gr.*, p. 691.
MOZAMBIQUE :   *A-kala mtu*, there was a man (= Swahili *Pa-li ku-wa na mtu*). Rankin's *Arab Tales*, p. 4.
*Ku-kala malimu mulubale* (= Swahili *A-ka-wa shekh mkuu*). Ibid.

**1032.** — In Chwana there are two verbs which mean " to sit ", viz. *-dula* and *-nna*. The one used for the copula is *-nna*. Its perfect is *-ntse*. Ex. : —

*Go-tla nna sentle*, it will be nice.
*Ga ke-a nna jalo*, I am not so.
*Ke-ntse jalo*, I am so (= Tonga *ndi-kede nawo*, Kafir *ndi-hleli nje*).

**1033.** — We find in Angola, Lower Congo, and Kaguru, the verb *ku-ina*, which probably is etymologically one with the Chwana *go-nna*. It means " to be habitually ". Cf. 945-947. In Angola it seems to be used exclusively in its perfect form *-ine* or *-ene*. In Kaguru the form *kw-ina* means " because ", exactly as *ku-ba* in Kafir (982). Ex. : —

LOWER CONGO: *K-ina vava* or *ki-na vava*, it is here. Bentley's *Gr.*, p. 690-691.
MODERN ANGOLA: *Eme ng-ene*..., I am... Chatelain's *Kimbundu Gr.*, p. 107.
OLD ANGOLA: *Ku-ine ringi mulonga?* Is there anything else? *Cat.*, p. 10.
*N. B.* Hence probably the suffix *-ene* " self, same ", n. 825.

## § 5. THE VERB *-ENDA* USED AS THE COPULA.

**1034.** — The verb *-enda* "to go" in Tonga, and its equivalents in other languages, are used for the copula in some instances. Ex.: —
TONGA: *U-enda maya*, he is naked, lit. he goes naked.
KAFIR: *U-hamba ze*, do. do.

## § 6. VARIOUS COPULATIVE PARTICLES.

**1035.** — Looking back to the various copulative particles which have been mentioned in previous chapters, we may now consider most of them as being more contractions or modifications of the various forms which have just been described. Thus: —

1° The Swahili copula *ni*, e. g. in *ni Sultani*, it is the Sultan (590), is probably a modification either of the copula *li* (1022) or of the copula *-ine* (1033). The same may be said of the Tonga copula *ni* or *n* (583), e. g. in *ni-ngombe*, it is a cow. *Ndi* before pronouns in Swahili and Tonga, as in *ndi-ue* " it is thou ", stands probably for *n-di = n-li = ni-li*, in which *n* or *ni* is the copula proper, while *li* is a kind of article or classifier. Cf. 661.

2° The Senna and Karanga copulative particle *ndi*, as in *ndi moto* " it is fire ", is probably directly derived from the perfect of *-enda*, and thus stands also in close relation to the copula *li* (1022).

3° In Kafir, *ngu mntu*, *nga bantu*, and *nga matanga* (583), probably stand for *ni u mntu*, *ni-ba bantu*, *ni-a matanga = li-u mntu*, *li-ba bantu*, *li-a matanga*. On the contrary, in such expressions as *si si-tulo* " it is a chair ", etc., the copula is dropped, but its subjective pronoun is retained. Hence *si si-tulo = si-(li) si-tulo*.

4° The Chwana copulative particle *ke* (= *nge*, 190) might be thought to have been originally identical with the Senna *ndi*, Mozambique *thi*. But this would be the only example of the phonetic change of *th* or *nd* to *k*. More probably it stands for *ntse*, the perfect of *-nna* " to sit " (1032), as we find in Chwana *tse* interchanging in some instances with *ke*, as in *-kena* or *-tsena* (Tonga *-njila*, Kafir *-kena*, 52*) " to go in ".

## § 7. THE COPULA IN NEGATIVE CLAUSES.

**1036.** — In negative clauses the copula is rendered in some cases, principally when the clause is not in the present indicative tense, by the regular verbs *-ba*, *-kala*, *-enda*, etc., and then it presents no special difficulty.

In other cases it is rendered by the negative auxiliaries which have been mentioned above (875-891), with or without other particles, and then we have to notice some peculiar constructions. In Tonga particularly we have to notice the regular use of the auxiliary *-insi* together with the negative particle *ta* or *si* (976). In Mpongwe we may remark, among other constructions, the use of the form *-jele* (= Tonga *-kede*, perfect of *-kala*), before which the negative particle is understood. In Chwana, Swahili, Angola, Herero, etc., the negative particle by itself does duty as the negative copula. In Ganda the copula *li* is retained together with the negative particle. In Kafir the auxiliary *si* (875) is sometimes used together with the other negative auxiliary *a* or *nge*, etc., etc. Ex. : —

TONGA : *Ti insi ndi mulozi*, I am not a sorcerer, lit. it is not (that) I am a sorcerer.
*Ei nyika ti insi mbotu*, this ground is not good.
*S'insi nyika i-li kule*, this ground is not far, lit. it is not a ground which is far.

GANDA : *Si-li-ko kie n-jogera*, there is nothing for me to say, lit. it is not there what I may say.

SWAHILI : *Si-ye*, it is not he ; *si-mi*, it is not I ; *si-mo*, it is not therein, etc.

HERERO : *O nganda ka-yo*, this is not the village.

KAFIR : *A si mntu* or *a si ye mntu*, he is not a man ; *a ka ko*, he is not therein ; ... *e-nge mntu*, ... not being a man (cf. 851) ; ... *e-nge ko*, not being there. (N. B. Notice that *nga* is thus changed to *nge* before the words which are not verbs.)

CHWANA : *Ga ke motho*, I am not a man, lit. not I (am) a man.
*Motse ga o montle*, the town is not pretty.
*Ke-ne ke-se molemo*, I was not good.

ANGOLA : *O tat'enu ki sob'e*, your father is not a chief.
*Eme ngi mutu ami* (negative particle understood, = *eme* **ki** *ngi mutu ami*), I am not a man. Cf. Chatelain's *Kimbundu Gr.*, pp. 51-56.

MPONGWE : *Ga mie*, it is not I ; *ga we*, it is not thou.
*Mi a-jele...*, I am not...; *o-jele...*, thou art not..., etc.
Cf. Mgr Le Berre's *Grammaire Pongouée*, pp. 108-121.

## § 8. The Verb " To Have. "

**1037.** — It may be laid down as a general principle that in Bantu the verb " to have " is rendered by the copula followed by a preposition which means " with ", viz. *a* in Tonga, *ya* in Congo, *ni* in Angola, *na* in Swahili, Kafir, Karanga, etc., etc. Cf. 570. The copula is sometimes understood, according to n. 1020. The preposition itself is generally not understood in any language, except in Lower Congo. Ex. : —

TONGA : *Ndi-li a baana*, I have children, lit. I am with children.
GANDA : *Miti tu-li na gio*, we have trees, lit. trees we are with them.
CHWANA : *Ke-na le pitse ( = ke-nna le pitse)*, I have a horse.
ANGOLA : *Etu tu-ala ni tunzo*, we have little houses (at present).
*Etu tu-ene ni tunzo*, we have little houses (habitually).
Cf. Héli Chatelain's *Kimbundu Grammar*, p. 107.
MOZAMBIQUE : *A-kala na muhaku minjeni*, he had much property.
SWAHILI : *A na maneno makubwa*, he has great words.
KARANGA : *Ndi na tunyuni*, I have little birds.
HERERO : *U no vanatye ( = u na o...)*, he has children.
KAFIR : *Ndi no mfazi ( = ndi na u...)*, I have a wife.
CONGO : *Ba-kedi yo madia mengi*, ( = *ya o madia*), they had much food.
*Mbele zam ng-ina zau*, I have my knives, lit. my knives I am (with) them.
Cf. Bentley's *Congo Gr.*, p. 691.

*N. B.* In Kafir affirmative clauses the preposition *na* is generally understood when the substantive which follows it is followed itself by a determinative. Then also this substantive takes no article. Ex. : *Yinto e zandla zimnyama*, he is a man whose hands are black, lit. he is a thing which (has) hands which (are) black. This is the usual construction in Kafir for " whose, of which ". Cf. 740, 741.

**1038.** — As " to have " is generally rendered into Bantu by " to be with ", so " not to have " is generally rendered by " not to be with ". Tonga seems to prove an exception to this principle, since in the clauses which contain " not to have " we generally find that peculiar verb *kui* which we have already seen coupled with negative particles to render our " never " (964). Ex. : —

TONGA : *Ta-ba-kue ngubo*, they have no clothes.
*Ei nzila ti i-kue bantu pe mu-li ei*, lit. this road it has no men at all in it, i. e. there is nobody on this road.
SWAHILI : *Si na chuma*, I have no iron, lit. not (I am with iron).
*Hu na*, thou hast not ; *ha tu na*, we have not, etc.
ANGOLA : *Ki tu-eny-etu* ( = *ki tu-ene etu*) *ni kitari*, we have no money (habitually).
*Ki tu-al'etu ni kitari*, we have no money (at present). Cf. 1037.

HERERO : *Hi no ruveze,* I have no time, lit. not I (am) with time.
  *Ka pe no mundu,* there is no man, lit. not there has a man.
KAFIR : *A ka na hashe,* he has no horse, lit. not he (is) with horse.
CHWANA : *Ga ke na pitse* (not *ga ke na le pitse,* 1037), I have no horse.
  *Ke-ne ke-se na sepe,* I had nothing.
  *Ga go na sepe,* there is nothing, lit. the place has nothing.
CONGO : *Ke bena* ( = *ba-ina*) *ya madia ko,* they have no food.
MPONGWE : *Mi a-jele ni...,* I have not..., Cf. 1036.
  etc., etc.

**1039.** — Sometimes, in Tonga and Ganda, the verb *lia* " to eat " is used with the meaning of " to have, to possess ". Ex. : —

TONGA : *Miaka koci kede, koci lia buame,* lit. (all) the years you live, eat the kingdom so long, h. e. possess the kingdom till the end of your life.

*N. B.* In this sentence, if the verb " possess " were rendered by " be with ", in Tonga one would say *koci ba a buame* (= *ka u-ci ba a muame*) instead of *koci lia buame* (= *ka u-ci lia buame*).

GANDA : *O Buganda buno mu-bu-lie,* lit. this Buganda eat it (ye), h. e. possess (ye) this Buganda. (*Grammaire Ruganda,* p. 83).

### § 9. THE VERBS " TO BE " AND " TO HAVE " IN LOCATIVE EXPRESSIONS.

**1040.** — We find in Bantu some quite idiomatic constructions for locative expressions when their locative particle (*pa, ku, mu,* etc.) is followed by a pronoun, or by a substantive without classifier, such as *Leza* " God ". For such expressions as " to me, from me, near God, to God, " etc. are rendered in several languages by " where I am, where God is ", etc., and in a few others by " the place which has myself, the place which has God ", etc. This principle explains a large number of very puzzling expressions. In Lower Congo and some other languages it is extended to all sorts of substantives. Ex. : —

**1041.** — TONGA :
*Uaka fugama ku-li Leza,* he knelt down to God, lit. where is God.
*Ukede ku-li uise,* he lives near his father, lit. where is his father.
*Mu-li ei nzila,* on this road, lit. wherein-is this road.

*N. B.* In Tonga one may also hear : *Mu-zoo-ba mbu-li Leza* " you shall be like unto God ", lit. " like as is God ", and other similar expressions.

**1042.** — MODERN ANGOLA (Héli Chatelain's *Kimbundu Gr.,* p. 113) :
*Ngondo kuiza ku-al'enu,* I shall come to you, lit. where are you.
*...ku-al-eme,* by, from, to me, lit. where am I.

*N. B.* Hence, even after passive and quasi-passive verbs : *Riosoneke ku-al'eme*, it has been written by me.

**1043.** — SENNA, etc. :
SENNA : *Pida ficei pa-li sulo*, when he came near the hare, lit. where is the hare.
GANDA : *Bagenda e-ri lubare*, they went to a doctor, lit. where is a doctor.

**1044.** — KARANGA, etc. :
KARANGA : *Ugere pa-na tate* ( = Tonga *ukede kuli uise*), he lives near his father, lit. (at the place) which has his father.
*Iakeja ku-no Eva*, it came to Eve, lit. to (the place) which has Eva.
SWAHILI : *Pali kuwa na mtu*..., there was a man..., lit. a place had a man...
KAFIR : *Mkulu ku na we*, he is taller than you, lit. he is tall at (the place) which has you.

**1045.** — CONGO :
*Mu-na nzo*, in a house, lit. within (the place) which is the house.

*N. B.* The original meaning of the particle *na* in such expressions seems to be entirely obliterated in Lower Congo.

**1046.** — CHWANA :
*Ea kwa go 'mago*, go to your mother, lit. go where your mother (is).
*Tla mo go nna*, come to me, lit. come inside where I (am).

Cf. Crisp's *Chwana Gr.*, pp. 70-71. The view which this author has taken of certain locative expressions does not seem to be altogether correct. Thus, among other things, he has not sufficiently attended to the fact that *mo* implies the notion " inside ", which *kwa* does not. Cf. 563.

## IV. — Derivative Verbs.

### § 1. PASSIVE VERBS.

**1047.** — Leaving aside Angola and Mozambique, the general law in Bantu for the formation of the principal parts of the verbs in the passive voice is to insert *-u-* or *-w-* before the final vowel of the active voice. Ex. in Tonga: *ku-luma* " to bite ", pass. *ku-lumua* " to be bitten ".

The principal exceptions to this law are the following : —

**1048.** — 1° In Tonga the full element inserted is generally *-igu-*. Ex. *ku-jatigua* " to be seized ", from *ku-jata* " to seize. " The insertion of the simple *-u-* seems to be admitted nearly exclusively for the verbs which end in *la*, *da*, or *ma*.

**1049.** — 2° In Ganda the element inserted is generally *-ibw-* or *-ebw-*, according as the preceding syllable contains a short vowel

## Derivative Verbs. 273

(*a*, *i*, or *u*) or a long one (*e*, or *o*). Ex. *ku-sulibwa* " to be cast ", from *ku-sula* " to cast "; *ku-temebwa* " to be felled ", from *ku-tema* " to fell ". The insertion of the simple -*w*- seems to be admitted exclusively for certain verbs ending in *la* or *ra*, and this only in certain tenses.

**1050.** — 3° In Boondei the element inserted is -*igw*- for verbs ending in two vowels and a few others. (Woodward's *Gr.*, p. 41.)

**1051.** — 4° In Yao the element inserted is -*ilw*- for certain verbs. (Which ?). Hetherwick's *Gr.*, p. 40.

**1052.** — 5° In Kafir the element inserted is generally -*iw*- for monosyllabic verbs, and for such dissyllabic verbs as begin with a vowel. In the same language the passive form corresponding to the active *bonanga* is *bonwanga*, that corresponding to the active *bonile* is *boniwe*, and that corresponding to the active *boni* is *bonwa*. Cf. 833.

**1053.** — 6° In some languages, principally in Chwana and Kafir, the addition to the verbal stem of the suffixes *wa*, *we*, or *iwa*, *iwe*, causes in certain verbs considerable phonetic changes, according to nn. 122 and 202-207. Ex. : —

| KAFIR : | | | CHWANA : | | |
|---|---|---|---|---|---|
| To send : | *u ku-tuma*, | pass. *u ku-tunywa* | *go-roma*, | pass. | *go-rongwa* |
| To stab : | *u ku-hlaba*, | „ *u ku-hlatywa* | *go-tlhaba*, | „ | *go-tlhaywa* |
| To shape : | *u ku-bumba*, | „ *u ku-bunjwa* | *go-bopa*, | „ | *go-bocwa* |
| To turn out : | *u ku-kupa*, | „ *u ku-kutshwa* | ... | ... | ... |
| To forget : | *u ku-libala*, | „ *u ku-lityalwa* | *go-lebala* | „ | ? |
| To beat : | *u ku-beta*, | „ (*u ku-betwa*) | *go-betsa* | „ | *go-bediwa* |
| etc., etc. | | | | | |

**1054.** — Examples : —

| Active Forms : | bona | bonanga | bonaga | boni | bone | bonide |
|---|---|---|---|---|---|---|
| Passive Forms: Tonga | bonigua | ... | ... | bonigui | bonigue | bonidue |
| Ganda { Act. | *sala*, to beget | *zalanga* | | *sala* | *zale* | *zadde* |
| Ganda { Pas. | *zal-* { wa / ibwa | *zalibwanga* (?) | | *zal-* { wa / ibwa | *zalibwe* | *zaliddwa* |
| Boondei | onwa | ... | ... | onwa | onwe | ... |
| Kaguru | langwa | ... | langagwa | langwe | langwe | langigwa |
| Yao | wonwa | ... | wonagwa | wonwa (?) | wonwe | ... |
| Nyamwezi | wonwa | ... | wonagwa | wonwe | wonwe | wonilwe |
| Swahili | onwa | ... | ... | onwi | onwe | ... |
| Kafir | bonwa | bonwanga | ... | bonwa | bonwe | boniwe |
| L. Congo | monwa | monangwa (?) | ... | monwa (?) | monwe | mwenwe (?) |
| Chwana | bonwa | ... | ... | ... | bonwe | boncwe (?) |

etc., etc.

**1055.** — A somewhat different kind of passive verbs is obtained by suffixing to the verbal stem *-ika*, or simply *-ka*, a suffix which changes regularly to *-ike, iki, ikide*, etc., according to tense and mood. This suffix is pronounced *ia* or *ea* in Mozambique, according to n. 175. In Kafir and some other languages the same suffix has generally the form *-eka*, and in a few verbs the form *-kala* (Chwana *-fala* or *-hala*, Angola *-ala* or *-ana*).

**1056.** — Properly speaking, the difference between passive verbs ending in *ua* and those ending in *ka* is that the former suppose a personal or external agent, while the latter suppose either a natural or internal agent, or that the act expressed by the verb is done naturally. For instance, in Tonga *bonigua* would be used properly when speaking of a person who brings himself into view, while *bonika* would better be said of a mountain or something else which from its very position naturally comes into view. The same distinction exists in Kafir between *bonwa* and *bonakala*. This distinction does not seem to be so well observed in some other languages.

**1057.** — *N. B.* 1. When active verbs end in *-ula* or *-una* this sort of passive form is generally obtained by changing the final *la* or *na* into *ka*. Ex. in Tonga: *ku-anduia* " to break open ", pass. *ku-anduka*.

2. In Mozambique and Angola there seems to be no other regular way of forming passive verbs than the one here described. However, we may notice in Angola another passive ending, viz. *-ama*, principally for verbs which in the active voice have the ending *-eka*.

**1058.** — Tonga :
*Ku-nvua* " to hear ". Pass. *ku-nvuika* " to be heard ".
*Ku-amba* " to speak ". Pass. *Citonga cila ambika*, Tonga is easy to be spoken.

Kafir :
*U ku-tanda* " to love ". Pass. *U mntwana o-tandwayo ngu nina*, a child which is loved by his mother. — *Umntwana o-tandekileyo*, a lovely child, (a child that is naturally loved).
*U ku-bona* " to see ". Pass. *u ku-bonwa...* " to be seen by... ", *u ku-bonakala* " to appear, to come into view ".

**1059.** — Angola :
*Ku-jikula* " to open ". Pass. *ku-jikuka* " to be opened ".
*Ku-mona* " to see ". Pass. *ku-moneka* " to appear ".
*Ku-bengeleka* " to render crooked ". Pass. *ku-bengalala* " to get crooked ". Notice that this ending *-ala* causes the vowel of the preceding syllable to be changed from *e* to *a*. The ending *-ana*, which is only a phonetic modification of *-ala* (280), has the same effect. Ex. *ku-temeneka* " to provoke ", pass. *ku-temanana* " to get angry ". Cf. Héli Chatelain's *Kimbundu Gr.*, p. 98.

**1060.** — MOZAMBIQUE :
*U-abela* " to cook for… ". Pass. *u-abelia* or *u-abelea* " to be cooked for… ".
*U-ona* " to see ". Pass. *u-onia* or *u-onea* " to appear ".
GANDA :
*Ku-labba* " to see ". Pass. *ku-labbika* (perfect *-labbise* " to appear ", etc., etc.)

**1061.** — *Etymologies.* The passive suffixes *-ika, -eka, -ea, -kala, -ala, -ana,* are nothing else than the verb *-ekala,* or *-kala,* " to sit " (52\*). It may thus be seen what considerable changes one and the same theme may undergo according as one or other of its consonants is dropped or weakened. A little short retrospect also will show what important parts the theme *ekala* plays in Bantu languages. We have just seen it used as a passive suffix. We had seen it a little before acting as the copula (1031), and as an auxiliary, in the various forms *-ala, kana,* and probably *ci, ki,* etc. (Cf. 941, 994, etc.). We have also found it giving us the classifier *ka* (527), and perhaps the classifier *ci* (502). Finally the word *-eka* " self " probably belongs to the same theme.

**1062.** — With regard to the passive endings *-gua, -bua, -ua,* phonetic laws do not allow us to see in them any other verb than *gua* or *bua* or *ua* " to fall " (52 \*), as if in the Bantu mind the act of " falling " were convertible with a passive notion.

**1063.** — In all probability the passive ending *-ma,* which has been mentioned particularly for Angola, though it might be found as well in several other languages, is radically identical with the verb *-ma* " to stand. "

*N. B.* Concerning the construction of the name of the agent after passive verbs, see n. 589.

## § 2. OTHER DERIVATIVE VERBS.

**1064.** — One of the main causes why Bantu is at the same time simple, clear, and wonderfully rich, is the facility with which derivatives are obtained from the various roots. I cannot go here into a particular study of this subject, as to do so would be to undertake no less than a complete analysis of these languages. I will only call the student's attention to five kinds of derivative verbs obtained in nearly all of them somewhat regularly from most verbal stems. These may be termed the applicative, the causative, the intensive, the reversive, and the reciprocal verbs. With the reversive may be coupled certain expansive verbs.

## I. — Applicative verbs.

**1065.** — The applicative verb adds to the simple the meaning of one of our relational prepositions *for, to, into, round*, etc. Its proper suffix is *-ila* or *-ela*, *-ira* or *-era*, (Swahili *-ia*, 88), which in certain cases is changed to *-ena* according to n. 280. In some instances it is strengthened to *-elela*, or *-erera*, or *-ella*.

**1066.** — In Tonga, Karanga, Angola, Congo, and some other languages, the initial vowel of these applicative suffixes is distinctly pronounced *e* (*ela*) when the preceding vowel is *e* or *o*. In most other cases it sounds more like *i*, and then in Tonga the sound of the following *l* approaches that of *r* (17).

Examples : —

**1067.** — TONGA :
*Ku-tila*, to pour water. *Ku-tilila*, to pour water *into*...
*Ku-leta*, to bring. *Ku-letela*, to bring *for* (some one or some purpose).
*Ku-ua*, to fall. *Ku-uila*, to fall *upon*...
*Ku-fugama*, to kneel down, *Ku-fugamena*, to kneel down *for*...
*Uletela nzi inyama ?* What are you bringing meat *for ?*
*Ka mutulapelela*, Pray ye *for* us, (from *-lapela*, pray).
*Ndiwe uaka ndiloela muana*, It is you who bewitched my child, lit. it is you who bewitched *to* me the child. (From *-loa*, bewitch.)
*Matezi utilila paa Ceezia*, The River Matezi flows *into* the Zambezi near Ceezia's place, lit... pours (its waters) *into* (the Zambezi)... (From *-tila*, to pour water).

*N. B.* The applicative form of *-za* "to come " is *-zida* " to come for ". Ex. *Muazida nzi ?* What have you come for ?

**1068.** — KARANGA :
*U-ja*, to come. *U-jira*, to come *for*...
*U-ta*, to do, to make. *U-tira*, to make *for*...
*U-tanga*, to begin. *U-tangira*, to begin *for*...
*U-leba*, to speak. *U-lebera*, to speak *for*...
*U-xoba*, to call. *U-xobera*, to call *for*...

**1069.** — KAFIR :
*Ku-lala*, to lie down. *Ku-lalela*, to lie in wait *for*...
*Ku-peka*, to cook. *Ku-pekela*, to cook *for*...
*Ku fa*, to die. *Ku-fela*, to die *for*.... Hence the passive *ku-felwa*, to be dead-*for*..., i. e. to lose by death... Ex. *Wafelwa ngu nina*, He lost his mother, lit. he was dead-*for* by his mother.

**1070.** — ANGOLA :
*Ku-sumba*, to buy. *Ku-sumbila*, to buy *for*...
*Ku tuma*, to send. *Ku-tumina*, to send *for*...

## Derivative Verbs.

*Ku-banga*, to do. *Ku-bangela*, to do *for*...
*Ku-soneka*, to write. *Ku-sonekena*, to write *for*...

**1071.** — LOWER CONGO:
*(Ku-)sumba*, to buy. *(Ku-)sumbila*, to buy *for*...
*(Ku-)boka*, to call. *(Ku-)bokela*, to call *for*...
*(Ku-)noka*, to rain. *(Ku-)nokena*, to rain *on*...

**1072.** — OTHER LANGUAGES:
SENNA: *Ku-lima*, to till. *Ku-limira*, to till *for*...
YAO: *Ku-tola*, to carry. *Ku-tolela*, to carry *for*...
BOONDEI: *Ku-leta*, to bring. *Ku-letela*, to bring *for*...
NYAMWEZI: *Ku-enha*, to bring. *Ku-enhela*, to bring *for*...
etc., etc.

### II. — Causative verbs.

**1073.** — Causative verbs are properly expressive of the efficient cause that determines an act. The most common causative suffix is *-isia*, *-isa*, or *-ixa*, according to the different languages. In Mozambique it is *-iha*, according to n. 174. In Yao, Boondei, Congo, and Angola, it is *-isa* after short vowels (*i*, *u*, *a*), *esa* after long vowels (*e*, *o*, *ā*). Ex.: —

TONGA: *Ku-(g)ua*, to fall. *Ku-guisia*, to cause to fall, to bring down.
*Ku-nyua*, to drink. *Ku-nyuisia*, to force to drink.
Ex. *Babue bala guisia meno imbooma*, The Bue knock out the teeth of boas, lit. cause to fall the teeth (to) boas.
*Balozui bala nyuisia muade balozi*, The Rotse force sorcerers to drink *muade* (a kind of poison).
YAO: *Ku-tenda*, to do. *Ku-tendesia*, to cause to do.
*Ku-kamula*, to seize. *Ku-kamulisia*, to cause to seize.
CONGO and ANGOLA: *Ku-sumba*, to buy. *Ku-sumbisa*, to cause to buy.
*Ku-zola*, to love. *Ku-zolesa*, to cause to love.
LUNDA: *Ku-sota*, to look for... *Ku-sotexa*, to tell to look for...
*Kukuata*, to hold. *Ku-kuatexa*, to help.
*Ku-xika*, to arrive. *Ku-xikixa*, to cause to arrive.
BOONDEI: *Ku-hela*, to cease. *Ku-helesa*, to cause to cease.
*Ku-gua*, to fall. *Ku-guisa*, to cause to fall.
KAGURU: *Ku-gala*, to bring. *Ku-galisa*, to cause to bring.
KAFIR: *Ku-buya*, to come back. *Ku-buyisa*, to bring back.
*Ku-anya*, to suck (milk). *Ku-anyisa*, to suckle.
CHWANA: *Go-loma*, to bite. *Go-lomisa*, to cause to bite.
SWAHILI: *Ku-panda*, to climb up. *Ku-pandisha*, to take up.
MOZAMBIQUE: *U-thepa*, to increase. *U-thepiha*, to cause to increase.
etc., etc.

*N. B.* The Nyamwezi equivalent of this suffix *-isia* seems to be *-ia*. Ex. *ku-zima* " to go out ", *ku-zimia* " to extinguish "; *ku-oha* " to suck ", *ku-ohia* " to suckle ". (Steere's *Collections*, p. 73).

**1074.** — The endings *-ka* (Chwana *-ga*), and *-ta* (Chwana *-ra*), in most languages become *-sia* or *-sa* in the causative form. Ex. : —

TONGA : *Ku-kunka*, to flow. *Ku-kunsia*, to cause to flow.
*Ku-oluka*, to fly. *Ku-olusia*, to take up in a flight.
*Ku-kuata*, to marry. *Ku-kuasia*, to cause to marry.
BOONDEI : *Ku-eguta*, to be satiated. *Ku-egusa*, to satisfy.
YAO : *Ku-sauka*, to suffer. *Ku-sausia*, to punish.
KAFIR : *Ku-goduka*, to return home. *Ku-godusa*, to send home back.
*Ku-ambata*, to put on a dress. *Ku-ambesa*, to clothe (some one).
CHWANA : *Go-coga*, to awake. *Go-cosa*, to awaken.
*Go-apara*, to put on a dress. *Go-apesa*, to clothe (some one).
SWAHILI : *Ku-anguka*, to fall. *Ku-angusa*, to cause to fall.
*Ku-fuata*, to follow. *Ku-fuasa*, to cause to follow.
etc., etc.

**1075.** — The ending *-la* in several languages becomes *-zia* or *za* (Chwana *tsa*) in the causative form, as if the influence of the *l* softened the harder sounds *-sia* or *-sa*. Ex.: —

TONGA : *Ku-njila*, to go in. *Ku-njizia*, to bring in.
*Ku-lila*, to weep, to cry. *Ku-lizia*, to play (an instrument), lit. to cause to cry.
GANDA : *Ku-agala*, to love. *Ku-agaza*, to cause to love.
NYAMWEZI : *Ku-manila*, to be accustomed. *Ku-maniza*, to accustom.
SWAHILI : *Ku-tembea* (= *ku-tembela*, 88), to walk. *Ku-tembeza*, to bring out for a walk.
KAFIR : *Ku-sondela*, to come near. *Ku-sondeza*, to bring near.
SENNA : *Ku-lila*, to cry, to sound. *Ku-lidza*, to cause to sound.
CHWANA : *Go-gakala*, to be provoked. *Go-gakatsa*, to provoke.
etc., etc.

**1076.** — Likewise, in some languages the causative suffix corresponding to *-na* is regularly *-nya*. Ex. : —

YAO : *Ku-songana*, to come together. *Ku-songanya*, to gather together.
NYAMWEZI : *Ku-lina*, to rise. *Ku-linya*, to raise.
GANDA : *Ku-wona*, to recover. *Ku-wonya*, to cure.
CHWANA : *Go-tlhakana*, to meet. *Go-tlhakanya*, to bring together.
etc., etc.

**1077.** — The suffix- *ika* " to set " also appears in some words as a causative suffix. It then causes various phonetic changes. Examples in Tonga : —

*Ku-kala*, to sit. *Ku-kazika*, to put some one in a sitting posture.
*Ku-ma*, to stand. *Ku-bika*, to set a thing standing, i. e. to place.
*Ku-pia*, to boil, to burn. *Ku-jika* (= *ku-pika*, 52\*), to cook, to boil (trans.).

N. B. *Ku-zika* " to bury " seems to be a causative form of the non-reduplicative form of *-lala* " to lie down ", just as *-kazika* is the causative of *-kala*.

**1078.** — *Etymologies.* The suffix *-ika*, though active in meaning, probably is related to the verb *-kala* " to sit ", no less than the passive suffix *-ika* (1061).

The suffix *-isia* seems to be the same as the verb *-sia* " to leave, to part with (52\*) ". From this meaning is naturally derived the causative one of " imparting ". It may be noticed by the way that the causative word *u-ise* " his father " (748), lit. " the one who leaves him behind ", also contains the element *sia*.

### III. — Intensive verbs.

**1079.** — In Tonga and a few other languages we find intensive, or quasi-superlative, verbs, which imply that a thing is done with great attention, or well, or with persistency. In form they much resemble causative verbs ; in many instances the context alone will tell whether a verb is causative or intensive. Their regular ending is *-isia* in Tonga and Yao, *-idza* in Senna, *-isa* in Chwana, etc. More expressive endings are *-isisia* in Tonga, *-ichisia* (?) in Yao, *-isidza* in Senna, *-isisa* in Chwana, etc. Ex. : —

TONGA : *Ku-amba*, to say. *Ku-ambisia*, to say well. Ex. *Uaambisia, muame,* You have said well, sir. — *Ku-ambisisia*, to speak with perfection.
*Ku-langa*, to look. *Ku-langisia*, to look attentively, to compare. *Ku-langisisia*, to consider very carefully. Ex. *Uazilangisisia inkaba,* He looks at the dice, studying them very attentively.

YAO : *Ku-gumilisia*, to cry aloud exceedingly. (From *ku-gumila* ?)

SENNA : *Ku-lira*, to cry. *Ku-liridza*, to cry perseveringly. *Ku-lirisidza*, to be most obstrusive, importunate.

LUNDA : *Ku-tala*, to look. *Ku-talexa*, to compare.
*Ku-londa*, to speak. *Ku-lon-dexa*, to explain.

CHWANA : *Go-feta*, to surpass. *Go-fetisa* or *go-fetisisa*, to be much above. etc., etc.

We may couple with intensive verbs such reduplicative forms as *ku-endenda*, to walk about, to journey. (From *ku-enda*, to go, to walk.)

### IV. — Reversive and expansive verbs.

**1080.** — Reversive verbs express the undoing of what is expressed by the simple, as " to tie — to untie " in English. Expansive verbs imply expansion, or dilatation, or ejection. Reversive and expansive verbs agree in taking identical suffixes.

Their active ending is *-ula*, or, in a reduplicated form, *-ulula*

(Chwana -*ola*, -*olola*). These according to certain phonetic laws become respectively in some instances -*ola* or -*olola*, and in other instances -*una* or -*ununa*, -*ona* or -*onona*.

Their regular passive ending is -*uka* (Chwana -*oka*), according to n. 1057, or -*uluka* (Chwana -*oloka*).

Examples : —

**1081.** — TONGA :
*Ku-lima*, to dig. *Ku-limula* or *ku-limuna*, to dig a crop out.
*Ku-zua* ( = *ku-rua*), to come out. *Ku-vula*, to breed, to multiply.
*Ku-zuata*, to dress, to tie the dress. *Ku-zula*, to undress.
*Ku-jala*, to shut. *Ku-jula*, to open ; *ku-juka*, to be opened.
*Ku-fuanda*, (?). *Ku-fuandula*, to open a spout. *Ku-fuanduluka*, to spout out.

**1082.** — ANGOLA (Héli Chatelain's *Kimbundu Gr.*, pp. 101-102) :
*Ku-beteka*, to incline. *Ku-betula*, to raise.
*Ku-bandeka*, to unite. *Ku-bandulula*, to separate.
*Ku-jitika*, to tie. *Ku-jituna*, to untie.
*Ku-kuta*, to bind. *Ku-kutununa*, to unbind.
*Ku-sokeka*, to join. *Ku-sokola*, to disjoin.
*Ku-fomeka*, to sheathe. *Ku-fomona*, to unsheathe.

**1083.** — OTHER LANGUAGES :
LUNDA : *Ku-sala*, to do. *Ku-salununa*, to undo.
KAFIR : *Ku-hlamba*, to wash. *Ku-hlambulula*, to wash out all dirt. *Ku-hlambuluka*, to be cleansed.
CHWANA : *Go-bofa*, to bind. *Go-bofolola*, to unbind.
*Go-huna*, to tie. *Go-hunolola*, to untie.
etc., etc.

### V. — Reciprocal verbs.

**1084.** — In nearly all the Bantu languages reciprocal verbs are derived from the others by appending to them the suffix -*ana*. Ex. : —

TONGA : *Ku-nvua*, to hear. *Ku-nvuana*, to hear one another, to agree.
CHWANA : *Go-ama*, to touch. *Go-amana*, to touch one another.
YAO : *Ku-suma*, to trade. *Ku-sumana*, to trade with one another.
KAFIR : *Ku-tanda*, to love. *Ku-tandana*, to love one another.
GANDA : *Kw-agala*, to love. *Kw-agalana*, to love one another.
BOONDEI : *Ku-kunda*, to like. *Ku-kundana*, to like one another.
LOWER CONGO : *(Ku-)tonda*, to love. *(Ku-)tondana*, to love one another.
SWAHILI : *Ku-penda*, to love. *Ku-pendana*, to love one another.

**1085.** — CONCLUSION. There is unmistakably an essential difference between the general notion implied by verbal suffixes and that implied by auxiliaries. But, until we have somewhat more abundant data to go by, it will be no easy task to define this difference exactly. If however I am not mistaken, auxiliaries generally imply a notion of *time*. Respectively they imply that an action is taking place now or took place before, lasts a long or a short time, was never done or was done once, still lasts or is already accomplished, etc., all of them notions which come under that of difference of time. Verbal suffixes, on the contrary, are rather either *relational or include relation*, and cannot be said to contain the notion of either time or duration. Passive verbs, for instance, suppose an agent and a patient; applicative verbs suppose a subject and an object; causative verbs suppose an efficient cause acting upon a subordinate agent; intensive verbs, being superlative, imply comparison with what is usual and common; expansive and reversive verbs bring back the mind to a contrary action; reciprocal verbs suppose at least two agents acting one upon the other, all of them notions which come under the head of relation.

## Retrospect

on

### Adverbs, Prepositions, and Conjunctions.

**1086.**— The student might have expected to find here a chapter on adverbs, prepositions, and conjunctions. But the analytical method which we have followed throughout has already brought under his notice most of the particles which might have found their place in a chapter thus headed. Those which have not been mentioned are for the most part found only in a few languages, and I do not know of any which may not be readily explained by the principles laid down in the preceding pages.

To sum up all that refers to those which we have come across, the notions which we render in English by prepositions are expressed in Bantu partly by particles, which may also be termed prepositions (569-578), partly by locative classifiers (563-567), partly by verbal suffixes (1065-1071). Our adverbs for the most part are not rendered in Bantu by invariable particles, but partly by locative expressions (533\*), partly by locative pronouns (693), partly by auxiliaries subject to the same changes as other verbs (873-1018), partly by variable verbal suffixes (1079). A few conjunctions exist in Bantu, but most of them have retained something of the nature of auxiliaries (939, 940, 944, 958, 984, 985). Of the other particles which correspond to our conjunctions, part are still auxiliaries proper (943, 955-958, 972, 978, 982, 1008, etc.), part are relative particles (784-788).

Hence the student who wishes to take a correct view of any Bantu language must, as it were, first forget all that he knew concerning the division of the parts of the speech in classical languages. Other minds and other shapes of thought entail other grammatical systems.

# First Appendix.

## ETHNOGRAPHICAL NOTES IN TONGA
## DICTATED BY NATIVES.

The following pages cannot claim to be considered as good specimens of the Tonga style in general, because my informants were not the best I could have wished for, and still more because my slow writing under their dictation naturally made them shorten both narratives and sentences. I am, however, encouraged to give them here by the fact that they contain a large number of sentences in which the thought is shaped otherwise than it would be in English, and thus well deserve the student's attention.

The italics between brackets (*a*, *b*, etc.) refer to notes at the end of this appendix.

### I. ON THE ROTSE.

Malozui nga akede mu Luizi, kutala a Basubia. Bayanda mulilo. Baame baao m-Balumbu. Mbabo banyuisia balozi muade.

*The sorcerers.* Aba balozi mbantu baloa, bali a masaku, bazua masaku. Mbuli ci tubeleka, ci tuzuete ezi ngubo, umue muntu uakubona, uati " Nguazuata ngubo zinono oulia muntu." Ualangisia, uati " Uerede kufua ", ko kuti " Afue oulia muntu." Oyu ta amunvuide uaambola nabo, uainka, uafua mu nganda iakue. Bantu baamuzika li bucia, baamulila. Oyu mulozi mansiku mbuli lino ua kutola mo inzule iakue.

*The accusation.* Beenzinyina baati " Ualumua a nzi muntu ulia a afua? Caa mpoo uabona isaku caafua." Umue muntu uati ku umue muntu

The Rotse (*a*) are the people who live on the Zambezi, above the Subia (*b*). They are fire-worshippers. Their chiefs are Lumbu (*c*). It is these who give sorcerers to drink the poison called *muade*.

These sorcerers are people who kill by charms. They have devils, they let out devils. It is as if, (for instance), while we are working, wearing these clothes, some one had seen you and said : " That is a man who has fine clothes on. " He looks fixedly and says : " Be thou bewitched for death. " That is : " May he die yonder man ! " This (other man) did not hear him speaking thus ; he goes off, and dies in his house. People bury him in the morning and weep over him. He, the sorcerer, at night, just as now, goes to dig out his clothes.

The parents say : " What was that man bitten by (*d*) the day he died ? It is because he saw a devil that he died. " One man says to another :

"Ndiue uaka ndiloela muana uaka fua." Ue uati "Pe, tinsi ndime." Ue uati "Tuia ku baame, ku Balumbu." Bala inka a ue ku Balumbu.

*The ordeal.* Baasika, Balumbu bala mubika mu julu, a busanza. Baabika tusamo, tumue tuasimbua, tumue tuayalua etala. Kunsi a busanza baabika mulilo. Ue uli kede a busanza.

Balumbu baati "Ue 'mulozi." Ue uakasia uati "Pe, tinsi ndi mulozi." Baati "Unyue musamo oyu, muade."

Muade ula tuba, ubed 'anga ni ncefo. Uabueza (?) muntu, uenyua. Ka ali mubotu, ta aci fui pe, ula luka; ka ali mulozi, muade uamukola, uaandula mutue. Ula cisa, uci zezela, uci ua.

Mulilo ula pia, bala mutenda. Muntu ta anvuide mulilo, uaka fua.

*Ordeals with thieves.* Baati ku muntu umue "Uaka ba." Uati "Pe, tinsi ndime pe, nguumbi." Baati "Tunjizie maanza mu manzi." Baajika manzi aapia. Beense baanjila maanza. Uasupuka lukanda mubi, bo pe, tinsi lutete luboko.

*The kings of the Rotse.* Muame ua Balumbu ngu Liuanika. Sebitunyana nguaka sanguna. Uali kufua, kuanjila muana uakue Segeletu. Uali kufua Segeletu, ueza Sipopo a Malozui uati "Ndime Sipopo", uanjila mu buame. Uali mubotu, uaka cita miaka njisano e inne, ua kujayigua. Muciu uakue

"It is you who bewitched my child who is dead." The other says: "No, it is not I." The other says: "We go to the Lords, the Lumbu." They go with him to the Lumbu.

When they arrive, the Lumbu put the man up in the air on a scaffold. They put poles, some fixed in the ground, others laid above. Under the scaffold they place fire. He (the accused) is sitting on the scaffold.

The Lumbu say: "You are a sorcerer." The (man) denies emphatically, and says: "No, I am no sorcerer." They say: "Drink this poison, (this) *muade.*"

The *muade* is white, it looks like arsenic. The man takes the cup (?), and drinks. If he is good, he will not die of it, he will vomit; if he is a sorcerer, the *muade* contracts his face, and breaks his head: he burns with pain, totters, and falls.

The fire then blazes, and they burn him. The man did not feel the fire, he was dead.

They say to some one: "You have stolen (such a thing)." He says: "No, it is not I, it is some one else." They say: "Let us put our hands into water." They heat water until it boils. They all (the accusers and the accused) put their hands into it. The thief's skin blisters, the others (feel) nothing, their skin is not even softened.

The king of the Lumbu is Liwanika. Sebituane (') was the first. When he died, his son Sekeletu came on. When Sekeletu died, Sipopo came with Rotse warriors, saying: "I am Sipopo", and he came into power. He was a good man, he reigned nine years ('), and then was killed. It was nguaka mujaya. Uaka cija uanjila mu buato, ua kufuida mu kasua afui a munzi uakue. Uayasigua e intobolo.

Pa akafua Sipopo, baainka ku Cilumbu, baamubuzia kabati " Ube muame." Baati "Ucite itatu." Kabe baati "Miaka k'oci kede, k'oci lia buame. "Cilumbu uati " Pe, ta ndiyandi buame buenu. "

Mpawo kuanjila Muanaena. Uati " Ndime Muanaena. " Uaka cita muaka ngumue, baamujaya. Muanaena nguaka yasana a Bambala, pa aka fua Sipopo. Bambala bakede kunsi a Babue, pa lutilila a Kafuefui, ku Buzungu. Bapalua meno. Muzungu uabo ngu Manuele. Boonse baayasana a bukali, boonse baakafua ua kumana musili uabo. Mpawo baaka kala. Masotane nguali muame ua Beciseke. Uci li muumi.

Mpa aka fua Muanaena, baanjizia Liuanika. Ngoci li wo.

*The Mambunda.* Makuango ali bantu ba Liuanika. Bakede mu talel' elino ku Mababe, ka bajaya mansui a li mu manzi. Bali a tuato tunini, bala njira mukati a manzi, ka bajaya insui a mazui (?), ka bazitola kuli Liuanika. Kuategua balala kunsi kua manzi. Ngaongao nga Mambunda.

*Depredations of the Rotse.* Balumbu bamue bakede ku Ciseke, bamue bakede kutala a Basubia. Balatola ku Kangombe baana baa Balea a baana

his nephew who sought his death. He (Sepopo) fled, got into a boat, and went to die on an island near his city. He was shot with a gun.

When Sipopo died, they went to Cilumbu ([5]), and asked him, saying : " Be king." They added : " Try three years. " Again they said : " (All) the years you shall live keep the power. " Cilumbu said : " No, I do not want any kingship over you. "

Then it was that Muanaena came in. He said : " I am Muanaena." He reigned one year, (then) they killed him. Muanaena was (the king) who had a quarrel with the Mbala after Sipopo's death. The Mbala live below the Bue, where the Zambezi receives the Kafuefue, in the Portuguese territory. They file their teeth. Their lord is Manuel ([k]). They fought furiously on both sides, and died in great numbers, until their powder was exhausted. Then they sat down. Masotane was at the head of the people of Sesheke. He is still alive.

When Muanaena died, they elected Liwanika. It is he who is still there (as king).

The Kuango are subjects of Liwanika. They live on this side (of the Zambezi), on the Mababe (river and flats), killing the large fish that is in the water. They have small canoes, (with which) they go into the water and kill fish with a special kind of assegai (?), taking them (then) to Liwanika. It is said that they can sleep at the bottom of the water. It is they that are called Mbunda ([i]).

Of the Lumbu some live at Sesheke, others above the Subia. They take children of the Lea ([j]) and the Ngete ([k]) to the white people of the

baa Mangete ku bantu batuba, ka baula ntobolo, ka beza a maato ka baza ku jaya bantu. Bakalanga balakomba, Masukulumbue ala yasana, Batonga tabakombi ta bayasani, bala zubuka a maato, ka baza kukala mu talel'elino, ka bati, a bata ci yowi Balumbu, baye kubola ku minzi iabo.

Bihe, and sell them for guns; then they come in canoes to kill people. The Karanga submit (to their exactions), the Shukulumbue ([1]) fight, the Tonga neither submit nor fight, but they cross (the Zambezi) in canoes, and come to live on this side (the southern bank of the Middle Zambezi), returning (afterwards) to their homes, when they no longer fear the Lumbu.

## II. ON THE KARANGA.

*The Karanga chiefs.* Bakalanga bamue bakede ku Bulumbu, bali a baame Taalimui a Nyamezi, baanza kunvua cigululu. Bamue bakede ku Bupunu. Mbavumbe aba, mbabua baa Nguaru. Bamue bakede ku Butonga, ngu Zuanga muame uabo. Oyu muame ta akue uaka komba kuli ngumue kusanguna. Monze, muame ua Batonga, uati " Ukombe kuli ndime. " Oyu Zuanga uaka kaka, uati " Kana nkufua, ndila fua. Sikue ndila komba. " Monze uatuma balavu kuli Zuanga. Balavu baaluma bantu baa Zuanga, uakomba.

Oyu Zuanga nguise uali muame mupati ua Bunyayi boonse. Uise ua Nguaru nguamubeja ua mujaya.

*Wange's priests.* Zuanga uli a bakajoaxa ([1]). Leza nguaka ti " Aba mbakajoaxa baako, Banerukoba, Netombo, Bampire. " Bo mbapati, bali baame. Beeza kuli Zuanga, baati " Sue tuaba bakazi baako, ta tuzi kuyasana, ta tukue sumo. " Mba-

Part of the Karanga nation live in the Rotse territory, they have as chiefs Taalimui and Nyamezi; they are beginning to understand the Kololo language. Others live in the Tebele territory. These are the Vumbe, they are the dogs ([m]) of Lobengula. Others live in the Tonga territory, they have Wange ([n]) as chief. This chief did not submit to any one at first. Monze, a king of the Tonga, said: " Pay homage to me. " This Wange refused (to do) saying: " If it is death, I can die. Never will I submit. " Monze sent lions against Wange, the lions bit Wange's men, he submitted.

This Wange's father was the paramount chief of the whole Nyayi territory (= Monomotapa). The father of Lobengula deceived and killed him.

Wange has *cacices* ([o]). It is God who said: " These are thy *cacices*, the families of Nerukoba, Netombo, and Mpire. " They are old men and chiefs. They came to Wange, and said: " We have become your *cacices*, we will not fight, we have no spears. "

---

1. *Bakajoaxa* is a Karanga word. If it were adapted to the Tonga pronunciation it would be sounded *Bakazoasa*.

bonya bo bacita milia imvula iue ; bala icita kabili muaka ( = mu muaka ?) ngumue, imue mu mpewo, imue ejinza ; ie impewo njia kusanguna.

*The seasons.* Umue muezi uati uze, oyu ufue, libe jinza, bacite milia, ipe kulia bantu, balime : ie jinza miezi njisano a umue. Liamana jinza, iaba mpewo ; njinne : oyu upola bantu, oyu ngua milia, ei nimpeo luzutu. Liamana mpewo, ciaba cilimo ; njibili. Eciamana cilimo, liaba jinza, ia ua mvula, liadilima mvula.

*The feasts.* Mpa a milia boonse baame baa Makalanga beza kuli Zuanga bazoolapela mvula. Baana baakue bala lizia ngoma, ka baziana. Zilila ziti kdíndili-kdíndili-kdíndili lingandanda-lingandanda-lingandanda kdi-kdi-kdi kdíndili...... Zuanga uasandula uazuata zimue ngubo zia muzimo zi alapela a nzio. Ula njila mu nganda ili a muzimo ia Ciloba. Oyu 'muntu mubotu uaka fua ciindi : uaka ziala banyena baa Zuanga. Ngue unjira muakale Zuanga, ngue aalike a bakazi baakue. Ta tuzi ci nyamanzi ci ocita mukati a nganda. Uazua uafugama ansi, uati guada ([1]), ula lapela Leza, ka ati " *To kubomberera, tate bedu, su bana babo* " ; ko kuti " Tula kukombelela, tuli baana baako, kootupa ([2]) mvula. "

It is these same (people) who offer the feasts (sacrifices ?) to bring down rain ; they offer them twice a year, the first in winter, the second in summer; the winter ones are the first.

When another moon comes and this one is dead, it will be the rainy season ([?]) (summer and autumn), when feasts will take place to give food to the people, and they will till the ground : the moons of the rainy season are five and one (in number). When the rainy season is over, winter comes, it lasts four (moons) : this (the first) refreshes the people, this (the second) is that of the feasts, these (the third and fourth) are only wind. Winter over, spring comes ; it lasts two (moons). Spring over, the rainy season comes (again), rain comes, the (sky) showers (copious) falls of rain.

It is on feast-days that all the chiefs of the Karanga come to Wange to pray for rain. His children ([?]) (= people) play musical instruments, and dance. The (instruments) sound like kdíndili-kdíndili-kdíndili lingandanda-lingandanda-lingandanda kdi-kdi-kdi kdíndili...... Wange then puts on other clothes, those of a spirit, in which he offers his prayers. He goes into the house which contains the spirit of Ciloba. This was a good man who died long ago, he begot the mother (ancestors ([?]) ?) of Wange. Wange alone goes inside, he and his *cacices*. We do not know what he does inside the house. He comes out, kneels down, prostrates himself, and prays God, saying (in Karanga) : " *To kubomberera, Tate bedu,*

---

1. *Guada*, from -*gua* " fall ", *a* " on " and *ida* " belly ". Hence " to fall on one's belly, to prostrate oneself ".
2. = *ka u-tu-pa*.

Bakajoaxa baakue mba bayasa mbelele e isumo, imbelele ia kupaila (kupa ila?), ka baisinza, ka babika mu ndido, ka baitenda, ka bapaila, ka babanda Leza. Oku nkupaila kuabo: bala tila manzi a bukande, ka bati " Inyweno muaka fua ciindi, muaka ya kuli Leza, ka mutufugamena kuli ngue, ka mutukombelela, ka mutulapelela bubotu. " Mpawo balia ka bati " Tulia mubili ua Leza. " Ta ulii koozuete (²) oyu hosi, uauzoola, uaubika ansı, *su bana babo* " (lit. " We adore Thee, our Father(¹), we are Thy children);" that is to say: " We adore Thee, we are Thy children, give us rain. "

They are his *cacices* who slaughter a sheep with an assegai for the sacrifice (remission of sins?). Then they skin it, put it on the fire, roast it, and offer up the sacrifice to propitiate God. This is their manner of offering the sacrifice: they pour water and beer (upon the roasted sheep?) (³), saying: " You who died long ago, and who went to God, kneel down for us before him, pay homage for us, and ask happiness for us. " Then they eat saying: " We eat the body of God " (⁴). You do not eat with your hat on, you take it off and put it down.

Bakajoaxa luzutu baaka kala ku kupaila, abalike. Zuanga aalike ula langa. Baana baakue bala lizia ngoma. Bakajoaxa bala lia ei nyama, Zuanga ta ailii pe.

(All this time) the *cacices* have been there alone to offer the sacrifice. Wange alone is present (lit. looking). His children are playing music. The *cacices* eat this meat, Wange does not eat of it.

### 3. ON THE TONGA.

*How the Tonga obtain rain.* Batonga ta bakue milia, bala pundula. Bala inka ku Monze, ka batola mbelele e impongo, ka bati " Moōnze! Tuaka komba kuli ndiue, tu baana baako. Siabulongo! Sikazimena! Mpandayo! Muana ua Leza! Muana ua Mpande! " Mpnze ualapelela baana baakue kuli Leza, imvula iaua.

*Monze, a favourite of the Son of God.* Oyu Mpande ngue Muana ua

The Tonga have no sacrifices, they are heathens. They go to their chiefs and bow down for rain. Many chiefs go to Monze (*), taking to him sheep and goats, and saying: " Moōnze! We have paid homage to you, we are your children! Siabulongo! Sikazimena! Mpandayo! Child of God! Child of Mpande! " Monze prays to God for his children, and rain falls.

This Mpande is the Son of God He lives in the air, in the rain-bow.

---

1. Lit. "our fathers", plural of dignity.
2. = *ka uzuete.*

Leza. Ukede mu julu, mu mpini-ciongue. Uaka tola Monze ka aci lusabila, uamuolusia, uamukazika mujulu. Kabe uamuselezia ansi; uauakuti po, wati " Ndila leta mvula, ndaambolana a Leza, uati ' Ka mundilapela kutede; ta mucite citede, caamuima kulia, caaka cila mvula ', ko kuti ' caaikasia imvula '. Mucite nabo, zintu zi ayanda Leza, ula mupa mvula." Mpawo baacita, imvula iaua.

*God's abode.* Batonga bati Leza ukede 'u manzi, mu Siongo. Munari, Munkua, Munjilisimane, uaka ya kuli ngue, uanjila muakale, uaka zua. Uati " Ndime muana a Leza, ndila njila awa ". Bo baati " Pe, t'insi ula njila, ula fua. " Ue uati " Pe, t'insi ndila fua. " Mpawo uanjila, uayala a buenga, pa akaselelela, uanjila 'u manzi, uazua.

*God's justice.* Leza uli muzimo, ta tumuboni. Ula nvua zintu zionse: uaamba zintu zibotu, uanvua: uaamba zintu zibi, uanvua. Bo baamba zintu zibotu, uya kubabika bubotu kojulu. Inzila nzibili: ei njitola bantu bacita zibi, njili a mulilo; ei njitola bantu bacita zibotu, bayanda, njili a bubotu, njili a kukondua.

*Prayers to the dead.* Bantu baaka fua ciindi baaka ba kuli Leza, baaka ba a baana baakue. Baame bala lapela kuli mbabo mu minzi iabo, bala lapela ka tuenda a bubotu kuakale, ka bati " Ka mutulapelela kuli Leza, ka mutufugamena kuli ngue, asuebo

He once took up Monze when still a baby, he made him fly up and remain in the air. Afterwards he let him down. He fell with a sound like *po*, and said: " I bring rain; I have spoken with God who said: ' Pray to me in such a manner; do not do such a thing; this has stood in the way of your food, this has made rain scarce ', that is to say: this has prevented rain. Do thus, (do) the things God wants, he will give you rain. " Then they did so, and rain fell.

The Tonga say that God lives in the water at Siongo (\*) (= Victoria Falls). Livingstone, a white man, an Englishman, once went to him, he went in to the bottom, and came out. He had said: " I am a child of God, I can enter therein. " The people said: " No, you cannot enter therein, you will die. " He said: " No, I shall not die. " Then he went in, he went along the bank up to where the water rushes down, he went into the water, and came out.

God is a spirit, we do not see Him. He hears all things: if you say good things, he hears (them); if you say bad things, he hears (them). To those who say good things he will give happiness in heaven. There are two roads: this is the one which takes people who do evil, it has fire; this is that which takes people who do good, who love; it has happiness, it has rejoicings.

The people who are dead long ago have gone to God, they have been received among his children. The chiefs pray to them in their villages, they pray that we may go with happiness to the end, saying: " Pray ye for us before God, kneel down tuzooende nzila mbotu ili a kukondua."

*Monze raising the dead.* Monze ula busia bantu baaka fua, ingombe, imbelele... Uati " A muze, a muzoolange bantu beenda bee ciindi, ndizoobabusia ba ndaamba. " Uama nkolia (?) ansi, inyika iaanduka. Ino bo baakeza bantu baalanga ansi ka basondela.

Bala bona bantu baaka fua bali mu kuendenda, imbelele, beense banyama, balavu, inyati, ingombe...

Monze uati " Ka mugona mansiku ", uati " A ta buci, muazua anze, ka mucibuka, muazoojana baakasika inyue ka mulilede, ka bali baciabuka anze. Mujike kulia, muzoolie a mbabo. "

Bo baazicita ezi zintu, baajika kulia, baabika mu ndido, boonse baati " A tulie toonse tusonone maala ", ko kuti " Tuanjilile a amue. " Baabuzia boumi ka bati " Muta no zui muoyo ", ko kuti " Muta no yowi kua kufua. "

*The Tonga doctors.* Muntu usonda ninganga. Pa aka fua muntu beenzinyina baakue baati " Tuende ku kusonda. " Baainka, beeza ku nganga, baabuzia baati "Tuyandal 'ube(?) anze. " Ni nganga iazua anze, iya kusondela a mbabo, iasonda, iasonda. Ka ali afuefui muntu uaka loa, inganga iati " Oyu mulozi. " Iati " Iue mulozi, uaka loa utede, uakede

for us before him, that we also we may go (by) the good road which has happiness (?). "

Monze can raise dead people, cattle, sheep, (etc.). He says: " Come and look at men of former times walking, I will raise up those I mention (i. e. So-and-So). " He then strikes on the ground with a stick (?), and the ground opens. Then the people who have come look down, coming near the edge.

They see people who were dead walking, (as well as) sheep, all sorts of animals, lions, buffaloes, cattle, (etc.).

Monze says: " Sleep during the night ", and he adds: " Before daybreak, if you come out when just getting up, you will find that they have come (up here) while you were sleeping, and that some are still rising up (?) outside. Do you cook some food, that you may eat with them. "

The men do these things, they cook food, they put it on the fire, they all (the living and the risen) say: " Let us eat together, and mix our nails"; that is to say: " Let us throw them (our nails) one with another." They (the risen) encourage the living, saying: " Do no let out your hearts "; that is to say: " Do not fear to die. "

A man who smells is (called) a *nganga* (') ( = doctor). When a man is dead, his parents say: " Let us go to smell. " Then they go, they come to a *nganga*, and ask him (out), saying: " We wish you to come outside ". Then the *nganga* comes out, and, approaching close to them, he smells and smells. If the man who has bewitched (the dead person) is kutede. Ka ali kule, iati " Awa ta akue mulozi, muaka musia ko 'u munzi uenu. Muinke kuabede. " Ila baambila izina, iati " Ngu ndaba, u- tede. " .

Mpawo baainka kuabede, baya kumuita, baəmunanga, baati " Ndiue mulozi, ndiwe uaka loa ndaba. " Iue uakasia, uati " T'insi ndime mulozi. " Bo baati " A tuende. " Iue ta akaki kuinka. Mpawo baainka a ue ku nganga.

Beeza ka lici zua izuba, ta bezi e isikati. Mpe eza i nganga iabualila nkaba nzisano a imue. Jio, jio, kua, ziaua, ziya ziti ka. Iati " A muzijate, a muzibuabile. " Boonse bala zijata, bala zibualila, inganga ia kuzifunda inkaba. Iakanyua misamo iazio, ia zooba nganga. Bamue ta baizi pe. Iati inganga " Ndiue mulozi. " Ue uti " Ndime t'insi ndi mulozi. " Iati " Uzibualile aebo. " Nguenya mulozi ula zijata, uazibualila katatu. Uazilangisisia munganga, uli mu kubualila muntu. Ni baaka mana kubualila, inganga iabalemba mpemba ba t'insi balozi, mulozi iamulemba masizi. Mpawo bo bala tuba nkumu, iue ula sia ntaamu.

near, the *nganga* says: " This is the sorcerer. " And (to him) he says: " You are the sorcerer, you have bewitched (that man) in such a manner, you were sitting in such a place. " If he be far, the *nganga* says: " There is no sorcerer here, you have left him there in your village. Go back to such a place. " He tells them his name, saying: " It is So-and-So, such a person. "

Then the people go to the said place, going to call him, they get hold (?) of him, and say: " You are the sorcerer, it is you who have bewitched So-and-So."The man denies strongly, saying: " It is not I (who am) the sorcerer. " The men say: " Let us go. " He does not refuse to go. Then they go with him to the *nganga*.

They come when the sun is just rising, they do not come in the middle of the day. When he (the sorcerer) comes, the *nganga* shakes dice five and one (in number). Jio! Jio! Kua! They fall, they disperse, they stop. He says: " Take them yourselves and shake them. " They all take them and shake them, while the *nganga* studies them. He has formerly drunk their science (lit. their trees or medicines, 378) in order to become a *nganga*. The other people understand nothing of it. The *nganga* says: " You are the sorcerer. " The man says: " I am no sorcerer. " The *nganga* says: " Do you also shake them. " Then the sorcerer also takes them, and shakes them three times. The *nganga* looks fixedly while the man is shaking them. And when they have finished shaking, the *nganga* paints in white those who are no

*Tame snakes, pythons, and crocodiles.* Babue mBatonga bakede kutala a Bambala. Ta bazuati ngubo, beenda maya. Bati, iajatigua imbooma, baaipumbaila a mubili, baaizambaila zambi zambi, mutue uazoosondela nabo. Bala ialila bantu, baati " Inka uka lume ndaba muntu. "

Bamue baabika inzoka mu nkomo, baaituma ko kuluma bantu.

Bamue, baajata intale a musamo, ta baijayi, baaibuzia, baati " Ka ijate muntu u bata muyandi. " Muntu uteka manzi, intale imujata.

Bamue bali a nzoka anga (?) babua. Baabika nzoka mu nkomo a muliango. Uaisia uainka ku mpompo, muntu bu eza uanjila mukati uazooba, inzoka iamusingila azoomujane muini ue inganda.

sorcerers; as to the sorcerer, he paints him (with) charcoal. Then they have their forehead all white, and he, he is quite (?) black.

The Bue are those Tonga who live above the Mbala. They wear no clothes, they go naked. When they have caught a boa, they coil it up round their body, they coil it round and round, so that its head should be near by so (as shown by a gesture). They throw it on people, saying : " Go and bite So-and-So. "

Some put a snake in their wallet (*ᵃᵃ*), and send it to bite people.

Others, when they have caught a crocodile by means of a charm, do not kill it, but ask him to catch a man whom they do not like. This man draws water, the crocodile catches him.

Others use snakes as dogs (*ᵇᵇ*). They put a snake in a bag at the door (of their hut). They leave it and go somewhere : (then), if a man comes inside to steal, the snake keeps him in until the master of the house may find him.

NOTES.

(*a*) *The Rotse*. — The Rotse, or Ma-rotse, or Ba-rotse, are well known from the descriptions of Livingstone, Holub, and Father Depelchin. According to Livingstone they call themselves *Ba-loi*, or *Ba-loiana*. *Ba-rotse* is the Chwana pronunciation of the same word. The Tonga call them *Ma-lozui*. It is not without interest to find them described by the Tonga as fire-worshippers. We know from ancient Arab geographers that the fire-worshippers of Siraf on the Persian Gulf used to trade with South-Africa at least as early as the 9th century of the Christian Era, and we still find the Parsees all over the east coast, principally at Mozambique. Putting these facts together, I am inclined to think that Parsee traders or slave dealers, starting at an unknown time from the East Coast, have pushed their way as far as the Upper Zambezi, and grouped together those blacks who now form the Rotse nation. I should not even be astonished if the word *Ba-rotse* were merely a phonetic adaptation of the word *Parsee* to Chwana pronunciation.

(*b*) *The Subia*. — The Subia are a Tonga tribe that used to be found between the Victoria and the Gonye Falls. Incorporated into the Kololo Empire about the year 1840, they have naturally become the subjects of the Rotse ever since these destroyed the Kololo. But ill-treated, and continually robbed of their children by their new masters in their old homes, they began to seek new ones. They are now found in great numbers, mixed up with other tribes, between Lake Ngami and the Zambezi, principally on the Mababe River.

(*c*) *Their chiefs are Lumbu.* — Whenever I meet in Tonga that Bantu sound which is intermediary between *l* and *r*, I adopt the *l*. Otherwise the word *Lumbu* might as well be spelt *Rumbu*. The word *Ba-lumbu*, or *Ba-rumbu*, seems to mean " white people ", or more exactly " yellow people ". Hence, if it be correct to say that the Rotse nation has been formed by Parsees from the East, the modern Lumbu mentioned in these notes are probably no other than their descendants. The *Ba-lumbu* of my Tonga informants are probably the same as the white *A Ba-lamba* repeatedly alluded to by the traveller Anderson in his " *Twenty-five Years in a Waggon* " (Vol. I, p. 247 ; vol. II, p. 200, etc.).

(*d*) *What was the man bitten by?* — On the Zambezi whoever dies young, unless killed in battle, is by the natives supposed to have been bewitched or poisoned, as they cannot imagine that a man may die a natural death before he has reached a good old age. This execrable notion dooms to death every year hundreds of imaginary sorcerers. A sorcerer is called *mu-lozi* in Tonga, *un-doi* in Karanga, *mo-roi* in Chwana, *u m-tagati* in Tebele, *u m-takati* in Xosa, *un-firi* in Senna, etc.

(*e*) *Sebituane.* — As is well known from Livingstone's Travels, this truly great man was the founder of the Kololo Empire. He died in 1851. My informants knew no distinction between the Kololo and the Rotse Empire.

(*f*) *He reigned nine years.* — Sipopo, *alias* Sipopa, was not a Kololo, but a Rotse. A short time after the death of Sekeletu, which occurred in 1864, he came down upon the Kololo, destroyed them all, and reigned paramount on the Upper Zambezi.

(*g*) *Cilumbu.* — I do not know who this Cilumbu is who has so much influence among the Rotse, but I suspect that he is a black from the Bihe.

(*h*) *Manuel.* — This must be Manuel Antonio de Souza, capitaõ mõr, formerly of Zumbo, now of Gorongoza. In the Portuguese East-African possessions, the chiefs are called *Ba-zungu*, which, whatever its etymology may be, is a synonym of Baptized Christians, baptism being considered as the mark of a chief, or child of God. The name of *Ba-mbala*, or *Ba-mbara*, which is given by the Tonga to the subjects of the *Ba-zungu*, must probably be identified with *Amhara*, which in Abyssinia is a synonym of Christian.

(*i*) *The Mbunda.* — As has been mentioned in a previous note (p. 30), the word *Mbunda* is applied to many different tribes. This word properly means " people of the back ", i. e. "the West " (See Introduction, I). The word *Kwango* has been misspelt *Kwengo* at pp. 30, 31, and 10-14, of this work, as I now find that the *Ma-kwengo* of my informants are different from their *Ma-kwango*, and probably are not even a Bantu tribe.

(*j*) *The Lea.* — The Lea are a Tonga tribe dwelling round the Victoria Falls. They have submitted to the Rotse. One of my informants was a Lea.

(*k*) *The Ngete.* — The Ngete, also known as *Nkete, N'keta, Kheta, K'hete, Ngeti,* whence, with the classifiers *MA-* and *BA-*, *Ma-nketa, Ma-ngete, Ba-ngeti*, etc., are a very industrious tribe inhabiting the Rotse Valley from the Gonye Falls to near the confluence of the Nyengo River with the Zambezi. They are particularly remarkable for their works in iron and wood. If I may believe my native informants, their language differs less from Rotse than from Tonga. In all probability they are related as a tribe to the no less industrious *Ba-kete* of the Lu-lua Valley, whose beautiful plantations have been described by Bateman in the " *First ascent of the Kasai* ".

(*l*) *The Shukulumbue.* — This tribe is located on the Upper Kafuefue River. They were described by my Zambezi informants as being very fierce. They will allow no white man to visit their country. Dr. Holub, the only European who ever reached it, was robbed by them of all his effects, and forced to retrace his steps southwards.

(*m*) *They are the dogs of Lobengula.* — Wherever Mohammedan customs have penetrated in South Africa, the native chiefs divide their subjects into " children " and " dogs ".

As a consequence of their being mere " dogs ", those Karanga who have accepted Lobengula's rule, are not allowed to possess cattle. Fine herds of these may well be seen under their care, but they all belong to the king.

(*n*) *Wange.* — This chief, also called Wankie, was repeatedly said by my informants to be the legitimate representative of the house that ruled for centuries over the whole *Bu-nyai*, or the Empire of the Monomotapa. I cannot conciliate this with the claims to the same honour of the chief Catoloza, or Cataloze, who in Livingstone's time had his residence at some distance to the west of Tette, unless these opposite claims be the result of an ancient scission of the Karanga nation, which has not been recorded by history. Wange's chief town is situated at the southernmost point of the Upper Zambezi. He is said to be a very good man. But, pressed on one side by the Rotse, on another by the Tebele, and on another by the Tonga, whose territory he has invaded, he has none of the power of his forefathers.

(*o*) *Wange has cacices.* — When, on the first day of January 1561, the venerable Father Gonçalo da Sylveira, S. J., reached the court of the Monomotapa,

> Onde Gonçalo morte e vituperio
> Padecera pela Fé sancta sua,
> *(Lusiads*, X, 93),

he found the place already occupied by Mohammedan emissaries, called *cacices*, the very men who by dint of calumnies soon caused him to be put to death by the so-called Emperor. This readily explains why the customs of the Karanga, who in those times were the ruling tribe in those parts, are mostly borrowed from the Mohammedans. For, though the emperor, repenting of having sacrificed Father Sylveira to the hatred of the Mohammedans, is said to have driven them out of his Empire in the year 1569, and to have then sincerely desired to live as a Christian, nevertheless, from want of Christian teachers he retained most of his Mohammedan practices.

(*p*) *When this moon is dead, it will be the rainy season.* — This was written on September 3, 1884, the 13th day of the moon. Therefore, as the Karanga year begins with winter, it must be said to commence in March or the beginning of April.

(*q*) *His children* — Wange, being a good chief, calls all his subjects " his children ".

(*r*) *He begot the mother (ancestors?) of Wange.* — I do not know whether *ba-nyena*, lit. " mothers ", is here a plural of respect (cf. n. 343), or a real plural. If it be a plural of respect, Ciloba must be said to have been the grandfather of Wange.

(*s*) *Upon the roasted sheep (?)* — It may be that they pour it simply on the ground. Old Kafirs used to make such libations round the enclosure in which the sacrifices took place.

(*t*) *We eat the body of God.* — This remnant of Father Gonçalo da Sylveira's short stay at the court of the Monomotapa is a good specimen of the religious eclectism of the Karanga. I also find that ever since the days of this glorious Martyr, the kings of those parts were never recognized as such until they had received something like baptism. *(Der Neue Welt-Bot*, 1748, n. 555, p. 106).

(*u*) *Monze.* — This chief went to meet Livingstone on his first journey from Sesheke to the East Coast. After having saluted the great traveller according to the Tonga fashion by throwing himself on his back and rolling from side to side, he made him several presents, and passed a whole day in his company. Livingstone thought him to be as good-natured a man as could be. (*Missionary Travels*, pp. 552-555). His sacred animal is the buffalo, as that of the old Karanga kings was the hippopotamus [n. 461 (10)].

(*v*) *Child of God!* — Lest more importance should be attached to this expression than it has in reality, it may be remarked that it is here a mere compliment, or " name ", as Kafirs say, just as the other expressions *Sikazimena, Mpandayo*, etc., the meaning of which is not clear to me. Chiefs are very generally termed Children of God, as are Christians in general, and whoever is considered to be of white, or the divine, race. It happened to me once, after having given a loaf of bread to a poor old Kafir woman, to hear her burst into the following expressions of thanks: *Nkosi! Dade! Mta ka Tixo! Mta ka Rulumente! Solotomana!* that is: " Lord! Father! Child of God! Child of the Government! Solotomana!" The last expression was considered by Kafirs as my proper name.

(*x*) *God lives at Siongo.* — " At three spots near these falls", says Livingstone, " three " Ba-toka (= Ba-tonga) chiefs offered up prayers and sacrifices to the *Ba-rimo* (= Tonga " *Mi-zimo*). They chose their places of prayer within the sound of the roar of the cata-" ract, and in sight of the bright bows in the clouds... The play of colours of the double " iris on the cloud, seen by them elsewhere only as the rainbow, may have led them to " the idea that this was the abode of the Deity." (*Missionary Travels*, London, 1857, p. 523.)

(*y*) *The road which has happiness.* — These to all appearances are prayers to ask for material, not eternal, happiness.

(*z*) *A man who smells is a nganga.* — The Bantu practice of smelling described in this passage (Tonga *ku-sonda*, Kafir *ku-nuka*) exists in the larger number of the Bantu tribes. In the hands of the chiefs it is the most powerful arm for getting rid of the men who are in their way.

(*aa*) *In their wallet.* — No Kafir ever goes about without his little bag or wallet made out of the skin of some little animal. He puts together in it tobacco, pipe, knife, small tools, and in general whatever he can pick up for his use. One of the worst kinds of un politeness is considered to be that of asking a man what he has in his bag.

(*bb*) *Others use snakes as dogs.* — This singular custom of using snakes as dogs has its counterpart in the use of snakes as cats among the Kafirs of Gazaland. We read in Father Depelchin's " *Trois ans dans l'Afrique Australe* ", p. 71, that in the hut in which Father Law died, " there lived two snakes, the one a cobra three feet long, thick as " an arm, the other smaller, which used to fulfil the duties of our cats in Europe by keep-" ing at a distance the mice and rats which would make their appearance at every " corner ".

# Second Appendix.

## SPECIMENS OF KAFIR FOLK-LORE.

Kafirs are in possession of a large number of traditional tales in which the heroes are not animals, but human beings. No such tales seem to be known by the other Bantu tribes. Neither do I find anything like them in any version of Pilpay's Fables. One of the most remarkable features of most of them is that they contain parts that are sung. It might even be thought that in several of them the story is merely the frame of the song.

*N. B.* 1. The division of the short melodies that occur in these tales into intermixed bars of 3, 2, or 4, beats each, is not intended to express a rigorous rhythm as in European music, but merely to set off those notes which bear the musical accent. Hence, though the relative value of the notes must be kept at least approximately in rendering these tunes, what is more important is that the first beat of each bar be accented.

2. The italics between brackets (*a, b, c,* etc.) refer to notes at the end of each tale.

## First Tale.

### INTAKA ENYA A MASI.

Wati u mfo, ngo mnye u mhla, wati e mfazini, ma kaye e masimini, alime. Waya ke, wafika, walima, wagoduka. Yafika i ntaka ku la ndawo ayilimileyo, yati : —

### THE BIRD THAT MADE MILK (*a*).

Once upon a time a man told his wife to go to hoe in the gardens (*b*). So she went, she arrived, she hoed, and came home back. Then a bird went to the place which had been hoed, and sang :

Tya - ni    ba   le   ntsi - mi,   ci - di - di!
Tya - ni    ba   le   nta - ka,   ci - di - di!

" Tyani ba le ntsimi, cididi !
Tyani ba le ntaka, cididi ! "

" Grass of this garden, shoot up.
Grass of this bird, shoot up. "

Bapuma u tyani, kwa ngati be kungalinywanga. Yafika i ndoda yati : " Ulime pi ? " Wati u mfazi : " Ndilime apa. " Yati i ndoda : " Uyaxoka, a kulimanga. "

Yatsho, ya se imbeta ngo mpini. Walila. Yambiza i ndoda yati : " Yiza

And the grass came up: it was as if no spot had been hoed. The husband came and said : " Where did you hoe ? " The woman said : " I hoed here ". The husband said : " You lie, you did not hoe ".

So he said, and then he struck her with the handle. And she cried. Her

silime." Waya ke, balima, balima, bagoduka.

Yafika i ntaka, yati : —
"Tyani ba le ntsimi, cididi!
Tyani ba le ntaka, cididi!"
Betu, kwa ngati be kungalinywanga.
Bati ke baya kusasa, a bayibona i ndima. Wati u mfazi : " I pina ke i ndima?" Yati i ndoda : " O ndibonile, mfazi, ub' unyanisile ; uz' undimbele ke uvelise i sandla sodwa." Wayenza ke lo nto u mfazi, wagoduka.

Yafika i ntaka yati citi citi, yanyatela e sandleni se ndoda, yayibamba.

Yati i ntaka: " Ndiyeke, ndi yi ntakana enya a masi." Yati i ndoda: " Ka wenze ke, ntak'am, ndibone." Yati pudlu i ngqaka e sandleni.

Yagoduka nayo, yafika, yati ku mfazi ma kahlambe u mpanda ayifake kuwo. Wayifaka ke u mfazi. Wati akugqiba u kuwuhlamba yazalisa u mpanda nga masi. Bavuya kakulu, kuba ba belamba, bafumana u kuhluta.

Baya kulima, bashiya a bantwana e kaya. Aba bantwana a magama abo o mkulu waye ngu Ngencu, o mncinane waye ngu Notuncu. Wati u Ngencu : " Ma siye kwa bantwana, sibaxelele le ntaka." Wati u Notuncu: " Ubawo ub 'ete ze singa baxeleli, uya kusibulala." Wati u Ngencu : " Hlal' uti tu, ntwanandini inolwini." Wayeka u Notuncu, kuba uyoyiswa.

husband then called her and said: "Come, let us hoe." So she went; they hoed and hoed, and then went back home.

The bird came then, and sang:
"Grass of this garden, shoot up.
Grass of this bird, shoot up."
Dear me! it was as if no spot had been hoed.

So, when they came in the morning, they saw no place hoed. The woman said : "Where is the work done (yesterday)?" The husband said : "Oh! I see how it is, my wife : bury me then in the ground, so as to leave the hand alone out." The woman did so, and went back home.

The bird came, and picked here and there, till it trod upon the man's hand, and he got hold of it.

The bird said : " Leave me, I am a bird that makes milk." The man said : " Make some then, my bird, that I may see." So it made thick milk on his hand.

He went home with it, and when he arrived he told his wife to wash a milkpail and to put it into it. So the woman put it there, and when she had finished washing the milkpail, the bird filled it with milk. And they rejoiced greatly, because they were hungry and they had found plenty.

They went to work in the field, and left the children at home. The names of these children were Ngencu for the elder, and Notuncu for the younger. Ngencu said : " Let us go to other children, to tell them of this bird." Notuncu said : " Our father told us not to mention it to them, otherwise he would kill us." Ngencu said : " Hold your tongue,

Waya kubaxelela.

Wati ke, akubaxelela, bati : " Ma siye. " Baya kufika, bayirola e mpandeni. Wavakala u Ngencu esiti : " Ka wukangele i ntaka ya ko kwetu. " Yati i ntaka : " U kuba ndi yi ntaka ya ko kwenu, hamba uyo kundibeka e buhlanti. " Wayitata waya kuyibeka e buhlanti. Yafika yati e buhlanti, ma kayibeke e lusaseni, wayibeka. Yesuka yapapazela yemka.

Wavakala u Notuncu esiti : " Nantso i nto e nda ndiyixelela, ndisiti siya kubetwa. Uya yibona na ke imka nje ? " Basuka babaleka aba bantwana be bezo kuyiboniswa, bemka.

Yavakala i ntaka ihamba esiti : " Ndiyekwe ngu Ngencu no Notuncu. " Yatsho yada ya malunga ngo yise lowo. Wavakala u mfazi : " Nantso i ntaka yako isiti " iyekwe ngu Ngencu no Notuncu. " Yati i ndoda : " Ms'u kuyinyebelela i ntak'am. A bantwana bam bangati ni u kuba ndibayala kangaka, kanti ba kwenza i nto embi kangaka ? "

Bagoduke bafike ekaya. U mfazi akangele e mpandeni, afike ingeko o kunene. I ndoda i sel' ibiza a bantwana : " Ngencu no Notuncu ! ", basabele. Iti : " Yizani apa. " Baye. Iti bakufika, ibuze i ntaka. Ati u Notuncu : " Ib' ikutshwe ngu Ngencu. " Ati ke u yise, akutsho u Notuncu, arole i ntambo, ati " uya kubabulala. " Bakale a bantwana. Avakale u mfazi esiti : " Yinina, Songencu, ungade ubulale a bantwana nga masi?"

you lying little creature. " So Notuncu yielded, as she was frightened. And he went to tell them.

So when he had told them, they said : " Let us go. " When they came, they took it out of the milkpail. Ngencu shouted out, saying : " Look at the bird of our place. " The bird said : " If I am a bird of your place, go and put me in the kraal ". He took it, and went to put it in the kraal. When in the kraal, it said he should put it on the fence, and he put it there. Straightway the bird took to flight, and went off.

Notuncu then cried out, saying : " There is just what I told you, when I said we should be beaten. Do you see it now going off thus ? " Straightway the children who had come to see it began to run, and went off.

The bird was heard saying while going : " I have been let off by Ngencu and Notuncu. " It kept saying so till it passed near that father of theirs. The woman cried out : " There is your bird saying it has been let off by Ngencu and Notuncu." The husband said : " Don't you speak ill of my bird. How could my children have received from me so strict instructions and yet do so bad a thing?"

Then they go back and arrive. The wife looks in the milkpail, and finds no bird in it certainly. The husband then calls out for the children : " Ngencu and Notuncu ! " ; they answer. He says : " Come here you. " They go, and when they come he inquires for the bird. Notuncu says : " It has been let off by Ngencu. " The father, when Notuncu has said this, draws a rope, and says he is going to kill them. The children cry.

Ivakale isiti i ndoda : " Nda kukubulala wena ke, u kuba utsho. " Ayeke u mfazi, alile. Ifake i ntambo, iyo kubaxoma e mlanjeni e mtini o pezu kwe siziba. Emke, ibaxome. Iti i ntambo iqauke. Bawe e sizibeni apo batshone kona, be nga bantu bo mlambo. Bakwazi u kuzalisa.

Kwati, nge linye i xesha, kwafika i lizwe, baya kuwela a bafazi. Bawuzalisa. Bavakala a bafazi besiti : " Vulela, Ngencu no Notuncu. " Babavulele, a bafazi bawele. Bati ba kuwela bawuzalisa.

Afika a madoda, bawuzalisa. Avakala esiti : " Vulela, Ngencu no Notuncu. " Apela ke a manzi, angena ke a madoda. Ati, akubona ukuba a pakati, wafika uyise lowa way'ebabulele. Bawuzalisa. Avakala a manye a madoda : " Puma, mfondini, wa ubulela ntonina wena a bantwana ? " Wapuma wauta ke u mlambo. Awela ke lo madoda ; wasala yedwa lo mntu way'ebabulele a bantwana bake.

Yada yabonakala i vela i mpi. Wavakala esiti : " Vulela, Ngencu no Notuncu. " Bati : " Oko wa usibulala ! " Wavakala ekala, yafika i mpi, yambulala, wafa ke kwapela.

The woman cries out, saying : " What is that, father of Ngencu ? Would you go so far as to kill children for milk ? " The man bursts forth, saying : " Then I shall kill you yourself, if you speak thus. " The woman insists no more, and sheds tears. The man ties (the children) with the rope, intending to go and hang them up near the river on a tree that is over a pool. He goes and hangs them up. But the rope breaks, and the children fall into the pool. There they disappear, they are turned into river-men, with power to produce floods.

Then, at one time, there happened to be an invasion of the enemy ; the women went to cross the river, but the rivermen filled it up. The women then cried out, saying : " Let us pass, Ngencu and Notuncu. " And they opened a way through, and the women crossed over the river. When these had crossed, they filled up the river again.

The men came also, then the rivermen filled the river. The men cried out, saying : " Let us pass, Ngencu and Notuncu. " So the water disappeared, and the men went in. But, when they were half-way, the father who had killed them arrived. They filled the river again. Then the other men shouted out : " Get out, you man, why did you kill your children ? " He went out, and the river dried up. Those men then crossed the river, and he remained alone, the man who had killed his children.

At last the invading army was seen to appear. The man raised his voice, saying : " Open for me, Ngencu and Notuncu. " They said : " Why ! You who killed us ! " He burst out shout-

Kwaba njalo u kufa kwa lo mfo wabulala a bantwana bake nge nxa ya masi. Bati ke bona, bapuma e manzini, bafuna u nina. Bamfumana, bahlala naye, ba se besiya ngo kuhamba e mlanjeni.

Ndiya pela apo.

ing. The enemy came, slew him, and he died; that was the end of him.

Such was the death of that man who had killed his children for the sake of milk. As to them, they came out of the river, and went to look for their mother. They found her, and remained with her, but kept the power of going into the river.

I stop there (*c*).

### NOTES.

(*a*) Two other versions of this tale have been published by Geo. M<sup>c</sup> Call Theal in his delicious little work, entitled " *Kafir Folk-Lore* ". Both of them want the interesting conclusion of the one here given, but they complete it in some other parts.

(*b*) *A man told his wife to go to hoe in the gardens.* — Among the Xosa-Kafirs the work was formerly so divided that men had the care of the cattle, and women that of the gardens. The introduction of the plough has naturally thrown upon the men part of the garden-work.

(*c*) I wonder whether this tale has not its parallel in Stanley's Legend of the Tanganyika (*Dark Continent*, ch. XIX). In both we first see gardens cultivated by a man and a woman; then a marvellous supply of food, heaven-sent fish on the Tanganyika, heaven-sent milk among the Kafirs; then the precious secret betrayed to a visitor, in the one case by the woman, in the other by the children of the house; then punishments by the loss of the treasure and further calamities, a flood on the Tanganyika, a flood and war together among the Kafirs.

## Second Tale.

### U MLONJALONJANI NO DADE WABO NE MBULU.

Kwati ke kaloku kwako u Mlonjalonjani e ne singqi. Wati ke u dade wabo : " Uhleli nje, u ne singqi na ? " Wati : " Yiza, ndokuqaqe lonto. " Wati yena : " Hayi, nda kufa. " Wati : " Hayi, mnta ka mama, uya kuti nina, uza kwaluka nje ? " Wati ke : " Ewe, ndiqaqe. "

Wati ke qaqa qaqa nge zembe. Wati yena : " Shushushu ! ndafa,

### MLONJALONJANI, HIS SISTER, AND A MBULU (*a*).

Once upon a time there was (a boy called) Mlonjalonjani, who was hunch-backed. His sister said to him : " Such as you are, are you really hunch-backed ? " She added : " Come that I cut that hump off you. " He said : " No, I should die. " She said : " No, child of my mother. What will you do, as you are going to be circumcised ? " He said : " Well, cut it off ".

So she cut, and cut, with an axe. He said : " Oh dear ! Oh dear ! I am

mnta ka bawo." Wati ke: "Yima, se yiza kumka." Wati ke qaqa qaqa. Wati: "Shushushu, ndafa." Wati ke: "Se yiza kugqitywa, se yiza kumka." Wati qaqaqa. Yawa ke.

Wati ke, ya kuwa, wasuka wafa.

Wabaleka ke u dade wabo, waya kuxela ku yise no nina u kuba u Mlonjalonjani ufile. Beza ke u yise no nina, beza belila. Bafika batshisa ke i ndlu, bazifaka e ndlini, bazitshisa nayo

Zati ke i ntombazana zemka zilila, zaquba i nkomo za ko wazo, zahamba ke zaya ku lo nina.

Wasuka u mhlaba wahlangana, kwasuka kwa mnyama.

Bati ke:—

dying, child of my father." She said: "Patience! It is nearly off." So she cut again. He said: "Oh dear! Oh dear! I am dying." So she said: "It is nearly finished, it is nearly off." She cut again and the hump fell down.

But when it fell down, he died.

Then his sister ran, and went to tell her father and mother that Mlonjalonjani was dead. So the father and the mother came shedding tears. When they reached their hut, they set fire to it, shut themselves in it, and burnt themselves with it.

So the girls went away crying. They drove before them the cattle of the place, and went in search of their mother.

Suddenly the earth was covered with a thick fog, and it got dark.

So they sang:

"Qabuka, mgada (¹), mbangambanga!
Sifele (²) ma (³) wetu, mbangambanga!
Uzitshise ne ndlu yake, mbangambanga!
Sibulele Mlonjalonjani, mbangambanga!
Simqaqa singqi sake, mbangambanga!"

Wasuka u mhlaba waqabuka.

Bahamba ke, bahamba, bahamba, bahamba, bava kusiti roqo roqo roqo

"Open out, earth, alas! alas!
We have lost our mother, alas! alas!
She has burnt herself with her hut, alas! alas!
We had killed Mlonjalonjani, alas! alas!
By cutting off his hump, alas! alas!"

Then the earth opened out.

So they went and went; they went and went, until they heard a sound

---

1. *Mgada* is a word used only by women for *m-hlaba*.
2. Regularly we should have *felwe*, not *-fele*; but, as I never could perceive the *w*, I have thought it better not to insert it. Possibly also *si-fele* is for *u-si-fele*, lit. "she is dead for us."
3. *Ma*, poetical for *ngu ma*, if *si-fele* stands for *si-felwe*; for *u ma*, if *si-fele* stands for *u-si-fele*.

roqo pantsi kwe lityc e sidulini. Ya puma ke le nto yati: " Nifuna nto nina? " Bati bona: —

" Sifele ma wetu, mbangambanga !
etc. (as above). "

Yi mbulu lo nto. Yati : " Hambani ndinikape, ndinise ku lo nyoko. " Bahamba ke. Yati yakufika e zibukweni e likulu, yati : " Na kuhlamba, u kuba nowavile (¹) (a manzi). " Ba cancata ke e matyeni, bacancata. Yasuka i mbulu yati ngcu ngo msila, yati ke tshizi. Yati : " Hlambani ke, niwavile nje. "

Bahlamba ke, watata i mpahla zabo, wazingxiba zona. Bati ke : " Zis'i mpahla zetu. " Wati : " O! ka nihambe, nina mbuka wa nina? " Ba hamba ke, bafika ke nga ku lo mzi. Bati ke : " Yis'i mpahla zetu. " Wati ke : " Ni na mbuka wa nina ? "

Basika ke baziqab' u daka. Bahamba ke.

Bafika ke ku lo mzi. Yati ke le nto, le mbulu i no msila, yati : " Yipani o mgodwanja (²) u kutya. " Bapiwa ke. Kwatiwa : " Ma bayo ku linda a masimi atyiwa zi ntaka. " Bahamba ke kusasa, baya ku linda.

Lati i xego : " Tsayitsayibom ! Nanzo, mgodwanga. " Zati i ntomba-

like roqo, roqo, roqo, coming from under a stone in a hill. So that thing came out, and said : " What are you looking for ? " They sang :

" We have lost our mother, alas ! alas !
etc. (as above) ".

That thing was a mbulu. It said : " Go on, I will lead you the (right) way, and bring you to that mother of yours. " So they went on. When the mbulu came to a great ford, it said : " If you are touched by water, you must go in and bathe. " So they walked on tottering and tottering from stone to stone. Suddenly the mbulu struck the water with its tail, and splashed it. Then it said : " Go in, and bathe, since you have been touched by water. "

So they went in. Then the mbulu took their clothes and put them on himself. They said : " Let us have our clothes. " It answered : " Just go on. What can you complain of ? " So they went on. When they came near that village, they said : " Let us have our clothes. " It said : " What can you complain of ? "

Then they smeared their body with clay, and they went on.

They reached that village. Then that thing, that mbulu with a tail, said : " Give food to these offsprings of dogs. " They received food. Then they were told to go and watch the gardens that were being eaten by birds. So they went to watch in the morning.

An old man said : " Tsayitsayibom (ᵇ) ! There they (the birds) are

---

1. *Nowavile* = *ni-wa-vile*. The change of *i* to *o* is the result of a partial assimilation with the following *w*.
2. *U mgodwanja*, pl. *o mgodwanja*, is a compound word derived from *u m-godo* " breed " and *i nja* " dog. "

zana: "Tsayitsayibom! Nanzo, Mabelengambonge (¹): —

"Sifele ma wetu, mbangambanga!
etc.". *(the same as before).*

Lati i xego: "He!" Bagoduka ke baya e kaya ngo kuhlwa. Alaxela ela xego.

Yona ke i mbulu yahlala e kaya. Kwabuzwa i ndaba, yati "Kusapiliwe," benga boni ingesiyo ntombazana ke, iyi mbulu. Yapuma ne nkosi ke, yaya kulala e ndlini yayo. Yati i ne sisu, yati: " Ncincinu, ndifun'i qwili (²)." Yafika ke i mpuku. La lise ko i xego ke, lati: " Yi mbulu le, u msila lo ufun' i mpuku wona." Alaxela noko.

Kwasa ke, zapinda ke i ntombazana, zaya kulinda kanjako. Lati i xego: "Tsayitsayibom! nanzo, mgodwanga. Zayidla i ntsimi kakade, zayitshitshela." Bati bona: "Tsayitsayibom! Nanzo, Mabelengambonge: —

near you, breed of dogs." The girls said: "Tsayitsayibom! There they are near you, Mabelengambonge:

"We have lost our mother, alas! alas!
etc." *(the same as before).*

The old man said: "What is that?" So they went home in the evening. The old man said nothing.

As to the mbulu, it had stayed at home. They asked it the news. It said: "Our health is good yet." They did not see it was not a girl, but a mbulu. So it came out with the chief, and went to sleep with him in his hut. It said it had a belly-ache. Then it said: "Ncincinu (³), I want a medicine." Then a mouse came. The old man was still there. He said: "That is a mbulu, that tail wants mice (⁴)." But he did not tell anybody.

Morning came; the girls went again to watch. The old man said: "Tsayitsayibom! there they are, breed of dogs. It is a long time already that they are eating off the garden. They are going to finish it altogether." They said: "Tsayitsayibom! there they are near you, Mabelengambonge:

Si - fe - le - ma we - tu, mba - nga - mba - nga!

U - zi - tshi - se ne ndlu ya - ke, mba - nga - mba - nga!
Si - bu - le le Mlo - nja - lo - nja - ni, mba - nga - mba - nga!
Si - m - qa - qa si - ngqi sa - ke, mba - nga - mba - nga!
Sa - ha - mba si - fu - na ma, mba - nga - mba - nga!
Sa - hla - nga - na ne mbu - lu, mba - nga - mba - nga!
Wa - si - hlu - ta mpa - hla ze - tu, mba - nga - mba - nga!
Si - hle - li zi - tye - ni ze zi - nja, mba - nga - mba - nga!

1. *Mabelengambonge* is the proper name of the old man.
2. *I qwili*, a word seldom used, is a synonym of *i yeza*.
3. *Ncincinu* seems to be the proper name of the chief.

Sifele ma wetu, mbangambanga !
Uzitshise ne ndlu yake, mbangambanga !
Sibulele Mlonjalonjani, mbangambanga !
Simqaqa singqi sake, mbangambanga !
Sahamba sifuna ma, mbangambanga !
Sahlangana ne mbulu, mbangambanga !
Wasihluta mpahla zetu, mbangambanga !
Sihleli zityeni (¹) ze zinja, mbangambanga ! "

We have lost our mother, alas ! alas !
She has burnt herself with her hut, alas! alas!
We had killed Mlonjalonjani, alas ! alas !
By cutting off his hump, alas ! alas !
We went in search of our mother, alas ! alas!
We met with a mbulu, alas ! alas !
He robbed us of our clothes, alas ! alas !
We now sit in the mangers of dogs, alas! alas!"

Bagoduka. Wati u Mabelengambonge e nkosini : " Ungandinika nto nina, ndokuxelela i nto ? " Yati i nkosi : " Ndinga kunika i nkomo. " Wati : " Ndi na mazinywana apina o kutya i nkomo? " Yati : " Ndokunika i bokwe. " Wati : " Ndi na mazinywana apina o kutya i bokwe ? " Yati : " Ndokunika i nqwemesha ? " Lati ke i xego : " Ndi na singqana sipina so kungxiba i nqwemesha ? " Yati ke : " Ndokunika u kobo. " Wati ke : " Kauti sibone. " Balugalela ke, walutya ke.

They went home. Mabelengambonge said to the king : " What will you give me, and I will tell you a thing ? " The king said : " I shall give you a cow. " The man said : " What remnants of teeth are left to me for eating a cow ? " The king said : " I shall give you a goat. " The man said : " What remnants of teeth are left to me for eating a goat ? " The king said : " I shall give you a loin-cloth. " The man said : " What loins are left to me to gird them with a loin-cloth ? " The king said : " I shall give you millet. " The man said : " Let us see. " So they poured out the millet, and he ate it.

Wati ke : " Eza ntombazana ziti zifelwe ngu ma wazo, zahlangana ne mbulu, yazihluta i ngubo zazo. " Kwatwa ke ku la mbulu : " Ma u dimbaze. " Yangena ke e si seleni. Agalelwa ke a manzi ashushu kuyo. Yasuka yati pundlu e siseleni, yati : " Ndiwadle kade a we nkonazana. "

Then he said : " Those girls say that, having lost their mother, they went in search of her, and met with a mbulu which robbed them of their clothes." So they said to that mbulu : " Go and take Kafir corn out of the pit." Then it went into the pit. Hot water was poured over it. But it jumped out of the pit, saying : " I have more than once played tricks of young girls. "

Kukupela kwayo ke.

That is the end of it.

### NOTES.

Another version of this tale has been given by Mr. G. Mc Call Theal in his " *Kafir Folk-Lore.* " It contains no song.

(*a*) *Mbulu.* — The mbulu is a fabulous being, supposed to live near the rivers and to

---

1. *Zityeni,* poetical for *e zityeni.* Likewise, In the preceding lines, several articles are poetically omitted. Thus, *Mlonjalonjani* stands for *u Mlonjalonjani, singci* for *i singci, ma* for *u ma,* and *mpahla* for *i mpahla.*

be fond of playing tricks on young girls. Its essential feature is a tail. In all other respects it has the appearance of a human being. Some Kafirs identify it with the *Gqongqo*, described in the following tale.

(*b*) *Tsayitsayibom*. — In Kafirland the principal occupation of women in summer time is to watch over the gardens, so as to prevent the birds, principally a small kind of finch, from eating the Kafir corn which is then ripening. Their usual stratagem for driving the birds away is merely to make a noise by clapping the hands. The exclamation " Tsayitsayibom ! " is what they are often heard to shout out when they wish to warn one another of the presence of birds in various quarters of the field.

(*c*) *That tail wants mice*. — In Kafir lore the tail of the mbulu is supposed to be particulary fond of mice. In Mr. Theal's version, the episode of the mouse comes, perhaps more naturally than here, only at the end of the tale. The people of the place, having then been told already by the old man that the supposed girl is a *mbulu*, wish to ascertain the truth of the assertion, and, to obtain their purpose set snares, in which the mbulu's tail gets fast while pursuing mice.

## Third Tale.

### A MAGQONGQO NO QAJANA.

Kwati ke kaloku i nkomo ze nkosi zamita (¹). Za li shumi. Zazal'e zinye, a yazala e nye. Yasika, lo mhla yazala, yazala i nkwenkwe. Ngu Qajana i gama la le nkwenkwe. Kwatiwa ma kaaluse i nkomo.

Zati ke i nkomo kusasa zapuma e buhlanti. Yati le nkwenkwe : —

*Allegretto (quasi Allegro).*

" Roqozani, roqozani u kuhamba (*bis*) ".

Zahamba ke i nkomo, zaya e hlatini.

Kwati, nxa zityayo, kwafika a magqongqo beza kuziba. Wati o mnye : " Kodwa uyazazi na ? " Wati o mnye : " A ndizazi, siqelile u kudla a banye a bantu tina. " Wati o mnye : " Mna ndiya zazi. "

Afika ke la magqongqo, aziquba,

### THE GQONGQOS (*a*) AND QAJANA (*b*).

Once upon a time ten cows of the king conceived. All of them calved except one. But the day she calved, she bore a boy, who received the name of Qajana. He was told to herd the cattle.

So in the morning the cattle went out of the kraal, and the boy sang :

Ro - qo - za - ni, ro - qo - za - ni u ku - ha - mba (*bis*)

" Range yourselves to go, range yourselves (*bis*) ".

So the cattle left the place, and went to the kloof (*c*).

While they were grazing, there came gqongqos, who wanted to steal them. One of them said : " But do you know how to manage cattle ? " Another said : " I don't know, our own custom is to eat other people. " Another said : " I do know. "

So they came, those gqongqos ;

---

1. With some Kafir tribes a more usual form of this word is *semita* (Gr. n. 274).

azahamba. Azibeta, azibeta, azibeta, azibeta, ada asika ancama agoduka.

Yiyo le nkwenkwe yazigodusa i nkomo, isiti :—

Ro - qo - za - ni, ro - qo - za - ni u ku - ha - mba *(bis)*.
Ni - ya bon' u ku - ba ni - fi - le *(bis)*.

" Roqozani, roqozani u kuhamba *(bis)*.
Niyabon' u kuba nifile *(bis)*. "

Utsho e zinkomeni za ko wabo. Zahamba ke zaya e kaya zafika. Kwasengwa ngo kuhlwa ke, kwasengwa i ntlazana. A zapuma i nkomo. Yati ke :—

" Roqozani, roqozani u kuhamba *(bis)*"
*(Sung as before)*.

Zahamba ke zaya e hlatini, zafika ke, zatya ke e hlatini.

Afika a magqongqo kanjako, azibeta, azibeta, azibeta, azibeta. A zahamba. Yati i nkosi ya magqongqo : " Kanifune e zi nkomeni, zingabi zi no mntu ozitetelayo. " Bafuna ke, basuke ke babona le nkwenkwe i ku nina. Bati : " Bonga. " Yati yona : " A ndikwazi. " Wati o mnye : " Bonga, ndokuhlaba ngo mkonto lo. " Wati ke :—

they tried to drive off the cattle ; they beat and beat them, they beat and beat, until at last they gave up resisting, and went homewards.

It is that boy who made them go home by singing :

" Range yourselves to go, range yourselves *(bis)*.
You see that you are killed *(bis)*. "

Thus he spoke to the cattle belonging to his village. So they went homewards, and arrived (safely). The evening milk was drawn, and the morning milk was drawn [d]. They did not go out. So the boy sang (as before) :

" Range yourselves to go, range yourselves *(bis)*".

Then they started, and went to the kloof, where they began to graze.

Again came the gqongqos, they beat and beat them, they beat and beat. They refused to go. Then the chief of the gqongqos said : " Just look well among these cows, may be there is somebody who directs them." So they looked and found that boy near his mother. They said : " Spell. " He said : " I do not know how to spell ". One of them said : " Spell, or I shall stab you with this spear. " Then he sang :

Ro - qo - za - ni ro - qo - za - ni u - ku - ha - mba *(bis)*.
Ni - ya - bon' u ku - ba ndi - fi - le *(bis)*.

" Roqozani, roqozani u kuhamba *(bis)*.

Niya bona u kuba ndifile *(bis)*. "

Zahamba ke i nkomo zitinjwa nga magqongqo. Yasuka e nye i nkabi e nkulu a yahamba. Bati ke: " Kwedini, bonga le nkabi." Yati le nkwenkwe: " A ndikwazi." Bati ke bona: " U ya kwazi." Yati ke le nkwenkwe :—

" Range yourselves to go, range yourselves *(bis)*.

You see that I am dead *(bis)*. "

Then the cattle went, being driven away by the gqongqos. But one old ox refused to go. So they said: " Boy, spell this ox." The boy said: " I don't know how to do so." They said: " You do know." Then the boy sang,

" Waqeqeza (¹), waqeqeza u kuhamba *(bis)*.

Uya bon' u kuba ndifile *(bis)*. "

Yahamba ke le nkabi, yema kwe nye i ndawo, bati: " Bonga, kwedini." Yati :—

" Waqeqeza, etc. *(the same as before)*. "

Yahamba ke, yafika e mlanjeni, yafika yema. Bati ke : " Bonga, kwedini." Yati ke :—

" Waqeqeza, waqeqeza u kuwela *(bis)*.

Uya bon' u kuba ndifile *(bis)*. "

Yawela ke, yahamba, bayiquba. Yati ya kufika nga se buhlanti, a yangena. Bati ke: " Bonga, kwedini." Yati ke le nkwenkwe :—

" Waqeqeza, waqeqeza u kungena *(bis)*.

Uya bon' u kuba ndifile *(bis)*. "

*(Sung as the previous spells.)*

Yangena ke. Batata i ntambo, beza kuyixela. Bayirintyela. Yasuka, a yarintyeleka. Bati : " Bonga, kwedini." Yati ke :—

" Take the trouble to go, take that trouble *(bis)*.

Thou seest that I am killed *(bis)*. "

So the ox went, but it stopped at another place. They said : " Spell, boy." He sang :

" Take the trouble, etc. *(the same as before)*".

So the ox went on ; but, when it came to the river, it stopped. They said : " Spell, boy." So he sang: —

" Take the trouble to cross, take that trouble *(bis)*.

Thou seest that I am killed *(bis)*. "

So the ox crossed the river and went on. They drove it before them. But when it came near the kraal, it refused to go in. They said : " Spell, boy." So he sang :

" Take the trouble to go in, take that trouble *(bis)*.

Thou seest that I am killed *(bis)*. "

So it went in. They took a riem (*e*), in order to go and slaughter it. They pulled. But it could not be drawn. They said : " Spell, boy." So he sang :

---

1. In another version of this tale I heard *u-ya-qeqeza*, which is more regular, but not so well adapted to the rhythm.

"Waqeqeza, waqeqeza u kurintyeleka (*bis*).
Uya bon' u kuba ndifile (*bis*). "

Yarintyeleka ke. Bayihlaba apa e siswini ngo mkonto, a wangena u mkonto. Bati : " Bonga, kwedini. " Yati ke : —

" Waqeqeza, waqeqeza u kuhlatywa (*bis*).
Uy abon' u kuba ndifile (*bis*). "
(*Sung as the previous spells.*)

Wangena ke u mkonto e siswini. Bayihlinza ke bayigqiba. A kwatyiwa ne ntwana e ngcingci, baya kuyibeka e ndlini. Bona baza kumka. Bati baya kuhlamba i sisu e lwandle, bobuya ngo kuhlwa.

Bemka ke, bashiya i xekwazana (¹) e kaya, liza kugcina i nyama na la nkwenkwe.

Yasuke ke le nkwenkwe, ba kumka, yatata (²) a mafuta, yawapeka e ziko, anyibilika. Yasuke yatata u mcepe, yaka e mafuteni, yawanika eli xekwazana e shushu. Lati lona : " Ndakutsha. " Yati yona : " Sela. " Lasela, lati : " Ashushu. " Yati le nkwenkwe : " Sela, " ngo msindo. Lasela. Yati yona : " Kwazà. " Lati i xekwazana : " Hu ! i nkomo ziyemka. " Yapinda yaka kanjako, ingxamele u kuba ze linga kwazi u kuteta. Yalita a mafuta, yati : " Kwazà. "

" Take the trouble to be drawn, take that trouble (*bis*).
Thou seest that I am killed (*bis*). "

So the ox was drawn. They tried to stab it here in the belly with a spear. But the spear could not go in. They said : " Spell, boy. " He sang :

" Take the trouble to be stabbed, take that trouble (*bis*).
Thou seest that I am killed (*bis*). "

So the spear went in into the belly. They skinned the ox and prepared it. But not the least bit of it was eaten then, they only went to put it down in a hut. Then they left the place, saying that they were going to wash the tripe ⁽¹⁾ in the sea ⁽²⁾, and that they would be back at sunset.

So they started, leaving a little old woman at home to watch over the meat and over that boy.

As soon as they had left, the boy took fat, and cooked it at the fireplace until it melted. Then taking a large spoon, he took out some of it, and presented it quite hot to the old woman. The woman said : " I shall be burnt. " The boy said : " Drink. " She then began to drink, but she stopped, saying : " It is too hot. " The boy said with an angry tone : " Drink. " She drank. The boy said : " Scream (now). " The old woman said : " Whew ! the cattle are going

---

1. It seems that the right spelling of this word should be *i xegwazana*, not *i xekwazana*, but I have thought better to spell it as I heard it pronounced. It is derived from *i xego* " an old man ", with the feminine suffix *-azi* an l the diminutive suffix *-ana* (591 and 592).

2. *Tata* is the usual pronunciation of the word which is commonly written *tabata*.

Lati: " Awu! " Yapinda kanjako, yati: " Kwazà. " La linga kwazi u kukwaza, litshile nga mafuta. Yasuke ke le nkwenkwe, yati: —

off. " He dipped again into the fat, wishing to make her unable to utter a sound. He poured it into her (throat), then said: " Scream. " She said: " Au! " He did the same once more, then said: " Scream. " She could not scream, she had been burnt by the fat. Then that boy sang:

" Waqeqeza, waqeqeza u kuvuka *(bis)*.
Uya bon' u kuba bemkile *(bis)*. "

" Take the trouble to rise again, take that trouble *(bis)*.
Thou seest that they are gone *(bis)*. "

Yavuka ke le nkabi ixeliweyo. Yaziquba ke le nkwenkwe i nkomo zonke, igoduka nazo.

So that ox which had been slaughtered rose again. Then the boy drove all the cattle before him, and went home with them.

Yati, ya kufika nazo e kaya, kwatiwa: " Be ziye pina lo nyaka wonke? " Yati ke yona: " Za zibiwe. " Kwatiwa ke: " Ulibele (¹) yi nto nina wena? " Yati ke: " Nam be ndimkile nam. " Kwatiwa ke: " Kulungile. "

When he got home, the people said: " Where have the cattle been all this long time? " He said: " They had been stolen. " The people said: " Where were you then? " He said: " I too, I had gone with them. " So they said: " All right. "

Wona a magqongqo afika e kaya, inkomo zingeko. Ati: " Madlebedlumbi (²), i nkomo ziye pina? " A kakwazi u kuteta.

As to the gqongqos, when they came home, they did not find the cattle there. They said (to the old woman): " Madlebedlumbi, where are the cattle? " But she could not speak.

Asuke ke la magqongqo enz' i zibata. Yaya ke le nkwenkwe, yaya e zi bateni, yafika kubanjisiwe i ntaka. Yati ke yakulula ke e nye i ntaka, yabanjiswa ke ngo mnwe. Yati: " I ! ub' i sandla sam siye pina? " Yatiwa go ke nga so, oko kukuti, ziti i zibata

So they went and laid snares. That boy then went where the snares had been laid, and found birds caught in them, but, while he loosened one of them, he was caught himself by one finger. He said: " Hee! Where do you want to take my hand to (³)? "

---
1. This is a participle. It means lit. " You having delayed... "
2. This is the proper name of the old woman. It means lit.: " Ears that eat another person ", i. e. " Long-ears ".
3. Lit. " You steal my hand that it may go whither? "

zimbambe. Yati : " I ! ub 'e sinye i sandla sam siye pi ? " Yatiwa go ngesi sandla. Yati : " I ! ub' u mlenze wam uye pi ! " Yatiwa go ngo mnye u mlenze. Yati : " I ! ub' o mnye u mlenze wam uye pi ? " Yatiwa go nga lo mlenze. Yati : " I ! ub' i ntlokw'am iye pi ? " Yatiwa go nga yo. Yati : " I ! ub' u mlomo wam uye pi ? " Yatiwa go nga wo.

But that hand did " *gv* ", that is to say, it was caught in the snares. He said : " Hee ! Where do you want to take my other hand to ? " He was caught by that hand. He said : " Hee ! Where do you want to take my leg to ? " He was caught by that leg. He said : " Hee ! where do you want to take my other leg to ? " He was caught by that leg. He said : " Hee ! where do you want to take my head to ? " He was caught by the head. He said : " Hee ! where do you want to take my lips to ? " He was caught by the lips.

Afika ke a magqongqo a mabini, ati : " E ! siya mfumana namhlanje u Qajana. " Wati : " Ndikululeni ize ndife. " Ati : " Hayi, uya kubaleka. " Wati yena : " Hayi, a ndisa kubaleka. " Bamkulula ke. Wati : " Basani i nyanda ze nkuni zibe mbini, ize ndife. " Bati : " Hayi, uya kubaleka. " Wati : " Hayi, a ndukubaleka (¹). " Bavuma ke bazibasa ke. Wati : " Vutelani no babini, ize ndife. " Bati : " Yi nto nina lo nto ? Ungxamele u kuze ubaleke. " Wati : " Hayi, a ndukubaleka. " Bati ke, bavutela ke, wabafaka bo babini e mlilweni i ntloko.

Thereupon came two gqongqos, who said : " Aha ! we have caught him to-day, this Qajana. " He said : " Loosen me, that I may die. " They said : " No, you would run away. " He said : " No, I shall no more run away. " So they loosened him. He said : " Set fire to two bundles of wood that I may die. " They said : " No, you would run away. " He said : " No, I shall not run away. " So they consented and lit the fire. He said : " Blow, both of you, that I may die. " They said : " What is that ? You only want to run away. " So they blew the fire ; then he sent them both into it head-forward.

Wati ke e zinkomeni za ko wabo : —

Then he said to the cattle of his own village :

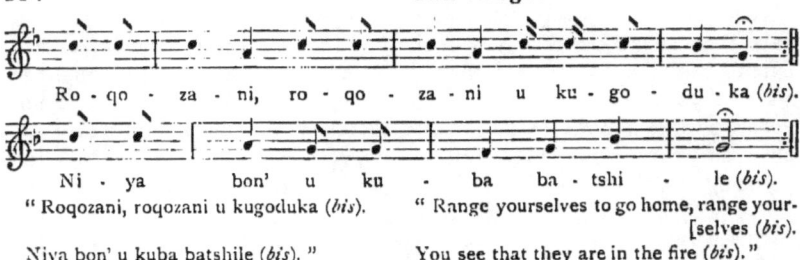

Ro - qo - za - ni, ro - qo - za - ni u ku - go - du - ka (*bis*).

Ni - ya bon' u ku - ba ba - tshi - le (*bis*).

" Roqozani, roqozani u kugoduka (*bis*).

Niya bon' u kuba batshile (*bis*). "

" Range yourselves to go home, range your-
[selves (*bis*).

You see that they are in the fire (*bis*). "

---

1. This is for *a ndiyi kubaleka*.

Zagoduka ke. Zona i nkomo za zibiwe nga magqongqo, waziquba, waya nazo e mzini we nkosi ya magqongqo. Wafika wati : " Ndafumana ezi nkomo zibaleka. Ndazinqanda ke, ngabi zezenu." Kwatiwa : " Ewe." Yati ke i nkosi : " Ma ke uye kuzalusa." Wemka nazo ke u kuya kuzalusa. Wati ke, a kumka nazo ke, wazityoba, wazityoba e mitini, wazityoba, wazityoba, wazityoba. Wabuya ke wati : " Nkosi, le nkomo yandihlaba, ma yixelwe." Yaxelwa ke. Yati ke i nkosi : " Hamba uhlambe eli tumbu e mlanjeni." Wahamba ke, wati ke yena kruntsu, kratya, wati : " Qweqwedē! Bonela, sele, i tumbu le nkosi a ndilityi." Wemka ke nalo walisa e nkosini, wahamba esiti : " Eyi! Eyi! isele yandipanga." Walinika ke i nkosi, wemka ke, wati uya e zinkomeni.

Wahamba ke, wabona u msi uquma nga se hlatini. Waya ke, wafika kungeko madoda, i li xekwazana lodwa lipeka e nye i nyamakazi. Wati: " Molo, makulu! " Wati : " Makulu, yopula i nyama le." Layopula ke, bayitya. Wayitya u Qajana le nyama ; wati, a kuyitya, wati : " Makulu, kunjanina? Ma senze i ntlonde yo kupekapekana." Lati i xekwazana : " Ewe." Lamfaka ke lafaka u Qajana e mbizweni. Wavakala u Qajana esiti : " Makulu, ndopule." Wamopula ke uninakulu. Walitata ke u Qajana eli xekwazana, waliti fungu, walifaka ke nge ntloko e ma-

So they went home. As to the cows which had been stolen by the gqongqos, he drove them before him, and went with them to the kraal of the king of the gqongqos. When he came to the place, he said : " I have found these cows running away, I have brought them back, thinking they might be yours." The people said : " Yes." Then the king said : " Go and herd them." So he went to herd them. When he had gone, he drove them deep into the bush, he drove them deeper and deeper. Then he came back (with one cow), and said : " King, this cow is vicious, it should be slaughtered." It was slaughtered. The king said : " Go and wash this tripe in the river." He went and bit off a piece ; he found it raw ; then he said : " Qweqwede! See here, frog, the tripe belonging to the king, I cannot eat it." He took back to the king what was left, saying on the way : " Oh dear! dear! a frog has robbed me." So he handed it back to the king, and went away, saying that he was going to see the cattle.

On his way, he saw smoke coming up from the direction of the forest. So he went in that direction. When he came, he found no men there, but only a little old woman who was cooking venison. He said : " Good morning, grandmother." He added : " Grandmother, take the meat out of the pot." So she took it out, and they sat down to eat it. Qajana ate most of it. When he had done, he said : " Grandmother, what do you think of this? Let us play at cooking one another." The old woman said : " Yes." So she put Qajana into the pot. Soon he cried out, saying :

nzini ashushu. Lati : " Shu ! ndatsha, ndopule, Qajana. " Wati : " Yitsha. " Lati : " Hu ! ndatsha, mntan'am Qajana. " Wati yena : " Vutwa. " Kade lisitsha, wafuna i siciko, wacika. Lasike lavutwa ke. Walopula ke, waligcuba, wafaka le nyama yalo e mbizeni kanjako. Le mpahla yalo walitata, wambata ke, wahlala ke.

Afika ke a madodana, ati : " Yopula, ma. " Wati : " Hayi, yopulani, bantwana bam. " Bayopula ke, bayigqiba, bayitya. Wati ke wapuma wati : " Ndzebe, badla nina. " Basuka, ba kuva lo nto, bamfunza nge zinja. Wafika u mlambo uzele, wasuka wazenza i sikuni. Afika ke a magqongqo, lati ke e linye : "Ma ke sigibisele i zikuni. " Bazitata ke, bazigibisela pesheya. U Qajana wagibiselwa naye. Wafika nga pesheya, wazenza i nkwenkwe ke kanjako, wati ke : " Ndzebe, nandiweza. "

" Grandmother, take me out. " The grandmother took him out. Then Qajana took her and thrust her head forward into the boiling water. She said : " Oh dear ! I am burning, take me out of the pot, Qajana. " He said : " Burn on. " She said : " Oh dear ! My child Qajana, I am burning. " He said : " Get done. " When she had been burning a long time, he looked for the lid, and covered the pot. So the woman got done. Then he took her out, peeled off her skin, and put the meat back into the pot. He also took her clothes, put them on, and sat down.

When the young men came, they said : " Mother, take the meat out of the pot. " He said : " Take it out yourselves, my children. " So they took the meat out of the pot and ate it. Then he went out, saying : " The fools ! they have eaten their mother. " As soon as they heard this, they chased him, setting dogs after him. He came to a river which was full, he then transformed himself into a log of wood. When the Gqongqos came, one of them said : " Let us throw logs of wood across. " So they took the logs, and threw them over to the other side. Qajana was thrown also, and thus came to the other side. Then he turned himself into a boy again, and said : " Fools ! you have helped me across " (*a*).

## NOTES.

(*a*) — *The Gqongqos*. — In Kafir lore the *Gqongqo* (or *Kongo*, or *Qongqongqo*) is a sort of wild man of the woods with ears as long as a man's hand, always described as a maneater. He is distinguished from the ordinary cannibal, who in Kafir is called *i zim*. It strikes me that probably the notion of the Gqongqo is not purely fabulous. My Tonga informants used to designate certain Bushmen tribes which are still in existence under the name of *Ma- ngoko*, and as there are no clicks in the Tonga language, there is every appearance that this word was originally identical with the Kafir noun *a Ma-gqongqo*. This again may have some connection with the double fact that in ancient Arabic geographies several South-African tribes are described under the name of *Wa-kwakwa* (¹), and that in these same geographies the *Wa-kwakwa* are considered as being related to the Chinese (²), who go themselves by the name of *Gog* and *Ma-gog*. Further in the same line of analogies, the Cape colonists used to call certain semi-Hottentot and semi-Bushmen tribes " Hottentot Chinese "; and the most remarkable feature of the language of the Bushmen is that the words generally change their meanings by admitting different accents somewhat as Chinese does. I wish to draw no conclusion from these coincidences; I only notice them as being not devoid of interest, and as giving some weight to the thought that the notion of the Gqongqo may be derived from history. Pursuing the same range of ideas, I wonder whether these various words *Gqongqo, Ngoko, Kwakwa, Gog*, etc., are not related themselves to the name of the *Gogo* tribe *(Ma-gogo)*, which is found inland from Zanzibar, all the more as the Chinese once occupied an island near the Zanzibar coast, and it would be astonishing if their name of *Gog* and *Magog* had not been preserved by one or other of the tribes that had more intimate connections with them at that time. — The long ears of the Gqongqos remind one of the custom which some South-African tribes have of stretching the lobes of their ears by means of copper weights.

(*b*) *Qajana* is one of the most popular heroes of Kafir lore. The facts related here are only a few of his exploits. The very same stories which are told of Qajana are sometimes attributed to *Hlakanyana*. Possibly these two heroes are in reality one and the same. They are as it were the Samsons of Kafir lore. The characteristic feature of Qajana is cunning and love of revenge. He is not precisely a specimen of courage, and his revenge falls mostly on poor old women. This represents unfortunately one of the worst traits in the Kafir character. For, as a rule, these people cannot be said to be very respectful or kind to old women. They told me themselves that in former times it was not uncommon, when women were getting incapable of doing any more work, to send them to draw water from the river, and then to make them jump into it.

(*c*) *The cattle... went to the kloof*. — In South-Africa we term *kloof* a sheltered valley bedecked with trees. This is properly a Dutch word.

(*d*) *The evening milk... and the morning milk:* — These are common expressions to mark the two most important times of the day (cf. Homer's νυκτὸς ἀμολγῷ, *Iliad*, XXII, 317; *Od.*, IV, 841). In Kafirland cows are generally milked first at sunset when they come from grazing : they are not milked at dawn, but they are then generally let out of the kraal for one or two hours to enjoy in its neighbourhood the short grass that has been refreshed by the dew of the night, and it is only after this that they are milked again to be led afterwards to more remote and richer grazing grounds. Hence the word *i ntlazane*, or *i ntlazana*, which means properly " small grass, " has come to be applied to the time of milking cows in the morning. The word *kraal* is of Dutch origin. The Kafir kraal, *u buhlanti*, is an open round inclosure, sometimes built with stones without mortar between them, but more commonly made only with thorn-bushes.

(*e*) *A riem*. — This is another Dutch word. Kafirs have nothing like European ropes. The only strong thing of some length they know of for tying or dragging anything is a kind of thong or leather strap prepared in a special manner, and in South-Africa called a riem.

(*f*) Kafirs are particularly fond of the tripe of clean animals. But even those among them who make light of the old custom of not eating unclean food, such as pork, monkeys, eels, etc., would never for anything in the world touch pig's tripe.

(*g*) *In the sea*. — I have three different versions of this tale in my hands, and in all

---

1. *Kwakwa* is now the name of that arm of the Zambezi on which Kilimane is built. There is also in Gazaland south of Sofala a tribe still known under the name of *Wa-kwakwa*.

2. Cf. Introduction.

(h) The conclusion of this tale is common to several others. It is somewhat abrupt. But this is one of the characteristic features of most Kafir tales that they are brought to an end precisely when the hearers would be glad to hear something more about their heroes.

## Fourth Tale.

### TANGA-LO-MLIBO (¹).

Kwaka kwako u mfazi enga hambi e mini, aze ahambe e busuku. La li ngu Tanga-lo-mlibo i gama lake la ko wabo. Wati eya kuzekwa yi ndoda, wati "a kahambi e mini." Yati i ndoda: " Mziseni noko, anga hamba e mini, ahambe ngo kuhlwa." Yamzeka ke. Waze ke wazala u mntana.

Yati i ndoda yake nge nye i mini, yaya kuzingela. Washiyeka ke lo mfazi e kaya, ne xego, ne ntombazana. Lati i xego: " Hamba undikelele a manzi e mlanjeni." Wati yena: " A ndihambi nge mini, ndihamba e busuku u kuya e mlanjeni." Wati u yise: " Ndincede, mntan'am, ndaqauka li ngxano, ndiyafa." Wati ke yena: " Nanga a masi." Lati i xego: " A ndiwafuni, ashushu." Wati: " Nabu u tywala." Lati: " A ndibufuni, bushushu." Wati ke watuma i ntombazana u kuya kuka e mlanjeni, wati: " A ndihambi e mini mna." Yeza nawo ke a manzi i ntombazana. Lati i xego: " Ashushu." Lati: " Hamba undikelele wena, mntan'am." Wati: " A ndihambi e mini."

### TANGA-LO-MLIBO (ᵃ).

There was once a woman who used never to go out by day, but to go out afterwards at night. Her name at home (ᵇ) was Tanga-lo-mlibo. As she was about to be married to a man, she said she could not go out by day. The man said: " Bring her all the same to me: she will not go out in the daytime, but only after sunset." So he married her, and in time she bore him a child.

One day her husband went to hunt. She was left at home with the old man (i. e. her father-in-law) and a young girl. The old man said: " Go to draw water for me from the river." She said: " I never go out by day, I go to the river at night only." Her father (-in-law) said: " Have pity on me, my child, I am panting with thirst, I am dying." She said: " Here is sour milk (ᶜ)." The old man said: " I do not want it, it is too hot." She said: " Here is Kafir beer (ᵈ)." He said: " I do not want it, it is too hot." So she sent the little girl to go and draw from the river, saying: " I cannot go myself by day." So the girl came back bringing water. But the old man said: " It is too hot. Go and draw for me yourself, my child." She said: " I cannot go out by day."

---

1. Proper name. It means properly " pumpkin of the tender shoot ", i. e. " first pumpkin ", as if the name had been given at the time the first pumpkins of the year were to be seen in the fields.

Wade wahamba u Si-hamba-nge-nyanga, washiya usana e kaya. Waya ke ecatazela, wafika e mlanjeni. Waka ngo mcepe, wasuke watshona. Waka nge mbiza, yasuke yatshona. Waka nge sitya, sasuke satshona. Waka ngo mpanda, wasuke watshona. Waka nge qiya, yasuke yatshona. Waka nge sikaka, sasuke satshona. Wasuke wenjenje waka nge sandl' esi, watshona naye wonke.

Ushiye u sana lwake e ndlini e ntombazaneni. Waze ke wavakala lo mntana elila. Yasuke i ntombazana yamsa e mlanjeni. Yafika, a yabona u nina. Yema nga pezu ko mlambo, yati : —

At last Si-hamba-nge-nyanga (the walker by moon-light) went, leaving her babe at home. She went tottering all the way. When she reached the river, she tried to draw with a large spoon; it sank. She tried to draw with a pot; it sank. She tried to draw with a basket (e); it sank. She tried to draw with a jug; it sank. She tried to draw with her kerchief; it sank. She tried to draw with her apron; it sank. Finally she did thus, dipping this hand of hers; she sank herself with her whole body.

She had left her babe at home in the hands of the little girl. After a time the child was heard crying. Then the girl took it to the river, but she did not see the mother. She then stood on the bank of the river, and sang thus :

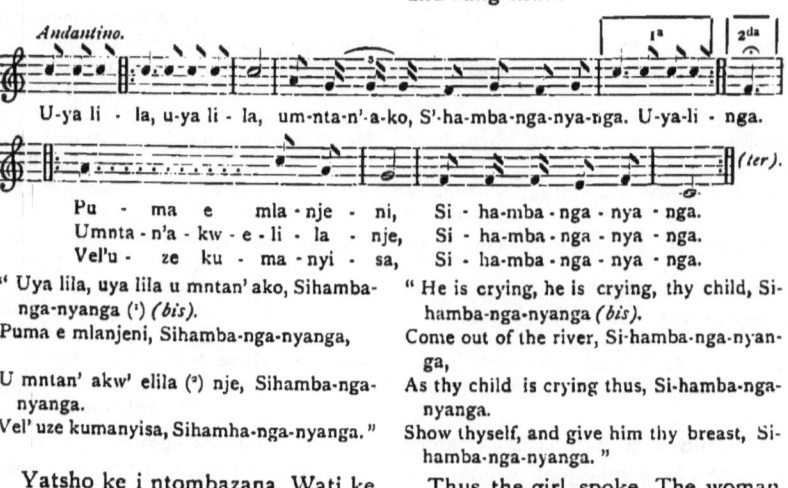

" Uya lila, uya lila u mntan' ako, Sihamba-nga-nyanga (¹) (bis).
Puma e mlanjeni, Sihamba-nga-nyanga,

U mntan' akw' elila (²) nje, Sihamba-nga-nyanga.
Vel' uze kumanyisa, Sihamba-nga-nyanga."

Yatsho ke i ntombazana. Wati ke yena u mfazi, wavela ke e sizibeni. Wati, nx' aza kupuma e mlanjeni, wati : —

" He is crying, he is crying, thy child, Sihamba-nga-nyanga (bis).
Come out of the river, Si-hamba-nga-nyanga,
As thy child is crying thus, Si-hamba-nga-nyanga,
Show thyself, and give him thy breast, Si-hamba-nga-nyanga."

Thus the girl spoke. The woman then showed herself in the pool, and before coming out of the river, she sang thus :

---

1. Here *nyanga* is used without its article *i*. Hence *Si-hamba-nga-nyanga*, whereas we had above *Si-hamba-nge-nyanga* (= *Si-hamba nga i nyanga*).
2. Contraction for *u mntana wako elila*.

(11 times).

| | | |
|---|---|---|
| U - ti ma ndi - ti ni, | No - ta - nda - la - ndlo - vu? |
| Ndi - pu - me e mla - nje - ni, | No - ta - nda - la - ndlo -. vu? |

| | | |
|---|---|---|
| Nde - nzi - we nga - bom, | No - ta-nda - la-ndlo - vu. |
| Pe - zu - lu pe - zu - lu, | No - ta-nda - la-ndlo - vu. |
| Nde - nzi - we ngu- ba - wo, | No - ta-nda - la-ndlo - vu. |
| Pe - zu - lu pe - zu - lu, | No - ta-nda - la-ndlo - vu. |
| U-ndi-tu-me a ma-nzi e - mi - ni, | No - ta-nda - la-ndlo - vu. |
| A-ndi S'ha - mba nga-nya - nga, | No - ta-nda - la-ndlo - vu? |
| U-ndi tu - me nga-ngo ca, | No - ta-nda - la-ndlo - vu. |
| Pe - zu - lu pe - zu - lu, | No - ta-nda - la-ndlo - vu. |
| Be - ta ngo ca - na, | No - ta-nda - la-ndlo - vu. |
| Pe - zu - lu pe - zu - lu, | No - ta-nda - la-ndlo - vu. |
| A - ku - m - si ku yi - se, | No - ta-nda - la-ndlo - vu? |

" Uti ma nditi ni, Notanda-la-ndlovu (¹)?

Ndipume e mlanjeni, Notanda-la-ndlovu?

Ndenziwe ngabom, Notanda-la-ndlovu,

Pezulu pezulu, Notanda-la-ndlovu.
Ndenziwe ngu bawo, Notanda-la-ndlovu.

Pezulu pezulu, Notanda-la-ndlovu.
Unditume a manzi e mini, Notanda-la-
        [ndlovu.
A ndi Sihamba-nga-nyanga, Notanda-la-
        [ndlovu?
Unditume nga ngoca, Notanda-la-ndlovu,

Pezulu pezulu, Notanda-la-ndlovu.
Beta ngo cana, Notanda-la-ndlovu,

Pezulu pezulu, Notanda-la-ndlovu.
A kumsi ku yise, Notanda-la-ndlovu ? "

Watsho u Si-hamba-nge-nyanga.
Wapuma ke e mlanjeni, wamanyisa lo mntana, wabe wangena e manzini. Wati : " Uz' unga baxeleli a bantu b'e kaya u kuba lo mntana ke ndamanyisa. "

Yagoduka ke le ntombazana.

" What dost thou want me to do, Notanda-
        [la-ndlovu?
That I should come out of the river, No-
        [tanda-la-ndlovu?
My fate has been brought about intention-
        [ally, No-tanda-la-ndlovu,
Above and above, No-tanda-la-ndlovu.
It has been brought about by my father,
        [No-tanda-la-ndlovu.
Above and above, No-tanda-la-ndlovu.
He sent me for water in the daytime, No-
        [tanda-la-ndlovu.
Am I not the Walker-by-moonlight, No-
        [tanda-la-ndlovu?
He sent me as if with a stick, No-tanda-la-
        [ndlovu,
Above and above, No-tanda-la-ndlovu.
Beat the child with rushes, No-tandla-la
        [ndlovu,
Above and above, No-tanda-la-ndlovu.
Why dost thou not take him to his father,
        [No-tanda-la-ndlovu ? "

Thus Si-hamba-nge-nyanga spoke. Then she came out of the river, gave her breast to the child, and went back into the water. She said : " Do not tell the people at home that I did give my breast to the child. "

The girl went home back. Night

---

1. This is the proper name of the girl. It means " Mother of Elephant-track ".

Kwahlwa ke, kwasa i mini, kwaba nge ntlazane, walila u mntana. Yamsa ke i ntombazana ku nina kanjako. Yema nga pezu ko mlambo, yati:—

"Uyalila, uyalila, etc. *(the same as before)*."

Wavela ke u nina e sizibeni, wati:
—
"Uti ma nditi ni, etc. *(the same as before)*."

Wapuma ke, wamanyisa lo mntana, wabe wangena e manzini, wati: "Uz' ungatsho u kuti ndamanyisa e kaya."

Yagoduka ke i ntombazana, yaya e kaya no mntana. Kwabuzwa: "Lo mntana umnika nto nina?" Yati: "Ndimnika u kutya." Kwatiwa: "Hayi, xela." Yati ke yona i ntombazana: "Wanyisiwe ngu nina." Wati ke u yise: "Ub' epumile e mlanjeni?" Yati ke yona: "Ewe." Yatsho ke yalila no yise. Wati u yise: "Ze sihambe ne ntambo ngo mso, siye kumrola, simrolele apa."

Kwati ke, kwa kusa, yahamba i ntombazana na madoda, yaya e mlanjeni. Yema pezu ko mlambo kanjako, yati:—

came, then dawn, then full daylight, and then the child began to cry. So the girl took him back to his mother. Again she stood on the bank, and sang (as before):

"He is crying, he is crying, etc."

So the mother showed herself in the pool, and sang (as before):

"What dost thou want me to do, etc."

Then she came out, gave her breast to the child, and went back into the water, saying: "Do not tell anybody at home that I have given him the breast."

So the girl went home back carrying the child. This question was asked: "What do you give to that child?" She said: "I give him food to eat." The people said: "Impossible, tell the truth." Then the girl said: "He has been suckled by his mother." So the father said: "Then she came out of the river?" The girl said "Yes", and she shed tears together with the father. The father said: "Let us go with riems to-morrow, to drag her hither."

So on the following morning the girl went with the men in the direction of the river. Once more she stood on the bank and sang thus:

U-ya li - la, u-ya li - la, um-nta-n'-a-ko, S'-ha-mba-nga-nya-nga. U-ya-li - nga.

(6 times).

| Pu - ma | e | mla-nje - ni, | Si - ha-mba-nga - nya - nga. |
| We - nzi - | we nga - | bom, | Si - ha-mba-nga - nya - nga. |
| Pe - zu - lu | | pe - zu - lu, | Si - ha-mba-nga - nya - nga. |
| Wa-tu-nywa | a | ma-nzi e mi - ni, | Si - ha-mba-nga - nya - nga. |
| Ka-nt'u-ngu | S'ha-mba nge nya - nga, | | Si - ha-mba-nga - nya - nga. |
| U mntan' | ak'u - ya - li - la, | | Si - ha-mba-nga - nya - nga. |

" Uya lila, uya lila, u mntan' ako, Sihamba-nga-nyanga *(bis)*.
Puma e mlanjeni, Sihamba-nga-nyanga.

Wenziwe ngabom, Sihamba-nga-nyanga,

Pezulu pezulu, Sihamba-nga-nyanga.
Watunywa a manzi e mini, Sihamba-nga-nyanga.
Kanti u ngu Sihamba-nga-nyanga, Sihamba-nga-nyanga.
U mtan' ako uya lila, Sihamba-nga-nyanga."

Akapuma. Emka ke a madoda. Yasala i ntombazana, yati: —

" He is crying, he is crying, thy child, Si-hamba-nga-nyanga *(bis)*.
Come out of the river, Si-hamba-nga-nyanga.
Thy fate has been brought about intentionally, Si-hamba-nga-nyanga,
Above and above, Si-hamba-nga-nyanga.
Thou wast sent for water in the daytime, Si-hamba-nga-nyanga.
Yet thou art the Walker-by-moonlight, Si-hamba-nga-nyanga.
Thy child is crying, Si-hamba-nga-nyanga."

The mother did not come out. So the men went away. The girl remained behind, and sang again:

U mntan' ak'    u - ya li - la,     Si - ha - mba-nga - nya - nga.
Vel'   u - ze   ku - ma - nyi - sa.   Si - ha - mba-nga - nya - nga.

" U mntan' ako uyalila, Sihamba nga [nyanga.
Vel' uze kumanyisa, Sihamba-nga-nyanga."

Wapuma wamanyisa u nina, wabe wangena e manzini. Yagoduka ke le ntombazana.

Yafika yati: " Uke wapuma e mva kwenu."

Kwasa ke, yaya i ntombazana, yaya na madoda kanjako. I ntombazana yahamba pambili, a madoda ahamba nge mva kwe ntombazana. Afika ke a madoda, azimela. Yema i ntombazana nga pezu ko mlambo kanjako, yati: —

" Uyalila, uyalila, etc. *(the same as the day [before).*

Wavela u Si-hamba-nge-nyanga, wati: " Ndi ma manwele. Ndiyoyika ngati uze na bantu. " Yati le ntombazana: " Hayi, andizanga na bantu. " Wapuma ke wamanyisa. Wabonwa esamanyisa nga madoda. Yasuke i ndoda yake yati ruquruku

" Thy child is crying, Si-hamba-nga-nyan- [ga,
Show thyself, and come to give him the [breast, Si-hamba-nga-nyanga. "

The mother then came out, gave her breast to the child, and went back into the water. The girl went back home.

When the girl came, she said: " She (the mother of the child) came out after you had gone. "

Morning came. The girl went back with the men as before. She walked in front, and the men walked behind her. When these came near the river, they hid themselves. The girl stood again on the bank of the river, and sang:

" He is crying, he is crying, etc. *(as on the [preceding day).*

Si - hamba - nge - nyanga showed herself and said: " I feel my hair standing on end upon my head. I fear you have come with other people. " The girl said: " I have not come with anybody. " Then the mother came out and gave her breast to the nge ntambo e mqaleni. Bamrola ke bambekisa e kaya e ndlini.

Kwa u mlambo wahamba nawo, ulandela lo mntu ubanjweyo. Seza i siziba sahlala e zantsi ko mzi. Kwaya kutengwa i zinto e zintsha, ne zikotile, ne qiya, ne lokwe, ne kumtye. Zabekwa ke e mlanjeni. Sahlala, asemka. Yati yeza i nkomo e bomvu ibaleka, yaya e sizibeni, yabuya le nkomo. Sahlala ke i siziba.

Wati u Si-hamba-nge-nyanga : " Tumani u mntu u kumxelela u ma u kuba ndatshona e mlanjeni. "

Kwatunywa i nkabi. Yati ya kufika, yati i ndoda ka Si-hamba-nge-nyanga : " Nkabi, ndikutume na ? " Yati " Mmō. " Kwatiwa nku, yabetwa yapuma ke.

Yatunywa i bokwe. Kwatiwa, ya kufika : " Bokwe, ndikutume na ? " Yati : " Mē. " Kwatiwa nku, yabetwa, yapuma ke.

Yatunywa i nkuku. Kwatiwa : " Nkuku, ndikutume na ? " Yati : " Ewe. " Kwatiwa : " Uye kuti nina ? " Yati : " Ndiya kuti : —

child. She was then seen by the men. Her husband rushed up, and threw a rope round her neck. So they dragged her, and brought her home into the hut.

But the river also went along, following the person who had been seized. The pool went to fix itself at the foot of the kraal. The people went to buy new things (¹), tinvessels, an apron, women's clothes, and crockery. They were put into the river. But it remained there, and would not go away. Then a red cow came running, and went into the pool ; but it came back, and the river did not move.

Si-hamba-nge-nyanga said : " Send somebody to tell my mother that I sank down into the river. "

The people wanted to send an ox. When it came, the husband of Si-hamba-nge-nyanga said : " Bullock, shall I send thee ? " The ox only bellowed. So they struck it, and it went out.

Then they wanted to send a goat. As it came, somebody said : " Goat, shall I send thee ? " It only said : " Bay! " They struck it, and it went out.

Then they wanted to send a cock. Somebody said : " Cock, shall I send thee ? " The cock said " Yes. " The people said : " And what wilt thou say ? " The cock said : " I shall say :

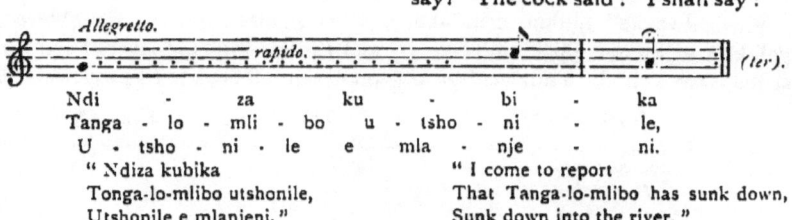

Ndi - za ku - bi - ka
Tanga - lo - mli - bo u - tsho - ni - le,
U - tsho - ni - le e mla - nje - ni.

" Ndiza kubika
Tonga-lo-mlibo utshonile,
Utshonile e mlanjeni. "

" I come to report
That Tanga-lo-mlibo has sunk down,
Sunk down into the river. "

Kwatiwa : " Kulungile." Yahamba ke. Yati ya kufika ku lo mzi ka Si-hamba-nge-nyanga, kwatiwa : " Uti nina ? " Yati : —

They said : " All right." So it went away. When it reached the birth-place of Si-hamba-nge-nyanga, the people said : " What hast thou to say ? " It sang :

Ku - lu - ku   ku   ku! (¹)        Ndi - nku - ku - nje.

A - ndi nku - ku   ya   ku - be - twa.
Ndi -   zo   ku - bi - ka.
Tanga - lo - mlibo   u - tsho - ni - le.
U -   tshonile   e   mla - nje - ni.

U - nga   ndi - bu - la - li   nje (*bis*).

" Kulukukūku !
Ndi nkuku (²) nje,
A ndi nkuku ya kubetwa.
Ndizo kubika
Tanga-lo-mlibo utshonile,
Utshonile e mlanjeni.
Unga ndibulali nje (*bis*). "

" Kulukukūku !
I am a cock as you see.
I am not a cock to be beaten.
I have come to report
That Tanga-lo-mlibo has sunk down,
Sunk down into the river.
Do not chase me in this way (*bis*). "

Yatsho ke i nkuku, walila u yise ka Si-hamba-nge-nyanga. Wati u nina, a kuva, wati : " Hamba siye e mlanjeni ku lo mntana wetu, sikangele u kuba simtenge nga nto nina." Bahamba ke, bafika ku lo ndoda ka Si-hamba-nge-nyanga, bati : " Kuxelwe i nkomo e mdaka, ifakwe e mlanjeni. "

Thus the cock spoke. The father of Si-hamba-nge-nyanga shed tears. Her mother, when she heard this, said : " Let us go towards the river to that child of ours, that we may see how we may buy her back. " So they went. When they came to the place of that husband of Si-hamba-nge-nyanga, they said : " A black cow must be slaughtered, and thrown into the river. "

Kwaxelwa ke i nkomo e mdaka, yafakwa ke e mlanjeni. Semka ke i siziba, saya kuhlala e ndaweni yaso.

Then a black cow was slaughtered, and thrown into the river. Then the pool went off back to its proper place.

Ipelile ke.

That is the end of the story.

1. Imitation of the cock's crow.
2. Poetical for *ndi yi nkuku*.

## NOTES.

(*a*) *Tanga-lo-mlibo.* — This is one of the most popular tales in Kafirland. I have myself collected six different versions of it. Here I give the fullest of the six. A version different from every one of mine has been published by Mr. Theal in his " *Kafir Folk-Lore,* " pp. 56-66. The most peculiar feature of Mr. Theal's version is an introduction explaining how it happened that Tanga-lo-mlibo could not go out in the daytime.

(*b*) *Her name at home.* — This name is opposed to that of *Si-hamba-nge-nyanga*, which this woman is going to receive at her new home. It is very common with Kafirs to have different names in different places. They are particulary careful to assume a new name when they go to work for white people, in order that their master may know as little as possible concerning their antecedents. Hence, among other causes, the great difficulty which is sometimes experienced in identifying thieves.

(*c*) *Sour milk.* — This is the principal food of every Kafir who has a sufficient number of cattle. It is nothing else than coagulated milk from which the whey has not been removed. It is kept in skin-bags, which men alone are allowed to touch, and which are well shaken in order to break the little lumps, whenever milk is poured out of them. Every time the cows are milked, the fresh milk is poured into these bags, where, mixed with the old milk, it ferments rapidly without any further trouble. Sour milk is the most refreshing drink Europeans can have in South-Afrika.

(*d*) *Kafir beer.* — Kafir beer is the same as the Abyssinian *doorah*. The ordinary kind is made out of Kafir corn, which is a kind of sorgho. The corn is first soaked in water, then left to sprout until the sprouts are nearly half an inch long. Then it is spread out in the sun to dry. When quite dry, it is mixed with an equal quantity of corn that has not sprouted. The women then kneeling before a flat stone a little hollowed out pound this corn on it with a small oval stone. The malt thus obtained is cooked in water till it boils, and left to stand in barrels for a day or two. Over night a little malt that has been kept is thrown over the liquid, to set it into fermentation. The following day the beer is strained through a small bag of wicker-work, which allows most of the substantial elements of the flour to pass with the liquid. The beer thus prepared, though a little sour, is a beverage not to be despised. Of course it cannot be kept more than two or three days. Kafir women are often valued as wives according to the quality of the beer they make. Some Kafirs have the bad taste to pour some bottles of brandy into their barrels of beer. This certainly does not improve it.

(*e*) *She dipped a basket.* — Kafirs know how to make wicker-work baskets, which, not leaking in the least, may be used to hold not only milk, but even water.

(*f*) *The people went to buy new things.* — Undoubtedly this is a sentence that does not belong to the original version of this tale, as it mentions several objects which the natives have learned to know of only through Europeans. It shows how Kafir lore is being transformed under new conditions of life.

# Alphabetical Index.

**N. B.** The numbers which are preceded by **p.** refer to the pages in the Appendices. Those in *italics* refer to the paragraphs in the Introduction. The others refer to the paragraphs in the Grammar. Those which are accompanied by an asterisk (*) refer to the comparative tables subjoined to various paragraphs.

*A*, how pronounced, 6.
— = *U*, 273.
— how changed before a vowel, 249.
— when accented, 309.
*a*, article, 317.
*a*, classifier, 337, 535.
*a*, pronoun, 639*, 650, 651, 737, 858, 995-1003.
*a*, relative particle, 718, 723, 724, 781.
*a*, auxiliary, 875, 892-910.
*a*, preposition, 570, 573, 743, 746.
*a*, conjunction, 785.
*a*, prefixed to various pronouns, 812, 814, 820, 821.
-*a*, verbal ending, 833, 842-854.
above, 133, 530, 533*, 541, 581(4).
Abulfeda, 110.
abundant, 601*.
Abyssinian tribes, origin of, *72*.
ACCENT, 301-312.
— its influence on the forms of the words, 444.
— its effect when transposed, 468(1), 559.
accustomed, 1075.
actions, 454.
ADJECTIVES, 600-634.
— rendered by relative, or possessive expressions, 778-780.
ADVERBS, 873, 1086.
affinity, how close between the various Bantu languages, 246.
affirmative clauses, 832.
afterwards, 1016.
-*aga*, verbal suffix, 870.
again, 1012-1015.
aged, 67.
agent, name of, after passive verbs, 589, 1042 (*N. B.*).
agglutinative languages, 108.
Agisumba, Agisymba, *9*.
agree, to, 1084.
agriculture, 454.
air, 377.
*a-ka*, auxiliary, 966.
-*aka*, verbal suffix, 870.
-*ala*, verbal suffix, 1031, 1037.
alive, 601*.
all, 136, 194, 250, 810-812.

alone, 250, 814-818.
along, 564.
ALPHABET, 3-38.
already, 987, 991, 992, 1016, 1017.
also, 691, 819-823.
always, 810.
amidst, 758-763.
among, 554, 563, 565, 758-763.
-*ana*, nominal suffix, 518, 590.
-*ana*, verbal suffix, 1057, 1084.
ancient, 601*, 236.
and, 570, 971, 972, 939.
Anderson, on certain ruins, *18*.
-*ang*?, 803.
*anga*, preposition, 576.
-*anga*, verbal suffix, 833, 870.
Angazidja language, 212.
Angola cluster of languages, *14*.
— sources for its study, *53*.
Angola language, —
— its phonetic features, 146-158.
— its article, 317, 321.
— how its purity has been preserved, *98*.
*ani*?, 803, 804.
animal, 525.
animals, names of, 358, 401, 483.
ankle, 402.
another, 827-829.
answer, to, 128.
ant-hill, 491, 503(9).
any one, 813.
-*anyi*?, 803.
appear, to, 1058-1061.
APPLICATIVE VERBS, 1065-1072.
Arabic words in Swahili, 85.
Arabs in Africa, *83-93*.
-*ari*, nominal suffix, 592.
arm, arms, 81, 179, 230, 232, 414, 462*, 468, (2), 484.
armlet, 482.
arrive, to, 52*, 105.
arrow, arrows, 99, 186, 372, 525.
ARTICLE —
— its forms and use, 317-321
— before relative clauses, 774, 776, 777.
— in Herero, 616, 623.
— in Ganda, 111.
— in Nyambu, 119.
— not found in Swahili, 84.
— how combined with other

particles, 572.
— its origin, 830.
artificial objects, 372 404.
as, 576, 944.
as if, 786.
ashes, 420.
ask, to, 126, 206.
aspiration, replacing a suppressed consonant, 298.
assimilation of vowels, 249-255, 263, 276, 277, 290, 612.
assimilation, predominant in Bantu, 299.
at, 565.
at last, 929.
at night, 556.
-*ati*, nominal suffix, 592.
augmentative nouns, 425-428, 430.
authority, 458.
AUXILIARIES, 873-1018.
— their general meaning, 1085.
— when they must be separated from the principal verb, 892 (*N. B.*)
Avatime language, 598.
awake, to, 173, 179, 1074.
axe, 504*, 525.
Azania, *83*.
-*azi*, nominal suffix, 592.
*azwe*, personal pronoun, 639*.

*B*, how pronounced, 7.
— = *C*, 179.
— = *J*, 221.
— = *M*, 240, 804.
— = *Nd*, 479.
— = *P*, 143.
— = *W*, 214.
— suppressed, 81, 95, 100, 139, 179, 182, 232, 279.
*ba*, classifier, 322-365.
— its transformations, 334-361.
— its use, 342-354, 357-360.
— its etymology, 362-364.
*ba*, locative classifier, 538.
*ba*, pronoun, 639, 718*.
*ba*, auxiliary, 977, 978, 983, 1012.
*ba*, copula, 1028.
Ba-bue, Ba-mbala, Ba-nsundu, Ba-rotse, etc., **see** Bue, Mbala, Nsundu, Rotse, etc.

baby, 480, 504, 525.
back, 174, 208, 366*, 384 (5).
back, adv., 1012-1015.
bad, 94, 129, 131, 139, 161, 214, 601*.
bad names, 432.
bake, to, 836.
Bangala language, 157.
Bantu languages —
— why so termed, 7, 365 (1).
— where spoken, *11*.
— their classification, *12-15*.
— their close affinity to one another, *15*.
— their purity, *100*.
— their elegance, *75*.
— their literature, *16-70*.
— their difference from Hottentot, *5*.
Bantu people, origin of the, *71-100*.
baobab-tree, 366.
*bar*, Semitic word, 364.
baskets among Kafirs, p. 321.
*BE = J*, 202.
*be*, classifier, 339, 496.
*be*, connective pronoun, 139*.
*be*, relative particle, 718*.
*be*, auxiliary, 977, 978, 983, 1012.
*be*, copula, 1028.
be, to, 1019, *sqq.*, 1028-1037.
beak, 223, 233, 365*, 384 (4).
beard, 66, 126, 137, 173, 232, 402, 502, 385*, 409 (1).
because, 977, 978.
become, to, 1028.
*bede*, copula, 1028.
bee, 471.
*be-ense*, 250.
beer, 122, 378, 440*, 461 (3), 446.
beer, Kafir, p. 321.
before, 533*, 581 (1), 1065.
beget, to, 52*, 88, 96, 108, 173.
behind, 533*, 581 (10).
belly, 107.
below, 151, 530, 533*, 581 (1).
*Be-lungu*, 365.
Bemba language, 62-65.
*Ben*, Semitic word, 364.
beneath, 533*, 581 (1).
Benga language, 227-228.
Benguela cluster of languages, *14*.
— sources for its study, *49*.
between, 180.
beverage, 378.
between, 533*, 581 (5).
bewitch, to, 480, 1057.
bewitching, p. 282.
*fa*, classifier, 537.
*bfa*, pronoun, 639*.
*BI = J*, 179.
= *TY*, 122.
*bi*, classifier, 369, 496.
*bi*, connective pronoun, 639*.
*bi*, auxiliary, 1012.
*bi*, copula, 1028.
Bihe, slave trade at, p. 285.

Bihe language, *14, 49*.
— its phonetic features, 62-65.
— compared with Nywema, 164-165.
— its article, 321 (2).
*bile*, auxiliary, 1012, 1014.
— *bili*, 792*.
bind, to, 1082, 1083.
bird, 68, 129, 133, 236, 358, 425, 500, 504, 520, 522, 523.
birds in the Kafir gardens, p. 305.
Bisa language, 62-65.
bite, to, 52*.
black, 624, 626, 778.
black man, 235.
blanket, 404.
Bleek, *5, 7, passim*.
— his Comparative Grammar, *25*.
blind, 128.
blood, 229, 455.
*BO = JW* or *J*, 202.
*bo*, classifier, 328, 352, 367, 446.
*bo*, pronoun, 639*.
*bo*, conjunction, 786.
*bo*, auxiliary, 1012, 1014.
boa, 235, 401.
boas, charmed, p. 292.
boat, 440*, 461 (7), see canoe.
body, 96, 219, 366*, 384 (1), 373, 402.
bone, 75, 77, 79, 99, 128, 143, 147, 180, 410*, 419, 439 (6), 491*, 503 (5).
Boondei language, *14*, 78.
both, 794 (*N. B.*)
bottom, 782.
bow, 72, 443, 453, 459.
bowels, 455.
brains, 440*, 459, 455, 461 (4).
branch, 504*, 526.
break open, to, 1057.
breast, 105, 143, 161, 217, 233, 419.
breath, 72, 377.
breed, to, 37, 1081.
bring, to, 52*, 126, 1057, 1072, 1073.
bring down, to, 1073.
bring in, to, 1075.
broom, 372.
Brusciotto a Vetralla (Father), *22*, 156.
*BU = TY* and *TYW*, 122.
— = *J*, 202.
*BU-MA* class of substantives, 440-461.
*BU-ZIN* sub-class of substantives, 452-453.
*bu*, classifier, 440-461, 507, 508, 538.
— its transformations, 445-451.
— its use, 454-459.
— its etymology, 450.
— dropped, 154, 450.
*bu*, connective pronoun, 639*.
*bu*, relative particle, 718*.
*bu*, referring to a substantive

understood, 781.
*bu*, conjunction, 785.
*bu*, copulative prefix, 583.
*bua*, prefix, 538.
Bue tribe, p. 292.
buffalo, 69, 94, 197, 215.
Buma language, *14*, 66, 159-162.
bunch, 491*.
Bunda, see Mbunda.
bury, to, 115, 1077.
Bushman (Hottentot =) languages, *2-5*.
Bushmen, description of the, *2*.
— their drawings on rocks, *18*.
buy, to, 52*, 81, 133, 1070, 1071.
*buya*, auxiliary, 1012-1015.
*bwe*, conjunction, 785.
by, 571, 573, 575, 589.
by himself, 814-819.
by means of, 573.
*bzi*, *bzi*, classifier, 496.

C, how pronounced, 8.
— = *B*, 179.
— = *G*, or *K*, 150.
— = *NV*, 186.
— = *S*, 176.
— = *T*, 139.
— = *TS*, 206.
— suppressed, 176.
cacice, p. 294.
calf, 418.
call, to, 52*, 139, 1070.
Cameron, 145.
Candlestick, 500.
Cannecattim, Father Bernardo Maria de, *24*.
cannibals, *72*, p. 305, p. 312.
canoe, 118, 161, 215, 220, 230, 238, 440*, 459, 461 (7), 583.
Capello and Ivens, 141, 148.
Cardozo, Father, *20*.
carry, to, 528, 1072.
Carvalho, Henrique Augusto Dias de, 788[bis].
castor-oil, 378.
cattle, 385*, see cow.
cattle, dealing with, p. 305, *sqq*.
causative notion, 502.
CAUSATIVE VERBS, 1073-1078.
cause, to, 1073-1078.
cave, 499.
cease, to, 1073.
center, 504*.
Ceylon, *96*.
*CH = NSH*, 479.
— = *T*, 90.
Chagga, see Tshagga.
characteristic features of Bantu, 39-59.
characteristics, 314.
Charibael, *83*.
charmed animals, p. 292.
Chatelain (Héli), *21*, and *passim*.
-*che*, suffix, 519, 593.
cheek, 172, 414, 419.

## Alphabetical Index.

chest, 147, 491*, 503 (5).
*chi*, classifier, 492.
*chi*, nominal prefix, 354.
*chi*, pronoun, 639*.
chickens, 456.
chief, chiefs, 322*, 365 (1, 2), 502.
chiefs (deceased), 365 (6).
chieftain, 131.
chief-town, 9.
child, children, 122, 161, 210, 229, 322*, 332, 365 (5), 512, 554, p. 294 (y).
chin, 131, 491*, 500, 502, 503 (3).
chinaware in South-Africa, 94.
Chinese in South-Africa, 94, p. 313.
*CHIW = PHE*, 203.
Chwana cluster of languages, 14.
— sources for its study, 61.
Chwana language, *passim*.
— its phonetic features, 169-208.
— its affinity with Mozambique and Mpongwe, 12.
— its peculiar sounds, 32.
— its suppressed nasals, 59, 419.
— its want of purity, 581 (1).
Chwana tribes, origin of, 97.
*CI = SI = SE*, 138.
*CI-ZI* class of substantives, 491-503.
*ci*, classifier, 491-503.
— its transformation, 492-495.
— its use, 497-501.
— its original meaning, 502, 994.
*ci*, connective pronoun, 639*.
*ci*, relative particle, 718*.
*ci*, referring to a substantive understood, 781.
*ci*, conjunction, 787.
*ci*, auxiliary, 986, 987, 994.
Ciboko cluster of languages, 14.
— sources for its study, 52.
Ciloba, p. 294 (r).
Cilumbu, the chief, p. 285.
circumcision, 86, p. 300.
CLASSES OF SUBSTANTIVES, 313, 314.
classification of the Bantu languages, 12-15.
CLASSIFIERS —
— their nature, 314, 830.
— their number, 41.
— their forms, 314, *sqq*.
— their importance, 39, 42.
— their obliteration in Mpongwe, 218.
— their use before adjectives and numbers, 604.
— understood, 389, 390.
clay, 440*, 461 (4).
clay, red, 626.
cleanse, to, 1082.
clicks, *4*, 4, 35-38, 120.

cliff, 485.
climb, to, 70.
climb up, to, 1073.
close to, 563.
cloth, clothes, 162, 372, 404.
clothe, to, 1074, **see dress**.
cloud, 420.
cob, 491*, 500.
cock, 358 (**misspelt coq**).
cock's comb, 484.
cocoanut, 419.
cocoanut tree, 371.
coffee, 406.
cold, 69, 73, 77, 137, 142, 405.
come, to, 52*, 94, 126, 129, 136, 141 (2), 225, 837.
come back, to, 1012.
come for, to, 1067.
come near, to, 1075.
come out, to, 115, 173, 489, 1081.
come together, to, 1076.
Comoro cluster of languages, 14.
— sources for its study, 64.
Comoro islands, 89, 169, 246.
Comoro languages, 14.
— their phonetic features, 211, 212.
COMPARATIVES, 629-631.
compared to, 563.
compress, to, 122.
CONCORD, how established, 39-43.
conditional tenses, 932, 995, *sqq*.
Congo dictionaries, MSS., 23.
Congo forest, 242.
Congo, Lower, 14, and *passim*.
— sources for its study.
— compared with Karanga, 154.
— compared with Angola, 146-155.
— its article, 317-321.
Congo, Middle, languages, 14.
— their phonetic features, 159-162.
Congo tribes, their nose-rings, and incisors chipped, 50.
CONJUGATION, 831, *sqq*.
— its difficulty, 831.
— its general principles, 832-834.
CONJUNCTIONS, 784-788, 873, 939, 943, 944, 1086.
CONNECTIVE PRONOUNS, 637-655.
— their nature, 830.
— in relative clauses, 717-742.
— in possessive expressions, 743-768.
— before numbers, 793.
— referring to substantives understood, 781-788.
— understood, 736, 747, 767, 874.
consecutive actions, 959.
continue, to, 1016.
continuative past, 909, 910, 917.

continuative present, 913, 914, 920-928, 930.
continuative, various, tenses, 942, 945, 972, 977.
contraction of vowels, 249-254, 263, 290, 612.
contrast, how to express, 663.
cook, to, 52*, 89, 1060, 1069.
COPULA, 1019, *sqq*.
— before adjectives, 618-623.
— understood, 620, 621, 1020, 1021.
— before pronouns, 656, 662, 685, 707.
— before relative clauses, 769-775.
copulative prefixes, 582-588, 1035.
Cosmas Indicopleustes, 80, 87, 96.
coughing, 423.
counting in Bantu, 789.
country, 147, 161.
countries, names of, 440*.
cow, 131, 189, 198, 210, 385*.
cow-dung, 455.
— how used, 460.
crocodiles, charmed, p. 292.
crooked, 1059.
cross, 372.
cross a river, to, 115, 116.
cry, to, 52*, 224, 1075, 1079.
cup, 627.
cure, to, 1076.
Cust, Dr. Robert Needham, —
— his classification of the Bantu languages, 13.
— his " Sketch of the Modern Languages of Africa ", 26.
*CW = PO*, 203.
— = *LU = LO*, 205.

D, how pronounced, 9.
— = *L = IL* or *LI*, 287.
— = *L* after *N*, 286.
— = *L* after *I*, 287.
— = *NZ*, 195.
— = *S*, 136.
**D**, how pronounced, 9.
— its use, 82, 133.
*da*, auxiliary, 918, 926, 929, 1003.
dances, p. 287.
danger, 405.
dawn, to, 52*, 150, 502.
day, days, 232, 410*, 421, 439 (3), 781 (*N.B.*).
de Coueto, Father, 21, and *passim*.
de Laborde, 18.
dead, 94.
dead, prayers to the, p. 288, p. 289.
dead people raised by Monze, p. 290.
death, 161.
deep, 624, 626.
DEMONSTRATIVE PRONOUNS, 693-716.

— their predominance in Bantu, 830.
DERIVATIVE VERBS, 1047-1084.
— their general meaning, 1085.
descriptive turn of mind of the Bantu, 830.
desert, 403.
destroy, to, 136.
devil, 105, 410*, 418, 431, p. 283.
DI = TS, 205.
di, classifier, 395, 411, 473, 496.
di, pronoun, 639*.
di, negative auxiliary, 875, *sqq*.
dialects, *15*.
Dias, Father Pedro, *23*, 158, 502, 904.
dice, when used, p. 291.
die, to, 52*, 128, 133, 177, 233, 404, 1069.
different, 826-827.
dig, to, 174, 1081.
Dikele, see Kele.
DIMINUTIVES, 504-529, 475, 488, 501, 509, 513, 517, 518.
*din*, classifier, 395.
diphthongs, not found in Bantu, 299.
disjoin, to, 1082.
*dji*, pronoun, 639*.
DL, how pronounced, 33.
— its use in Kafir, 121.
do, to, 834, 1070, 1073.
doctor, doctors, 139, 142, 161, 235, 385*, 400, 409 (¹), p. 290, p. 295.
dog, dogs, 105, 122, 143, 161, 243, 358, 390, 504*, *3*, p. 293 *(m)*.
doorah, p. 321.
doorway, 96, 178, 190, 377.
double consonants, 99, 105.
down, 57, 136, 147, 180, 533*, 581(1).
drawings on rocks in South-Africa, *18*.
dress, to, 52*, 99, 1081.
drink, to, 52*, 216, 841.
drinking, beer-, among Kafirs, p. 321.
drop, 420.
drum, 74, 76, 161, 190, 404.
*dsa*, auxiliary, 948, 963.
*du*, classifier, 490.
dual in Ganda, 692.
Dualla cluster of languages, *14*.
— sources for its study, *68*.
Dualla language, *14*.
— its phonetic features, 219-230.
Dualla people, origin of the, 226.
duck, 410*, 418, 439(3).
duration, 986.
dust, 420, 485.
dwarfs, *2*, 243, 244.
— their language, 4, 242.
DY, euphonic, 294.
DZ = Z after N, 288.

*dza*, auxiliary, 948.
-*dza*, verbal suffix, 1075, 1079.
*dzi*, classifier, 496.
*dzi*, reflexive pronoun, 655.

E, how pronounced, 10, 271, 272, 1066.
— how changed before vowels, 252.
— = A, 274.
— = A-I, 249.
— = I, 200.
*e*, article, 317.
*e*, classifier, 331, 367, 369, 390, 411, 492, 493.
*e*, locative classifier and preposition, 543.
*e*, reflexive pronoun, 655.
*e*, connective pronoun, 639*.
*e*, relative particle, 718*, 723, 724.
*e*, indefinite pronoun, 955.
-*e*, verbal ending, 833, 862, 872, 874.
-*ea*, verbal suffix, 1055, 1060.
ear, ears, 72, 143, 161, 211, 232, 243, 462*, 465, 468(1).
ear-ring, 525.
earth, 89, 90, 147.
eat, to, 52*, 178, 838, 841.
*eci*?, 801.
-*ede*, verbal suffix, 860.
Edrisi, *91*, 110.
egg, 67, 161, 419.
eight, 789, 796.
*ej*, classifier, 492.
-*eka*, verbal suffix, 1055, 1061.
-*ela*, verbal suffix, 1065-1072.
eland, 358.
elder, 153.
*ele*, copula, 1022.
-*elela*, verbal suffix, 1065-1072.
elements, 374.
elephant, 126, 133, 208, 214, 233, 385*.
elision of vowels, 249, 255, 256, 612.
embers, 504*.
emphasis, 302, 663, 704-706.
empire, 458.
-*ena*, verbal suffix, 1065-1072.
enclitics, 656.
end, 471.
*enda*, auxiliary, 918-940.
*enda*, copula, 1034.
endings of the verbal forms, 833.
-*ene*, 825, 1033.
*enja*, *enje* = *enza*, *enze*, 289.
enjoyment, 487.
enter, to, 191, 221.
*enyo*, auxiliary, 947.
*eo*, locative pronoun, 682.
epithets, adjectives as, 613-617.
-*era*, verbal suffix, 1065-1072.
-*erera*, verbal suffix, 1065-1072.
*eri*, copula, 1026.
*ese*, auxiliary, 992.
euphonic letters, 641 (3).
evil spirit, 410*, p. 283.

evening, 421.
ever, for, 782.
EXPANSIVE VERBS, 1080-1083.
extinguish, to, 147, 1073.
eye, eyes, 76, 89, 126, 133, 136, 143, 174, 194, 208, 228, 230, 236, 410*, 414, 419, 439(4).
eyelids, 99.

F, how pronounced, 11.
— = G, 77, 77.
— = H, 177.
— = K, 177, 233.
— = P, 180.
— = PF, 99.
— = SH, 177.
— = T, 128, 133.
— suppressed, 66, 225, 233.
*fa*, classifier, 537.
face, 228, 230, 414, 440*, 453, 457, 461 (1).
fall, to, 462*, 1067, 1073, 1074.
family, 482.
Fan language, *69*.
— its phonetic features, 231-237.
far, 96, 533*, 764.
Farini's description of certain ruins, *18*.
fat, 66, 75, 80, 93, 133, 177, 220, 225, 440*, 461 (11).
fat, adj., 601*.
father, 126, 228, 322*, 342, 365 (7), 748-753, 1078.
feasts, 379, p. 287.
feather, 373.
female, 136, 164, 211, see woman.
fermented drink, 440*, 461 (3).
Fernandian group of languages, *14*.
— sources for its study, *70*.
Fernando Po languages, *14*.
— their phonetic features, 238-241.
*fi*, classifier, 496, 520, 521.
field, 464.
fifth, 797.
Fiji islands, *95*, 815.
file, to, 236.
finally, 929, 1016.
fine, 601*.
finger, fingers, 133, 164, 230, 373.
finish, to, 1016, 1017.
Fiote language, see Congo (Lower).
fire, 162, 211, 232, 239, 366*, 374, 384 (8), 504*.
firewood, 73, 80, 188.
fire-worshippers, *93*, p. 283.
fish, 136, 161.
first, 797.
five, 789, 792*.
flame, 232, 529 (5).
flaton, 563.
flea, 471, 528.
flesh, 385*, 402.
flour, 440*, 455, 461 (6).
flow, to, 1074.

## Alphabetical Index. 327

fluids, 454.
fly, 523.
fly, to, 1074.
*fo*, auxiliary, 1012, 1015.
FOLK-LORE of the Kafirs, pp. 296-321.
follow, to, 1074.
food, 176.
foot, 81, 88, 233, 243, 462, 468(3).
for, 1065.
force, to, 1073-1078.
ford, 499.
forehead, 402.
foreign, 826, 827.
foreign, words, 406.
form, to, 185.
four, 789, 792*.
fourth, 797.
fowl, 233, 385*, 409 (4).
from, 563, 575.
fruit, fruits, 419, 439.
full, to become, 52*, 67, 94, 99, 173.
future tenses, 907, 908, 912-916, 920-928, 930, 937, 946, 967.

G, ⏆, how pronounced, 12.
G = F, 75, 77.
— = J, 221.
— = K, 175.
— euphonic, 113, 294, 295, 297.
*ga*, pronoun, 639*.
*ga*, before possessive expressions, 783.
*ga*, negative auxiliary, 875, *sqq*.
-*ga*, verbal suffix, 836, 920.
Gabún River, 246.
Ganda cluster of languages, *14*.*
... sources for its study, 37.
Ganda language, *passim*.
— its phonetic features, 111-118.
— its article, 317-319.
Gangi cluster of languages, *14*.
— sources for its study, *32*.
garden, 374.
gardens, Kafir, p. 296, p. 300.
gather, to, 77, 1076.
GC, how pronounced, 36.
genders in Bantu, 313.
genuine, 632 (2), 780.
*gi*, pronoun, 639*.
Gindo language, 103.
give, to, 147.
*go*, classifier, 465, 543.
*go*, pronoun, 639*.
— in locative expressions, 579, 1046.
go, to, 193, 250, 839*-841, 843, 911-939.
go in, to, 52*, 250.
Goa, 246.
Goanese in South-Africa, *96*, 246 (foot-note).
goat, 139, 142, 162, 164, 185, 205, 220, 385.
*gobane*, 982.
God, *86*, 105, 322*, 339, 365 (6).
— how described, p. 289.
— his abode, p. 289.
— eating his body, p. 294 (*t*).

Gog, p. 313.
Gogo language, *passim*.
— its phonetic features, 77.
Gogo tribes, p. 313.
gold-trade, 80-96.
Golden Meadows, 362 (2), *72*.
Gonçalo da Sylveira, Father, *92*, p. 294.
good, 220, 601*, 624, 628, 779.
*gore*, 1004-1012.
gothic letters, 5.
GQ, how pronounced, 37.
Gqongqo, pp. 305-313.
grass, 105, 440*, 456, 461 (2).
gravel, 485.
great, 601*, 779.
greatly, 633.
greedy, 780.
green, see grass, 440*.
grinding-stone, 517.
ground, 502, 581 (1), 626.
grow, to, 468.
*gu*, pronoun, 639*.
Guha cluster of languages, *14*.
— sources for its study, 56.
Guinea languages, related to Bantu, 588.
gulley, 207.
gun, 404.
Gunda language, 97.
gutta percha, 83.
Gwamba language, 210.
Gwamba tribe, *29* (foot-note).
Gweno language, 212.
GX, how pronounced, 38.

H, how pronounced, 13.
— = D, 73.
— = F, 177.
— = K, 73, 123, 177, 211.
— = N, 284.
— = NS, 194.
— = P, 73, 177, 148.
— = S, 123.
— = T, 73, 93, 114.
*ha*, classifier, 535, 537.
*ha*, pronoun, 639*.
habitual tenses, 947.
hailstorm, 498.
hair, 139, 174.
-*hala*, verbal suffix, 1061.
half, 500.
hammer, 404.
hand, 77, 415, 419.
handle, 180, 372.
happiness, 457.
hatchet, 522.
*hatta*, conjunction, 958.
have, to, 904, 1037-1039.
he, 637, 639*, 656*.
he who, 718.
head, 131, 144, 161, 164, 211, 229, 232, 238, 366*, 384 (3), 468 (1), 471.
heal, to, 77.
healthy, 67.
hear, to, 133, 137, 152, 186, 238, 250, 1058, 1084.
heart, 139, 209, 223, 366*, 384 (6).

heifer, 418.
hen, 126, 139, 188, 214, 358.
here, 211, 693, 693*.
Herero cluster of languages, *14*.
— sources for its study, *48*.
Herero language, *passim*.
— its article, 317-319.
— its phonetic features, 125-130, 133.
— its peculiar accentuation, 304.
Herodotus, on South-Africa, *81*.
*hi*, negative auxiliary, 875, *sqq*.
hide, 491*, 500, 503 (7).
high, 425.
hill, 126, 491*, 500, 503 (8).
him, 639*, 653, 656*.
Hinzua language, 211.
hippopotamus, 99, 161, 233.
— a sacred animal, 461 (10).
his, 211, 745, *sqq*., 768-777.
HL, how pronounced, 33.
— its use in Kafir, 121.
— = TLH = S, 208.
Hlakanyana, p. 313.
hoe, 410*, 422.
hoe, to, 52*.
Homer, on South-Africa, *81*.
hold, to, 172.
honey, 118, 455.
honey-bee, 471.
hoof, 194, 471.
horn, 419, 484.
horse, 401, 454.
horses in South-Africa, *72*.
hot, 778.
Hottentot-Bushman languages, 2-5.
Hottentots, *3*.
house, 243, 385*, 390, 409(4), 533*.
how many?, 211, 800.
hundred, 789, 792*.
hunger, 66, 88, 96, 97, 115, 126, 195, 208.
husband, 96, 214, 223, 235, 241, 322*, 365(2).
hut, 133, 500.
hut, burning one's, p. 301.
hyaena, 128, 139.

I, how pronounced, 14.
— = E, 200.
— = N, 198, 285, 414.
— = U, 275, 276.
— combined with a consonant, 257-258.
— how changed before vowels, 255-258.
— change to Y before vowels, 255.
— elided before vowels, 255-256.
— transposed, 285.
— initial, dropped, 250.
J, how pronounced, 14.
— when used, 271.
— how changed before vowels, 251.
*i*, article, 317.
*i*, classifier, 369, 390, 411, 492, 495, 496, 522.

*i*, connective pronoun, 639*.
*i*, reflexive pronoun, 655.
*i*, relative particle, 718.
*i*, indefinite pronoun, 955.
-*i*, negative ending, 872.
I, 637, 639*, 656*.
-*ia*, verbal suffix, 1065-1072, 1073 *(N. B.)*
Ibo cluster of languages, *14.*
— sources for its study, *44.*
-*ibwa*, passive suffix, 1049, 1062.
-*ichisia*, verbal suffix, 1079.
-*ide*, verbal suffix, 860.
if, 786, 787, 788, 943, 963, 970, 997, 1001, 1002.
-*igua*, -*igwa*, passive suffix, 1048, 1050, 1062.
-*iha*, verbal suffix, 1073-1078.
-*ika*, verbal suffix, 1055, 1061, 1077.
-*ike*, nominal suffix, 593.
-*ila*, copula, 1022, 1023.
-*ila*, verbal suffix, 1065-1072.
-*ile*, verbal suffix, 860.
*im*, classifier, 388.
immediately, 690.
imperative mood and tenses, 832, 835-841, 855-859, 859, 873, 880, 906, 938, 968.
*IN-MA* sub-class of substantives, 385.
*IN-ZIN* class of substantives, 385-409.
*in*, classifier, —
— its transformations, 386-390.
— its etymology, 407.
— its use, 399-406.
in, 533, 564, 565, 544.
in front, 533*, 542, 581(9).
in the air, 533*, 541, 581(4).
in the house, 533*, 553, 561.
in the mouth, 554.
in the road, 552.
in the river, 554.
in the sky, 553.
*ina*, copula, 1031.
incline, to, 1082.
increase, to, 1073.
indefinite pronouns, 809.
Indians in South-Africa, *96.*
indicative clauses, 842, *sqq.*, 832, 876, *sqq.*
infinitive forms, 466, 832, 853-854.
*inga*, preposition, 576.
-*ini*, locative suffix, 532, 548, 554.
— compared with -*yo*, 723.
inscriptions in South-Africa, *18.*
*insi*, auxiliary, 976.
— copula, 1036.
inside, 533*, 549, 581 (1, 5).
instrument, 573.
intensive adjectives, 632.
intensive notion, 502.
INTENSIVE VERBS, 1079.
INTERROGATIVE PRONOUNS, 799-809.

INTERJECTIONS, 596.
into, 566, 1065.
*inza*, auxiliary, 976.
-*ira*, verbal suffix, 1065-1072.
iron, 403.
iron ore, 455.
-*isa*, -*isha*, -*isia*, verbal suffixes, 1073-1079.
*isha*, auxiliary, 1017.
-*isidza*, -*isisa*, -*isisia*, verbal suffixes, 1079.
island, 525.
Isubu language, 227, 229.
it, 637, 639*, 653, 656*.
it is, 582-588, 656*, 662, 685, 707.
its, 745, *sqq.*, 768-777.
-*iwa*, passive suffix, 1052, 1062.
-*iza*, auxiliary, 948, 949, 952.

J, how pronounced, 15.
— = *BE, BI, BO, BU*, 122, 202, 178, 445.
— = *LE, LI*, 178, 205.
— = Z, 52*, 63, 89, 106.
— euphonic, 294, 295.
— suppressed, 81.
— a favourite in Yao, 68.
— *ja*, auxiliary, 948, 949, 951, 963, 964.
jackal, 358.
*jaka*, preposition, 576.
Javanese in South-Africa, *95.*
*ji*, classifier, 394.
*ji*, connective pronoun, 639*.
*ji*, reflexive pronoun, 655.
*ji*, relative particle, 718*.
*jin*, classifier, 394.
Jinga tribes, 76.
join, to, 1082.
joint of the arm, 524.
Jorge (Father), *20.*
journey, 454.
just, 974, 987.
*JW = BW*, 202, 1053.

K, how pronounced, 16.
— = C, 150.
— = F, 177, 233.
— = G, 175, 214.
— = H, 123, 211.
— = NG, 190, 479.
— = NJ, 191.
— = SH, 175.
— = T, 244.
— = TS, 1035.
— = TY, 214.
— = V, 233.
— = W, 175.
— suppressed, 175, 211, 225, 233, 290, 292, 559.
ℳ, how pronounced, 16.
— its use, 106, 133.
*KA-TU* class of substantives, 504-529.
*ka*, classifier, 504-529.
— its use, 524-527.
— its original meaning, 527.
*ka*, non-classifying prefix, 345, 347, 350, 527.

*ka*, connective pronoun, 639*.
*ka*, relative particle, 718*.
*ka*, before possessive expression, 783.
*ka*, auxiliary, 875, *sqq.*, 965-975, 1000.
*ka*, conjunction, 788, 970.
*ka*, preposition, 573, 574.
- *ka*, suffix in numbers, 792.
- *ka*, verbal suffix, 1055, 1061.
Kafir beer, p. 321.
Kafir cluster of languages, *14.*
— sources for its study, *27.*
Kafir folk-lore, pp. 396-321.
Kafir language, *passim.*
— its article, 317, 318.
— its peculiar sounds, 33-38.
— its phonetic features, 120-124.
*kala*, auxiliary, 941-947.
*kala*, copula, 1031.
*kala*, conjunction, 943, 944.
*kala*, preposition, 576.
- *kala*, verbal suffix, 1055, 1061.
Kamba cluster of languages, *14.*
— sources for its study, *41.*
Kamba language, *passim.*
— its phonetic features, 81-83.
*kana*, conjunction, 943-944.
*ka-nga*, before nouns, 515.
*Kangombe*, p. 285.
Karanga cluster of languages, *14.*
— sources for its study, *28.*
Karanga language, *passim.*
— agglutination in it, 254.
— compared with Kamba, 303.
— its phonetic features, 104-108, 133.
Karanga nation, pp. 286-288.
*kati ka*, 758-760, 763.
- *kazi*, nominal suffix, 592.
*ke*, pronoun, 639.
*ke*, copulative particle, 587, 1035.
*ke*, auxiliary, 875, *sqq.*, 965-975.
- *ke*, nominal suffix, 593.
Keish, the prince of, *91.*
Kele language, 227, 230.
key, 404.
*KG = NK*, 188.
— = *NG*, 189.
*KH = NF*, 187.
*KI = CI = TYI = SI = SE*, etc., 260, 492.
*KI*, changed to C or *CH*, 258-259.
*ki*, for *ka*, 250.
*ki*, classifier, 462.
*ki*, connective pronoun, 639*.
*ki*, relative particle, 718*.
*ki*, auxiliary, 986, 993, 994.
*ki ?*, 801.
*kia*, auxiliary, 989, 994.
kid, 418.
*kile*, auxiliary, 992.
*Kilima Njaro*, 246.
kill, to, 81.
kindness, 457.
king, *72* (foot-note), **see** chief.
*Ki-rimba, Ki-zimba*, *9.*
kloof, p. 313.

## Alphabetical Index.    329

knee, 500.
kneel, to, 1067.
knife, 404, 512.
know, to, 834.
*ko*, pronoun, 674 (*c*), 675-681, 1020.
Koelle, 83.
Kololo language, 131 (3), 169.
Kololo tribes, p. 293.
Konde language, *14*.
— sources for its study, *46*.
Kongo, *13*, see Congo.
*koo = ke-ku*, 967.
kraal, p. 313 (*d*).
*KU-MA* class of substantives, 462-468.
*ku*, classifier and preposition, 462-468, 533-581.
— its transformations, 463-465, 542-546.
— its use, 466-467, 562-568.
— its original meaning, 468, 581.
— dropped, 154.
*ku*, connective pronoun, 639*.
*ku*, relative particle, 718*.
*ku*, referring to a substantive understood, 781.
*ku*, copulative prefix, 583.
*kua*, locative particle, 783.
Kua group of languages, *12*.
— its divisions, and subdivisions, *14*.
— its proper features, 169, and *passim*.
— its origin, 97, 246.
Kua tribes, their origin, 97. .
*kuba*, 982.
*kui*, auxiliary, 964.
—, negative copula, 964, 1038.
*kuila, kuina*, 1023.
*kuli*, 580, 1004-1012.
· *kulu*, nominal suffix, 591.
Kumbi tribes, 50.
*kumi*, 792*.
*kuna*, 580, 1004-1012.
Kush, 72, 75-77.
*kwa*, locative particle, 543, 546, 691 (2), 783.
*kwa*, preposition, 573.
Kwakwa River and tribes, p. 313.
Kwana tribe, 246.
Kwango language, *14*.
— sources for its study, *50*.
— its phonetic features, 132-133.
Kwango tribes, 108, p. 293.
Kwengo, see Kwango.

*L*, how pronounced, 17.
— = *N*, 280.
— = *R*, 214.
— = *T*, 220.
— = *Z*, 165.
— suppressed, 81, 88, 96, 97, 123, 224, 233.
*la*, classifier, 471, 545.
*la*, auxiliary, 918-922.
*la*, demonstrative suffix, 698.
lake, 499.

land, 389.
LANGUAGES OF SOUTH-AFRICA
— their general division, *1*.
— their elegance, 75.
— their names, 484, 491*, 497, 503 (2), *14*.
large, 215, 425, 427, 601*.
last night, 533, 581 (7).
Last, J. T., 145, and *passim*.
laugh, to, 82, 133, 136, 174.
*LE = J*, 205.
*le*, classifier, 411.
*le*, pronoun, 639*.
*le*, auxiliary, 918, 930-936.
*le*, copula, 1022.
*le*, preposition, 570, 940.
- *le*, element in words, 409(2).
*le*, suffix of demonst. pron. 698.
Le Roy, Father, *94*.
Lea tribe, p. 285, p. 293.
lean, 601*.
leave, to, 52*, 136.
leave behind, to, 174.
lest, 974.
*LI = JI*, 143, 178.
*li*, for *la*, 250.
*LI-MA* class of substantives, 410-439.
*li*, classifier, 395, 410-415, 426.
— its transformations, 410-415.
— its use, 417-418.
— its original meaning, 429-435.
— omitted, 411.
— omitted before adjectives, 614.
*li*, connective pronoun, 639*.
— referring to a substantive understood, 781.
*li*, relative particle, 718*.
*li*, auxiliary, 918, 930-936.
*li*, copula, 619, 1022, 1024, 1025.
*li*, particle in locative expressions, 579, 1040-1043.
*li*, conjunction, 784.
*li?*, 806.
*lia* «to have », 1039.
- *lia*, suffix of demonst. pron. 698.
· *lia*, 401.
lie down, to, 52*, 1069.
life, 440*, 461 (9).
light-hole, 491*, 503 (10).
*liji*, copula, 1022.
like, 576, 944.
like, to, 1084.
Limpopo River, 246.
lion, 358.
lip, 366*, 384 (4).
lip-rings, phonetic effects of, 50, 210.
LITERATURE, BANTU, 16-70.
liver, 500.
living-place, 374.
Livingstone, p. 289, p. 294, p. 295.
— his spelling, 141.
Liwanika, p. 284, p. 285.
*lo*, classifier, 476, 490, 511.

*lo*, pronoun, 639*.
Lobengula, p. 286.
LOCATIVE EXPRESSIONS, 530-581.
— containing adjectives, 605.
— how emphasized, 704-705.
— requiring certain particles inserted, 1040-1046.
— their peculiar value, 43.
— used as comparatives, 630.
— what concord they require, 643, 674, 675, 755-767.
loins, 389, 390.
Lojazi language, 132-133.
*lon*, classifier, 398.
long, 214, 601*.
lord, 502, see chief.
look, to, 1079.
loud, 423.
Lower Congo, see Congo.
love, to, 1058, 1073, 1075, 1084.
*LU = CW*, 205.
*LU-ZIN* class of substantives, 469-490.
*lu*, common classifier, 469-490.
— its transformations, 470-473.
— its use, 475-476, 481- 488.
— its original meaning, 489.
— dropped, 472.
*lu*, connective pronoun, 639*.
*lu*, relative particle, 718*.
*lu*, referring to a substantive understood, 781.
*lu*, copulative prefix, 583.
Luba language, *14*.
— sources for its study, *59*.
— its phonetic features, 143.
Luiana language, 141.
Lumbu people, pp. 283-286, p. 293.
Lunda language, *14*, 788bis.
— sources for its study, *55*.
— its phonetic features, 143-144, 788bis.

*M*, how pronounced, 18.
— = *B*, 240, 804.
— = *MO* = *MU*, 279, 240, 560.
— = *N*, 281, 607.
— = dropped, 292, 640.
'*M* = *MOB*, 279.
*m*, classifier, 328, 367, 551-553.
— for *n*, 389.
*m*, connective pronoun, 639*.
*m*, copulative prefix, 583.
*MA* sub-class of substantives, 442-444.
*ma*, classifier, 322, 338, 355-356, 416-438, 442-480.
— its transformations, 416, 442-444.
— its use, 355-356, 417-428, 454, 480.
— its original meaning, 436-438.
*ma*, pronoun, 639*.
*ma*, auxiliary, 977, 978, 980, 981.

# South-African Bantu Languages.

*ma*, verbal suffix, 1063.
Macrobians, *81*, *82*.
*madze* = *madzi*, 272.
Magog, p. 313.
Ma-gqongqo, Ma-kalanga, Ma-kua, etc., see Gqongqo, Kalanga, Kua, etc.,
maize, 500.
*mala*, auxiliary, 1016.
Malays in South-Africa, *95*.
man, 322\*, 340, 365.
*mana*, auxiliary, 1016.
*mang?*, 804.
Manuel Antonio de Souza. p. 285, p. 293.
many, 454, 601\*.
mark, national, 490.
marry, to, 1074.
Marvels of India, Book of the, *90*.
Masai languages, *6*.
Masai tribes, *79*.
Mashonaland, *73*, see Shona.
Mas'oudi —
— on the name of the king of the Zindj, 365 (2).
— on the origins of the Bantu, *72*, *89*, *93*.
— his trustworthiness, *75*.
Matapa-metsi, 461 (10).
match, 504\*.
may, 966, *sqq*.
*MB* = *P*, 185.
*mba*, relative particle, 718\*, 721, 771.
*mba*, auxiliary, 984.
Mbala language, 102.
Mbala tribes, 50.
Mbamba language, 146-151.
Mbangala language, 157.
Mbara, see Mbala.
*mbu*, relative particle, 718\*, 721, 771.
*mbulu*, pp. 300-305.
Mbunda, Mbundu, *13*, 132.
Mbunda languages, *14*.
— sources for their study, 50-53.
Mbunda tribes, 77, p. 285, p. 293.
*me*, classifier, 369.
*me*, pronoun, 639\*.
*me*, auxiliary, 977, 979, 980.
*me*, conjunction, 910, 985.
me, 639\*, 653, 656\*.
meal, 487.
meat, 73, 196, 385.
medicine, 378.
meet, to, 1076.
Melanesian languages, *95*.
*melekh*, Semitic word, 339.
metal, 403.
metempsychosis, p. 114 (footnote).
*m-falme*, *72*, 365 (2).
*MI* = *VI* = *E*, 164.
*mi*, classifier, 366-384.
— its transformations, 369-370.
— its etymology, 384.
*mi*, pronoun, 639\*.
'*mi*, conjunction, 985.
mice, how the *mbulu* is fond of, p. 305.
midday, 136.
middle, 139, 504\*.
milk, sour, 454, p. 321.
milking among Kafirs, p. 313, p. 321.
mimosa-tree, 371.
mine, 768-777.
mines, gold-, *80-82*, *84*.
*Mi-zimo*, *86*.
*Mlonjalonjani*, the tale of, pp. 300-305.
*MO* = *NGW*, 204, 207.
*mo*, classifier, 328, 367.
*mo*, pronoun, 639\*.
Molokh, *86*, 339, 365 (6).
monkey, 358.
Monomotapa, 461 (10), p. 294.
MONOSYLLABIC STEMS —
— how accented, 45, 310.
— their peculiar laws, 44, 45, 283, 284, 310, 325, 368, 413, 444, 464, 478, 561, 608, 652, 661, 832, 837, 841, 843, 851, 853, 866, 867.
Monze, the chief, p. 286, pp. 288-290, p. 294.
MOODS, 832.
moon, 81, 126, 136, 164, 173, 214, 232, 366\*, 374, 384 (10), 481.
Moon, mountains of the, *82*, 266.
morning, 533\*, 581 (8).
mother, 126, 322\*, 342, 365 (7), 748-753.
motions of the hand, 362, 789, 830.
mountain, 425, 491\*, 503 (8).
mouth, 164, 223, 366\*, 384 (4, 10), 504\*.
Mozambique cluster of languages, *14*.
— sources for its study, *63*.
Mozambique language, *passim*.
— its affinity with Chwana and Mpongwe, *12*, 169.
— its phonetic features, 169-208.
Mozambique tribes, 50 (footnote).
*mpa*, relative particle, 718\*, 721, 771.
Mpongwe cluster of languages, *14*.
— sources for its study, 67.
Mpongwe language, *passim*.
— compared with Nywema, 164-167.
— its affinity with Chwana and Mozambique, *12*, 169, 213.
— its phonetic features, 59, 213-218.
— its traces of an article, 321 (3).
*MU* = *NI* = *NY*, 122, 581, 792.
— = *O*, 164.
*MU-BA* class of substantives, 322-365.

*MU-MI* class of substantives, 366-384.
*MU*, locative class, 533-581.
*mu*, classifier —
— its transformations, 323-332, 367-368, 547-555.
— its use, 357-360, 371-380, 562-568.
— its original meanings, 361, 381, 581.
— weakened, 559, 560.
*mu*, connective pronoun, 639\*.
*mu*, relative particle, 718.
*MUA* = *NYA*, 268.
*muade*, poison, 378, p. 284.
Muanaena, p. 285.
*muave*, see *muade*.
-*mue*, 792\*, 820.
-*mue*, relative suffix, 725.
— = *yo* = *ng*, 725.
*muene*, 825.
*mwenyewe*, *mwenyi*, 825.
multiplied, to be, 137.
multiply, to, 1081.
Mulungu, Muungu, 339.
*muna*, 580.
murder, 423.
musical instruments, p. 287.
*muv*, classifier, 326, 367.
my, 745, *sqq*.

*N*, 𝔅, how pronounced, 19.
*N* = *I*, 152, 198, 285.
— = *L*, 280.
— = *M*, 551, 552.
— = *MU*, 101, 107, 153, 559.
— = *NY*, 196.
— = *Z*, 232.
— suppressed, or half-suppressed, 282, 551, 584, 640.
*N* class of substantives, see *IN-ZIN* class.
*n* = *un* = *mu*, classifier, 327, 367, 551.
*n* (= *in*) classifier, 388-389, 391, 477-480.
*n* pronoun, 639\*.
*n*, copulative prefix, 583, 1035.
*na*, prefix in substantives, 347, 350.
*na*, auxiliary, 918-929, 946.
*na*, preposition, 570, 573, 578, 682, 704, 940, 1037.
*na*, in locative expressions, 579, 1040-1046.
— in Congo, 537, 542, 549.
*na*, conjunction in Ganda, 111, 939.
*na* " to have ", 1037.
- *na*, locative suffix, 553.
- *na*, pronominal suffix, 689, 698.
nail, 525.
naked, 1034.
name, 99, 115, 147, 173, 220, 410\*, 423.
Nano language, 132, 133.
— its article, 321 (2).
NASALS —
— suppressed, or half-suppressed,

# Alphabetical Index. 331

77, 78, 151, 166, 183-196, 225, 283, 607.
— their peculiar influence on following consonants, 51, 52, 55-59, 67, 69, 73, 77, 78, 80, 83, 93, 94, 95, 114, 127, 129, 140, 170-198, 214-216, 283, 412, 479, 608, 609, 649.
nations, names of, 322*, 365 (5).
*nci*, 773.
$ND = T, TH$, 193.
*ndi*, connective pronoun, 639*.
*ndi*, relative particle, 718*, 721, 771.
*ndi*, copulative prefix, 583, 587, 1035.
*ndi*, preposition, 570, 573, 940.
*-ndini*, vocative suffix, 595.
$NDL = TL = NZ$, 208.
Ndonga language, 132-133.
*ndu*, relative particle, 718*, 721, 771.
*ndyi*, pronoun, 639*.
*ne*, auxiliary, 918, 930-931.
*ne*, copulative particle, 588, 1035.
*ne*, ne, preposition, 570, 573, 940.
*ne*, conjunction, 939.
near, 533*, 541, 581 (2), 764.
neck, 136, 142.
negative auxiliaries, 875-891.
negative clauses and tenses, 832, 833, 872, 875-891, 964, 967, 976.
— containing the copula, 1036.
— containing the verb "to have," 1038.
negative particle before numbers, 798.
negative notion, 502.
Negro languages, 830.
nest, 500.
nestling, 418.
never, 946, 960-962, 964.
new, 94, 105, 127, 129, 137, 147, 601*, 779.
$NF = KH$, 187.
$NG = K$, 190.
— dropped, 210.
$NG = MU$, 1053.
— = $NI$, 200.
*-ng*, relative and locative suffix, 532, 552, 718*, 727, 734, 802.
*nga*, relative particle, 718*, 721, 771.
*nga*, auxiliary, 875, *sqq.*, 995-1003.
*nga*, copulative prefix, 583, 1035.
*nga*, preposition, 573, 574, 576.
*-nga*, suffix in the number "one", 792.
*-nga*, verbal suffix, 920.
*ngai?*, 800.
*nganga*, 385*, 409 (1), p. 290, p. 295.
*nyanga*, preposition and conjunction, 576.
*-ngapi?*, 800.
*nge*, auxiliary, 995, *sqq.*

Ngete tribe, p. 286, p. 923.
*-ngi*, locative suffix, 553.
*ngu*, relative particle, 718*, 773.
*ngu*, copulative particle, 583, 1035.
$NGW = MO$, 204, 207.
$NI = MU = NG$, 581, 200.
*ni*, classifier, 387, 411.
*ni*, pronoun, 639*.
*ni*, copulative particle, 583, 587, 1035.
*ni*, preposition, 1037.
*ni*, conjunction, 939.
*ni*, 801, 803.
*-ni*, locative suffix, 532, 548, 553, 555, 590.
*-ni*, pronoun suffixed, 855.
nice, 601.
Niger languages, related to Bantu, 598.
night, 128, 174, 440*, 443, 453, 456, 461 (5).
night, at, 556.
Nika cluster of languages, *14*.
— sources for its study, 39.
Nika language, *passim*.
— its phonetic features, 92-96.
Nika tribes, 110.
Nile, sources of the, *80-82*.
nine, 789, 796.
$NJ = K = TS$, 191.
Njenji language, 141 (3).
*nji*, relative particle, 718*, 721, 771, 773.
$NJW = MBW$, 1053.
*nka*, nominal prefix, 527.
*nki?*, 801.
*nle*, conjunction, 939.
*nna*, auxiliary, 929, 941-947.
*nna*, copula, 1031.
*-nna*, pronominal suffix, 689.
*-nne*, 792*.
*no*, nominal prefix, 347.
no, not, 872, 875-891, 1036.
no longer, 987, 991.
no more, 987.
no one, 798.
*-no*, demonstrative suffix, 698.
*noo = ne-ku*, 946.
non-quantitative adjectives, 601, 624-628.
North-African languages, 5.
nose, 133, 402.
not at all, 964, 989.
not yet, 929, 960, 963, 974, 987, 992.
nothing, 798.
now, 421.
nowhere, 798.
Northern traders in South-Africa, *79-82*.
$NS = H$, 194.
— = $T = TH = TLH = X$, 194.
Nsundu people, *10*.
$NT = T = TH$, 192.
*ntss*, auxiliary, 945.
NUMERALS, 789-798.
numeration in Bantu, 789, 830.
$NV = C$, 186.
$NY = MU$, 122, 581, 1053.

— = $N$, 196.
*ny*, classifier, 478.
$NYA = MUA$, 268.
*nya*, nominal prefix, 465.
*-nya*, pronominal suffix, 689.
Nyambane cluster of languages, *14*.
— sources for its study, *62*.
Nyambane language, 210.
Nyambu language, 119.
Nyamwezi cluster of languages, *14*.
— sources for its study, *35*.
Nyamwezi language, *passim*.
— its phonetic features, 73-76
Nyamwezi tribes, 50 (foot-note).
*-nyana*, nominal suffix, 518, 590.
Nyanja, or Nyassa, language, see Senna.
*nye*, 829.
Nyengo language, 142.
*nyi*, pronoun, 639*.
Nyika, see Nika.
*-nyo*, pronominal suffix, 689.
Nywema cluster of languages, *14*.
— sources for its study, *57*.
Nywema language, *passim*.
— its phonetic features, 163-168.
$NZ = D = TH = T = TL$, 210, 195.
— = $DZ$, 211.
— = $N = NY$, 196, 197.
— = $X$, 195.
*nzi*, relative particle, 718*, 721, 771.
*nzi?*, 801.

O, Ø, how pronounced, 20.
— = $A-U$, or $A-O$, 249.
— = $A-KU$, 907.
— = $MU$, 164.
— = $U$, 200, 262.
— = $UA, WA, UE, WE$, 265, 270, 659.
— = $UO$, 263.
*o*, article, 317, 352, 353.
*o*, classifier, 330, 331, 367, 449, 465, 480.
*o*, connective pronoun, 639*.
*o*, relative particle, 718*, 723, 724.
*-o*, pronominal suffix, 659, 698.
*oba*, 982.
object of a verb, how expressed, 653.
— in relative clauses, 735-742.
OBJECTIVE VERBS, see APPLICATIVE.
of, 577, 589.
Ogowe River, 246.
oil, 66, 75, 177, 220, see fat.
*ojo*, auxiliary, 949.
*-oka, -ola, -olola, -oloka*, verbal suffixes, 1080-1083.
old, 601*.
old man, 139, 500.
old women among Kafirs, p. 313.
*olo*, auxiliary, 920, 942.

on, 544, 563, 564, 565, 1065.
once, 525, 797, 974.
*ondo*, auxiliary, 918, 937, 949.
one, 122, 235, 789, 792*.
one... another, 828-829.
one who, the, 718.
O'Neil, on South-African inscriptions, *18*.
ONOMATOPOETIC WORDS, 596.
open, to, 1059, 1081.
Ophir, *85*.
ordeals for sorcerers and thieves, pp. 283-285.
ordinal numbers, 797.
ore, 455.
ORIGIN OF THE BANTU, *71-100*.
ORTHOGRAPHY, regarding the separation of the words, 892 *(N. B.)*.
ostrich, 388, 390, 401.
other, 826-829.
our, 745, *sqq*.
ours, 768-777.
outside, 136, 195, 208, 533*, 581 (3).
over, 531, 563, 564.
ox, 202, see cow.
oxen, pack-, *72*.

P, how pronounced, 21.
— = *B* = *V* = *H*, 137, 138, 166, 180, 211, 215.
— = *BF*, 94.
— = *F*, 180.
— = *J*, 89.
— = *MB*, 185, 479.
— = *MP* = *PH*, 184.
— = *NV*, 186.
— weakened, or suppressed, 64, 69, 73, 74, 77, 117, 148, 292.
*pa*, locative classifier, 533-581.
— its transformations, 534-541.
— its use, 562-568.
— its meaning, 581.
*pa*, connective pronoun, 639*.
*pa*, relative particle, 718*.
*pa*, negative auxiliary, 875, *sqq*.
*pa*, conjunction, 785.
paddle, 142, 500.
palm-leaf, 500.
*pana*, 580.
Papuan languages, *95*.
Parsees in South-Africa, *93*, p. 292.
participles, 851, 910, 931-935, 979, 980, 993.
particles changing their forms, 291-298.
Paruain, *85*.
PASSIVE VERBS, 1047-1063.
— the name of the agent after them, 589, 1042.
past, 498.
past tenses, 892-907, 930-936, 909, 910, 917, 966.
path, 97, 142, 147, 385*, 409 (4), see road.
Paz, *85*.
*pe*, pronoun, 639.

*pe*, negative particle, 872.
pebble, 504*.
Pedro Dias, Father, see Dias.
people, 210, 232, 322*, 340.
perfect forms and tenses, 70, 860-871, 892, 904, 905, 981.
permanently, 810.
Persians in South-Africa, *93*, p. 292.
person, 133, 139, 142, 192, 223, 241, 243, 244, 322*, 340, 365 (1).
PERSONAL PRONOUNS, 635-692.
persons, names of, 357.
personified, things, 360.
*PH* = *MB* = *P*, 184.
*PHE* = *CHW*, 203.
PHONETIC CHANGES —
— their general laws, 47-59, 247-300.
— their main cause, 50.
— specimens, 52*, and *passim*.
— in the various languages, 60-246.
— in the perfect form, 861.
— caused by suffixes, 596, 1053.
*PI* = *TSH*, 122.
*pi ?* 800.
pierce, to, 202.
pig, 233.
pipe, 404.
pit, 193, 377.
place, 403, 537, 556, 782, 783.
place, to, 1077.
plain, 374.
plant, to, 122.
pleasant, 601*.
plural, for the singular, 343, 344, 750.
*PO* = *CW*, 203.
point, 389.
Pokomo cluster of languages, *14*.
— sources for its study, *40*.
Pokomo language, *passim*.
— its phonetic features, 92-96.
Polynesian languages, *95*.
pool, 374.
poor, the, 554, 601*.
porridge, 404.
POSSESSIVE ADJECTIVES AND EXPRESSIONS, 577, 659, 684, 743-780.
pot, 500, 525.
potato, 500.
pot-clay, 455, 525.
pour water, to, 1066.
powder, 378.
Prasos, Cape, *96*.
pray, to, 1067.
prayer, 487.
prayers of the Bantu, 365 (6), pp. 287-290.
predicates, adjectives as, 618-623.
Prefixes of the substantives, see CLASSIFIERS.
PREPOSITIONS, 530-581, 674-688, 940, 1086.

present tenses, 930-936, *sqq*.
priest, see cacice.
privative notion, 502.
productive notion, 502.
PRONOUNS, 635-830.
proper names of persons, 346.
provoke, to, 1059.
*PU* = *TSH*, 122.
pumpkin, 415.
Pun, land of, *84*.
put out a light, to, 147.

Q, how pronounced, 37.
*qa*, 792, 794.
Qajana, the tale of, p. 305, p. 313.
quantitative adjectives, 601.
question, 206.

*R*, how pronounced, 23.
— = *T*, 172, 210, 211, 214.
— = *Z* = *D*, 173.
*ra*, nominal prefix in Timneh, 471.
-*ra*, suffix, 594.
race, 482.
raft, 482.
rain, 66, 73, 79, 107, 114, 116, 123, 143, 186, 224, 243, 385*, 403, 409(4).
rain, how obtained, pp. 287-290.
rain, to, 1071.
rain-bow, 375.
raise, to, 1076, 1082.
raising the dead, Monze, p. 290.
razor, 478.
*RE* = *TSH*, 206.
*re*, pronoun, 639*.
*re*, auxiliary, 875, *sqq*., 1004-1012.
Rebmann's mode of spelling, 92, 101.
— his enthusiasm for the Nyassa language, 98.
RECIPROCAL VERBS, 1084.
recover, to, 52*, 1076.
red, 624.
red clay, red ground, 626.
reduplicative forms, 632(2), 1079.
REFLEXIVE PRONOUN, 655, 198.
Regga language, *14*.
— sources for its study, *36*.
RELATIVE CLAUSES AND EXPRESSIONS. —
— used substantively, 768-777.
— negative, 878.
— their construction, 717-742.
— forms of the verb in them, 844.
RELATIVE PARTICLES, 718-746.
— in what they differ from relative pronouns, 718.
— their forms, 719.
— their etymology and nature, 830.
— their use before relative clauses, 728, 731-742, 769-777.

## Alphabetical Index. 333

— their use before possessive expressions, 769-777.
— their use before adjectives, 605, 616-617.
RELATIVE PRONOUNS, 717-746.
remain, to, 52*, 126, 941-947, 1031-1033.
repetitive tenses, 946.
return, to, 1074.
REVERSIVE VERBS, 1080-1083.
rhinoceros, 500, 502.
*ri*, classifier, 411.
*ri*, connective pronoun, 639*.
*ri*, reflexive pronoun, 655.
*ri*, copula, 1022, 1024, 1026.
rich, 233.
riem, p. 313.
*rile*, auxiliary, 1008.
*rire*, copula, 1022, 1026.
ring, 404.
rise, to, 1076.
river, 203, 366*, 374, 384(9), 470*, 490(2), 525.
rivers, names of, 466, 470*, 486.
Roa, or Rwa, people, *3*.
road, 72, 88, 97, 126, 142, 147, 187, 195, 224, 239.
rod, 404.
roof, 482.
rope, 470*, 485, 490(3).
ropes, how made, 490(3).
Rotse cluster of languages, *14*.
— sources for its study, *51*.
Rotse language, *passim*.
— its phonetic features, 135-141.
Rotse nation, *93*, pp. 283-286, p. 292.
round, 564, 1065.
rouse, to, 174.
row, 482.
*ru*, classifier, 490, 509.
*ru*, pronoun, 639.
Rua language, *14*.
— sources for its study, *58*.
— its phonetic features, 145.
ruins in South-Africa, *18*.
Runda, see Lunda.

S, ⸿, how pronounced, 24.
— = C, 176.
— = D, = J, 136.
— = Đ, 82.
— = F, 410*, 656*.
— = H, 123, 174.
— = W, 105.
— = T, 90, 128, 174, 239.
— = TLH, 174.
— = TSH, 174.
— = TY, 214.
— = X, 106, 133, 136.
— = Z, 214.
— suppressed, 174.
*sa*, nominal prefix, 347.
*sa*, auxiliary, 875, *sqq*., 986, 991, 992, 994.
Saba, the queen of, *85*.
Sabæans, *83-86*, 365(6).
sacrifices, pp. 286-288, p. 294.
saddle, 500.

Sagara cluster of languages, *14*.
— sources for its study, *34*.
Sagara language, *passim*.
— its phonetic features, 77.
Sagaraland, *82*.
same, 825.
sand, 485.
sandy ground, 420.
-*sano*, 792*.
Sasos, *80*, *85*.
satisfied, to be, 1074.
saw, 422.
say, to, 834, 1004-1011, 1079.
*se*, common classifier, 492.
*se*, locative prefix, 583.
*se*, nominal prefix, 348.
*se*, pronoun, 639*.
*se*, auxiliary, 875, *sqq*. 991, 992.
sea, 470*, 478, 486, 488.
sea-cow, 99, see hippopotamus.
seasons, p. 287, p. 294.
seat, 491*, 500, 503(4).
Sebituane, p. 284, p. 293.
Se-chwana, Se-kololo, Se-suto, etc., see Chwana, Kololo, Suto, etc.
second, 797.
see, to, 52*, 126, 179, 835.
seeds, 185.
seize, to, 107, 108, 1048, 1073.
Sekeletu, 1095.
self, 689, 816, 824-825.
Semi-Bantu, 598, 830.
Semitic languages, distantly related to Bantu, 599.
send, to, 52*, 172, 216, 232, 220, 1070.
Senegambia languages, related to Bantu, 598.
Senna, *73*, 110 (foot-note).
Senna cluster of languages, *14*.
— sources for its study, *30*.
Senna language, *passim*.
— its importance, 103.
— its partial loss of the classifiers *LI* and *LU*, 380.
— its suppressed nasals and double consonants, 94, 412.
sensations, 405.
separation of the words, 892 (*N. B.*).
servant, 211, 322*, 363(2).
Sesheke, p. 285.
seven, 789, 796.
shadow, 375.
shaft, 478.
Shambala cluster of languages, *14*.
— sources for its study, *43*.
Shambala language, *passim*.
— its phonetic features, 78.
shame, 79, 82, 126. 151, 194, 208, 214, 385*, 409 (4).
shape, to, 52*.
sheathe, to, 1082.
sheep, 390, 401.
shield, 192, 202, 404, 500.
shoe, 194, 208, 404.
Shona country, identified with Siyuna, 110.

Shona language, 110.
Shona tribes, 50 (foot-note).
short, 187, 500, 502, 601*, 632 (1).
should, 395, *sqq*.
shoulder, 468, (2).
shout, to, 175.
Shukulumbue nation, p. 286, p. 293.
shut, to, 1081.
*SI* — *N*, 174.
*si*, classifier, 396, 492. 523.
*si*, nominal prefix, 347.
*si*, pronoun, 639*.
*si*, auxiliary, 875, *sqq*., 986, 990, 994.
*si* copulative prefix, 583.
side, 83.
side of a river, 421.
*sin*, classifier, 396.
*singa*, *sinka*, auxiliary, 1001.
Siongo, 74, 499, p. 289, p. 295.
Sipopo, p. 284, p. 285, p. 293.
Siraf, *93*.
sit, to, 52*, 70, 941-947, 1031-1033.
six, 789, 792*, 796.
Siyuna, *73*, 110.
skeleton, 161.
skin, 419, 484.
sky, 115, 126, 410*, 420, 439 (7).
slave, 143, 418.
small, 228, 525, 595, 601*, 632 (1).
small-pox, 455.
smoke, 147, 455.
snake, 68, 162, 175, 195, 197, 233, 385*, 427.
snakes, charmed, p. 292.
snakes, used as dogs, p. 292, p. 295.
snow, 454.
Sofala, *73*, *85*.
Sofala language, 102.
soil, 374.
Solomon, *85*.
some, 828-829.
son, 322*, 364, 365 (3), 747, 753, see child.
soon, 1018.
sorcerers, p. 283, pp. 290-295.
soul, 232, 365 (6), 375.
sound, 423.
sound, to, 1075.
soup, 378.
SOURCES FOR THE STUDY OF THE BANTU LANGUAGES, *16-70*.
Souza, Manuel Antonio de, p. 285, p. 293.
sow, to, 179.
speak, to, 113, 1004-1011, 1058, 1079.
spear, 80, 410*, 422, 439 (5).
spirit, 232, 365 (6).
spirit, pernicious, 410*.
spit, to, 80.
springbock, 203.
stand, to, 977, 1016.

## 334 South-African Bantu Languages.

Stanley, 168.
star, 403, 525.
start, to, 527, 965.
steal, to, 52*, 139.
stick, 504*.
still, 987, 989, 990, 991.
sting, 389.
stone, 72, 122, 126, 133, 139, 141 (2), 243, 380, 410*, 414, 415, 420, 438, 439 (7); 485.
stool, 491*, 503 (4).
stop, to, 977, 1016.
story, 69, 80.
straight, 220, 625, 626, 778.
straightway, 971, 1018.
stranger, 825.
straw, 443.
strength, 173.
string, 470*, 478, 490 (3).
strong, 624, 626.
stump, 491*, 503 (6).
*su*, classifier, 478.
*su*, nominal prefix, 348.
sub-classes of substantives, 315.
Subia language, 65.
Subia tribe, p. 285, p. 292.
subject, how expressed, 638, 644.
subjunctive mood and tenses, 832, 855-859, 955-958, 969.
SUBSTANTIVES, 313-599.
SUBSTANTIVE PERSONAL PRONOUNS, 656-692, 830.
SUBSTANTIVE VERB, 1018, *sqq*.
such, 498, 628.
such, to, 1073.
suckle, to, 1073.
suffer, to, 1074.
suffixes of substantives, 590-595.
summer, 499.
sun, 136, 141 (2), 162, 211, 239, 243, 410*, 421, 430, 438, 439 (2).
Sun, Table of the, *81, 82*.
Sundi tribe, *10*.
SUPERLATIVES, 632-634, 1079.
superlative, quasi-, pronouns. 813.
suppose that, supposing that, 786, 988.
surpass, to, 631, 1079.
Suto language, 169.
Suto nation, 365 (5), *10*.
Swahili cluster of languages, *14*.
— sources for its study, *42*.
Swahili language, *passim*.
— its phonetic features, 84-91.
swallow, 151.
sweep, to, 122.
Sylveira, Father Gonçalo da, p. 294.

*T*, how pronounced, 25.
— = *C*, or *CH*, 90, 139.
— = *H*, 93.
— = *K*, 244.
— = *L*, 220, 232.
— = *ND*, or *NL*, 193, 479.
— = *NH*, 479.
— = *NT*, 192.

— = *NZ*, 210.
— = *R*, 172, 198, 210, 211, 214.
— = *S*, 90, 174, 239.
— = *TLH*, 949.
— = *Z*, 136, 239.
*ta*, auxiliary, 875, *sqq*., 948, 949, 953.
Tabele, see Tebele.
table, 422, 500.
Table of the Sun, *81, 82*.
tail, 96, 150, 153, 176, 366*, 384 (2).
Taita cluster of languages, *14*.
— sources for its study, *38*.
Taita language, *passim*.
— its phonetic features, 80.
take, to, 528.
tall, 601*.
*tankhara, 80*.
-*tano*, 792*.
-*talu*, 792.
*te*, auxiliary, 1010.
tear, tears, 126, 136.
Tebele language, see Kafir.
Tebele nation, p. 286.
tear, 105.
teeth, see tooth.
teeth, filed, or knocked out, *72*, 50, 209, 210.
Teke language, 159-162.
Tekeza language, 200.
ten, 131, 175, 225, 789, 792*.
Tette, see Senna.
*TH = NT*, 192.
— = *NZ*, 195.
that, 693-716.
Theal, M^c Call, p. 300.
thee, 639*, 653, 656*.
their, 745, *sqq*.
theirs, 768-777.
them, 639*, 653, 656*.
then, 1016, 1018.
there, 693, 693*.
these, 693-716.
they, 637, 639*, 656*.
thick, 500, 502.
thieves, ordeals for, p. 284.
thine, 175, 211, 768-777.
thing, 176, 491*, 497, 502, 503 (1), 781 (1), 782 (2).
third, 797.
this, 693-716.
thorn, 525.
those, 693-716.
those who, 718.
thou, 637, 639*, 656*.
three, 172, 198, 210, 211, 214, 220, 232, 238, 244, 789, 792*.
throat, 484.
through, 637.
thunderclap, 425.
thy, 745, sqq.
*ti*, classifier, 512.
*ti*, pronoun, 639*.
*ti*, peculiar verb in Bantu, 596, 834, 1004-1011.
*ti*, negative auxiliary, 875, *sqq*.
tie, to, 1082.

tiger, 517.
till, 955-959, 971.
till, to, 52* (*lima*), 1072.
time, 504, 787.
times, 3, 4, etc., 797.
Timneh language, 471.
Titles of dignity, 356.
*TL*, how pronounced, 32, 33.
— = *NDL = NZ*, 195, 208.
— = *TLH*, 208.
— its use in Kafir, 121.
*TLH*, how pronounced, 32.
— = *S = NS = T*, 174, 949.
*tla, tlha*, auxiliary, 948, 955, 958.
Tlhaping language, 169.
to, 563, 1065.
tobacco, 632.
together, 533*, 541, 581 (6), 810.
to-morrow, 142, 421, 533*, 581 (8).
Tonga cluster of languages, *14*.
— sources for its study, *29*.
Tonga language, *passim*.
— its phonetic features, 62-64.
— taken as standard, 2.
Tonga tribes, *29* (foot-note), 50, pp. 288-295.
tongue, 133, 143, 145, 243, 470*, 478, 484, 488, 490 (1), 583.
tools, 372.
tooth, teeth, 126, 143, 145, 205, 233, 235, 243, 410*, 419.
tortoise, 205, 418, 500.
touch, to, 1084.
town, 136, 142, 147, 229.
trade, to, 1084.
Trade in South-Africa, 79-99.
transient actions, 832.
transitory tenses, 971, 972, 974.
tree, 153, 164, 206, 210, 211, 366*, 371, 425, 526.
tribal names, 322*, 376.
tripe, p. 313.
Troglodytes, *3*.
Troglodytica, *80*.
true, 780.
*TS = C*, 206.
— = *DJ*, 205.
— = *K*, 1037.
— = *NJ*, 191.
— = *NZ*, 195.
— = *S* after *N*, 288.
*TSH = PU*, or *PI*, 222.
— = *RE*, 206.
— = *S*, 174.
Tshagga cluster of languages, *14*.
— sources for its study, *65*.
Tshagga language, 211.
*tsho*, peculiar verb, 834.
*TU = TSH*, 144.
*tu*, connective pronoun, 639*.
*tu*, relative particle, 718*.
Tua people, *3*.
tusk, 419, 484.
*tu-nga*, nominal prefix, 515.
twice, 504* (a second time), 797.
two, 131, 145, 217, 233, 789, 792*.

# Alphabetical Index. 335

*TY* = *BU*, or *RI*, 122, 445.
-*tye*, nominal suffix, 519, 593.
*tyi*, classifier, 492.
*tyi*, pronoun, 639*.
*tyi*, conjunction, 787.
*tyi?*, 801.
*tyu*, pronoun, 639.
*TYlV* = *BU*, 122.

*U*, how pronounced, 26.
— = *A*, 273.
— = *I*, 276.
— = *MU*, 279, 560.
— = *O*, 200.
— = *UA*, 332.
— = *UE*, or *IVE*, 266.
— = *UI*, 267.
— = *IV*, 261.
— elided, 264.
— how changed before vowels, 261-268.
— suppressed, 278.
*u*, article, 317.
*u*, common classifier, 329, 367, 448, 465, 490, 509.
*u*, locative classifier, 543.
*u*, connective pronoun, 639*.
*u*, relative particle, 718*.
*UA* = *OA*, 262.
-*ua*, passive suffix, 1047, 1053, 1062.
*uba*, 1007.
*UE* = *O*, 265, 659.
-*ue*, pronominal suffix, 660.
-*uka*, verbal suffix, 1050, 1083.
*u kuba*, 982, 1007.
*u kuti*, 1007.
*u kuze*, 959.
-*ula*,-*ulula*,-*uluka*, *una*, -*ununa*, verbal suffixes, 1057, 1080-1083.
*un*, pronoun, 639*.
unbind, to, 1082, 1083.
undo, to, 1083.
undress, to, 1081.
Ungu cluster of languages, *14*.
— sources for its study, *33*.
unite, to, 1082.
unproductive animals, 418.
unsheathe, to, 1082.
untie, to, 1082.
until, 955-959, 1016.
up, 562.
Upaz, *85*.
upon, 533*, 541, 581 (4).
us, 653, 639*, 656*.

*V*, *U*, how pronounced, 27.
*V* = *BV*, 94, 99.
— = *K*, 233.
— = *P*, 137, 148, 180, 211, 215.
— = *Z*, 91, 63.
— = suppressed, 66.
*va*, common classifier, 338.
*va*, locative classifier, 537.
*va*, pronoun, 639*.
Vasco de Gama, *92*.
*ve*, pronoun, 639*.
vein, 402.

verbal suffixes, 1047-1084.
VERBS, 831-1085.
very, 633, 689, 824.
very far, 533*.
*vi*, classifier, 369, 494, 496, 510, 522.
*vi*, pronoun, 639*.
*vi?*, 801.
Victoria Falls, *74*, 499, p. 289, p. 295.
village, 136, 142, 147, **see** town.
Viti cluster of languages, *14*.
— sources for its study, *31*.
Viti tribes, *95*.
*vo*, auxiliary, 1012, 1015.
VOWELS, changed, 559.
— elided, 49, 76.
— indifferent, 833.
— remarkably firm in Bantu, 48.
— weakened, 235, 892, 904, 905.
VOWEL-STEMS, or stems which begin with a vowel, 46 (3).
— their peculiar laws, 46 (2), 67, 87, 113, 415, 478, 611, 648, 832, 837-841, 843, 851.
*VU*, meaning of the element, 409(2).
vulture, 358.
Vumbe tribe, p. 286.

*W*, how pronounced, 28.
— = *K*, 175.
— = *P*, 272.
— = *U*, 28.
— euphonic, 295.
*w*, classifier, 448, 465, 490.
*w*, pronoun, 642.
*wa*, common classifier, 336.
*wa*, locative classifier, 536.
*wa*, pronoun, 447.
-*wa*, passive suffix, 1047, 1053, 1062. '
Wakwak, *72*, *84*, *93*, p. 312.
walk, to, 52*, 1075.
wallets, p. 295.
Wange, the chief, pp. 286-288, p. 294.
Wangwana, 246.
Wankie, **see** Wange.
wash, to, 174, 208, 1082.
watch over, to, 193.
watching over gardens, p. 305.
water, 89, 115, 133, 136, 143, 195, 210, 211, 440*, 454, 461(10).
watercourse, 470*, 490(2).
*we*, pronoun, 639*, 656*.
we, 128, 214, 637, 639*, 656*.
well, 499.
what?, 801-803.
whatever, 813.
when, 784, 785, 787, 788, 902, 970, 993, 1008-1012.
when?, 808.
whence?, 533*, 581(11).
whenever, 993.
where?, 533*, 581(11).
where, wherein, 785.

which, 717-746.
which?, 806-807.
while, 787, 788, 970, 988, 989.
white, 624, 628, 778.
white man, 355, 365(1), 432.
whither?, 533*, 581(11).
who, 717-746.
who?, 804.
whoever, 813.
whole, 601*, 810-812.
whom, 717-746.
whose?, 740-741, 805.
*wi*, pronoun, 639*.
wicker-work among Kafirs, p. 321.
wide, 624.
wife, 173, 322*, **see** woman.
wild beast, 502.
wind, 69, 73, 77, 79, 137, 142, 149, 184, 405.
window, 503(6).
wine, 440*, 455, 461(3).
wing, 419.
winter, 137, 142, 405, **see** wind.
wish, to, 126, 995, 1003.
with, 570, 573, 575.
within, 194, 533, 533*, 581(1).
wizard, 143, **see** sorcerer.
Wolof language, 830.
woman, 142, 143, 211, 239, 243, 322*, 365(4).
wool, 139, 440*.
work, 379.
would, 995, *sqq*.
wound, 423.
write, to, 1070.
writing, 487.
writing in South-Africa, *16*, *17*.
written language, when differing from the spoken, 253.
*wu*, classifier, 447.
*wu*, pronoun, 639*.

*X*, how pronounced, 29, 38.
— = *NS*, 194.
— = *NZ*, 195.
— = *SI*, 174.
Xosa language, *passim*, **see** Kafir.
— its peculiar sounds, 33-38.
— its phonetic features, 120-124.

*Y*, how pronounced, 30.
— = *L*, 96, 97.
— = *M*, or *N*, 295.
*y*, classifier, 496.
*y*, pronoun, 639, 642.
*ya*, pronoun, 639*.
*ya*, auxiliary, 911-917, 920.
*ya*, preposition, 570.
-*ya*, demonstrative suffix, 698.
Yansi cluster of languages, *14*.
Yansi language, 159-162.
Yao language, *14*.
— sources for its study, *47*.
— its phonetic features, 66-72.
— its peculiar plurals, 354.
— its relation to Chwana, 72.

ye, auxiliary, 916, 917.
year, 366*, 379, 384(11).
yesterday, 421, 533*, 581(7).
yet, 991.
Yeye language, 109.
yi, pronoun, 639*.
yo, suffixed to verbs in relative clauses, 723, 734.
yonder, 693, 693*.
you, 637, 639*, 656*.
young, 601*.
young of animal, 418.
your, 745, *sqq*.
yours, 768-777.
youth, 504*.
yo = ye, 916.
yu, pronoun, 639*, 652.

Z, how pronounced, 31.
— = *BZ* = *BV*, 99.
— = *D*, or *R*, 173, 220.
— = *D*, or *T*. 136.
— = *DY*, 123, 214.
— = *DZ*, 94, 99.
— = *J*, 89, 106, 115, 143, 147.
— = *L*, 165, 173 (cf. 9), 211, 214, 232.
— = *N*, 232.
— = *T*, 239.
— = *V*, 91, 115.
— = *J*, 126, 225.
— suppressed, 66, 81.
3, how pronounced, 31.
— its use, 105, 123, 133.
ʒa, classifier, 490.
ʒa, auxiliary, 948, 950.
-ʒa, verbal suffix, 1079.
Zambezi, 486.
Zaramo language, *14*.
— sources for its study, *45*.
ze, auxiliary, 955.
zebra, 133, 136, 401.
Zendj, **see** Zindj.
zi, classifier, 491-503.
— its transformations, 496.
— its use, 497-501.
— its original meaning, 502.
zi, connective pronoun, 639*.
zi, reflexive pronoun, 655.
zi, relative particle, 718*.
zi, copulative prefix, 583.
-zi, suffix in the number "one", 792.
-zia, verbal suffix, 1079.

Zimba, Zimbawe, Zimbabye, Zimbaze, 9.
Zimbabye, or Zimbaze, ruins. —
— inscriptions found on them, *18*.
— their description, *73*.
— their origin, *73-74*.
zin, classifier, 385-409.
— its transformations, 391-398.
— its use, 399-406, 477-480.
— its original meaning, 408.
Zindj, who they are, *8*.
— their ancient trade, *80*.
— their origin, *72*.
zon, classifier, 397.
zo-o = za-ku, 950.
zu, meaning of the element, 409(2).
Zulu language, **see** Kafir.
— its difference from Xosa, 124.
— its peculiar sounds, 33-38.
Zulu tribes, origin of the, 95, 365(5).
Zumbo language, 102.
ʒwi, classifier, 496.
ʒwi, pronoun, 639*.

A. M. D. G.

Desclée, De Brouwer, and Cᵒ., Bruges, Belgium.

# Additions and Corrections.

## NGONI LANGUAGE.

Sources: *Introductory Grammar of the Ngony language*, by W. A. Elmslie, M. B., 1891.
*Ikatekisma la Hari...*, ngu W. A. Elmslie, 1890.
*Izindaba zombuso ka Mlungu*, 1890.

There are in South Africa several different tribes which go by the name of Ngoni. Those among which the Rev. W. A. Elmslie has passed several years live under the rule of Mombera, on the western side of Lake Nyassa. Their language must not be coupled with Bunga (p. xix of this work), but with Mfengu, Zulu, Xosa, and Tebele, in the Kafir cluster. In the sources mentioned above I have scarcely found more than two or three words which may not be heard among the Kafirs of Cape Colony and Natal.

The demonstrative pronouns and a few other forms are the same as in Zulu, not as in Xosa (n. 124). A few grammatical forms are proper to Ngoni, or borrowed from the dialects of the Nyassa region. Thus the classifiers *ci* and *vi* replace *si* and *zi* of Kafir (*ci* and *zi* of Tonga); and the connective pronouns of the plural number in the 1st and 2d person are *ti* "we" instead of the Kafir *si*; *mu* or *li* "you" instead of the Kafir *ni*. Consequently, the substantive pronoun *mwena* or *lina* "you" replaces *nina*. (See pp. 153 and 160). Were it not for these few differences, all good Zulu and Kafir books might be used among the Ngoni of Nyassaland.

## KAFIR.

The Xosa auxiliary *ba* (Zulu *ma*, nn. 977 and 978) in some of its uses, though not in all, is certainly the same verb as the Chwana *-bwa*, to say (Tonga *-amba*). Thus a Kafir in a letter, speaking of the animals *(i zilwanyana)* set up in a museum, says of them: *E zinye ungake wotuke u-*be *zisa pilile*, of some of these you would say in your surprise that they were alive. This explains why in Kafir *u ku-ba* (Zulu *u-ma*) and *u ku-ti* "to say" may be used indifferently after several verbs of saying, thinking, and willing.

## BIHE.

New source: *New Testament*, A. B. C. F. M., 1889.

The *z* of the main group of the Bantu languages is not always changed to *l* in Bihe (n. 131); in some words it is dropped, in others it is changed to *y*. Ex.: *m-bia*, a pot (Kafir *im-biza*); *ku-i*, to know (Tonga *ku-zi*); *u-kae*, a woman (Tonga *mu-kazi*); *ku-yela*, to be white (Angola *ku-zela*).

The influence of the nasal on some consonants reminds one of Nyamwezi. Thus *n* replaces *nt*, as in *mu-nu*, a person (Tonga *mu-ntu*), *vi-na*, things (T *zi-ntu*); hence, e. g., *n-uma*, I send, for *n-tuma*; *n-ava*, I believe, for *n-tava*; *n-embele*, a temple, for *n-tempele*. *M* replaces *mp* and *np*; hence, e. g., *m-anga*, I wish, for *n-panga*; *m-inga*, I ask, for *n-pinga*; *m-opia*, I say, for *n-popia*. *H* and *ñ* replace *nk*, as in *hali*, a hard thing, (Tonga *in-kali*); hence *huatela* or *ñuatela*, I hold, for *n-kuatela*; *huami* or *ñuami*, follow me, for *n-kuami*. *Mbw* replaces *nw* as in *wa-m-bwaveka*, he anointed me, from *ku-waveka*, to anoint. *Nd* replaces *nl* as in most other Bantu languages.

In the same language the article seems to be regularly dropped before vowels, as in *i-so*, the eye, for *e i-so*; *u-tima*, the heart, for *o u-tima*; *i-tima*, the hearts, for *o i-tima*. The locative classifier corresponding to *mu* is *vu*, as in *v-u-tima*, in the heart, for *vu u-tima*. The reflexive pronoun is *li*, as in Yao. Ex.: *Li-lekise*, show thyself. The pronouns *u* "thou" and *vu* "you" are generally used before nouns in the vocative. *Nundepo konyima*, **u** *Satana*, Go behind me, Satan (Marc. 8. 33). **Vu** *pata lio lomata!*

O incredulous generation ! (Marc, 9-18). The copulative prefix before nouns and pronouns is *ha* (= Chwana *ke*). Ex.: *ha situ*, it is meat. We find " to be " rendered sometimes by *na*, sometimes by *kasi*, which is the perfect of *kala*, in sentences which in other respects are identical. Ex. *Isiene u*kasi *ko vailu*, or *Isiene u*na *ko vailu*, Your Father who is in Heaven (Mat., 5, 46 ; 6, 1, etc.).

The Bihe equivalent of the puzzling Tonga verb *kue* or *kui* (964 and 1038) is *kuete*, pft. of *ku-kuata*, to hold. Ex. *O vinyu ka va-kuete*, they have no wine. This shows that the Swahili and Pokomo form *si-kw-ona*, I have not seen, is essentially different from the Tonga form *si kue ndaka bona*, I never saw.

## BOKO.

Source: *Essai sur la langue congolaise*, par le R. P. Cambier, C. C. I. M., 1891.

The Boko (I-boko) language is that of some tribes living on the Congo near and north of the Equator. It belongs to the main group of the Bantu languages, and is particularly related to Yansi.

It drops *s* in many words, as in *angu*, my father (Yansi *sangu*), *-atu*, three (Yansi *-satu*), *i-anga*, an island (Yansi *ki-sanga*), *-umba*, to buy (*-sumba* in several languages), *jiu*, an eye (Yansi *disu*), *bo*, the forehead (*buso* in many languages). It also drops *k* in some cases, *z* before *i*, and *f* before *u*. Ex.: *njo*, a snake (*njoka* or *nyoka* in several languages), *ma-i*, water (*ma-nzi, ma-zi, ma-dzi*, etc., in various languages), *-eba*, to know (Tonga *-ziba*), *-ua*, to die (Tonga *-fua*), *ma-uta*, oil (Tonga *ma-futa*).The vowel *e* is often interchanged with *i*, and *o* with *u*, as in several other Bantu languages.

These phonetic peculiarities account for the following changes in the forms of the classifiers. The classifier *si* of Kafir (Tonga *ci*) is pronounced *e* or *i* in Boko. The locative classifier *ku* is reduced to *o*. The other classifier *ku* has disappeared even before the infinitive forms of verbs. It is replaced by the classifier *e ( = ci, si, ki)* in the two words *e-boko*, an arm (Tonga *ku-boko*), and *e-kolo*, a leg (Tonga *ku-ulu*). The plural classifier *zin* of Tonga is not only reduced to *n* before substantives as in several other languages, but drops its *z* even in personal and demonstrative pronouns.

The only traces that I find in Boko of the locative classifier *pa* are the demonstrative particles *wa*, here, *wana*, there, and *wai ?*, where ? The locative classifier *mu* seems to be reduced to *o*. Ex. *o bo-atu*, in a canoe (Tonga *mu bu-ato*). The regular ending of the present indicative tense seems to be *i* instead of *a*. Ex. *na-jibi*, I shut.

## FANG.

Source: *Dictionnaire Français-Fang*, par le R. P. Lejeune, C. S. E., 1892.

This is the language which has been termed Fan in the course of this work, but wrongly, as may now be judged from the work of Father Lejeune.

The most remarkable transitions of sounds in this language are given correctly on p. 48, with but one exception. Namely, in n. 233 the two lines referring to *l*=*s* (?) must be left out, as, etymologically speaking, *en-soon*, mouth, is not the same word as *mu-lomo*, and *a-son*, a tooth, more correctly *a-song* or *a-shong*, is related, not to the Tonga *li-no*, but to the Dualla *i-sunga*. It must also be remarked that *k* in *en-sok*, an elephant, and, in general, wherever it occupies the place of the Tonga syllable *vu*, is pronounced like the German *ch* in *nach*. In n. 232 *kaba* and *doa* do not seem to be the same word as the Guha *ka-bia*, a flame, pl. *tu-bia*.

In the chapter on substantives I considered as doubtful the forms of several Fang classifiers. They are now certain, and for the most part very interesting. Thus :

CLASS MU-BA. — In Fang this class includes the nouns which require the same concord as *m-ur*, or *m-oru*, a person, pl. *b-ur*, or *b-oru*. When the stem of these words begins with a vowel, their classifier is *m* in the singular, *b-* in the plural, as in *m-one*, a child, pl. *b-one* (p. 67). When their stem begins with a consonant, their classifier is.

generally speaking, *m* before labials, *n* before other consonants. In the plural their classifier *be* in most words keeps the *m* or *n* of the singular, which gives *bem* or *ben*. When they do not keep this nasal, the initial consonant of their stem generally undergoes a phonetic change. Ex.: *n-dji*, a man who eats, pl. *be-n-dji*; *m-vong*, a kind of fish, pl. *be-m-vong*; *n-gal*, a female, pl. *be-yal*.

CLASS MU-MI. — In Fang the classifiers of this class are *n* in the singular (*m* before *b*), *mi* in the plural (*min*, when the *n* of the singular is kept). Ex.: *n-lu* or *n-nu*, the head, pl. *mi-lu*, or *mi-n-lu*; *n-lem* or *n-nem*, the heart, pl. *mi-lem* or *mi-n-lem*; *n-lo* or *n-no*, a river, pl. *mi-lo* or *mi-n-lo*. If these words be compared with those given in pp. 76-78, one should bear in mind that Fang changes to *l* the *t* of the main group of Bantu languages (n. 232).

CLASS IN-ZIN. — In the singular the classifier *n* of this class is dropped in Fang before hard consonants, such as *k*, *f*, *s*, as in several other Bantu languages. In the plural this class generally borrows the classifier *be* of cl. MU-BA, as it borrows the classifier *wa* in Swahili. In a few words it borrows the classifier *me*. The nasal sound of the singular is always kept in the plural. Ex.: *n-go*, a dress, pl. *be-n-go*; *n-zoh* or *n-joh*, an elephant, pl. *be-n-zoh* or *be-n-joh*; *n-gan*, a doctor, pl. *be-n-gan*; *khuma*, a chief, pl. *be-khuma*; *n-gon*, a month, pl. *me-n-gon*; *n-gana*, a story, pl. *me-n-gana*.

CLASS LI-MA. — It cannot be doubted that in Fang the classifier of this class in the singular is *a* before consonants. Before vowels its form is generally *dy*, in some cases *dz*. The plural classifier is *me*, in some words *ma*, *m* before vowels. Ex : *a shong*, a tooth, pl. *me-shong* (p. 89); *a-gum*, ten, pl. *me-gum* (p. 205); *a-bi*, a woman's breast, pl. *ma-bi*; *a-kong*, a spear, pl. *me-kong* (p. 89); *dy-ise*, or *dy-is*, or *dy-it*, an eye, pl. *m-ise*, or *m-is* or *m-it* (p. 88); *dz-am*, a thing, pl. *m-am* (*l-ambo*, pl. *m-ambo* in Dualla).

CLASS BU-MA. — I find in Fang only one word belonging to this class, viz. *bi-al*, a canoe, pl. *m-al* (p. 97); but several examples may be given of words which are used only with the classifier *me*, such as *me-djim*, water (p. 98); *me-li*, saliva; *me-ki*, blood (Dualla *ma-kiya*).

CLASS KU-MA. — This is not found in Fang. Some trace of it may perhaps be seen in the word *w-o*, an arm, pl. *m-o* (Tonga *ku-boko*, pl. *ma-boko*). Before the infinitive forms of verbs we find *e* instead of the Bantu *ku*.

CLASS CI-ZI. — In Fang its classifiers are *e* or *i* before consonants, *j* before vowels in the singular, *bi* in all cases in the plural. Ex.: *e-li*, a tree, pl. *bi-li*; *j-um*, a thing, pl. *bi-um* (p. 109); *e-bma*, or *e-buma*, a fruit, pl. *bi-bma* or *bi-buma* (Dualla *e-puma*. pl. *be-puma*; Benga *e-buma*, pl. *be-buma*).

CLASS KA-TU. — To this corresponds in Fang the class VI-LO. Ex.: *vi-ong*, an antelope, pl. *l-ong*; *vi-o*, a bit of grass, pl. *l-o*. Etymologically speaking, the classifier *lo* is the same as the Tonga *tu* (n. 511). With regard to *vi* see nn. 520-523.

CLASS LU-ZIN. — To this seems to correspond in Fang the class O-A. Ex.: *o-non*, a bird, pl. *a-non*; *o-kee*, a leaf, pl. *a-kee*; *o-bon*, or *u-bon*, a collar, pl. *a-bon*; *o-nu*, a finger, pl. *a-nu*. The change of *lu* to *o* is regular (n. 232). The change of *zin* to *a* is more puzzling. But it should be noticed that this Fang classifier *a* gives us the possessive pronouns *dam*, mine, *di-na*, yours, etc., the demonstrative pronouns *edi*, *edina*, *edine*, and before verbs the pronoun *do*. Whence we may infer that this classifier *a* stands for *da*, or *di*, which corresponds regularly to *zi*. And we have seen above that Fang gives the form *a* to the classifier which in the other Bantu languages is variously pronounced *i*, *li*, or *di*. Therefore the change of *i* to *a* is not entirely new.

LOCATIVE EXPRESSIONS. — These in Fang have nothing of the nature of substantives, that is to say, their first element, which generally is *o* (= Mpongwe *go*) or *e*, is not a classifier, but merely a preposition without any governing power. Ex.: *o shu Nzame*, before God, not *o shu o Nzame* (cf. in Mpongwe *g'ojo* w'*Anyambie*).

*Adjectives.* — In adjectives proper, Fang has kept better than in substantives the distinction between the classifiers *n* = *mu* and *n* = *in*. For in this language, as in several others, *n* = *in* disappears before hard consonants, and, when it comes before a soft consonant, in some cases it dentalizes it, in others it strengthens it. On the contrary, *n* = *mu* disappears only before *n*, and does not strengthen the following consonant. It, however, changes *v* to *b*. Thus, with the classifier *n* = *in*, we find *n-ati n-den*, a large gun, for *n-zali n-nen ; n-zali fork*, another gun, for *n-sali n-vork ; nyul tork*, a small body, for *nyul n-tork ;* while the classifier *n* = *mu* gives us *m-ua-nen*, a great leader, for *n-jue n-nen ; m-ur n-tork*, a small man ; *n-nu m-bork*, another kind for *n-nu n-vork*.

I also notice that the classifier *vi* requires the same concord as the classifier *n*: *vi-ong o-tork*, a small antelope, instead of *vi-ong vi-tork*.

*Verbs.* — The forms corresponding to the Tonga *ndi-bona, ndi-bone, and bonide*, are respectively *m-a yen* (without the final *a*), *me yen-ege* (with the subjunctive ending *-ege* instead of the simple *-e*), and *me yen* or *me yena* (with no ending, or the ending *-a*, instead of *-ide* or *-ile*).

The auxiliary of the future tense is the verb *-ke*, to go. This confirms the opinion given in n. 965, that the auxiliary *ka*, which in several languages is expressive of future, is related to the verb *-inka*, to go. It would be surprising that the various forms of derivative verbs should not be found in Fang. Father Lejeune, however, mentions only two of these, viz., the passive and the reciprocal. The passive ending is *-i* in the present, *-ea* in the perfect. Ex. : *me yen-eba*, I am seen, *me yen-ea*, I have been seen. The reciprocal ending is *-ana*, as in the other Bantu languages. Some however reduce this to *-a*. Ex. : *enyeghana*, or *enyegha*, to love one another.

*Conclusion.* — Judging from the work of Father Lejeune, the Fang language differs considerably from the Bantu languages of the main group. The difference, on the whole, may even be said to amount to something like the difference between Greek and Latin. But it has much in common with Mpongwe, Benga, Kele, and Dualla. Hence these languages, together with some others that are not so well known, may be said to form a special group in the classification of the Bantu languages. I am thus be led now to divide this family of languages, inasmuch as I know them, into four groups, viz. 1) the main group, 2) the Kua or Kuana group, including Chuana, Tebele and the dialects of the coast of Mozambique, etc., 3) the north-western group, including Mpongwe, Fang, etc., 4) The Fernandian group.

---

## NEW SOURCES TO HAND ON VARIOUS LANGUAGES.

NYASSA.  *A Grammar of Chinyanja*, by George Henry, M. A., Aberdeen, 1891.
— *Chinyanja Dictionary. Tentative edition.*
TUMBUKA (West of Lake Nyassa) : *Notes on the Tumbuka Language*, by the Rev. W. A. Elmslie, M. A., Aberdeen, 1891.
KONDE.  *Collections for a Handbook of the Makonde Language*, Zanzibar, 1876.
SWAHILI.  *Dictionnaire Français-Swahili*, par le R. P. Ch. Sacleux, C. S. E., Zanzibar, 1891.
—  *African Aphorisms*, by the Rev. W. E. Taylor, M. A., S. P. C. K., 1891.
GIRYAMA (Nika cluster). *Vocabulary and Collections*, by the Rev. W. E. Taylor, M. A., S. P. C. K., 1891.
GANDA.  *Collections for a Lexicon*, by Rev. P. O'Flaherty, C. M. S., S. P. C. K.
—  *Kitabu ky'esala*, Alger, 1891.
—  *Hymns*, by G. L. P., B. A., S. P. C. K.
—  *Ngero za mu Kitabu*, S. P. C. K.
ANGOLA.  *Jisabu....*, by Jakim ria Matta, Lisboa, 1891.
FERNANDIAN. *Primer paso á la lengua Bubi*, por el Rdo P. Joaquin Juanola, Madrid, 1890.
TSWA (a dialect of Gwamba). *Ti-vangeli...*, Amer. B. S., 1891.
PEDI (a Chwana dialect). New Testament, B. F. B. S., 1890.
KAFIR.  New Testament (revised translation), B. F. B. S., 1888.
ZULU.  St John and Acts (revised translation), B. F. B. S. 1890.
DUALLA.  New Testament, translated by Rev. A. Saker, B. T. S., 1882.
BENGA.  Gospels and Acts, B. F. B. S., 1881.
BOONDEI.  *Anjili kua Mattayo*, B. F. B. S., 1890.
GOGO.  *Mattayo...*, B. F. B. S., 1891.
YAO.  *Johanna...*, B. F. B. S., 1889.   *May 18, 1892.*

www.ingramcontent.com/pod-product-compliance
Lightning Source LLC
Chambersburg PA
CBHW032026220426
43664CB00006B/381